Deploying Next G Multicast-Enabled Applications

Deploying Next Generation Multicast-Enabled Applications

Label Switched Multicast for MPLS VPNs, VPLS, and Wholesale Ethernet

Vinod Joseph

Srinivas Mulugu

AMSTERDAM • BOSTON • HEIDELBERG • LONDON
NEW YORK • OXFORD • PARIS • SAN DIEGO
SAN FRANCISCO • SINGAPORE • SYDNEY • TOKYO
Morgan Kaufmann is an imprint of Elsevier

Acquiring Editor: Todd Green
Development Editor: Robyn Day
Project Manager: Jessica Vaughan
Designer: Eric DeCicco

Morgan Kaufmann is an imprint of Elsevier
225 Wyman Street, Waltham, MA 02451, USA

Library of Congress Cataloging-in-Publication Data
Joseph, Vinod.
  Deploying next generation multicast-enabled applications : label switched multicast for MPLS VPNs,
VPLS, and wholesale Ethernet / Vinod Joseph, with Srinivas Mulugu.
      p. cm.
  Summary: "Provides detailed information on existing Multicast and MVPN standards, referred to as
Next-Generation Multicast based standards, Multicast Applications, and case studies with detailed
configurations"— Provided by publisher.
  Includes bibliographical references and index.
  ISBN 978-0-12-384923-6 (hardback)
  1. Multicasting (Computer networks) 2. Extranets (Computer networks)   I. Mulugu, Srinivas. II. Title.
  TK5105.887.J67 2011
  004.6'6—dc23   2011011965

British Library Cataloguing-in-Publication Data
A catalogue record for this book is available from the British Library

ISBN: 978-0-12-384923-6

For information on all MK publications visit our website at www.mkp.com

Praise for *Deploying Next Generation Multicast-Enabled Applications*

"Service Providers/carriers have been consistently challenged to keep abreast with requirements of next-generation multicast Enabled Applications in Mobility/IPTV arena and in deploying a video optimized core transport supporting this stringent applications demands. Finally here is a practical, comprehensive approach to deploy Next Generation Multicast, this book addresses. IP Multicast is destined to become more and more of a fundamentally important technology to address the Zettabyte era and this book provides a practical insight to field on how to deploy the Next Generation implementation of multicast by being vendor agnostic. Vinod Joseph's first book on deploying next-Generation QoS has already gained significant accolades and has been well received in the networking community and I heartily endorse this book as a useful guide to all Network Design/Optimization engineers and Network Consultants who are looking forward to deploy Next Generation IP Multicast in a multi-vendor environment"

—Mahesh Kumar Jothi–Head, World Wide Service Provider – IOX-XR Centre of Excellence, Cisco Systems Inc.

"Vinod has a great eye for detail and this is demonstrated in his book where he has looked at the design considerations in great depth, providing the reader with clear insight into the issue being discussed. In his book *Deploying Next Generation Multicast-Enabled Applications*, Vinod demonstrates his unique combination of deep technical understanding of Next Generation Multicast whilst being able to step back and take the reader through his logic is a very systematic manner. This is coupled with his very humble nature which is evident in the way the book has been written. I have seen Vinod develop over the years both in terms of his technical expertise and leadership as his ability to distil a deeply technical subject into a very concise approach designing some of the world's most complex networks."

—Ran Kalsi–Global Engineering Head and Executive Vice President of Fixed Mobile Convergence at Vodafone

"More and more networks require multicast capabilities to optimize the traffic in-line with business demands. The industry has come up with several mechanisms to provide a multicast enabled network, using IP and/or MPLS techniques. This book, written by Vinod Joseph and Srinivas Mulugu, addresses the different available solutions allowing people to have a good understanding of the available technologies. After reading this book, architects and operational people will get a good understanding of the different technologies available such that they can make the right design choices and implications of one solutions or another. The book is an excellent reference for different people to get a good inside into this complex technology."

—Wim Henderickx – Senior Director Consulting Engineering IP Division at Alcatel Lucent

"Communication Service Providers (CSP) is making the transition to IP/MPLS infrastructures to deliver video. This move offers significant economic and operational advantages, but it also comes with challenges. The introduction of new high speed access technologies in mobile and fixed is increasing the consumer demand for the video content anytime, anywhere. So CSPs are always looking for effective and efficient methods to deliver content to different devices. The volume of multicast traffic has been increasing mainly based on the emergence of video-based applications. The significant interest in IPTV services is driving the need to consider more scalable ways to deliver multicast services. One of the main challenges is to make sure that the quality of the video is adequately high to attract and retain subscribers. CSP must be able to deliver a better quality of experience (QoE) to drive adoption of IP video. This book by Vinod Joseph will provide an excellent insight on the deployment of Next Generation Multicast Technology and will also include detailed practical information which will be extremely helpful for the service providers."

—Jogesh Ajay – Vice President Technology Strategy & Planning at DU (An Emirates Integrated Telecommunications Company).

"Vinod has provided the first book that describes in detail the newest multicast technology available on the internet. He clearly lays out the pros and cons and deployment considerations for each of the technologies. This is the first and only book to give guidance to a network operator how to design and deploy multicast with tight SLAs and full protection."

—CTO (IPG) of Juniper Networks

"First put forward in 1988, Multicast has been developed for more than twenty years. Several international organizations have devoted a large amount of work to the technical research and deployment of Multicast. With the rapid development of Internet and continuous emergence of new services based on Video, Multicast has become driving technology for future network evolution. Many operators have already deployed different Multicast services. Major ISPs have run inter-domain Multicast routing protocols to exchange multicast routes and Multicast peers have been formed. In the context of increasingly more and more multimedia services on IP networks, Multicast has huge market potential. The Next Generation Model of Multicast based on MPLS technology is clearly explained in this book and different aspects of choosing appropriate architecture and migration strategies are considered and recommended. This book provides a good guidance for any Multicast-specific environments including architectural nuances and practical deployment case studies with specific details. I recommend this book to any network professional who is involved in architecting, designing or troubleshooting Multicast-enabled data networks."

—Oleg Zharov – Network Architect – Huawei

"This book will provide a comprehensive and insightful examination of this important topic, which is applicable to carriers and enterprises alike. It should prove extremely valuable to both engineers and visionaries involved in building Next Generation Multicast infrastructures".

—Luke Broome–CTO of COLT

"There have been many books in the market of addressing the topic of native multicast. However with the emergence of newer Video applications and Label Switched Multicast, there are no comprehensive collateral or books available. The topic of newer technologies such as Label Switched Multicast is no more in the experimental stage, and there are large deployments of these technologies, both in the enterprise and Service provider networks. The idea of providing a transitional approach, from legacy to the newer technologies is extremely impressive. Moving from Rosen Draft to Next-Generation Multicast would be a key highlight, since many customers have deployed the legacy architecture and are interested in moving to the newer options. I would rate this book, as the "G To" reference for Next Generation Multicast and VPNs. Vinod Joseph and Srinivas Mulugu are well known industry experts on emerging technologies and I would believe this book would make a significant contribution in providing an in-depth insight into an already mature technology, but relatively new to end users and customers alike."

—Shanmugasundaram – Global Head of IP Engineering and Strategy – Dell Inc.

"The necessity and use of multicast protocols in service provider's networks is today truistic. The Internet will not scale without a wide adoption of multicast. At the same time, over the last few years, standard bodies have crafted significant changes to the protocols and the industry has brought its shades and nuances in their implementations. The effort of synthesis made by Vinod Joseph and Srinivas Mulugu in this book is therefore timely and very valuable. The basics and history of multicast are covered in such a manner to build a robust understanding of today's standards and implementations. The book addresses a wide audience. Architects will find the philosophy behind the protocol's evolution to support today's applications of multicast; designers, the meticulous dissections of the protocols and its workings; operation and support staff, profuse practical illustrations of the multicast implementations. *Deploying Next Generation Multicast-enabled Applications* is an enjoyable and easy read written by two experts who have contributed to the IETF's standards, and are assisting service providers in this field. It is a good reference in the library of any IT professionals."

—Laurent Lavallee – Head of Strategy and Architecture of BSKYB (Sky Broadband)

This book provides good insight about the Multicast deployment in SP scenarios. Today, when the enterprises are looking for innovative ways to connect, collaborative and communicate globally, multicast is the technology which needs to be exploited to its core.

Deploying multicast VPN with an optimized backbone for creating a stable, scalable backbone with defined SLA is a key requirement of our customers. This book is one source whereby it provides the crisp details and configuration best practices for deployment of the same and provides detailed insight to various scenarios and techniques. With the growth of business video applications, enterprise collaboration and more services on cloud there will be an inherent push to Service providers to offer multicast based solutions and service sets. This book covers careful planning of the core network of SP and I congratulate Vinod Joseph for taking time and pen down his experience and expertise to share the knowledge.

—Manish Gupta – Senior Director British Telecom Asia Pacific

Contents

Acknowledgements

I would like to thank God for the opportunity to publish my second book, without whom I would not have been able to handle the personal challenges and barriers of accomplishing such a task.

I dedicate this book to my little angel Rochelle, who has been my strength and lucky charm through everything; her smile gave me the perseverance to deliver this publication, which is very close to my heart. This book is also dedicated to my two little boys Rocky and Zinger, to whom I owe a great deal, for I have learnt so much from them.

In every accomplishment, I remember my mother Tanis and my grandparents Hylda and Harry, for without them I would never have written this. A special thanks to Jos Bazelmans, my manager and a great friend, who has professionally and personally supported me during the challenges of making this publication a reality.

And lastly, a sincere and special mention of Rahul Aggarwal and Yakov Rekhter, for without whom this technology would never be a reality. Their support all through this process was a blessing, and is greatly appreciated.

–Vinod Joseph

Any significant venture such as writing a book entails a lot of support from family and friends. First and foremost, thanks to Vinod, my friend and co-author for reaching out to me with the idea. The need for a book such as this was clear, and the task of writing significant and challenging. Vinod's confidence and persuasion were the basis for this collaborative effort.

My gratitude goes out to Swati, my wife, for her constant encouragement and support, and for getting a lot of mundane things out of my way during this writing process. And thanks to my friend Amit Kumar Dash, for his assistance in the course of this project.

–Srinivas Mulugu

Overview of IP Multicast

1.1 INTRODUCTION

Welcome to the world of IP Multicast and more important Multicast-based Virtual Private Networks (MVPNs). The objective of this book is to provide detailed information about existing Multicast and MVPN standards—the most recent are referred to as next-generation Multicast-based standards, Multicast Applications, and case studies with detailed configurations. Whenever a given topic of an advanced nature is discussed, the best way to relate to it is by looking at a relevant piece of configuration or a case study. That is exactly what we have done in this book with the three vendors: Juniper, Cisco, and Alcatel-Lucent. Therefore, a given illustration might contain a configuration of JUNOS, TiMOS (Alcatel's OS), or Cisco IOS, and each of the configurations will be explained in great detail. The reason we chose various vendor configurations instead of just one is to provide diversity. Also, the intent of this book is to tell you where the industry at large is moving to, not to be vendor centric. As engineers, technical managers, and visionaries in building next-generation IP Multicast infrastructures, we are more interested in standards and areas where there is consensus rather than looking at proprietary implementations. The illustrations provided in this book do not represent a given vendor's hardware or software unless explicitly mentioned. Therefore, do not assume that a particular illustration is relevant to any one vendor. Similarly, a configuration template provided regarding a solution/technology does not necessarily indicate that the implementation is only supported by that vendor. Specific details on a vendor's unique implementation of a standard or Internet Engineering Task Force (IETF) draft will be explicitly mentioned. With this short introduction, We will continue on with this interesting journey.

1.1.1 Overview of IP Multicast

Some of the information provided in this chapter will be repeated in other chapters to refresh our memories and provide the relevance needed for that specific chapter. Traditional IP communications allow a host to send packets to another host (unicast transmissions) or to all hosts (broadcast transmissions). IP Multicast provides a third communication alternative—allowing a host to send packets to a group made up of a subset of the hosts on the network. IP Multicast is a bandwidth-conserving technology specifically designed to reduce traffic by simultaneously delivering a single stream of information to potentially thousands of corporate recipients or homes. There are three modes of communication: Unicast, Broadcast, and Multicast (see Figure 1.1).

By replacing copies for all recipients with the delivery of a single stream of information, IP Multicast is able to minimize the burden on both sending and receiving hosts and reduce overall network traffic. Within a multicast network, routers are responsible for replicating and distributing multicast content to all hosts listening to a particular multicast group. Routers employ Protocol

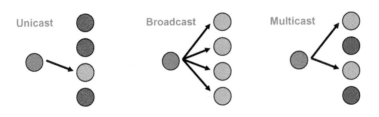

FIGURE 1.1

Independent Multicast (PIM) to build distribution trees for transmitting multicast content, resulting in the most efficient delivery of data to multiple receivers. Alternatives to IP Multicast require the source to send more than one copy of the data. Traditional application-level unicast, for example, requires the source to transmit one copy for each individual receiver in the group. There are two scenarios: without Multicast in the network and traffic delivery with Multicast (see Figure 1.2).

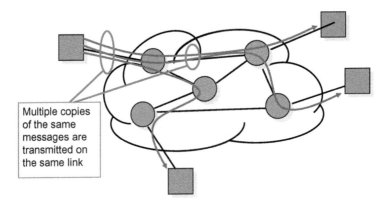

FIGURE 1.2

The same scenario changes when there is Multicast in the network. This is illustrated in Figure 1.3. IP Multicast solutions offer benefits relating to the conservation of network bandwidth. In a high-bandwidth application, such as MPEG video, IP Multicast can benefit situations with only a few receivers, because video streams would otherwise consume a large portion of the available network bandwidth. Even for low-bandwidth applications, IP Multicast conserves resources when transmissions involve thousands of receivers. Additionally, IP Multicast is the only non-broadcasting alternative for situations that require simultaneously sending information to more than one receiver. For low-bandwidth applications, an alternative to IP Multicast could involve replicating data at the source. This solution, however, can deteriorate application performance, introduce latencies and variable delays that impact users and applications, and require expensive servers to manage the replications and data distribution. Such solutions also result in multiple transmissions of the same content, consuming an enormous amount of network bandwidth. For most high-bandwidth applications, these same issues make IP Multicast the only viable option. Today, many applications take advantage of multicast, as shown in Figure 1.4. Other applications that take advantage of IP Multicast include:

- Corporate communications
- Consumer television and music channel delivery
- Distance learning (e.g., e-learning) and white-boarding solutions
- IP surveillance systems
- Interactive gaming

With support for multicast at the network layer:

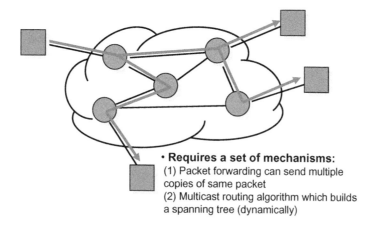

• **Requires a set of mechanisms:**
(1) Packet forwarding can send multiple copies of same packet
(2) Multicast routing algorithm which builds a spanning tree (dynamically)

FIGURE 1.3

	Real Time	Non-Real Time

Multimedia	• IPTV
	• Live Video
	• Videoconferencing
	• Live Internet Audio
		• Replication
		  – Video,
		    Web Servers,
		    Kiosks
		• Content Delivery

Data-Only	• Stock Quotes • News Feeds • White-Boarding • Interactive Gaming	• Information Delivery • Server to Server, Server to Desktop • Database Replication • Software Distribution

FIGURE 1.4

IP Multicast is also supported in

- IPv4 networks
- IPv6 networks
- Multiprotocol Label Switching (MPLS) VPNs
- Mobile and wireless networks

IP Multicast capabilities can be deployed using a variety of different protocols, conventions, and considerations suited to the different network environments just mentioned. Multicast services can also be deployed across multiple protocol platforms and domains within the same network. By implementing native IP Multicast functionality inside MPLS VPN networks, service providers can more efficiently deliver bandwidth-intensive streaming services such as telecommuting, videoconferencing, e-learning, and a host of other business applications. Multicast VPN technology eliminates the packet replication and performance issues associated with the traffic relating to these applications. Multicast MPLS VPNs further benefit service providers by

- Minimizing configuration time and complexity; configuration is required only at edge routers
- Ensuring transparency of the service provider network
- Providing the ability to easily build advanced enterprise-friendly services such as Virtual Multicast Networks
- Increasing network scalability

IP Multicast can work with Mobile Networks. An IP Mobility platform extends the network with traditional fixed-line access to an environment that supports mobile wireless access. Multicast, from the point of IP Mobility, is a network service or application. Within an IP Mobility environment, IP Multicast can be employed to deliver content to users with wireless devices.

Over the past decade, enterprise and public sector adoption of IP Multicast-enabled applications has skyrocketed, and service providers have responded by increasingly adding multicast VPNs to service portfolios. Today, any service provider with enterprise customers must support IP Multicast to remain competitive. The deployment of video services provides further incentives for the strengthening of a service provider's multicast platform, because it offers the most efficient, cost-effective means of supporting triple-play traffic (data, voice, and video).

1.1.2 Multicast Addressing
1.1.2.1 Layer 3 Multicast Addressing

IP multicast uses the Class D range of IP addresses (224.0.0.0 through 239.255.255.255; see Figure 1.5). Within the IP multicast Class D address range, there are a number of addresses reserved by the Internet Assigned Numbers Authority (IANA). These addresses are reserved for well-known multicast protocols and applications, such as routing protocol Hellos. Examples of special and reserved Class D addresses are given in Figure 1.6. Table 1.1 summarizes the IANA allocations for the Class D range and the recommendations as per RFC 2365.

The usage of these address ranges are as follows:

- The Local Link Scope (224.0.0.0) addresses have been reserved by IANA for use by network protocol. Packets using this range are local in scope and are not forwarded by Multicast routers regardless of the TTL.

•All Class D addresses are multicast addresses:

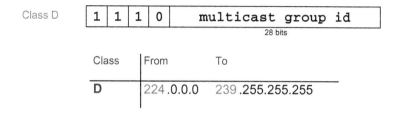

FIGURE 1.5

224.0.0.1 All systems on this subnet
224.0.0.2 All routers on this subnet
224.0.1.1 NTP (Network Time Protocol)
224.0.0.9 RIP-2 (a routing protocol)

FIGURE 1.6

Table 1.1 Summary of IANA Allocations and Recommendations for the Class D Range

Range	Usage
224.0.0.0/24	Local Link Scope
224.0.1.0–238.255.255.255	Global Scope
239.0.0.0/10	Greater than Organizational Scope (RFC 2365)
239.64.0.0/10	
239.128.0.0/10	
239.192.0.0/14	Organizational Local Scope (RFC 2365), used for MDTs [MVPN]
239.255.0.0/16	Site Local Scope (RFC 2365) used for VPN traffic

- The Global Scope (224.0.1.0–238.255.255.255) is reserved for network-wide protocols and commercial Internet multicast applications. These addresses can transit Administrative boundaries and are globally (Internet wide) unique.
- (RFC 2365) The ranges 239.0.0.0/10, 239.64.0.0/10, and 239.128.0.0/10 are unassigned and available for expansion of the Organizational Local Scope. However, these ranges should be left unassigned until the 239.192.0.0/14 space is no longer sufficient. This is to allow for the possibility that future revisions of RFC 2365 may define additional scopes on a scale larger than organizations (hence the name Greater than Organizational Scope)
- (RFC 2365) The Organizational Local Scope (239.192.0.0/14) is the space from which the Service Provider should allocate groups for the Default and Data MDTs to support multicast VPN. However, they should not be used outside the Service Provider, unless by agreement with

interconnected service providers. The multicast groups from these ranges will be used by all PE routers to identify associated MDTs for particular VPNs. The addresses in the Organizational Local Scope can be used across the Service Provider as defined by that service provider.
- (RFC 2365) The Site Local Scope (239.255.0.0/16) addresses represent applications that are confined to within local boundaries. For example, the same 239.255.0.0/16 range could be reused across all precincts in a Service Provider as long as the address was contained within that precinct. RFC 2365 states that the range must not be subdivided for use across sites; therefore all sources in that precinct will be uniquely identified within the range. The groups from this scope must not be advertised across the network into other precincts, as each precinct could use the same Site Local Scope to define local multicast services.

The following are some of the options available for the Multicast Address design within a Service Provider Network. More details on Source Specific Multicast (SSM) can be found in the following sections:

- SSM group range of 232.x.x.x
- Administratively scoped Multicast range of 239.x.x.x
- Private SSM range (part of admin scoped range) of 239.232.x.x

1.1.2.1.1 Ad Hoc Multicast Block
The multicast group range of 224.0.2.0 through 224.0.255.255 is the ad hoc multicast block. Historically, addresses in this range have been assigned to applications that do not clearly fall into the Local Network Control and Inter-Network Control categories. In general, the guidelines provided in RFC 3171bis for the assignment of addresses in this range state that the IANA should not assign addresses in this range except under very special circumstances. Even then, the assignment must undergo a strict Expert Review, IESG Approval, or Standards Action process before addresses are assigned.

1.1.2.1.2 SDP/SAP Multicast Block
The multicast group range of 224.2.0.0 through 224.2.255.255 (224.2/16) is the SDP/SAP Multicast Block, which is reserved for applications that send and receive multimedia session announcements via the Session Announcement Protocol (SAP) described in RFC 2974. An example of an application that uses SAP is the Session Directory tool (SDR), which transmits global scope SAP announcements on groups 224.2.127.254 and 224.2.127.255.

1.1.2.2 GLOP Multicast Block
This block of addresses has been assigned by the IANA as an experimental, statically assigned range of multicast addresses intended for use by Content Providers, ISPs, or anyone wishing to source content into the global Internet. This allocation methodology, called GLOP addressing, which is defined in RFC 2770, uses the multicast group range of 233.0.0.0 through 233.255.255.255 (233/8) and provides each Autonomous System (AS) with a block of 255 statically assigned multicast addresses. Content Providers who wish to transmit multicast traffic to their customers in the Internet and that have an assigned Autonomous System Number (ASN) can use multicast addresses from their block of 255 static GLOP addresses to transmit content. If the content provider does not have its own assigned ASN, it can usually lease static GLOP addresses from their ISP.

1.1.2.2.1 GLOP Addressing

In the late 1990s when native multicast was beginning to be deployed in the Internet, several Content Providers were looking to begin multicasting some of their audio and video content. Unfortunately, the state of dynamic address allocation at that time was such that no good solutions were available that permitted the Content Providers to uniquely allocate addresses. To work around this problem, an experimental form of static address allocation was proposed by the IETF. This allocation methodology, called GLOP addressing, which is defined in RFC 2770, uses the multicast group range of 233.0.0.0 through 233.255.255.255 (233/8). This block was assigned by the IANA and is an experimental, statically assigned range of multicast addresses intended for use by Content Providers, ISPs, or anyone wishing to source content into the global Internet.

GLOP addresses are constructed as follows: the high order octet is always 233 (decimal), followed by the next two octets that contain the 16-bit AS of the Content Provider, or ISP that is sourcing the multicast traffic (see Figure 1.7).

GLOP Addresses

Octet 1	Octet 2	Octet 3	Octet 4
233	16 bit AS		local bits

FIGURE 1.7

The advantage of this allocation mechanism should be obvious. For each registered AS that an entity owns, it automatically has a /24 worth of statically allocated multicast address space. No registration process is necessary since the allocation is already based on registered AS numbers.

What does the acronym GLOP stand for? It turns out that this is not an acronym at all. The original authors of this RFC needed to refer to this mechanism other than something besides "that address allocation method where you put your AS in the middle two octets." Lacking anything better to call it, one of the authors, David Meyer, simply began to refer to this as "GLOP" addressing and the name stuck.

As an example of GLOP addressing, let us assume that Company XYZ wishes to begin sourcing various live video and audio multicast streams to the global Internet as part of their service offering. If Company XYZ has a registered AS number of 2109, then they would be able to source this traffic using multicast addresses in the range of 233.8.61.0–233.8.61.255. (The decimal AS number 2109 converts to binary 100000111101, which in turn converts to 8.61. in dotted decimal format.)

It might also be the case that Company XYZ does not have a registered AS number. In that case, they could "lease" some GLOP address space from their ISP who would allocate the leased addresses from their pool of statically assigned GLOP addresses based on their registered AS number(s).

1.1.2.3 Layer 2 Multicast Addressing

The IEEE 802.2 specification makes provisions for the transmission of broadcast and/or multicast packets. As shown in Figure 1.8, Bit 0 of Octet 0 in an IEEE MAC address indicates whether the destination address is a broadcast/multicast address or a unicast address. If this bit is set, then the MAC frame is destined for either an arbitrary group of hosts or all hosts on the network (if the MAC destination address is the broadcast address, 0xFFFF.FFFF.FFFF). IP Multicasting at Layer 2 makes use of this ability to transmit IP Multicast packets to a group of hosts on an LAN segment. IP Multicast frames all use MAC layer addresses beginning with the 24-bit prefix of 0x0100.5Exx. xxxx. Unfortunately, only half of these MAC addresses are available for use by IP Multicast. This leaves 23 bits of MAC address space for mapping Layer 3 IP Multicast addresses into Layer 2 MAC addresses. Since all Layer 3 IP Multicast addresses have the first 4 of the 32 bits set to 0x1110, this leaves 28 bits of meaningful IP Multicast address information. These 28 bits must map into only 23 bits of the available MAC address. This mapping is shown graphically in Figure 1.9. Since all 28 bits of the Layer 3 IP Multicast address information cannot be mapped into the available 23 bits of MAC address space, 5 bits of address information are lost in the mapping process. This results in a 32:1 address ambiguity when a Layer 3 IP Multicast address is mapped to a Layer 2 IEEE MAC address. This means that each IEEE IP Multicast MAC address can represent 32 IP Multicast addresses as shown in Figure 1.10. It should be obvious that this 32:1 address ambiguity has the potential to cause

IEEE 802.2 MAC Address Format

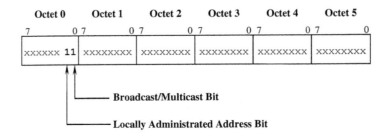

FIGURE 1.8

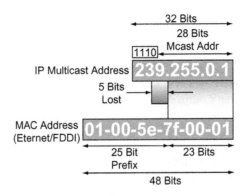

FIGURE 1.9

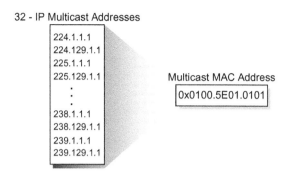

32 - IP Multicast Addresses

224.1.1.1
224.129.1.1
225.1.1.1
225.129.1.1
  :
  :
238.1.1.1
238.129.1.1
239.1.1.1
239.129.1.1

Multicast MAC Address

0x0100.5E01.0101

FIGURE 1.10

some problems. For example, a host that wishes to receive multicast group 224.1.1.1 will program the hardware registers in the network interface card (NIC) to interrupt the CPU when a frame with a destination multicast MAC address of 0x0100.5E00.0101 is received. Unfortunately, this same multicast MAC address is also used for 31 other IP Multicast groups. If any of these 31 other groups are also active on the LAN, the host's CPU will receive interrupts any time a frame is received for any of these other groups. The CPU will have to examine the IP portion of each of these received frames to determine if it is the desired group such as 224.1.1.1. This can have an impact on the host's available CPU power if the amount of "spurious" group traffic is high enough.

IGMP Snooping is normally used by Layer 2 switches to constrain multicast traffic to only those ports that have hosts attached and who have signaled their desire to join the multicast group by sending IGMP Membership Reports. However, it is important to note that most Layer 2 switches flood all multicast traffic that falls within the MAC address range of 0x0100.5E00.00xx (which corresponds to Layer 3 addresses in the Link-Local block) to all ports on the switch even if IGMP Snooping is enabled. The reason that this Link-Local multicast traffic is always flooded is that IGMP Membership Reports are normally never sent for multicast traffic in the Link-Local block. For example, routers do not send IGMP Membership Reports for the ALL-OSPF-ROUTERS group (224.0.0.5) when OSPF is enabled. Therefore, if Layer 2 switches were to constrain (i.e., not flood) Link-Local packets in the 224.0.0.0/24 (0x0100.5E00.00xx) range to only those ports where IGMP Membership reports were received, Link-Local protocols such as OSPF would break. The impact of this Link-Local flooding in combination with the 32:1 ambiguity that arises when Layer 3 multicast addresses are mapped to Layer 2 MAC addresses means that there are several multicast group ranges besides the 224.0.0.0/24 that will map to the 0x0100.5E00.00xx MAC address range and hence will be also be flooded by most Layer 2 switches. *It is therefore recommended that multicast addresses that map to the 0x0100.5E00.00xx MAC address range not be used.* The following lists all multicast address ranges that should not be used if Layer 2 flooding is to be avoided. These entire Multicast addresses map to 0x0100.5E00.00xx range

- 224.0.0.0/24 and 224.128.0.0/24
- 225.0.0.0/24 and 225.128.0.0/24
- 226.0.0.0/24 and 226.128.0.0/24

- 227.0.0.0/24 and 227.128.0.0/24
- 228.0.0.0/24 and 228.128.0.0/24
- 229.0.0.0/24 and 229.128.0.0/24
- 230.0.0.0/24 and 230.128.0.0/24
- 231.0.0.0/24 and 231.128.0.0/24
- 232.0.0.0/24 and 232.128.0.0/24
- 233.0.0.0/24 and 233.128.0.0/24
- 234.0.0.0/24 and 234.128.0.0/24
- 235.0.0.0/24 and 235.128.0.0/24
- 236.0.0.0/24 and 236.128.0.0/24
- 237.0.0.0/24 and 237.128.0.0/24
- 238.0.0.0/24 and 238.128.0.0/24
- 239.0.0.0/24 and 239.128.0.0/24

1.1.3 Internet Group Management Protocol

The Internet Group Management Protocol (IGMP) is an industry-standard protocol for managing IPv4 multicast group membership. It is used to dynamically register individual hosts in a multicast group on a particular LAN. Hosts identify group memberships by sending IGMP messages to their local multicast router. Under IGMP, routers listen to IGMP messages and periodically send out queries to discover which groups are active or inactive on a particular subnet. The various IGMP versions are

- IGMPv1—Provides host mechanisms for joining groups and reporting group membership, as well as a router mechanism for periodically querying for group membership
- IGMPv2—Provides all of the mechanisms of IGMPv1, as well as a host mechanism for leaving a multicast group, and a router mechanism for sending group-specific membership queries
- IGMPv3—Standard for managing multicast group membership, including support for SSM, which allows hosts to join multicast streams on a per-source basis

1.1.3.1 IGMP Join

IGMP reports/joins are the means by which end hosts such as set-top boxes (STBs) request broadcast channels on a particular Multicast address. Either IGMPv2 or IGMPv3 must be supported on IP STBs in an IPTV environment. An IGMPv2 join is a (*, G) join, whereas an IGMPv3 join also includes source information for the multicast group that is being joined.

1.1.3.2 IGMP Leave

IGMP leave reports are the means by which end hosts such as IP STBs inform the Layer 3 edge device that they are no longer interested in receiving a broadcast channel. When a channel is changed or selected on the STB, it sends an IGMP leave for the channel being watched and sends an IGMP join to the new channel.

1.1.3.3 IGMP Fast-Leave Processing

IGMP snooping fast-leave processing allows IGMP snooping to remove a Layer 2 LAN interface from the forwarding-table entry of a switch without first sending out IGMP group-specific queries.

This improves the leave latency, which helps reduce the channel-change time. This feature should be enabled only when there is just one receiver connected behind the Layer 2 interface. This is done because if more than one receiver is connected on this port and if both of them are watching the same channel, then a leave on one STB will cause a leave on the other STB. This feature may therefore be enabled on a residential gateway when there is only one receiver per port.

1.1.3.4 IGMP Proxy Reporting

IGMP supports proxy reporting for IGMP messages. In proxy reporting mode, the switch/DSLAM terminates the reports from the STB and forwards only one report for a channel to the upstream router. This feature is also enabled on the residential gateway (RG) in routed mode.

1.1.3.5 IGMP Host Tracking

IGMPv3 supports explicit tracking of membership information on any port. The explicit-tracking database is used for fast-leave processing for IGMPv3 hosts, proxy reporting, and statistics collection. The main benefit of this feature allows minimal leave latencies when a host leaves a multicast group or channel. A router configured with IGMPv3 and explicit tracking can immediately stop forwarding traffic if the last STB to request to receive a broadcast channel (multicast group) from the router indicates that it no longer wants to receive the channel. The leave latency is thus bound only by the packet transmission latencies in the multi-access network and the processing time in the router. In IGMP Version 2, when a router receives an IGMP leave message from a host, it must first send an IGMP group-specific query to learn if other hosts on the same multi-access network are still requesting to receive traffic. If after a specific time no host replies to the query, the router will then stop forwarding the traffic. This query process is required because, in IGMPv2, membership reports are suppressed if the same report has already been sent by another host in the network. Therefore, it is impossible for the router to reliably know how many hosts on a multi-access network are requesting to receive traffic. An IGMP query with a response is illustrated in Figure 1.11.

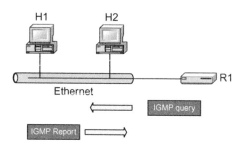

FIGURE 1.11

1.1.3.6 Static IGMP Joins

Static IGMP joins can enable at the network edge to enable the multicast stream to be always available at the respective location. This would help accelerate the channel change time. It is recommended that the Static IGMP configurations are performed only for the most frequently watched channels to ensure optimal bandwidth usage.

1.1.4 Protocol Independent Multicast

The most popular and widely deployed multicast protocol is PIM. Unlike other multicast routing protocols such as Distance Vector Multicast Routing Protocol (DVRMP) or Multicast Open Shortest Path First (MOSPF), PIM does not maintain a separate multicast routing table; instead it relies on the existing Internet Gateway Protocol (IGP) table when performing its Reverse Path Forwarding (RPF) check. Because PIM does not have to perform multicast routing updates, its overhead is significantly less when compared to other multicast protocols. The main versions of the PIM protocol are in current use, all of which are control plane protocols:

- PIM Dense Mode
- PIM Sparse Mode
- PIM Sparse-Dense Mode
- PIM SSM
- Bidirectional PIM

1.1.4.1 PIM Dense Mode

PIM Dense Mode (PIM-DM) uses a flood and prune mechanism. When a source sends to an IP Multicast group address, each router that receives the packet will create an (S, G) forwarding state entry. The receiving router will initially forward the multicast packet out eligible output interfaces that

- Pass the RPF check
- Have either IGMP receivers present or PIM neighbors

To pass the RPF check, an incoming multicast packet must be received on an interface that the IGP routing table indicates the source (of the multicast packet) is reachable from. Independence from a multicast routing protocol is where PIM derives its name. The concept of RPF is illustrated in Figure 1.12.

Note that multicast-enabled interfaces must have the corresponding unicast source routes in the IGP to avoid black holes. In a situation where equal cost paths exist, the unicast route with the highest upstream neighbor IP address is chosen. Also, when there are multiple routers sending on to the same subnet, a PIM assert process is triggered to elect a single designated router (DR) to be the sole forwarder to avoid duplicate frames. When a state is created according to the RPF check, a source tree or shortest path tree (SPT) is developed with the source at the root or first hop router. Multicast packets following the tree take the optimal path through a network and packets are not duplicated over the same subnets. The state created in the routers is referred to as "source comma group" or (S, G), and the routers forwarding interfaces are referred to as an outgoing interface list (OIL). Leaf routers or last hop routers with no receivers then prune back from the tree; however, OILs in the upstream neighbor are maintained. These entries periodically (every 3 minutes) move into a forwarding state and the prune process recurs. PIM-DM is usually not suitable for a large network deployment. PIM-DM is illustrated in Figure 1.13.

- RPF builds a shortest path tree in a distributed fashion by taking advantage of the unicast routing tables.
- **Main concept:** Given the address of the root of the tree (e.g., the sending host), a router selects as its upstream neighbor in the tree the router which is the next-hop neighbor for forwarding unicast packets to the root.

- This concept leads to a **reverse shortest path** from any router to the sending host. The union of reverse shortest paths builds a **reverse shortest path tree**.

  RPF Forwarding:
    Forward a packet
    only if it is received
    from an RPF neighbor

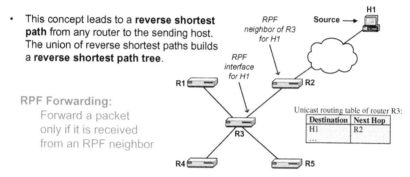

FIGURE 1.12

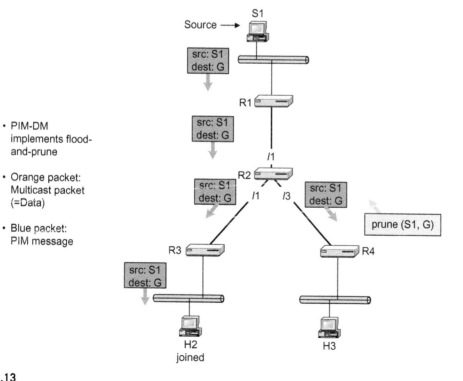

- PIM-DM implements flood-and-prune

- Orange packet: Multicast packet (=Data)

- Blue packet: PIM message

FIGURE 1.13

1.1.4.2 PIM Sparse Mode

PIM Sparse Mode (PIM-SM) uses an explicit join model, where only routers with active receivers will join multicast groups. This has obvious advantages over the flood and prune mechanism deployed in PIM-DM. PIM-SM uses a control point known as Rendezvous Point (RP), which can be viewed as an exchange where receivers and sources can meet. First hop designated routers (the routers with sources attached) register the sources to the RP. When the RP sees the source traffic coming in it will build an SPT back to the source; hence there will be (S, G) state entries between the RP and the source. The last hop designated routers (the routers with the receivers attached) join to the RP hop by hop, creating a shared tree (*, G) with the "*" meaning any source. The RPF check is modified to include the RP for (*, G) entries, whereas the source is used for (S, G) entries. When a source starts transmitting, the initial multicast traffic flows to the RP via an SPT and then down to the receivers for that group via a shared tree (with the RP being the root). This may result in a non-optimal path being created to a receiver depending where the RP is positioned. The operation of a shared tree is shown in Figure 1.14, and has the following characteristics:

- Root is a common point known as the Rendezvous Point (RP)
- The RP can support many multicast groups
- Receivers join RP to learn of sources
- Sources only transmit to RP
- RP forwards traffic from source to receivers

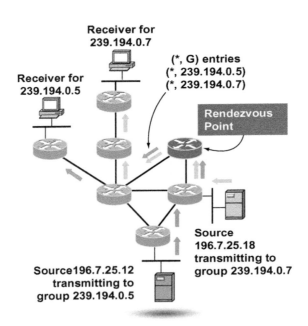

FIGURE 1.14

- Forwarding entries represented as (*, G)
- Less state required at the expense of optimal routing

In Figure 1.14, two receivers are listening for the groups 239.194.0.5 and 239.194.0.7, respectively. The receivers both join the same tree rooted at the source 196.7.25.12. The two groups are associated with different sources: 196.7.25.12 and 196.7.25.18. These sources will transmit their traffic to the RP which will then send the traffic down the shared tree to the receivers. An (*, G) entry in each router along the path represents the distribution tree for each multicast group. To address this problem, a mechanism known as SPT switchover can be used. The last hop router, depending on the traffic rate, sends an (S, G) join toward the source to create an optimal SPT forwarding path, and once established sends RP prunes toward the RP. The decision to create an SPT to the source is dependent upon the SPT-threshold in terms of bandwidth. Most routers have this threshold set to 0; therefore, all traffic received via the RP will be switched to an SPT to the source after the initial flood of packets. This facilitates the creation of a source tree. Source Trees are unidirectional trees rooted at the data source. Traffic flows from the source (at the root) to each receiver (at the leaves) using the shortest possible path. A source tree is also known as a shortest path tree. The operation of a source tree is shown in Figure 1.15 and has the following characteristics:

- Simplest form of tree, but receiver requires knowledge of source address
- Traffic travels from source (root) to receivers (leaves)
- Shortest path taken
- Packets replicated at each bifurcation point
- Forwarding entry states represented as (S, G)—(Source IP, Group IP)
- Provides optimal routing at the expense of more state (S, G)

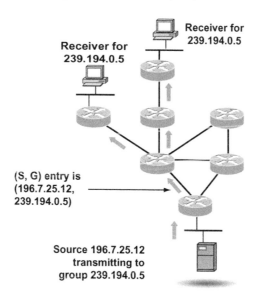

FIGURE 1.15

In Figure 1.15 two receivers are listening for the group 239.194.0.5. They both join the same tree rooted at the source 196.7.25.12. An (S, G) entry in each router along the path represents the distribution tree.

By using PIM-SM, the inefficient flood and prune of PIM-DM is not required. Some state maintenance is still required, albeit in a more controlled manner; for example, the RP sends periodic joins toward the source, and last hop routers send periodic joins/prunes toward the RP to maintain (S, G) entries.

1.1.4.3 PIM Sparse-Dense Mode

This mode is a combination of both of the previous modes. The decision to use sparse or dense mode for a particular multicast group depends on whether a group has a matching entry in the Group-to-RP mapping cache. If an entry exists in the cache, then that group operates in sparse mode on that interface. If the multicast group does not have a corresponding entry in the mapping cache, then that group operates in dense mode.

1.1.4.4 PIM Source Specific Multicast

The Source Specific Multicast feature is an extension of IP Multicast where datagram traffic is forwarded to receivers from only those multicast sources to which the receivers have explicitly joined. For multicast groups configured for SSM, only source-specific multicast distribution trees (no shared trees) are created, that is, (S, G) versus (*, G) state. The current IP Multicast infrastructure in the Internet and many enterprise intranets is based on the PIM-SM protocol and Multicast Source Discovery Protocol (MSDP; see Section 1.1.4.7.1). These protocols have proven to be reliable, extensive, and efficient. However, they are bound to the complexity and functionality limitations of the Internet Standard Multicast (ISM) service model. For example, with ISM, the network must maintain knowledge about which hosts in the network are actively sending multicast traffic. With SSM, this information is provided by receivers through the source address(es) relayed to the last hop routers by features such as IGMPv3lite or URL Rendezvous Directory (URD). It is also possible to utilize the SSM-map feature in the network devices, which allows a device to automatically determine the source of a given group, even when the received IGMP message is in the v2 format. SSM is the ideal choice for IPTV deployments. In SSM, delivery of datagrams is based on (S, G) channels. Traffic for one (S, G) channel consists of datagrams with an IP unicast source address S and the multicast group address G as the IP destination address. Systems will receive this traffic by becoming members of the (S, G) channel. In both SSM and ISM, no signaling is required to become a source. However, in SSM, receivers must subscribe or unsubscribe to (S, G) channels to receive or not receive traffic from specific sources. In other words, receivers can receive traffic only from (S, G) channels that they are subscribed to, whereas in ISM, receivers do not need to know the IP addresses of sources from which they receive their traffic. The proposed standard approach for channel subscription signaling utilizes IGMP INCLUDE mode membership reports, which are only supported in Version 3 of IGMP. The following benefits make SSM the preferred best practice for video-over-IP applications:

- Internet broadcast services can be provided through SSM without the need for unique IP Multicast addresses. This allows content providers to easily offer their service. IP Multicast address allocation has been a serious problem for Content Providers in the past, and SSM helps provide simpler address management.

- The large numbers of receivers make broadcast video a common target for attacks. SSM provides greater security and prevents Denial of Service (DoS) attacks due to explicit mapping of sources to Groups (as in the case of SSM with IGMPv3 and SSM-mapping for IGMPv2).
- SSM is relatively easy to implement and maintain (RP configuration not required). Additionally, the control plane for SSM is very simple, and mechanisms such as SPT switchover/threshold are not applicable.
- Inter-AS deployments are simpler when using PIM SSM and this assists in forwarding content between multiple independent PIM domains (because there is no need to manage MSDP for SSM between PIM domains).

PIM-SSM Mapping is required for hosts/PCs that do not support IGMPv3 but support IGMPv2. The operation is as follows. The Layer 3 edge router will implement the SSM Mapping feature to perform a proxy service on behalf of the host. In operation, the Layer 3 edge router will receive a (*, G) IGMP-Join from the DSLAM/Access Node. The (*, G) IGMP-Join will be translated into an (S,G) PIM-Join request. The source to be specified will be derived by static ACL mappings on each first hop router. The (S, G) PIM-Join will then be directed toward the relevant source and the Group's traffic will flow toward the receiver.

PIM-SSM for IGMPv2 could be done using either Static maps or using DNS configuration.

Static PIM-SSM mapping can be configured on the Layer 3 Access (or L3 PE Aggregation device if the Access is a Layer 2 device) of the IPTV network to convert the IGMPv2 joins to PIM joins to the respective Video source. PIM-SM is configured on the relevant interfaces on all devices in Core ring, Aggregation, Access rings, and the Video Headend routers. Some sample Cisco IOS configurations illustrating "Static SSM-Mapping" and "DNS SSM-Mapping" are provided below.

```
ip multicast-routing
ip multicast multipath
!
ip igmp ssm-map enable
no ip igmp ssm-map query dns
ip pim ssm range <ACL 10>
ip igmp ssm-map static <ACL 15> <Video Source Unicast Addr>
!
access-list 10 permit <Mcast Group range, say, 232.1.0.0 0.0.255.255>
access-list 15 permit <Mcast Group range, say, 232.1.1.0 0.0.0.255>
```

If DNS-based SSM mapping is configured, the router constructs a domain name that includes the group address and performs a lookup into the DNS. The router looks up IP A RR (IP address resource records) to be returned for this constructed domain name and uses the returned IP addresses as the source addresses associated with this group.

```
ip multicast-routing
ip multicast multipath
!
ip domain multicast <domain name>
ip domain-name <domain name>
ip name-server <DNS Server IP Addr>
!
```

```
ip multicast-routing
ip igmp ssm-map enable
ip igmp ssm-map query dns
!
ip pim ssm range <ACL 10>
!
access-list 10 permit <Group range, say, 232.1.0.0 0.0.255.255>
```

- The following configuration parameters needs to be added on the DNS Server: Resource records for the first multicast IP address associated with a source
- All other multicast IP addresses from the same source
- The multicast domain
- The time-out (optional)

The DNS server will have to be configured to be able to look up one or more source addresses for the Customer groups. The records shown in the following illustration below will need to be added to the configuration file of the appropriate zone. The time-out argument configures the length of time for which the router performing SSM mapping will cache the DNS lookup. This argument is optional and defaults to the time-out of the zone in which this entry is configured. The time-out indicates how long the router will keep the current mapping before querying the DNS server for this group. It is suggested to configure the time-out for each group, as it defaults to 86,400 seconds (1 day).

```
1.1.1.232.ssm-map <timeout> IN A <Video Source IP Addr1>
2.1.1.232.ssm-map <timeout> IN A <Video Source IP Addr2>
3.1.1.232.ssm-map <timeout> IN A <Video Source IP Addr3>
```

With SSM addressing the multicast group range of 232.0.0.0 through 232.255.255.255 (232/8) is the Source Specific Multicast Block, which is reserved for (oddly enough) Source Specific Multicast. SSM is a new extension to PIM-SM that eliminates the need for the RP and the Shared Tree and only uses the SPT to the desired source(s).

A key premise of SSM is that it is the host application program's responsibility to determine the active source IP address and group multicast address of the desired multicast flow. The host then signals the router via IGMPv3 exactly which specific source (hence the name Source Specific Multicast) and group that it wishes to receive. Since PIM-SM does not use an RP or a Shared Tree in the 232/8 range, a host will only receive traffic from sources that it has specifically requested. This eliminates interference or DoS attacks from unwanted sources sending to the same multicast group. Furthermore, the lack of Shared Trees in the SSM range means two different sources in the Internet can source traffic to the same group address in the 232/8 range and not have to worry about having a group address conflict. The reason there is no conflict is that the hosts join only the SPT of the desired source. Therefore, one host can receive Stock Quotes from (S1, 232.1.1.1) while another host can be watching live video from (S2, 232.1.1.1), since separate SPTs are being used and no common Shared Tree exists that might accidentally deliver the unwanted source.

1.1.4.4.1 Private Source Specific Mapping—Administratively Scoped

At the request of the IETF, the IANA has reserved the group range of 232/8 for SSM. Because this range falls outside the 239/8 private address space, it might be erroneously assumed that SSM was intended for use in only the global Internet scope. However, this is not true as SSM has numerous advantages that simplify and improve multicast security and scalability. Thus, application developers and network administrators should consider deploying SSM within the Enterprise network. Once the decision to deploy SSM within the Enterprise network has been made, the combination of SSM and Administrative Scope poses some interesting scenarios. First, the network administrator must decide which address range(s) is (are) to be enabled for SSM mode within the network. If we desire to either send or receive SSM traffic to/from the global Internet, the default range of 232/8 must be enabled for SSM. However, assume the network administrator also wishes to support SSM at some scope smaller than the global Internet scope, such as at the Enterprise (Organization-Local) scope or even smaller scopes within the Enterprise network. Due to the way SSM works, there is no reason that the same 232/8 SSM address range could not be used by SSM applications within the Enterprise network for a private, Enterprise-only SSM multicast. However, if this approach is taken it is very difficult to configure the boundary routers at the edge of the Enterprise to prevent hosts outside of the network from joining the SPT for an internal SSM session in the 232/8 range while allowing other public SSM sessions to cross the boundary. Therefore, it is better to dedicate a portion of the private 239/8 address space for an Organization-Local SSM scope for private SSM traffic inside the Enterprise network. This will allow the 239/8 multicast boundary that is normally configured at the edge of the Enterprise network to prevent private SSM traffic from leaving the network. Additionally, assume that the network administrator also wishes to establish other SSM scopes that are smaller than the Organization-Local SSM scope just described. These smaller SSM scopes would restrict SSM traffic from crossing an SSM scope boundary. The recommended method is to allocate the 239.232.0.0/16 address space from the Site-Local Expansion block for private SSM multicast. Continuing with our previous example, this results in the Private SSM block allocated as shown in the address map in Figure 1.16.

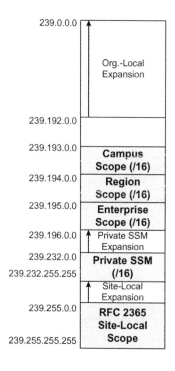

FIGURE 1.16

The Private SSM block can then be subdivided into smaller blocks for SSM scopes that correspond to our Region and Campus scopes as shown in Figure 1.16. Notice that the Enterprise SSM scope is allocated from the top of the Private SSM block at 239.255.0.0/24, and the Region and Campus scopes are also /24 ranges allocated from the Private SSM block immediately below the Enterprise SSM range. The approach used in this example has the advantage that the configuration for the SSM address range in each router in the network remains constant (ranges 232/8 and 239.232/16) even if new SSM scopes are defined later. The size of these SSM scope group ranges is only a suggestion and individual network administrators may use different group range sizes as desired. The choice of a /24 allocation for each of the SSM scopes was made to make the ranges fall on an octet boundary to keep the address masks simple. Smaller mask sizes can be used (i.e., /20 masks) if additional addresses are desired in each of the SSM scopes. However, keep in mind that one of the key advantages of SSM is that multiple sources can use the same group address without causing their traffic to be merged. (That is because SSM does not use a Shared Tree and only SPTs are used.) This means that the number of addresses in an SSM range is much less critical than for other PIM multicast modes such as classic PIM-SM (aka Any Source Multicast; ASM) or Bidirectional PIM.

Finally, Figure 1.17 illustrates the Enterprise, Region, and Campus SSM scope ranges in order according to their decreasing scope size. However, this is not mandatory and these SSM scope ranges may be allocated in any order.

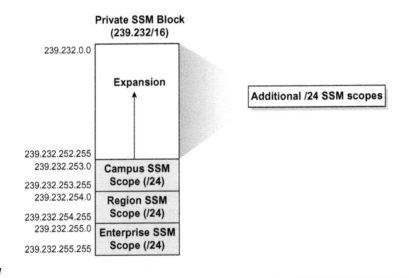

FIGURE 1.17

1.1.4.5 Bidirectional PIM

Normally, distribution trees are unidirectional, which means the data flows down the tree toward the receivers and control traffic flows up the tree toward the source. PIM Bi-Dir will create a two-way forwarding tree, which allows the efficient transmission of low bandwidth many-to-many communication (e.g., a financial trading application up and down the tree). This means that sources and receivers downstream from the RP do not have to transit the RP. Figure 1.18 shows an example of a bidirectional shared tree. Traffic from 196.7.25.18 and 239.194.0.7 can travel down the tree to the RP (and receivers beyond) and also up the tree away from the RP.

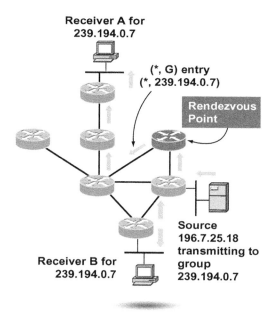

FIGURE 1.18

1.1.4.6 Rendezvous Points
Rendezvous Points are required to allow the receivers to find sources and join the shared tree in the multicast network.

1.1.4.6.1 Auto-RP
Auto-RP can be used to provide the RP to a multicast group discovery mechanism for the core multicast in a Service Provider network. Static RP configurations identifying RP to Group Mapping may also be used. Briefly, there are two parts to Auto-RP: Candidate RPs and Mapping Agents. Candidate RPs advertise their intention to be an RP for multicast groups using multicast messages. Mapping Agents see these multicast messages and are tasked with selecting the best RP to use (if more than one is advertising for a group or range of groups). Once the best RPs are selected (i.e., the one that has the highest IP address for the group advertised), the Mapping Agents multicast discovery messages to all multicast routers such as which RPs to use for which multicast groups. Each multicast router then builds a Group-to-RP mapping table.

1.1.4.6.2 RP Placement
As a general rule, RPs are usually located close to the sources, particularly if many sources are situated together. If the receivers are located close together then the RPs can be situated near them.

However, this is not an absolute requirement in multicast networks, and the default behavior for last hop routers (the ones closest to a receiver) will always build an SPT directly to the source after the initial receipt of multicast data from the RP.

This happens because the SPT-Threshold is set to 0 by default, which forces the last hop router to immediately join the SPT to the source. In many cases, the RP will not be part of the tree (between receiver and source), and its function is mainly as an exchange or meeting place between receiver and source.

1.1.4.7 Anycast RP

Anycast RP is a useful application of MSDP (explained in the next section) and can be used within a Service Provider network for scaling purposes. Originally developed for inter-domain multicast applications, MSDP used for Anycast RP is an intra-domain feature that provides redundancy and load-sharing capabilities for RPs. Service providers and Enterprise customers typically use Anycast RP for configuring a PIM-SM network to meet fault tolerance requirements within a single multicast domain. The following section includes a brief explanation of MSDP.

1.1.4.7.1 Multicast Source Distribution Protocol

Multicast Source Distribution Protocol (MSDP) is a mechanism that allows RPs to share information about active sources. RPs know about the receivers in their local domain. When RPs in remote domains hear about the active sources, they can pass on that information to their local receivers and multicast data can then be forwarded between the domains. A useful feature of MSDP is that it allows each domain to maintain an independent RP that does not rely on other domains but enables RPs to forward traffic between domains. PIM-SM is used to forward the traffic between the multicast domains. The RP in each domain establishes an MSDP peering session using a TCP connection with the RPs in other domains or with border routers leading to the other domains. When the RP learns about a new multicast source within its own domain (through the normal PIM register mechanism), the RP encapsulates the first data packet in a Source-Active (SA) message and sends the SA to all MSDP peers. The SA is forwarded by each receiving peer using a modified RPF check, until the SA reaches every MSDP router in the interconnected networks—theoretically the entire multicast Internet. If the receiving MSDP peer is an RP, and the RP has a (*, G) entry for the group in the SA (there is an interested receiver), the RP creates an (S, G) state for the source and joins to the SPT for the source. The encapsulated data is decapsulated and forwarded down the shared tree of that RP. When the packet is received by the last hop router of the receiver, the last hop router also may join the SPT to the source. The MSDP speaker periodically sends SAs that include all sources within the own domain of the RP. Figure 1.19 provides details about MSDP operations.

The operation that occurs when a receiver is interested is shown in Figure 1.20.

1.1.4.7.2 MSDP Application in Anycast RP

As discussed in the previous section, MSDP was developed to allow RPs in different domains (e.g., domains between service providers) to learn about active global sources inside those domains. By using MSDP, a service provider only has to manage its own RPs. MSDP is primarily used in an *inter-domain* environment; however, it can also be applied in an *intra-domain* environment to provide redundancy and load-sharing capabilities to RPs. This feature is referred to as Anycast RP. Essentially Anycast RP allows a group of RPs on the same network (e.g., Service Provider) to use the *same* loopback address. The loopback address of the RPs will be learned by multicast routers using the normal

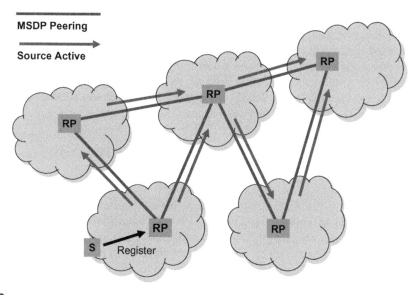

FIGURE 1.19

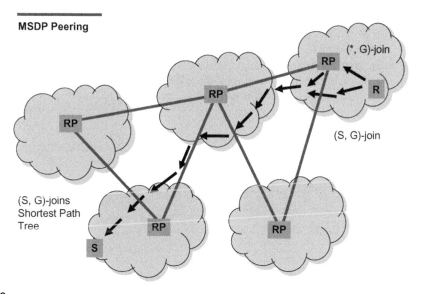

FIGURE 1.20

methods of static configurations or Auto-RP. The result is that all multicast routers will receive one RP address group regardless of the number of RPs that are advertising these groups. Although there will be more than one RP using the same IP address, the routing protocol will choose the RP closest to each source and/or receiver. Using a common RP address across many RPs allows sources and receivers to be evenly distributed across the network therefore providing a form of load sharing. Because it is possible that a source may register with one RP and a receiver may join a different RP, MSDP must be used between the RPs to indicate an active source to receivers. In Anycast RP, the RPs are configured to be peers of each other. When a source registers with one RP, an SA message will be sent to other RPs. The result is that all RPs will be aware of the sources that are active. In the event of a failure of an RP, the routing protocol will converge and the next closest RP would be selected for subsequent source register and receiver join requests.

1.1.5 Multicast Admission Control Mechanisms

1.1.5.1 IGMP Limit

A Service Provider can enforce a maximum broadcast bandwidth limit by limiting the number of IGMP joins on the ranges of multicast addresses associated with broadcast video to a configured maximum on the aggregation links that the router controls. Once again, we look at a Cisco IOS configuration for illustrative purposes. The `ip igmp limit` command can be used to configure a limit on the number of IGMP states resulting from IGMP membership reports on a per-system or per-interface basis. It controls the maximum number of IGMP states allowed on a router or interface. Membership reports sent after the configured limits have been exceeded are not entered in the IGMP cache, and traffic for the excess membership reports is not forwarded. Per-interface and per-system limits operate independently of each other and can enforce different configured limits. A membership state will be ignored if it exceeds either the per-interface limit or global limit. If you do not configure the `except access-list` keyword and argument, all IGMP states resulting from IGMP are counted toward the configured cache limit on an interface. The `except access-list` keyword and argument exclude particular groups or channels from counting toward the IGMP cache limit. An IGMP membership report is counted against the per-interface limit if it is permitted by the extended access list specified by the `except access-list` keyword and argument.

```
!
ip igmp limit <number> [except access-list] (Enables per-system IGMP limit)
!
interface GigE x/y (Enables per-interface IGMP limit. DSLAM-facing intf)
      ip igmp limit <number> [except access-list]
!
```

1.1.5.2 IP Mroute Limit

The per interface mroute state limit feature provides the ability to limit the number of mroute states on an interface for different ACL-classified sets of multicast traffic. This feature can be used to prevent DoS attacks, or to provide a multicast CAC mechanism when all of the multicast flows roughly utilize the same amount of bandwidth.

The per interface mroute state limit feature essentially is a complete superset of the IGMP State Limit feature (except that it does not support a global limit). Moreover, it is more flexible and powerful (albeit more complex) than the IGMP State Limit feature, but it is not intended to be a replacement for it because there are applications that suit both features.

The per interface mroute state limit feature can be used in conjunction with the IGMP State Limit feature. If both the per interface mroute state limit feature and IGMP State Limit feature are configured on an interface, routers generally enforce both limits.

The main differences between the per interface mroute state limit feature and the IGMP Limit feature are

- The per interface mroute state limit feature allows multiple limits to be configured on an interface, whereas the IGMP state limit feature allows only one limit to be configured on an interface. The per interface mroute state limit feature, thus, is more flexible than the IGMP State Limit feature because it allows multiple limits to be configured for different sets of multicast traffic on an interface.
- The per interface mroute state limit feature can be used to limit both IGMP and PIM joins, whereas the IGMP State Limit feature can only be used to limit IGMP joins. The IGMP State Limit feature, thus, is more limited in application because it is best suited to be configured on an edge router to limit the number of groups that receivers can join on an outgoing interface. The per interface mroute state limit feature has a wider application because it can be configured to limit IGMP joins on an outgoing interface, to limit PIM joins (for ASM groups or SSM channels) on an outgoing interface connected to other routers, to limit sources behind an incoming interface from sending multicast traffic, or to limit sources directly connected to an incoming interface from sending multicast traffic.

Although the PIM Interface Mroute State Limit feature allows you to limit both IGMP and PIM joins, it does not provide the ability to limit PIM or IGMP joins separately because it does not take into account whether a state is created as a result of an IGMP or PIM join. As such, the IGMP State Limit feature is more specific in application because it specifically limits IGMP joins.

The per interface mroute state limit feature allows you to specify limits according to the direction of traffic; that is, it allows you to specify limits for outgoing interfaces, incoming interfaces, and for incoming interfaces having directly connected multicast sources. The IGMP State Limit feature, however, can only be used to limit outgoing interfaces. The Per Interface State Mroute State Limit feature, thus, is wider in scope because it can be used to limit mroute states for both incoming and outgoing interfaces from both sources and receivers. The IGMP State Limit feature is narrower in scope because it can only be used to limit mroute states for receivers on a LAN by limiting the number of IGMP joins on an outgoing interface.

Both the IGMP State Limit and the per interface mroute state limit features provide a rudimentary multicast CAC mechanism that can be used to provision bandwidth utilization on an interface when all multicast flows roughly utilize the same amount of bandwidth. The Bandwidth-based CAC for IP Multicast feature, however, offers a more flexible and powerful alternative for providing multicast CAC in network environments where IP Multicast flows utilize different amounts of bandwidth.

1.1.5.3 Bandwidth-Based Multicast CAC

The Bandwidth-based CAC for IP Multicast features enhances the per interface mroute state limit feature by implementing a way to count per interface mroute state limiters using cost multipliers. This feature can be used to provide Bandwidth-based multicast CAC on a per interface basis in network environments where the multicast flows utilize different amounts of bandwidth. Once again referring to a Cisco IOS-based implementation/configuration: Bandwidth-based CAC policies are configured using the `ip multicast limit cost` command in global configuration mode. The syntax of the `ip multicast limit cost` command is as follows:

```
!
ip multicast limit cost access-list cost-multiplier
!
```

ACLs are used with this command to define the IP Multicast traffic for which to apply a cost. Standard ACLs can be used to define the (*, G) state. Extended ACLs can be used to define the (S, G) state. Extended ACLs also can be used to define the (*, G) state by specifying 0.0.0.0 for the source address and source wildcard—referred to as (0, G)—in the permit or deny statements that compose the extended access list.

1.1.5.3.1 Mechanics of the Bandwidth-Based CAC for IP Multicast Feature
The mechanics of the Bandwidth-based CAC for IP Multicast feature are as follows:

- Once an mroute matches an ACL configured for an mroute state limiter, a router performs a top-down search from the global list of configured Bandwidth-based CAC policies to determine if a cost should be applied to the mroute.
- A cost is applied to the first Bandwidth-based CAC policy that matches the mroute. A match is found when the ACL applied to the Bandwidth-based CAC policy permits the mroute state.
- The counter for the mroute state limiter either adds or subtracts the cost configured for the cost-multiplier argument. If no costs are configured or if the mroute does not match any of the configured Bandwidth-based CAC polices, the default cost of 1 is used.

1.1.5.3.2 Case Study 1
The following example shows how to configure mroute state limiters on interfaces to provide multicast CAC in a network environment where all the multicast flows roughly utilize the same amount of bandwidth. The case study uses a Cisco IOS configuration shown in Figure 1.21. In this example, a service provider is offering 300 Standard Definition (SD) TV channels. The SD channels are offered to customers in three service bundles (Basic, Premium, and Gold), which are available to customers on a subscription basis. Each bundle offers 100 channels to subscribers, and each channel utilizes approximately 4 Mbps of bandwidth. The service provider must provision the Gigabit Ethernet interfaces on the provider edge (PE) router connected to Digital Subscriber Line Access Multiplexers (DSLAMs) as follows: 50% of the link's bandwidth (500 Mbps) must be available to subscribers of their Internet, voice, and video on demand (VoD) service offerings while the remaining 50% (500 Mbps) of the link's bandwidth must be available to subscribers of their SD channel bundle service offerings. For the 500 Mbps of the link's bandwidth that must always be available to (but must never be exceeded by) the subscribers of the SD channel bundles, the interface must be further provisioned as follows:

- 60% of the bandwidth must be available to subscribers of the basic service (300 Mbps).
- 20% of the bandwidth must be available to subscribers of the premium service (100 Mbps).
- 20% of the bandwidth must be available to subscribers of the gold service (100 Mbps).

Because each SD channel utilizes the same amount of bandwidth (4 Mbps), the per interface mroute state limit feature can be used to provide the necessary CAC to provision the services offered by the service provider. To determine the required CAC needed per interface, the number of channels

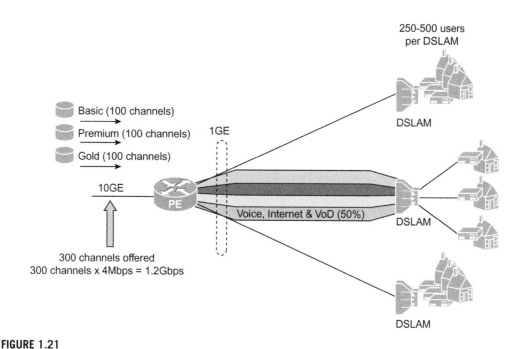

FIGURE 1.21

for each bundle is divided by 4 (because each channel utilizes 4 Mbps of bandwidth). The required CAC needed per interface, therefore, is as follows:

- Basic Services: 300/4 = 75
- Premium Services: 100/4 = 25
- Gold Services: 100/4 = 25

Three ACLs are created for each of the mroute state limiters in the following way and applied to the interface (GigE in this case):

- An mroute state limit of 75 for the SD channels that match acl-basic.
- An mroute state limit of 25 for the SD channels that match acl-premium.
- An mroute state limit of 25 for the SD channels that match acl-gold.

```
!
interface GigabitEthernet X/y
      description — Interface towards the DSLAM—

        .

        .
      ip multicast limit out 75 acl-basic
      ip multicast limit out 25 acl-premium
      ip multicast limit out 25 acl-gold
!
!
```

1.1.5.3.3 Case Study 2

The following example shows how to configure per interface mroute state limiters with Bandwidth-based CAC policies to provide multicast CAC in a network environment where the multicast flows utilize the different amounts of bandwidth. The case study uses a Cisco IOS configuration for illustrative purposes (see Figure 1.22). In this example, three content providers are providing TV services across a service provider core. The content providers are broadcasting TV channels that utilize different amounts of bandwidth:

- MPEG-2 SDTV channels—4 Mbps per channel
- MPEG-2 HDTV channels—18 Mbps per channel
- MPEG-4 SDTV channels—1.6 Mbps per channel
- MPEG-4 HDTV channels—6 Mbps per channel

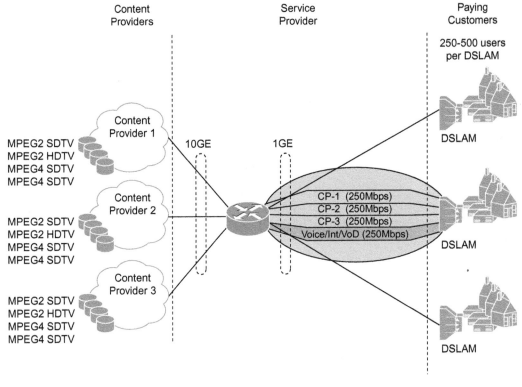

FIGURE 1.22

The Service Provider needs to provision the fair sharing of bandwidth between these three content providers to its subscribers across Gigabit Ethernet interfaces. The Service Provider, thus, determines that it needs to provision each Gigabit Ethernet interface on the PE router connected to the DSLAMs as follows:

- 250 Mbps per content provider
- 250 Mbps for Internet, voice, and VoD services

The Service Provider then configures three ACLs:

- acl-CP1-channels: Defines the channels being offered by the content provider CP1
- acl-CP2-channels: Defines the channels being offered by the content provider CP2
- acl-CP3-channels: Defines the channels being offered by the content provider CP3

Because the Content Providers are broadcasting TV channels that utilize different amounts of bandwidth, the Service Provider needs to determine the values that need to be configured for the mroute state limiters and Bandwidth-based CAC policies to provide the fair sharing of bandwidth required between the Content Providers.

Prior to the introduction of the Bandwidth-Based CAC for IP Multicast feature, the mroute state limiters were based strictly on the number of flows. The introduction of cost multipliers by the Bandwidth-Based CAC for IP Multicast feature expands how mroute state limiters can be defined. Instead of defining the mroute state limiters based on the number of multicast flows, the service provider looks for a common unit of measure and decides to represent the mroute state limiters in Kbps. The service provider then configures three mroute states, one mroute state limiter per Content Provider. Because the link is a Gigabit, the service provider sets each limit to 250,000 (because 250,000 Kbps equals 250 Mbps, the number of bits that the service provider needs to provision per content provider).

The service provider needs to further provision the fair sharing of bandwidth between the content providers, which can be achieved by configuring Bandwidth-based CAC policies. The Service Provider decides to create four Bandwidth-based CAC policies, one policy per channel based on bandwidth. For these policies, the Service Provider configures the following ACLs:

- acl-MP2SD-channels: Defines all the MPEG-2 SD channels offered by the three Content Providers.
- acl-MP2HD-channels: Defines all the MPEG-2 HD channels offered by the three Content Providers.
- acl-MP4SD-channels: Defines all the MPEG-4 SD channels offered by the three Content Providers.
- acl-MP4HD-channels: Defines all the MPEG-4 HD channels offered by the three Content Providers.

For each policy, a cost multiplier (represented in Kbps) is defined for each ACL based on the bandwidth of the channels defined in the ACL:

- 4000—represents the 4 Mbps MPEG-2 SD channels
- 18000—represents the 18 Mbps MPEG-2 HD channels
- 1600—represents the 1.6 Mbps MPEG-4 SD channels
- 6000—Represents the 6 Mbps MPEG-4 HD channels

The following configuration example shows how the Service Provider used mroute state limiters with Bandwidth-based CAC policies to provision Gigabit Ethernet interface for the fair sharing of bandwidth required between the three content providers:

```
!
ip multicast limit cost acl-MP2SD-channels 4000
ip multicast limit cost acl-MP2HD-channels 18000
ip multicast limit cost acl-MP4SD-channels 1600
ip multicast limit cost acl-MP4HD-channels 6000
!
.
.
!
```

```
interface GigabitEthernet X/y
 ip multicast limit out acl-CP1-channels 250000
 ip multicast limit out acl-CP2-channels 250000
 ip multicast limit out acl-CP3-channels 250000
 !
```

1.2 GUIDELINES ON ADDRESSES ALLOCATIONS

The allocation of IP Multicast group addresses is a complex process. Allocation of addresses needs to take into account multiple factors such as:

- *Size of the organization now and in the future.* Sufficient address allocation or expansion should be allowed to accommodate future growth and acquisitions or mergers.
- *Organizational structure and relations between Business Units.* There may be specific demarcation points of administrative control within an organization that need to be considered when allocating addresses. Each Business Unit may require its own address range.
- *Scale of the IP Multicast deployment currently and in the future.* Many organizations underestimate the growth of multicast throughout the business and do not create a comprehensive addressing scheme from the beginning. This can often lead to re-addressing at a later stage (in the same way as we have seen with unicast addressing).
- *Internal policies on the control and deployment of network applications.* Depending on the network topology, certain constraints and protection mechanisms may need to be put in place to protect network resources. A well-summarized address range can help to simplify this process.
- *Scope of the applications.* Will they mainly be local to a site, city, or country? How does this relate to the network topology? Will QoS need to be put in place for specific application?
- *Security policy.* Many multicast applications lack any form of real security. Organizations may find the need to impose restrictions via other means. A carefully designed addressing plan and RP scoping will aid the implementation of these restrictions if required. Also by using the administratively scoped addresses defined in RFC 2365 then these addresses cannot traverse the Internet. This will prevent outside sources from accessing organization data via multicast addresses.
- *Application flexibility.* It is an unfortunate fact that some multicast applications that are clearly not intended to be run Enterprise wide (much less the global Internet) often make use of hard-coded multicast addresses, and have no provision to reconfigure the application to use another multicast address that is more applicable in scope. This can create some serious issues when attempting to develop a rational address scoping plan particularly if the application is hard-coded to use an address that does not fall within the desired scope.
- *Avoiding problematic address ranges.* Multicast addresses that map to MAC addresses in the 0x0100.5E00.00xx range are normally flooded by Layer 2 switches. These addresses should be avoided.
- *Readiness for future use of new multicast delivery methods such as Bidirectional PIM and SSM.*

Overall, there are many different requirements that need to be considered. There is no single "best" way to allocate multicast addresses for all organizations. Each administrator needs to take his or her own unique requirements into account and design the best addressing policy for his or her needs.

1.3 CONCLUSION

In this section we went through the building blocks or basics of IP Multicast. The upcoming chapters will detail the applications and emerging trends including vendor adoptions, as well as the future for Multicast.

Draft-Rosen Multicast Virtual Private Networks

2

2.1 INTRODUCTION

Chapter 1 discussed the building blocks of IP Multicast and the need for IP Multicast in general. We went into great depth of analyzing the various applications that benefited from using Multicast for transport, and their requirements from the underlying network infrastructure. In this chapter we move to the next level in understanding how IP Multicast can be extended to BGP- and MPLS-based Layer 3 Virtual Private Networks (VPNs); in other words, enabling an organization or enterprise to deploy a private Multicast infrastructure across a shared carrier MPLS network.

2.2 DRAFT-ROSEN MULTICAST VIRTUAL PRIVATE NETWORKS

Before we get into the details of Multicast-based VPNs, a discussion of Unicast-based VPNs and their operation would present a detailed insight into how the Multicast VPN infrastructure fits into our scheme of things. So let us start with the details on BGP- and MPLS-based (RFC 2547bis) VPNs.

2.2.1 Unicast VPNs

RFC 2547bis defines a mechanism that allows service providers to use their IP backbone to provide VPN services to their customers. RFC 2547bis VPNs are also known as BGP/MPLS VPNs because BGP is used to distribute VPN routing information across the provider's backbone and because MPLS is used to forward VPN traffic from one VPN site to another.

The primary objectives of this approach are to

- Make the service very simple for customers to use even if they lack experience in IP routing.
- Make the service very scalable and flexible to facilitate large-scale deployment.
- Allow the policies used to create a VPN to be implemented by the service provider alone, or by the service provider working together with the customer.
- Allow the service provider to deliver a critical value-added service that galvanizes customer loyalty.

2.2.1.1 Network Components

In the context of RFC2547bis, a VPN is a collection of policies, and these policies control connectivity among a set of sites. A customer site is connected to the service provider network by one or more ports, where the service provider associates each port with a VPN routing table. In RFC 2547bis terms, the VPN routing table is called a VPN routing and forwarding (VRF) table.

Figure 2.1 illustrates the fundamental building blocks of a BGP/MPLS VPN.

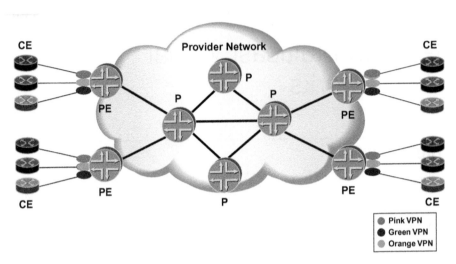

FIGURE 2.1

2.2.1.1.1 Customer Edge Routers

A customer edge (CE) device provides customer access to the service provider network over a data link to one or more provider edge (PE) routers. While the CE device can be a host or a Layer 2 switch, typically the CE device is an IP router that establishes an adjacency with its directly connected PE routers. After the adjacency is established, the CE router advertises the site's local VPN routes to the PE router and learns remote VPN routes from the PE router.

2.2.1.1.2 Provider Edge Routers

Provider edge (PE) routers exchange routing information with CE routers using static routing, RIPv2, OSPF, or EBGP. Although a PE router maintains VPN routing information, it is only required to maintain VPN routes for those VPNs to which it is directly attached. This design enhances the scalability of the RFC 2547bis model because it eliminates the need for PE routers to maintain all of the service provider's VPN routes.

Each PE router maintains a VRF for each of its directly connected sites. Each customer connection (such as Frame Relay PVC, ATM PVC, and VLAN) is mapped to a specific VRF. Thus, it is a port on the PE router and not a site that is associated with a VRF. Note that multiple ports on a PE router can be associated with a single VRF. It is the ability of PE routers to maintain multiple forwarding tables that supports the per-VPN segregation of routing information.

After learning local VPN routes from CE routers, a PE router exchanges VPN routing information with other PE routers using an Internal Border Gateway Protocol (IBGP). PE routers can maintain IBGP sessions to route reflectors as an alternative to a full mesh of IBGP sessions. Deploying multiple route reflectors enhances the scalability of the RFC 2547bis model because it eliminates the need for any single network component to maintain all VPN routes.

Finally, when using MPLS to forward VPN data traffic across the provider's backbone, the ingress PE router functions as the ingress LSR and the egress PE router functions as the egress LSR.

2.2.1.1.3 Provider Routers

A provider (P) router is any router in the provider's network that does not attach to CE devices. P routers function as MPLS transit Label Switching Routers (LSRs) when forwarding VPN data traffic between PE routers. Since traffic is forwarded across the MPLS backbone using a two-layer label stack, P routers are only required to maintain routes to the provider's PE routers; they are not required to maintain specific VPN routing information for each customer site.

2.2.1.2 *Operational Model*

Two fundamental traffic flows occur in a BGP/MPLS VPN:

- A control flow that is used for VPN route distribution and Label Switched Path (LSP) establishment
- A data flow that is used to forward customer data traffic

2.2.1.2.1 Sample Network Topology

Figure 2.2 provides a sample network topology where a single service provider delivers a BGP/MPLS VPN service to different enterprises customers. In this network there are two PE routers connected to four different customer sites.

The inter-site connectivity can be described by the following policies.

- Any host in Site 1 can communicate with any host in Site 2.
- Any host in Site 2 can communicate with any host in Site 1.
- Any host in Site 3 can communicate with any host in Site 4.
- Any host in Site 4 can communicate with any host in Site 3.

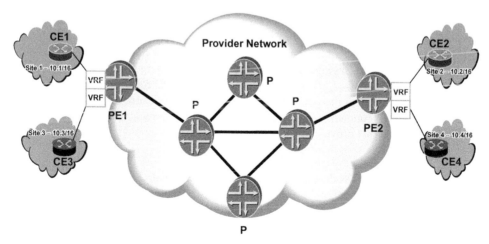

FIGURE 2.2

2.2.1.2.2 Control Flow

In a BGP/MPLS VPN, the control flow consists of two subflows:

1. Responsible for the exchange of routing information between the CE and PE routers at the edges of the provider's backbone and between the PE routers across the provider's backbone.
2. Responsible for the establishment of LSPs across the provider's backbone between PE routers.

In Figure 2.2, PE1 is configured to associate VRF GREEN with the interface or subinterface over which it learns routes from CE1. When CE1 advertises the route for prefix 10.1/16 to PE1, PE1 installs a local route to 10.1/16 in VRF GREEN. PE1 advertises the route for 10.1/16 to PE2 using IBGP. Before advertising the route, PE1 selects an MPLS label (for this example, 222) to advertise with the route and assigns its loopback address as the BGP next hop for the route.

RFC 2547bis supports overlapping address spaces (private addressing defined in RFC 1918) by the use of route distinguishers (RDs) and the VPN-IPv4 address family.

RFC 2547bis constrains the distribution of routing information among PE routers by the use of route filtering based on BGP extended community attributes (route targets). When PE2 receives PE1's route advertisement, it determines if it should install the route to prefix 10.1/16 into VRF GREEN by performing route filtering based on the BGP extended community attributes carried with the route. If PE2 decides to install the route in VRF GREEN, it then advertises the route to prefix 10.1/16 to CE2. The same process is followed for VRF ORANGE.

2.2.1.2.3 LSP Establishment

To use MPLS to forward VPN traffic across the provider's backbone, MPLS LSPs must be established between the PE router that learns the route and the PE router that advertises the route (Figure 2.3).

MPLS LSPs can be established and maintained across the service provider's network using either Label Distribution Protocol (LDP) or Resource Reservation Protocol (RSVP). The provider uses RSVP if it wants to MPLS Fast Reroute for ~50 ms convergence in the case of link/node failures in the Provider network. RSVP LSPs also offer the option to either assign bandwidth to the LSP or use Traffic Engineering—a technique used to select an explicit path for the LSP within the network. RSVP-based LSPs support specific quality of service (QoS) guarantees and/or specific traffic engineering objectives. It is also possible to use both LDP and RSVP LSPs: LDP for basic MPLS forwarding and RSVP for Traffic Engineering and Fast-Reroute depending on the network architecture.

Where LDP- and RSVP-based LSPs exist between a pair of PE routers, the ingress LSR selects the RSVP-based LSP instead of the LDP-based LSP. This occurs because RSVP LSPs have a higher preference than their LDP counterparts. This model supports the incremental configuration of RSVP-based LSPs across the service provider's backbone.

2.2.1.2.4 Data Flow

Figure 2.4 shows the flow of VPN data traffic across the service provider's backbone from one customer site to another. Assume that Host 10.2.3.4 at Site 2 wants to communicate with Server 10.1.3.8 at Site 1.

Host 10.2.3.4 forwards all data packets for Server 10.1.3.8 to its default gateway. When a packet arrives at CE2, it performs a longest-match-route lookup and forwards the IPv4 packet to PE2. PE2 receives the packet, performs a route lookup in VRF GREEN, and obtains the following information:

- MPLS label that was advertised by PE1 with the route (label = 222)
- BGP next hop for the route (the loopback address of PE1)

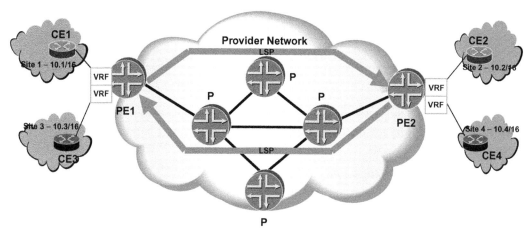

FIGURE 2.3

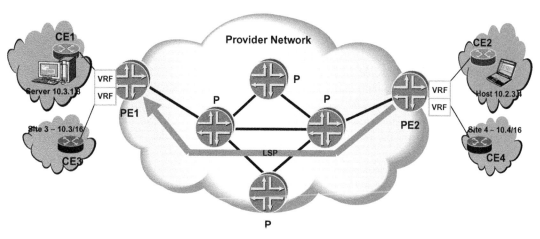

FIGURE 2.4

- Outgoing subinterface for the LSP from PE2 to PE1
- Initial MPLS label for the LSP from PE2 to PE1

User traffic is forwarded from PE2 to PE1 using MPLS with a label stack containing two labels. For this data flow, PE2 is the ingress LSR for the LSP and PE1 is the egress LSR for the LSP. Before transmitting a packet, PE2 pushes the label 222 onto the label stack, making it the bottom (or inner) label. This label is originally installed in VRF GREEN when PE2 receives PE1's IBGP advertisement for the route to 10.1/16. Next, PE2 pushes the label associated with the LDP- or

RSVP-based LSP to PE1 (the route's BGP next hop) onto the label stack, making it the top (or outer) label. After creating the label stack, PE2 forwards the MPLS packet on the outgoing interface to the first P router along the LSP from PE2 to PE1. P routers switch packets across the core of the provider's backbone network based on the top label, which is exchanged using LDP/RSVP. The penultimate router to PE1 pops the top label (exposing the bottom or inner label) and forwards the packet to PE1.

When PE1 receives the packet, it pops the label, creating a native IPv4 packet. PE1 uses the bottom label (222) to identify the directly attached CE, which is the next hop to 10.1/16. Finally, PE1 forwards the native IPv4 packet to CE1, which forwards the packet to Server 10.1.3.8 at Site 1.

2.2.1.3 Benefits of BGP/MPLS VPNs

The major objective of BGP/MPLS VPNs is to simplify network operations for customers while allowing the service provider to offer scalable, revenue-generating, value-added services. BGP/MPLS VPNs have many benefits, including:

- There are no constraints on the address plan used by each VPN customer. The customer can use either globally unique or private IP address spaces. From the service provider's perspective, different customers can have overlapping address spaces.
- The CE router at each customer site does not directly exchange routing information with other CE routers. Customers do not have to deal with inter-site routing issues because they are the responsibility of the service provider.
- VPN customers do not have a backbone or a virtual backbone to administer. Thus, customers do not need management access to PE or P routers.
- Providers do not have a separate backbone or virtual backbone to administer for each customer VPN. Thus, providers do not require management access to CE routers.
- The policies that determine whether a specific site is a member of a particular VPN are the policies of the customer. The administrative model for RFC 2547bis VPNs allows customer policies to be implemented by the provider alone or by the service provider working together with the customer.
- The VPN can span multiple service providers.
- Without the use of cryptographic techniques, security is equivalent to that supported by existing Layer 2 (ATM or Frame Relay) backbone networks.
- Service providers can use a common infrastructure to deliver both VPN and Internet connectivity services.
- Flexible and scalable QoS for customer VPN services is supported through the use of the experimental bits in the MPLS shim header or by the use of traffic engineered LSPs (signaled by RSVP).
- The RFC 2547bis model is link layer (Layer 2) independent.

2.2.1.4 Challenges and Solutions

RFC 2547bis uses several mechanisms to enhance the scalability of the approach and solve specific VPN operational issues. These challenges include:

- Supporting overlapping Customer Address Spaces
- Constraining network connectivity

- Maintaining updated VPN routing information
- Conserving backbone bandwidth and PE router packet processing resources
- Overlapping Customer Address Spaces

VPN customers often manage their own networks and use the RFC 1918 private address space. If customers do not use globally unique IP addresses, the same 32-bit IPv4 address can be used to identify different systems in different VPNs. The result can be routing difficulties because BGP assumes that each IPv4 address it carries is globally unique. To solve this problem, BGP/MPLS VPNs support a mechanism that converts non-unique IP addresses into globally unique addresses by combining the use of the VPN-IPv4 address family with the deployment of Multiprotocol BGP Extensions (MP-BGP).

2.2.1.4.1 The VPN-IPv4 Address Family

One challenge posed by overlapping address spaces is that if a conventional BGP sees two different routes to the same IPv4 address prefix (where the prefix is assigned to systems in different VPNs), BGP treats the prefixes as if they are equivalent and installs only one route. As a result, the other system is unreachable. Eliminating this problem requires a mechanism that allows BGP to disambiguate the prefixes so that it is possible to install two completely different routes to that address, one for each VPN. RFC 2547bis supports this capability by defining the VPN-IPv4 address family.

A VPN-IPv4 address is a 12-byte quantity composed of an 8-byte RD followed by a 4-byte IPv4 address prefix. Figure 2.5 shows the structure of a VPN-IPv4 address.

The 8-byte RD is composed of a 2-byte Type field and a 6-byte Value field. The Type field determines the lengths of the Value field's two subfields (Administrator and Assigned Number), as well as the semantics of the Administrator field. Currently, there are two values defined for the Type field: 0 and 1.

- For Type 0, the Administrator subfield contains 2 bytes and the Assigned Number subfield contains 4 bytes. The Administrator subfield holds an Autonomous System Number (ASN). The use of an ASN from the private ASN space is strongly discouraged. The Assigned Number subfield holds a value from the numbering space administered by the service provider that offers the VPN service and to which the ASN has been assigned.

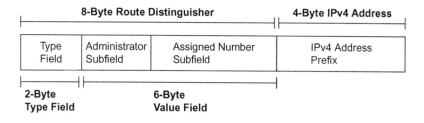

FIGURE 2.5

- For Type 1, the Administrator subfield contains 4 bytes and the Assigned Number subfield contains 2 bytes. The Administrator subfield holds an IPv4 address. The use of an IP address from the private IP address space is strongly discouraged. The Assigned Number subfield holds a value from the numbering space administered by the service provider that offers the VPN service and to which the ASN has been assigned. A configuration option for Type 1 RDs is to use the loopback address of the PE router that originates the route for the 4-byte Administrator subfield and to select a number local to that PE router for the 2-byte Assigned Number subfield.

When configuring RDs on PE routers, RFC 2547bis does not require that all the routes within a VPN use the same RD; each VRF within a VPN can use its own RD. However, the service provider must ensure that each RD is globally unique. For this reason, the use of the private ASN space or the private IP address space when defining RDs is strongly discouraged. The use of the public ASN space or the public IP address space guarantees that each RD is globally unique. Globally unique RDs provide a mechanism that allows each service provider to administer its own address space and create globally unique VPN-IPv4 addresses without conflicting with the RD assignments made by other service providers. The use of globally unique RDs supports the

- Creation of distinct routes to a common IPv4 prefix
- Creation of multiple, globally unique routes to the same system
- Use of policy to decide which packets use which route

Finally, note these few observations to help avoid confusion concerning how VPN-IPv4 addresses are used in a BGP/MPLS VPN:

- VPN-IPv4 addresses are used only within the service provider network.
- VPN customers are not aware of the use of VPN-IPv4 addresses.
- VPN-IPv4 addresses are carried only in routing protocols that run across the provider's backbone.
- VPN-IPv4 addresses are not carried in the packet headers of VPN data traffic as it crosses the provider's backbone.

2.2.1.4.2 Multiprotocol BGP Extensions

Another limitation of using conventional BGP4 to support BGP/MPLS VPNs is that it was originally designed to carry routing information only for the IPv4 address family. Realizing this limitation, the IETF is working to standardize the Multiprotocol Extensions for BGP4. These extensions were originally defined in RFC 2283 (February 1998) and later updated in RFC 2858 (June 2000). The extensions allow BGP4 to carry routing information for multiple Network Layer Protocols (IPv6, IPX, VPN-IPv4, etc.). Therefore, to deploy BGP/MPLS VPNs and support the distribution of VPN-IPv4 routes, PE routers are required to support the MP-BGP extensions and not just conventional BGP.

Before exchanging VPN-IPv4 routing information, RFC 2547bis requires that BGP capabilities negotiation takes place to ensure that the BGP peers are both capable of processing the VPN-IPv4 address family. Note that the MP-BGP extensions are backward compatible, so a router that supports these extensions can still interoperate with a router that does not support these extensions using conventional BGP4 (however, conventional BGP4 does not support RFC 2547bis VPNs).

2.2.1.5 Challenges and Solutions

Assuming a routing table does not contain a default route, a basic assumption of IP routing is that if the route to a specific network is not installed in a router's forwarding table, the network is unreachable from that router. By constraining the flow of routing information, service providers can efficiently control the flow of customer VPN data traffic. The BGP/MPLS VPN model constrains the flow of routing information using two mechanisms:

1. Multiple forwarding tables
2. BGP extended community attributes

2.2.1.5.1 Multiple Forwarding Tables

Each PE router maintains one or more per-site forwarding tables known as VRFs. When a PE router is configured, each of its VRFs is associated with one or more ports (interfaces/subinterfaces) on the PE router that connects directly to the service provider's customers. If a given site contains hosts that are members of multiple VPNs, the VRF associated with the customer site contains routes for all VPNs of which the site is a member. When receiving an outbound customer data packet from a directly attached CE router, the PE router performs a route lookup in the VRF associated with that site. The specific VRF is determined by the subinterface over which the data packet is received. Support for multiple forwarding tables makes it easy for the PE router to provide the per-VPN segregation of routing information. Figure 2.6 illustrates how PE1 populates VRF GREEN.

- PE1 learns Site 1's VPN GREEN routes from CE1 and installs them into VRF GREEN.
- Remote routes are learned via MP-IBGP from other PE routers that are directly connected to sites with hosts that are members of VPN GREEN. PE1 learns Site 2's VPN Red routes from CE2 and installs them into VRF GREEN. The import of remote routes into VRF GREEN is managed by the use of BGP extended community route target attributes.

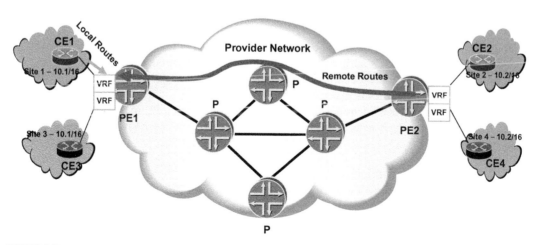

FIGURE 2.6

- Local VPN ORANGE routes at Site 4 and remote VPN ORANGE routes at Site 3 are not associated with VPN GREEN and are not imported into VRF GREEN.

There are a number of benefits derived from having PE routers support multiple forwarding tables.

- Different VPN sites served by the same PE router can use overlapping address spaces.
- Selection of the specific forwarding table for data traffic is determined by policy (the mapping of a router subinterface to a VRF), not by the user content of the packet.
- Multiple forwarding tables prevent communication between sites that have no VPNs in common.
- Scalability is enhanced because PE routers are not required to maintain a dedicated VRF for all of the VPNs supported by the provider's network. Each PE router is only required to maintain a VRF for each of its directly connected sites.
- Finally, the backbone network can support multiple different routes to the same system where the route for a specific packet is determined by the site from which the packet enters the provider's backbone.

2.2.1.5.2 BGP Extended Community Attributes

The distribution of VPN routing information is constrained through the use of BGP extended community attributes. Extended community attributes are carried in BGP messages as attributes of the route. They identify the route as belonging to a specific collection of routes, all of which are treated the same with respect to routing policy. Each BGP extended community must be globally unique (contains either a public IP address or ASN) and can be used by only one VPN. However, a given customer VPN can make use of multiple globally unique BGP extended communities to help control the distribution of routing information. BGP/MPLS VPNs use 32-bit BGP extended community attributes instead of conventional 16-bit BGP community attributes. The use of 32-bit extended community attributes enhances scalability, because a single service provider can support a maximum of 232 communities (not just 216). Since each community attribute contains the provider's globally unique ASN, the service provider can control local assignment while also maintaining the global uniqueness of that assignment.

RFC 2547bis VPNs can use up to three different types of BGP extended community attributes:

- The route target attribute identifies a collection of sites (VRFs) to which a PE router distributes routes. A PE router uses this attribute to constrain the import of remote routes into its VRFs.
- The VPN-of-origin attribute identifies a collection of sites and establishes the associated route as coming from one of the sites in that set.
- The site-of-origin attribute identifies the specific site from which a PE router learns a route. It is encoded as a route origin extended community attribute, which can be used to prevent routing loops.

2.2.1.5.3 Operational Model

Before distributing local routes to other PE routers, the ingress PE router attaches a route target attribute to each route learned from directly connected sites. The route target attached to the route is based on the value of the VRFs configured export target policy. This approach provides a tremendous amount of flexibility in the way a PE router can assign a route target attribute to a route.

- The ingress PE router can be configured to assign a single route target attribute to all routes learned from a given site.

- The ingress PE router can be configured to assign one route target attribute to a set of routes learned from a site and other route target attributes to other sets of routes learned from a site.
- If the CE router communicates with the PE router via EBGP, then the CE router can specify one or more route targets for each route. This approach shifts the control of implementing VPN policies from the service provider to the customer.

Before installing remote routes that have been distributed by another PE router, each VRF on an egress PE router is configured with an import target policy. A PE router can only install a VPN-IPv4 route in a VRF if the route target attribute carried with the route matches one of the important targets of the PE router VRFs.

This approach allows a service provider to use a single mechanism to support VPN customers that have a wide range of inter-site connectivity policies. By careful configuration of export target and import target policies, service providers can construct different types of VPN topologies. The mechanisms that implement the VPN topologies can be completely restricted to the service provider so VPN customers are not aware of this process.

2.2.1.6 BGP/MPLS VPN Topologies

In this section, there are various topologies that can be created for the customer network by virtue of establishing policies in route population within a given VRF table.

2.2.1.6.1 Full-Mesh VPN Topology

Assume that Corporation GREEN (VPN GREEN) wants its BGP/MPLS VPN service provider to create a VPN that supports full-mesh site connectivity (Figure 2.7). Each of Corporation GREEN's sites can send traffic directly to another Corporation GREEN site, but sites of Corporation ORANGE (VPN ORANGE) receiving BGP/MPLS VPN service from the same service provider cannot send traffic to or receive traffic from Corporation GREEN sites.

Each Corporation GREEN site is associated with VRF GREEN on its PE router. A single globally unique route target (GREEN) is configured for each VRF GREEN as both the import target and the export target. This route target (GREEN) is not assigned to any other VRF as the import or the export target. The result is full-mesh connectivity among Corporation GREEN sites. The same applies to Corporation ORANGE as well.

2.2.1.6.2 Hub-and-Spoke VPN Topology

Assume that Corporation GREEN wants its BGP/MPLS VPN service provider to create a VPN that supports hub-and-spoke site connectivity (Figure 2.8). The inter-site connectivity for Corporation GREEN can be described by the following policies:

- Site 1 can communicate directly with Site 5, but not directly with Site 2. If Site 1 wants to communicate with Site 2, it must send traffic by way of Site 5.
- Site 2 can communicate directly with Site 5, but not directly with Site 1. If Site 2 wants to communicate with Site 1, it must send traffic by way of Site 5.
- Site 5 can communicate directly with Site 1 and Site 2.

Privacy requires that Corporation GREEN sites and Corporation ORANGE sites cannot send traffic to or receive traffic from each other.

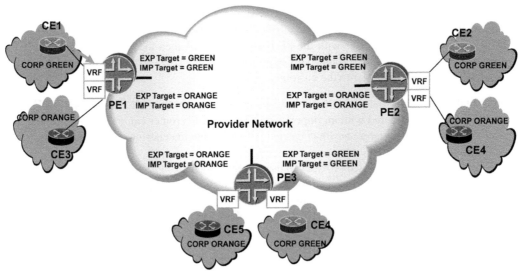

FIGURE 2.7

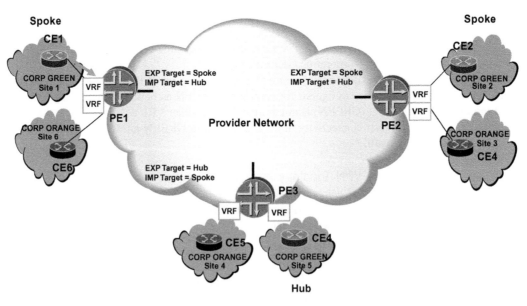

FIGURE 2.8

Hub-and-spoke topology is created using two globally unique route target values: the hub and the spoke.

- The hub site's VRF is configured with an `export target = hub` and an `import target = spoke`. The VRF at the hub site distributes all of the routes in its VRF with a hub attribute that causes the routes to be imported by the spoke sites. The VRF at the hub site imports all remote routes with a spoke attribute.
- The VRF at each spoke site is configured with an `export target = spoke` and an `import target = hub`. The VRF at each spoke site distributes its routes with a spoke attribute, which causes the routes to be imported by the hub site, but dropped by other spoke sites. The VRF at a spoke site imports only routes with a hub attribute, which causes its VRF to be populated only with routes advertised by the hub site.

2.2.1.7 Maintaining Updated VPN Routing Information

When the configuration of a PE router is changed by creating a new VRF or by adding one or more new import target policies to an existing VRF, the PE router might need to obtain the VPN-IPv4 routes that it previously discarded. The speed of delivering updated routing information can present a problem with conventional BGP4 because it is a stateful protocol and does not support the exchange of route refresh request messages and the subsequent re-advertisement of routes. Once BGP peers synchronize their routing tables, they do not exchange routing information until there is a change in that routing information.

A solution to this design feature is provided by the BGP route refresh capability. During the establishment of an MP-IBGP session, a BGP speaker that wants to receive a route refresh message from its peer or route reflector advertises the BGP route refresh capability using a BGP capabilities advertisement. The BGP route refresh capability states that a BGP speaker can send a route refresh message to a peer or route reflector only if it has received a route refresh capabilities advertisement from that peer or route reflector. Whenever the configuration of a PE router is changed, the PE router can request the retransmission of routing information from its MP-IBGP peers to obtain routing information it previously discarded. When the routes are re-advertised, the updated import target policy is applied as the PE router populates its VRFs.

2.2.1.8 Conserving Backbone B/W and PE Router Packet Processing Resources

During the process of populating its VRFs, a BGP speaker often receives and then filters unwanted routes from peers based on each VRF's import target policy. Since the generation, transmission, and processing of routing updates consumes backbone bandwidth and router packet processing resources, these assets can be conserved by eliminating the transmission of unnecessary routing updates.

The number of BGP routing updates can be reduced by enabling BGP cooperative route filtering capability. During the establishment of the MP-IBGP session, a BGP speaker that wants to send or receive outbound route filters (ORFs) to or from its peer or route reflector advertises the cooperative route filtering capability using a BGP capabilities advertisement. The BGP speaker sends its peer a set of ORFs that are expressed in terms of BGP communities. The ORF entries are carried in BGP route refresh messages. The peer applies the received ORFs, in addition to its locally configured export target policy, to constrain and filter outbound routing updates to the BGP speaker. Note that a BGP peer might not honor the ORFs received from a BGP speaker. By implementing this mechanism, BGP cooperative route filtering can be used to conserve service provider backbone bandwidth and PE router packet processing resources.

2.2.1.9 Case Study

Assume a single service provider has an IP/MPLS backbone to deliver BGP/MPLS VPN services to different enterprises. There are three PE routers in the network connected to seven different customer sites (Figure 2.9).

The following policies describe the desired inter-site connectivity for this case study.

- Any host in Site 1 can communicate with any host in Site 4.
- Any host in Site 2 can communicate with any host in Site 5.
- Any host in Site 3 can communicate with any host in Site 6 and Site 7.
- Any host in Site 4 can communicate with any host in Site 1.
- Any host in Site 5 can communicate with any host in Site 2.
- Any host in Site 6 can communicate with any host in Site 3 and Site 7.
- Any host in Site 7 can communicate with any host in Site 3 and Site 6.

Assume that the service provider uses RSVP to establish the following LSPs across its backbone (Figure 2.10). The label displayed at the ingress of each LSP is the label that the PE router associates with the route that it uses to forward traffic to the remote PE router (see Figures 2.11–2.13).

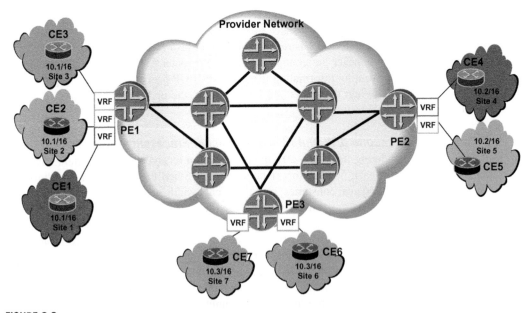

FIGURE 2.9

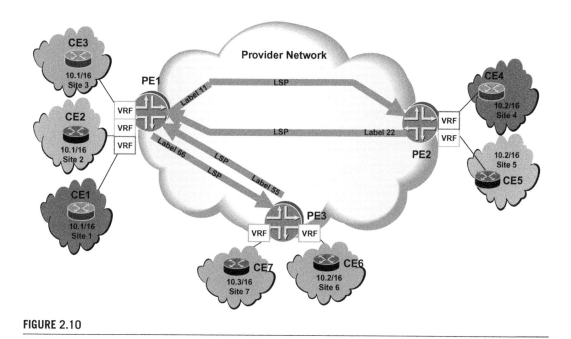

FIGURE 2.10

2.2.1.9.1 Generic Configuration for PE1

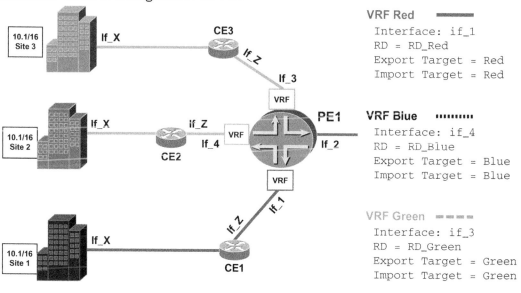

FIGURE 2.11

2.2.1.9.2 Generic Configuration for PE2

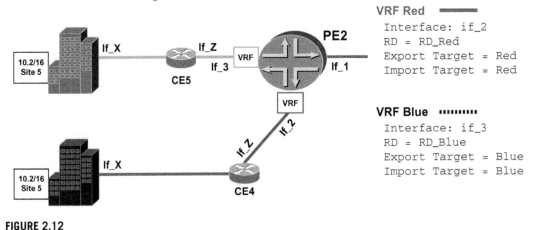

VRF Red ━━━━
```
Interface: if_2
RD = RD_Red
Export Target = Red
Import Target = Red
```

VRF Blue •••••••••
```
Interface: if_3
RD = RD_Blue
Export Target = Blue
Import Target = Blue
```

FIGURE 2.12

2.2.1.9.3 Generic Configuration for PE3

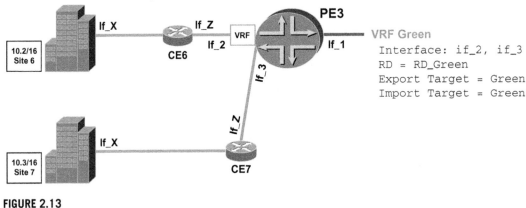

VRF Green
```
Interface: if_2, if_3
RD = RD_Green
Export Target = Green
Import Target = Green
```

FIGURE 2.13

2.2.1.10 Distribution of VPN Routing Information

Before a customer site can forward VPN traffic to a remote site, VPN routing information must be distributed from each customer site across the backbone to other customer sites.

2.2.1.10.1 CE Router-to-Ingress PE Route Distribution

The CE router advertises IPv4 route prefixes to its PE router. There are several mechanisms that a PE router can use to learn routes from each of its directly connected CE routers.

- Static routing
- Running an IGP (e.g., RIPv2, OSPF) with the CE router
- Establishing an EBGP connection with the CE router

In the CE-to-ingress PE flow of routing information, the PE router performs a number of functions. It creates and maintains a VRF for each of its directly connected sites. Note that in this example, PE3 is configured to associate multiple sites (Site 6 and Site 7) with a single VRF. The PE checks all routes against the locally configured import policy for the routing protocol running between the PE router and the CE router. If the route passes the import policy, the prefix is installed in the VRF as an IPv4 route. The PE must be careful that the routes it learns from each CE (via an IGP connection) are not leaked into the provider's backbone IGP. Before advertising a route, the PE assigns an MPLS label to the route.

2.2.1.10.2 Router PE1

Now back to our case study. Assume that PE1 assigns the label 1001 to the routes learned from Site 1, the label 1002 to routes learned from Site 2, and the label 1003 to routes learned from Site 3. PE1 installs three MPLS routes such that when a packet with a label 1001, 1002, or 1003 is received from the backbone, it can simply pop the label and forward the IPv4 packet directly to CE1, CE2, or CE3 based on the packet's label (Figure 2.14).

As a result of these operations, the VRFs in PE1 contain the following local routes (Figure 2.15).

2.2.1.10.3 Router PE2

Assume that PE2 assigns the label 1004 to routes learned from Site 4, and the label 1005 to routes learned from Site 5. PE2 installs two MPLS routes such that when a packet with a label 1004 or 1005 is received from the backbone, it can simply pop the label and send the IPv4 packet directly to CE4 or CE5 based on the packet's label (see Figure 2.16).

As a result of these operations, the VRFs in PE2 contain the following local routes as given below in Figure 2.17.

```
                    MPLS Forwarding Table (PE1)

           Input                                 Output
         Interface      Label      Action      Interface
           If_2         1001        Pop          If_1
           If_2         1002        Pop          If_4
           If_2         1003        Pop          If_3
```

FIGURE 2.14

```
VRF Red
                        BGP                      Bottom   Top
Destination             Next-Hop   Interface     Label    Label
10.1/16                 Direct     if_1          1001     -


VRF Blue
                        BGP                      Bottom   Top
Destination             Next-Hop   Interface     Label    Label
10.1/16                 Direct     if_4          1002     -


VRF Green
                        BGP                      Bottom   Top
Destination             Next-Hop   Interface     Label    Label
10.1/16                 Direct     if_3          1003     -
```

FIGURE 2.15

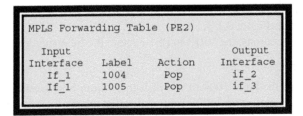

```
MPLS Forwarding Table (PE2)

  Input                             Output
Interface   Label    Action       Interface
  If_1      1004     Pop            if_2
  If_1      1005     Pop            if_3
```

FIGURE 2.16

```
VRF Red
                        BGP                      Bottom   Top
Destination             Next-Hop   Interface     Label    Label
10.2/16                 Direct     if_2          1004     -


VRF Blue
                        BGP                      Bottom   Top
Destination             Next-Hop   Interface     Label    Label
10.2/16                 Direct     if_3          1005     -
```

FIGURE 2.17

2.2.1.10.4 Router PE3

Assume that PE3 assigns the label 1006 to routes learned from Site 6 and the label 1007 to routes learned from Site 7. PE3 installs two MPLS routes such that when a packet with a label 1006 or 1007 is received from the backbone, it can simply pop the label and forward the IPv4 packet directly to CE6 or CE7 based on the packet's label (Figure 2.18).

As a result of these operations, the VRFs in PE3 contain the following local routes (Figure 2.19).

```
MPLS Forwarding Table (PE3)

  Input                              Output
Interface    Label    Action     Interface
  If_1       1006      Pop         if_2
  If_1       1007      Pop         if_3
```

FIGURE 2.18

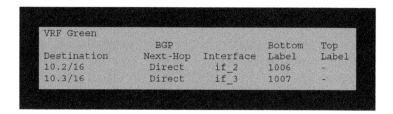

```
VRF Green
                    BGP                 Bottom    Top
Destination      Next-Hop   Interface   Label     Label
10.2/16          Direct      if_2       1006       -
10.3/16          Direct      if_3       1007       -
```

FIGURE 2.19

2.2.1.10.5 Ingress PE to Egress PE Route Distribution Across the Backbone

Ingress PE routers use MP-IBGP to distribute routes received from directly connected sites to egress PE routers. PE routers are required to maintain an MP-IBGP mesh or use route reflectors to ensure that routing information can be distributed to all PE routers. Before the ingress PE router distributes local VPN routes to its MP-IBGP peers, it converts each IPv4 prefix into a VPN-IPv4 prefix using the RDs configured for the VRF that contains the route. The advertisement for each route contains the following:

- The VPN-IPv4 address prefix for the route.
- A BGP next hop that contains the loopback address of the ingress PE router. The address is encoded as a VPN-IPv4 address with an RD = 0, because MP-BGP requires that the next hop be a member of the same address family as the route being advertised.
- The MPLS label that was assigned to the route by the ingress PE router when it learned the local route from the directly attached CE router.
- A route target attribute based on the locally configured export target policy for the VRF containing the local route. Recall that all of the PE routers in this example have been configured to assign a route

`target` = `Red` when advertising VPN Red routes, a `route target` = `Blue` when advertising VPN Blue routes, and a `route target` = `Green` when advertising VPN Green routes.

- Optionally, the site-of-origin attribute could be encoded as a route origin extended community.

When an ingress PE router advertises its local VPN-IPv4 routes to its MP-IBGP peers, it can either send all of the routes in its VRFs to all of its MP-IBGP peers or it can construct a distinct advertisement for each peer that excludes the specific VPN routes that it does not share with a given peer. This is accomplished by the use of ORFs that allow a BGP speaker to announce to its peer or route reflector the set of routes that can be imported into one or more VRFs maintained by the PE router.

When an egress PE router receives a VPN-IPv4 route from a peer, it compares the route to all of the VRF import policies for all of the VPNs that are directly attached to the egress PE router. If the route target carried with the route matches the import target policy of at least one of the egress PE's VRFs, the VPN-IPv4 route is installed in its VPN_IPv4 routing table.

The VPN routing table contains all routes that satisfy the import policy of at least one of the egress PE router's VRFs. This table is the only one that relies on the RD to disambiguate routes, because it is the table that contains all of the routes from all of the VPNs directly connected to the given PE router. The routes in this table should be globally unique because overlapping IPv4 addresses will have been assigned globally unique RDs. BGP path selection occurs in this table before routes are exported to their target VRF. Note that user errors when configuring RDs can cause VPN-IPv4 routes in this table to have the same structure when they should be different. If this situation occurs, the BGP path selection is executed and only one of these routes is installed in its VRF. For this reason, RFC 2547bis recommends the use of globally unique public ASNs and IPv4 addresses when a service provider defines its RDs, which is critical if the BGP/MPLS VPN spans multiple service providers. The best route is selected for each VPN-IPv4 prefix and (based on the route target stored with the route) installed in the target VRF as an IPv4 route.

2.2.1.10.6 Ingress PE Route Advertisements
This section describes how the ingress PE routers in this case study advertise their local routes across the service provider's backbone to egress PE routers. Look the Route Advertisements for routers PE1, PE2, and PE3 (Figure 2.20).

2.2.1.10.7 Egress PE Route Installation
This section describes how the egress PE routers in this case study filter and then install remote routes received from ingress PE routers (Figure 2.21).

Finally, look at the various VRF tables that get created and populated on the three PE routers in our case study (Figure 2.22).

2.2.1.10.8 Egress PE Router to CE Route Distribution
If the egress PE router installs a route in the VRF used to route packets received from a directly connected CE router, the PE router can distribute that route to the CE router. There are several mechanisms that a CE router can use to learn VPN routes from its directly connected PE router.

- Run an IGP (RIPv2, OSPF) with the PE router.
- Establish an EBGP connection with the PE router.
- PE-to-CE routing protocol can distribute a default route pointing to the PE router.
- CE can be configured with a static default route pointing to the PE router.

PE2

```
Destination = RD_Red:10.2/16
Label = 1004
BGP Next Hop = PE2
Route Target = Red


Destination = RD_Blue:10.2/16
Label = 1005
BGP Next Hop = PE2
Route Target = Blue
```

PE1

```
Destination = RD_Red:10.1/16
Label = 1001
BGP Next Hop = PE1
Route Target = Red


Destination = RD_Blue:10.1/16
Label = 1002
BGP Next Hop = PE1
Route Target = Blue


Destination = RD_Green:10.1/16
Label = 1003
BGP Next Hop = PE1
Route Target = Green
```

PE3

```
Destination = RD_Green:10.2/16
Label = 1006
BGP Next Hop = PE3
Route Target = Green


Destination = RD_Green:10.3/16
Label = 1007
BGP Next Hop = PE3
Route Target = Green
```

FIGURE 2.20

PE1

```
Destination = RD_Red:10.2/16
Label = 1004
BGP Next Hop = PE2
Route Target = Red
```

```
Destination = RD_Blue:10.2/16
Label = 1005
BGP Next Hop = PE2
Route Target = Blue
```

```
Destination = RD_Green:10.2/16
Label = 1006
BGP Next Hop = PE3
Route Target = Green


Destination = RD_Green:10.3/16
Label = 1007
BGP Next Hop = PE3
Route Target = Green
```

PE2

```
Destination = RD_Red:10.1/16
Label = 1001
BGP Next Hop = PE1
Route Target = Red
```

```
Destination = RS_Blue:10.1/16
Label = 1002
BGP Next Hop = PE1
Route Target = Blue
```

PE3

```
Destination = RD_Green:10.1/16
Label = 1003
BGP Next Hop = PE1
Route Target = Green
```

FIGURE 2.21

PE1

```
VRF Red
                       BGP                    Bottom   Top
    Destination        Next-Hop   Interface   Label    Label
    10.1/16            Direct     if_1        1001     -
    10.2/16            PE-2       if_2        1004     11


VRF Blue
                       BGP                    Bottom   Top
    Destination        Next-Hop   Interface   Label    Label
    10.1/16            Direct     if_4        1002     -
    10.2/16            PE-2       if_2        1005     11


VRF Green
                       BGP                    Bottom   Top
    Destination        Next-Hop   Interface   Label    Label
    10.1/16            Direct     if_3        1003     -
    10.2/16            PE-3       if_2        1006     11
    10.3/16            PE-3       if_2        1007     66
```

PE2

```
VRF Red
                       BGP                    Bottom   Top
    Destination        Next-Hop   Interface   Label    Label
    10.1/16            PE-1       if_1        1001     22
    10.2/16            Direct     if_2        1004     -

VRF Blue
                       BGP                    Bottom   Top
    Destination        Next-Hop   Interface   Label    Label
    10.1/16            PE 1       if_1        1002     22
    10.2/16            Direct     if_2        1005     -
```

PE3

```
VRF Green
                       BGP                    Bottom   Top
    Destination        Next-Hop   Interface   Label    Label
    10.1/16            PE-1       if_1        1003     55
    10.2/16            Direct     if_2        1006     -
    10.3/16            Direct     if_3        1007     -
```

FIGURE 2.22

After all routes are distributed from the egress PE routers to CE routers, the CE routing tables contain the following (see Figure 2.23).

2.2.1.10.9 Forwarding Customer VPN Traffic Across the BGP/MPLS Backbone

Transmitting customer traffic from one VPN site to another VPN site involves a number of different forwarding decisions.

- Source CE router to ingress PE router forwarding
- Ingress PE router forwarding
- Forwarding at each P router
- Egress PE router to destination CE router forwarding

```
CE 1 Routing Table
Destination     Next-Hop    Interface
10.1/16         Direct       if_x
10.2/16         PE1          if_z


CE 2 Routing Table
Destination     Next-Hop    Interface
10.1/16         Direct       if_x
10.2/16         PE1          if_z


CE 3 Routing Table
Destination     Next-Hop    Interface
10.1/16         Direct       if_x
10.2/16         PE1          if_z
10.3/16         PE1          if_z


CE 4 Routing Table
Destination     Next-Hop    Interface
10.1/16         PE2          if_z
10.2/16         Direct       if_x


CE 5 Routing Table
Destination     Next-Hop    Interface
10.1/16         PE2          if_z
10.2/16         Direct       if_x


CE 6 Routing Table
Destination     Next-Hop    Interface
10.1/16         PE3          if_z
10.2/16         Direct       if_x
10.3/16         PE3          if_z


CE 7 Routing Table
Destination     Next-Hop    Interface
10.1/16         PE3          if_z
10.2/16         PE3          if_z
10.3/16         Direct       if_x
```

FIGURE 2.23

2.2.1.10.10 Source CE Router to Ingress PE Router Forwarding

When a CE router receives an outbound IPv4 data packet from a system in its site, the CE router performs a traditional longest-match-route lookup and forwards the native IPv4 packet to its directly attached PE router.

Ingress PE Router Forwarding When a PE router receives an IPv4 data packet from a CE router, the PE router performs a route lookup in the VRF for the site based on the packet's incoming subinterface. The packet's destination address is matched against the IPv4 prefix. If a match is found in the VRF, the route lookup returns a next hop and an outgoing subinterface. If the packet's outgoing subinterface is associated with the same VRF as the incoming packet, the next hop is either another CE device located at the same site or a CE from a different directly connected site that is a member of the same VPN. Recall that a single VRF in a PE router maintains the routes from all directly connected sites of a given VPN.

If the packet's outgoing subinterface and incoming subinterface are associated with two different VRFs, they are directly attached sites that have at least one VPN in common and that each has a separate forwarding table. To forward the packet, it might be necessary to look up the packet's destination address in the VRF associated with the outgoing interface.

If the packet's outgoing subinterface is not associated with a VRF, then the packet must travel at least one hop across the provider's backbone to reach a remote PE router. If the packet must cross the provider's backbone then it has two next hops: a BGP next hop and an IGP next hop.

- The BGP next hop is the ingress PE router that initially advertises the VPN-IPv4 route. The BGP next hop assigns and distributes a label with the route via MP-IBGP that it subsequently uses to identify the directly connected site that advertised the route. The PE router pushes this label onto the packet's label stack, and it becomes the bottom (or inner) label.
- The IGP next hop is the first hop in the LPS to the BGP next hop. The IGP next hop will have assigned a label (via LDP or RSVP) for the LSP that leads to the BGP next-hop router. This label is pushed onto the packet's label stack and becomes the top (or outer) label. For this case, the PE router that receives the packet from the CE and creates the label stack is the ingress LSR, and the BGP next hop is the egress LSR for the LSP across the service provider's network. If the BGP next hop and the IGP next hop are the same routers, and if penultimate hop popping is used, the packet can be transmitted with only the BGP-supplied bottom (or inner) label.

P Router Forwarding The MPLS backbone switches the labeled packet, swapping the top label at each hop until it reaches the penultimate router to the PE router to which the packet is sent. At the penultimate router, the top label is popped and the packet is sent to the target PE router.

PE Router to Destination CE Router Forwarding When the PE router receives the packet, it looks for a matching MPLS route (label, subinterface) for the bottom label. If there is a match, the bottom label is popped and a native IPv4 packet is sent directly to the CE router associated with the label. Note that the VRF for the directly connected site does not have to be consulted. A snapshot of the process is given in Figure 2.24.

2.2.1.10.11 Actual VPN Forwarding Based on the Case Study

Assume that Host 10.1.2.3 at Site 1 wants to transmit a packet to Server 10.2.9.3 at Site 4, based on our case study provided earlier in this chapter. Figure 2.25 illustrates a detailed deep-dive.

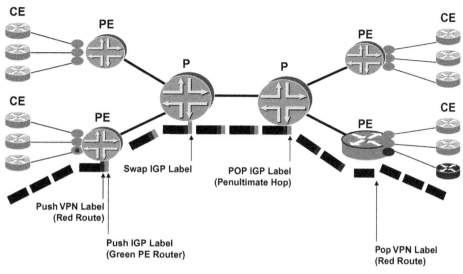

FIGURE 2.24

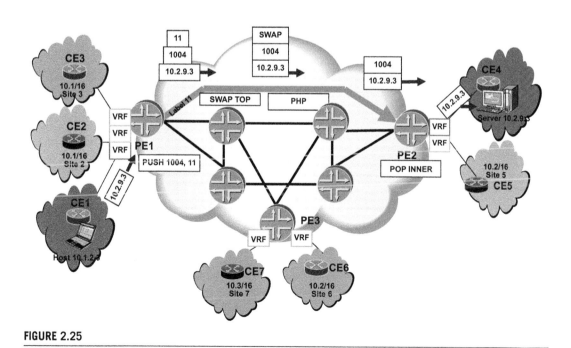

FIGURE 2.25

When the native IPv4 packet arrives at CE1, it performs a longest-match route lookup in its IP forwarding table. The entry in CE1's forwarding table that best matches the packet's destination address is as seen in Figure 2.26.

As a result of this lookup, CE1 forwards the native IPv4 packet to PE1. PE1 receives the native IPv4 packet on the CE interface. Since all packets that arrive on the given interface are associated with VRF RED, PE1 performs a longest-match route lookup in VRF RED. The entry in VRF RED that best matches the packet's destination address is seen in Figure 2.27.

Since the packet's outgoing subinterface (if_2) is not associated with a local VRF, the packet must travel at least one hop across the provider's MPLS backbone. PE1 creates an MPLS header for the packet and then pushes the label 1004 (assigned by PE2 when it originally advertised the route to 10.2/16) onto the packet's label stack, making it the bottom label. PE1 then pushes the first label (11) for the LSP from PE1 to PE2 onto the packet's label stack, making it the top label. The packet is then forwarded to the first transit router in the LSP from PE1 to PE2. The MPLS backbone switches the labeled packet along the LSP, swapping the top label at each hop, until it reaches the penultimate router to PE2. At the penultimate router, the top label is popped and the packet with a single label (1004) is sent to PE2. When PE2 receives the labeled packet on if_1, it performs an exact match lookup in its MPLS forwarding table. The entry in the MPLS forwarding table that matches the packet's label is seen in Figure 2.28.

As a result of this lookup, PE2 pops the label and forwards the native IPv4 packet over if_2 to CE4. When the native IPv4 packet arrives at CE4, it performs a longest-match route lookup in its IP forwarding table. The entry in CE4's forwarding table that best matches the packet's destination address is seen in Figure 2.29.

Finally, as a result of this lookup, CE4 forwards the packet to Server 10.2.9.3 at Site 4.

Destination	Next-Hop	Interface
10.2/16	PE1	if_z

FIGURE 2.26

Destination	BGP Next-Hop	Interface	Bottom Label	Top Label
10.2/16	PE2	if_2	1004	11

FIGURE 2.27

Input Interface	Label	Action	Output Interface
if_1	1004	Pop	if_2

FIGURE 2.28

```
Destination    Next-Hop    Interface
10.2/16         Direct        if_x
```

FIGURE 2.29

2.2.1.11 Summary

Having discussed the operation of a BGP/MPLS VPN, some of the important aspects that help in achieving scalability for operations are summarized in the following list.

- BGP/MPLS VPNs are not constructed as an overlay network that sits on top of the service provider's network. Hence, the n-squared scalability issues typically associated with the overlay model do not exist.
- If there are multiple attachments between a customer site and a PE router, all of the attachments are mapped to a single forwarding table to conserve PE router resources.
- Overlapping address spaces are supported, thus allowing customers to efficiently use the private IP address space.
- PE routers are required to maintain VPN routes, but only for those VPNs to which they are directly attached.
- Route targets constrain the distribution of routing information, making policy enforcement easy. Also PE routers do not maintain routes to remote CE routers, only to other PE routers.
- P routers do not maintain any VPN routing information due to the use of a two-level label stack.
- No single system in the provider's backbone is required to maintain routing information for all of the VPNs supported by the service provider.
- Network management is simplified because service providers do not have a backbone or virtual backbone to administer for each customer VPN.
- RDs are structured to ensure that every service provider can administer its own numbering space and create globally unique RDs that do not conflict with the RDs assigned by any other service provider.
- ORFs reduce the amount of routing information distributed across the provider's backbone and conserve PE router packet processing resources.
- The challenge of maintaining a full mesh of MP-IBGP connections is eliminated through the use of route reflectors.
- Route reflectors are the only systems in the network that are required to maintain VPN routing information for sites to which they are not directly connected. Segmented route reflection enhances scalability because no single route reflector has to maintain routing information for all VPN-IPv4 routes deployed across the provider's network.
- RSVP-based traffic engineered LSPs optimize connectivity between PE routers.
- Finally, BGP/MPLS VPNs are the foundation on which Draft-Rosen Multicast VPNs will be created, which will be discussed in the following sections.

For the sake of completeness of this section, Figure 2.30 illustrates a summary of the MPLS VPN operation.

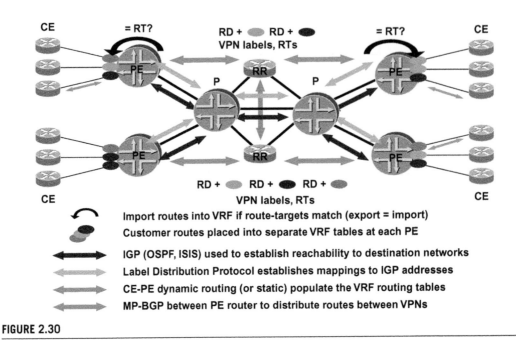

FIGURE 2.30

2.2.2 Multicast VPNs

The previous sections presented a detailed overview of BGP/MPLS-based Unicast VPN services, and one of the primary advantages for enterprises subscribing to this service is "outsourcing." In other words, it offers enterprises the opportunity to off-load the complexity of deploying and maintaining large networks to carriers who specialize in such functions. This facilitates the enablement of focusing on core competencies for end user organizations. IP Multicast has become an integral part of any corporation in today's environment, and it is imperative for the carrier to offer a mechanism to transport end customers' multicast traffic over BGP/MPLS-based VPNs and offer the same amount of distinction and segregation between any two customers' multicast traffic within a shared carrier infrastructure.

Draft-Rosen `http://www.ietf.org/internet-drafts/draft-rosen-vpn-mcast-xx.txt` defined a mechanism to carry multicast traffic within the context of BGP MPLS VPNs and enable the transport of multicast traffic between VRFs of a participating VPN. We will call this Multicast VPN for the rest of this chapter. Transporting customer multicast traffic over a shared carrier infrastructure brings its own set of complexities:

- Ensuring that multicast protocols used by the customer are supported by the carrier.
- The subscription to the Multicast VPN service should not require any redesign to the customer multicast infrastructure—unless it is mutually agreed—for benefits that are evident to the customer.

2.2.2.1 Multicast Domains

The `Draft-rosen-vpn-mcast-xx.txt` extends the IETF VPN specification by describing the protocols and procedures required to support a multicast in an MPLS-VPN. In particular, the multicast domain proposal of this draft is the solution that the industry has adopted, and it will be discussed in the following sections.

It is necessary to be familiar with these terms as they are essentially the building blocks of this solution.

- *Multicast domain*: A set of BGP/MPLS VPNs (VRFs) that can send multicast traffic to each other, that is, within the context of their respective sites that are part of the same VPN.
- *Multicast VPN*: A VRF that supports both uni- and multicast forwarding tables.
- *Multicast Distribution Tree*: Used to carry customer multicast traffic (C-MCAST packets) among PE routers in a common Multicast Domain.

Some of the important aspects of the Multicast Domain operation within the context of a Multicast VPN are detailed in the following:

- A MVPN is assigned to a Multicast Domain.
- A P-Group address is defined per Multicast Domain, and this address needs to be unique.
- C-PACKETS are encapsulated on the PE routers connected to the customer sites and sent on the MDT as P-packets. This ensures that the carrier network does not need to possess any knowledge of customer multicast routing information.
    - The source address of the P-packet is always the address of the MP-BGP source.
    - Destination Address is the P-Group address (this address is assigned during the configuration of the MVPN and is also known as the VPN-Group-Address).
    - The encapsulation is typically GRE.

2.2.2.2 Multicast Distribution Trees

As previously mentioned, a Multicast Distribution Tree (MDT) is used to carry the customer multicast traffic in a distinct manner—over a shared carrier infrastructure. In simple terms, an MDT is a unique multicast tree that is created per MVPN. The two most commonly deployed models are Shared Trees using PIM-SM, also referred to as the Any Source Multicast (ASM) model, and Source Trees using PIM-SSM. An MDT for a given customer can use the ASM, SSM, or a combination of both the models. This is predominantly a design-related decision taken by the carrier based on various factors that are beneficial to both the carrier and in certain cases to the customer as well. Most of the questions that arise when reading this section will be addressed as we progress through the chapter.

The MDTs consists of three components:

- Default MDT—An MVPN uses this MDT to send low-bandwidth multicast traffic or traffic that is destined to a widely distributed set of receivers. It is always used to send multicast control traffic between PE routers in a multicast domain and is created for every MVPN on a PE router.
- Data MDT—This type of MDT is used to tunnel high-bandwidth source traffic through the P-network to interested PE routers. They avoid unnecessary flooding of customer multicast traffic to all PE routers in a multicast domain.
- Multicast Tunnel Interface (MTI)—It is a representation of access to the multicast domain.

2.2.2.3 Default MDT

When a Multicast VPN is created, it must also be associated with a Default-MDT. The PE router always builds a Default MDT to peer PE routers that have MVPNs with the same configured MDT-Group address, which is also known as the VPN group address. (Note: Terms will be used interchangeably within this chapter. For instance, MDT group address and VPN group address identify the Default MDT).

Every MVPN is connected to a Default MDT. An MDT is created and maintained in the P-network by using standard PIM mechanisms. For example, if PIM-SM (ASM Mode) was used in the P-network, PE routers in a particular multicast domain would discover each other by joining the shared tree for the MDT-Group that is rooted at the service provider's Rendezvous Point (RP). After a Default MDT is configured for the MVPN, an MTI is created within the specific MVPN, which provides access to the configured MDT-Group. If other PE routers in the network are configured with the same group, then a Default MDT is built between those PE routers. Enabling multicast on a VRF does not guarantee that there is any multicast activity on a CE router interface, only that there is a potential for sources and receivers to exist. After multicast is enabled on a VRF and a Default MDT is configured, the PE router joins the Default MDT for that domain regardless of whether sources or receivers are active. This is necessary so the PE router can build PIM adjacencies to other PE routers in the same domain and that, at the very least, MVPN control information can be exchanged.

When a PE router joins an MDT, it becomes the root of that tree, and the remote peer PE routers become leaves of the MDT. Conversely, the local PE router becomes a leaf of the MDT that is rooted at remote PE routers. Being a root and a leaf of the same tree allows the PE router to participate in a multicast domain as both a sender and receiver. Look at the state information that gets created in the carrier network core via Figure 2.31.

In our illustration, there are a total of 17 PE routers and each of these PE routers hosts three MVPNs (VRF RED, VRF BLUE, and VRF GREEN). Since the Default MDT is created on a per-PE and per-MVPN basis—there are a total of 17 (S, G) states per VPN that need to be maintained in the carrier core—each PE can be a sender site and receiver site at the same time. This multiplied by 3 (number of MVPNs in Figure 2.31) makes it 51 in total. This number will greatly increase in proportion to the number of MVPNs deployed in the network.

Before we move to the next stage, it is worthwhile mentioning that the CE router within the MVPN would still use PIM on its interface toward the PE router for exchanging its multicast routing information. Now this information needs to be propagated to the remote CE routers at each site of the same customer or MVPN. This information is exchanged between PE routers via the MTI and using GRE encapsulation, as discussed earlier. The MTI ensures that the customer multicast routing information is masked from the provider core (P routers). The VPN group address used for the default MDT encapsulates all C-MCAST traffic. Therefore the provider network associates all C-MCAST traffic (irrespective of the number of customer sources/groups) using only this single VPN group address. Therefore all PE routers establish PIM adjacencies with the provider routers inside the carrier core, which is completely separate from the PE-CE and PE-PE (MTI) PIM adjacencies. Figure 2.32 explains this in more detail.

Examine the actual traffic flow in a Multicast VPN environment to better understand the concepts that have been discussed so far. In our example, there is a C-MCAST (Customer Multicast) source with an IPv4 address "192.1.1.1" sending traffic to a C-MCAST group at address "239.1.1.1." The VPN Group address assigned for this MVPN in the provider network is "239.2.2.2." Therefore, in Figure 2.33 the customer multicast packet gets encapsulated, using GRE encapsulation, into a

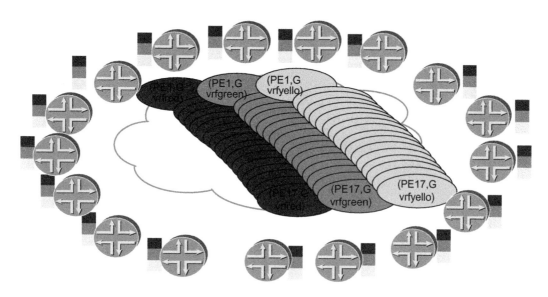

- One state per VRF per PE in global table
- 51 in total in this example

FIGURE 2.31

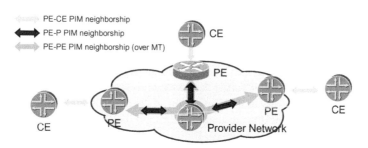

Multicast Distribution Tree is established between PE routers in Provider Network

CE router forms PIM neighborship with VRF instance on PE router

PE routers form PIM neighborship with other PE routers over MDT. This is a VRF specific neighborship using the MTI

PE routers form PIM neighborship with P routers. This is a global neighborship

Multicast packets from CE routers will be forwarded over MDT

FIGURE 2.32

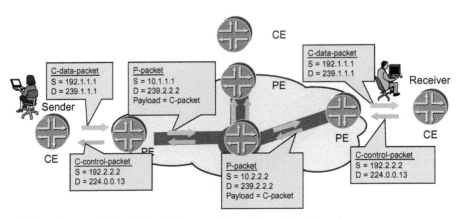

Both customer control and data traffic are sent over the multicast tunnel

P routers only see P packets, so they won't build state for traffic inside the VPN

P packets will go to each PE router that is in the multicast domain

FIGURE 2.33

.

P-packet and the source address is the ingress PE (connected to the C-MCAST source) and the multicast group address is the VPN group address.

As mentioned previously, when a PE router forwards a customer multicast packet onto an MDT, it is encapsulated with GRE. This is so that the multicast group of a particular VPN can be mapped to a single MDT-Group in the P-network. The source address of the outer IP header is the PE Multiprotocol BGP local peering address, and the destination address is the MDT-Group address assigned to the multicast domain. Therefore, the P-network is only concerned with the IP addresses in the GRE header (allocated by the service provider), not the customer-specific addressing.

The packet is then forwarded in the P-network by using the MDT-Group multicast address just like any other multicast packet with normal RPF checks being done on the source address (the originating PE). When the packet arrives at a PE router from an MDT, the encapsulation is removed and the original customer multicast packet is forwarded to the corresponding MVPN. The target MVPN is derived from the MDT-Group address in the destination of the encapsulation header. Therefore, using this process, customer multicast packets are tunneled through the P-network to the appropriate MDT leaves. Each MDT is a mesh of multicast tunnels forming the multicast domain.

Figure 2.33 provides two traffic flows between the two sites within the MVPN. The first flow is the multicast traffic, which is being sent from the sender to the receiver (and indicated as C-data-packet for the ease of reading). The egress PE removes the P-packet in order to forward the multicast traffic into the customer domain. The second flow is control traffic, which is encapsulated into a P-packet in the carrier core. The second flow is a PIM Hello message sent from the CE to discover neighboring PIM routers to 224.0.0.13 (ALL-PIM-ROUTERS-group).

The MDT on all PE routers is connected in a fully meshed manner. This means that traffic flowing on the Default MDT inevitably reaches all the participating PE routers. Figures 2.34 and 2.35 illustrate this concept in more detail.

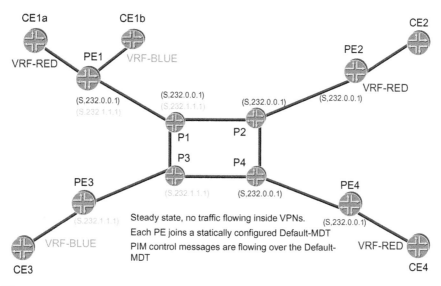

Steady state, no traffic flowing inside VPNs.
Each PE joins a statically configured Default-MDT
PIM control messages are flowing over the Default-MDT

FIGURE 2.34

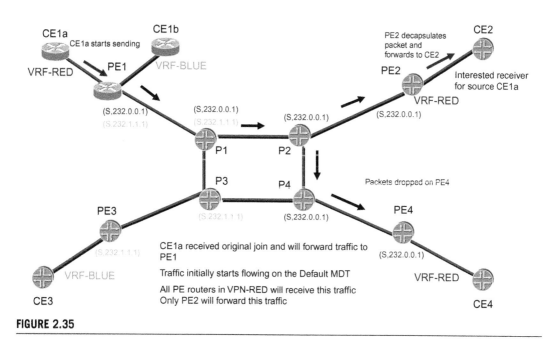

CE1a received original join and will forward traffic to PE1

Traffic initially starts flowing on the Default MDT

All PE routers in VPN-RED will receive this traffic
Only PE2 will forward this traffic

FIGURE 2.35

Figure 2.34 is an indication of the provider network, when the MVPN is just deployed or when there is no activity (PIM joins, Prunes, multicast traffic flow, etc.) in the network. In our example, there are two MVPNs (VPN RED and VPN BLUE). The MDT address for VPN RED is "232.0.0.1," and the address for VPN BLUE is "232.1.1.1." Each PE router joins the respective MDT groups that they are hosting, For instance, PE1 joins the MDT created for both VPN BLUE and VPN RED, while PE4 only joins the MDT for VPN RED (since PE4 only has VPN RED connected to itself). At this point, there is no user traffic flowing on the MDT; however, the infrastructure is ready for C-MAST transport. In Figure 2.35 the activity that follows once customer traffic is originated is illustrated.

In Figure 2.36, the moment CE1 starts sending traffic, PE1 sends the traffic over the Default MDT. Therefore the traffic reaches every other PE router that is part of this MDT. This can be very suboptimal and is a serious limitation, especially if there are large volumes of traffic and few interested receivers. This model can result in potentially large volumes of bandwidth being utilized, since PE routers without interested receivers would still be receiving traffic only to be dropped. So it is better to have a more optimal way to have traffic delivered only to interested receivers, yet over a shared tree; in other words, to emulate an SSM model without the cost of much state information injected into the network. Remember that an SSM model requires unique multicast groups to distinguish between traffic flows, whereas we only use a single VPN group address within the context of the Default MDT.

2.2.2.4 Data MDT

To overcome the limitations of the Default MDT, a special MDT group called a Data MDT can be created within the MVPN to minimize the flooding by sending data only to PE routers that have active VPN receivers. The Data MDT can be created dynamically if a particular customer multicast stream exceeds a bandwidth threshold. Each MVPN can have a pool (group range) of Data MDT groups allocated to it. Note that the Data MDT is only created for data traffic. All multicast control traffic travels on the Default MDT to ensure that all PE routers receive control information.

When a traffic threshold is exceeded on the Default MDT, the PE router connected to the VPN source of the multicast traffic can switch the (S, G) from the Default MDT to a group associated with the Data MDT. The rate the threshold is checked is a fixed value, which is user configurable. The bandwidth threshold is checked by the PE router on the basis of (S, G) customer multicast streams rather than an aggregate of all traffic on the Default MDT. The group selected for the Data MDT is taken from a pool that has been configured on the MVPN. For each source that exceeds the configured bandwidth threshold, a new Data MDT is created from the available pool for that MVPN. If there are

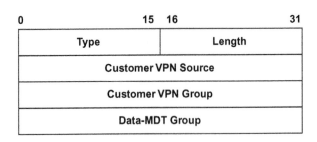

FIGURE 2.36

more high-bandwidth sources than groups available in the pool, then the group that has been referenced the least is selected and reused. This implies that if the pool contains a small number of groups, then a Data MDT might have more than one high-bandwidth source using it. A small Data MDT pool ensures that the amount of state information in the P-network is minimized. A large Data MDT pool allows more optimal routing (less likely for sources to share the same Data MDT) at the expense of increased state information in the P-network (carrier network).

When a PE router creates a Data MDT, the multicast source traffic is encapsulated in the same manner as the Default MDT, but the destination group is taken from the Data MDT pool. Any PE router that has interested receivers needs to issue a P-join for the Data MDT; otherwise, the receivers cannot see the C-packets because they are no longer active on the Default MDT. For this to occur, the source PE router must inform all other PE routers in the multicast domain of the existence of the newly created Data MDT. This is achieved by transmitting a special PIM-like control message on the Default MDT containing the customer's (S, G) to Data MDT group mapping. This message is called a Data MDT join. It is an invitation to peer PE routers to join the new Data MDT if they have interested receivers in the corresponding MVPN. The message is carried in a UDP packet destined to the ALL-PIM-ROUTERS group (224.0.0.13) with UDP port number 3232. The (S, G, Data MDT) mapping is advertised by using the type, length, value (TLV) format, as shown in Figure 2.36.

Any PE router that receives the (S, G, Data MDT) mapping joins the Data MDT if they have receivers in the MVPN for G. The source PE router that initiated the Data MDT waits several seconds before sending the multicast stream onto the Data MDT. The delay is necessary to allow receiving PE routers time to build a path back to the Data MDT root and avoid packet loss when switching from the Default MDT. The Data MDT is a transient entity that exists as long as the bandwidth threshold is exceeded. If the traffic bandwidth falls below the threshold, the source is switched back to the Default MDT. To avoid transitions between the MDTs, traffic only reverts to the Default MDT if the Data MDT is at least one minute old. PE routers that do not have MVPN receivers for the Data MDT will cache the (S, G, Data MDT) mappings in an internal table so that the join latency can be minimized if a receiver appears at some given point in time. Figures 2.37–2.39 are examples of the Data MDT setup.

In the previous example, MVPN RED has a Default MDT on group address "232.0.0.1," and MVPN BLUE has a group address of 232.1.1.1. This state information is maintained on all of the routers in the carrier network. Now traffic from a given C-MCAST source exceeds the threshold configured. (Remember, it was mentioned that the Data MDT can be initiated based on a given traffic threshold of a multicast stream.) PE1 is the source from which PE immediately signals to all of the other PEs that are part of the Default MDT by using Data MDT. The subsequent steps are seen in more detail in Figure 2.38.

The Data MDT address chosen in this example is "232.0.0.2," which is signaled to all the PEs. Now only PE2 chooses to join the Data MDT, since it has interested receivers for the group to which the multicast stream is being sent. PE4, on the contrary, does not join the stream and only caches the information, which can be reused in the event of future interests received from its connected CE router. The next set of events is illustrated in Figure 2.39 where traffic now actually starts flowing on the Data-MDT (Group 232.0.0.2), and only PE2 is actually receiving the traffic.

2.2.2.5 Multicast Tunnel Interface

The MTI appears in the MVPN as an interface called "Tunnelx" or "MT" depending on the vendor and platform used. For every multicast domain in which an MVPN participates, there is a

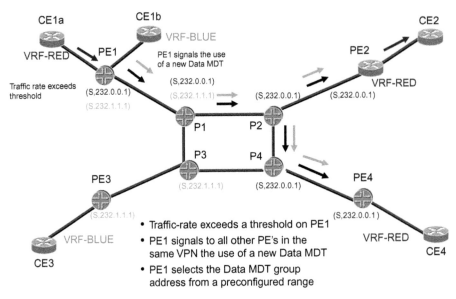

- Traffic-rate exceeds a threshold on PE1
- PE1 signals to all other PE's in the same VPN the use of a new Data MDT
- PE1 selects the Data MDT group address from a preconfigured range

FIGURE 2.37

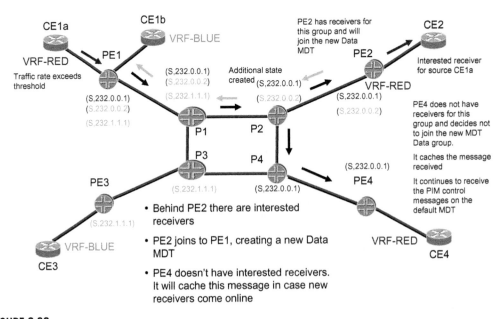

- Behind PE2 there are interested receivers
- PE2 joins to PE1, creating a new Data MDT
- PE4 doesn't have interested receivers. It will cache this message in case new receivers come online

FIGURE 2.38

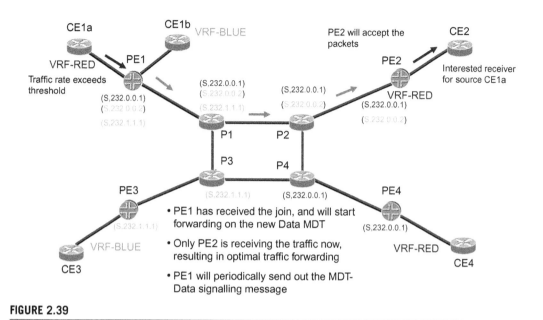

FIGURE 2.39

corresponding MTI. An MTI is essentially a gateway that connects the customer environment (MVPN) to the carrier's global environment (MDT). Any C-packets sent to the MTI are encapsulated into a P-packet (using GRE) and forwarded along the MDT. When the PE router sends to the MTI, it is the root of that MDT; when the PE router receives traffic from an MTI, it is the leaf of that MDT. PIM adjacencies are formed to all other PE routers in the multicast domain via the MTI. Therefore, for a specific MVPN, the PIM neighbors of the PE routers are all seen as reachable via the same MTI. The MTI is treated by an MVPN PIM instance as if it were a LAN interface: therefore all PIM LAN procedures are valid over the MTI.

The PE router sends PIM control messages across the MTI so that multicast forwarding trees can be created between customer sites separated by the P-network. The forwarding trees referred to here are visible only in the C-network, not the P-network. To allow multicast forwarding between a customer's sites, the MTI is part of the outgoing interface list for the (S, G) or (*, G) states that originate from the MVPN. The MTI is created dynamically upon configuration of the Default-MDT and cannot be explicitly configured. PIM Sparse-Dense (PIM-SD) mode is automatically enabled so that various customer group modes can be supported. For example, if the customer was using PIM-DM exclusively, then the MTI would be added to the outgoing list (olist) in the MVPN with the entry marked Forward/Dense to allow distribution of traffic to other customer sites. If the PE router neighbors all sent a prune message back, and no prune override was received, then the MTI in the olist entry would be set to Prune/Dense exactly as if it were a LAN interface. If the customer network was running PIM-SM, then the MTI would be added to the olist only on the reception of an explicit join from a remote PE router in the multicast domain.

The MTI is not accessible or visible to the IGP (such as OSPF or ISIS) operating in the customer network. In other words, no unicast routing is forwarded over the MTI because the interface does not appear in the unicast routing table of the associated VRF. Because the RPF check is performed on the unicast routing table for PIM, traffic received through an MTI has direct implications on current RPF procedures.

2.2.2.6 RPF

RPF is a fundamental requirement of multicast routing. The RPF check ensures that multicast traffic has arrived from the correct interface that leads back to the source. If this check passes, the multicast packets can be distributed out the appropriate interfaces away from the source. RPF consists of two pieces of information: the RPF interface and the RPF neighbor. The RPF interface is used to perform the RPF check by making sure that the multicast packet arrives on the interface it is supposed to, as determined by the unicast routing table. The RPF neighbor is the IP address of the PIM adjacency. It is used to forward messages such as PIM joins or prunes for the (*, G) or (S, G) entries (back toward the root of the tree where the source or RP resides). The RPF interface and neighbor are created during control plane setup of an (*, G) or (S, G) entry. During data forwarding, the RPF check is executed using the RPF interface cached in the state entry. In an MVPN environment, the RPF check can be categorized into three types of multicast packets:

- C-packets received from a PE router customer interface in the MVPN
- P-packets received from a PE router or P router interface in the global routing table
- C-packets received from a multicast tunnel interface in the MVPN

The RPF check for the first two categories is performed as per legacy RPF procedures. The interface information is gleaned from the unicast routing table and cached in a state entry. For C-packets, the C-source lookup in the VRF unicast routing table returns a PE router interface associated with that VRF. For P-packets, the P-source lookup in the global routing table returns an interface connected to another P router or PE router. The results of these lookups are used as the RPF interface.

The third category, where C-packets that are received from an MTI, is treated a little differently and requires some modification to the way the (S, G) or (*, G) state is created. C-packets in this category have originated from remote PE routers in the network and have traveled across the P-network via the MDT. Therefore, from the MVPN's perspective, these C-packets must have been received on the MTI. However, because the MTI does not participate in unicast routing, a lookup of the C-source in the VRF does not return the tunnel interface. Instead, the route to the C-source will have been distributed by Multiprotocol BGP as a VPNv4 prefix from the remote PE router. This implies that the receiving interface is actually in the P-network. In this case, the RPF procedure has been modified so that if Multiprotocol BGP has learned a prefix that contains the C-source address then the RPF interface is set to the MTI associated with that MVPN.

The procedure for determining the RPF neighbor has also been modified. If the RPF interface is set to the MTI, then the RPF neighbor must be a remote PE router. (Remember, a PE router forms PIM adjacencies to other PE routers via the MTI.) The RPF neighbor is selected according to two criteria. First, the RPF neighbor must be the BGP next hop to the C-source, as appears in the routing table for that VRF. Second, the same BGP next hop address must appear as a PIM neighbor in the adjacency table for the MVPN. This is the reason that PIM must use the local BGP peering address when it sends Hello packets across the MDT. Referencing the BGP table is done once during setup in the control plane (to create the RPF entries). When multicast data is forwarded, verification only needs to take place on the cached RPF information.

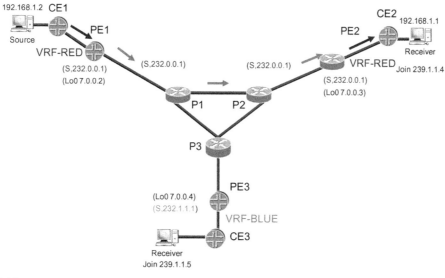

FIGURE 2.40

2.2.2.7 Case Study and Configurations

In this section various case studies of Draft-Rosen MVPNs are reviewed along with some sample configurations to understand the implementation in more detail. In our case study, the equipment from two vendors is chosen (Juniper and Cisco) for illustrative purposes. This provides the reader with details specific to either vendor's configuration details, aspects related to interoperability, and finally, to ensure diversity in our case study and examples. Therefore, each example and case study that follows may have different hardware (Juniper/Cisco) to ensure adequate interest in reading. Certain examples may use hardware from a single vendor for all illustrative purposes. This ensures diversity as previously mentioned and prevents any vendor bias.

2.2.2.8 ASM Mode Using Only Default MDT—Static RP

In this example, there are three PE routers (PE1, PE2, and PE3) and two MVPNs (VPN RED and VPN BLUE). PE1 and PE2 are connected to VPN RED, whereas PE3 is connected to VPN BLUE. There is a source with IP address "192.168.1.2" and a destination at address "192.168.1.1." The receiver is interested in traffic to group "239.1.1.4," and this is a C-MAST group address. Source 192.168.1.2 is in the process of sending multicast traffic to group "239.1.1.4." There is a Default MDT created for MVPN RED using group address 232.0.0.1 and 232.1.1.1 for MVPN BLUE. Routers PE1 and PE3 are Juniper PE routers and PE2 is a Cisco PE router. Similarly, all P routers are Cisco IOS based. All of the relevant configurations are displayed in Figure 2.40.

In this section, the configurations for the MVPNs are demonstrated, which are configured for Static RPs. Command explanations are provided wherever needed and relevant. (Note: Only the relevant portions of the configurations are displayed below.)

2.2.2.9 PE1 Router Configuration

On PE1, the appropriate MVPN configured with the Default MDT address and the RP configured for the VRF instance is seen (Figure 2.41). In this case PE1 acts as the RP for the C-MCAST network. BGP is configured to send and receive IPv4 and VPNv4 prefixes, facilitating BGP/MPLS connectivity and optionally IPv4 prefixes to be exchanged. PIM is configured in the global routing instance for carrying P-Groups and PE1 is configured to be the RP for the master PIM instance (Global table).

```
interfaces {
lo0 {
      unit 0 {
          family inet {
              address 7.0.0.2/32;
          }
      }
    unit 1 {
          family inet {
              address 7.0.0.2/32;
          }
      }
    }
  }
routing-instances {
vpn-red {
    instance-type vrf;
    interface ge-2/0/1.0;
    interface lo0.1;
    route-distinguisher 100:1;
    vrf-target target:100:1;
    protocols {
        pim {
            vpn-group-address 232.0.0.1;  ------→ Default MDT Address
            rp {
                local { ----------→ PE1 is configured as RP for MVPN RED
                    address 7.0.0.2;  ---------→ Loopback address of PE1
                }
            }
            interface ge-2/0/1.0 {
                mode sparse-dense;
                version 2;
            }
            interface lo0.1 {
                mode sparse-dense;
                version 2;
            }
        }
      }
    }
  }
}
```

FIGURE 2.41

PE1 router configuration—JUNOS.

```
        protocols {
        bgp {
            group carrier-ibgp {
                type internal;
                local-address 7.0.0.2;
                family inet { ---→ IPv4 support
                    any;
                }
                family inet-vpn { ---→ VPNv4 support
                    any;
                }
                peer-as 100;
                neighbor 7.0.0.3;
                neighbor 7.0.0.4;
            }
        }
        pim {
            rp {
                local {
                    family inet {
                        address 7.0.0.2; ---→ PE1 is RP for the Global PIM instance
                    }
                }
            }
            interface all {
                mode sparse;
                version 2;
            }
            interface fxp0.0 {
                disable;
            }
        }
    }
```

FIGURE 2.41

(Continued)

2.2.2.10 PE2 Router Configuration

On PE2, the configuration remains identical to PE1 with the exception of the RP addresses (Figure 2.42). Both the VRF instance and Master routing instances of PIM are configured to identify PE as the RP.

2.2.2.11 PE3 Router Configuration

PE3 does not host VPN RED, and only has a local VPN called VPN BLUE. The idea of this configuration was to demonstrate that each MVPN within a provider network can have its own distinct multicast infrastructure to support a given customer multicast network. In Figure 2.43, PE3 acts as the RP for MVPN BLUE; however, the Master instance still uses PE1 as the RP.

2.2.2.12 P Router Configuration

Provider routers only have the PIM configuration for the Master instance (Global table), and as provided in Figure 2.44, have no visibility to any C-MCAST routing or MVPN information.

```
!
ip vrf forwarding
!
ip vrf vpn-red
 rd 100:1
 route-target export 100:1
 route-target import 100:1
 mdt default 232.0.0.1 ----------→ Default MDT Group Address

!
!
!
ip multicast-routing
ip multicast-routing vrf vpn-red
!
!
!
interface Loopback0
 ip address 7.0.0.3 255.255.255.255
 ip pim sparse-mode
!
interface Loopback1
 ip vrf forwarding vpn-red
 ip address 7.0.0.3 255.255.255.255
 ip pim sparse-mode
!
interface GigabitEthernet4/1
 ip vrf forwarding vpn-red
 ip address 10.13.91.1 255.255.255.0
 ip pim sparse-mode
 !
router bgp 100 --→ BGP configured to support IPv4 and VPNv4 address
family
 no synchronization
 bgp log-neighbor-changes
 neighbor 7.0.0.2 remote-as 100
 neighbor 7.0.0.2 update-source Loopback0
 neighbor 7.0.0.2 next-hop-self
 neighbor 7.0.0.4 remote-as 100
 neighbor 7.0.0.4 update-source Loopback0
 neighbor 7.0.0.4 next-hop-self
 !
 address-family vpnv4
  neighbor 7.0.0.2 activate
  neighbor 7.0.0.2 send-community both
  neighbor 7.0.0.4 activate
  neighbor 7.0.0.4 send-community both
  exit-address-family
 !
ip pim vrf vpn-red rp-address 7.0.0.2 -→ Pointing to PE1 as MVPN RP
ip pim rp-address 7.0.0.2 --→PE1 is the RP for the master instance
 !
end
```

FIGURE 2.42

PE2 router configuration—Cisco IOS.

```
interfaces {
lo0 {
      unit 0 {
          family inet {
              address 7.0.0.4/32;
          }
        }
        unit 1 {
            family inet {
                address 7.0.0.4/32;
            }
          }
        }
      }
routing-instances {
vpn-blue {
    instance-type vrf;
    interface ge-2/1/1.0;
    interface lo0.1;
    route-distinguisher 100:2;
    vrf-target target:100:2;
    protocols {
        pim {
            vpn-group-address 232.1.1.1;  ------> Default MDT Address
            rp {
                local {  ----------> PE3 is configured as RP for MVPN BLUE
                    address 7.0.0.4;  --------> Loopback address of PE3
                }
            }
            interface ge-2/1/1.0 {
                mode sparse-dense;
                version 2;
            }
            interface lo0.1 {
                mode sparse-dense;
                version 2;
            }
        }
      }
    }
  }
protocols {
bgp {
    group carrier-ibgp {
        type internal;
        local-address 7.0.0.4;
        family inet {
            any;
        }
        family inet-vpn {
            any;
        }
```

FIGURE 2.43

PE3 router configuration—JUNOS.

```
            peer-as 100;
            neighbor 7.0.0.2;
            neighbor 7.0.0.3;
        }
    }
    pim {
        rp {
            local {
                family inet {
                    address 7.0.0.2; ---→ PE1 is RP for the Global PIM instance
                }
            }
        }
        interface all {
            mode sparse;
            version 2;
        }
        interface fxp0.0 {
            disable;
        }
    }
}
```

FIGURE 2.43

(Continued)

```
!
ip multicast-routing -→ Enable global multicast routing.

ip cef
mpls label protocol ldp
tag-switching tdp router-id Loopback0
!
!
!
interface Loopback0
 ip address 7.0.0.1 255.255.255.255
 ip pim sparse-dense-mode
!
!
interface GigabitEthernet4/3
 ip address 10.2.0.3 255.255.255.0
 ip pim sparse-mode

!--- Enable multicast on links to PE routers
!--- which have MVPNs configured.
!
ip pim ssm default
ip pim rp-address 7.0.0.2 --→ PE1 is the RP for the master instance
!
end
```

FIGURE 2.44

P Router configuration—IOS.

2.2.2.13 CE1 Router Configuration

```
operator@CE1# show protocols pim
rp {
    static {
        address 7.0.0.2;
    }
}
interface all {
    mode sparse-dense;
    version 2;
}
interface fxp0.0 {
    disable;
}
```

FIGURE 2.45

CE1 router configuration—JUNOS.

2.2.2.14 CE2 Router Configuration

Both routers CE1 and CE2 have identical configurations, with PIM enabled on interfaces facing the
PE router (Figures 2.45 and 2.46). The RP address is defined and points to PE1. CE2 has a configuration under the protocol's "sap" hierarchy. This configuration directs the JUNOS kernel to register a
PIM join toward the PE router for the group specified (239.1.1.4). The other distinct functionality it
brings is to respond to ping messages directed to the group specified under this context. Using IGMP
instead of SAP would register a PIM join with the appropriate group configured; however, a PING
response would not be achievable. The "SAP" protocol configuration is only available in JUNOS.
If the CE was a Cisco IOS-based device, then an IGMP join would serve the purpose both in terms

```
operator@CE2# show protocols pim
rp {
    static {
        address 7.0.0.2;
    }
}
interface all {
    mode sparse-dense;
    version 2;
}
interface fxp0.0 {
    disable;
}

operator@CE1# show protocols sap
listen 239.1.1.4;
```

FIGURE 2.46

CE1 router configuration—JUNOS.

of the join and the response to a multicast ping as well. Our validation of the multicast transport discussed later will use "PING" for verification.

2.2.2.15 PE1 Router Outputs

In all of the outputs seen in Figure 2.47, assume that traffic is generated from C-MCAST source "192.168.1.2" to C-MCAST group "239.1.1.4."

```
operator@PE1# run show pim join instance vpn-red
Instance: PIM.vpn-red Family: INET
R = Rendezvous Point Tree, S = Sparse, W = Wildcard

Group: 239.1.1.4 ------------------> Join from the receiver via PE2
Source: *
    RP: 7.0.0.2
    Flags: sparse,rptree,wildcard
    Upstream interface: Local ---------> Indicates the path towards Source

Instance: PIM.vpn-red Family: INET6
R = Rendezvous Point Tree, S = Sparse, W = Wildcard
```

FIGURE 2.47

Verifying PIM joins on PE1 via the VPN instance.

This output verifies that the PIM joins received for C-MCAST groups. In this case, since the upstream interface points as "LOCAL," it indicates that the join has been received from a remote PE (leaf PE).

This output verifies the C-MCAST routing instance for VPN RED (Figure 2.48). Here the (S, G) entry in the routing entry, indicating that a source has started sending multicast traffic to a group, is "239.1.1.4."

This output provides details on PIM neighbors via the MTI for a given MVPN, details on the PIM Mode used, and finally interfaces that are part of the MVPN PIM instance (Figure 2.49).

In Figure 2.50 details on the MDT for VPN RED are provided. Details of importance are the MDT address (Default) and the MTI (outgoing) used for exchanging C-MCAST control and data traffic to a remote PE that is part of the same MDT.

```
operator@PE1# run show multicast route instance vpn-red
Family: INET

Group: 239.1.1.4 --> Indicates an entry for the C-MCAST group
    Source: 192.168.1.2/32 ----> Source sending traffic to C-MCAST group
    Upstream interface: ge-2/0/1.0 -> Path to the source (Via CE1)
    Downstream interface list:
        mt-2/1/0.32768        ---> MTI towards PE2 and the receiver
```

FIGURE 2.48

Verifying the multicast routing table on the VPN instance on PE1.

```
operator@PE1# run show pim neighbors instance vpn-red detail
Instance: PIM.vpn-red
Interface: ge-2/0/1.0
    Address: 76.76.76.1,IPv4, PIM v2, Mode: SparseDense, Join Count: 0
        Hello Option Holdtime: 65535 seconds
        Hello Option DR Priority: 1
        Hello Option Generation ID: 922248608
        Hello Option LAN Prune Delay: delay 500 ms override 2000 ms

    Address: 76.76.76.2,IPv4, PIM v2, Join Count: 0 -------> Router CE1
        BFD: Disabled
        Hello Option Holdtime: 105 seconds 98 remaining
        Hello Option DR Priority: 1
        Hello Option Generation ID: 1154995986
        Hello Option LAN Prune Delay: delay 500 ms override 2000 ms
    Rx Join: Group           Source           Timeout

Interface: lo0.1
    Address: 7.0.0.2,    IPv4, PIM v2, Mode: SparseDense, Join Count: 0
        Hello Option Holdtime: 65535 seconds
        Hello Option DR Priority: 1
        Hello Option Generation ID: 272385923
        Hello Option LAN Prune Delay: delay 500 ms override 2000 ms

Interface: mt-2/1/0.32768 -------> MTI towards PE2 for VPN RED
    Address: 7.0.0.2,    IPv4, PIM v2, Mode: SparseDense, Join Count: 0
        Hello Option Holdtime: 65535 seconds
        Hello Option DR Priority: 1
        Hello Option Generation ID: 395850892
        Hello Option LAN Prune Delay: delay 500 ms override 2000 ms
    Rx Join: Group           Source           Timeout
             239.1.1.1       7.0.0.2            0
             239.1.1.1       7.0.0.3            0

    Address: 7.0.0.3,    IPv4, PIM v2, Join Count: 0 ------------> PE2
        BFD: Disabled
        Hello Option Holdtime: 105 seconds 104 remaining
        Hello Option DR Priority: 1
        Hello Option Generation ID: 217423569
        Hello Option LAN Prune Delay: delay 500 ms override 2000 ms
    Rx Join: Group           Source           Timeout
             239.1.1.4                          164 --> Join for Group

Interface: mt-2/1/0.49152 ---------> MTI originating from PE2 towards PE1
    Address: 7.0.0.2,    IPv4, PIM v2, Mode: SparseDense, Join Count: 0
        Hello Option Holdtime: 65535 seconds
        Hello Option DR Priority: 1
        Hello Option Generation ID: 2069425206
        Hello Option LAN Prune Delay: delay 500 ms override 2000 ms
```

FIGURE 2.49

Verifying PIM neighbors under the routing instance on PE1.

```
Interface: pd-0/1/0.32770 -→ PIM Decapsulation Interface as PE1 is RP
    Address: 0.0.0.0,    IPv4, PIM v2, Mode: Sparse, Join Count: 0
        Hello Option Holdtime: 65535 seconds
        Hello Option DR Priority: 0
        Hello Option Generation ID: 669598265
        Hello Option LAN Prune Delay: delay 500 ms override 2000 ms
```

FIGURE 2.49

(Continued)

```
operator@PE1# run show pim mdt extensive outgoing instance vpn-red
Instance: PIM.vpn-red
Tunnel direction: Outgoing
Default group address: 232.0.0.1 -→ Default MDT Address
Default tunnel interface: mt-2/1/0.32768 -→ MTI towards the remote PE
```

FIGURE 2.50

Verifying the outgoing MTI on PE1.

```
operator@PE1# run show pim mdt extensive incoming instance vpn-red
Instance: PIM.vpn-red
Tunnel direction: Incoming
Default group address: 232.0.0.1
Default tunnel interface: mt-2/1/0.49152
```

FIGURE 2.51

Verifying the incoming MTI on PE1.

It is important to note that JUNOS creates two tunnel interfaces (in either direction) toward a given PE for C-MCAST traffic (Figure 2.51). In other words, when PIM is configured within a routing instance, two mt interfaces are created. PIM is run only on the mt-encapsulation interface. The mt-decapsulation interface is used to populate downstream interface information. It is worthwhile to note that JUNOS would use the same interface numbers (e.g., mt-x/x/x.32768) toward all PE routers for a given MVPN. Remember, a default MDT is like a LAN with all PE routers sharing a common MDT.

- mt-xxxxx range is 32768 through 49151 for mt-encapsulation.
- mt-yyyyy range is 49152 through 65535 for mt-decapsulation.

In Figure 2.52 the RP database for the MVPN instance is seen. The C-MCAST group "239.1.1.4" is registered in the RP. The join has come via PE2, which has an interested receiver.

This command displays the various interfaces (PIM) for a given MVPN (Figure 2.53). The MT encapsulation and decapsulation interfaces along with the PIM Decapsulation interface (displayed as "pd") are seen.

2.2.2.16 PE2 Router Outputs

In the outputs seen in Figures 2.54 and 2.55, a PIM neighborship for the MVPN has been established between the PE-CE and between the two PE routers over the MTI interfaces. Tunnel0 identifies the MTI interface on Cisco PE routers. Similarly the multicast routing table also has the required entry for the PIM join received from the CE router.

```
operator@PE1# run show pim source instance vpn-red detail
Instance: PIM.vpn-red Family: INET
Source 7.0.0.2
    Prefix 7.0.0.2/32
    Upstream interface Local
    Upstream neighbor Local
    Active groups:
        239.1.1.4
```

FIGURE 2.52

Verifying the RP database on the VPN instance on PE1.

```
operator@PE1# run show pim interfaces instance vpn-red
Instance: PIM.vpn-red

Name              Stat Mode        IP V State NbrCnt JoinCnt DR address
ge-2/0/1.0        Up   SparseDense 4 2 NotDR    1      0 76.76.76.2
lo0.1             Up   SparseDense 4 2 DR       0      0 7.0.0.2
mt-2/1/0.32768    Up   SparseDense 4 2 NotDR    1      0 7.0.0.3
mt-2/1/0.49152    Up   SparseDense 4 2 DR       0      0 7.0.0.2
pd-0/1/0.32770    Up   Sparse      4 2 DR       0      0
```

FIGURE 2.53

Verifying the PIM interfaces under the VPN instance on PE1.

```
PE2#show ip mroute vrf vpn-red
IP Multicast Routing Table
Flags: D - Dense, S - Sparse, B - Bidir Group, s - SSM Group, C - Connected,
       L - Local, P - Pruned, R - RP-bit set, F - Register flag,
       T - SPT-bit set, J - Join SPT, M - MSDP created entry,
       X - Proxy Join Timer Running, A - Candidate for MSDP Advertisement,
       U - URD, I - Received Source Specific Host Report, Z - Multicast
Tunnel,
       Y - Joined MDT-data group, y - Sending to MDT-data group
Outgoing interface flags: H - Hardware switched
 Timers: Uptime/Expires
 Interface state: Interface, Next-Hop or VCD, State/Mode
 (*, 239.1.1.4), 00:11:20/00:03:26, RP 7.0.0.2, flags: S  --→Mroute entry
 Incoming interface: Tunnel0
 Outgoing interface list:
       GigabitEthernet4/1, Forward/Sparse-Dense, 00:11:20/00:02:51
 [output truncated]
```

FIGURE 2.54

Verifying Multicast routing table on PE2.

```
PE2#show ip pim vrf vpn-red neighbor
PIM Neighbor Table
Neighbor        Interface    Uptime/Expires         Ver   DR
Address                                                    Priority/Mode
20.0.1.2          Gig4/1          00:18:30/00:01:27   v2    1 / DR
7.0.0.2           Tunnel0         00:17:40/00:01:18   v2    1 / DR
```

FIGURE 2.55

Verifying the PIM interfaces under the VPN instance on PE2.

```
*Mar 5 00:48:55.567: PIM(1): Received v2 Join/Prune on Ethernet 0/0 from
172.16.200.17, to us
*Mar 5 00:48:55.567: PIM(1): Join-list: (*, 239.1.1.4) RP 7.0.0.2
*Mar 5 00:48:55.567: MRT(1): Create (*, 239.1.1.4), RPF Null, PC
0x607573F4
*Mar 5 00:48:55.567: PIM(1): Check RP 20.0.1.2 into the (*, 239.1.1.4)
entry, RPT-bit set, WC-bit set, S-bit set
*Mar 5 00:48:55.571: MRT(1): Add/Update GigabitEthernet 4/1/224.0.0.2 to
the olist of (*, 239.1.1.4), Forward state
*Mar 5 00:48:55.571: PIM(1): Add GigabitEthernet4/1/172.16.200.17 to (*,
239.1.1.4), Forward state
*Mar 5 00:48:55.571: PIM(1): Send v2 Join on Tunnel0 to 7.0.0.2 for
(172.16.0.17/32, 239.1.1.4), WC-bit, RPT-bit, S-bit
```

FIGURE 2.56

Log messages on PE2—a sequence of events on the MTI.

In the outputs in Figure 2.56, the sequence of events from the PIM joins are received by PE2 until the join is encapsulated and sent toward PE1.

2.2.2.17 Validation

Assume the carrier has configured the multicast VPN for a given customer and would like to verify connectivity between the sites for multicast transport. One of the easiest methods of verifying whether or not multicast traffic forwarding is working is to use multicast pings to the multicast groups to which leaf nodes have expressed an interest. In a way this validates multicast reachability between the CE routers. Once this is successful, the carrier can confirm a functional setup and do a handover to the customer for production usage. There are more complex and advanced ways to verify multicast reachability by using traffic generators or real-time applications. However, for our illustration, we would use the simplest approach.

In Figure 2.57 there is a reply from the remote CE for the multicast ping. If CE1 was a Cisco IOS-based device, the same command would be used as seen in Figure 2.58.

2.2.2.18 ASM Mode Using Only Default- and Data MDTs—Static RP

Next, look at the Data MDT setup and relevant configuration based on our case study. In this section, we make a small change as compared to our previous illustration, which only used the Default MDT. The change is that PE3 is connected with a new site for VPN RED and has an interested receiver for C-MCAST group address "239.1.1.4." This is further illustrated in Figure 2.59. Note that all of the other parameters such as PIM RP and group addresses remain the same.

```
operator@CE1#run ping ttl 5 bypass-routing interface ge-4/0/0.0 239.1.1.4
PING 239.1.1.4 (239.1.1.4): 56 data bytes
64 bytes from 20.0.1.2: icmp_seq=0 ttl=62 time=51.361 ms → Remote CE
64 bytes from 20.0.1.2: icmp_seq=0 ttl=62 time=51.361 ms
64 bytes from 20.0.1.2: icmp_seq=0 ttl=62 time=51.361 ms
64 bytes from 20.0.1.2: icmp_seq=0 ttl=62 time=51.361 ms
64 bytes from 20.0.1.2: icmp_seq=0 ttl=62 time=51.361 ms
64 bytes from 20.0.1.2: icmp_seq=0 ttl=62 time=51.361 ms
64 bytes from 20.0.1.2: icmp_seq=0 ttl=62 time=51.361 ms
64 bytes from 20.0.1.2: icmp_seq=0 ttl=62 time=51.361 ms
64 bytes from 20.0.1.2: icmp_seq=0 ttl=62 time=51.361 ms
64 bytes from 20.0.1.2: icmp_seq=0 ttl=62 time=51.361 ms
```

FIGURE 2.57

Verifying reachability from CE1—JUNOS.

```
CE1#ping 239.1.1.4
Type escape sequence to abort.
Sending 1, 100-byte ICMP Echos to 239.1.1.4, timeout is 2 seconds:

Reply to request 0 from 20.0.1.2, 4 ms         --→ Response received
Reply to request 0 from 20.0.1.2, 4 ms
```

FIGURE 2.58

Verifying reachability from CE1—IOS.

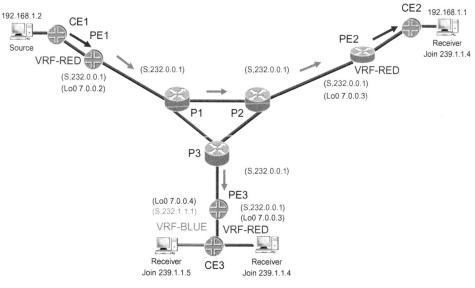

FIGURE 2.59

2.2.2.19 PE1 Router Configuration

In Figure 2.60, a criterion is defined for the Data MDT setup. As per the criteria, a C-MCAST Source with an IPv4 address "192.168.1.2" transmitting to C-MCAST group "239.1.1.4" exceeding a threshold of 10 Kbps is eligible for its traffic to be switched to a Data MDT. The definition of a C-MCAST (S, G) in JUNOS allows a carrier to define which traffic that belongs to the customer network could be allocated a Data MDT. Note that Multicast addresses in the carrier core are considered a costly resource due to the available address space and scale of customers to be supported. Also important is the amount of state information the carrier network is to host; therefore the allocations of Data MDT addresses are always allotted after careful consideration.

2.2.2.20 Data MDT Criteria—To Only Include Bandwidth Rate

Note: In a scenario where the carrier is not particularly interested in defining an (S, G) criterion for allotment of the Data MDTs and would like to provision Data MDTs for any (S, G) pair that exceeds a given bandwidth rate (say, 10 Kbps), the configuration in Figure 2.61 may be used. In this configuration, it is specified that any multicast address group range (indicated as 224.0.0.0/3) and any

```
interfaces {
lo0 {
        unit 0 {
            family inet {
                address 7.0.0.2/32;
            }
        }
        unit 1 {
            family inet {
                address 7.0.0.2/32;
              }
            }
          }
        }
routing-instances {
vpn-red {
    instance-type vrf;
    interface ge-2/0/1.0;
    interface lo0.1;
    route-distinguisher 100:1;
    vrf-target target:100:1;
    protocols {
        pim {
            vpn-group-address 232.0.0.1; ------> Default MDT Address
            rp {
                local { ---------->PE1 is configured as RP for MVPN RED
                    address 7.0.0.2; --------> Loopback address of PE1
                }
            }
            interface ge-2/0/1.0 {
                mode sparse-dense;
                version 2;
            }
```

FIGURE 2.60

PE1 router configuration—JUNOS.

```
                interface lo0.1 {
                    mode sparse-dense;
                    version 2;
                }
            mdt {
                    threshold {
                        group 239.1.1.4/32 {
                            source 192.168.1.2/32 {
                                rate 10;
                            }
                        }
                    }
                    tunnel-limit 255; ------> Maximum no. of Data MDTs allowed
                    group-range 232.13.13.0/24; ------> Data MDT Group Address
                }
            }
        }
    }
}
protocols {
bgp {
    group carrier-ibgp {
        type internal;
        local-address 7.0.0.2;
        family inet { ---> IPv4 support
            any;
        }
        family inet-vpn { ---> VPNv4 support
            any;
        }
        peer-as 100;
        neighbor 7.0.0.3;
        neighbor 7.0.0.4;
    }
}
pim {
    rp {
        local {
            family inet {
                address 7.0.0.2; ---> PE1 is RP for the Global PIM instance
            }
        }
    }
    interface all {
        mode sparse;
        version 2;
    }
    interface fxp0.0 {
        disable;
    }
}
}
```

FIGURE 2.60

(Continued)

```
routing-instances {
vpn-red {
    instance-type vrf;
    interface ge-2/0/1.0;
    interface lo0.1;
    route-distinguisher 100:1;
    vrf-target target:100:1;
    protocols {
        pim {
            vpn-group-address 232.0.0.1; ------→Default MDT Address
            rp {
                local { ----------→PE1 is configured as RP for MVPN RED
                    address 7.0.0.2; ---------→ Loopback address of PE1
                }
            }
            interface ge-2/0/1.0 {
                mode sparse-dense;
                version 2;
            }
            interface lo0.1 {
                mode sparse-dense;
                version 2;
            }
        mdt {
            threshold {
                group 224.0.0.0/3 {
                    source 0.0.0.0/0 {
                        rate 10;
                    }
                }
            }
            tunnel-limit 255; ------→Maximum no. of Data MDTs allowed
            group-range 232.13.13.0/24; ------→Data MDT Group Address
        }
      }
    }
  }
}
```

FIGURE 2.61

PE1 router configuration—JUNOS.

source (indicated as 0.0.0.0/0) exceeding a threshold of 10 Kbps would have its traffic switched to a Data MDT address.

2.2.2.21 PE2 Router Configuration

As per our case study, PE2 does not have any active sources at the moment. Therefore the Data MDT command is not mandatory. However, the command has been used to enable PE2 to switch to a Data MDT if it would have sources connected to its VPN site in the future (see Figure 2.62).

```
!
ip vrf forwarding
!
ip vrf vpn-red
 rd 100:1
 route-target export 100:1
 route-target import 100:1
 mdt default 232.0.0.1 ----------→ Default MDT Group Address
 mdt data 232.13.14.0 0.0.0.255 threshold 10 -→ Data MDT address range
 !
 !
 !
ip multicast-routing
ip multicast-routing vrf vpn-red
 !
 !
 !
interface Loopback0
 ip address 7.0.0.3 255.255.255.255
 ip pim sparse-mode
 !
interface Loopback1
 ip vrf forwarding vpn-red
 ip address 7.0.0.3 255.255.255.255
 ip pim sparse-mode
 !
interface GigabitEthernet4/1
 ip vrf forwarding vpn-red
 ip address 10.13.91.1 255.255.255.0
 ip pim sparse-mode
 !
router bgp 100 --→ BGP configured to support IPv4 and VPNv4 address family
 no synchronization
 bgp log-neighbor-changes
 neighbor 7.0.0.2 remote-as 100
 neighbor 7.0.0.2 update-source Loopback0
 neighbor 7.0.0.2 next-hop-self
 neighbor 7.0.0.4 remote-as 100
 neighbor 7.0.0.4 update-source Loopback0
 neighbor 7.0.0.4 next-hop-self
 !
 address-family vpnv4
  neighbor 7.0.0.2 activate
  neighbor 7.0.0.2 send-community both
  neighbor 7.0.0.4 activate
  neighbor 7.0.0.4 send-community both
  exit-address-family
 !
ip pim vrf vpn-red rp-address 7.0.0.2 -→ Pointing to PE1 as MVPN RP
ip pim rp-address 7.0.0.2 --→ PE1 is the RP for the master instance
ip pim ssm default
 !
end
```

FIGURE 2.62

PE2 router configuration—Cisco IOS.

2.2.2.22 Provider Routers, PE3, and Customer Edge Router Configurations

P and CE router configurations remain the same as the previous instance where only Default MDT was used. Data MDT configurations are not required on PE3, since it would not be initiating an MDT switchover from Default to Data MDTs as per our case study. The only difference would be that the MVPN (VPN RED) would need to be created on PE3 as seen in Figure 2.63.

2.2.2.23 PE3 Router Configuration

```
interfaces {
lo0 {
        unit 0 {
            family inet {
                address 7.0.0.4/32;
            }
        }
        unit 1 {
            family inet {
                address 7.0.0.4/32;
            }
        }
    unit 2 {
            family inet {
                address 7.0.0.4/32;
            }
        }


        }
    }
routing-instances {
vpn-red {
    instance-type vrf;
    interface ge-2/1/0.0;
    interface lo0.1;
    route-distinguisher 100:1;
    vrf-target target:100:1;
    protocols {
        pim {
            vpn-group-address 232.0.0.1;  ------> Default MDT Address
            rp {
                static {  ----------> PE1 is configured as RP for MVPN RED
                    address 7.0.0.2;  ---------> Loopback address of PE1
                }
            }
            interface ge-2/1/0.0 {
                mode sparse-dense;
                version 2;
            }
            interface lo0.1 {
                mode sparse-dense;
                version 2;
```

FIGURE 2.63

PE3 router configuration—JUNOS.

```
                }
            }
        }
    }
    vpn-blue {
        instance-type vrf;
        interface ge-2/1/1.0;
        interface lo0.2;
        route-distinguisher 100:2;
        vrf-target target:100:2;
        protocols {
            pim {
                vpn-group-address 232.1.1.1; ------> Default MDT Address
                rp {
                    local { ----------> PE3 is configured as RP for MVPN BLUE
                        address 7.0.0.4; --------> Loopback address of PE3
                    }
                }
                interface ge-2/1/1.0 {
                    mode sparse-dense;
                    version 2;
                }
                interface lo0.2 {
                    mode sparse-dense;
                    version 2;
                }
            }
        }
    }
}
protocols {
bgp {
    group carrier-ibgp {
        type internal;
        local-address 7.0.0.4;
        family inet {
            any;
        }
        family inet-vpn {
            any;
        }
        peer-as 100;
        neighbor 7.0.0.2;
        neighbor 7.0.0.3;
    }
}
pim {
    rp {
        local {
            family inet {
                address 7.0.0.2; ---> PE1 is RP for the Global PIM instance
```

FIGURE 2.63

(Continued)

```
                }
              }
            }
            interface all {
                mode sparse;
                version 2;
            }
            interface fxp0.0 {
                disable;
            }
        }
    }
```

FIGURE 2.63

(Continued)

2.2.2.24 PE1 Router Outputs

The assumption here is that the traffic from the source in MVPN RED has exceeded the configured threshold of 10 Kbps; therefore, the relevant commands will validate the setup and usage of the Data MDTs.

The output in Figure 2.64 provides details on the Data MDT address (232.13.13.0) allocated for C-MCAST Source "192.168.1.2" and group "239.1.1.4." This ensures that traffic is only sent to PE routers that have interested receivers.

2.2.2.25 PE2 Router Outputs

In all the outputs in Figure 2.65, assume that traffic is generated from C-MCAST source "192.168.1.2" to C-MCAST group "239.1.1.4."

The output in Figure 2.65 provides details on PE2 joining the Data MDT, which is announced by PE1. The big Y flag indicates that we are receiving on this Data MDT. Use show ip mroute on the receiving PE router (PE2) to verify that the Data MDT created state inside the Global table and that the Z flag are set and the outgoing interface is pointing to the correct MVPN.

```
operator@PE1# run show pim mdt outgoing instance vpn-red detail
Instance: PIM.vpn-red
Tunnel direction: Outgoing
Default group address: 232.0.0.1
Default tunnel interface: mt-2/1/0.32768

C-Group: 239.1.1.4
    C-Source: 192.168.1.2
    P-Group : 232.13.13.0
    Data tunnel interface       : mt-0/1/0.32769
    Last known forwarding rate  : 48 kbps (2 kBps)
    Configured threshold rate   : 10 kbps
    Tunnel uptime               : 00:00:31
```

FIGURE 2.64

Verifying Data MDTs in the VPN instance.

```
PE2#show ip pim vrf vpn-red mdt receive detail
Flags:D - Dense, S - Sparse, B - Bidir Group, s - SSM Group, C - Connected,
      L - Local, P - Pruned, R - RP-bit set, F - Register flag,
      T - SPT-bit set, J - Join SPT, M - MSDP created entry,
      X - Proxy Join Timer Running, A - Candidate for MSDP Advertisement,
      U - URD, I - Received Source Specific Host Report, Z - Multicast
Tunnel,
      Y - Joined MDT-data group, y - Sending to MDT-data group
Joined MDT-data [group : source] uptime/expires for VRF: vpn-red
  [232.13.13.0 : 7.0.0.2] 00:11:20/00:02:35
        (192.168.1.2, 239.1.1.4), 00:11:20/00:03:26/00:02:35, OIF count: 1,
 flags: TY
```

FIGURE 2.65

Verifying Data MDTs in the VPN instance for the receiving PE-PE2.

The output in Figure 2.66 validates that the outgoing interface list points to the correct MVPN. In Figure 2.67, it is MVPN RED.

We also use the command show ip mroute vrf vpn-red to verify the correct state inside the VPN. Again verify the big Y flag to indicate that we are receiving on a Data MDT.

2.2.2.26 The Final Picture of the Data MDT
Figure 2.68 provides insight into how the Data MDTs would in effect help a carrier network and when the number of PEs and MVPNs scale.

2.2.2.27 An Important Note on PIM-SM in Conjunction with MVPNs
As mentioned earlier, all the C-MCAST control traffic such as PIM joins, registers, and so forth are forwarded by transparently end-end by the concerned PE routers. Multicast infrastructure operates

```
PE2#show ip mroute
IP Multicast Routing Table
Flags:D - Dense, S - Sparse, B - Bidir Group, s - SSM Group, C - Connected,
      L - Local, P - Pruned, R - RP-bit set, F - Register flag,
      T - SPT-bit set, J - Join SPT, M - MSDP created entry,
      X - Proxy Join Timer Running, A - Candidate for MSDP Advertisement,
      U - URD, I - Received Source Specific Host Report, Z - Multicast
Tunnel,
      Y - Joined MDT-data group, y - Sending to MDT-data group
Outgoing interface flags: H - Hardware switched
 Timers: Uptime/Expires
 Interface state: Interface, Next-Hop or VCD, State/Mode
(7.0.0.2, 232.13.13.0), 00:11:20/00:02:56, flags: sTIZ
 Outgoing interface list:
      MVRF vpn-red, Forward/Sparse, 00:11:20/00:00:00
[output truncated]
```

FIGURE 2.66

Verifying Data MDT outgoing interface points to MVPN RED.

```
PE2#show ip mroute vrf vpn-red
IP Multicast Routing Table
Flags:D - Dense, S - Sparse, B - Bidir Group, s - SSM Group, C - Connected,
      L - Local, P - Pruned, R - RP-bit set, F - Register flag,
      T - SPT-bit set, J - Join SPT, M - MSDP created entry,
      X - Proxy Join Timer Running, A - Candidate for MSDP Advertisement,
      U - URD, I - Received Source Specific Host Report, Z - Multicast
Tunnel,
      Y - Joined MDT-data group, y - Sending to MDT-data group
Outgoing interface flags: H - Hardware switched
 Timers: Uptime/Expires
 Interface state: Interface, Next-Hop or VCD, State/Mode
(*, 239.1.1.4), 00:11:20/stopped, RP 7.0.0.2, flags: S
 Incoming interface: Tunnel0
 Outgoing interface list:
       GigabitEthernet4/1, Forward/Sparse-Dense, 00:11:20/00:02:51
(192.168.1.2, 239.1.1.4), 00:11:20/00:03:26, flags: TY
 Incoming interface: Tunnel0
 Outgoing interface list:
       GigabitEthernet4/1, Forward/Sparse-Dense, 00:11:20/00:02:51
[output truncated]
```

FIGURE 2.67

Verifying Data MDT state in the MVPN to ensure that Data MDT is used.

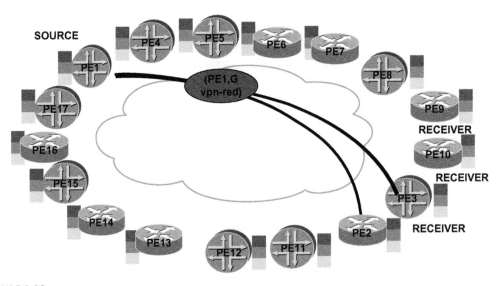

FIGURE 2.68

```
protocols {
pim {
dense-groups {
    224.0.1.39/32;
    224.0.1.40/32;
}
rp {
    local {
        family inet {
            address 7.0.0.2;
        }
    }
    auto-rp mapping;
}
interface all {
    mode sparse-dense;
    version 2;
}
interface fxp0.0 {
    disable;
}
```

FIGURE 2.69

PE1 router configuration—JUNOS.

unaltered and in an optimal fashion. For instance, a PIM PRUNE message from a receiver in the C-MCAST domain needs to be propagated to the DR connected to the source directly or via the RP. This is necessary to instruct the source to stop sending traffic into the network. However, note that the traffic path or the data plane for C-MCAST traffic within the carrier core is subject to the configuration of PIM-SM within the core—Shared Tree always versus Shortest Path Tree. Therefore, the carrier PIM-SM policies override the patterns of C-MCAST flows.

2.2.2.28 ASM Mode Using AutoRP for the PIM Master Instance
In this section we still follow the same case study as in the Data MDT section; however, we made a small change in the configuration. We used AutoRP for the PIM Master instance in the carrier core. The C-MCAST domain still uses Static RP. Relevant configurations on the PE and P routers are seen in Figure 2.69. Only the relevant portions of the configurations are displayed.

If the router combines the local RP function to send announcements and also perform the mapping function, configure the router as a local RP and include the `auto-rp` mapping statement at the hierarchy level. In this case PE1 performs these functions.

PE2 is configured with the RP configuration to enable it to listen to AUTO-RP mapping messages (see Figure 2.70).

2.2.2.29 PE2 Router Configuration
Cisco IOS does not require any additional configuration, since it automatically listens to AUTO-RP mapping messages (see Figure 2.71).

Note: All Cisco IOS-based Provider routers do not require any additional configuration, and may follow the same template used for router PE2.

```
protocols {
pim {
dense-groups {
    224.0.1.39/32;
    224.0.1.40/32;
}
rp {
    auto-rp discovery;
    }
interface all {
    mode sparse-dense;
    version 2;
}
interface fxp0.0 {
    disable;
}
```

FIGURE 2.70

PE3 router configuration—JUNOS.

```
ip multicast-routing
!
!
!
!
interface GigabitEthernet5/1
description #Interface to Carrier Core #
 ip address 10.3.91.1 255.255.255.252
 ip pim sparse-dense-mode
 !
ip pim ssm default
 !
End
```

FIGURE 2.71

PE2 router configuration—Cisco IOS.

2.2.2.30 Verifying the Outputs on PE3

Figure 2.72 provides the details on the P-Group address "232.0.0.1" learned from the RP at address 7.0.0.2. Also, the RP address has been learned via Auto-RP.

CE router configurations remain the same, since they use Static RP as per this example.

2.2.2.31 ASM Mode—Inter-Provider Multicast VPNs

Inter-Provider-based MVPNs using an ASM deployment model are seen in Figure 2.73. The configurations for each router would depict only the MVPN-specific information; for instance, generic VRF-specific information such as Route distinguishers would be omitted. The network topology used for this case study is provided below.

```
operator@PE3# run show pim rps extensive
Instance: PIM.master
Address family INET
RP: 7.0.0.2
Learned from 7.0.0.2 via: auto-rp
Time Active: 00:06:48
Holdtime: 150 with 146 remaining
Device Index: 179
Subunit: 32768
Interface: pe-4/2/0.32769
Active groups using RP:
        232.0.0.1
        total 1 groups active
```

FIGURE 2.72

Outputs on PE3 verifying RP information.

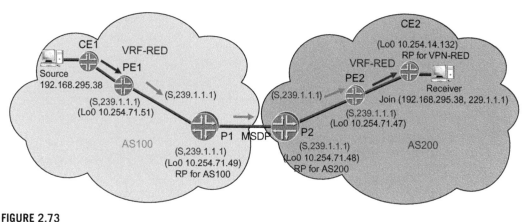

FIGURE 2.73

In our case study, we have two Autonomous Systems (ASs): AS100 & AS200. A BGP/MPLS VPN that belongs to VPN RED is spread across both ASs; in other words, two sites of the same VPN span the two ASs. The objective here is to provide Multicast VPN transport for VPN RED. The RP for the PIM Master instance in AS100 is router P1, and the RP in AS200 is P2. To enable exchange of group information between the two RPs, MSDP is used. The RP for VPN RED is router CE2, and a Static RP configuration is used both within the two Master instances in the two ASs as well as within the MVPN instance. We have a source connected to CE1 in AS100, which sends traffic to an interested receiver connected to CE2 at AS200. This would validate in the Inter-Provider transport of MVPN traffic. The configuration and validation templates are provided in Figure 2.74.

2.2.2.32 PE1 Router Configuration

```
protocols {
  pim {
    rp {
      static {
        address 10.254.71.49;---→ P1 is the RP for Master PIM instance
      }
    }
      interface all {
        mode sparse;
        version 2;
}
      interface fxp0.0 {
disable;
      }
    }
  }
routing-instances {
    vpn-red {
      protocols {
        pim {
          dense-groups {
            229.0.0.0/8;
          }
          vpn-group-address 239.1.1.1;  --→ Default MDT
          rp {
            static {
              address 10.254.14.132; → CE2 is the RP for PIM VPN instance
            }
          }
            interface t1-1/0/0:0.0 {
            mode sparse-dense;
             version 2;
          }
            interface lo0.1 {
            mode sparse-dense;
            version 2;
        }
      }
    }
  }
}
```

FIGURE 2.74

PE1 router configuration—JUNOS.

2.2.2.33 P1 Router Configuration

```
protocols {
  msdp {
     peer 10.254.71.48 { ---------→ Peer RP in the neighboring AS200
      local-address 10.254.71.49; → RP for local AS100
    }
  }
 pim {
  rp {
   local {
     address 10.254.71.49;
   }
  }
   interface all {
     mode sparse;
     version 2;
  }
   interface fxp0.0 {
    disable;
  }
 }
}
```

FIGURE 2.75

P1 router configuration—JUNOS.

2.2.2.34 CE1 Router Configuration

```
protocols {
   pim {
     rp {
        dense-groups {
          229.0.0.0/8;
       }
        static {
          address 10.254.14.132; --→ CE2 is the RP
      }
    }
       interface all {
        mode sparse-dense;
        version 2;
    }
      interface fxp0.0 {
       disable;
    }
   }
}
```

FIGURE 2.76

CE1 router configuration—JUNOS.

2.2.2.35 PE2 Router Configuration

```
protocols {
  pim {
    rp {
     static {
      address 10.254.71.48;  --------→ P2 is the RP
     }
  }
     interface all {
     mode sparse;
     version 2;
     }
     interface fxp0.0 {
     disable;
  }
 }
 }
routing-instances {
    vpn-red {
      protocols {
       pim {
        dense-groups {
         229.0.0.0/8;
         }
       vpn-group-address 239.1.1.1;
        rp {
          static {
            address 10.254.14.132;  ----→ CE2 is the RP
        }
    }
          interface t1-1/0/0:0.0 {
          mode sparse-dense;
          version 2;
    }
          interface lo0.1 {
          mode sparse-dense;
          version 2;
     }
    }
   }
  }
 }
```

FIGURE 2.77

PE2 router configuration—JUNOS.

2.2.2.36 P2 Router Configuration

```
protocols {
  msdp {
    peer 10.254.71.49 {
    local-address 10.254.71.48;
    }
  }
  pim {
    rp {
     local {
     address 10.254.71.48;
    }
  }
        interface all {
          mode sparse;
          version 2;
      }
        interface fxp0.0 {
        disable;
      }
    }
  }
}
```

FIGURE 2.78

P2 router configuration—JUNOS.

2.2.2.37 CE2 Router Configuration

```
protocols {
    pim {
       dense-groups {
          229.0.0.0/8;
    }
    rp {
       local {
          address 10.254.14.132;
      }
    }
   interface all {
    mode sparse-dense;
    version 2;
   }
   interface fxp0.0 {
    disable;
   }
  }
}
```

FIGURE 2.79

CE2 router configuration—JUNOS.

2.2.2.38 Verifying the Outputs on CE1

Figure 2.80 shows a source interested in sending multicast traffic to group "229.1.1.1," and a join has been received by CE1.

2.2.2.39 Verifying the Outputs on PE1

In this output we verify the RP association between PE1 and P1 (which is the RP for the Master instance) along with the groups that have been registered (Figure. 2.81). In this case "239.1.1.1," which is the P-Group address (Default MDT), is registered. The register state also indicates that PE1 (IPv4 address 10.254.71.51) has made the registration.

Check for the PIM joins under the PIM Master instance. Note the (S, G) entries for the P-Group address, which has each of the unicast addresses for the PE routers (PE2 with address 10.254.71.47, and PE1 with 10.254.71.51). The upstream state Local source indicates that PE1 is the local source for state (PE1, 239.1.1.1). The upstream state Join to source indicates an MDT is set up between PE1 and PE2 (see Figure 2.82).

A source Registration is visible in this output for C-MCAST group 229.1.1.1 (see Figure 2.83).

```
operator@CE1> show pim join extensive
Instance: PIM.master Family: INET
Group: 229.1.1.1 --→ C-MCAST Group
      Source: 192.168.295.38 ------→ Source IPv4 address
      Flags: dense
      Upstream interface: fe-3/0/2.0
      Downstream interfaces:
          t1-7/0/0:0.0
```

FIGURE 2.80

Verifying PIM joins.

```
operator@PE1> show pim rps extensive
Instance: PIM.master
Family: INET
RP: 10.254.71.49
Learned via: static configuration
Time Active: 00:22:07
Holdtime: 0
Device Index: 34
Subunit: 32769
Interface: pe-1/1/0.32769
Group Ranges:
      224.0.0.0/4
Active groups using RP:
      239.1.1.1
      total 1 groups active
Register State for RP:
```

Group	Source	FirstHop	RP Address	State	Timeout
239.1.1.1	10.254.71.51	10.254.71.51	10.254.71.49	Suppress	20

FIGURE 2.81

RP registration details.

```
operator@PE1> show pim join extensive
Instance: PIM.master Family: INET
Group: 239.1.1.1
    Source: *
    RP: 10.254.71.49
    Flags: sparse,rptree,wildcard
    Upstream interface: so-0/0/0.0
    Upstream State: Join to RP
    Downstream Neighbors:
        Interface: mt-1/1/0.32769
            0.0.0.0 State: Join   Flags: SRW  Timeout: Infinity
Group: 239.1.1.1
    Source: 10.254.71.47
    Flags: sparse,spt-pending
    Upstream interface: so-0/0/0.0
    Upstream State: Join to Source ----→ Join to PE1
    Keepalive timeout: 198
    Downstream Neighbors:
        Interface: mt-1/1/0.32769
            0.0.0.0 State: Join   Flags: S    Timeout: Infinity
Group: 239.1.1.1
    Source: 10.254.71.51
    Flags: sparse
    Upstream interface: local
    Upstream State: Local Source, Prune to RP --→ Source is PE1
    Keepalive timeout: 198
    Downstream Neighbors:
        Interface: so-0/0/0.0
            192.168.296.42 State: Join   Flags: S    Timeout: 176
Instance: PIM.master
```

FIGURE 2.82

Verifying PIM joins.

```
operator@PE1> show pim join extensive instance VPN-A
Instance: PIM.VPN-A Family: INET
Group: 229.1.1.1 -→ C-MCAST Group
    Source: 192.168.295.38 ---→ C-MCAST Source
    Flags: dense
    Upstream interface: t1-1/0/0:0.0
    Downstream interfaces:
        mt-1/1/0.32769
Instance: PIM.vpn-red
```

FIGURE 2.83

PIM joins under the routing instance.

```
operator@P1> show pim rps extensive
Instance: PIM.master
Family: INET
RP: 10.254.71.49
Learned via: static configuration
Time Active: 00:30:43
Holdtime: 0
Device Index: 33
Subunit: 32768
Interface: pd-1/1/0.32768
Group Ranges:
        224.0.0.0/4
Active groups using RP:
        239.1.1.1 ---------> P-Group for vpn-red
        total 1 groups active
Register State for RP:
Group           Source          FirstHop        RP Address      State      Timeout
239.1.1.1       10.254.71.51    10.254.71.51    10.254.71.49    Receive
```

FIGURE 2.84

RP details.

2.2.2.40 Verifying the Outputs on P1

The (S, G) registration entries for both PE1 and PE2 to MDT group address "239.1.1.1" is visible, with each of the PE routers to form the Default MDT. They form the MTI directly with each other (see Figures 2.84 and 2.85).

```
operator@P1> show pim join extensive
Instance: PIM.master Family: INET
Group: 239.1.1.1
    Source: *
    RP: 10.254.71.49
    Flags: sparse,rptree,wildcard
    Upstream interface: local
    Upstream State: Local RP
    Downstream Neighbors:
        Interface: so-0/1/0.0
            192.168.296.41 State: Join   Flags: SRW  Timeout: 184
Group: 239.1.1.1
    Source: 10.254.71.47
    Flags: sparse,spt-pending
    Upstream interface: so-0/0/2.0 ------> Interface to AS200
    Upstream State: Local RP, Join to Source
    Keepalive timeout: 207
    Downstream Neighbors:
        Interface: so-0/1/0.0
            192.168.296.41 State: Join   Flags: S    Timeout: 184
```

FIGURE 2.85

PIM Joins on the RP.

```
Group: 239.1.1.1
    Source: 10.254.71.51
    Flags: sparse,spt
    Upstream interface: so-0/1/0.0
    Upstream State: Local RP, Join to Source
    Keepalive timeout: 207
    Downstream Neighbors:
        Interface: so-0/0/2.0
            192.168.296.73 State: Join    Flags: S     Timeout: 186
        Interface: so-0/1/0.0              (pruned)
            192.168.296.41 State: Prune  Flags: SR    Timeout: 184
Instance: PIM.master
```

FIGURE 2.85

(Continued)

2.2.2.41 *Verifying the Outputs on P2*

```
operator@P2> show pim rps extensive
Instance: PIM.master
Family: INET
RP: 10.254.71.48
Learned via: static configuration
Time Active: 06:26:56
Holdtime: 0
Device Index: 32
Subunit: 32768
Interface: pd-1/1/0.32768
Group Ranges:
        224.0.0.0/4
Active groups using RP:
        239.1.1.1
        total 1 groups active
Register State for RP:
Group          Source        FirstHop       RP Address     State    Timeout
239.1.1.1      10.254.71.47  10.254.71.47   10.254.71.48   Receive        0
```

FIGURE 2.86

RP details.

2.2.2.42 *Verifying the Outputs on PE2*

```
operator@PE2> show pim rps extensive
Instance: PIM.master
Family: INET
RP: 10.254.71.48
Learned via: static configuration
Time Active: 06:26:56
Holdtime: 0
```

FIGURE 2.87

RP Registration from PE2.

```
Device Index: 34
Subunit: 32770
Interface: pe-1/1/0.32770
Group Ranges:
        224.0.0.0/4
Active groups using RP:
        239.1.1.1
        total 1 groups active
Register State for RP:
Group            Source          FirstHop         RP Address        State      Timeout
239.1.1.1        10.254.71.47    10.254.71.47     10.254.71.48      Suppress       42
```

FIGURE 2.87

(Continued)

```
operator@PE2> show pim join extensive
Instance: PIM.master Family: INET
Group: 239.1.1.1
    Source: *
    RP: 10.254.71.48
    Flags: sparse,rptree,wildcard
    Upstream interface: so-0/0/3.0
    Upstream State: Join to RP
    Downstream Neighbors:
        Interface: mt-1/1/0.32769
            0.0.0.0 State: Join    Flags: SRW  Timeout: Infinity
Group: 239.1.1.1
    Source: 10.254.71.47
    Flags: sparse
    Upstream interface: local
    Upstream State: Local Source, Prune to RP
    Keepalive timeout: 173
    Downstream Neighbors:
        Interface: so-0/0/3.0
            192.168.296.49 State: Join   Flags: S    Timeout: 199
Group: 239.1.1.1
    Source: 10.254.71.51
    Flags: sparse,spt-pending
    Upstream interface: so-0/0/3.0
    Upstream State: Join to Source
    Keepalive timeout: 173
    Downstream Neighbors:
        Interface: mt-1/1/0.32769
            0.0.0.0 State: Join    Flags: S    Timeout: Infinity
Instance: PIM.master
```

FIGURE 2.88

Verifying PIM joins.

```
operator@PE2> show pim join extensive instance VPN-A
Instance: PIM.VPN-A Family: INET
Group: 229.1.1.1
    Source: 192.168.295.38
    Flags: dense
    Upstream interface: mt-1/1/0.32769
    Downstream interfaces:
        t1-1/0/0:0.0
Instance: PIM.VPN-A Family: INET6
```

FIGURE 2.89

PIM Joins under the routing instance.

2.2.2.43 Verifying the Outputs on CE2

```
operator@CE2> show pim join extensive
Instance: PIM.master Family: INET
Group: 229.1.1.1
    Source: 192.168.295.38
    Flags: dense
    Upstream interface: t1-2/0/0:0.0
    Downstream interfaces:
        fe-2/2/0.0
Instance: PIM.master
```

FIGURE 2.90

Verifying PIM joins.

2.2.2.44 SSM Mode—Using BGP-Based MDT Subaddress Family Identifier Information

In a single AS environment, if the Default MDT is using PIM-SM) with Rendezvous Points (RPs), then PIM over the MTI will establish adjacencies because the source PE and receiver PE discover each other via the RP. In this case, the local PE (source PE) sends Register messages to the RP, which then builds a Shortest Path Tree (SPT) toward the source PE. The remote PE, which acts as a receiver for the MDT multicast group, sends *, G joins toward the RP and joins the distribution tree for that group.

A Draft-Rosen MVPN with service provider tunnels operating in SSM mode uses BGP signaling for autodiscovery of the PE routers. Each PE sends an MDT subsequent address family identifier (MDT-SAFI) BGP network layer reachability information (NLRI) advertisement. The advertisement contains the following:

- Route distinguisher
- Unicast address of the PE router to which the source site is attached (usually the loopback)
- Multicast group address
- Route target extended community attribute

Each remote PE router imports the MDT-SAFI advertisements from each of the other PE routers if the route target matches. Each PE router then joins the (S, G) tree rooted at each of the other PE

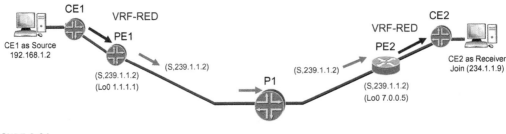

FIGURE 2.91

routers. After a PE router discovers the other PE routers, the source and group are bound to the VRF through the multicast tunnel de-encapsulation interface. After the PE routers are discovered, PIM is notified of the multicast source and group addresses. PIM binds the (S, G) state to the `mti` interface and sends a join message for that group. Autodiscovery for a Draft-Rosen MVPN with service provider tunnels operating in SSM mode uses some of the facilities of the BGP-based MVPN control plane software module. Therefore, the BGP-based MVPN control plane must be enabled.

Next is a case study demonstrating this functionality. In this example, two PE routers (PE1 is a JUNOS-based PE and PE2 a Cisco IOS-based PE device) are used, each connected to a single site using BGP/MPLS VPNs. In this example, PIM-SSM is used for both the Default and Data MDT setup. This setup uses PE1 as the RP for the MVPN instance. Note that the Provide core does not use an RP, since only SSM for both Default and Data MDTs are now used. In our setup, CE1 generates traffic to two groups (234.1.1.2) and (234.1.1.9) for which CE2 has joined. In this example, we demonstrate the outputs (later in this section) based on the scenario where CE1 is sending multicast traffic to CE2 (see Figure 2.91).

2.2.2.45 PE1 Router Configuration
The configuration in Figure 2.92 displays a few additional statements that define the mode of operation as SSM. BGP Address families are enabled for MDT-SAFI NLRI and Autodiscovery, respectively. Other parameters remain the same with the exception that the PIM infrastructure in the carrier core does not use an RP anymore.

2.2.2.46 PE2 Router Configuration
JUNOS imports MDT-SAFI family prefixes into the VRF based upon the extended community Route Targets attached to the packet. Therefore, it is mandatory to configure the Cisco PE to send the right Route-Target attached to the MDT-SAFI packet so that PE1 can import the MDT-SAFI prefix into its VRF. The route-map named send-community on PE2 does exactly this function (see Figure 2.93).

2.2.2.47 CE and Provider Router Configurations
The CE routers still use ASM, and hence the configurations from previous sections can be substituted. The P router configurations only use PIM in the core, and have no additional configuration required; hence these configurations are not provided in this section.

```
protocol{
bgp { --------------→ BGP enabled for SAFI Type 66
    group INTERNAL {
        type internal;
        family inet-vpn {
            any;
        }
        family inet-mvpn { --→ BGP Control plane for PE Autodiscovery
            signaling;
        }
        family inet-mdt { ------→ MDT SAFI NLRI enabled
            signaling;
        }
        neighbor 7.0.0.5 {
            local-address 1.1.1.
            peer-as 65100;
        }
    }
}
pim {
    interface all {
        mode sparse;
        version 2;
    }
    interface fxp0.0 {
        disable;
    }
  }
}
routing-instances{
vpn-red {
    instance-type vrf;
    interface ge-5/2/0.100;
    interface lo0.1;
    route-distinguisher 100:1;
    provider-tunnel {-----------→ Definition of the Forwarding plane
        pim-ssm {{-----------→ SSM used for the MVPN
            group-address 239.1.1.2; {-----------→ Default MDT
            }
        mdt {
            threshold {
                group 224.0.0.0/3 {
                    source 0.0.0.0/0 {
                        rate 10;
                    }
                }
            }
            tunnel-limit 25; -→ Maximum number of Data MDTs for this MVRF
            group-range 239.2.2.192/26; -> Address for the Data MDT
        }
    }
}
```

FIGURE 2.92

PE1 router configuration—JUNOS.

```
vrf-target target:100:1;
vrf-table-label;
routing-options {
    multicast {
        ssm-groups 239.0.0.0/8;
    }
    auto-export;
}
protocols {
    bgp { -----------------→ ebgp session to the CE
        family inet {
            unicast;
        }
        export bgp;
        group peer {
            type external;
            peer-as 65001;
            neighbor 192.168.1.2; --→ Address of CE1
        }
    }
    pim {
        mvpn {
            autodiscovery {
                inet-mdt; →Use MDT SAFI for PE Autodiscovery
            }
        }
        rp {
            local {
                address 1.1.1.1; -→ PE1 is the RP for the MVPN
            }
        }
        interface lo0.1 {
            mode sparse;


            version 2;
        }
        interface ge-5/2/0.100 {
            mode sparse;
            version 2;
        }
    }
    mvpn {-----→ Use BGP-based control plane for Autodiscovery only
        autodiscovery-only {--→ Not to use BGP for PIM-based operations
            intra-as { →Enabled only for Intra-AS routes
                inclusive; -----→Over a PMSI (Default MDT)
            }
        }
    }
}
}
}
```

FIGURE 2.92

(Continued)

```
routing-options{
 autonomous-system 65100;
  multicast {
    ssm-groups 239.0.0.0/8; -→ Use this group as an SSM Group
 }
}
```

FIGURE 2.92

(Continued)

```
ip vrf forwarding
!
ip vrf vpna
 rd 100:1
 route-target export 100:1
 route-target import 100:1
 mdt default 239.1.1.2
 mdt data 239.2.1.0 0.0.0.255 threshold 10 -→ Data MDT address range
 !
 !
 !
ip multicast-routing
ip multicast-routing vrf vpn-red
 !
 !
 !
interface Loopback0
 ip address 7.0.0.5 255.255.255.255
 ip pim sparse-mode
 !
interface Loopback1
 ip vrf forwarding vpn-red
 ip address 7.0.0.5 255.255.255.255
 ip pim sparse-mode
 !
 !
interface GigabitEthernet4/1
 ip vrf forwarding vpna
 ip address 13.13.13.2 255.255.255.252
 ip pim sparse-mode
 !
router bgp 65100
  no synchronization
  bgp log-neighbor-changes
  neighbor 1.1.1.1 remote-as 65100
  neighbor 1.1.1.1 update-source Loopback0
  neighbor 1.1.1.1 next-hop-self
  no auto-summary  !
  address-family vpnv4
  neighbor 1.1.1.1 activate
  neighbor 1.1.1.1 send-community both
  exit-address-family
 !
```

FIGURE 2.93

PE2 router configuration—IOS.

```
!
ip pim ssm range 10
ip pim vrf vpna rp-address 1.1.1.1
!
access-list 10 permit 239.0.0.0
!
route-map send-community permit 10 --→ Extended community attributes
 set extcommunity rt  100:1
!
end
```

FIGURE 2.93

(Continued)

2.2.2.48 Verifying the Outputs on PE1

The output in Figure 2.94 provides a snapshot of the C-MCAST (S, G) groups currently active and the traffic rate and statistics per (S, G) pair.

```
operator@PE1# run show multicast route instance vpn-red extensive
Family: INET

Group: 234.1.1.2 ------------→ C-MCAST Group
    Source: 192.168.1.2/32 ------------→ C-MCAST Source (CE1)
    Upstream interface: ge-5/2/0.100
    Downstream interface list:
        mt-5/0/0.32768 -----→ Multicast Tunnel Interface to the remote PE
    Session description: Unknown
    Statistics: 0 kBps, 0 pps, 29022 packets ------------→ Packets
    transmitted
    Next-hop ID: 262145
    Upstream protocol: PIM
    Route state: Active
    Forwarding state: Forwarding
    Cache lifetime/timeout: 335 seconds
    Wrong incoming interface notifications: 0

Group: 234.1.1.9 ------------→ C-MCAST Group
    Source: 192.168.1.2/32 ------------→ C-MCAST Source (CE1)
    Upstream interface: ge-5/2/0.100
    Downstream interface list:
        mt-5/0/0.32768
    Session description: Unknown
    Statistics: 30 kBps, 360 pps, 32082 packets ------------→ Packets
    Next-hop ID: 262145
    Upstream protocol: PIM
    Route state: Active
    Forwarding state: Forwarding
    Cache lifetime/timeout: 360 seconds
    Wrong incoming interface notifications: 0
```

FIGURE 2.94

Verifying Multicast Route Table for the MVPN.

The output in Figure 2.95 provides a snapshot of the traffic statistics using the Default MDT for a given MVPN.

```
operator@PE1# run show multicast route extensive
Family: INET

Group: 239.1.1.2 --→ Default MDT
    Source: 1.1.1.1/32 -→ PE1
    Upstream interface: local
    Downstream interface list:
        ge-3/1/0.0 ---------------------------→ Interface to carrier core
    Session description: Administratively Scoped
    Statistics: 91 kBps, 847 pps, 353716 packets ------→ Traffic using the
P-Group Address
    Next-hop ID: 262143
    Upstream protocol: PIM
    Route state: Active
    Forwarding state: Forwarding ---→ Traffic is currently being forwarded
    Cache lifetime/timeout: 360 seconds
    Wrong incoming interface notifications: 0

Group: 239.1.1.2
    Source: 7.0.0.5/32 ---→ PE2
    Upstream interface: ge-3/1/0.0
    Downstream interface list:
        mt-5/0/0.49152
    Session description: Administratively Scoped
    Statistics: 0 kBps, 0 pps, 1494 packets
    Next-hop ID: 262144
    Upstream protocol: PIM
    Route state: Active
    Forwarding state: Forwarding
    Cache lifetime/timeout: 360 seconds
    Wrong incoming interface notifications: 0
```

FIGURE 2.95

Verifying the Global Multicast Table.

The output in Figure 2.96 validates that PE1 has discovered PE2 via BGP, and this information is now available to PIM for the forwarding plane to function correctly.

```
operator@PE1 # run show pim join extensive
Instance: PIM.master Family: INET
R = Rendezvous Point Tree, S = Sparse, W = Wildcard

Group: 239.1.1.2
    Source: 1.1.1.1 -----------→ Local PE
    Flags: sparse,spt
    Upstream interface: Local
```

FIGURE 2.96

Verifying PIM joins on the Global Instance of PIM.

```
        Upstream neighbor: Local
        Upstream state: Local Source
        Keepalive timeout: 320
        Downstream neighbors:
            Interface: ge-3/1/0.0
                11.11.3.2 State: Join Flags: S Timeout: 174

Group: 239.1.1.2
    Source: 7.0.0.5 ------> Join for Provider core SSM group PE2
    Flags: sparse,spt
    Upstream interface: ge-3/1/0.0 -> Facing the carrier core
    Upstream neighbor: 11.11.3.2
    Upstream state: Join to Source
    Keepalive timeout:
    Downstream neighbors:
        Interface: mt-5/0/0.32768
            1.1.1.1 State: Join Flags: S   Timeout: Infinity
Instance: PIM.master Family: INET6
R = Rendezvous Point Tree, S = Sparse, W = Wildcard
```

FIGURE 2.96

(Continued)

```
operator@PE1# run show pim join extensive instance vpn-red
Instance: PIM.vpn-red Family: INET
R = Rendezvous Point Tree, S = Sparse, W = Wildcard

Group: 234.1.1.2 -----> Joins for Group
 Source: *
 RP: 1.1.1.1
 Flags: sparse,rptree,wildcard
 Upstream interface: Local
 Upstream neighbor: Local
 Upstream state: Local RP
 Downstream neighbors:
 Interface: mt-5/0/0.32768
 7.0.0.5 State: Join Flags: SRW Timeout: 198

Group: 234.1.1.9 ------> Joins for Group
 Source: *
 RP: 1.1.1.1
 Flags: sparse,rptree,wildcard
 Upstream interface: Local
 Upstream neighbor: Local
 Upstream state: Local RP
 Downstream neighbors:
     Interface: mt-5/0/0.32768
         7.0.0.5 State: Join Flags: SRW Timeout: 198

Group: 234.1.1.9 -----> (S,G) Entry
 Source: 192.168.1.2
 Flags: sparse,spt
 Upstream interface: ge-5/2/0.100
```

FIGURE 2.97

Verifying PIM joins on the MVPN instance.

```
Upstream neighbor: 192.168.1.2
Upstream state: Local Source, Local RP
Keepalive timeout: 312
Downstream neighbors:
    Interface: mt-5/0/0.32768
        7.0.0.5 State: Join Flags: S Timeout: 198
Instance: PIM.vpn-red Family: INET6
R = Rendezvous Point Tree, S = Sparse, W = Wildcard
```

FIGURE 2.97

(Continued)

The output in Figure 2.98 lists the contents of the MDT database, which essentially lists the BGP updates received from neighboring PE routers via BGP MDT signaling to aid the auto discovery process. In Figure 2.98, an update from PE2 is received with the appropriate P-group address attached and extended community attributes, which makes it worthwhile to be passed onto the PIM process associated with MVPN RED.

```
operator@PE1# run show route table vpn-red.mdt extensive
vpn-red.mdt.0: 2 destinations, 2 routes (2 active, 0 holddown, 0 hidden)
1:100:1:1.1.1.1:239.1.1.2/144 (1 entry, 1 announced)
Page 0 idx 0 Type 1 val 8d56d38
        *MVPN   Preference: 70
                Next hop type: Indirect
                Next-hop reference count: 2
                Protocol next hop: 1.1.1.1
                Indirect next hop: 0 -
                State: <Active Int Ext>
                Age: 22:51:52   Metric2: 1
                Task: mvpn global task
              Announcement bits (2): 0-mvpn global task 1-BGP RT Background
                AS path: I

1:100:1:7.0.0.5:239.1.1.2/144 (1 entry,1 announced)-→ Announcement from PE2
        *BGP    Preference: 170/-101
                Route Distinguisher: 100:1
                Next hop type: Indirect
                Next-hop reference count: 2
                Source: 7.0.0.5
                Protocol next hop: 7.0.0.5
                Indirect next hop: 2 no-forward
                State: <Secondary Active Int Ext>
                Local AS: 65100 Peer AS: 65100
                Age: 8:13:44    Metric2: 1
                Task: BGP_65100.7.0.0.5+61713
                Announcement bits (1): 0-mvpn global task
                AS path: I
                Communities: target:100:1 )-→ Extended community
                Import Accepted --→ Update Accepted
```

FIGURE 2.98

Checking the BGP table for MDT updates.

```
Localpref: 100
Router ID: 7.0.0.5
Primary Routing Table bgp.mdt.0
        Indirect next hops: 1
        Protocol next hop: 7.0.0.5 Metric: 1
        Indirect next hop: 2 no-forward
        Indirect path forwarding next hops: 1
                Next hop type: Router
                Next hop: 11.11.3.2 via ge-3/1/0.0
        7.0.0.5/32 Originating RIB: inet.3
          Metric: 1                        Node path count: 1
            Forwarding nexthops: 1
                Nexthop: 11.11.3.2 via ge-3/1/0.0
```

FIGURE 2.98

(Continued)

The output in Figure 2.99 indicates that a Data MDT is set up the moment the traffic threshold from CE1 (source) to CE (receiver) for group "234.1.1.9" exceeds 10 Kbps. In our case, the output shows that the current traffic threshold is 26 Kbps.

```
operator@PE1# run show pim mdt outgoing instance vpn-red detail
Instance: PIM.vpn-red
Tunnel direction: Outgoing
Tunnel mode: PIM-SSM
Default group address: 239.1.1.2   → Default MDT
Default source address: 1.1.1.1 → IPv4 Source Address of PE1
Default tunnel interface: mt-1/3/0.32768 -→ MTI
Default tunnel source: 0.0.0.0

C-Group: 234.1.1.9 → C-MCAST Group
    C-Source: 192.168.1.2 → Customer Source Address
    P-Group : 239.2.2.192 → Data MDT is Triggered
    Data tunnel interface     : mt-1/3/0.32769 → MTI for Data MDT
    Last known forwarding rate : 192 kbps (24 kBps)
    Configured threshold rate  : 10 kbps → Threshold for the DATA MDT
    Tunnel uptime              : 00:00:26
```

FIGURE 2.99

Verifying the Data MDT.

The output in Figure 2.100 shows events that are triggered to set up the Data MDT when the threshold for C-MCAST traffic flowing over the Default MDT is exceeded.

2.2.2.49 Verifying the Outputs on PE2
The output in Figure 2.101 shows that the receiving PE (PE2) has joined the Data MDT for vpn-red.

2.2.2.50 SSM Mode—Using BGP-Based MDT-SAFI for Inter-AS MVPN Deployments
This deployment allows Multicast traffic within a VRF to pass between two or more sites located in different ASs (very similar to the PIM-SM model seen earlier); however, BGP MDT signaling is

```
operator@PE1# Jun  4 14:58:14.040729 PIM mt-1/3/0.32768 SENT 1.1.1.1 ->
224.0.0.13+3232 DATA-MDT UDP C-Source 192.168.1.2 C-Group 234.1.1.9 P-Group
239.2.2.192

Jun  4 14:59:14.042423 PIM mt-1/3/0.32768 SENT 1.1.1.1 -> 224.0.0.13+3232
DATA-MDT UDP C-Source 192.168.1.2 C-Group 234.1.1.9 P-Group 239.2.2.192

Jun  4 15:00:14.044127 PIM mt-1/3/0.32768 SENT 1.1.1.1 -> 224.0.0.13+3232
DATA-MDT UDP C-Source 192.168.1.2 C-Group 234.1.1.9 P-Group 239.2.2.192
```

FIGURE 2.100

Debug outputs verifying the Data MDT setup.

```
PE2#show ip pim vrf vpn-red mdt receive
Flags: D - Dense, S - Sparse, B - Bidir Group, s - SSM Group, C - Connected,
       L - Local, P - Pruned, R - RP-bit set, F - Register flag,
       T - SPT-bit set, J - Join SPT, M - MSDP created entry,
       X - Proxy Join Timer Running, A - Candidate MSDP Advertisement,
       U - URD, I - Received Source Specific Host Report, Z - Multicast
Tunnel
       Y - Joined MDT-data group, y - Sending to MDT-data group
Joined MDT-data groups for VRF: vpn-red
   group: 239.2.2.192
```

FIGURE 2.101

Verifying the Data MDT.

used here. The model allows MDTs (Default or Data) to be provisioned between PE routers across Autonomous System Boundary Routers (ASBRs) without the PE or P routers in either AS requiring knowledge of reachability information (usually loopbacks) of the remote AS. The implementation details provided here are only applicable to Cisco devices.

A reference network is illustrated in Figure 2.102. This network consists of a customer with two sites connected via two service provider networks, AS200 and AS300. To connect the two VPN sites to pass *unicast* (VPNv4) traffic, one of the options described in Section 10 of RFC 4364 would be used:

- Option A: Back-to-Back VRFs
- Option B: ABSR-to-ASBR passing eBGP + VPNv4 + Label (this is used in Figure 2.102)
- Option C: RR-to-RR passing eBGP + VPNv4 + Label (VPN addresses)
- Option D: ASBR-to-ASBR passing eBGP + IPv4 + Label (PE loopbacks)

In this case study we focus on an Option B deployment in conjunction with MVPN.

Figure 2.102 also shows a Multicast receiver in AS300 wishing to join a stream originating from a source in AS200. Before the detailed discussion, this would be rather problematic to accomplish in the reference network where the two ASs are interconnected with ASBRs using Option B (eBGP passing VPNv4 routes plus VPN Label). The problem basically revolves around several areas associated with the creation and use of the MDTs between the ASs as follows:

- The ability to successfully do a reverse path forwarding check for the VPN source at the receiver VRF when the MPLS-VPN Inter-AS Option B is used. This is addressed by the **BGP Connector Attribute**.

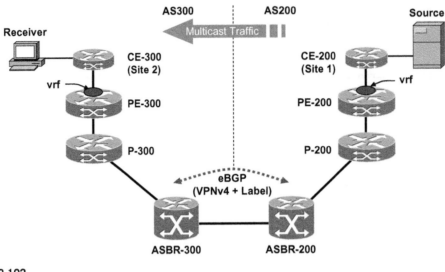

FIGURE 2.102

- The ability for the last hop PE router (PE-300) to issue a PIM join to the MDT rooted in the remote AS and for the RPF check to operate successfully for traffic passing along the MDT. This is only relevant if the local AS P routers have no knowledge of the routes from the remote AS (external routes). For example, if PE-300 does not know about PE-200, then an MDT cannot be built. This is addressed by the **PIM Vector**.

2.2.2.51 BGP MDT SAFI Across AS Boundaries

BGP MDT SAFI can be propagated across AS boundaries as shown below and summarized as follows (see Figure 2.103):

1. PE-200 sends an MDT update (AFI = 1, SAFI = 66) for the Default MDT (RD, S:PE-200, G:RED) to ASBR-200 using iBGP.
2. ABSR-200 propagates the received MDT message to ASBR-300 using eBGP.
3. This allows PE-300 in the remote AS to learn of the (S, G) for the Default MDT RED from ASBR-300 using iBGP.
4. Hence, for PIM-SSM, a PIM Join for (PE-200, RED) can be issued by PE-300 to join the Default MDT.

2.2.2.52 BGP Connector Attribute

The BGP connector attribute essentially defines a way, if required, for an NLRI destination to be forwarded over a tunnel by identifying the tunnel endpoint in the connector attribute. The BGP connector is a transitive attribute that preserves the PE router address (most certainly the loopback) across an Inter-AS boundary for all originating VPNv4 routes to ensure that the RPF check for a source address within a given mVPN will succeed. It does this by "connecting" the VPNv4 prefix of the source to the PIM Neighbor on the MDT; hence, it removes the dependence on the BGP next hop.

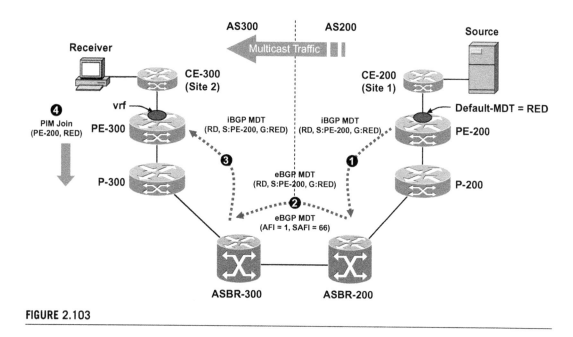

FIGURE 2.103

For Multicast VPN, the BGP connector is an optional transitive attribute that is carried in a BGP VPNv4 Update. In the local AS, this attribute has no purpose, and it will always be the same value as the next hop attribute that identifies the PE router. However, it is when MPLS-VPN Inter-AS Option B is used where one or both of the ASBRs rewrite the BGP next hop that the BGP connector is used. **This is required only for Inter-AS Option B, where the BGP Next-Hop is changed.**

Consider the next scenario (see Figure 2.104). Assume Default MDT has been successfully created between PE-200 and PE-300. In the Multicast VPN solution, a PIM adjacency will be established between the two PE routers over the MDT to transport customer Multicast information. PE-300 sees 166.50.10.3 (PE-200) as its adjacency. The MVPN in PE-300 will be populated with the customer VPN routes including the address of Source (X) in AS200 by way of MP-BGP VPNv4 updates as follows:

1. PE-200 will send a BGP VPNv4 update to ASBR-200 with the NLRI = (X) and BGP next hop = PE-200.
2. ASBR-200 has an eBGP session with ASBR-300; therefore, it will always rewrite the BGP next hop of any local VPNv4 route it receives to the value of its interface/loopback before passing it to ASBR-300. ABSR-200 sends NLRI = (X) and BGP next hop = ASBR-200.
3. The behavior of ASBR-300 will depend on whether next-hop-self is set on the peering session to PE-300. If next-hop-self is not set, then the VPNv4 update for (X) will be passed as it was received with a BGP next hop of ASBR-200. In our example, the next-hop-self has been set; therefore, the BGP next hop in the VPNv4 at PE-300 update will be set to ASBR-300.
4. This process breaks the RPF check for the Source (X) inside the MVPN (and any other source address in that VRF). For the mVPN RPF check to succeed, the rule is that the next hop of the

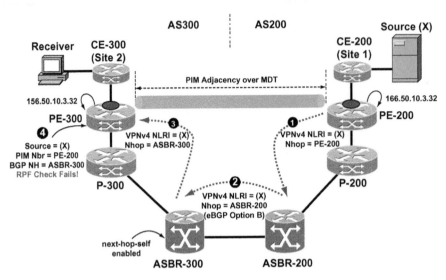

FIGURE 2.104

Source in the VRF routing table must = the PIM adjacency address. In our example, for the RPF check to succeed for X, the BGP next hop *must be* 166.50.10.3, and the PIM Neighbor must be 166.50.10.3. This is not the case as the PIM Neighbor is 166.50.10.3 (PE-200) but the BGP next hop for X is ASBR-300; therefore, Multicast traffic from Source X to the receiver in AS300 will be dropped.

The BGP connector attribute rectifies this problem by preserving the originating PE router address across the Inter-AS boundary as illustrated in Figure 2.105. The connector attribute is a little similar to the Originator ID attribute used by an RR, which preserves the originator of the route in the local AS; however, the Originator ID is a non-transitive attribute.

Figure 2.105 shows that the VPNv4 updates now include the BGP connector attribute that carries the value PE-200. Because this attribute is transitive, it will be carried across the AS boundary. Therefore, the process is the same as it was in the Figure 2.104 except that the connector preserves the originating PE router across the AS boundary, whereas the BGP next hop changes to the value of the ABSR. Therefore, PE-300 receives two pieces of information relating to the VPNv4 source address; the BGP next hop is its own AS, and the originating PE router address is in the remote AS.

When PE-300 receives the update, it will use the BGP connector value (if present) in the RPF check instead of the BGP next hop. Figure 2.106 details the logic involved.

As it is not possible to know whether a VPNv4 update will go across an AS boundary or not, every VPNv4 update in a Multicast-enabled VRF must carry the BGP connector attribute. Figure 2.107 shows the BGP connector attribute for address 192.168.2.3 (the (X) in our previous diagrams) on a VRF called VPN_RECEIVER. As you can see, the connector has the value 166.50.10.3 (PE-200) while the BGP next hop is 156.50.10.1 (which is ASBR-300). The RPF check has been modified so that it will give precedence to the BGP Connector if present instead of the BGP next hop.

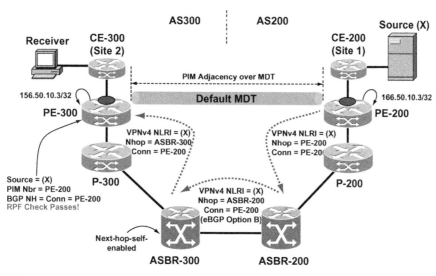

FIGURE 2.105

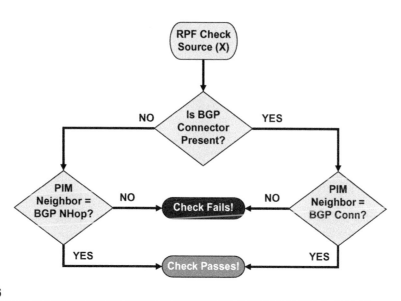

FIGURE 2.106

2.2.2.53 PIM RPF Vector

The PIM RPF Vector is a mechanism that allows a Multicast tree to be built in a local AS or between ASs in the situation where the P routers *do not* possess the routing information indicating the location of the root or source of the tree. Normally, if a router does not possess the IGP information for the

```
PE-300#sho ip bgp vpnv4 vrf VPN_RECEIVER 192.168.2.3
BGP routing table entry for 300:1:192.168.2.0/24, version 30
Paths: (1 available, best #1, table VPN_RECEIVER)
  Not advertised to any peer
  200, imported path from 200:1:192.168.2.0/24
    156.50.10.1 (metric 59) from 156.50.10.1 (156.50.10.1)
      Origin incomplete, metric 0, localpref 100, valid, internal, best
      Extended Community: RT:200:1 RT:200:777
        OSPF DOMAIN ID:0x0005:0x000000010200 OSPF RT:0.0.0.0:2:0
        OSPF ROUTER ID:2.1.1.1:512
      Connector Attribute: count=1
       type 1 len 12 value 200:1:166.50.10.3,
      mpls labels in/out nolabel/28
```

FIGURE 2.107

BGP connector attribute.

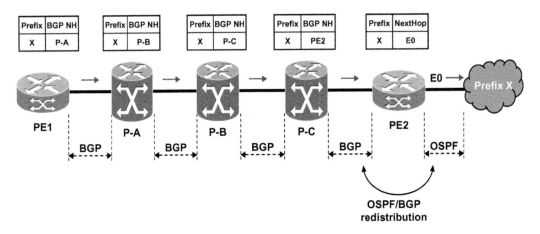

FIGURE 2.108

Multicast source, then a PIM Join cannot be issued toward the root and an RPF check cannot be done on traffic traveling down the tree toward the receivers.

There are two scenarios where the use of the PIM Vector is required:

- When a "BGP Free Core" is deployed in an MPLS environment
- In certain MPLS-VPN Inter-AS scenarios (Option B and Option C using BGP Free Core)

2.2.2.53.1 BGP Free Core

Figure 2.108 shows a classic routed network. In this example, for router PE1 to reach prefix X attached to router PE2 every router in the path between PE1 and PE2 must hold prefix X in its routing table. Typically, if prefix X represented an external route that was not part of the service provider's infrastructure (e.g., a customer enterprise network), it would most likely be advertised to the service

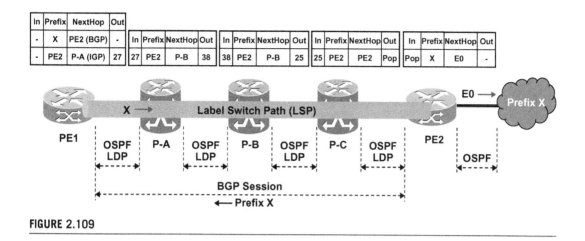

In	Prefix	NextHop	Out
-	X	PE2 (BGP)	-
-	PE2	P-A (IGP)	27

In	Prefix	NextHop	Out
27	PE2	P-B	38

In	Prefix	NextHop	Out
38	PE2	P-B	25

In	Prefix	NextHop	Out
25	PE2	PE2	Pop

In	Prefix	NextHop	Out
Pop	X	E0	-

FIGURE 2.109

provider edge router (PE2) using OSPF or another enterprise-preferred IGP (if the PE2 were an Internet peering point, it would be BGP).

It is not good practice to propagate external customer routes within the service provider IGP; therefore, prefix X would normally be distributed into BGP at PE2. Each core router (P-A, P-B, P-C) along the path between PE1/PE2 would then use BGP to advertise the customer prefixes to its upstream neighbor. Hence, a packet destined for X originating at PE1 would be routed on a per-hop basis via P-A → P-B → P-C → PE2. Obviously, all routers must have knowledge of the location of prefix X for this to occur. The same goes for external Internet routes. Without MPLS, every P router in the network would require a BGP peering session (typically to an RR) and would need to hold all or part of the Internet routing table for traffic to pass from edge to edge.

One of the great benefits of MPLS is that it separates the *forwarding plane* from the *routing plane*. This essentially means the core routers do not need to know about every external prefix available from edge routers to forward the packets. Instead, MPLS allows an LSP to be created between PE routers across the core. The P routers only need to know how to forward a labeled packet toward the egress PE router instead of having to know all about the external prefixes behind it. A simplistic demonstration of MPLS and a BGP Free Core is shown in Figure 2.109.

In this figure, the external/customer prefix X is still injected into PE2 using OSPF. However, prefix X is not redistributed into the service provider IGP; instead it is passed by a BGP session to PE1. The core P routers do not run BGP; they use OSPF and Label Distribution Protocol (LDP) to advertise the IP addresses of the core infrastructure only (PE loopbacks, link addresses, etc.). Each PE loopback will be allocated a label, for example, PE1 will use {27} to access PE2 at the opposite edge of the network. The in/out labels at each router hop are used to form a tunnel or LSP between the PE routers. Therefore, at PE1, we know that prefix X is reachable via BGP next hop PE2. By looking up the label forwarding table for PE2, label {27} is pushed on to the label stack. From that point on, the P routers only look at the incoming label to determine the outgoing label and interface. The P routers do not need to have any knowledge of prefix X to get the packet to PE2. This is a BGP Free Core, and as you can see, we are *forwarding* on the label, not routing on the IP address.

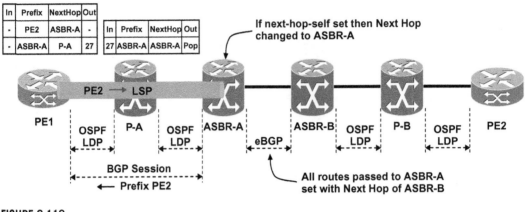

FIGURE 2.110

This is beneficial because it minimizes the amount of routing information and configuration a P router requires. However, if PE1 needed to join a Multicast tree rooted at X, there would be a problem because none of the P routers would have any knowledge of where prefix X is and the tree could not be joined from PE1. Remember, PIM relies on the IGP for RPF checks and to forward joins.

2.2.2.53.2 MPLS VPN Inter-AS

The PIM Vector may be necessary depending on the way the MPLS-VPN Inter-AS solution is implemented in conjunction with mVPN. A simple rule would be if a router in the local AS does not know the address of the PE router in the remote AS, that is, the root of an MDT, then the PIM Vector is needed. This would occur when Option B is used for MPLS-VPN Inter-AS (the ASBR becomes the next hop) and also for Option C where the "BGP Routes Method" is used resulting in a BGP Free Core. Figure 2.110 shows the Inter-AS Option B scenario where all VPNv4 and IGP routing information travels via the ASBRs. When routes are exchanged between the two ASs, the ASBRs become the next hop for the eBGP session. In our example, ASBR-A has next-hop-self set and is passing the loopback address of PE2 to PE1. PE1 then sees that PE2 is reachable with the BGP next hop of ASBR-A and uses an LSP to get to ASBR-A (BGP Free Core) and then onward to PE2 in the other ASs. We cannot build an MDT to PE2 across the AS boundary because the P-A router does not know where PE2 is (remember that an mVPN is based on native Multicast PIM + IGP). This problem is similar to the one that the mVPN Inter-AS RPF check faces in Option B (where the PIM neighbor and VPNv4 BGP neighbor are not the same), which is addressed by the BGP connector attribute.

The PIM Vector solves the problem in the previous scenarios by enabling PIM to build Multicast trees through an MPLS-enabled network, even if that network's IGP does not have a route to the source of the tree (remote PE router). The PIM Vector allows the core routers to correctly process join messages for the multicast group and forward the join message toward the root of the tree via the ASBR (in the Inter-AS example). It is to be noted that all routers in the Multicast Path must support the PIM Vector for an MDT to be set up.

Figure 2.111 shows a new PIM Join format that includes the PIM Vector and is encoded as part of the source address in a PIM Join/Prune message. This PIM source encoding has a special Encoding

0	8	16		24
Address Family	Encoding Type	Reserved	Flags	Mask Length
Source Address				
RPF Vector				
RD				

FIGURE 2.111

Type to distinguish itself from the normal encoded source. A new join format was necessary as there was no space to include the Vector in the default PIM Join.

The RPF Vector contains the IP address of the egress router (ASBR-A in our previous example) that has reachability to the source address (PE2). If a PIM Vector is present, the RPF check resolves the address in the RPF Vector to determine the egress upstream interface and neighbor to whom the Join is forwarded. Hence, a core router that supports the RPF Vector only requires reachability information to the address in the RPF Vector, not the source address. If present in the PIM Join message, the PIM Vector takes precedence over the source address for RPF check processing.

The PIM source message also contains a route distinguisher (RD) value. In the case of an MDT Join, this is the RD carried in the BGP MDT update message. When an ASBR receives a PIM join with a vector that is one of ASBR's local interfaces (most likely the loopback), then it must discard the Vector and do a normal RPF lookup. In an MVPN environment, the source address will be a PE router whose address has been learned via a BGP MDT update. It will not be kept in the normal IGP or BGP table, but will reside in a special table known as the BGP MDT table, which is indexed by the RD. Therefore, the RD value must be included in the Join message to ensure that the correct PE source address is used in the BGP MDT table for the MDT Join.

Because the PIM Vector uses a completely new source-encoding type, the upstream routers (i.e., toward the source) must be able to receive and parse the Join. A new PIM Hello option has been introduced to signal PIM Vector capability. The PIM Vector will only be included in the Join message if all neighbors on an interface possess the PIM Vector capability.

A router originating a PIM Join needs to know if it should include the RPF Vector in the Join message. In an MVPN, the originating router will be a PE router that is the leaf of an MDT. Currently, there is no dynamic mechanism to include the PIM Vector; there is no way of telling whether the upstream router knows how to reach the source or whether it runs BGP to other upstream routers or is part of a BGP Free Core. Therefore, the simplest way to include the RPF Vector is by way of configuration, which is discussed next.

If the Multicast source originates from a BGP next hop, then the originating router will use this address as the PIM Vector. Therefore, the PIM Vector is always learned via BGP via using the BGP MDT update (MDT SAFI) in an MVPN environment.

A router receiving an RPF Vector will store it so that a periodic/triggered RPF check can be done, and the RPF Vector can be advertised upstream. P routers in a BGP Free Core learn about the RPF Vector via the Join messages. A Vector can be seen using the `show ip mr proxy` command. If a router receives the same Vector from multiple sources, the one with the lower originator address is preferred.

An RPF Vector always takes priority in the RPF check over a source address that might be present in the IGP. Multiple P routers may be connected to each other, and the PIM vector needs to be

```
!
! Multicast VPN Traffic
!
ip multicast vrf VPN_RECEIVER rpf proxy rd vector
```

FIGURE 2.112

PIM RPF Vector configuration.

advertised to these routers as well. If the router receives a Vector associated with one of its interfaces, the Vector is ignored, and a normal RPF lookup is done on the source (this would be the case for an ASBR or an edge router of a BGP Free Core). As previously mentioned, if the receiving router is an ASBR in an mVPN environment, then the RD in the Join message will be used to look up the correct source address in the BGP MDT table.

The rd keyword enables the RD value to be included with the RPF Vector for processing at the ASBR (see Figure 2.112).

2.2.2.54 PIM RPF Vector Operation

Figure 2.113 shows the PIM Vector in operation using option B when creating a multicast tree from PE200 to PE-300 for the Default MDT. The steps are as follows:

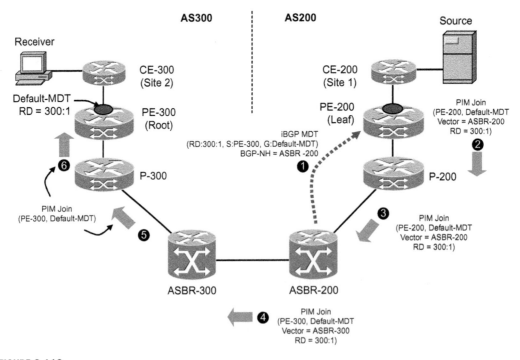

FIGURE 2.113

- PE-200 receives the BGP MDT Update from ASBR-200 identifying the Default MDT from PE-300. The IP address of PE-300 is not redistributed into AS200; therefore, it will not appear in the global routing table of any AS200 routers. PE-200 will be configured manually to use the PIM Vector when necessary.
- To create the Default MDT, PE-200 must issue a PIM Join toward PE-300. The route for PE-300 was received in the MDT update with a BGP next hop of ASBR-200. Therefore, PE-200 can issue a PIM Join using the Vector of ASBR-200 and RD of 300:1 (from the MDT update) toward P-200 for the S, G (PE-300, Default MDT). PE-200 will only include the Vector if P-200 indicated support via the PIM Hello.
- When P-200 receives the PIM Join, it notices the presence of the Vector and will use the address of ASBR-200 to forward the PIM Join. It will also use the Vector to process RPF checks on Multicast packets arriving from source PE-300 (traffic travels PE-300 → PE-200). P-200 then forwards the PIM Join to ABSR-200.
- When ASBR-200 receives the PIM Join, it checks the Vector. Because the value of the Vector contains one of its own addresses, it will discard the Vector and look at the value of the source address (PE-300). Because route to PE-300 does not exist in the global routing table (it was not distributed across AS), ASBR-200 will use the RD value in the PIM Join to look up the BGP MDT table to find the relevant RPF information. Because there is no IGP route for PE-300, the BGP next hop for PE-300 in the MDT update, which is ASBR-300, will be used as the PIM Vector. The PIM Join will then be forwarded across the AS boundary to ASBR-300 (PIM must be enabled on the Inter-AS link).
- When ASBR-300 receives the PIM Join, it sees that the PIM Vector is a local router address. Therefore, the Vector will be discarded, and the IGP table will be used to derive where to send the PIM Join. From this point onward, the PIM Join is processed in the normal manner (no PIM Vector is necessary).

Figure 2.114 shows an example output from a Multicast entry that uses the PIM Vector. In this example, the Vector used is 156.50.10.1, which is ASBR 300.

2.2.2.55 Configurations and the Example Environment

In this section, there are more details in the example case study along with the configurations of the devices used. The topology and details are provided in this section (see Figure 2.115).

The following list summarizes the test setup that will be used for this case study:

- There are two BGP ASs, AS200 and AS300, with a VPN source (Site 1) in AS200 multicasting to a VPN receiver (Site 2) in AS300.
- OSPF is used as the routing protocol in the global table and also on the PE/CE circuits.
- The Multicast source is attached to **CE-200**, which is in VRF VPN_SOURCE on **PE-200.**
- The Multicast receiver is attached to **CE-300**, which is in VRF VPN_RECEIVER on **PE-300.**
- **PE-200** and **PE-300** have two iBGP sessions, one to each of their respective ASBRs, to exchange VPNv4 routing information.
- The VPNv4 routes (source and receiver subnets) in both VRFs are exchanged across an eBGP session between **ABSR-A200** and **ABSR-A300.** Only VPNv4 routes holding the route-target 300:777 or 200:777 will be allowed across the AS boundary.
- Both of the ASBRs have next-hop-self set; therefore, VPNv4 routes learned from the remote ASs will have the next hop address set to the local ASBR.

```
PE-300#show ip mroute 166.50.10.3 239.232.0.1
IP Multicast Routing Table
Flags: D - Dense, S - Sparse, B - Bidir Group, s - SSM Group, C - Connected,
       L - Local, P - Pruned, R - RP-bit set, F - Register flag,
       T - SPT-bit set, J - Join SPT, M - MSDP created entry,
       X - Proxy Join Timer Running, A - Candidate for MSDP Advertisement,
       U - URD, I - Received Source Specific Host Report, Z - Multicast
Tunnel,
       Y - Joined MDT-data group, y - Sending to MDT-data group
       V - RD & Vector, v - Vector
Outgoing interface flags: H - Hardware switched, A - Assert winner
 Timers: Uptime/Expires
 Interface state: Interface, Next-Hop or VCD, State/Mode

(166.50.10.3, 239.232.0.1), 03:17:29/00:02:38, flags: sTIZV
   Incoming interface: Ethernet0/0, RPF nbr 3.3.3.5, vector 156.50.10.1
   Outgoing interface list:
     MVRF VPN_RECEIVER, Forward/Sparse, 03:17:29/00:00:00
```

FIGURE 2.114

PIM Vector example.

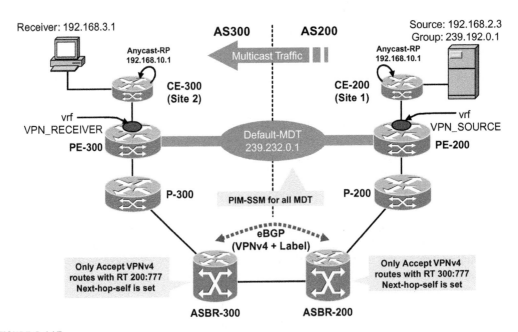

FIGURE 2.115

- No local infrastructure routes (loopbacks and interfaces) are passed to the remote AS. Therefore, the ASs are completely hidden from each other.
- **CE-200** and **CE-300** are part of the customer Multicast network (as are the VRFs on the PE routers) and are using Anycast RP. There is an MSDP session between both CE routers (across the ASBRs) to pass source discovery information within the VRFs. The Anycast RP configuration means that Multicast routers within the customer network will always use the closest RP, that is, within their own AS (unless it is unavailable).
- The customer network is not aware of the underlying Inter-AS mechanisms to provide Multicast connectivity across the AS boundary.
- The PE routers establish a Default MDT between each other across the ASBRs using the group **239.232.0.1**.
- The global Multicast has been configured to use PIM-SSM for all MDTs while the customer network is configured to use PIM-SM.
- Once Multicast traffic begins to flow from **PE-200** to **PE-300**, a Data MDT will be created (not shown) using the group **239.232.3.0**.

Figure 2.116 illustrates the logical layout of the test network for reference when examining the command outputs.

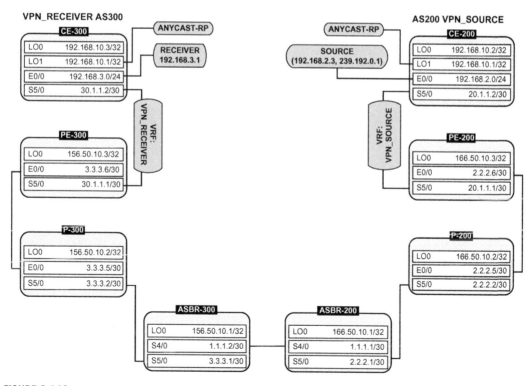

FIGURE 2.116

```
ip vrf VPN_SOURCE
 rd 200:1
 route-target export 200:1
 route-target export 200:777
 route-target import 200:1
 route-target import 300:1
 mdt default 239.232.0.1
 mdt data 239.232.2.0 0.0.0.255 threshold 10
!
ip multicast-routing
ip multicast-routing vrf VPN_SOURCE
```

FIGURE 2.117

VPN_SOURCE on PE-200.

```
ip vrf VPN_RECEIVER
 rd 300:1
 route-target export 300:1
 route-target export 300:777
 route-target import 300:1
 route-target import 200:1
 mdt default 239.232.0.1
 mdt data 239.232.3.0 0.0.0.255 threshold 10
!
ip multicast-routing
ip multicast-routing vrf VPN_RECEIVER
```

FIGURE 2.118

VPN_RECEIVER on PE-300.

2.2.2.56 Operational Analysis

This section analyzes the way the Default/Data MDT is built across an Inter-AS boundary that has been configured using Option B. Full configuration listings of all the routers can be found later in this section.

2.2.2.57 VRF and MDT Definitions

There are two VRFs defined—VPN_SOURCE on PE-200 and VPN_RECEIVER on PE-300—shown in Figures 2.117 and 2.118.

The VRF configurations include the Default (239.232.0.1) and Data MDTs with their respective groups. The route-target xxx:777 on each of the VRFs ensures that the VPNv4 routes are passed across the ASBR (they have a match statement denying access to non-compliant routes).

2.2.2.58 BGP MDT Update

Once the Default MDT has been configured, it will be propagated to all other relevant PE routers via a BGP MDT update. Figure 2.119 shows the BGP configuration on PE-200. The mdt address family configures a peer with 166.50.10.1, which is ASBR-200. This means that as soon as the Default MDT is configured on a VRF (i.e., VPN_SOURCE), an update will be sent to ASBR-200, which will then relay it to ASBR-300.

```
router bgp 200
 !
 [snip]
 !
 address-family ipv4 mdt
 neighbor 166.50.10.1 activate
 neighbor 166.50.10.1 send-community both
 exit-address-family
 !
 [snip]
!
 exit-address-family
```

FIGURE 2.119

BGP configuration on PE-200.

```
PE-200#show ip bgp ipv4 mdt all
BGP table version is 4, local router ID is 166.50.10.3
Status codes: s suppressed, d damped, h history, * valid, > best, i -
internal,
              r RIB-failure, S Stale
Origin codes: i - IGP, e - EGP, ? - incomplete

   Network            Next Hop            Metric LocPrf Weight Path
   Route Distinguisher: 200:1 (default for vrf VPN_SOURCE)
   *> 166.50.10.3/32   0.0.0.0                               0 ?
   Route Distinguisher: 300:1
   *>i156.50.10.3/32   166.50.10.1            0    100      0 300 ?
```

FIGURE 2.120

MDT table on PE-200.

```
PE-200#show ip bgp ipv4 mdt all 156.50.10.3
BGP routing table entry for 300:1:156.50.10.3/32, version 2
Paths: (1 available, best #1, table IPv4-MDT-BGP-Table)
  Not advertised to any peer
  300
    166.50.10.1 (metric 59) from 166.50.10.1 (166.50.10.1)
      Origin incomplete, metric 0, localpref 100, valid, internal, best,
      MDT group address: 239.232.0.1
```

FIGURE 2.121

Detail of Default MDT entry on PE-200.

The BGP MDT update is kept in a separate table from VPNv4 and IPv4 routes distributed by BGP. Figure 2.120 illustrates the MDT table on PE-200, which has two entries. The first entry is the MDT update that originates locally while the second entry 156.50.10.3 is the MDT update from PE-300 in the other AS (where the receiver is). This update is propagated from ASBR-300 → ASBR-200 → PE-200; therefore, in the text network, only the two ASBR and PE routers will hold the MDT table.

Figure 2.121 shows the detail on the Default MDT update received from PE-300.

```
ip pim ssm range MDT-Groups
ip pim vrf VPN_SOURCE rp-address 192.168.10.1
!
!
ip access-list standard MDT-Groups
 permit 239.232.0.0 0.0.255.255
```

FIGURE 2.122

Global PIM-SSM configuration.

2.2.2.59 PIM-SSM

PIM-SSM has been configured on all the core routers (P + PE); therefore, the MDT update is very important so that an (S, G) Join can be issued from PE-200, which is the leaf toward PE-300 and the root of the MDT (this process also happens in reverse where PE-300 is the leaf and PE-200 is the root). Without it, an explicit (S, G) could not be issued as PE-200 would not know the value of (S) (see Figure 2.122).

PE-200 will issue a (156.50.10.3, 239.232.0.1) Join along the path toward PE-300 in the remote AS.

2.2.2.60 Default MDT with PIM Vector

This section describes how the Default MDT is created using the PIM Vector. The process for creating Data MDTs between the two ASs would be exactly the same. The group 239.232.0.1 is used by both PE routers to create two MDT trees: one with PE-200 as the root, and the other with PE-300 as the root. For purposes of clarity, we will only look at the process that takes place to build the Default MDT between PE-200 (leaf) to PE-300 (root). The same process happens in the opposite direction. For PE-200 to issue the (156.50.10.3, 239.232.0.1) Join request, PIM needs to know the whereabouts of the next hop of 156.50.10.3. If we look at the routing table in PE-200 shown in Figure 2.123, we can see that there is no routing entry for 156.50.10.3 as the ASBRs are configured not to propagate any remote routing information (they only pass VPNv4 routes). This normally would cause a problem with the RPF check and the ability to issue an (S, G) Join for the Default MDT.

```
PE-200#show ip route
[snip]
Gateway of last resort is not set

     2.0.0.0/30 is subnetted, 2 subnets
O       2.2.2.0 [110/58] via 2.2.2.5, 03:37:04, Ethernet0/0
C       2.2.2.4 is directly connected, Ethernet0/0
     166.50.0.0/32 is subnetted, 3 subnets
O       166.50.10.2 [110/11] via 2.2.2.5, 03:37:04, Ethernet0/0
C       166.50.10.3 is directly connected, Loopback0
O       166.50.10.1 [110/59] via 2.2.2.5, 03:37:04, Ethernet0/0
```

FIGURE 2.123

Routing table PE-200.

```
ip multicast vrf VPN_SOURCE rpf proxy rd vector
```

FIGURE 2.124

PIM Vector configuration on PE-200.

```
PE-200#show ip bgp ipv4 mdt all
BGP table version is 4, local router ID is 166.50.10.3
Status codes: s suppressed, d damped, h history, * valid, > best, i - internal,
              r RIB-failure, S Stale
Origin codes: i - IGP, e - EGP, ? - incomplete

   Network          Next Hop          Metric LocPrf Weight Path
Route Distinguisher: 200:1 (default for vrf VPN_SOURCE)
*> 166.50.10.3/32   0.0.0.0                             0 ?
Route Distinguisher: 300:1
*>i156.50.10.3/32   166.50.10.1          0    100      0 300 ?
```

FIGURE 2.125

MDT entry for PE-300.

The ABSRs have been configured not to redistribute any routing information from their remote AS; hence, normally a Join could not be issued. This is where the PIM Vector solves the problem by configuring the command shown in Figure 2.124 on PE-200 (and also PE-300 for the reverse direction).

This command causes PE-200 to look into the BGP MDT table to decide if the Multicast source (PE-300) is reachable via a BGP next hop. The table in Figure 2.125 illustrates that the BGP next hop for the MDT source 156.50.10.3 (PE-300) is 166.50.10.1 (ASBR-200).

For PE-200 to issue a Default MDT Join toward PE-300, it will use 166.50.10.1 (ASBR-200) as the PIM Vector as seen in Figure 2.126.

```
PE-200#show ip mroute 156.50.10.3 239.232.0.1
IP Multicast Routing Table
Flags: D - Dense, S - Sparse, B - Bidir Group, s - SSM Group, C - Connected,
       L - Local, P - Pruned, R - RP-bit set, F - Register flag,
       T - SPT-bit set, J - Join SPT, M - MSDP created entry,
       X - Proxy Join Timer Running, A - Candidate for MSDP Advertisement,
       U - URD, I - Received Source Specific Host Report, Z - Multicast Tunnel,
       Y - Joined MDT-data group, y - Sending to MDT-data group
       V - RD & Vector, v - Vector
Outgoing interface flags: H - Hardware switched, A - Assert winner
 Timers: Uptime/Expires
 Interface state: Interface, Next-Hop or VCD, State/Mode

(156.50.10.3, 239.232.0.1), 1w5d/00:02:59, flags: sTIZV
  Incoming interface: Ethernet0/0, RPF nbr 2.2.2.5, vector 166.50.10.1
  Outgoing interface list:
    MVRF VPN_SOURCE, Forward/Sparse, 1w5d/00:00:00
```

FIGURE 2.126

Default MDT Mroute entry on PE-200.

```
PE-200#show ip rpf 166.50.10.1
RPF information for ASBR-200 (166.50.10.1)
  RPF interface: Ethernet0/0
  RPF neighbor: P-200 (2.2.2.5)
  RPF route/mask: 166.50.10.1/32
  RPF type: unicast (ospf 200)
  RPF recursion count: 0
  Doing distance-preferred lookups across tables
```

FIGURE 2.127

RPF information for ASBR-200.

```
P-200#show ip mroute proxy
(156.50.10.3, 239.232.0.1)
  Proxy                    Assigner        Origin      Uptime/Expire
  300:1/166.50.10.1        2.2.2.6         PIM         1w5d/00:02:20
```

FIGURE 2.128

PIM Vector table on P-200.

This figure shows that PE-200 will send the (156.50.10.3, 239.232.0.1) Join message toward 166.50.10.1, which is reachable via the upstream RPF interface Ethernet0/0, PIM neighbor 2.2.2.5 (P-200) as verified in Figure 2.127. Also in Figure 2.126, note the V flag indicating the presence of PIM Vector using the RD and Vector (or IP address), although the RD is not shown in the output (RD can be seen using the show ip mroute proxy command).

2.2.2.60.1 A Closer Look from P-200
The PIM Vector will only be used if the upstream neighbor, in this case P-200, has advertised PIM Vector capability. Hence the disadvantage of using the PIM Vector is that all routers in the path must be upgraded to an appropriate release of Cisco IOS. No special configuration is necessary on P-200 to process the PIM Vector. On the other hand, PE-200, which is the original assigner of the vector (PE-200), will only do so if manually configured.

In our test example, P-200 receives the PIM Vector from PE-200 and stores it for use in RPF check as shown in Figure 2.128. In this example, P-200 has learned the vector via PIM from the assigner 2.2.26, which is PE-200.

Compare the PIM Vector table on P-200 to the PIM Vector table for PE-200 as seen in Figure 2.129. PE-200 learned the vector via BGP MDT update, and the assigner is 0.0.0.0, which means itself.

```
PE-200#show ip mroute proxy
(156.50.10.3, 239.232.0.1)
  Proxy                    Assigner        Origin      Uptime/Expire
  300:1/166.50.10.1        0.0.0.0         BGP MDT     1w5d/stopped
```

FIGURE 2.129

PIM Vector table on PE-200.

```
P-200#show ip mroute 156.50.10.3 239.232.0.1
IP Multicast Routing Table
Flags: D - Dense, S - Sparse, B - Bidir Group, s - SSM Group, C - Connected,
       L - Local, P - Pruned, R - RP-bit set, F - Register flag,
       T - SPT-bit set, J - Join SPT, M - MSDP created entry,
       X - Proxy Join Timer Running, A - Candidate for MSDP Advertisement,
       U - URD, I - Received Source Specific Host Report, Z - Multicast Tunnel,
       Y - Joined MDT-data group, y - Sending to MDT-data group
       V - RD & Vector, v - Vector
Outgoing interface flags: H - Hardware switched, A - Assert winner
 Timers: Uptime/Expires
 Interface state: Interface, Next-Hop or VCD, State/Mode

(156.50.10.3, 239.232.0.1), 1w5d/00:03:29, flags: sty
  Incoming interface: Serial5/0, RPF nbr 2.2.2.1, vector 166.50.10.1
  Outgoing interface list:
    Ethernet0/0, Forward/Sparse, 1w5d/00:03:29
```

FIGURE 2.130

Default MDT Mroute entry on P-200.

P-200 will use the RPF Vector (166.50.10.1) received in the join message for the RPF check over the source address (156.50.10.3) that may or may not (as in our case) be present in the IGP. In Figure 2.130, which shows the Default MDT entry on P-200, the PIM Vector will be passed upstream to 2.2.2.1, which is the ingress interface on ASBR-200. This is interesting as the vector 166.50.10.1 is also a loopback on ASBR-200. Therefore, when ASBR-200 receives the PIM join with a vector that is on its own address, the process will be slightly different, as discussed in the next section.

2.2.2.60.2 A Closer Look from ASBR-200

When ABSR-200 receives the (156.50.10.3, 239.232.0.1) Default MDT join, it will see that the PIM Vector (166.50.10.1) is a local interface Loopback0; therefore, it must process it differently. Figure 2.131 illustrates the PIM Vector table. The first entry 300:1/local is the vector received from P-200 (2.2.2.2), and the local signifies an address on ASBR-200. You may notice a second entry 200:1/local; this is the PIM Vector for Default MDT in the opposite direction from PE-300 to PE-200, which has been assigned by ASBR-300 (1.1.1.2). We will discover why this second entry exists as we follow the path of (156.50.10.3, 239.232.0.1) to ASBR-300 in the next section.

```
ABSR-200#show ip mroute proxy
(156.50.10.3, 239.232.0.1)
  Proxy                    Assigner        Origin    Uptime/Expire
  300:1/local              2.2.2.2         PIM       2w1d/00:02:57

(166.50.10.3, 239.232.0.1)
  Proxy                    Assigner        Origin    Uptime/Expire
  200:1/local              1.1.1.2         PIM       2w1d/00:02:42
```

FIGURE 2.131

PIM Vector table on ASBR-200.

```
ABSR-200#show ip route
[snip]

    1.0.0.0/8 is variably subnetted, 2 subnets, 2 masks
C      1.1.1.0/30 is directly connected, Serial4/0
C      1.1.1.2/32 is directly connected, Serial4/0
    2.0.0.0/30 is subnetted, 2 subnets
C      2.2.2.0 is directly connected, Serial5/0
O      2.2.2.4 [110/58] via 2.2.2.2, 2w1d, Serial5/0
    166.50.0.0/32 is subnetted, 3 subnets
O      166.50.10.2 [110/49] via 2.2.2.2, 2w1d, Serial5/0
O      166.50.10.3 [110/59] via 2.2.2.2, 2w1d, Serial5/0
C      166.50.10.1 is directly connected, Loopback0
```

FIGURE 2.132

Routing table on ASBR-200.

Both ASBRs have been configured so they do not pass infrastructure routes across the AS boundary. Figure 2.132 shows that the routing table on ASBR-200 does not contain a route to 156.50.10.3; therefore, the next hop for the join must be derived from another table.

Because there is no routing entry in the IGP table, the BGP MDT table is consulted as seen in Figure 2.133. ASBR-200 will use the RD (300:1) as an index into the MDT table to find the correct entry.

The BGP MDT table in Figure 2.133 shows that the source 156.50.10.3 is reachable via the BGP next hop 1.1.1.2 (ASBR-300). If the multicast source originates from a BGP next hop, then the originating router will use this address as the PIM Vector. Therefore, 1.1.1.2 will be used as the PIM Vector by ASBR-200 to forward the join as seen in Figure 2.134.

```
ABSR-200#show ip bgp ipv4 mdt all
BGP table version is 3, local router ID is 166.50.10.1
Status codes: s suppressed, d damped, h history, * valid, > best, i -
internal,
           r RIB-failure, S Stale
Origin codes: i - IGP, e - EGP, ? - incomplete

   Network          Next Hop          Metric LocPrf Weight Path
Route Distinguisher: 200:1
*>i166.50.10.3/32   166.50.10.3            0    100      0 ?
Route Distinguisher: 300:1
*>  156.50.10.3/32   1.1.1.2                              0 300 ?
```

FIGURE 2.133

BGP MDT table on ASBR-200.

```
ABSR-200#show ip mroute 156.50.10.3 239.232.0.1
[snip]
(156.50.10.3, 239.232.0.1), 2w1d/00:03:24, flags: sTV
  Incoming interface: Serial4/0, RPF nbr 1.1.1.2, vector 1.1.1.2
  Outgoing interface list:
    Serial5/0, Forward/Sparse, 2w1d/00:02:46
```

FIGURE 2.134

Changed PIM Vector.

2.2.2.60.3 A Closer Look from ASBR-300

The way ASBR-300 processes (156.50.10.3, 239.232.0.1) is similar to ASBR-200. The PIM join with vector 1.1.1.2 is received from ASBR-300 (1.1.1.1) and determined to be a local address. Therefore, ASBR-300 must look up one of its tables to determine where to send the PIM join. Note that the 200:1 entry is the PIM Vector for the Default MDT in the opposite direction from PE-300 (leaf) to PE-200 (root). That is why there are two vector entries in each ASBR (each representing one of the MDTs; see Figure 2.135).

Because 156.50.10.3 originates within the local AS, it will appear in the IGP table as shown in Figure 2.136; therefore, it is not necessary to add a PIM Vector to the join.

From this point on, within AS300, the PIM join will operate normally on a hop-by-hop basis from ASBR-300 to P-300 to PE-300 (see Figure 2.137).

2.2.2.60.4 A Closer Look from PE-300

Once the join reaches PE-300, the Default MDT will be created between PE-300 (root) and PE-200 (leaf). The same process occurs for the Default MDT between PE-200 (root) and PE-300 (leaf). Figure 2.138 shows the Default MDT entries on PE-300. The first entry (156.50.10.3, 239.232.0.1) is the MDT where PE-300 is the root. The second entry (166.50.10.3, 239.232.0.1) is the MDT where PE-300 is the leaf—notice it has a PIM Vector 156.50.10.1 (ASBR-300) so that P-300 knows where to send the join when it receives it. Therefore, the MDT + PIM Vector process is repeated in the opposite direction.

```
ASBR-300#show ip mroute proxy
(156.50.10.3, 239.232.0.1)
   Proxy                    Assigner         Origin      Uptime/Expire
   300:1/local              1.1.1.1          PIM         2w2d/00:02:58

(166.50.10.3, 239.232.0.1)
   Proxy                    Assigner         Origin      Uptime/Expire
   200:1/local              3.3.3.2          PIM         2w2d/00:02:04
```

FIGURE 2.135

PIM Vector table on ASBR-300.

```
ASBR-300#show ip route
[snip]

    1.0.0.0/8 is variably subnetted, 2 subnets, 2 masks
C      1.1.1.1/32 is directly connected, Serial4/0
C      1.1.1.0/30 is directly connected, Serial4/0
    3.0.0.0/30 is subnetted, 2 subnets
C      3.3.3.0 is directly connected, Serial5/0
O      3.3.3.4 [110/58] via 3.3.3.2, 2w2d, Serial5/0
    156.50.0.0/32 is subnetted, 3 subnets
C      156.50.10.1 is directly connected, Loopback0
O      156.50.10.2 [110/49] via 3.3.3.2, 2w2d, Serial5/0
O      156.50.10.3 [110/59] via 3.3.3.2, 2w2d, Serial5/0
```

FIGURE 2.136

Routing table on ASBR-300.

```
ASBR-300#show ip mroute 156.50.10.3 239.232.0.1
[snip]

(156.50.10.3, 239.232.0.1), 2w2d/00:03:25, flags: sT
  Incoming interface: Serial5/0, RPF nbr 3.3.3.2
  Outgoing interface list:
    Serial4/0, Forward/Sparse, 2w2d/00:02:40
```

FIGURE 2.137

Normal Mroute entry.

```
PE-300#show ip mroute
IP Multicast Routing Table
Flags: D - Dense, S - Sparse, B - Bidir Group, s - SSM Group, C - Connected,
       L - Local, P - Pruned, R - RP-bit set, F - Register flag,
       T - SPT-bit set, J - Join SPT, M - MSDP created entry,
       X - Proxy Join Timer Running, A - Candidate for MSDP Advertisement,
       U - URD, I - Received Source Specific Host Report, Z - Multicast Tunnel,
       Y - Joined MDT-data group, y - Sending to MDT-data group
       V - RD & Vector, v - Vector
Outgoing interface flags: H - Hardware switched, A - Assert winner
 Timers: Uptime/Expires
 Interface state: Interface, Next-Hop or VCD, State/Mode

(156.50.10.3, 239.232.0.1), 2w2d/00:03:17, flags: sTZ
  Incoming interface: Loopback0, RPF nbr 0.0.0.0
  Outgoing interface list:
    Ethernet0/0, Forward/Sparse, 2w2d/00:02:36

(166.50.10.3, 239.232.0.1), 2w2d/00:02:56, flags: sTIZV
  Incoming interface: Ethernet0/0, RPF nbr 3.3.3.5, vector 156.50.10.1
  Outgoing interface list:
    MVRF VPN_RECEIVER, Forward/Sparse, 2w2d/00:00:00

[snip]
```

FIGURE 2.138

Multicast cache entries on PE-300.

As discussed earlier, the BGP Connector attribute is only necessary when the BGP next hop is changed for a VPNv4 address. In our example, this is applicable as ASBR-200 and ASBR-300 both rewrite the next hop for VPNv4 addresses passing across the AS boundary.

As per Figure 2.139, The BGP next hop for 192.168.2.0/24 is 156.50.10.1 (ASBR-300). However, when we look at the PIM neighbors within the VRF, we can see that the PIM neighbor over the MDT tunnel is 166.50.10.3, which is the BGP loopback address on PE-200. The RPF check for a source address within a VRF states that the PIM neighbor must equal the BGP next hop of source. In our case, we are comparing 166.50.10.3 (PIM neighbor) with 156.50.10.1 (BGP next hop); therefore, any multicast traffic received from source VPN 192.168.2.3 will be dropped as the RPF check will fail (see Figure 2.140).

```
PE-300#show ip route vrf VPN_RECEIVER

Routing Table: VPN_RECEIVER
[snip]

    2.0.0.0/30 is subnetted, 1 subnets
B      2.1.1.0 [200/0] via 156.50.10.1, 00:01:59
    192.168.10.0/32 is subnetted, 3 subnets
B      192.168.10.2 [200/0] via 156.50.10.1, 00:01:59
O      192.168.10.3 [110/49] via 30.1.1.2, 00:03:30, Serial5/0
O      192.168.10.1 [110/49] via 30.1.1.2, 00:03:30, Serial5/0
B   192.168.2.0/24 [200/0] via 156.50.10.1, 00:01:59
O      192.168.3.0/24 [110/58] via 30.1.1.2, 00:03:30, Serial5/0
    30.0.0.0/30 is subnetted, 1 subnets
C      30.1.1.0 is directly connected, Serial5/0
```

FIGURE 2.139

VPN_RECEIVER routing table.

```
PE-300#show ip pim vrf VPN_RECEIVER neighbour
PIM Neighbor Table
Neighbor         Interface              Uptime/Expires    Ver   DR
Address                                                        Priority/Mode
30.1.1.2         Serial5/0              00:10:05/00:01:30 v2  1 / P
166.50.10.3      Tunnel0                00:07:35/00:01:33 v2  1 / DR P
```

FIGURE 2.140

PIM neighbors in VPN_RECEIVER.

However, because the BGP next hop has been preserved by the BGP connector as shown in Figure 2.141, PE-300 can successfully complete the RPF check by comparing the PIM neighbor with the BGP connector.

```
PE-300#show ip bgp vpnv4 vrf VPN_RECEIVER 192.168.2.3
BGP routing table entry for 300:1:192.168.2.0/24, version 15
Paths: (1 available, best #1, table VPN_RECEIVER)
  Not advertised to any peer
  200, imported path from 200:1:192.168.2.0/24
    156.50.10.1 (metric 59) from 156.50.10.1 (156.50.10.1)
      Origin incomplete, metric 0, localpref 100, valid, internal, best
      Extended Community: RT:200:1 RT:200:777
        OSPF DOMAIN ID:0x0005:0x000000010200 OSPF RT:0.0.0.0:2:0
        OSPF ROUTER ID:2.1.1.1:512
      Connector Attribute: count=1
        type 1 len 12 value 200:1:166.50.10.3,
      mpls labels in/out nolabel/25
```

FIGURE 2.141

BGP connector for VPN source.

```
PE-300#show ip rpf vrf VPN_RECEIVER 192.168.2.3
RPF information for Source-200 (192.168.2.3)
  RPF interface: Tunnel0
  RPF neighbor: PE-200 (166.50.10.3)
  RPF route/mask: 192.168.2.0/24
  RPF type: unicast (bgp 300)
  RPF recursion count: 0
  Doing distance-preferred lookups across tables
  BGP originator: 166.50.10.3
```

FIGURE 2.142

RPF check with BGP connector.

The modified RPF check can be seen in Figure 2.142, where the BGP originator is stored for reference (takes precedence over the BGP next hop).

2.2.2.61 Data MDT with PIM Vector

The creation of the Data MDT across the Inter-AS boundary using a PIM Vector is identical to creating a Default MDT. When the source at PE-200 begins to transmit traffic along the Default MDT toward PE-300, at some point, PE-300 may receive a Data MDT join message (over the Default MDT) when a certain bandwidth threshold is reached. When this occurs, PE-300 will then switch from the Default MDT to a Data MDT by issuing a new join request to (166.50.10.3, 239.232.2.0) with a PIM Vector as shown in Figure 2.143. The group (166.50.10.3, 239.232.2.0) is joined using the PIM Vector 156.50.10.1 (ASBR-300), which is then forwarded to P-300, then to ASBR-300.

```
PE-300#show ip mroute
[snip]

(156.50.10.3, 239.232.0.1), 00:51:51/00:03:29, flags: sTZ
  Incoming interface: Loopback0, RPF nbr 0.0.0.0
  Outgoing interface list:
    Ethernet0/0, Forward/Sparse, 00:51:50/00:02:54

(166.50.10.3, 239.232.0.1), 00:51:50/00:02:59, flags: sTIZV
  Incoming interface: Ethernet0/0, RPF nbr 3.3.3.5, vector 156.50.10.1
  Outgoing interface list:
    MVRF VPN_RECEIVER, Forward/Sparse, 00:51:50/00:00:00

(166.50.10.3, 239.232.2.0), 00:25:17/00:02:52, flags: sTIZV
  Incoming interface: Ethernet0/0, RPF nbr 3.3.3.5, vector 156.50.10.1
  Outgoing interface list:
    MVRF VPN_RECEIVER, Forward/Sparse, 00:25:17/00:00:00
[snip]
```

FIGURE 2.143

Data MDT with PIM Vector.

If we look at the PIM Vector cache on ABSR-300 (Figure 2.144), we can see three entries: the first entry is the Default MDT for PE-300 (leaf) to PE-200 (root), the second entry is the Default MDT PE-200 (leaf) to PE-300 (root), and the third entry is the Data MDT PE-300 (leaf) to PE-200 (root) for high-bandwidth source traffic to travel downward toward PE-300.

Last, Figure 2.145 illustrates the mroute entries within the VPN_RECEIVER VPN on PE-200. The entry (192.168.2.3, 239.192.0.1) is the customer source traffic traveling inside the Data MDT (166.50.10.3, 239.232.2.0). The "Y" flag indicates this (S, G) has switched to a Data MDT.

```
ASBR-300#show ip mroute proxy
(166.50.10.3, 239.232.2.0) ← PE-200 Root for Default-MDT
  Proxy                     Assigner        Origin     Uptime/Expire
  200:1/local               3.3.3.2         PIM        00:38:50/00:02:51

(156.50.10.3, 239.232.0.1) ← PE-300 Root for Default-MDT
  Proxy                     Assigner        Origin     Uptime/Expire
  300:1/local               1.1.1.1         PIM        01:05:24/00:02:54

(166.50.10.3, 239.232.0.1) ← PE-300 Root for Data-MDT
  Proxy                     Assigner        Origin     Uptime/Expire
  200:1/local               3.3.3.2         PIM        01:05:24/00:02:54
```

FIGURE 2.144

PIM Vectors on ASBR-300.

```
PE-300#show ip mroute vrf VPN_RECEIVER
[snip]
Outgoing interface flags: H - Hardware switched, A - Assert winner
 Timers: Uptime/Expires
 Interface state: Interface, Next-Hop or VCD, State/Mode

(*, 239.192.0.1), 00:01:22/stopped, RP 192.168.10.1, flags: SP
  Incoming interface: Serial5/0, RPF nbr 30.1.1.2
  Outgoing interface list: Null

(192.168.2.3, 239.192.0.1), 00:01:22/00:03:25, flags: TY
  Incoming interface: Tunnel0, RPF nbr 166.50.10.3,
MDT:[166.50.10.3,239.232.2.0]/00:02:01
  Outgoing interface list:
    Serial5/0, Forward/Sparse, 00:01:22/00:02:43

(*, 224.0.1.40), 00:29:54/stopped, RP 192.168.10.1, flags: SJPCL
  Incoming interface: Serial5/0, RPF nbr 30.1.1.2
  Outgoing interface list: Null
```

FIGURE 2.145

mRoute entries in VPN_RECEIVER.

2.2.2.62 PE-200 Configuration Template

```
service timestamps debug uptime
service timestamps log uptime
no service password-encryption
!
hostname PE-200
!
!
ip subnet-zero
ip cef
ip host CE-200-RP 192.168.10.1
ip host ASBR-200 166.50.10.1
ip host P-200 2.2.2.5
ip vrf VPN_SOURCE
 rd 200:1
 route-target export 200:1
 route-target export 200:777
 route-target import 200:1
 route-target import 300:1
 mdt default 239.232.0.1
 mdt data 239.232.2.0 0.0.0.255 threshold 10
!
ip multicast-routing
ip multicast-routing vrf VPN_SOURCE
ip multicast vrf VPN_SOURCE rpf proxy rd vector
mpls label protocol ldp
tag-switching tdp router-id Loopback0
!
interface Loopback0
 ip address 166.50.10.3 255.255.255.255
 no ip directed-broadcast
 ip pim sparse-mode
!
interface Ethernet0/0
 ip address 2.2.2.6 255.255.255.252
 no ip directed-broadcast
 ip pim sparse-mode
 tag-switching ip
!
interface Serial5/0
 ip vrf forwarding VPN_SOURCE
 ip address 2.1.1.1 255.255.255.252
```

FIGURE 2.146

PE-200 configuration.

```
 no ip directed-broadcast
 ip pim sparse-mode
!
router ospf 1 vrf VPN_SOURCE
 log-adjacency-changes
 redistribute bgp 200 subnets
 network 2.0.0.0 0.255.255.255 area 0
!
router ospf 200
 log-adjacency-changes
 network 2.2.2.0 0.0.0.255 area 0
 network 166.50.10.0 0.0.0.255 area 0
!
router bgp 200
 no bgp default ipv4-unicast
 bgp log-neighbor-changes
 neighbor 166.50.10.1 remote-as 200
 neighbor 166.50.10.1 update-source Loopback0
 !
 address-family ipv4 mdt
 neighbor 166.50.10.1 activate
 neighbor 166.50.10.1 send-community both
 exit-address-family
 !
 address-family vpnv4
 neighbor 166.50.10.1 activate
 neighbor 166.50.10.1 send-community extended
 exit-address-family
 !
 address-family ipv4 vrf VPN_SOURCE
 redistribute ospf 1 vrf VPN_SOURCE match internal external 1 external 2
 no auto-summary
 no synchronization
 exit-address-family
!
ip classless
!
ip pim ssm range MDT-Groups
ip pim vrf VPN_SOURCE rp-address 192.168.10.1
!
!
ip access-list standard MDT-Groups
 permit 239.232.0.0 0.0.255.255
!
end
```

FIGURE 2.146

(Continued)

2.2.2.63 P-200 Configuration Template

```
service timestamps debug uptime
service timestamps log uptime
no service password-encryption
!
hostname P-200
!
!
ip subnet-zero
ip cef
ip multicast-routing
mpls label protocol ldp
tag-switching tdp router-id Loopback0
!
interface Loopback0
 ip address 166.50.10.2 255.255.255.255
 no ip directed-broadcast
 ip pim sparse-mode
!
interface Ethernet0/0
 ip address 2.2.2.5 255.255.255.252
 no ip directed-broadcast
 ip pim sparse-mode
 tag-switching ip
!
interface Serial5/0
 description To ASBR-200
 ip address 2.2.2.2 255.255.255.252
 no ip directed-broadcast
 ip pim sparse-mode
 tag-switching ip
!
router ospf 300
 log-adjacency-changes
 network 2.2.2.0 0.0.0.255 area 0
 network 166.50.10.0 0.0.0.255 area 0
!
ip classless
!
ip pim ssm range MDT-Groups
!
ip access-list standard MDT-Groups
 permit 239.232.0.0 0.0.255.255
!
end
```

FIGURE 2.147

P-200 configuration.

2.2.2.64 ASBR-200 Configuration Template

```
service timestamps debug uptime
service timestamps log uptime
no service password-encryption
!
hostname ABSR-200
!
ip subnet-zero
ip cef
ip multicast-routing
mpls label protocol ldp
tag-switching tdp router-id Loopback0
!
interface Loopback0
 ip address 166.50.10.1 255.255.255.255
 no ip directed-broadcast
 ip pim sparse-mode
!
interface Serial4/0
 ip address 1.1.1.1 255.255.255.252
 no ip directed-broadcast
 ip pim sparse-mode
 mpls bgp forwarding
 no fair-queue
!
interface Serial5/0
 ip address 2.2.2.1 255.255.255.252
 no ip directed-broadcast
 ip pim sparse-mode
 tag-switching ip
!
router ospf 200
 log-adjacency-changes
 network 2.2.2.0 0.0.0.255 area 0
 network 166.50.10.0 0.0.0.255 area 0
!
router bgp 200
 no bgp default ipv4-unicast
 no bgp default route-target filter
 bgp log-neighbor-changes
 neighbor 1.1.1.2 remote-as 300
 neighbor 166.50.10.3 remote-as 200
 neighbor 166.50.10.3 update-source Loopback0
 !
 address-family ipv4 mdt
 neighbor 1.1.1.2 activate
 neighbor 1.1.1.2 send-community both
```

FIGURE 2.148

ASBR-200 configuration.

```
 neighbor 166.50.10.3 activate
 neighbor 166.50.10.3 send-community both
 neighbor 166.50.10.3 next-hop-self
 exit-address-family
 !
 address-family vpnv4
 address-family vpnv4
 neighbor 1.1.1.2 activate
 neighbor 1.1.1.2 send-community extended
 neighbor 1.1.1.2 route-map INTER-AS in
 neighbor 166.50.10.3 activate
 neighbor 166.50.10.3 send-community extended
 neighbor 166.50.10.3 next-hop-self
 exit-address-family
!
ip classless
!
ip extcommunity-list 10 permit rt 300:777
ip pim ssm range MDT-Groups
!
!
ip access-list standard MDT-Groups
 permit 239.232.0.0 0.0.255.255
route-map INTER-AS permit 10
 match extcommunity 10
!
end
```

FIGURE 2.148

(Continued)

2.2.2.65 CE-200 Configuration Template

```
service timestamps debug uptime
service timestamps log uptime
no service password-encryption
!
hostname CE-200
!
ip subnet-zero
ip host CE-200-RP 192.168.10.1
ip host CE-300 192.168.10.3
ip multicast-routing
!
interface Loopback0
 ip address 192.168.10.2 255.255.255.255
 no ip directed-broadcast
!
```

FIGURE 2.149

CE-200 configuration.

```
interface Loopback1
 description ANYCAST-RP
 ip address 192.168.10.1 255.255.255.255
 no ip directed-broadcast
!
interface Ethernet0/0
 ip address 192.168.2.1 255.255.255.0
 no ip directed-broadcast
 ip pim sparse-mode
 no keepalive
!
interface Serial5/0
 ip address 2.1.1.2 255.255.255.252
 no ip directed-broadcast
 ip pim sparse-mode
!
router ospf 1
 log-adjacency-changes
 passive-interface Loopback0
 passive-interface Loopback1
 network 2.0.0.0 0.255.255.255 area 0
 network 192.168.0.0 0.0.255.255 area 0
!
ip classless
!
ip pim rp-address 192.168.10.1
ip msdp peer 192.168.10.3 connect-source Loopback0
ip msdp cache-sa-state
ip msdp originator-id Loopback0
!
end
```

FIGURE 2.149

(Continued)

2.2.2.66 PE-300 Configuration Template

```
service timestamps debug uptime
service timestamps log uptime
no service password-encryption
!
hostname PE-300
!
ip subnet-zero
ip cef
ip host PE-200 166.50.10.3
ip host IP_Source 20.1.1.1
ip host CE-300-RP 192.168.10.1
ip host Source-200 192.168.2.3
ip vrf VPN_RECEIVER
```

FIGURE 2.150

PE-300 configuration.

```
 rd 300:1
 route-target export 300:1
 route-target export 300:777
 route-target import 300:1
 route-target import 200:1
 mdt default 239.232.0.1
 mdt data 239.232.3.0 0.0.0.255 threshold 10
!
ip vrf VPN_SOURCE
!
ip multicast-routing
ip multicast-routing vrf VPN_RECEIVER
ip multicast vrf VPN_RECEIVER rpf proxy rd vector
mpls label protocol ldp
tag-switching tdp router-id Loopback0
!
interface Loopback0
 ip address 156.50.10.3 255.255.255.255
 no ip directed-broadcast
 ip pim sparse-mode
!
interface Ethernet0/0
 ip address 3.3.3.6 255.255.255.252
 no ip directed-broadcast
 ip pim sparse-mode
 tag-switching ip
!
interface Serial5/0
 ip vrf forwarding VPN_RECEIVER
 ip address 30.1.1.1 255.255.255.252
 no ip directed-broadcast
 ip pim sparse-mode
!
router ospf 1 vrf VPN_RECEIVER
 log-adjacency-changes
 redistribute bgp 300 subnets
 network 30.0.0.0 0.255.255.255 area 0
!
router ospf 300
 log-adjacency-changes
 network 3.3.3.0 0.0.0.255 area 0
 network 156.50.10.0 0.0.0.255 area 0
!
router bgp 300
 no bgp default ipv4-unicast
 bgp log-neighbor-changes
 neighbor 156.50.10.1 remote-as 300
 neighbor 156.50.10.1 update-source Loopback0
 !
 address-family ipv4 mdt
 neighbor 156.50.10.1 activate
 neighbor 156.50.10.1 send-community both
 exit-address-family
```

FIGURE 2.150

(Continued)

```
!
address-family vpnv4
neighbor 156.50.10.1 activate
neighbor 156.50.10.1 send-community extended
exit-address-family
!
address-family ipv4 vrf VPN_SOURCE
no auto-summary
no synchronization
exit-address-family
!
address-family ipv4 vrf VPN_RECEIVER
redistribute ospf 1 vrf VPN_RECEIVER match internal external 1 external 2
no auto-summary
no synchronization
exit-address-family
!
ip classless
!
ip pim ssm range MDT-Groups
ip pim vrf VPN_RECEIVER rp-address 192.168.10.1
!
!
ip access-list standard MDT-Groups
 permit 239.232.0.0 0.0.255.255
!
end
```

FIGURE 2.150

(Continued)

2.2.2.67 P-300 Configuration Template

```
service timestamps debug uptime
service timestamps log uptime
no service password-encryption
!
hostname P-300
!
ip subnet-zero
ip cef
ip multicast-routing
mpls label protocol ldp
tag-switching tdp router-id Loopback0
!
interface Loopback0
 ip address 156.50.10.2 255.255.255.255
 no ip directed-broadcast
 ip pim sparse-mode
!
interface Ethernet0/0
 ip address 3.3.3.5 255.255.255.252
 no ip directed-broadcast
```

FIGURE 2.151

P-300 configuration.

```
 ip pim sparse-mode
 tag-switching ip
!
interface Serial5/0
 ip address 3.3.3.2 255.255.255.252
 no ip directed-broadcast
 ip pim sparse-mode
 tag-switching ip
!
interface Serial6/0
 ip address 3.3.3.9 255.255.255.252
 no ip directed-broadcast
 shutdown
!
router ospf 300
 log-adjacency-changes
 network 3.3.3.0 0.0.0.255 area 0
 network 156.50.10.0 0.0.0.255 area 0
!
ip pim ssm range MDT-Groups
!
ip access-list standard MDT-Groups
 permit 239.232.0.0 0.0.255.255
!
end
```

FIGURE 2.151

(Continued)

2.2.2.68 ASBR-300 Configuration Template

```
service timestamps debug uptime
service timestamps log uptime
no service password-encryption
!
hostname ASBR-300
!
ip subnet-zero
ip cef
ip multicast-routing
mpls label protocol ldp
tag-switching tdp router-id Loopback0
!
interface Loopback0
 ip address 156.50.10.1 255.255.255.255
 no ip directed-broadcast
 ip pim sparse-mode
!
interface Serial4/0
 ip address 1.1.1.2 255.255.255.252
 no ip directed-broadcast
 ip pim sparse-mode
 mpls bgp forwarding
 no fair-queue
!
```

FIGURE 2.152

ASBR-300 configuration.

```
interface Serial5/0
 ip address 3.3.3.1 255.255.255.252
 no ip directed-broadcast
 ip pim sparse-mode
 tag-switching ip
!
router ospf 300
 log-adjacency-changes
 redistribute connected subnets
 network 3.3.3.0 0.0.0.255 area 0
 network 156.50.10.0 0.0.0.255 area 0
!
router bgp 300
 no bgp default ipv4-unicast
 no bgp default route-target filter
 bgp log-neighbor-changes
 neighbor 1.1.1.1 remote-as 200
 neighbor 156.50.10.3 remote-as 300
 neighbor 156.50.10.3 update-source Loopback0
 !
 address-family ipv4 mdt
 neighbor 1.1.1.1 activate
 neighbor 1.1.1.1 send-community both
 neighbor 156.50.10.3 activate
 neighbor 156.50.10.3 send-community both
 neighbor 156.50.10.3 next-hop-self
 exit-address-family
 !
 address-family vpnv4
 neighbor 1.1.1.1 activate
 neighbor 1.1.1.1 send-community extended
 neighbor 1.1.1.1 route-map INTER-AS in
 neighbor 156.50.10.3 activate
 neighbor 156.50.10.3 send-community extended
 neighbor 156.50.10.3 next-hop-self
 exit-address-family
!
ip extcommunity-list 10 permit rt 200:777
ip pim ssm range MDT-Groups
!
ip access-list standard MDT-Groups
 permit 239.232.0.0 0.0.255.255
route-map INTER-AS permit 10
 match extcommunity 10
 !
end
```

FIGURE 2.152

(Continued)

2.2.2.69 CE-300 Configuration Template

```
service timestamps debug uptime
service timestamps log uptime
no service password-encryption
!
hostname CE-300
!
ip subnet-zero
ip host CE-200 192.168.10.2
ip host ANYCAST-RP 192.168.10.1
ip multicast-routing
!
interface Loopback0
 ip address 192.168.10.3 255.255.255.255
 no ip directed-broadcast
!
interface Loopback1
 description ANYCAST-RP
 ip address 192.168.10.1 255.255.255.255
 no ip directed-broadcast
!
interface Ethernet0/0
 ip address 192.168.3.1 255.255.255.0
 no ip directed-broadcast
 ip pim sparse-mode
 ip igmp join-group 239.192.0.1
 no keepalive
!
interface Serial5/0
 ip address 30.1.1.2 255.255.255.252
 no ip directed-broadcast
 ip pim sparse-mode
!
interface Serial6/0
 no ip address
 no ip directed-broadcast
 shutdown
!
interface Serial7/0
 no ip address
 no ip directed-broadcast
 shutdown
!
router ospf 1
 log-adjacency-changes
 passive-interface Loopback0
 passive-interface Loopback1
 network 30.0.0.0 0.255.255.255 area 0
 network 192.168.0.0 0.0.255.255 area 0
!
ip classless
!
ip pim rp-address 192.168.10.1
ip msdp peer 192.168.10.2 connect-source Loopback0
ip msdp cache-sa-state
ip msdp originator-id Loopback0
!
end
```

FIGURE 2.153

CE-300 configuration.

2.3 **SUMMARY**

As we have discussed in this chapter, Draft-Rosen MVPNs use a combination of PIM and GRE encapsulation for the control plane and forwarding plane, respectively. P-Group addresses, Data MDTs, and BGP MDT support do offer some amount of scalability in the carrier network, without flooding customer multicast information (signaling) into the Provider routers, but there are still some limitations that need to be considered.

- At least one multicast tree is needed per customer in the core and there is no option to aggregate multicast streams over a Data MDT, especially if the carrier transports high volumes of C-MCAST traffic.
- Flooded multicast streams over the per MVPN MDT "emulated LAN." This happens with the Default MDT.
- Per MVPN (S, G) states to maintain in the P router. This was discussed early in the chapter.

  - Explosion of C-PIM adjacencies over the emulated LAN/MDT.
  - Multicast traffic is GRE (not MPLS) encapsulated. The carrier has to address the encapsulation/decapsulation cost in the form of separate hardware possibly.
  - Operational costs with different multicast and unicast data planes.
  - PIM is the only fully described way to build core trees, but it may not ideally suit all environments. This will be discussed in future chapters.
  - The PE-PE exchange of C-MCAST routes is by using per-customer PIM instances. This is a different protocol compared to Unicast VPN(s).
  - No administrative scoping of multicast topology is possible.
  - Inter-AS challenges include PIM Overlay extending beyond the AS boundary.

Next-Generation Multicast VPNS

3

3.1 INTRODUCTION

The previous chapter introduced us to BGP/MPLS Layer 3 VPNs, and various flavors of Draft-Rosen based Multicast VPNs. Draft-Rosen based MVPNs offer an operator the ability to provide a customer-specific multicast infrastructure that could extend a customer multicast domain across a provider backbone. However, certain inherent limitations with the Draft-Rosen approach, as detailed in the next section, made technologists think about alternates to this approach. In other words, the new approach would be the Next-Generation of Multicast VPNs, which addresses limitations seen with Draft-Rosen and offers closer integration with the transport and control plane.

3.1.1 Draft-Rosen Limitations

RFC 4364 describes BGP/MPLS VPNs addresses, unicast traffic, and a scheme for building an infrastructure for MPLS-based Layer 3 VPNs. Multicast does not figure in this scheme; therefore Draft-Rosen for Multicast VPNs evolved from addressing multicast traffic.

Draft-Rosen essentially built a parallel infrastructure over a carrier IP/MPLS network for extending customer multicast traffic over the network core, which was discussed in detail in Chapter 2. In other words, a GRE-based infrastructure was built between the Provider Edge and Provider layers of the network. This resulted in the creation of an overlay infrastructure for facilitating both the customer multicast signaling information and transporting customer multicast traffic. Therefore the benefits of MPLS are not extended, since Draft-Rosen based Multicast traffic is transported as native IP traffic that is GRE encapsulated. Therefore an operator would need to view VPN traffic in two categories: one for unicast and the other for multicast. This actually results in more than one overhead for an operator, for example, Quality of Service (QoS) schemes would essentially now need classification and marking for two sets of traffic within the same VPN—one for unicast, which is label switched, and the other, which is not label switched. The end result is increased bandwidth/encapsulation + decapsulation cost and operational costs for maintaining two data and control planes (PIM + GRE for Multicast and MPLS + BGP for Unicast).

Draft-Rosen MVPNs are represented as an emulated LAN. Each MVPN has a logical PIM interface, and will form an adjacency to every other PIM interface across PE routers within the same MVPN. This is illustrated in Figure 3.1.

This results in an explosion in the number of PIM adjacencies over the Emulated LAN that PIM creates, which has a direct bearing on the scalability of the network. Explosion in Customer PIM joins that need to be transported across the network core can add further burden. For instance, if a CE on the top left side of Figure 3.1 issued a PIM (*, G) join, and assuming the source for the given

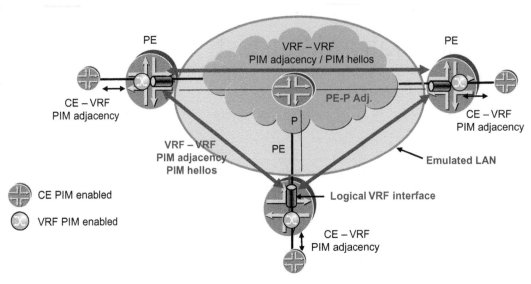

FIGURE 3.1

group is behind the PE on the top left right, this join would be flooded to both PE routers since we are dealing with an emulated LAN in this context.

The provider routers need to maintain state information for individual customer traffic flows over a Data MDT. This results in more state information on Provider routers, because most operators prefer the Provider layer to be free of any state machinery. Most operators have BGP Free Cores, enabling the Provider Layer to ONLY label switch traffic.

Traffic over a Default MDT is inherently flooded to all PE routers within the same MVPN, causing increased ineffective bandwidth utilization. Data MDTs and Draft-Rosen Version 8 (using special BGP SAFI types) offer an alternative to this situation; however, Data MDTs, as seen earlier, increase state information within the provider core. Therefore the solution for flooding is a double-edged sword.

Finally, Draft-Rosen does not offer any scope for aggregating multicast trees; therefore each MVPN results in dedicated multicast trees created in the network depending on the deployment (Default-MDT + Total of Data MDTs used).

3.2 NEXT-GENERATION MULTICAST VPNS

Having discussed the limitations of Draft-Rosen, we can now make a small wish list for enhancements in particular areas, especially related to the needs of a Next-Generation Multicast VPN infrastructure.

1. Single layer for both MPLS VPN unicast and multicast traffic. This ideally means that we now want to label switch multicast traffic within a VPN.
2. Single or unified control plane for both unicast and multicast traffic. In other words, use BGP for unicast and multicast traffic instead of relying on additional protocol machinery.

3. Overcome the limitations of using an Emulated LAN for each customer multicast VPN negating the limitations of PIM.
4. Have the ability to choose more than one data plane mechanism. We are now looking at using schemes other than or in addition to GRE encapsulation. Free the Provider layer from any sort of state machinery needed for the transport of multicast VPNs.
5. Provide an option to have traffic transported to the intended receiver only. This would be similar to Data MDT in Draft-Rosen without the need for a Data MDT.
6. Provide a road map for aggregation of customer multicast traffic.
7. Create a standards-based and interoperable solution.

Our wish list is increasingly relevant for all Service Provider environments, primarily because carriers have adopted their operations infrastructure, including Operations Support Systems (OSSs) and operations processes, to support MPLS-based service provisioning and troubleshooting. Because of an increasing shift in revenue mix from voice to data, with an increasing emphasis on real-time service connectivity requirements, the majority of carriers have started to put more focus on network resilience, performance, and scale to ensure reliable and predictable end-to-end service connectivity. So far, resiliency efforts have primarily been focused on protecting unicast IP traffic carried across MPLS networks. Various unicast traffic protection mechanisms are available, such as fast convergence and Traffic Engineering (TE)/Resource Reservation Protocol (RSVP) Fast Reroute (FRR), which are deployed by a significant number of carrier customers. Emerging network applications, such as video transport, have been the key drivers for new connectivity requirements for Multicast VPN traffic similar to their unicast counterparts.

This warrants a paradigm shift in the evolution of Next-Generation architecture, since we are now looking at changes to the control plane and data plane infrastructures with more flexibility in terms of options to choose from for data plane deployment. The good news is that the earlier wish list is an achievable reality with the Next-Generation VPN framework. This chapter focuses on the Next-Generation MVPN (NG-MVPN) framework and the various building blocks that help achieve the goals outlined in our wish list.

3.2.1 **Terminology**

The following terms will be used throughout this chapter, and their definitions are provided in this section. Detailed explanations for each of these terms will be provided in the subsequent sections of this chapter.

- **Branch LSR:** A label switching router (LSR) with more than one directly connected downstream LSR.
- **Bud LSR:** An egress LSR with one or more directly connected downstream LSRs.
- **Egress LSR:** One of many potential destinations of the P2MP Data plane (LSP). Egress LSRs may also be referred to as leaf nodes or leaves.
- **Ingress LSR:** LSR connected to the C-MCAST Source.
- **P2MP tree:** Ordered set of LSRs that comprise the path of a P2MP LSP between the ingress LSR to all of its egress LSRs.
- **P2MP-ID (P2ID):** A unique identifier of a P2MP TE LSP, which is constant for the whole LSP regardless of the number of branches and/or leaves.

- **Receiver:** A recipient of traffic carried on a P2MP service supported by a P2MP LSP. A receiver is not necessarily an egress LSR of the P2MP LSP. One or more receivers may receive data through a given egress LSR.
- **Source:** The sender of traffic that is carried on a P2MP service supported by a P2MP LSP. The sender can be other than the ingress LSR of the P2MP LSP.

3.3 NG-MVPN CONTROL PLANE

The NG-MVPN framework is based on the following Internet drafts:

- BGP encodings and procedures for multicast in BGP/MPLS VPNs (draft-ietf-l3vpn-2547bis-mcast-bgp).
- Multicast in BGP/MPLS VPNs (draft-ietf-l3vpn-2547bis-mcast).

The NG-MVPN control plane within the Provider network is based on BGP signaling. In other words, BGP is used for exchanging both VPNv4 unicast and multicast information, thus replacing the need for PIM with the Provider IP/MPLS network. The use of a single control plane protocol for invariably all IP/MPLS-based services such as IPv4 Internet prefixes, VPNv4 for both unicast and multicast, and IPv6 results in decreased operational overhead and also offers a simplified and converged control plane infrastructure. In the context of NG-MVPNs, BGP is used for the following functions:

- Auto-discovery of PE routers within a given NG-MVPN instance.
- Exchange of Data plane (from this point onward the Data plane will be referred to as Provider-Tunnel or P-tunnel) information between Provider Edge routers. In the context of NG-MVPN, details on the type and identifier of the tunnel used for transmitting C-MCAST traffic is advertised from the ingress PE to all relevant egress PE routers.
- Exchange of C-MCAST routing information. All joins from the Customer domain (CE routers) are announced to the relevant PE routers within a context of a given NG-MVPN.

The introduction of the BGP control plane does not impose any restrictions in the customer multicast domain. CE routers continue to use PIM between the CE-PE links similar to Draft-Rosen. Therefore the introduction of NG-MVPNs or migration of customers using Draft-Rosen to the NG-MVPN scheme (which will be discussed in detail later in this chapter) does not warrant any redesign or changes to the customer infrastructure. One of the advantages that NG-MVPN offers is a seamless migration for customer multicast infrastructures. Coming back to the BGP control plane, the 2547bis-mcast-bgp draft introduces a new BGP address family called MCAST-VPN for supporting NG-MVPN control plane operations. The new address family is assigned the subsequent address family identifier (SAFI) of 5 by IANA.

A PE router that participates in a BGP-based NG-MVPN network is required to send a BGP update message that contains an MCAST-VPN NLRI, which contains route type, length, and variable fields (illustrated in detail a little later in this chapter). The value of the variable field depends on the route type. Seven types of NG-MVPN BGP routes, also known as MVPN routes, are specified. The first five route types are called auto-discovery (AD) MVPN routes. This chapter also refers to Type 1–5 routes as non-C-multicast MVPN routes. Type 6 and Type 7 routes are called C-multicast MVPN routes.

The table below provides details about the various MVPN routes used:

Table 3.1

Route	Definition
Type 1 Intra-AS I-PMSI AD	Originated by all PE routers and used for advertising and learning Intra-AS MVPN membership information.
Type 2 Inter-AS I-PMSI AD	Originated by NG-MVPN ASBR routers and used for advertising and learning Inter-AS MVPN membership information.
Type 3 S-PMSI AD	Originated by Ingress PE routers and used for initiating a selective P-tunnel for a given C-Source and C-Group multicast stream.
Type 4 Leaf AD	Originated by Egress PE routers in response to a Type 3 announcement. It is used for indicating interest for a given C-Source and C-Group multicast stream.
Type 5 Source Active AD	Originated by a PE router (Ingress PE) when it learns about an active Multicast Source. The Type 5 route is announced to all Egress PE that belongs to a given NG-MVPN.
Type 6 Shared Tree Join	Originated by an Egress PE when it receives a PIM Shared Tree join (C-*, C-G) from the CE device.
Type 7 Source Tree Join	Originated by an Egress PE when it receives a Source Tree Join or when it receives a Type 5 route announcement from an Ingress PE.

3.3.1 Ingress and Egress PE Routers

The term Ingress PE router refers to a PE router that has an active C-MCAST source for a given NG-MVPN. Egress PE routers are referred also as leaf nodes. This indicates that they are end points for a given C-MCAST traffic flow. One of the advantages of the NG-MVPN architecture is the ability to designate a PE router as a "Sender and Receiver" site or "Receiver Only" site. The former is an indication of the specified PE router to be able to both originate and receive C-MCAST traffic, while the latter is only able to receive traffic. This will be discussed in greater detail in subsequent sections of this chapter.

3.3.2 Provider Multicast Service Interface

While looking at the various BGP route types for NG-MVPNs, references were made to a term known as PMSI (Provider Multicast Service Interface). Let us discuss this concept further, since it forms a key part of the MVPN architecture.

The NG-MVPN architecture uses a PMSI to simplify and generalize different options for the MVPN solution. The PMSI distinguishes between services and the transport mechanism (P-tunnels) that support and realize the concept. When a PE gives a packet to PMSI, the underlying transport mechanism, P-tunnels, delivers the packet to some or all of the other PEs. A PMSI is a conceptual "overlay" on the Provider network with the following property: a PE in a given MVPN can give a packet to the PMSI, and the packet will be delivered to some or all of the other PEs in the MVPN, such that any PE receiving the packet will be able to determine the MVPN to which the packet belongs. For instance, an Ingress PE router may wish to send C-MCAST traffic only to given set of

PE routers who express interest for the traffic or send it to all PE routers that participate in a given MVPN—irrespective of whether they have interested receivers or not. This is achieved by attaching an appropriate PMSI attribute to the BGP routes.

The various PMSI types are

- Inclusive PMSI (I-PMSI)
- Selective PMSI (S-PMSI)

I-PMSI may be considered as a unidirectional P2MP connection between an Ingress PE and all Egress PE routers. Therefore, if a BGP route announcement has an attached I-PMSI attribute (e.g., a Type 1 BGP route used for auto-discovery may have an I-PSMI attribute attached), all traffic from the Ingress PE router is delivered to every other PE router participating in a given NG-MVPN. This behavior can be compared to the operation of the Default MDT in a Draft-Rosen MVPN.

Selective PMSI (S-PMSI) may be considered to be a subset of the I-PMSI, because a packet is delivered to a subset of PE routers that is participating in a given MVPN. This behavior can be compared to the Data MDT in Draft-Rosen.

The format of the PMSI Tunnel Attribute is displayed in Figure 3.2.

Carried in BGP MCAST-VPN A-D route Updates to identify PMSI Tunnels

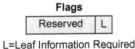

PMSI Tunnel Attribute

| Flags (1 octet) |
| Tunnel Type (1 octet) |
| MPLS Label (3 octets) |
| Tunnel Identifier (variable) |

Flags

| Reserved | L |

L=Leaf Information Required

Tunnel Type: RSVP-TE P2MP,LDP P2MP,PIM-SSM, PIM-SM, PIM-BIDIR, Ingress Replication, LDP MP2MP

MPLS Label (high order 20 bits): the de-multiplexer value on aggregate trees (or zero)

Tunnel Identifier (format dependent on tunnel type):

RSVP-TE: contents of SESSION object, <P2MP ID, Tunnel ID, Extended Tunnel ID>

PIM: <sender IP address, P-multicast address>

Leaf information flag used to solicit Leaf auto-discovery routes for explicit tracking

E.g., from remote PEs with interest in <C-S,C-G> when setting up an S-PMSI

FIGURE 3.2

The Tunnel type indicates the various options available within the context of NG-MVPNs. Compared to Draft-Rosen where PIM-GRE was the only option available for transport of multicast traffic, the NG-MVPN provides options including RSVP-TE, MLDP, and also traditional PIM GRE-based schemes as options for Provider Tunnels (transport mechanisms). Each of these options will be discussed in subsequent sections.

The MPLS Label indicates the Label assigned. It is always set to "zero," since both I-PMSI and S-PMSI tunnels always correspond to a single MVPN instance. MVPN differentiation is actually based on other values used in the BGP MVPN routes such as RD values, which uniquely identify a BGP/MPLS VPN.

The Tunnel identifier uniquely identifies the P-tunnel. In Figure 3.2 we use RSVP-TE as an example for indicating the construct of a Tunnel Identifier.

A flag indicates whether the PMSI is an I-PMSI or S-PMSI. A flag value of "0" is an indication of an I-PMSI and "1" indicates an S-PMSI. In the case of an S-PMSI, interested leaf nodes need to identify themselves (similar to a Default MDT in Draft-Rosen); hence the only available flag is "Leaf Information Required." An example of an I-PMSI attribute attached to a BGP Type 1 route is provided in Figure 3.3.

```
operator@PE1# run show route table FOO-MVPN.mvpn.0 detail
1:100:1:7.0.0.1/240 (1 entry, 1 announced)
*BGP       Preference: 170/-101
PMSI: Flags 0:RSVP-TE:label[0:0:0]:Session_13[7.0.0.1:0:28754:7.0.0.1]
[Output is Truncated]
```

FIGURE 3.3

I-PMSI Attribute.

Note: This chapter will focus on the JUNOS CLI and related configurations and outputs. However, this does not indicate that any or all of the information provided here will vary on other vendor implementations since the JUNOS implementation completely adheres to the NG-MVPN IEFT draft. Other vendor implementations are covered in the subsequent chapters.

3.3.3 BGP MVPN Routes

Let us look at the various BGP MVPN routes in more detail just to understand their usage.

3.3.3.1 BGP Type 1 AD Routes

Every NG-MVPN Provider Edge router advertises a BGP Type 1 route for each NG-MVPN hosted. For instance, if a PE router is connected to three NG-MVPN customer sites, then a total of three BGP Type 1 routes are created and announced to every NG-MVPN PE in the network. The format for a Type 1 AD route is illustrated in Figure 3.4.

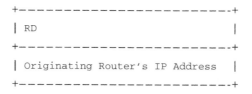

FIGURE 3.4

The RD field indicates that the Route Distinguisher is configured under the BGP/MPLS VPN and is set to this value when the PE announces a Type 1 route. The field "Originating Router IP Address" is always set to the IPv4 loopback address of the originating PE router. There is a sample output from a JUNOS-based PE router that displays a BGP Type 1 route. In this example there are a total of three PE routers, including the local PE router.

The first entry displayed in Figure 3.5 is "1:100:1:7.0.0.1/240." The entry "1"indicates a BGP Type 1 AD Route type. The next part, 100:1, indicates the configured RD for the given BGP/MPLS NG-MVPN. 7.0.0.1 indicates the loopback IPv4 address of the PE. Finally, the field BGP indicates that this route was learned via BGP. The third entry in Figure 3.5 indicates that the local PE router with address 7.0.0.5 has created a Type 1 route entry for itself, which is ready to be announced to other participating PE routers within the context of the same NG-MVPN instance. Each of these concepts will become clearer as we progress through the chapter.

```
operator@PE1# run show route
1:100:1:7.0.0.1/240
                    *[BGP/170] 3d 02:04:45, localpref 100, from 7.0.0.1
                       AS path: I
                     > to 172.16.1.1 via ge-1/0/1.0, Push 300144
1:100:1:7.0.0.4/240
                    *[BGP/170] 5d 03:21:21, localpref 100, from 7.0.0.4
                       AS path: I
                     > to 172.16.1.1 via ge-1/0/1.0
1:100:1:7.0.0.5/240
                    *[MVPN/70] 5d 03:42:50, metric2 1
                       Indirect
[Output is Truncated]
```

FIGURE 3.5

BGP Type 1 AD route.

3.3.3.2 BGP Type 3 and Type 4 S-PMSI Routes

An Ingress PE router signals a Type 3 BGP route for the creation of the S-PMSI. The creation of the S-PMSI can be defined based on a variety of criteria such as traffic thresholds (as used in the Draft-Rosen Data MDT creation). Upon receipt of the Type 3 BGP routes, Egress PE routers with interested receivers will respond to the announcement by advertising a Type 4 route. After this step, an Ingress PE router creates the appropriate P-tunnel. Type 3 and Type 4 routes on an Ingress PE are seen in Figure 3.6).

3.3.3.3 BGP Type 5 Source Active Routes

Type 5 routes carry information about active VPN sources and the groups to which they are transmitting data. These routes can be generated by any PE router that becomes aware of an active source. Type 5 routes apply only for PIM-SM (ASM) when the inter-site source-tree-only mode is used (see Figures 3.7 and 3.8).

```
operator@PE1# run show route
3:100:1:32:192.168.1.9:32:236.1.1.1:7.0.0.1/240
        *MVPN    Preference: 70
                 Next hop type: Indirect
                 Next-hop reference count: 4
                 Protocol next hop: 7.0.0.1
                 Indirect next hop: 0 -

4:3:100:1:32:192.168.1.9:32:236.1.1.1:7.0.0.1:7.0.0.4/240
        *BGP     Preference: 170/-101
                 Next hop type: Indirect
                 Source: 7.0.0.4
                 Protocol next hop: 7.0.0.4
[Output is Truncated]
```

FIGURE 3.6

Type 3 and 4 routes displayed on the Ingress PE router.

```
operator@PE1# run show route
5:100:1:32:192.168.1.9:32:236.1.1.1/240 (1 entry, 1 announced)
        *PIM     Preference: 105
                 Next hop type: Multicast (IPv4)
                 State: <Active Int>
[Output is Truncated]
```

FIGURE 3.7

Type 5 routes displayed on the Ingress PE router.

```
operator@PE1# run show route
5:100:1:32:192.168.1.9:32:236.1.1.1/240 (1 entry, 1 announced)
        *BGP     Preference: 170/-101
                 Next hop type: Indirect
                 Next-hop reference count: 6
                 Source: 7.0.0.1
                 Protocol next hop: 7.0.0.1
                 Indirect next hop: 2 no-forward
                 State: <Secondary Active Int Ext>
                 Local AS:    100 Peer AS:    100
                 Localpref: 100
                 Router ID: 7.0.0.1
   [Output is Truncated]
```

FIGURE 3.8

Type 5 routes displayed on the Egress PE router.

3.3.3.4 BGP Type 6 and Type 7 Routes

The C-multicast route exchange between PE routers refers to the propagation of C-joins from receiver PEs to the sender PEs. In an NG-MVPN, C-joins are translated into (or encoded as) BGP C-multicast MVPN routes and advertised via a BGP MCAST-VPN address family toward the sender PEs. Two types of C-multicast MVPN routes are specified.

- Type 6 C-multicast routes are used in representing information contained in a Shared Tree (C-*, C-G) join.
- Type 7 C-multicast routes are used in representing information contained in a source tree (C-S, C-G) join.

NG-MVPN provides an optimization in handling additional state information created in a Shared Tree environment. In a Shared Tree environment, every C-MCAST Source needs to register itself with the C-RP and the receivers need to join the shared tree via the RP. Therefore traffic initially flows over this shared tree prior to moving to the SPT or shortest path to the Source. Prior to joining the SPT, the receivers send PRUNE messages to the RP to stop the traffic flowing through it for the group they have joined via the SPT. The RP further triggers another PRUNE toward the source, and now traffic flows via the Source Tree or SPT. This process increases the state information in the network and involves additional complexity, which adds no value since traffic eventually ends up flowing via the SPT.

NG-MVPN by default provides a solution for this RPT to SPT switchover. Whenever an egress PE router generates a Type 6 BGP route for every PIM join (C-*, C-G) it receives a multicast domain from the customer; it does not advertise this route to remote PE routers unless it receives information of an active source via a Type 5 route. Sources by default do not register themselves with the RP; it is their locally connected router (CE device for NG-MVPN) that sends a unicast packet to the RP with the source's data packets encapsulated within. For the PE routers to learn about active sources, two conditions need to be met:

1. One of the PE routers needs to be designated as the Customer-RP.
2. An MSDP session needs to be established between the PE router and customer RP.

It is only through one of the above procedures that a PE router (e.g., RP-PE) will learn of an active source and generate a BGP Type 5 route. PE routers with interested receivers will generate a Type 7 route toward the Ingress PE (and not toward the RP) forming the SPT. Figure 3.9 is a sample output taken from a PE router designated as a C-RP with PIM register messages from a C-MCAST source. In Figure 3.9 we see that a PIM Register message has been sent from a PE router with the address "7.0.0.1" for a Source "192.168.1.9" at Group "235.1.1.12" to the RP at address "7.0.0.4."

```
operator@PE1# run show pim rps extensive instance NG-MVPN
Instance: PIM.NG-MVPN
RP: 7.0.0.4
Learned via: static configuration
Time Active: 01:59:32
Holdtime: 0

Register State for RP:
Group          Source         FirstHop       RP Address     State
235.1.1.1      192.168.1.9    7.0.0.1        7.0.0.4        Receive
[Output is Truncated]
```

FIGURE 3.9

PIM Register Messages received by PE acting as C-RP.

Now that the RP knows about an active source, a BGP Type 5 route will be originated. Figure 3.10 is an example of a Type 5 route format.

```
+-----------------------+
| RD (8 octets)         |
+-----------------------+
| Multicast Source Length (1 octet) |
+-----------------------+
| Multicast Source (variable)   |
+-----------------------+
| Multicast Group Length (1 octet)  |
+-----------------------+
| Multicast Group (variable)    |
+-----------------------+
```

FIGURE 3.10

To understand each field in more detail review Figure 3.11; it is a real-life example.

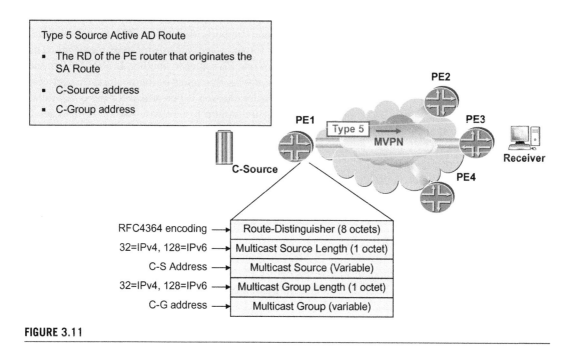

FIGURE 3.11

Figure 3.12 illustrates a corresponding Type 7 route generated by the Egress PE received at the Ingress PE.

```
operator@PE1# run show route
7:100:1:100:32:192.168.1.9:32:235.1.1.1/240
*[PIM/105] 00:00:05
Multicast (IPv4)
[BGP/170] 00:00:05, localpref 100, from 7.0.0.4 ----------> Type 7 received from
Egress PE router PE2.
AS path: I
> to 172.16.1.5 via ge-4/0/0.0
[Output is Truncated]
```

FIGURE 3.12

Type 7 route at the Ingress PE.

As seen in this section, the default mode of operation provides advantages but requires the Customer Rendezvous Point (C-RP) to be located on a PE router or the Multicast Source Discovery Protocol (MSDP) to be used between the C-RP and a PE router so the PE router can learn about active sources advertised by other PE routers.

If the default mode is not suitable for a given environment, configure an RPT-SPT mode (also known as shared-tree data distribution), as documented in Section 13 of the BGP-MVPN draft (draft-ietf-l3vpn-2547bis-mcast-bgp.txt). RPT-SPT mode supports the native PIM model of transmitting (*, G) messages from the receiver to the RP for inter-site shared-tree join messages. This means that the Type 6 (*, G) routes get transmitted from one PE router to another. In RPT-SPT mode, the shared-tree multicast routes are advertised from an egress PE router to the upstream router connected to the VPN site with the C-RP. The single-forwarder election is performed for the C-RP rather than for the source. The egress PE router takes the upstream hop to advertise the (*, G) and sends the Type 6 route toward the upstream PE router. After these data start flowing on the RPT, the last hop router switches to SPT mode, unless you include the "spt-threshold infinity" statements in the configuration.

The switch to SPT mode is performed by PIM and not by MVPN Type 5 and Type 6 routes. After the last hop router switches to SPT mode, the SPT (S, G) join messages follow the same rules as the SPT-only default mode.

The advantage of RPT-SPT mode is that it provides a method for PE routers to discover sources in the multicast VPN when the C-RP is located on the customer site instead of on a PE router. Because the shared C-tree is established between VPN sites, there is no need to run MSDP between the C-RP and the PE routers. RPT-SPT mode also enables egress PE routers to switch to receiving data from the PE connected to the source after the source information is learned, instead of receiving data from the RP. Figure 3.13 is an illustration of a Type 6 route. Here we note the announcement of Type 6 routes from PE routers with C-MCAST (C-*, C-G) joins sent to the upstream PE (PE closest to the RP). These routes are further announced as PIM joins toward the C-RP.

```
operator@PE1# run show route
6:100:1:100:32:8.0.0.4:32:237.1.1.1/240
                     *[PIM/105] 00:00:06
                      Multicast (IPv4)
                      [BGP/170] 00:00:06, localpref 100, from 7.0.0.5
                      AS path: I
                     > to 172.16.1.2 via ge-4/0/0.0
6:100:1:100:32:8.0.0.4:32:238.1.1.1/240
                     *[PIM/105] 00:00:06
                      Multicast (IPv4)
                      [BGP/170] 00:00:06, localpref 100, from 7.0.0.5
                      AS path: I
                     > to 172.16.1.2 via ge-4/0/0.0
6:100:1:100:32:8.0.0.4:32:239.1.1.2/240
                     *[PIM/105] 00:00:06
                      Multicast (IPv4)
                      [BGP/170] 00:00:06, localpref 100, from 7.0.0.5
                      AS path: I
                     > to 172.16.1.2 via ge-4/0/0.0
   [Output is Truncated]
```

FIGURE 3.13

Type 6 routes displayed on the PE router connected to the C-RP (CE).

3.3.3.5 Customer Multicast Routing Information and Route Targets

Based on the details discussed in the previous sections, it is now clear that C-multicast MVPN routes (Type 6 and Type 7) are only useful to the PE router connected to the active C-S or C-RP. Therefore, C-multicast routes need to be installed only in the VRF table on the active sender PE for a given C-G in the case of SPT in the PE router closest to the C-RP or acting as the C-RP in the RPT mode where Type 6 routes are installed.

To accomplish this, 2547bis-mcast proposes to attach a special and dynamic RT to C-multicast MVPN routes (see Figure 3.14).

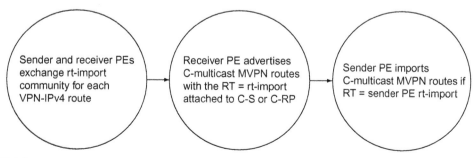

FIGURE 3.14

The RT attached to C-multicast routes is also referred to as C-multicast import RT and should not to be confused with the rt-import used for importing Unicast routing information. Note that C-multicast MVPN routes differ from other MVPN routes in one essential way: they carry a dynamic RT whose value depends on the identity of the active sender PE at a given time and may change if the active PE changes.

A PE router that receives a local C-join determines the identity of the active sender PE router by performing a unicast route lookup for the C-S or C-RP in the unicast VRF table. It chooses the appropriate upstream PE also known as the active sender. After the active sender (upstream) PE is selected, the receiver PE constructs the C-multicast MVPN route corresponding to the local C-join. Once the C-multicast route is constructed, the receiver PE needs to attach the correct RT to this route, targeting the active sender PE. As mentioned, each PE router creates a unique VRF route import (rt-import) community and attaches it to the VPN-IPv4 routes. When the receiver PE does a route lookup for C-S or C-RP, it can extract the value of the rt-import associated with this route and set the value of C-multicast import RT to the value of rt-import. On the active sender PE, C-multicast routes are imported only if they carry an RT whose value is the same as the rt-import that the sender PE generated. Let us look at an output of this value, displayed on a sender PE.

In the output in Figure 3.15, there is a field Communities: target: 7.0.0.1:5. This indicates the import RT set by the PE router with an IPv4 address of "7.0.0.1" and "5" is a random value chosen. Therefore any Type 6 or Type 7 route with this target attached will be accepted by the PE. Other PE routers receiving this route will ignore the route, since the import target does not match.

```
operator@PE1# run show route
7:100:1:100:32:192.168.1.9:32:236.1.1.1/240 (2 entries, 2 announced)
                BGP     Preference: 170/-101
                Next hop type: Indirect
                Next-hop reference count: 4
                Source: 7.0.0.4
                Protocol next hop: 7.0.0.4
                Local AS:    100 Peer AS:     100
                Age: 4:30       Metric2: 1
                Task: BGP_100.7.0.0.4+51285
                AS path: I
                Communities: target:7.0.0.1:5
                Import Accepted
                Localpref: 100
                Router ID: 7.0.0.4
    [Output is Truncated]
```

FIGURE 3.15

RT Import community on the Ingress or Sender PE.

The fields set by the Egress PE for this update are seen in Figures 3.16 and 3.17.

The fields that constitute a C-MCAST route used in NG-MVPNs are seen in Figure 3.18. Here we see that the Multicast Source field would be set to either C-Source or C-RP depending on whether it is a Source Tree Join or Shared Tree Join. For a Source Tree Join (Type 7 route), the source address is known by means of a Type route announcement; therefore, this address is used in

```
operator@PE2# run show route
7:100:1:100:32:192.168.1.9:32:236.1.1.1/240 (2 entries, 2 announced)
*MVPN    Preference: 70
Next hop type: Multicast (IPv4), Next hop index: 1048575
Next-hop reference count: 19
Communities: target:7.0.0.1:5 ----→ Appropriate Target set
  [Output is Truncated]
```

FIGURE 3.16

RT Import community on the Egress or Receiver PE.

```
operator@PE1# run show route
6:100:1:100:32:8.0.0.4:32:230.1.1.1/240
                BGP     Preference: 170/-101
                Next hop type: Indirect
                Next-hop reference count: 4
                Source: 7.0.0.4
                Protocol next hop: 7.0.0.4
                Communities: target:7.0.0.1:5
                Import Accepted
                Localpref: 100
                Router ID: 7.0.0.4
  [Output is Truncated]
```

FIGURE 3.17

Type 6 route with the RT Import community on the PE closest to C-RP.

BGP Control Plane with MVPN Address Family

- Type of C-Multicast route (Shared/Source Tree Join)

- The RD of the route that advertises the multicast source into the VPN, or C-RP which is set to the Upstream PE router

- The multicast source AS

- C-Group address

- C-Source address or C-RP address

- The C-multicast route should also carry a Route Target Extended Community identifying the Selected Upstream Multicast Hop

- To remove (prune) itself from the C-multicast tree, the PE withdraws the corresponding BGP update (MP_UNREACH_NLRI)

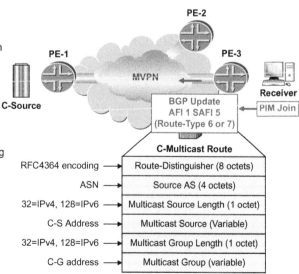

FIGURE 3.18

this field. On the other hand, a Type 6 route does not know the source for a given group; hence the RP address is entered in this field. Type 6 and Type 7 routes for validating this understanding are seen in Figure 3.19).

```
operator@PE2# run show route
6:100:1:100:32:8.0.0.4:32:230.1.1.1/240 (2 entries, 2 announced)
                BGP     Preference: 170/-101
                Next hop type: Indirect
                Next-hop reference count: 6
                Source: 7.0.0.1
                Protocol next hop: 7.0.0.1
                Local AS:    100 Peer AS:    100
                Age: 55         Metric2: 1
                Task: BGP_100.7.0.0.1+179
                Communities: target:7.0.0.4:5
                Import Accepted
                Localpref: 100
                Router ID: 7.0.0.1
   [Output is Truncated]
```

FIGURE 3.19

Type 6 route with the Source field set to the C-RP.

The address "8.0.0.4" indicated in the first line of the output is the address of a C-RP, since this is a Shared Tree Join. The same field will have an IP Address of the C-Source if it is a Source Tree Join, such as the Type 7 route as shown in Figure 3.20.

```
operator@PE2# run show route
7:100:1:100:32:192.168.1.9:32:230.1.1.1/240 (2 entries, 2 announced)
                BGP     Preference: 170/-101
                Next hop type: Indirect
                Next-hop reference count: 4
                Source: 7.0.0.1
                Protocol next hop: 7.0.0.1
                Indirect next hop: 2 no-forward
                State: <Secondary Int Ext>
                Inactive reason: Route Preference
                Local AS:    100 Peer AS:    100
                Age: 4:30       Metric2: 1
                AS path: I
                Communities: target:7.0.0.4:5
                Import Accepted
                Localpref: 100
                Router ID: 7.0.0.1
   [Output is Truncated]
```

FIGURE 3.20

Type 7 route with the Source field set to the C-Source.

The address "192.168.1.9" indicated in the first line of the output is the address of a C-Source.

3.3.3.6 Putting the Building Blocks into Perspective

The following list is a summary of the various steps involved in the BGP control plane used to enable multicast traffic flows within an NG-MVPN.

1. MVPN Membership and Autodiscovery
2. MVPN Membership and Autodiscovery + I-PMSI setup. In Figure 3.21 we use PIM-SM as the P-tunnel, since we have yet to introduce other MPLS-based P-tunnels such as RSVP-TE.

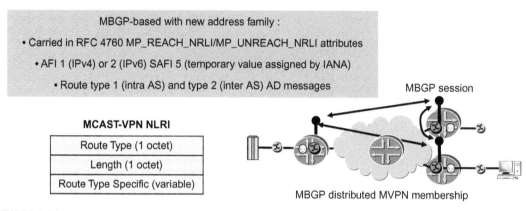

FIGURE 3.21

A PIM-SM P-tunnel uses an ASM Group Address (similar to Default MDT in Draft-Rosen), such as 239.1.1.1, which we used earlier. An NG-MVPN with PIM-SM or PIM-SSM uses GRE encapsulation and is similar to Draft-Rosen with the exception of using the superior BGP control plane. Some providers opt for this model as a first step to migrate to NG-MVPNs, wherein the control plane is changed and the Data plane is still preserved. It can be considered as an option for a phased migration. However, Figure 3.22 demonstrates the setup of a BGP Type 1 route along with the I-PMSI setup.

An I-PMSI field with a PIM-SM P-tunnel (see Figures 3.23 and 3.24) includes the following:

1. Receivers come online and C-JOIN messages are sent to the Receiver PE routers. The Receiver PE routers perform a route lookup for C-S and C-RP, respectively, and extract the RD, rt-import, and src-as associated with each route. PE with an interested receiver for a given group originates a Type 7 route upon receipt of a Type 5 route carrying RT information (value matching rt-import); PE without an interested receiver creates a Type 6 route, but does not advertise it.
2. The Ingress PE compares the received Type 7 routes with its import-RT and, based on a match, the route gets accepted and passed onto the C-PIM infrastructure.

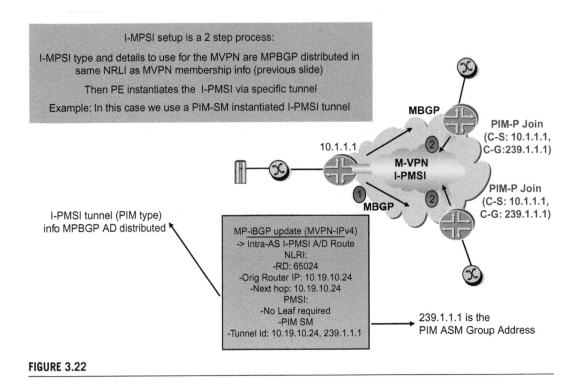

I-MPSI setup is a 2 step process:

I-MPSI type and details to use for the MVPN are MPBGP distributed in same NRLI as MVPN membership info (previous slide)

Then PE instantiates the I-PMSI via specific tunnel

Example: In this case we use a PIM-SM instantiated I-PMSI tunnel

MBGP

10.1.1.1

M-VPN I-PMSI

MBGP

PIM-P Join
(C-S: 10.1.1.1,
C-G:239.1.1.1)

PIM-P Join
(C-S: 10.1.1.1,
C-G: 239.1.1.1)

I-PMSI tunnel (PIM type) info MPBGP AD distributed

MP-iBGP update (MVPN-IPv4)
-> Intra-AS I-PMSI A/D Route
NLRI:
-RD: 65024
-Orig Router IP: 10.19.10.24
-Next hop: 10.19.10.24
PMSI:
-No Leaf required
-PIM SM
-Tunnel Id: 10.19.10.24, 239.1.1.1

239.1.1.1 is the
PIM ASM Group Address

FIGURE 3.22

```
PMSI: 0:PIM-SM:label[0:0:0]:Sender10.1.1.1 Group 239.1.1.1
```

FIGURE 3.23

Route type 6 (share tree join), route type 7 (source tree join)

MCAST-VPN NLRI

Route Type (1 octet)
Length (1 octet)
Route Type Specific (variable)

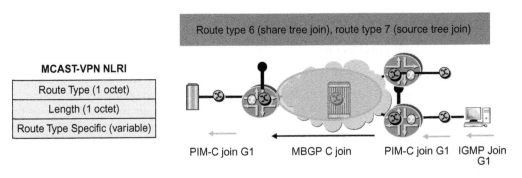

PIM-C join G1   MBGP C join   PIM-C join G1   IGMP Join
                                                                 G1

FIGURE 3.24

3.4 NG-MVPN DATA PLANE—PROVIDER TUNNELS

In this section, we move on to the Data plane setup, where one of the various supported options may be used for setting up Provider Tunnels in the network to facilitate C-MCAST traffic flows. The NG-MVPN framework currently provides support for the Provider Tunnels seen in Figure 3.25.

Tunnel Type 0 = No Tunnel Information Is Present
Tunnel Type 1 = RSVP-TE Point-to-Multipoint LSP
Tunnel Type 2 = MLDP Point-to-Multipoint LSP
Tunnel Type 3 = PIM-Source Specific Multicast
Tunnel Type 4 = PIM-Sparse Mode Tree
Tunnel Type 5 = PIM-Bidirectional Tree
Tunnel Type 6 = Ingress Replication
Tunnel Type 7 = MLDP MP2MPLSP

FIGURE 3.25

In theory, each NG-MVPN can be set up to use a different Provider Tunnel or Data plane. However, this is very unlikely since an operator would prefer to use a Provider Tunnel because all unicast traffic uses a single Data plane such as RSVP-TE. The NG-MVPN framework permits an operator to use different Data plane protocols for unicast and multicast traffic, respectively. P-tunnels are rooted at the Ingress PE (Sender) and receiver PEs join a given P-tunnel that signaled based on the NG-MVPN they belong to or based on C-MCAST receiver interest.

It is worthy to note that the sender PE goes through two steps when setting up the Data plane. One step includes using the PMSI attribute; it advertises the P-tunnel it will be using via BGP using a Type 1 route. In step two it actually signals the tunnel using whatever tunnel signaling protocol is configured for that VPN. This allows receiver PE routers to bind the tunnel signaled to the VPN that imported the Type 1 intra-AS AD route. Binding a P-tunnel to a VRF table enables a receiver PE router to map the incoming traffic from the core network on the P-tunnel to the local target VRF table.

3.4.1 Point-to-Multipoint LSPs

In Figure 3.25 there is a reference to P2MP LSPs. In the beginning of this chapter, the need for an MPLS-based transport for MVPN traffic against PIM GRE used as an overlay was reviewed. One of the key benefits discussed was the need for a converged platform for all traffic types such as Multicast and Unicast, which uses MPLS-based transport and a PIM free core. From an NG-MVPN point of view, there are two Provider Tunnel options that use MPLS as a transport mechanism: RSVP-TE and MLDP (Multicast LDP). All of the other Provider Tunnels use GRE-based transport similar to Draft

Rosen, with the exception of the control plane, which is based on BGP (except ingress replication, which we would discuss later in this chapter).

The hierarchy from an NG-MVPN BGP-based control plane with P2MP LSPs is illustrated in Figure 3.26.

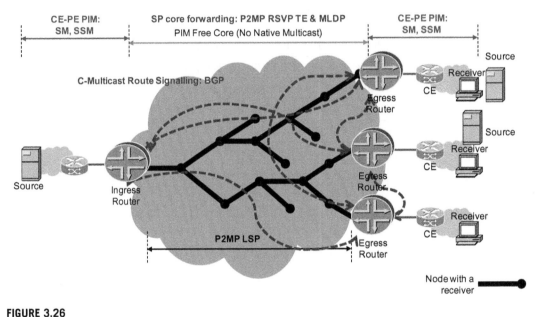

FIGURE 3.26

The signaling and setup of P2MP LSPs will be discussed in the following sections.

3.4.2 MVPN Routing Tables in JUNOS

As mentioned earlier in this section, NG-MVPNs are presently supported only on Juniper platforms. Therefore all of our practical examples of NG-MVPN will be focused on JUNOS; hence it is important to understand the routing table infrastructure that JUNOS uses for NG-MVPN. The various components are illustrated in Figure 3.27.

3.4.3 RSVP-TE Provider Tunnels

In this section we discuss the actual setup of Provider Tunnels and their signaling. RSVP-TE-based P-tunnels enable P2MP LSPs for an NG-MVPN, providing all the benefits of P2MP replication as seen in the previous section. In addition, all standards for RSVP-TE functionality such as MPLS TE Fast Reroute (Only Link Protection) can be used for protecting both unicast and multicast traffic and resource reservation.

Automatically Generated Routing Table	Description
`bgp.l3vpn.0`	Populated with VPN-IPv4 routes received from remote PE routers via INET-VPN address family. The routes in the `bgp.l3vpn.0` table are in the form of `RD:IPv4-Address` and carry one or more RT communities. In an NG MVPN network, these routes also carry `rt-import` and `src-as` communities.
`bgp.mvpn.0`	Populated by `mvpn` routes (Type 1 – Type 7) received from remote PE routers via the MCAST-VPN address family. Routes in this table carry one or more RT communities.
`<routing-instance-name>.inet.0`	Populated by local and remote VPN unicast routes. The local VPN routes are typically learned from local CE routers via protocols like BGP, OSPF, and RIP, or via a static configuration. The remote VPN routes are imported from the `bgp.l3vpn.0` table if their RT matches one of the import RTs configured for the VPN. When remote VPN routes are imported from the `bgp.l3vpn.0` table, their RD is removed, leaving them as regular unicast IPv4 addresses.
`<routing-instance-name>.mvpn.0`	Populated by local and remote `mvpn` routes. The local `mvpn` routes are typically the locally originated routes, such as Type 1 intra-AS AD routes, or Type 7 C-multicast routes. The remote `mvpn` routes are imported from the `bgp.mvpn.0` table based on their RT. The import RT used for accepting `mvpn` routes into the `<routing-instance-name>.mvpn.0` table is different for C-multicast `mvpn` routes (Type 6 and Type 7) versus non-C-multicast `mvpn` routes (Type 1 – Type 5).

FIGURE 3.27

RSVP-TE P2MP LSPs can be used to signal both I-PMSI and S-PMSI tunnels. If you configure a VPN to use an inclusive P-tunnel, the sender PE signals one P2MP LSP for the VPN. If you configure a VPN to use selective P-tunnels, the sender PE signals a P2MP LSP for each selective tunnel configured. Sender (ingress) PEs and receiver (egress) PEs play different roles in the P2MP LSP setup. Sender PEs are mainly responsible for initiating the parent P2MP LSP and the sub-LSPs associated with it. Receiver PEs are responsible for setting up a state from which they can forward packets received over a sub-LSP to the correct VRF table (binding P-tunnel to the VRF).

3.4.3.1 Inclusive Tunnel P2MP LSP Setup

The P2MP LSP and associated sub-LSPs are signaled by the ingress PE router. The information about the P2MP LSP is advertised to egress PEs in the PMSI attribute via BGP. The ingress PE router signals P2MP sub-LSPs by originating P2MP RSVP PATH messages toward egress PE routers. The ingress PE learns the identity of the egress PEs from Type 1 routes installed in its <routing-instance-name>.mvpn.0 table. Each RSVP PATH message carries an S2L_Sub_LSP Object along with the P2MP Session Object. The S2L_Sub_LSP Object carries a 4-byte sub-LSP destination (egress) IP address. Sub-LSPs associated with a P2MP LSP can be signaled automatically by the system or via a static sub-LSP configuration. When they are automatically signaled, the system chooses a name for the P2MP LSP and each sub-LSP associated with it using the following naming convention (see Figure 3.28).

```
operator@PE1-re0# run show mpls lsp p2mp
Ingress LSP: 1 sessions
P2MP name: 100:1:mvpn:FOO-MVPN,  P2MP branch count: 2
To            From           State Rt P     ActivePath      LSPname
7.0.0.5       7.0.0.1        Up    0 *                      7.0.0.5:100:1:mvpn:FOO-MVPN
7.0.0.4       7.0.0.1        Up    0 *                      7.0.0.4:100:1:mvpn:FOO-MVPN
Total 2 displayed, Up 2, Down 0
```

FIGURE 3.28

- P2MP LSPs naming convention: **<ingress PE rid>:<a per VRF unique number>:mvpn: <routing-instance-name>**
- Sub-LSPs naming convention: **<egress PE rid>:<ingress PE rid>:<a per VRF unique>:mvpn: <routing-instance-name>**

Looking at the output in this list, the Parent LSP and the two Sub-LSPs are created. The first Sub-LSP is toward an Egress PE router "7.0.0.5" and the next to "7.0.0.4." The remaining fields identify the MVPN to which the Sub-LSPs are associated. To understand the Parent LSP and Sub-LSP, see Figure 3.29.

A P2MP Tunnel

- Comprises one or more P2MP LSPs sharing same root and leaf nodes
- Supports resource reservation
- Unidirectional

S2L sub-LSP is one path of P2MP LSP
– From the root node to a leaf node

A P2MP LSP comprises multiple S2L sub-LSPs, one per leaf node

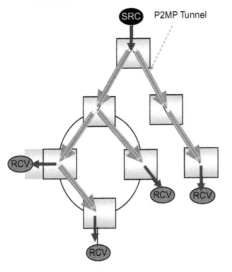
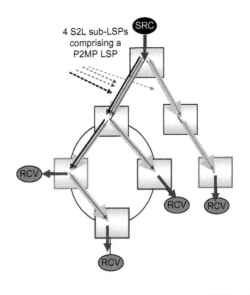

FIGURE 3.29

In Figure 3.29, there is a Sub-LSP created from each Ingress PE to an Egress PE that belongs to the same MVPN. This is from the RSVP-TE signaling perspective.

Figure 3.30 illustrates the PATH and RESV messages exchanged between the Ingress and Egress PE routers.

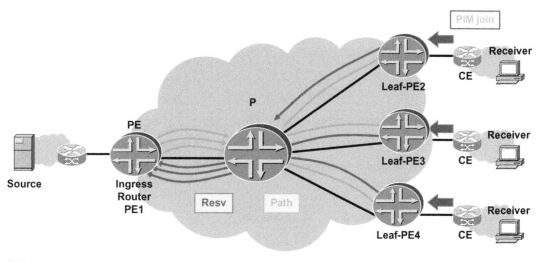

FIGURE 3.30

As per Figure 3.30, a total of three Sub-LSPs are created from the Ingress PE router; however, there is a Branch LSR in the form of a Provider router. Going back to the discussion in our previous section on P2MP LSPs, we note that the Branch LSR would be creating multiple copies (replication) of the same traffic stream to interested receiver PE routers. From a Data plane perspective, we expect the merge of three Sub-LSPs into a single P2MP RSVP-TE LSP; therefore, the Ingress PE would only send one copy of the multicast stream, which will replicate to the three LEAF Nodes by the Branch LSR (Router P) (see Figure 3.31).

The outputs of the RSVP-TE LSPs on both the Ingress PE and the Branch LSR (Provider router) are shown in Figure 3.32.

The ingress PE has signaled three RSVP-TE LSPs to the three Egress PE routers (Figure 3.32). In the outputs, each of these Ingress LSPs has an associated P2MP LSP name that identifies the NG-MVPN configured on the Ingress PE router. From an RSVP-TE signaling perspective, there are a total of three RSVP-TE Sub-LSPs signaled as P2MP. The "Label out" values indicate the label allocated by the downstream LSR. In Figure 3.33, the output is the same for all the three LSPs, since the same branch LSR (Provider router in the figure) connects to the three leaf nodes. See the output on the Provider router in Figure 3.33.

In Figure 3.33 there are three LSPs signaled from the Ingress PE displayed as P2MP LSPs on the Provider router. The P-tunnel–NG-MVPN association is also displayed. The "Label OUT" field indicates the label announced by the egress PE routers for the Sub-LSP initiated by the ingress PE.

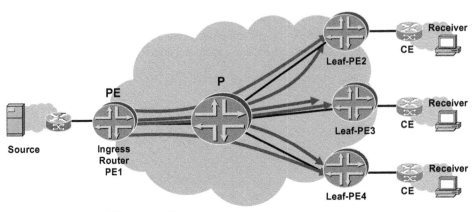

- From the Router "P"' perspective:

- Control Plane: **3 P2P sub-LSPs from the ingress to the leaves**

- Data Plane: The 3 sub-LSP are merged into **one P2MP for replication**

FIGURE 3.31

```
operator@PE1# run show rsvp session extensive
Ingress RSVP: 3 sessions
4.4.4.4 ------------------------> PE2
  From: 1.1.1.1, LSPstate: Up, ActiveRoute: 0
  LSPname: 4.4.4.4:100:1:mvpn:FOO-MVPN, LSPpath: Primary
  P2MP LSPname: 100:1:mvpn:FOO-MVPN -------> P2MP LSP associated with MVPN
  Resv style: 1 SE, Label in: -, Label out: 300992
  Port number: sender 17 receiver 27121 protocol 0
  PATH rcvfrom: localclient
  Adspec: sent MTU 1500
  Path MTU: received 1500
  PATH sentto: 7.7.7.2 (ge-0/1/0.0) 31 pkts
  RESV rcvfrom: 7.7.7.2 (ge-0/1/0.0) 31 pkts
  Explct route: 7.7.7.2 14.14.14.2
  Record route: <self> 7.7.7.2 8.8.8.2 14.14.14.2

  5.5.5.5 ------------------------> PE3
  From: 1.1.1.1, LSPstate: Up, ActiveRoute: 0
  LSPname: 5.5.5.5: 100:1:mvpn: FOO-MVPN, LSPpath: Primary
  P2MP LSPname: 100:1:mvpn: FOO-MVPN
  Resv style: 1 SE, Label in: -, Label out: 300992
  Port number: sender 17 receiver 27121 protocol 0
  PATH rcvfrom: localclient
  Adspec: sent MTU 1500
  Path MTU: received 1500
  PATH sentto: 7.7.7.2 (ge-0/1/0.0) 31 pkts
  RESV rcvfrom: 7.7.7.2 (ge-0/1/0.0) 32 pkts
  Explct route: 7.7.7.2 10.10.10.2
  Record route: <self> 7.7.7.2 10.10.10.2
```

FIGURE 3.32

RSVP-TE LSP outputs on the Ingress PE router.

```
6.6.6.6  -----------------------> PE4
  From: 1.1.1.1, LSPstate: Up, ActiveRoute: 0
  LSPname: 6.6.6.6: 100:1:mvpn: FOO-MVPN, LSPpath: Primary
  P2MP LSPname: 100:1:mvpn: FOO-MVPN
  Resv style: 1 SE, Label in: -, Label out: 300992
  Port number: sender 17 receiver 27121 protocol 0
  PATH rcvfrom: localclient
  Adspec: sent MTU 1500
  Path MTU: received 1500
  PATH sentto: 7.7.7.2 (ge-0/1/0.0) 31 pkts
  RESV rcvfrom: 7.7.7.2 (ge-0/1/0.0) 32 pkts
  Explct route: 7.7.7.2 8.8.8.2
  Record route: <self> 7.7.7.2 8.8.8.2
[Output Truncated]
```

FIGURE 3.32

(*Continued*)

```
operator@P# run show mpls lsp p2mp extensive
P2MP name: 100:1:mvpn:FOO-MVPN, P2MP branch count: 2
5.5.5.5 -----------------------> PE2
  From: 1.1.1.1, LSPstate: Up, ActiveRoute: 0
  LSPname: 5.5.5.5:100:1:mvpn: FOO-MVPN, LSPpath: Primary
  P2MP LSPname: 100:1:mvpn: FOO-MVPN
  Resv style: 1 SE, Label in: 300992, Label out: 18
  Tspec: rate 0bps size 0bps peak Infbps m 20 M 1500
  Port number: sender 1 receiver 27121 protocol 0
  PATH rcvfrom: 7.7.7.1 (ge-0/2/1.0) 83 pkts
  Adspec: received MTU 1500 sent MTU 1500
  PATH sentto: 10.10.10.2 (ge-0/0/1.0) 83 pkts
  RESV rcvfrom: 10.10.10.2 (ge-0/0/1.0) 82 pkts
  Explct route: 10.10.10.2
  Record route: 7.7.7.1 <self> 10.10.10.2

4.4.4.4 -----------------------> PE2
  From: 1.1.1.1, LSPstate: Up, ActiveRoute: 0
  LSPname: 4.4.4.4:100:1:mvpn: FOO-MVPN, LSPpath: Primary
  P2MP LSPname: 100:1:mvpn: FOO-MVPN -----------------------> MVPN
  Resv style: 1 SE, Label in: 300992, Label out: 16
  Tspec: rate 0bps size 0bps peak Infbps m 20 M 1500
  Port number: sender 1 receiver 27121 protocol 0
  PATH rcvfrom: 7.7.7.1 (ge-0/2/1.0) 80 pkts
  Adspec: received MTU 1500 sent MTU 1500
  PATH sentto: 9.9.9.2 (ge-0/0/0.0) 81 pkts
  RESV rcvfrom: 9.9.9.2 (ge-0/0/0.0) 81 pkts
  Explct route: 9.9.9.2
  Record route: 7.7.7.1 <self> 9.9.9.2
```

FIGURE 3.33

Provider router outputs for the RSVP-TE P2MP LSP.

```
6.6.6.6 ------------------------> PE2
  From: 1.1.1.1, LSPstate: Up, ActiveRoute: 0
  LSPname: 6.6.6.6:100:1:mvpn: FOO-MVPN, LSPpath: Primary
  P2MP LSPname: 100:1:mvpn: FOO-MVPN
  Resv style: 1 SE, Label in: 300992, Label out: 17
  Tspec: rate 0bps size 0bps peak Infbps m 20 M 1500
  Port number: sender 1 receiver 27121 protocol 0
  PATH rcvfrom: 7.7.7.1 (ge-0/2/1.0) 80 pkts
  Adspec: received MTU 1500 sent MTU 1500
  PATH sentto: 11.11.11.2 (ge-0/2/0.0) 81 pkts
  RESV rcvfrom: 11.11.11.2 (ge-0/2/0.0) 81 pkts
  Explct route: 11.11.11.2
  Record route: 7.7.7.1 <self> 11.11.11.2

Total 3 displayed, Up 3, Down 0
[Output Truncated]
```

FIGURE 3.33

(Continued)

There are three labels announced by each of the egress PE routers (16, 18, and 17). A snapshot of the detailed S2L Sub-LSP signaling is provided in Figure 3.34.

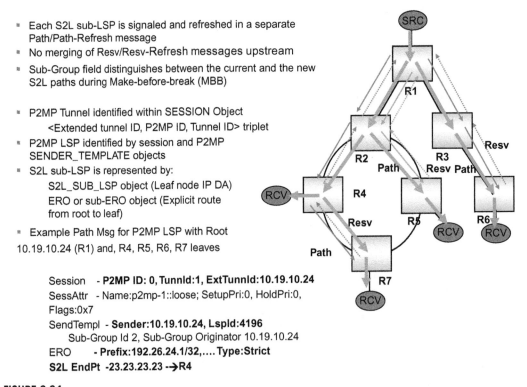

- Each S2L sub-LSP is signaled and refreshed in a separate Path/Path-Refresh message
- No merging of Resv/Resv-Refresh messages upstream
- Sub-Group field distinguishes between the current and the new S2L paths during Make-before-break (MBB)

- P2MP Tunnel identified within SESSION Object
    <Extended tunnel ID, P2MP ID, Tunnel ID> triplet
- P2MP LSP identified by session and P2MP SENDER_TEMPLATE objects
- S2L sub-LSP is represented by:
    S2L_SUB_LSP object (Leaf node IP DA)
    ERO or sub-ERO object (Explicit route from root to leaf)
- Example Path Msg for P2MP LSP with Root 10.19.10.24 (R1) and, R4, R5, R6, R7 leaves

    Session   - P2MP ID: 0, Tunnld:1, ExtTunnld:10.19.10.24
    SessAttr - Name:p2mp-1::loose; SetupPri:0, HoldPri:0,
    Flags:0x7
    SendTempl - Sender:10.19.10.24, Lspld:4196
        Sub-Group Id 2, Sub-Group Originator 10.19.10.24
    ERO   - Prefix:192.26.24.1/32,.... Type:Strict
    S2L EndPt -23.23.23.23 -→R4

FIGURE 3.34

Each Egress PE router installs a forwarding entry in its "mpls forwarding table" for the label it has allocated for the sub-LSP. The MPLS label is installed with a Pop operation and the packet is passed on to the VRF table for a second route lookup. The second lookup on the egress PE is necessary for VPN multicast data packets to be processed inside the VRF table using normal C-PIM procedures. This is illustrated in Figure 3.35.

```
operator@PE2-re0# run show route table mpls label 18

mpls.0: 8 destinations, 8 routes (8 active, 0 holddown, 0 hidden)
+ = Active Route, - = Last Active, * = Both

18                    *[VPN/0] 00:16:48
                        to table FOO-MVPN.inet.0, Pop
 [Output Truncated]
```

FIGURE 3.35

Egress PE output for the label entry—Router PE2.

The Label "18" was announced by PE2 for the Sub-LSP from the Ingress PE. This could be verified in the output provided in Figure 3.35 for the P router indicated as "LABEL OUT" for the LSP terminating at PE2. In JUNOS, VPN multicast routing entries are stored in the <routing-instance-name>.inet.1 table, which is where the second route lookup occurs. In Figure 3.35, even though FOO-MVPN.inet.0 is listed as the routing table where the second lookup happens after the Pop operation, internally the lookup is pointed to the FOO-MVPN.inet.1 table.

In Figure 3.36, PE2 contains the following VPN multicast forwarding entry corresponding to the multicast routing entry for the Local join. The Upstream interface points to lsi.21 and the Downstream interface (OIL) points to ge-4/0/2.1000 (toward local receivers). The Upstream protocol is MVPN because the VPN multicast source is reachable via the NG-MVPN network. The lsi.21 interface is similar to the mt (GRE) interface used when PIM-based P-tunnels are used. The lsi.21 interface is used for removing the top MPLS header.

```
operator@PE2# run show multicast route instance FOO-MVPN extensive
Family: INET
Group: 239.1.1.1
    Source: 192.168.1.9/32
    Upstream interface: lsi.21
    Downstream interface list:
        ge-4/0/2.100
    Session description: Administratively Scoped
    Statistics: 64 kBps, 762 pps, 356396 packets --> Traffic Statistics
    Next-hop ID: 1048577
    Upstream protocol: MVPN
    Route state: Active
    Forwarding state: Forwarding
    Cache lifetime/timeout: forever
    Wrong incoming interface notifications: 0
```

FIGURE 3.36

Checking the Multicast forwarding table.

Since the top MPLS label used for the P2MP sub-LSP is actually tied to the VRF table on the egress PE routers, the penultimate-hop popping (PHP) operation must be disabled. PHP allows the penultimate router (router before the egress PE) to remove the top MPLS label. PHP works well for VPN unicast data packets because they typically carry two MPLS labels: one for the VPN and one for the transport LSP. Once the LSP label is removed, unicast VPN packets still have a VPN label that can be used for determining the VPN to which the packets belong. VPN multicast data packets, on the other hand, carry only one MPLS label directly tied to the VPN. Therefore, the MPLS label carried by VPN multicast packets must be preserved until the packets reach the egress PE. Normally, PHP must be disabled through manual configuration. To simplify configuration, PHP is disabled by default on Juniper PE routers when you configure the protocol's MVPN statement under the routing-instance hierarchy. You do not need to explicitly disable it.

After discussing the details of the P2MP Data plane infrastructure, we can now summarize the functions each device in the P2MP infrastructure performs (see Figure 3.37).

1. Ingress LER node
   Receives IP-MC traffic and maps the traffic to
   a P2MP LSP + performs MPLS-MC
   replication by swapping labels

2. LSR node
   Performs no replication, just label swap

3. Branch LSR node
   Performs MPLS-MC replication and label
   swapping.

4. Egress LER node
   Performs label pop and IP-MC replication.

5. BUD LSR
   Receives MPLS-MC traffic and performs IP-
   MC replication and MPLS-MC replication by
   swapping labels.

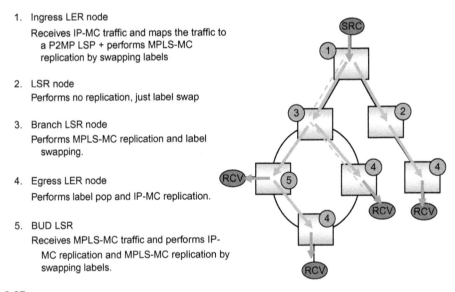

FIGURE 3.37

Figure 3.38 provides a detailed and descriptive depiction of the various nodes or devices within an NG-MVPN framework. It is worthwhile to note that an Ingress PE router may also be referred as the Root of a P2MP LSP.

An Ingress PE will perform replication only when it is a Branch LSR by itself. In Figure 3.38, the Ingress PE has two physical paths to two separate Branch LSRs; hence it will replicate traffic across the two paths.

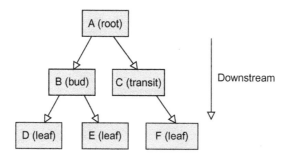

FIGURE 3.38

3.4.3.1.1 Label Allocation in RSVP-TE P2MP LSPs

It is important to understand the label announcements and exchange between LSRs in an RSVP-TE P2MP LSP deployment. So far we have the control plane operations, P2MP LSP, infrastructure from a replication standpoint, and the functions of each type of node in the P2MP Data plane infrastructure. These simple examples to will help us understand actual forwarding in more detail. The first step is the exchange of RSVP PATH Messages from the Ingress LSR to the Egress LSRs. Even though this aspect has been discussed in previous sections, Figure 3.39 is provided here for the sake of completeness.

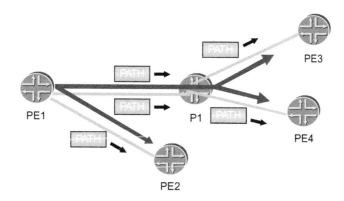

Head-end Router PE1 sends three path messages (one per destination)
First PATH message:	PE1 -> P1 -> PE3
Second PATH message:	PE1 -> P1 -> PE4
Third PATH message:	PE1 -> PE2

FIGURE 3.39

Upon receipt of the PATH Messages, Egress PE routers respond with RESV Messages with the appropriate labels for the creation of the P2MP LSP infrastructure, as illustrated in Figure 3.40.

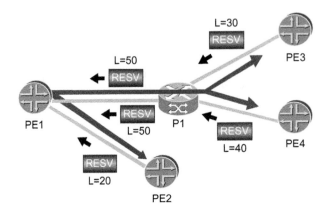

- PE3 advertises incoming "303", PE4 advertises "40", and PE2 advertises "20"
- Upon arrival of RESV from PE3 & PE4, P1 advertises incoming label "50" for the LSP destined for PE3 and PE4 - since it is a branch point.

FIGURE 3.40

Finally, we look at the traffic forwarding along with the process of Label imposition and SWAP operations, respectively (see Figure 3.41).

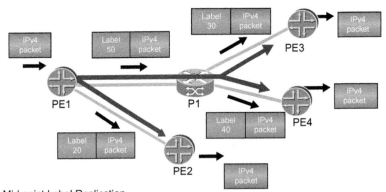

Mid-point Label Replication
- Advertise the same incoming label for LSP destined for PE3 and PE4
- This mechanism allows upstream LSR to perform label replication

Head-end Label Replication
- Sends one packet (outgoing label 50) for both LSP destined for PE3 and PE4

FIGURE 3.41

In summary, the P2MP RSVP-TE is ingress driven from initiating the tunnel setup. However, the label allocation is done by the Egress PE routers, so in that sense it is downstream label allocation.

However, an MPLS LSR can also perform upstream label allocation, and this technique is described in RFC 5331. An extract from the draft is given below:

> *When MPLS labels are upstream-assigned, the context of an MPLS label "L" is provided by the LSR that assigns the label and binds the label to an "FEC F" for a Label Switched Path (LSP) LSP1. The LSR that assigns the label distributes the binding and context to an LSR "Lr" that then receives MPLS packets on LSP1 with label L. When Lr receives an MPLS packet on LSP1, it MUST be able to determine the context of this packet. An example of such a context is a tunnel over which MPLS packets on LSP1 may be received. In this case, the top label of the MPLS packet, after tunnel Decapsulation, is looked up in a label space that is specific to the root of the tunnel. This does imply that Lr be able to determine the tunnel over which the packet was received. Therefore, if the tunnel is an MPLS tunnel, penultimate-hop-popping (PHP) MUST be disabled for the tunnel.*

This chapter does not discuss upstream label allocation, since the applications currently discussed within the context of this book do not need this method of label allocation. The need for this scheme will be discussed in Chapter 9.

The following draft "draft-ietf-mpls-rsvp-upstream" also discusses upstream label allocation within the context of RSVP-TE where upstream labels are allocated via RSVP-PATH messages.

3.4.3.2 *Case Study for an RSVP-TE-Based P2MP LSP—I-PMSI Setup*

In this section, we look at the actual configurations required for creating NG-MVPNs based on BGP Signaling using P2MP RSVP-TE LSPs. I-PMSI setup will be covered in this section (see Figure 3.42). The following topology will be used for all illustrations in this chapter.

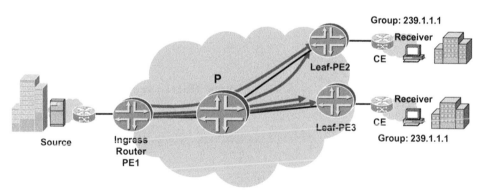

- The router "P" does not indicate a single Provider router, and indicates a Carrier Provider core that may contain many devices. A single device is just given ONLY for illustrative reasons.

FIGURE 3.42

3.4.3.2.1 Configurations

We have an Ingress PE router (PE1) and two Egress PE routers (PE2 and PE3) within a given NG-MVPN named "FOO-MVPN." Our customer FOO is a content provider who distributes video feeds (traffic) to the two remote sites connected via PE2 and PE3. Therefore in our setup, PE1 is the sender site and PE2 and PE3 will be "receiver only sites." Our configuration will focus on using RSVP-TE as the Provider Tunnel and traffic will flow via an I-PMSI.

Only the relevant portions of the configuration are provided (see Figure 3.43).

```
protocols {
    rsvp {
        interface ge-4/0/0.0;
        interface ge-0/1/0.0;
    }
    mpls {
        label-switched-path P2MP-RSVP-TE { -----→ Dynamic Template
            template;
            p2mp; -------------→ 2MP Flag
        }
        interface ge-4/0/0.0;
        interface ge-0/1/0.0;
    }
    bgp {
        group FOO {
            type internal;
            local-address 7.0.0.1;
            family inet-vpn {
                unicast;
            }
            family inet-mvpn {
                signaling;
            }
            neighbor 7.0.0.5 {
                peer-as 100;
            }
            neighbor 7.0.0.4 {
                peer-as 100;
            }
        }
    }
    ospf {
        traffic-engineering; ---→ Enables MPLS Traffic Engineering
        area 0.0.0.0 {
            interface lo0.0 {
                passive;
            }
            interface ge-4/0/0.0 {
                interface-type p2p;
            }
            interface ge-0/1/0.0 {
                interface-type p2p;
            }
        }
    }
    ldp {
        interface ge-0/1/0.0;
        interface ge-4/0/0.0;
    }
}
```

FIGURE 3.43

Ingress PE router configuration—PE1.

```
routing-instances {  ---------→ MPLS Layer 3 VPN
  FOO-MVPN {
    instance-type vrf;
    interface ge-0/1/0.0;  -----→ PE-CE interface
    interface ge-4/0/1.0;
    interface lo0.1;
    route-distinguisher 100:1;
    provider-tunnel {  -----→ P-Tunnel Configuration
        rsvp-te {  ------------------→ RSVP-TE P2MP LSP
            label-switched-path-template {  -→ Uses the Dynamic Template
                P2MP-RSVP-TE;
            }
        }
    }
    vrf-target target:100:1;
    vrf-table-label;
    protocols {
        bgp {  --------→ PE-CE Routing uses BGP
            family inet {
                unicast;
            }
            group peer {
                type external;
                peer-as 65005;
                neighbor 192.168.1.9;
                neighbor 192.168.1.17 {
                    peer-as 65010;
                }
            }
        }
        pim {  -------------→ PIM towards the CE Domain
            rp {
                local {
                    address 7.0.0.1;
                }
            }
            interface ge-4/0/1.0 {
                mode sparse;
                version 2;
            }
            interface lo0.1 {
                mode sparse;
                version 2;
            }
        }
        mvpn;
    }
  }
}
```

FIGURE 3.43

(Continued)

The first section of the configuration template enables the IGP, BGP, and MPLS Traffic Engineering. The PE router uses LDP for unicast traffic, while we are configuring RSVP-TE for multicast VPN traffic. As mentioned earlier in this chapter, this is a possible configuration option. In this example, RSVP-TE was chosen as the P-tunnel because it offers features such as MPLS Fast Re-route protection and Bandwidth guarantees, which can be used by the P2MP Multicast LSPs.

RSVP-TE Provider Tunnels can be created in two ways: (1) using a static configuration where the P2MP LSP will be established immediately even without an association with an MVPN instance and (2) using a Dynamic Template that will be established if it is associated with an MVPN instance and the membership information obtained. Dynamic LSP allows the constraints specified in the LSP template to be used for more than one MVPN, which reduces the configuration complexity. We use the Dynamic template in all of our examples.

The BGP configuration in the main instance (under protocols) is configured by the address family "inet-mvpn" in addition to "inet-vpn." The "inet-mvpn" address family allows PEs to enhance BGP capability to support multicast extensions to automatically discover MVPN membership information (autodiscovery) and exchange customer multicast routes without requiring full-mesh PIM adjacency among PE routers.

The "routing-instance" is the customer-specific VRF configuration for a given BGP/MPLS Layer 3 VPN. It is under this instance that customer-specific MVPN configurations are performed. Figure 3.43 depicts this in detail. The P-tunnel (RSVP-TE P2MP Template) is associated with the routing instance for multicast transport. Then we configure PIM as the CE-PE multicast routing protocol. In this example PE1 acts as the C-RP for the MVPN instance; hence that configuration is also reflected.

The final step is to enable the "MVPN" protocol on the Layer 3 VPN service instance. This configuration is also used to set the policies in order to correctly identify and process various BGP advertisements for the building of the multicast routing table (see Figure 3.44).

```
mvpn {
  route-target {
    import-target {
      unicast;
      target target:100:1;
  }
    export-target {
      unicast;
      target target:100:1;
    }
  }
}
…truncated…
```

FIGURE 3.44

MVPN policies.

However, if the import-target and export-target are the same, then there is no need to explicitly configure the route-targets for import and export as shown in Figure 3.44. Instead enabling the protocols for MVPN will be sufficient in all the PE routers. This is illustrated in our configuration template for PE1.

Next is the configuration of the Egress PE routers (see Figures 3.45 and 3.46). It would be exactly the same as PE1; however, the use of a Provider Tunnel is optional since these PE routers are designated as "receiver only PEs." In other words, they do not have any C-MCAST sources connected in their respective sites.

```
protocols {
    rsvp {
        interface so-4/1/0.0;
        interface ge-4/0/3.0;
        interface ge-4/0/0.0;
    }
    mpls {
        interface ge-4/0/0.0;
        interface ge-4/0/5.0;
        interface ge-4/0/3.0;
    }
    bgp {
        group FOO {
            type internal;
            local-address 7.0.0.4;
            family inet-vpn {
                unicast;
            }
            family inet-mvpn {
                signaling;
            }
            neighbor 7.0.0.5 {
                peer-as 100;
            }
            neighbor 7.0.0.1 {
                peer-as 100;
            }
        }
    }
    ospf {
        traffic-engineering;
        area 0.0.0.0 {
            interface lo0.0 {
                passive;
            }
            interface ge-4/0/0.0 {
                interface-type p2p;
            }
            interface ge-4/0/5.0 {
                interface-type p2p;
            }
            interface ge-4/0/3.0 {
                interface-type p2p;
            }
        }
    }
}
```

FIGURE 3.45

Egress PE router configuration—PE2.

```
        ldp {
            interface ge-4/0/0.0;
            interface ge-4/0/3.0;
            interface ge-4/0/5.0;
        }
    }
    routing-instances {  ---------> MPLS Layer 3 VPN
    FOO-MVPN {
            instance-type vrf;
            interface ge-4/0/2.100;
            interface lo0.1;
            route-distinguisher 100:1;
            vrf-target target:100:1;
            vrf-table-label;
            protocols {
                bgp {
                    family inet {
                        unicast;
                    }
                    group peer {
                        type external;
                        peer-as 65003;
                        neighbor 192.168.1.1;  ->
                    }
                }
                pim {
                    rp {
                        static {
                            address 7.0.0.1; --  PE1 is the C-RP
                        }
                    }
                    interface ge-4/0/2.100 {
                        mode sparse-dense;
                        version 2;
                    }
                    interface lo0.1 {
                        mode sparse-dense;
                        version 2;
                    }
                }
                mvpn;
            }
        }
    }
    [Output Truncated]
```

FIGURE 3.45

(*Continued*)

```
protocols {
    rsvp {
        interface ge-1/0/1.0;
    }
    mpls {
        interface ge-1/0/1.0;
        interface fe-1/1/0.0;
    }
    bgp {
        group FOO {
            type internal;
            local-address 7.0.0.5;
            family inet-vpn {
                unicast;
            }
            family inet-mvpn {
                signaling;
            }
            neighbor 7.0.0.4 {
                peer-as 100;
            }
            neighbor 7.0.0.1 {
                peer-as 100;
            }
        }
    }
    ospf {
        traffic-engineering;
        area 0.0.0.0 {
            interface ge-1/0/1.0 {
                interface-type p2p;
            }
            interface lo0.0 {
                passive;
            }
            interface fe-1/1/0.0;
        }
    }
    ldp {
        interface ge-1/0/1.0;
        interface fe-1/1/0.0;
    }
}
routing-instances { --------> MPLS Layer 3 VPN
    FOO-MVPN {
        instance-type vrf;
        interface ge-1/0/2.0;
        interface lo0.1;
        route-distinguisher 100:1;
        vrf-target target:100:1;
        vrf-table-label;
        protocols {
```

FIGURE 3.46

Egress PE router configuration—PE3.

```
bgp {
    family inet {
        unicast;
    }
    group peer {
        type external;
        peer-as 65004;
        neighbor 192.168.1.5;
    }
}
pim {
    rp {
        static {
            address 7.0.0.1;
        }
    }
    interface ge-1/0/2.0 {
        mode sparse-dense;
        version 2;
    }
    interface lo0.1 {
        mode sparse-dense;
        version 2;
    }
}
mvpn;
            }
        }
    }
```

FIGURE 3.46

(Continued)

Let us review the configurations needed on the MPLS Provider routers. Figure 3.47 is a template for the Provider core. The only sections required are the MPLS and IGP configurations. No PIM- or MVPN-specific configurations are needed.

3.4.3.2.2 Validations

In this section, we validate this functionality of the NG-MVPN by verifying both the BGP control plane and RSVP-TE-based Data Plane (only I-PMSI). Various commands are used to check the functionality at both the Ingress and Egress PE routers.

3.4.3.2.3 Validations at the Ingress PE Router—PE1

Start with the Ingress PE router. The auto-discovery process and the advertisements of BGP Type 1 routes will be reviewed first (see Figure 3.48).

In the detailed output (Figure 3.49), we can verify that there are no PMSI attributes attached to the Type 1 announcement by the egress PE routers. Remember, we have not configured all the egress PE routers with an RSVP-TE Provider Tunnel for I-PMSI usage.

Next we check the P-tunnel information and the status of the P2MP LSP, which was configured under the NG-MVPN instance. The command in Figure 3.50 validates the P2MP LSP setup and indicates a branch count (leaf nodes or egress PEs) of 2.

```
        Protocols {
        rsvp {
            interface ge-0/2/0.0;
            interface ge-0/0/0.0;
            interface ge-0/2/1.0;
            interface ge-0/0/1.0;
        }
        mpls {
            interface ge-0/2/0.0;
            interface ge-0/0/0.0;
            interface ge-0/2/1.0;
            interface ge-0/0/1.0;
        }
        ospf {
            traffic-engineering;
            area 0.0.0.0 {
                interface ge-0/2/0.0;
                interface ge-0/0/0.0;
                interface ge-0/2/1.0;
                interface ge-0/0/1.0;
                interface lo0.0;
            }
        }
    }
```

FIGURE 3.47

MPLS Provider router configurations.

```
operator@PE1# run show route table FOO-MVPN.mvpn.0
FOO-MVPN.mvpn.0: 3 destinations, 3 routes (3 active, 0 holddown, 0 hidden)
+ = Active Route, - = Last Active, * = Both

1:100:1:7.0.0.1/240     ---> Local Type 1 Route Generated
                  *[MVPN/70] 2d 06:46:56, metric2 1
                     Indirect
1:100:1:7.0.0.4/240             --------->   PE2
                  *[BGP/170] 00:01:14, localpref 100, from 7.0.0.4
                     AS path: I
                   > to 172.16.1.5 via ge-4/0/0.0
1:100:1:7.0.0.5/240             ------------->   PE3
                  *[BGP/170] 00:01:14, localpref 100, from 7.0.0.5
                     AS path: I
                   > to 172.16.1.5 via ge-4/0/0.0, Push 299792
```

FIGURE 3.48

Checking for BGP Type 1 route.

Moving on to a more detailed output (Figure 3.51), we can now check details on the P2MP LSP Path, Label assignments, and the associated NG-MVPN for a given P2MP LSP.

Now we generate the Video stream (Multicast Traffic) from the Source connected via PE1 toward the receivers connected to PE2 and PE3, respectively. Checking the MVPN routing table, as

```
operator@PE1# run show route table FOO-MVPN.mvpn.0 detail
FOO-MVPN.mvpn.0: 4 destinations, 4 routes (4 active, 0 holddown, 0 hidden)
1:100:1:7.0.0.1/240 (1 entry, 1 announced)
*MVPN    Preference: 70
                 Next hop type: Indirect
                 Next-hop reference count: 3
                 Protocol next hop: 7.0.0.1
                 Indirect next hop: 0 -
                 State: <Active Int Ext>
                 Age: 2d 6:49:20          Metric2: 1
                 Task: mvpn global task
        Announcement bits (3): 0-PIM.FOO-MVPN 1-mvpn global task 2-BGP RT Background
                 AS path: I


1:100:1:7.0.0.4/240 (1 entry, 1 announced)
*BGP     Preference: 170/-101
                 Next hop type: Indirect
                 Next-hop reference count: 2
                 Source: 7.0.0.4
                 Protocol next hop: 7.0.0.4
                 Indirect next hop: 2 no-forward
                 State: <Secondary Active Int Ext>
                 Local AS:    100 Peer AS:    100
                 Age: 3:38        Metric2: 1
                 Task: BGP_100.7.0.0.4+51389
                 Announcement bits (2): 0-PIM.FOO-MVPN 1-mvpn global task
                 AS path: I
                 Communities: target:100:1
                 Import Accepted
                 Localpref: 100
                 Router ID: 7.0.0.4
                 Primary Routing Table bgp.mvpn.0

1:100:1:7.0.0.5/240 (1 entry, 1 announced)
*BGP     Preference: 170/-101
                 Next hop type: Indirect
                 Next-hop reference count: 2
                 Source: 7.0.0.5
                 Protocol next hop: 7.0.0.5
                 Indirect next hop: 2 no-forward
                 State: <Secondary Active Int Ext>
                 Local AS:    100 Peer AS:    100
                 Age: 3:38        Metric2: 1
                 Task: BGP_100.7.0.0.5+58906
                 Announcement bits (2): 0-PIM.FOO-MVPN 1-mvpn global task
                 AS path: I
                 Communities: target:100:1
                 Import Accepted
                 Localpref: 100
                 Router ID: 7.0.0.5
                 Primary Routing Table bgp.mvpn.0
```

FIGURE 3.49

Checking for BGP Type 1 route—More detailed outputs.

```
operator@PE1# run show mpls lsp p2mp
Ingress LSP: 1 sessions
P2MP name: 100:1:mvpn:FOO-MVPN, P2MP branch count: 2
To              From            State Rt P    ActivePath         LSPname
7.0.0.5         7.0.0.1         Up    0 *     7.0.0.5:100:1:mvpn: FOO-MVPN
7.0.0.4         7.0.0.1         Up    0 *     7.0.0.4:100:1:mvpn: FOO-MVPN
Total 2 displayed, Up 2, Down 0
```

FIGURE 3.50

Checking the status of the P2MP LSP.

```
operator@PE1# run show rsvp session detail
Ingress RSVP: 2 sessions

7.0.0.5 ------------------------------------> To PE3
  From: 7.0.0.1, LSPstate: Up, ActiveRoute: 0
  LSPname: 7.0.0.5:100:1:mvpn:FOO-MVPN, LSPpath: Primary
  LSPtype: Dynamic Configured
  P2MP LSPname: 100:1:mvpn:FOO-MVPN --> LSP to MVPN association details
  Suggested label received: -, Suggested label sent: -
  Recovery label received: -, Recovery label sent: 300096
  Resv style: 1 SE, Label in: -, Label out: 300096
  Time left:     -, Since: Sun Sep 19 17:29:18 2010
  Tspec: rate 0bps size 0bps peak Infbps m 20 M 1500
  Port number: sender 1 receiver 6834 protocol 0
  PATH rcvfrom: localclient
  Adspec: sent MTU 1500
  Path MTU: received 1500
  PATH sentto: 172.16.1.5 (ge-4/0/0.0) 35 pkts
  RESV rcvfrom: 172.16.1.5 (ge-4/0/0.0) 35 pkts
  Explct route: 172.16.1.5 172.16.1.2
  Record route: <self> 172.16.1.5 172.16.1.2

7.0.0.4 ------------------------------------> To PE2
  From: 7.0.0.1, LSPstate: Up, ActiveRoute: 0
  LSPname: 7.0.0.4:100:1:mvpn:FOO-MVPN, LSPpath: Primary
  LSPtype: Dynamic Configured
  P2MP LSPname: 100:1:mvpn:FOO-MVPN --> LSP to MVPN association details
  Suggested label received: -, Suggested label sent: -
  Recovery label received: -, Recovery label sent: 37
  Resv style: 1 SE, Label in: -, Label out: 37
  Time left:     -, Since: Sun Sep 19 17:29:18 2010
  Tspec: rate 0bps size 0bps peak Infbps m 20 M 1500
  Port number: sender 1 receiver 6834 protocol 0
  PATH rcvfrom: localclient
  Adspec: sent MTU 1500
  Path MTU: received 1500
  PATH sentto: 172.16.1.5 (ge-4/0/0.0) 33 pkts
  RESV rcvfrom: 172.16.1.5 (ge-4/0/0.0) 39 pkts
  Explct route: 172.16.1.5
  Record route: <self> 172.16.1.5
Total 2 displayed, Up 2, Down 0
```

FIGURE 3.51

Checking the status of the P2MP LSP—Detailed outputs.

displayed in Figure 3.52, indicates that the PE1 has generated a Type 5 route, and PE2 and PE3 have responded with Type 7 routes.

```
operator@PE1# run show route table FOO-MVPN.mvpn.0

1:100:1:7.0.0.1/240
                     *[MVPN/70] 2d 09:37:05, metric2 1
                        Indirect
1:100:1:7.0.0.4/240
                     *[BGP/170] 02:34:30, localpref 100, from 7.0.0.4
                        AS path: I
                      > to 172.16.1.5 via ge-4/0/0.0
1:100:1:7.0.0.5/240
                     *[BGP/170] 02:34:18, localpref 100, from 7.0.0.5
                        AS path: I
                      > to 172.16.1.5 via ge-4/0/0.0, Push 299792
5:100:1:32:192.168.1.9:32:239.1.1.1/240   -> Originated by PE1
                     *[PIM/105] 00:00:03
                        Multicast (IPv4)
7:100:1:100:32:192.168.1.9:32:239.1.1.1/240
                   *[PIM/105] 00:00:03
                     Multicast (IPv4)
                     [BGP/170] 00:00:03, localpref 100, from 7.0.0.4
                     AS path: I
                     > to 172.16.1.5 via ge-4/0/0.0 --> Type 7 from PE2
                     [BGP/170] 00:00:03, localpref 100, from 7.0.0.5
                     AS path: I
                     > to 172.16.1.5 via ge-4/0/0.0, Push 299792 --> Type 7 from PE3
```

FIGURE 3.52

Checking the MVPN routing table for Type 5 and Type 7 routes.

Let us look at some detailed outputs of the same command, verifying the MVPN routing table information on PE1. Details on Target communities and the status of the announced routes are displayed in Figure 3.53.

Having checked the control plane for the Type 5 and Type 7 routes, the next steps involve verifying the Data plane to ensure that traffic is forwarded over the RSVP-TE P2MP LSPs. The output shows traffic forwarded via the LSP, which is verified by the increments of packet and byte counters. This can be validated as seen in Figure 3.54.

Next we check the multicast forwarding table for the MVPN instance. It indicates that the traffic is forwarded on a per C-MCAST-Source and C-MCAST-Group pair. The Group we are interested in is "239.1.1.1." Our output (Figure 3.55) indicates a Multicast forwarding entry for this Group identified with a C-MCAST source and traffic forwarding details. The traffic is forwarded and the statistics indicate an incrementing packet count while the route state is also in an "ACTIVE" state.

Another useful command is given in Figure 3.56. This verifies the C-MCAST traffic flows and the appropriate P-tunnel and the type it is using.

Let us verify the PIM source information on PE1, which is designated as the C-RP (see Figure 3.57).

```
operator@PE1# run show route table FOO-MVPN.mvpn.0 detail
1:100:1:7.0.0.1/240 (1 entry, 1 announced)
        *MVPN   Preference: 70
                Next hop type: Indirect
                Next-hop reference count: 3
                Protocol next hop: 7.0.0.1
                Indirect next hop: 0 -
                State: <Active Int Ext>
                Age: 2d 9:37:36          Metric2: 1
                Task: mvpn global task
Announcement bits (3): 0-PIM.FOO-MVPN 1-mvpn global task 2-BGP RT Background
                AS path: I

1:100:1:7.0.0.4/240 (1 entry, 1 announced)
        *BGP    Preference: 170/-101
                Next hop type: Indirect
                Next-hop reference count: 4
                Source: 7.0.0.4
                Protocol next hop: 7.0.0.4
                Indirect next hop: 2 no-forward
                State: <Secondary Active Int Ext>
                Local AS:   100 Peer AS:   100
                Age: 2:35:01    Metric2: 1
                Task: BGP_100.7.0.0.4+51389
                Announcement bits (2): 0-PIM. FOO-MVPN 1-mvpn global task
                AS path: I
                Communities: target:100:1
                Import Accepted
                Localpref: 100
                Router ID: 7.0.0.4
                Primary Routing Table bgp.mvpn.0

1:100:1:7.0.0.5/240 (1 entry, 1 announced)
        *BGP    Preference: 170/-101
                Next hop type: Indirect
                Next-hop reference count: 4
                Source: 7.0.0.5
                Protocol next hop: 7.0.0.5
                Indirect next hop: 2 no-forward
                State: <Secondary Active Int Ext>
                Local AS:   100 Peer AS:   100
                Age: 2:34:49    Metric2: 1
                Task: BGP_100.7.0.0.5+58906
                Announcement bits (2): 0-PIM. FOO-MVPN 1-mvpn global task
                AS path: I
                Communities: target:100:1
                Import Accepted
                Localpref: 100
                Router ID: 7.0.0.5
                Primary Routing Table bgp.mvpn.0

5:100:1:32:192.168.1.9:32:239.1.1.1/240 (1 entry, 1 announced)
        *PIM    Preference: 105
                Next hop type: Multicast (IPv4)
                Next-hop reference count: 4
```

FIGURE 3.53

Checking the MVPN routing table for Type 5 and Type 7 routes—Detailed outputs.

```
                    State: <Active Int>
                    Age: 34
                    Task: PIM.FOO-MVPN
        Announcement bits (3): 0-PIM. FOO-MVPN 1-mvpn global task 2-BGP RT Background
                    AS path: I

  7:100:1:100:32:192.168.1.9:32:239.1.1.1/240 (3 entries, 3 announced)
          *PIM      Preference: 105
                    Next hop type: Multicast (IPv4)
                    Next-hop reference count: 4
                    State: <Active Int>
                    Age: 34
                    Task: PIM. FOO-MVPN
                    Announcement bits (2): 0-PIM.FOO-MVPN 1-mvpn global task
                    AS path: I
                    Communities: no-advertise target:7.0.0.1:5
          BGP       Preference: 170/-101
                    Next hop type: Indirect
                    Next-hop reference count: 4
                    Source: 7.0.0.4
                    Protocol next hop: 7.0.0.4
                    Indirect next hop: 2 no-forward
                    State: <Secondary Int Ext>
                    Inactive reason: Route Preference
                    Local AS:    100 Peer AS:    100
                    Age: 34         Metric2: 1
                    Task: BGP_100.7.0.0.4+51389
                    Announcement bits (2): 0-PIM.FOO-MVPN 1-mvpn global task
                    AS path: I
                    Communities: target:7.0.0.1:5
                    Import Accepted
                    Localpref: 100
                    Router ID: 7.0.0.4
                    Primary Routing Table bgp.mvpn.0
          BGP       Preference: 170/-101
                    Next hop type: Indirect
                    Next-hop reference count: 4
                    Source: 7.0.0.5
                    Protocol next hop: 7.0.0.5
                    Indirect next hop: 2 no-forward
                    State: <Secondary NotBest Int Ext>
                    Inactive reason: Not Best in its group - Router ID
                    Local AS:    100 Peer AS:    100
                    Age: 34         Metric2: 1
                    Task: BGP_100.7.0.0.5+58906
                    Announcement bits (2): 0-PIM.FOO-MVPN 1-mvpn global task
                    AS path: I
                    Communities: target:7.0.0.1:5
                    Import Accepted
                    Localpref: 100
                    Router ID: 7.0.0.5
                    Primary Routing Table bgp.mvpn.0
```

FIGURE 3.53

(*Continued*)

```
operator@PE1# run show rsvp session statistics
Ingress RSVP: 2 sessions
To      From     State Packets Bytes      LSPname
7.0.0.5 7.0.0.1   Up    689803 60702664 7.0.0.5:100:1:mvpn:FOO-MVPN
7.0.0.4 7.0.0.1   Up    689803 60702664 7.0.0.4:100:1:mvpn:FOO-MVPN
Total 2 displayed,Up 2, Down 0
```

FIGURE 3.54

Checking the P2MP RSVP-TE statistics.

```
operator@PE1# run show multicast route instance FOO-MVPN extensive
Family: INET
Group: 239.1.1.1
        Source: 192.168.1.9/32 ----→ C-MCAST Source
        Upstream interface: ge-4/0/1.0 -→ Interface towards the Source
        Session description: Administratively Scoped
        Statistics: 68 kBps, 813 pps, 1083247 packets -→ Traffic forwarded
        Next-hop ID: 1048577
        Upstream protocol: MVPN
        Route state: Active
        Forwarding state: Forwarding -→ In Active forwarding state
        Cache lifetime/timeout: forever
        Wrong incoming interface notifications: 0
```

FIGURE 3.55

Checking the P2MP RSVP-TE statistics.

```
operator@PE1# run show mvpn instance
MVPN instance:
Legend for provider tunnel
I-P-tnl -- inclusive provider tunnel S-P-tnl -- selective provider tunnel
Legend for c-multicast routes properties (Pr)
DS -- derived from (*, c-g)          RM -- remote VPN route
Instance : FOO-MVPN
  MVPN Mode : SPT-ONLY ----→Indicates SPT-Mode, and no RPT.
  Provider tunnel: I-P-tnl:RSVP-TE P2MP:7.0.0.1, 6834,7.0.0.1
  Neighbor                    I-P-tnl
  7.0.0.4
  7.0.0.5
  C-mcast IPv4 (S:G)          Ptnl                              St
  192.168.1.9/32:239.1.1.1/32 RSVP-TE P2MP:7.0.0.1, 6834,7.0.0.1 RM
```

FIGURE 3.56

Checking the P-tunnel information.

3.4.3.2.4 Validations at the Egress PE Router—PE2

The same sequence of commands as seen in the previous section are followed on each of the Egress PE routers to first verify the control plane followed by the Data plane infrastructure. The only difference between the Ingress and Egress PE routers from the point of view of an MVPN routing table is the Type 6 routes. PE routers generate Type 6 routers based on C-PIM joins. A Type 6 route is generated for each PIM join received via the CE router. In Figure 3.58, a Type 6 route is generated for the group "239.1.1.1." The address "7.0.0.1" in the Type 6 route identifies the C-RP for the Ingress PE router PE1.

```
operator@PE1# run show pim source instance FOO-MVPN detail
Instance: PIM.FOO-MVPN Family: INET
Source 192.168.1.9
    Prefix 192.168.1.8/30
    Upstream interface ge-4/0/1.0
    Active groups:239.1.1.1
```

FIGURE 3.57

Checking the P-tunnel information.

```
operator@PE2# run show route table FOO-MVPN.mvpn.0
1:100:1:7.0.0.1/240      -----> PE1
                    *[BGP/170] 05:33:39, localpref 100, from 7.0.0.1
                      AS path: I
                    > to 172.16.1.6 via ge-4/0/3.0
1:100:1:7.0.0.4/240
                    *[MVPN/70] 05:16:47, metric2 1
                      Indirect
1:100:1:7.0.0.5/240      --------> PE3
                    *[BGP/170] 05:16:34, localpref 100, from 7.0.0.5
                      AS path: I
                    > to 172.16.1.2 via ge-4/0/0.0
5:100:1:32:192.168.1.9:32:239.1.1.1/240 -> Type 5 BGP route from PE1
                    *[BGP/170] 01:53:18, localpref 100, from 7.0.0.1
                      AS path: I
                    > to 172.16.1.6 via ge-4/0/3.0
6:100:1:100:32:7.0.0.1:32:239.1.1.1/240 ---> Type 6 based on PIM Joins
                    *[PIM/105] 05:33:39
                      Multicast (IPv4)
7:100:1:100:32:192.168.1.9:32:239.1.1.1/240--> Type 7 originated by PE2
                    *[MVPN/70] 01:53:18, metric2 1
                      Multicast (IPv4)
                    [PIM/105] 01:53:18
                      Multicast (IPv4)
```

FIGURE 3.58

Checking for MVPN routes.

Using the "detail" keyword, we can validate key information such as the I-PMSI attribute attached by the Ingress PE router. In the output seen in Figure 3.59, a PMSI attribute with a P-tunnel type "RSVP-TE" is seen. However, the Type 1 announcement from PE3 does not have an attached I-PMSI attribute, since it is configured as a "receiver only" site without any P-tunnel configuration.

In the next few illustrations, the multicast forwarding table and the PIM C-Join information received from locally connected CE routers are checked (see Figure 3.60).

The output shown in Figure 3.61 provides information on the PIM joins received by the Egress PE router. There are two entries here: (1) Shared Tree Join to the RP and (2) Source Tree Join to the 192.168.1.9 (C-MCAST source) sending traffic to the group "239.1.1.1."

Figure 3.62 illustrates the P-tunnel information—the P2MP RSVP-TE LSP on which PE2 is a Leaf Node. Only 7.0.0.1 (PE1) has P-tunnel information, since it is the ingress PE.

```
operator@PE2# run show route table FOO-MVPN.mvpn.0 detail
1:100:1:7.0.0.1/240 (1 entry, 1 announced)
*BGP     Preference: 170/-101
PMSI: Flags 0x0: Label[0:0:0]: RSVP-TE: Session_13[7.0.0.1:0:6834:7.0.0.1]
                Next hop type: Indirect
                Next-hop reference count: 4
                Source: 7.0.0.1
                Protocol next hop: 7.0.0.1
                Indirect next hop: 2 no-forward
                State: <Secondary Active Int Ext>
                Local AS:    100 Peer AS:    100
                Age: 5:47:09    Metric2: 1
                Task: BGP_100.7.0.0.1+179
                Announcement bits (2): 0-PIM.FOO-MVPN 1-mvpn global task
                AS path: I
                Communities: target:100:1
                Import Accepted
                Localpref: 100
                Router ID: 7.0.0.1
                Primary Routing Table bgp.mvpn.0

1:100:1:7.0.0.4/240 (1 entry, 1 announced)
       *MVPN    Preference: 70
                Next hop type: Indirect
                Next-hop reference count: 3
                Protocol next hop: 7.0.0.4
                Indirect next hop: 0 -
                State: <Active Int Ext>
                Age: 5:30:17    Metric2: 1
                Task: mvpn global task
Announcement bits (3): 0-PIM.FOO-MVPN 1-mvpn global task 2-BGP RT Background
                AS path: I

1:100:1:7.0.0.5/240 (1 entry, 1 announced)
       *BGP     Preference: 170/-101
                Next hop type: Indirect
                Next-hop reference count: 2
                Source: 7.0.0.5
                Protocol next hop: 7.0.0.5
                Indirect next hop: 2 no-forward
                State: <Secondary Active Int Ext>
                Local AS:    100 Peer AS:    100
                Age: 5:30:04    Metric2: 1
                Task: BGP_100.7.0.0.5+179
                Announcement bits (2): 0-PIM.FOO-MVPN 1-mvpn global task
                AS path: I
                Communities: target:100:1
                Import Accepted
                Localpref: 100
                Router ID: 7.0.0.5
                Primary Routing Table bgp.mvpn.0
```

FIGURE 3.59

Checking for MVPN routes—Detailed outputs.

```
5:100:1:32:192.168.1.9:32:239.1.1.1/240 (1 entry, 1 announced)
       *BGP     Preference: 170/-101
                Next hop type: Indirect
                Next-hop reference count: 4
                Source: 7.0.0.1
                Protocol next hop: 7.0.0.1
                Indirect next hop: 2 no-forward
                State: <Secondary Active Int Ext>
                Local AS:    100 Peer AS:    100
                Age: 5  Metric2: 1
                Task: BGP_100.7.0.0.1+179
                Announcement bits (2): 0-PIM.FOO-MVPN 1-mvpn global task
                AS path: I
                Communities: target:100:1
                Import Accepted
                Localpref: 100
                Router ID: 7.0.0.1
                Primary Routing Table bgp.mvpn.0

6:100:1:100:32:7.0.0.1:32:239.1.1.1/240 (1 entry, 1 announced)
       *PIM     Preference: 105
                Next hop type: Multicast (IPv4), Next hop index: 1048577
                Next-hop reference count: 16
                State: <Active Int>
                Age: 5:47:09
                Task: PIM.FOO-MVPN
                Announcement bits (2): 0-PIM.FOO-MVPN 1-mvpn global task
                AS path: I
                Communities: no-advertise target:7.0.0.1:5

7:100:1:100:32:192.168.1.9:32:239.1.1.1/240 (2 entries, 2 announced)
       *MVPN    Preference: 70
                Next hop type: Multicast (IPv4), Next hop index: 1048577
                Next-hop reference count: 16
                State: <Active Int Ext>
                Age: 5  Metric2: 1
                Task: mvpn global task
Announcement bits (3): 0-PIM.FOO-MVPN 1-mvpn global task 2-BGP RT Background
                AS path: I
                Communities: target:7.0.0.1:5
        PIM     Preference: 105
                Next hop type: Multicast (IPv4), Next hop index: 1048577
                Next-hop reference count: 16
                State: <Int>
                Inactive reason: Route Preference
                Age: 4
                Task: PIM.FOO-MVPN
                Announcement bits (2): 0-PIM.FOO-MVPN 1-mvpn global task
                AS path: I
                Communities: target:7.0.0.1:5
```

FIGURE 3.59

(*Continued*)

```
operator@PE2# run show multicast route instance FOO-MVPN extensive
Family: INET
Group: 239.1.1.1
    Source: 192.168.1.9/32
    Upstream interface: lsi.21
    Downstream interface list:
        ge-4/0/2.100
    Session description: Administratively Scoped
    Statistics: 64 kBps, 762 pps, 356396 packets --> Traffic Statistics
    Next-hop ID: 1048577
    Upstream protocol: MVPN
    Route state: Active
    Forwarding state: Forwarding
    Cache lifetime/timeout: forever
    Wrong incoming interface notifications: 0
```

FIGURE 3.60

Checking the Multicast forwarding table.

```
operator@PE2# run show pim join instance FOO-MVPN extensive
Instance: PIM.FOO-MVPN Family: INET
R = Rendezvous Point Tree, S = Sparse, W = Wildcard
Group: 239.1.1.1 -----> C-MCAST Group - Shared Tree Join
    Source: *
    RP: 7.0.0.1
    Flags: sparse,rptree,wildcard
    Upstream protcol: BGP
    Upstream interface: Through BGP
    Upstream neighbor: Through MVPN
    Upstream state: Join to RP
    Downstream neighbors:
        Interface: ge-4/0/2.100
            192.168.1.1 State: Join Flags: SRW Timeout: 184

Group: 239.1.1.1 -----> C-MCAST Group - Source Tree Join
    Source: 192.168.1.9
    Flags: sparse
    Upstream protcol: BGP
    Upstream interface: Through BGP
    Upstream neighbor: Through MVPN
    Upstream state: None, Join to Source
    Keepalive timeout:
    Downstream neighbors:
        Interface: ge-4/0/2.100
            192.168.1.1 State: Join Flags: S Timeout: 184

R = Rendezvous Point Tree, S = Sparse, W = Wildcard
```

FIGURE 3.61

Checking PIM Joins from the CE.

```
operator@PE2# run show mvpn instance
MVPN instance:
Legend for provider tunnel
I-P-tnl -- inclusive provider tunnel S-P-tnl -- selective provider tunnel
Legend for c-multicast routes properties (Pr)
DS -- derived from (*, c-g)         RM -- remote VPN route
Instance : FOO-MVPN
  MVPN Mode : SPT-ONLY
  Provider tunnel: I-P-tnl:invalid:
  Neighbor                     I-P-tnl
  7.0.0.1                      RSVP-TE P2MP:7.0.0.1, 6834,7.0.0.1
  7.0.0.5
  C-mcast IPv4 (S:G)           Ptnl                              St
  0.0.0.0/0:239.1.1.1/32
  192.168.1.9/32:239.1.1.1/32  RSVP-TE P2MP:7.0.0.1, 6834,7.0.0.1  DS
```

FIGURE 3.62

Checking the MVPN instance for P-tunnel information.

3.4.3.2.5 Validations at the Egress PE Router—PE3

Here we visit the outputs on PE3, which is the other Egress PE router (see Figures 3.63 to 3.67). All of the outputs are provided without explanations in this section, since the information here is exactly the same as that discussed in the previous section for PE router PE2.

```
operator@PE3# run show route table FOO-MVPN.mvpn.0
1:100:1:7.0.0.1/240
                    *[BGP/170] 06:11:50, localpref 100, from 7.0.0.1
                      AS path: I
                    > to 172.16.1.1 via ge-1/0/1.0, Push 299856
1:100:1:7.0.0.4/240
                    *[BGP/170] 05:54:58, localpref 100, from 7.0.0.4
                      AS path: I
                    > to 172.16.1.1 via ge-1/0/1.0
1:100:1:7.0.0.5/240
                    *[MVPN/70] 05:54:45, metric2 1
                      Indirect
5:100:1:32:192.168.1.9:32:239.1.1.1/240
                    *[BGP/170] 00:24:46, localpref 100, from 7.0.0.1
                      AS path: I
                    > to 172.16.1.1 via ge-1/0/1.0, Push 299856
6:100:1:100:32:7.0.0.1:32:239.1.1.1/240
                    *[PIM/105] 03:21:37
                      Multicast (IPv4)
7:100:1:100:32:192.168.1.9:32:239.1.1.1/240
                    *[MVPN/70] 00:24:46, metric2 1
                      Multicast (IPv4)
                    [PIM/105] 00:24:45
                      Multicast (IPv4)
```

FIGURE 3.63

Checking for MVPN routes.

```
operator@PE3# run show route table FOO-MVPN.mvpn.0 detail
1:100:1:7.0.0.1/240 (1 entry, 1 announced)
*BGP    Preference: 170/-101
PMSI: Flags 0x0: Label[0:0:0]: RSVP-TE: Session_13[7.0.0.1:0:6834:7.0.0.1]
                Next hop type: Indirect
                Next-hop reference count: 4
                Source: 7.0.0.1
                Protocol next hop: 7.0.0.1
                Indirect next hop: 2 no-forward
                State: <Secondary Active Int Ext>
                Local AS:   100 Peer AS:    100
                Age: 6:12:46    Metric2: 1
                Task: BGP_100.7.0.0.1+179
                Announcement bits (2): 0-PIM.FOO-MVPN 1-mvpn global task
                AS path: I
                Communities: target:100:1
                Import Accepted
                Localpref: 100
                Router ID: 7.0.0.1
                Primary Routing Table bgp.mvpn.0

1:100:1:7.0.0.4/240 (1 entry, 1 announced)
        *BGP    Preference: 170/-101
                Next hop type: Indirect
                Next-hop reference count: 2
                Source: 7.0.0.4
                Protocol next hop: 7.0.0.4
                Indirect next hop: 2 no-forward
                State: <Secondary Active Int Ext>
                Local AS:   100 Peer AS:    100
                Age: 5:55:54    Metric2: 1
                Task: BGP_100.7.0.0.4+63093
                Announcement bits (2): 0-PIM.FOO-MVPN 1-mvpn global task
                AS path: I
                Communities: target:100:1
                Import Accepted
                Localpref: 100
                Router ID: 7.0.0.4
                Primary Routing Table bgp.mvpn.0

1:100:1:7.0.0.5/240 (1 entry, 1 announced)
        *MVPN   Preference: 70
                Next hop type: Indirect
                Next-hop reference count: 3
                Protocol next hop: 7.0.0.5
                Indirect next hop: 0 -
                State: <Active Int Ext>
                Age: 5:55:41    Metric2: 1
                Task: mvpn global task
    Announcement bits (3): 0-PIM.FOO-MVPN 1-mvpn global task 2-BGP RT Background
                AS path: I
```

FIGURE 3.64

Checking for MVPN routes—Detailed outputs.

```
5:100:1:32:192.168.1.9:32:239.1.1.1/240 (1 entry, 1 announced)
        *BGP    Preference: 170/-101
                Next hop type: Indirect
                Next-hop reference count: 4
                Source: 7.0.0.1
                Protocol next hop: 7.0.0.1
                Indirect next hop: 2 no-forward
                State: <Secondary Active Int Ext>
                Local AS:    100 Peer AS:    100
                Age: 25:42      Metric2: 1
                Task: BGP_100.7.0.0.1+179
                Announcement bits (2): 0-PIM.FOO-MVPN 1-mvpn global task
                AS path: I
                Communities: target:100:1
                Import Accepted
                Localpref: 100
                Router ID: 7.0.0.1
                Primary Routing Table bgp.mvpn.0

6:100:1:100:32:7.0.0.1:32:239.1.1.1/240 (1 entry, 1 announced)
        *PIM    Preference: 105
                Next hop type: Multicast (IPv4), Next hop index: 1048577
                Next-hop reference count: 14
                State: <Active Int>
                Age: 3:22:33
                Task: PIM.FOO-MVPN
                Announcement bits (2): 0-PIM.FOO-MVPN 1-mvpn global task
                AS path: I
                Communities: no-advertise target:7.0.0.1:5

7:100:1:100:32:192.168.1.9:32:239.1.1.1/240 (2 entries, 2 announced)
        *MVPN   Preference: 70
                Next hop type: Multicast (IPv4), Next hop index: 1048577
                Next-hop reference count: 14
                State: <Active Int Ext>
                Age: 25:42      Metric2: 1
                Task: mvpn global task
    Announcement bits (3): 0-PIM.FOO-MVPN 1-mvpn global task 2-BGP RT Background
                AS path: I
                Communities: target:7.0.0.1:5
         PIM    Preference: 105
                Next hop type: Multicast (IPv4), Next hop index: 1048577
                Next-hop reference count: 14
                State: <Int>
                Inactive reason: Route Preference
                Age: 25:41
                Task: PIM.FOO-MVPN
                Announcement bits (2): 0-PIM.FOO-MVPN 1-mvpn global task
                AS path: I
                Communities: target:7.0.0.1:5
```

FIGURE 3.64

(*Continued*)

```
operator@PE3# run show multicast route instance FOO-MVPN extensive
Family: INET
Group: 239.1.1.1
    Source: 192.168.1.9/32
    Upstream interface: lsi.1
    Downstream interface list:
        ge-1/0/2.0
    Session description: Administratively Scoped
    Statistics: 67 kBps, 793 pps, 1467693 packets
    Next-hop ID: 1048577
    Upstream protocol: MVPN
    Route state: Active
    Forwarding state: Forwarding
    Cache lifetime/timeout: forever
    Wrong incoming interface notifications: 0
```

FIGURE 3.65

Checking the Multicast forwarding table.

```
operator@PE3# run show pim join instance FOO-MVPN extensive
Instance: PIM.FOO-MVPN Family: INET
R = Rendezvous Point Tree, S = Sparse, W = Wildcard
Group: 239.1.1.1
    Source: *
    RP: 7.0.0.1
    Flags: sparse,rptree,wildcard
    Upstream protcol: BGP
    Upstream interface: Through BGP
    Upstream neighbor: Through MVPN
    Upstream state: Join to RP
    Downstream neighbors:
        Interface: ge-1/0/2.0
            192.168.1.5 State: Join Flags: SRW Timeout: 165

Group: 239.1.1.1
    Source: 192.168.1.9
    Flags: sparse
    Upstream protcol: BGP
    Upstream interface: Through BGP
    Upstream neighbor: Through MVPN
    Upstream state: None, Join to Source
    Keepalive timeout:
    Downstream neighbors:
    Interface: ge-1/0/2.0
    192.168.1.5 State: Join Flags: S Timeout: 165
 R = Rendezvous Point Tree, S = Sparse, W = Wildcard
```

FIGURE 3.66

Checking PIM Joins from the CE.

```
operator@PE3# run show mvpn instance
MVPN instance:
Legend for provider tunnel
I-P-tnl -- inclusive provider tunnel S-P-tnl -- selective provider tunnel
Legend for c-multicast routes properties (Pr)
DS -- derived from (*, c-g)          RM -- remote VPN route
Instance : FOO-MVPN
  MVPN Mode : SPT-ONLY
  Provider tunnel: I-P-tnl:invalid:
  Neighbor                           I-P-tnl
  7.0.0.1                            RSVP-TE P2MP:7.0.0.1, 6834,7.0.0.1
  7.0.0.4
  C-mcast IPv4 (S:G)        Ptnl                                       St
  0.0.0.0/0:239.1.1.1/32
  192.168.1.9/32:239.1.1.1/32   RSVP-TE P2MP:7.0.0.1, 6834,7.0.0.1   DS
```

FIGURE 3.67

Checking the MVPN instance for P-tunnel information.

3.4.3.3 Case Study for an RSVP-TE-Based P2MP LSP—S-PMSI Setup

In this section, we look at the actual configurations required for creating an S-PMSI for certain multicast groups. One of the advantages of an S-PMSI over an I-PMSI is the ability to have traffic forwarded to PE routers "ONLY" with interested receivers. This is very similar to the Data MDT functionality within the Draft-Rosen implementation. In this case study, we construct a scenario where PE2 is interested in receiving traffic for C-MCAST group "238.1.1.1", however, PE3 does not have any interested receivers for "238.1.1.1." Therefore our objective is to have traffic delivered over an S-PMSI only to Egress PE router PE2. Traffic to group "239.1.1.1" is to be delivered to both of the Egress PE routers as usual (see Figure 3.68).

The following topology will be used for all illustrations in this chapter.

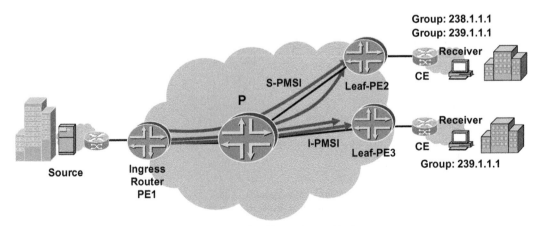

- The router "P" does not indicate a single Provider router, and indicates a Carrier Provider core that may contain many devices. A single device is just given ONLY for illustrative reasons.

FIGURE 3.68

3.4.3.3.1 S-PMSI Configuration Using a C-Source and C-Group Pair

Next we review the configurations for Ingress PE router PE1. The additional configuration for creating an S-PMSI for group "238.1.1.1" is provided under the section "Selective" in the routing-instance hierarchy. Only the routing-instance portion of the configuration is provided in Figure 3.69.

```
routing-instances {
FOO-MVPN {
    instance-type vrf;
    interface ge-4/0/1.0;
    interface lo0.1;
    route-distinguisher 100:1;
    provider-tunnel {
        rsvp-te {
            label-switched-path-template {
                P2MP-RSVP-TE;
            }
        }
        selective { ----------  S-PMSI Configuration
            group 238.1.1.1/32→{
                source 192.168.1.9/32 {
                    rsvp-te {
                        label-switched-path-template {
                            P2MP-RSVP-TE;
                        }
                    }
                }
            }
        }
    }
    vrf-target target:100:1;
    vrf-table-label;
    protocols {
        bgp {
            family inet {
                unicast;
            }
            group peer {
                type external;
                peer-as 65005;
                neighbor 192.168.1.9;
                neighbor 192.168.1.17 {
                    peer-as 65010;
                }
            }
        }
        pim {
            rp {
                local {
                    address 7.0.0.1;
                }
            }
            interface ge-4/0/1.0 {
                mode sparse;
                version 2;
            }
            interface lo0.1 {
                mode sparse;
                version 2;
            }
        }
        mvpn;
    }
}
}
```

FIGURE 3.69

Ingress PE router configuration—PE1.

Under the S-PMSI configuration, a C-MCAST Source and C-MCAST Group have been defined for which an S-PMSI is to be created. In our configuration, PE2 has an interested receiver for group "238.1.1.1"; therefore an S-PMSI is created for source "192.168.1.9" transmitting to this group. There are many combinations and criteria that can be defined under the S-PMSI hierarchy, and some of the key combinations that can be used will be discussed later in the chapter.

The configuration for PE2 and PE3 remain unchanged so they are not provided here.

3.4.3.3.2 Validations

In this section, the S-PMSI setup for Group "238.1.1.1" and the existing I-PMSI infrastructure for Group "239.1.1.1" will be validated.

3.4.3.3.3 Validations at the Ingress PE Router—PE1

Now let us look at the Ingress PE router. First we check the MVPN routing table. The PE1 has originated a Type 3 route (Source: 192.168.1.9 and Group: 238.1.1.1) and received a Type 4 announcement only from PE2 (7.0.0.4), and not from PE3. Therefore the S-PMSI is only created between PE1 and PE2. However, the I-PMSI setup for group "239.1.1.1" is still "UP" between PE1 to PE2/PE3 (see Figure 3.70).

```
operator@PE1# run show route table FOO-MVPN.mvpn.0
FOO-MVPN.mvpn.0: 9 destinations, 12 routes (9 active, 0 holddown, 0 hidden)
+ = Active Route, - = Last Active, * = Both

1:100:1:7.0.0.1/240
                    *[MVPN/70] 00:15:22, metric2 1
                       Indirect
1:100:1:7.0.0.4/240
                    *[BGP/170] 00:14:51, localpref 100, from 7.0.0.4
                       AS path: I
                     > to 172.16.1.5 via ge-4/0/0.0
1:100:1:7.0.0.5/240
                    *[BGP/170] 00:14:51, localpref 100, from 7.0.0.5
                       AS path: I
                     > to 172.16.1.5 via ge-4/0/0.0, Push 299792
3:100:1:32:192.168.1.9:32:238.1.1.1:7.0.0.1/240        --  Type 3 Route
                    *[MVPN/70] 00:00:03, metric2 1
                       Indirect                        →
4:3:100:1:32:192.168.1.9:32:238.1.1.1:7.0.0.1:7.0.0.4/240
                    *[BGP/170] 00:00:03, localpref 100, from 7.0.0.4
                       AS path: I --  Type 4 received from only PE2
                     > to 172.16.1.5 via ge-4/0/0.0
5:100:1:32:192.168.1.9:32:238.1.1.1/240
                    *[PIM/105] 00:00:03
                       Multicast (IPv4)
5:100:1:32:192.168.1.9:32:239.1.1.1/240
                    *[PIM/105] 00:00:06
                       Multicast (IPv4)
7:100:1:100:32:192.168.1.9:32:238.1.1.1/240
                    *[PIM/105] 00:00:03
                       Multicast (IPv4)
                     [BGP/170] 00:00:03, localpref 100, from 7.0.0.4
                       AS path: I
                     > to 172.16.1.5 via ge-4/0/0.0
7:100:1:100:32:192.168.1.9:32:239.1.1.1/240
                    *[PIM/105] 00:00:06
                       Multicast (IPv4)
                     [BGP/170] 00:00:06, localpref 100, from 7.0.0.4
                       AS path: I
                     > to 172.16.1.5 via ge-4/0/0.0
                     [BGP/170] 00:00:06, localpref 100, from 7.0.0.5
                       AS path: I
                     > to 172.16.1.5 via ge-4/0/0.0, Push 299792
```

FIGURE 3.70

Checking for BGP routes.

Let us check the detailed outputs in Figure 3.71.

```
operator@PE1# run show route table FOO-MVPN.mvpn.0  detail
FOO-MVPN.mvpn.0: 9 destinations, 12 routes (9 active, 0 holddown, 0 hidden)
1:100:1:7.0.0.1/240 (1 entry, 1 announced)
        *MVPN   Preference: 70
                Next hop type: Indirect
                Next-hop reference count: 4
                Protocol next hop: 7.0.0.1
                Indirect next hop: 0 -
                State: <Active Int Ext>
                Age: 15:24       Metric2: 1
                Task: mvpn `global task
Announcement bits (3): 0-PIM.FOO-MVPN 1-mvpn global task 2-BGP RT Background
                AS path: I

1:100:1:7.0.0.4/240 (1 entry, 1 announced)
        *BGP    Preference: 170/-101
                Next hop type: Indirect
                Next-hop reference count: 8
                Source: 7.0.0.4
                Protocol next hop: 7.0.0.4
                Indirect next hop: 2 no-forward
                State: <Secondary Active Int Ext>
                Local AS:    100 Peer AS:    100
                Age: 14:53       Metric2: 1
                Task: BGP_100.7.0.0.4+64153
                Announcement bits (2): 0-PIM.FOO-MVPN 1-mvpn global task
                AS path: I
                Communities: target:100:1
                Import Accepted
                Localpref: 100
                Router ID: 7.0.0.4
                Primary Routing Table bgp.mvpn.0

1:100:1:7.0.0.5/240 (1 entry, 1 announced)
        *BGP    Preference: 170/-101
                Next hop type: Indirect
                Next-hop reference count: 4
                Source: 7.0.0.5
                Protocol next hop: 7.0.0.5
                Indirect next hop: 2 no-forward
                State: <Secondary Active Int Ext>
                Local AS:    100 Peer AS:    100
                Age: 14:53       Metric2: 1
                Task: BGP_100.7.0.0.5+54984
                Announcement bits (2): 0-PIM.FOO-MVPN 1-mvpn global task
                AS path: I
                Communities: target:100:1
                Import Accepted
                Localpref: 100
                Router ID: 7.0.0.5
                Primary Routing Table bgp.mvpn.0
```

FIGURE 3.71

Checking for BGP routes—Detailed outputs.

```
3:100:1:32:192.168.1.9:32:238.1.1.1:7.0.0.1/240 (1 entry, 1 announced)
        *MVPN    Preference: 70
                 Next hop type: Indirect
                 Next-hop reference count: 4
                 Protocol next hop: 7.0.0.1
                 Indirect next hop: 0 -
                 State: <Active Int Ext>
                 Age: 5  Metric2: 1
                 Task: mvpn global task
Announcement bits (3): 0-PIM.FOO-MVPN 1-mvpn global task 2-BGP RT Background
                 AS path: I

4:3:100:1:32:192.168.1.9:32:238.1.1.1:7.0.0.1:7.0.0.4/240 (1 entry, 1
announced)
        *BGP     Preference: 170/-101
                 Next hop type: Indirect
                 Next-hop reference count: 8
                 Source: 7.0.0.4
                 Protocol next hop: 7.0.0.4
                 Indirect next hop: 2 no-forward
                 State: <Secondary Active Int Ext>
                 Local AS:    100 Peer AS:    100
                 Age: 5  Metric2: 1
                 Task: BGP_100.7.0.0.4+64153
                 Announcement bits (2): 0-PIM.FOO-MVPN 1-mvpn global task
                 AS path: I
                 Communities: target:7.0.0.1:0
                 Import Accepted
                 Localpref: 100
                 Router ID: 7.0.0.4
                 Primary Routing Table bgp.mvpn.0

5:100:1:32:192.168.1.9:32:238.1.1.1/240 (1 entry, 1 announced)
        *PIM     Preference: 105
                 Next hop type: Multicast (IPv4)
                 Next-hop reference count: 7
                 State: <Active Int>
                 Age: 5
                 Task: PIM.FOO-MVPN
Announcement bits (3): 0-PIM.FOO-MVPN 1-mvpn global task 2-BGP RT Background
                 AS path: I

5:100:1:32:192.168.1.9:32:239.1.1.1/240 (1 entry, 1 announced)
        *PIM     Preference: 105
                 Next hop type: Multicast (IPv4)
                 Next-hop reference count: 7
                 State: <Active Int>
                 Age: 8
                 Task: PIM.FOO-MVPN
Announcement bits (3): 0-PIM.FOO-MVPN 1-mvpn global task 2-BGP RT Background
                 AS path: I
```

FIGURE 3.71

(Continued)

```
7:100:1:100:32:192.168.1.9:32:238.1.1.1/240 (2 entries, 2 announced)
        *PIM     Preference: 105
                 Next hop type: Multicast (IPv4)
                 Next-hop reference count: 7
                 State: <Active Int>
                 Age: 5
                 Task: PIM.FOO-MVPN
                 Announcement bits (2): 0-PIM.FOO-MVPN 1-mvpn global task
                 AS path: I
                 Communities: no-advertise target:7.0.0.1:5
         BGP     Preference: 170/-101
                 Next hop type: Indirect
                 Next-hop reference count: 8
                 Source: 7.0.0.4
                 Protocol next hop: 7.0.0.4
                 Indirect next hop: 2 no-forward
                 State: <Secondary Int Ext>
                 Inactive reason: Route Preference
                 Local AS:    100 Peer AS:    100
                 Age: 5  Metric2: 1
                 Task: BGP_100.7.0.0.4+64153
                 Announcement bits (2): 0-PIM.FOO-MVPN 1-mvpn global task
                 AS path: I
                 Communities: target:7.0.0.1:5
                 Import Accepted
                 Localpref: 100
                 Router ID: 7.0.0.4
                 Primary Routing Table bgp.mvpn.0

7:100:1:100:32:192.168.1.9:32:239.1.1.1/240 (3 entries, 3 announced)
        *PIM     Preference: 105
                 Next hop type: Multicast (IPv4)
                 Next-hop reference count: 7
                 State: <Active Int>
                 Age: 8
                 Task: PIM.FOO-MVPN
                 Announcement bits (2): 0-PIM.FOO-MVPN 1-mvpn global task
                 AS path: I
                 Communities: no-advertise target:7.0.0.1:5
         BGP     Preference: 170/-101
                 Next hop type: Indirect
                 Next-hop reference count: 8
                 Source: 7.0.0.4
                 Protocol next hop: 7.0.0.4
                 Indirect next hop: 2 no-forward
                 State: <Secondary Int Ext>
                 Inactive reason: Route Preference
                 Local AS:    100 Peer AS:    100
                 Age: 8  Metric2: 1
                 Task: BGP_100.7.0.0.4+64153
                 Announcement bits (2): 0-PIM.FOO-MVPN 1-mvpn global task
                 AS path: I
```

FIGURE 3.71

(*Continued*)

```
                  Communities: target:7.0.0.1:5
                  Import Accepted
                  Localpref: 100
                  Router ID: 7.0.0.4
                  Primary Routing Table bgp.mvpn.0
        BGP       Preference: 170/-101
                  Next hop type: Indirect
                  Next-hop reference count: 4
                  Source: 7.0.0.5
                  Protocol next hop: 7.0.0.5
                  Indirect next hop: 2 no-forward
                  State: <Secondary NotBest Int Ext>
                  Inactive reason: Not Best in its group - Router ID
                  Local AS:    100 Peer AS:    100
                  Age: 8  Metric2: 1
                  Task: BGP_100.7.0.0.5+54984
                  Announcement bits (2): 0-PIM.FOO-MVPN 1-mvpn global task
                  AS path: I
                  Communities: target:7.0.0.1:5
                  Import Accepted
                  Localpref: 100
                  Router ID: 7.0.0.5
                  Primary Routing Table bgp.mvpn.0
```

FIGURE 3.71

(*Continued*)

Let us check the status of the Multicast forwarding table on Ingress PE router PE1. In the output seen in Figure 3.72 the router is forwarding traffic for groups (238.1.1.1 and 239.1.1.1).

The MVPN instance needs to be checked to verify whether the I-PMSI and S-PMSI have been correctly created for the configured groups and their forwarding state. In the output shown in Figure 3.73, two P-tunnels are seen. The first tunnel is indicated as "S-RSVP-TE," which is an S-PMSI, and the second one, "RSVP-TE," is an indication of an I-PMSI.

3.4.3.3.4 Validations at the Egress PE Router—PE2

The same set of steps performed for the I-PMSI validation is followed here. The first task is to check the MVPN routing table for Type 3 and Type 4 routing information, which is an indication of an S-PMSI signaling (see Figure 3.74).

We check the detailed outputs for validating the S-PMSI attribute, which is advertised by ingress PE router PE1. In the output illustrated in Figure 3.75, the following information is attached to the Type 3 BGP announcement "**PMSI: Flags 0x1: Label[0:0:0]: RSVP-TE: Session_13[7.0.0.1:0:47055:7.0.0.1].**" "**0x1**" indicates an S-PMSI attribute.

We now check the Multicast forwarding table, which indicates forwarding for two C-MCAST groups (238.1.1.1 and 239.1.1.1; Figure 3.76).

We now check the MVPN instance for P-tunnel information on PE2. The output displays both the I-PMSI and S-PMSI information (see Figure 3.77).

```
operator@PE1# run show multicast route instance FOO-MVPN extensive
Family: INET
Group: 238.1.1.1
    Source: 192.168.1.9/32
    Upstream interface: ge-4/0/1.0
    Session description: Unknown
    Statistics: 29 kBps, 345 pps, 220507 packets
    Next-hop ID: 1048577
    Upstream protocol: MVPN
    Route state: Active
    Forwarding state: Forwarding
    Cache lifetime/timeout: forever
    Wrong incoming interface notifications: 0

Group: 239.1.1.1
    Source: 192.168.1.9/32
    Upstream interface: ge-4/0/1.0
    Session description: Administratively Scoped
    Statistics: 89 kBps, 1063 pps, 685281 packets -> Traffic forwarded
    Next-hop ID: 1048576
    Upstream protocol: MVPN
    Route state: Active
    Forwarding state: Forwarding
    Cache lifetime/timeout: forever
    Wrong incoming interface notifications: 0
```

FIGURE 3.72

Checking the Multicast forwarding table.

```
operator@PE1# run show mvpn instance
MVPN instance:
Legend for provider tunnel
I-P-tnl -- inclusive provider tunnel S-P-tnl -- selective provider tunnel
Legend for c-multicast routes properties (Pr)
DS -- derived from (*, c-g)         RM -- remote VPN route
Instance : FOO-MVPN
  MVPN Mode : SPT-ONLY
  Provider tunnel: I-P-tnl:RSVP-TE P2MP:7.0.0.1, 47053,7.0.0.1
  Neighbor                        I-P-tnl
  7.0.0.4
  7.0.0.5
C-mcast IPv4 (S:G)              Ptnl                               St
192.168.1.9/32:238.1.1.1/32    S-RSVP-TE P2MP:7.0.0.1, 47055,7.0.0.1    RM
192.168.1.9/32:239.1.1.1/32    RSVP-TE P2MP:7.0.0.1,   47053,7.0.0.1    RM
```

FIGURE 3.73

Checking the Multicast forwarding table.

```
operator@PE2# run show route table FOO-MVPN.mvpn.0
FOO-MVPN.mvpn.0: 13 destinations, 15 routes (13 active, 0 holddown, 0 hidden)
+ = Active Route, - = Last Active, * = Both
1:100:1:7.0.0.1/240
                       *[BGP/170] 00:33:45, localpref 100, from 7.0.0.1
                         AS path: I
                        > to 172.16.1.6 via ge-4/0/3.0
1:100:1:7.0.0.4/240
                       *[MVPN/70] 1d 01:54:00, metric2 1
                         Indirect
1:100:1:7.0.0.5/240
                       *[BGP/170] 1d 01:53:47, localpref 100, from 7.0.0.5
                         AS path: I
                        > to 172.16.1.2 via ge-4/0/0.0
3:100:1:32:192.168.1.9:32:238.1.1.1:7.0.0.1/240   ---> From PE1
                       *[BGP/170] 00:18:57, localpref 100, from 7.0.0.1
                         AS path: I
                        > to 172.16.1.6 via ge-4/0/3.0
4:3:100:1:32:192.168.1.9:32:238.1.1.1:7.0.0.1:7.0.0.4/240 -> Originated
                       *[MVPN/70] 00:18:57, metric2 1
                         Indirect
5:100:1:32:192.168.1.9:32:238.1.1.1/240
                       *[BGP/170] 00:18:57, localpref 100, from 7.0.0.1
                         AS path: I
                        > to 172.16.1.6 via ge-4/0/3.0
5:100:1:32:192.168.1.9:32:239.1.1.1/240
                       *[BGP/170] 00:19:00, localpref 100, from 7.0.0.1
                         AS path: I
                        > to 172.16.1.6 via ge-4/0/3.0
6:100:1:100:32:7.0.0.1:32:238.1.1.1/240
                       *[PIM/105] 00:33:45
                         Multicast (IPv4)
6:100:1:100:32:7.0.0.1:32:239.1.1.1/240
                       *[PIM/105] 00:33:45
                         Multicast (IPv4)
7:100:1:100:32:192.168.1.9:32:238.1.1.1/240
                       *[MVPN/70] 00:18:57, metric2 1
                         Multicast (IPv4)
                        [PIM/105] 00:18:57
                         Multicast (IPv4)
7:100:1:100:32:192.168.1.9:32:239.1.1.1/240
                       *[MVPN/70] 00:19:00, metric2 1
                         Multicast (IPv4)
                        [PIM/105] 00:19:00
                         Multicast (IPv4)
```

FIGURE 3.74

Checking for BGP routes.

```
operator@PE2# run show route table FOO-MVPN.mvpn.0 detail
FOO-MVPN.mvpn.0: 13 destinations, 15 routes (13 active, 0 holddown, 0 hidden)
1:100:1:7.0.0.1/240 (1 entry, 1 announced)
        *BGP    Preference: 170/-101
PMSI: Flags 0x0: Label[0:0:0]: RSVP-TE: Session_13[7.0.0.1:0:47053:7.0.0.1]
                Next hop type: Indirect
                Next-hop reference count: 8
                Source: 7.0.0.1
                Protocol next hop: 7.0.0.1
                Indirect next hop: 2 no-forward
                State: <Secondary Active Int Ext>
                Local AS:    100 Peer AS:    100
                Age: 39:23      Metric2: 1
                Task: BGP_100.7.0.0.1+179
                Announcement bits (2): 0-PIM.FOO-MVPN 1-mvpn global task
                AS path: I
                Communities: target:100:1
                Import Accepted
                Localpref: 100
                Router ID: 7.0.0.1
                Primary Routing Table bgp.mvpn.0

1:100:1:7.0.0.4/240 (1 entry, 1 announced)
        *MVPN   Preference: 70
                Next hop type: Indirect
                Next-hop reference count: 4
                Protocol next hop: 7.0.0.4
                Indirect next hop: 0 -
                State: <Active Int Ext>
                Age: 1d 1:59:38         Metric2: 1
                Task: mvpn global task
        Announcement bits (3): 0-PIM.FOO-MVPN 1-mvpn global task 2-BGP RT Background
                AS path: I

1:100:1:7.0.0.5/240 (1 entry, 1 announced)
        *BGP    Preference: 170/-101
                Next hop type: Indirect
                Next-hop reference count: 2
                Source: 7.0.0.5
                Protocol next hop: 7.0.0.5
                Indirect next hop: 2 no-forward
                State: <Secondary Active Int Ext>
                Local AS:    100 Peer AS:    100
                Age: 1d 1:59:25         Metric2: 1
                Task: BGP_100.7.0.0.5+179
```

FIGURE 3.75

Checking for BGP routes—Detailed outputs.

```
Announcement bits (2): 0-PIM.FOO-MVPN 1-mvpn global task
                AS path: I
                Communities: target:100:1
                Import Accepted
                Localpref: 100
                Router ID: 7.0.0.5
                Primary Routing Table bgp.mvpn.0


3:100:1:32:192.168.1.9:32:238.1.1.1:7.0.0.1/240 (1 entry, 1 announced)
        *BGP    Preference: 170/-101
PMSI: Flags 0x1: Label[0:0:0]: RSVP-TE: Session_13[7.0.0.1:0:47055:7.0.0.1]
                Next hop type: Indirect
                Next-hop reference count: 8
                Source: 7.0.0.1
                Protocol next hop: 7.0.0.1
                Indirect next hop: 2 no-forward
                State: <Secondary Active Int Ext>
                Local AS:   100 Peer AS:    100
                Age: 24:35      Metric2: 1
                Task: BGP_100.7.0.0.1+179
                Announcement bits (2): 0-PIM.FOO-MVPN 1-mvpn global task
                AS path: I
                Communities: target:100:1
                Import Accepted
                Localpref: 100
                Router ID: 7.0.0.1
                Primary Routing Table bgp.mvpn.0


4:3:100:1:32:192.168.1.9:32:238.1.1.1:7.0.0.1:7.0.0.4/240 (1 entry, 1
announced)
        *MVPN   Preference: 70
                Next hop type: Indirect
                Next-hop reference count: 4
                Protocol next hop: 7.0.0.4
                Indirect next hop: 0 -
                State: <Active Int Ext>
                Age: 24:35      Metric2: 1
                Task: mvpn global task
                Announcement bits (3): 0-PIM.FOO-MVPN 1-mvpn global task 2-BGP
    RT Background
                AS path: I
                Communities: target:7.0.0.1:0


5:100:1:32:192.168.1.9:32:238.1.1.1/240 (1 entry, 1 announced)
        *BGP    Preference: 170/-101
                Next hop type: Indirect
                Next-hop reference count: 8
                Source: 7.0.0.1
```

FIGURE 3.75

(*Continued*)

```
                        Protocol next hop: 7.0.0.1
                        Indirect next hop: 2 no-forward
                        State: <Secondary Active Int Ext>
                        Local AS:    100 Peer AS:    100
                        Age: 24:35      Metric2: 1
                        Task: BGP_100.7.0.0.1+179
                        Announcement bits (2): 0-PIM.FOO-MVPN 1-mvpn global task
                        AS path: I
                        Communities: target:100:1
                        Import Accepted
                        Localpref: 100
                        Router ID: 7.0.0.1
                        Primary Routing Table bgp.mvpn.0

5:100:1:32:192.168.1.9:32:239.1.1.1/240 (1 entry, 1 announced)
        *BGP    Preference: 170/-101
                        Next hop type: Indirect
                        Next-hop reference count: 8
                        Source: 7.0.0.1
                        Protocol next hop: 7.0.0.1
                        Indirect next hop: 2 no-forward
                        State: <Secondary Active Int Ext>
                        Local AS:    100 Peer AS:    100
                        Age: 24:38      Metric2: 1
                        Task: BGP_100.7.0.0.1+179
                        Announcement bits (2): 0-PIM.FOO-MVPN 1-mvpn global task
                        AS path: I
                        Communities: target:100:1
                        Import Accepted
                        Localpref: 100
                        Router ID: 7.0.0.1
                        Primary Routing Table bgp.mvpn.0

6:100:1:100:32:7.0.0.1:32:238.1.1.1/240 (1 entry, 1 announced)
        *PIM    Preference: 105
                        Next hop type: Multicast (IPv4), Next hop index: 1048576
                        Next-hop reference count: 37
                        State: <Active Int>
                        Age: 39:23
                        Task: PIM.FOO-MVPN
                        Announcement bits (2): 0-PIM.FOO-MVPN 1-mvpn global task
                        AS path: I
                        Communities: no-advertise target:7.0.0.1:5

6:100:1:100:32:7.0.0.1:32:239.1.1.1/240 (1 entry, 1 announced)
        *PIM    Preference: 105
                        Next hop type: Multicast (IPv4), Next hop index: 1048576
                        Next-hop reference count: 37
                        State: <Active Int>
                        Age: 39:23
                        Task: PIM.FOO-MVPN
```

FIGURE 3.75

(Continued)

```
                        Announcement bits (2): 0-PIM.FOO-MVPN 1-mvpn global task
                        AS path: I
                        Communities: no-advertise target:7.0.0.1:5

     7:100:1:100:32:192.168.1.9:32:238.1.1.1/240 (2 entries, 2 announced)
             *MVPN    Preference: 70
                      Next hop type: Multicast (IPv4), Next hop index: 1048576
                      Next-hop reference count: 37
                      State: <Active Int Ext>
                      Age: 24:35      Metric2: 1
                      Task: mvpn global task
     Announcement bits (3): 0-PIM.FOO-MVPN 1-mvpn global task 2-BGP RT Background
                      AS path: I
                      Communities: target:7.0.0.1:5
             PIM      Preference: 105
                      Next hop type: Multicast (IPv4), Next hop index: 1048576
                      Next-hop reference count: 37
                      State: <Int>
                      Inactive reason: Route Preference
                      Age: 24:35
                      Task: PIM.FOO-MVPN
                      Announcement bits (2): 0-PIM.FOO-MVPN 1-mvpn global task
                      AS path: I
                      Communities: target:7.0.0.1:5

     7:100:1:100:32:192.168.1.9:32:239.1.1.1/240 (2 entries, 2 announced)
             *MVPN    Preference: 70
                      Next hop type: Multicast (IPv4), Next hop index: 1048576
                      Next-hop reference count: 37
                      State: <Active Int Ext>
                      Age: 24:38      Metric2: 1
                      Task: mvpn global task
     Announcement bits (3): 0-PIM.FOO-MVPN 1-mvpn global task 2-BGP RT Background
                      AS path: I
                      Communities: target:7.0.0.1:5
             PIM      Preference: 105
                      Next hop type: Multicast (IPv4), Next hop index: 1048576
                      Next-hop reference count: 37
                      State: <Int>
                      Inactive reason: Route Preference
                      Age: 24:38
                      Task: PIM.FOO-MVPN
                      Announcement bits (2): 0-PIM.FOO-MVPN 1-mvpn global task
                      AS path: I
                      Communities: target:7.0.0.1:5
```

FIGURE 3.75

(*Continued*)

```
operator@PE2# run show multicast route instance FOO-MVPN extensive
Family: INET
Group: 238.1.1.1
    Source: 192.168.1.9/32
    Upstream interface: lsi.21
    Downstream interface list:
        ge-4/0/2.100
    Session description: Unknown
    Statistics: 29 kBps, 342 pps, 717278 packets
    Next-hop ID: 1048576
    Upstream protocol: MVPN
    Route state: Active
    Forwarding state: Forwarding
    Cache lifetime/timeout: forever
    Wrong incoming interface notifications: 0

Group: 239.1.1.1
    Source: 192.168.1.9/32
    Upstream interface: lsi.21
    Downstream interface list:
        ge-4/0/2.100
    Session description: Administratively Scoped
    Statistics: 97 kBps, 1154 pps, 2246202 packets
    Next-hop ID: 1048576
    Upstream protocol: MVPN
    Route state: Active
    Forwarding state: Forwarding
    Cache lifetime/timeout: forever
    Wrong incoming interface notifications: 0
```

FIGURE 3.76

Checking the Multicast forwarding table.

```
operator@PE2# run show mvpn instance
MVPN instance:
Legend for provider tunnel
I-P-tnl -- inclusive provider tunnel S-P-tnl -- selective provider tunnel
Legend for c-multicast routes properties (Pr)
DS -- derived from (*, c-g)          RM -- remote VPN route
Instance : FOO-MVPN
  MVPN Mode : SPT-ONLY
  Provider tunnel: I-P-tnl:invalid:
  Neighbor                           I-P-tnl
  7.0.0.1                            RSVP-TE P2MP:7.0.0.1, 47053,7.0.0.1
  7.0.0.5
C-mcast IPv4 (S:G)           Ptnl                               St
192.168.1.9/32:238.1.1.1/32  S-RSVP-TE P2MP:7.0.0.1, 47055,7.0.0.1  DS
192.168.1.9/32:239.1.1.1/32  RSVP-TE P2MP:7.0.0.1,   47053,7.0.0.1  DS
```

FIGURE 3.77

Checking the MVPN instance.

3.4.3.3.5 Validations at the Egress PE Router—PE3

We follow the same set of steps as performed for the I-PMSI validation. The first task is to check the MVPN routing table for Type 3 and Type 4 routing information, which is an indication of an S-PMSI signaling. As seen in the output (Figure 3.78), PE3 installs the Type 3 announcement from PE1; however, it does not respond with a corresponding Type 4 route since there are no interested receivers for group 238.1.1.1.

```
operator@PE3# run show route table FOO-MVPN.mvpn.0
FOO-MVPN.mvpn.0: 9 destinations, 10 routes (9 active, 0 holddown, 0 hidden)
+ = Active Route, - = Last Active, * = Both
1:100:1:7.0.0.1/240
                   *[BGP/170] 00:54:22, localpref 100, from 7.0.0.1
                      AS path: I
                    > to 172.16.1.1 via ge-1/0/1.0, Push 299856
1:100:1:7.0.0.4/240
                   *[BGP/170] 1d 02:14:37, localpref 100, from 7.0.0.4
                      AS path: I
                    > to 172.16.1.1 via ge-1/0/1.0
1:100:1:7.0.0.5/240
                   *[MVPN/70] 1d 02:14:24, metric2 1
                      Indirect
3:100:1:32:192.168.1.9:32:238.1.1.1:7.0.0.1/240
                   *[BGP/170] 00:39:34, localpref 100, from 7.0.0.1
                      AS path: I
                    > to 172.16.1.1 via ge-1/0/1.0, Push 299856
5:100:1:32:192.168.1.9:32:238.1.1.1/240
                   *[BGP/170] 00:39:34, localpref 100, from 7.0.0.1
                      AS path: I
                    > to 172.16.1.1 via ge-1/0/1.0, Push 299856
5:100:1:32:192.168.1.9:32:239.1.1.1/240
                   *[BGP/170] 00:39:37, localpref 100, from 7.0.0.1
                      AS path: I
                    > to 172.16.1.1 via ge-1/0/1.0, Push 299856
6:100:1:100:32:7.0.0.1:32:239.1.1.1/240
                   *[PIM/105] 00:54:22
                      Multicast (IPv4)
7:100:1:100:32:192.168.1.9:32:239.1.1.1/240
                   *[MVPN/70] 00:39:37, metric2 1
                      Multicast (IPv4)
                    [PIM/105] 00:39:37
                      Multicast (IPv4)
```

FIGURE 3.78

Checking for BGP routes.

Next the detailed outputs on PE3 are checked (see Figure 3.79).

The next step is to verify the multicast forwarding state for the groups. In the output seen in Figure 3.80 we can verify the forwarding state only for group "239.1.1.1."

Checking the MVPN instance information is done next. The output seen in Figure 3.81 only shows the I-PMSI information, since PE3 does not have an S-PMSI setup.

```
operator@PE3# run show route table FOO-MVPN.mvpn.0 detail
FOO-MVPN.mvpn.0: 9 destinations, 10 routes (9 active, 0 holddown, 0 hidden)
1:100:1:7.0.0.1/240 (1 entry, 1 announced)
        *BGP      Preference: 170/-101
PMSI: Flags 0x0: Label[0:0:0]: RSVP-TE: Session_13[7.0.0.1:0:47053:7.0.0.1]
                  Next hop type: Indirect
                  Next-hop reference count: 8
                  Source: 7.0.0.1
                  Protocol next hop: 7.0.0.1
                  Indirect next hop: 2 no-forward
                  State: <Secondary Active Int Ext>
                  Local AS:    100 Peer AS:    100
                  Age: 1:01:01    Metric2: 1
                  Task: BGP_100.7.0.0.1+179
                  Announcement bits (2): 0-PIM.FOO-MVPN 1-mvpn global task
                  AS path: I
                  Communities: target:100:1
                  Import Accepted
                  Localpref: 100
                  Router ID: 7.0.0.1
                  Primary Routing Table bgp.mvpn.0

1:100:1:7.0.0.4/240 (1 entry, 1 announced)
        *BGP      Preference: 170/-101
                  Next hop type: Indirect
                  Next-hop reference count: 2
                  Source: 7.0.0.4
                  Protocol next hop: 7.0.0.4
                  Indirect next hop: 2 no-forward
                  State: <Secondary Active Int Ext>
                  Local AS:    100 Peer AS:    100
                  Age: 1d 2:21:16          Metric2: 1
                  Task: BGP_100.7.0.0.4+63093
                  Announcement bits (2): 0-PIM.FOO-MVPN 1-mvpn global task
                  AS path: I
                  Communities: target:100:1
                  Import Accepted
                  Localpref: 100
                  Router ID: 7.0.0.4
                  Primary Routing Table bgp.mvpn.0

1:100:1:7.0.0.5/240 (1 entry, 1 announced)
        *MVPN     Preference: 70
                  Next hop type: Indirect
                  Next-hop reference count: 3
                  Protocol next hop: 7.0.0.5
                  Indirect next hop: 0 -
                  State: <Active Int Ext>
                  Age: 1d 2:21:03          Metric2: 1
                  Task: mvpn global task
  Announcement bits (3): 0-PIM.FOO-MVPN 1-mvpn global task 2-BGP RT Background
                  AS path: I
```

FIGURE 3.79

Checking for BGP routes—detailed outputs.

```
3:100:1:32:192.168.1.9:32:238.1.1.1:7.0.0.1/240 (1 entry, 1 announced)
        *BGP     Preference: 170/-101
PMSI: Flags 0x1: Label[0:0:0]: RSVP-TE: Session_13[7.0.0.1:0:47055:7.0.0.1]
                 Next hop type: Indirect
                 Next-hop reference count: 8
                 Source: 7.0.0.1
                 Protocol next hop: 7.0.0.1
                 Indirect next hop: 2 no-forward
                 State: <Secondary Active Int Ext>
                 Local AS:    100 Peer AS:    100
                 Age: 46:13      Metric2: 1
                 Task: BGP_100.7.0.0.1+179
                 Announcement bits (2): 0-PIM.FOO-MVPN 1-mvpn global task
                 AS path: I
                 Communities: target:100:1
                 Import Accepted
                 Localpref: 100
                 Router ID: 7.0.0.1
                 Primary Routing Table bgp.mvpn.0

5:100:1:32:192.168.1.9:32:238.1.1.1/240 (1 entry, 1 announced)
        *BGP     Preference: 170/-101
                 Next hop type: Indirect
                 Next-hop reference count: 8
                 Source: 7.0.0.1
                 Protocol next hop: 7.0.0.1
                 Indirect next hop: 2 no-forward
                 State: <Secondary Active Int Ext>
                 Local AS:    100 Peer AS:    100
                 Age: 46:13      Metric2: 1
                 Task: BGP_100.7.0.0.1+179
                 Announcement bits (2): 0-PIM.FOO-MVPN 1-mvpn global task
                 AS path: I
                 Communities: target:100:1
                 Import Accepted
                 Localpref: 100
                 Router ID: 7.0.0.1
                 Primary Routing Table bgp.mvpn.0

5:100:1:32:192.168.1.9:32:239.1.1.1/240 (1 entry, 1 announced)
        *BGP     Preference: 170/-101
                 Next hop type: Indirect
                 Next-hop reference count: 8
                 Source: 7.0.0.1
                 Protocol next hop: 7.0.0.1
                 Indirect next hop: 2 no-forward
                 State: <Secondary Active Int Ext>
                 Local AS:    100 Peer AS:    100
                 Age: 46:16      Metric2: 1
```

FIGURE 3.79

(Continued)

```
                    Task: BGP_100.7.0.0.1+179
                    Announcement bits (2): 0-PIM.FOO-MVPN 1-mvpn global task
                    AS path: I
                    Communities: target:100:1
                    Import Accepted
                    Localpref: 100
                    Router ID: 7.0.0.1
                    Primary Routing Table bgp.mvpn.0

6:100:1:100:32:7.0.0.1:32:224.2.127.254/240 (1 entry, 1 announced)
        *PIM    Preference: 105
                    Next hop type: Multicast (IPv4), Next hop index: 1048577
                    Next-hop reference count: 19
                    State: <Active Int>
                    Age: 1:01:01
                    Task: PIM.FOO-MVPN
                    Announcement bits (2): 0-PIM.FOO-MVPN 1-mvpn global task
                    AS path: I
                    Communities: no-advertise target:7.0.0.1:5

6:100:1:100:32:7.0.0.1:32:239.1.1.1/240 (1 entry, 1 announced)
        *PIM    Preference: 105
                    Next hop type: Multicast (IPv4), Next hop index: 1048577
                    Next-hop reference count: 19
                    State: <Active Int>
                    Age: 1:01:01
                    Task: PIM.FOO-MVPN
                    Announcement bits (2): 0-PIM.FOO-MVPN 1-mvpn global task
                    AS path: I
                    Communities: no-advertise target:7.0.0.1:5

7:100:1:100:32:192.168.1.9:32:239.1.1.1/240 (2 entries, 2 announced)
        *MVPN   Preference: 70
                    Next hop type: Multicast (IPv4), Next hop index: 1048577
                    Next-hop reference count: 19
                    State: <Active Int Ext>
                    Age: 46:16        Metric2: 1
                    Task: mvpn global task
Announcement bits (3): 0-PIM.FOO-MVPN 1-mvpn global task 2-BGP RT Background
                    AS path: I
                    Communities: target:7.0.0.1:5
        PIM     Preference: 105
                    Next hop type: Multicast (IPv4), Next hop index: 1048577
                    Next-hop reference count: 19
                    State: <Int>
                    Inactive reason: Route Preference
                    Age: 46:16
                    Task: PIM.FOO-MVPN
                    Announcement bits (2): 0-PIM.FOO-MVPN 1-mvpn global task
                    AS path: I
                    Communities: target:7.0.0.1:5
```

FIGURE 3.79

(Continued)

```
operator@PE3# run show multicast route instance FOO-MVPN extensive
Family: INET
Group: 239.1.1.1
    Source: 192.168.1.9/32
    Upstream interface: lsi.1
    Downstream interface list:
        ge-1/0/2.0
    Session description: Administratively Scoped
    Statistics: 97 kBps, 1156 pps, 3375081 packets
    Next-hop ID: 1048577
    Upstream protocol: MVPN
    Route state: Active
    Forwarding state: Forwarding
    Cache lifetime/timeout: forever
    Wrong incoming interface notifications: 0
```

FIGURE 3.80

Checking the Multicast forwarding table.

```
operator@PE3# run show mvpn instance
MVPN instance:
Legend for provider tunnel
I-P-tnl -- inclusive provider tunnel S-P-tnl -- selective provider tunnel
Legend for c-multicast routes properties (Pr)
DS -- derived from (*, c-g)        RM -- remote VPN route
Instance : FOO-MVPN
  MVPN Mode : SPT-ONLY
  Provider tunnel: I-P-tnl:invalid:
  Neighbor                    I-P-tnl
  7.0.0.1                        RSVP-TE P2MP:7.0.0.1, 47053,7.0.0.1
  7.0.0.4
C-mcast IPv4 (S:G)          Ptnl                                     St
192.168.1.9/32:239.1.1.1/32 RSVP-TE P2MP:7.0.0.1, 47053,7.0.0.1     DS
```

FIGURE 3.81

Checking the MVPN instance.

3.4.3.3.6 S-PMSI Configuration Using a C-Source and C-Group with Traffic Threshold

While configuring an S-PMSI for a Source and Group, we can also configure a threshold value. The Threshold can be defined at a minimum rate of 10 Kbps until 1,000,000 Kbps. Traffic flows over an I-PMSI until the threshold is within the configured range. Upon exceeding the rate traffic is switched over to an S-PMSI. The relevant configuration is provided in Figure 3.82.

Now the MVPN instance information is checked and the values within the P-tunnels on PE1 are noted. The Tunnel ID information for the I-PMSI has a tag of "47053," and the S-PMSI has a value of "47056" attached.

```
routing-instances {
FOO-MVPN {
    instance-type vrf;
    interface ge-4/0/1.0;
    interface lo0.1;
    route-distinguisher 100:1;
    provider-tunnel {
        rsvp-te {
            label-switched-path-template {
                P2MP-RSVP-TE;
            }
        }
        selective {
            group 238.1.1.1/32 {
                source 192.168.1.9/32 {
                    rsvp-te {
                        label-switched-path-template {
                            P2MP-RSVP-TE;
                        }
                    }
                    threshold-rate 10; ----> 10Kbps Threshold defined
                }
            }
        }
    }
    vrf-target target:100:1;
    vrf-table-label;
    protocols {
        bgp {
            family inet {
                unicast;
            }
            group peer {
                type external;
                export export;
                peer-as 65005;
                neighbor 192.168.1.9;
                neighbor 192.168.1.17 {
                    peer-as 65010;
                }
            }
        }
        pim {
            rp {
                local {
                    address 7.0.0.1;
                }
            }
            interface ge-4/0/1.0 {
                mode sparse;
                version 2;
            }
```

FIGURE 3.82

Ingress PE router configuration—PE1.

```
            interface lo0.1 {
                mode sparse;
                version 2;
            }
        }
        mvpn {
            traceoptions {
                file MVPN size 1m world-readable;
                flag all;
            }
        }
    }
  }
}
```

FIGURE 3.82

(*Continued*)

```
operator@PE1# run show mvpn instance
MVPN instance:
Legend for provider tunnel
I-P-tnl -- inclusive provider tunnel S-P-tnl -- selective provider tunnel
Legend for c-multicast routes properties (Pr)
DS -- derived from (*, c-g)          RM -- remote VPN route
Instance : FOO-MVPN
  MVPN Mode : SPT-ONLY
  Provider tunnel: I-P-tnl:RSVP-TE P2MP:7.0.0.1, 47053,7.0.0.1
  Neighbor                          I-P-tnl
  7.0.0.4
  7.0.0.5
  C-mcast IPv4 (S:G)        Ptnl                                      St
  192.168.1.9/32:238.1.1.1/32   S-RSVP-TE P2MP:7.0.0.1, 47056,7.0.0.1 RM
```

FIGURE 3.83

Checking the MVPN instance.

To validate the S-PMSI setup, we actually enable some debugging (traceoptions) and the output of the traceoptions is illustrated in Figure 3.84. Note that the I-PMSI gets unbound from the C-MCAST Source and Group pair when the traffic rate exceeds the threshold. Also visible is the exchange of Type 3 and Type 4 routing information between PE1 and PE2 as indicated at the beginning of the output.

The last line of the output in Figure 3.84 indicates an RSVP-TE P-tunnel being set up, and a value of "47056" is visible. Compare this with the previous output and this value will match with the S-PMSI output displayed in the "MVPN instance."

3.4.3.3.7 S-PMSI Configuration Using Wild Cards

We would like all C-MCAST traffic to use an S-PMSI instead of using an I-PMSI. This is like stating we use only a Data MDT and no Default MDT ever in the context of a Draft-Rosen implementation,

```
Sep 20 20:27:35.746064 Checking SPMSI bw: threshold=10, mc=1056
Sep 20 20:27:35.746163 Add SPMSI AD route for mvpn
3:100:1:32:192.168.1.9:32:238.1.1.1:7.0.0.1
Sep 20 20:27:35.746352 Flash call for MVPN from FOO-MVPN.MVPN.0
Sep 20 20:27:35.746361 Flash processing complete for MVPN from FOO-MVPN.MVPN.0
Sep 20 20:27:35.758324 Flash call for MVPN from FOO-MVPN.MVPN.0
Sep 20 20:27:35.758337 Received LEAF-AD route from 4000007 for,
4:3:100:1:32:192.168.1.9:32:238.1.1.1:7.0.0.1:7.0.0.4 ----> PE2
Sep 20 20:27:35.758384 Flash processing complete for MVPN from FOO-MVPN.MVPN.0
Sep 20 20:28:05.747471 Instance FOO-MVPN: unbind cmcast 238.1.1.1.192.168.1.9
from ptnl 0x8EAE900 flags 0x4001 refcnt 1 type 0 root Flags 0x0: Label[0:0:0]:
RSVP-TE: Session_13[7.0.0.1:0:47053:7.0.0.1]
Sep 20 20:28:05.747540 mvpn_fw_get_cmcast_nh Evaluating RD 0x64:1 for cmcast
238.1.1.1.192.168.1.9 - fwd rt 0x900d8e8
Sep 20 20:28:05.747548 mvpn_fw_get_mcast_nh_source_rt done: add_ptnl (1/1), nh
empty 1
Sep 20 20:28:05.747554 mvpn_fw_get_mcast_nh_inherit_shrd_rt done: add_ptnl
(0/1), nh empty 1
Sep 20 20:28:05.747570 Instance FOO-MVPN: mvpn_ptnl_cmcast_fw_rt_upd for
238.1.1.1.192.168.1.9 on ptnl 0x8EAE900 flags 0x4001 refcnt 1 type 0 root Flags
0x0: Label[0:0:0]: RSVP-TE: Session_13[7.0.0.1:0:47053:7.0.0.1]: nh 0x9007688
Sep 20 20:28:05.747580 Instance FOO-MVPN: mvpn_fw_rt_update for
238.1.1.1.192.168.1.9 on ptnl 0x8EAE900 flags 0x4001 refcnt 1 type 0 root Flags
0x0: Label[0:0:0]: RSVP-TE: Session_13[7.0.0.1:0:47053:7.0.0.1]
Sep 20 20:28:05.747596 Instance FOO-MVPN: bind cmcast 238.1.1.1.192.168.1.9 to
ptnl 0x8EAEB80 flags 0x8001 refcnt 1 type 0 root Flags 0x1: Label[0:0:0]:
RSVP-TE: Session_13[7.0.0.1:0:47056:7.0.0.1]
Sep 20 20:28:05.758441 mvpn_fw_get_cmcast_nh Evaluating RD 0x64:1 for cmcast
238.1.1.1.192.168.1.9 - fwd rt 0x900d8e8
Sep 20 20:28:05.758448 mvpn_fw_get_mcast_nh_source_rt done: add_ptnl (1/1), nh
empty 1
Sep 20 20:28:05.758453 mvpn_fw_get_mcast_nh_inherit_shrd_rt done: add_ptnl
(0/1), nh empty 1
Sep 20 20:28:05.758464 Instance FOO-MVPN: mvpn_ptnl_cmcast_fw_rt_upd for
238.1.1.1.192.168.1.9 on ptnl 0x8EAEB80 flags 0x8021 refcnt 1 type 0 root Flags
0x1: Label[0:0:0]: RSVP-TE: Session_13[7.0.0.1:0:47056:7.0.0.1]: nh 0x9007b08
Sep 20 20:28:05.758473 Instance FOO-MVPN: mvpn_fw_rt_update for
238.1.1.1.192.168.1.9 on ptnl 0x8EAEB80 flags 0x8021 refcnt 1 type 0 root Flags
0x1: Label[0:0:0]: RSVP-TE: Session_13[7.0.0.1:0:47056:7.0.0.1]
```

FIGURE 3.84

Traceoptions output.

which is not possible in Draft-Rosen MVPNs. This could be a requirement for many operators who intend to save on bandwidth utilization and not toward the additional state information. In this case, wild cards can be used as follows.

The relevant configuration is provided in Figure 3.85.

```
routing-instances {
FOO-MVPN {
    instance-type vrf;
    interface ge-4/0/1.0;
    interface lo0.1;
    route-distinguisher 100:1;
    provider-tunnel {
        rsvp-te {
            label-switched-path-template {
                P2MP-RSVP-TE;
            }
        }
        selective {
            group 224.0.0.0/4 {
                source 0.0.0.0/0 {
                    rsvp-te {
                        label-switched-path-template {
                            P2MP-RSVP-TE;
                        }
                    }
                }
            }
        }
    }
    vrf-target target:100:1;
    vrf-table-label;
    protocols {
        bgp {
            family inet {
                unicast;
            }
            group peer {
                type external;
                peer-as 65005;
                neighbor 192.168.1.9;
                neighbor 192.168.1.17 {
                    peer-as 65010;
                }
            }
        }
        pim {
            rp {
                local {
                    address 7.0.0.1;
                }
            }
            interface ge-4/0/1.0 {
                mode sparse;
                version 2;
            }
            interface lo0.1 {
                mode sparse;
```

FIGURE 3.85

Ingress PE router configuration—PE1.

```
            version 2;
        }
    }
    mvpn {
        traceoptions {
            file MVPN size 1m world-readable;
            flag all;
        }
    }
}
}
}
```

FIGURE 3.85

(*Continued*)

A Group entry of "224.0.0.0/4" indicates all multicast groups and a source entry of "0.0.0.0/0" indicates any or all sources.

3.4.3.3.8 Validations at the Ingress PE Router—PE1

Check the MVPN routing table to ensure that Type 3 and Type 4 announcements have been originated and received for groups 238.1.1.1 and 239.1.1.1. We see two Type 4 route announcements from PE2 for groups 238.1.1.1 and 239.1.1.1, and one Type 4 announcement from PE3 for group 239.1.1.1, since PE3 does not have an interested receiver for the group 238.1.1.1.

The output in Figure 3.86 validates the same.

```
operator@PE1# run show route table FOO-MVPN.mvpn.0
FOO-MVPN.mvpn.0: 12 destinations, 15 routes (12 active, 0 holddown, 0 hidden)
+ = Active Route, - = Last Active, * = Both
1:100:1:7.0.0.1/240
                    *[MVPN/70] 02:00:57, metric2 1
                        Indirect
1:100:1:7.0.0.4/240
                    *[BGP/170] 00:07:50, localpref 100, from 7.0.0.4
                        AS path: I
                      > to 172.16.1.5 via ge-4/0/0.0
1:100:1:7.0.0.5/240
                    *[BGP/170] 00:07:50, localpref 100, from 7.0.0.5
                        AS path: I
                      > to 172.16.1.5 via ge-4/0/0.0, Push 299792
3:100:1:32:192.168.1.9:32:238.1.1.1:7.0.0.1/240
                    *[MVPN/70] 00:06:49, metric2 1
                        Indirect
3:100:1:32:192.168.1.9:32:239.1.1.1:7.0.0.1/240
                    *[MVPN/70] 00:06:54, metric2 1
                        Indirect
```

FIGURE 3.86

Checking the MVPN routing table.

```
4:3:100:1:32:192.168.1.9:32:238.1.1.1:7.0.0.1:7.0.0.4/240
                     *[BGP/170] 00:06:49, localpref 100, from 7.0.0.4
                        AS path: I
                        > to 172.16.1.5 via ge-4/0/0.0
4:3:100:1:32:192.168.1.9:32:239.1.1.1:7.0.0.1:7.0.0.4/240
                     *[BGP/170] 00:06:54, localpref 100, from 7.0.0.4
                        AS path: I
                        > to 172.16.1.5 via ge-4/0/0.0
4:3:100:1:32:192.168.1.9:32:239.1.1.1:7.0.0.1:7.0.0.5/240
                     *[BGP/170] 00:06:54, localpref 100, from 7.0.0.5
                        AS path: I
                        > to 172.16.1.5 via ge-4/0/0.0, Push 299792
5:100:1:32:192.168.1.9:32:238.1.1.1/240
                     *[PIM/105] 00:06:49
                        Multicast (IPv4)
5:100:1:32:192.168.1.9:32:239.1.1.1/240
                     *[PIM/105] 00:06:54
                        Multicast (IPv4)
7:100:1:100:32:192.168.1.9:32:238.1.1.1/240
                     *[PIM/105] 00:06:49
                        Multicast (IPv4)
                     [BGP/170] 00:06:49, localpref 100, from 7.0.0.4
                        AS path: I
                        > to 172.16.1.5 via ge-4/0/0.0
7:100:1:100:32:192.168.1.9:32:239.1.1.1/240
                     *[PIM/105] 00:06:54
                        Multicast (IPv4)
                     [BGP/170] 00:06:54, localpref 100, from 7.0.0.4
                        AS path: I
                        > to 172.16.1.5 via ge-4/0/0.0
                     [BGP/170] 00:06:54, localpref 100, from 7.0.0.5
                        AS path: I
                        > to 172.16.1.5 via ge-4/0/0.0, Push 299792
```

FIGURE 3.86

(*Continued*)

Some detailed outputs are seen in Figure 3.87.

```
operator@PE1# run show route table FOO-MVPN.mvpn.0 detail
FOO-MVPN.mvpn.0: 12 destinations, 15 routes (12 active, 0 holddown, 0 hidden)
1:100:1:7.0.0.1/240 (1 entry, 1 announced)
        *MVPN    Preference: 70
                 Next hop type: Indirect
                 Next-hop reference count: 5
                 Protocol next hop: 7.0.0.1
                 Indirect next hop: 0 -
                 State: <Active Int Ext>
                 Age: 2:04:39    Metric2: 1
                 Task: mvpn global task
                 Announcement bits (3): 0-PIM.FOO-MVPN 1-mvpn global task 2-BGP RT
Background
                 AS path: I
```

FIGURE 3.87

Checking the MVPN routing table.

```
1:100:1:7.0.0.4/240 (1 entry, 1 announced)
      *BGP     Preference: 170/-101
               Next hop type: Indirect
               Next-hop reference count: 10
               Source: 7.0.0.4
               Protocol next hop: 7.0.0.4
               Indirect next hop: 2 no-forward
               State: <Secondary Active Int Ext>
               Local AS:    100 Peer AS:    100
               Age: 11:32      Metric2: 1
               Task: BGP_100.7.0.0.4+57844
               Announcement bits (2): 0-PIM.FOO-MVPN 1-mvpn global task
               AS path: I
               Communities: target:100:1
               Import Accepted
               Localpref: 100
               Router ID: 7.0.0.4
               Primary Routing Table bgp.mvpn.0

1:100:1:7.0.0.5/240 (1 entry, 1 announced)
      *BGP     Preference: 170/-101
               Next hop type: Indirect
               Next-hop reference count: 6
               Source: 7.0.0.5
               Protocol next hop: 7.0.0.5
               Indirect next hop: 2 no-forward
               State: <Secondary Active Int Ext>
               Local AS:    100 Peer AS:    100
               Age: 11:32      Metric2: 1
               Task: BGP_100.7.0.0.5+61278
               Announcement bits (2): 0-PIM.FOO-MVPN 1-mvpn global task
               AS path: I
               Communities: target:100:1
               Import Accepted
               Localpref: 100
               Router ID: 7.0.0.5
               Primary Routing Table bgp.mvpn.0


3:100:1:32:192.168.1.9:32:238.1.1.1:7.0.0.1/240 (1 entry, 1 announced)
      *MVPN    Preference: 70
               Next hop type: Indirect
               Next-hop reference count: 5
               Protocol next hop: 7.0.0.1
               Indirect next hop: 0 -
               State: <Active Int Ext>
               Age: 10:31       Metric2: 1
               Task: mvpn global task
               Announcement bits (3): 0-PIM.FOO-MVPN 1-mvpn global task 2-BGP RT
Background
               AS path: I
```

FIGURE 3.87

(Continued)

```
3:100:1:32:192.168.1.9:32:239.1.1.1:7.0.0.1/240 (1 entry, 1 announced)
        *MVPN   Preference: 70
                Next hop type: Indirect
                Next-hop reference count: 5
                Protocol next hop: 7.0.0.1
                Indirect next hop: 0 -
                State: <Active Int Ext>
                Age: 10:36      Metric2: 1
                Task: mvpn global task
                Announcement bits (3): 0-PIM.FOO-MVPN 1-mvpn global task 2-BGP RT
Background
                AS path: I

4:3:100:1:32:192.168.1.9:32:238.1.1.1:7.0.0.1:7.0.0.4/240 (1 entry, 1 announced)
        *BGP    Preference: 170/-101
                Next hop type: Indirect
                Next-hop reference count: 10
                Source: 7.0.0.4
                Protocol next hop: 7.0.0.4
                Indirect next hop: 2 no-forward
                State: <Secondary Active Int Ext>
                Local AS:   100 Peer AS:    100
                Age: 10:31      Metric2: 1
                Task: BGP_100.7.0.0.4+57844
                Announcement bits (2): 0-PIM.FOO-MVPN 1-mvpn global task
                AS path: I
                Communities: target:7.0.0.1:0
                Import Accepted
                Localpref: 100
                Router ID: 7.0.0.4
                Primary Routing Table bgp.mvpn.0

4:3:100:1:32:192.168.1.9:32:239.1.1.1:7.0.0.1:7.0.0.4/240 (1 entry, 1 announced)
        *BGP    Preference: 170/-101
                Next hop type: Indirect
                Next-hop reference count: 10
                Source: 7.0.0.4
                Protocol next hop: 7.0.0.4
                Indirect next hop: 2 no-forward
                State: <Secondary Active Int Ext>
                Local AS:   100 Peer AS:    100
                Age: 10:36      Metric2: 1
                Task: BGP_100.7.0.0.4+57844
                Announcement bits (2): 0-PIM.FOO-MVPN 1-mvpn global task
                AS path: I
                Communities: target:7.0.0.1:0
                Import Accepted
                Localpref: 100
                Router ID: 7.0.0.4
                Primary Routing Table bgp.mvpn.0
```

FIGURE 3.87

(*Continued*)

```
4:3:100:1:32:192.168.1.9:32:239.1.1.1:7.0.0.1:7.0.0.5/240 (1 entry, 1 announced)
        *BGP    Preference: 170/-101
                Next hop type: Indirect
                Next-hop reference count: 6
                Source: 7.0.0.5
                Protocol next hop: 7.0.0.5
                Indirect next hop: 2 no-forward
                State: <Secondary Active Int Ext>
                Local AS:    100 Peer AS:    100
                Age: 10:36      Metric2: 1
                Task: BGP_100.7.0.0.5+61278
                Announcement bits (2): 0-PIM.FOO-MVPN 1-mvpn global task
                AS path: I
                Communities: target:7.0.0.1:0
                Import Accepted
                Localpref: 100
                Router ID: 7.0.0.5
                Primary Routing Table bgp.mvpn.0

5:100:1:32:192.168.1.9:32:238.1.1.1/240 (1 entry, 1 announced)
        *PIM    Preference: 105
                Next hop type: Multicast (IPv4)
                Next-hop reference count: 7
                State: <Active Int>
                Age: 10:31
                Task: PIM.FOO-MVPN
                Announcement bits (3): 0-PIM.FOO-MVPN 1-mvpn global task 2-BGP RT
Background
                AS path: I

5:100:1:32:192.168.1.9:32:239.1.1.1/240 (1 entry, 1 announced)
        *PIM    Preference: 105
                Next hop type: Multicast (IPv4)
                Next-hop reference count: 7
                State: <Active Int>
                Age: 10:36
                Task: PIM.FOO-MVPN

                Announcement bits (3): 0-PIM.FOO-MVPN 1-mvpn global task 2-BGP RT
Background
                AS path: I

7:100:1:100:32:192.168.1.9:32:238.1.1.1/240 (2 entries, 2 announced)
        *PIM    Preference: 105
                Next hop type: Multicast (IPv4)
                Next-hop reference count: 7
                State: <Active Int>
                Age: 10:31
                Task: PIM.FOO-MVPN
                Announcement bits (2): 0-PIM.FOO-MVPN 1-mvpn global task
                AS path: I
                Communities: no-advertise target:7.0.0.1:5
```

FIGURE 3.87

(*Continued*)

```
         BGP       Preference: 170/-101
                   Next hop type: Indirect
                   Next-hop reference count: 10
                   Source: 7.0.0.4
                   Protocol next hop: 7.0.0.4
                   Indirect next hop: 2 no-forward
                   State: <Secondary Int Ext>
                   Inactive reason: Route Preference
                   Local AS:    100 Peer AS:    100
                   Age: 10:31      Metric2: 1
                   Task: BGP_100.7.0.0.4+57844
                   Announcement bits (2): 0-PIM.FOO-MVPN 1-mvpn global task
                   AS path: I
                   Communities: target:7.0.0.1:5
                   Import Accepted
                   Localpref: 100
                   Router ID: 7.0.0.4
                   Primary Routing Table bgp.mvpn.0

7:100:1:100:32:192.168.1.9:32:239.1.1.1/240 (3 entries, 3 announced)
         *PIM      Preference: 105
                   Next hop type: Multicast (IPv4)
                   Next-hop reference count: 7
                   State: <Active Int>
                   Age: 10:36
                   Task: PIM.FOO-MVPN
                   Announcement bits (2): 0-PIM.FOO-MVPN 1-mvpn global task
                   AS path: I
                   Communities: no-advertise target:7.0.0.1:5
         BGP       Preference: 170/-101
                   Next hop type: Indirect
                   Next-hop reference count: 10
                   Source: 7.0.0.4
                   Protocol next hop: 7.0.0.4
                   Indirect next hop: 2 no-forward
                   State: <Secondary Int Ext>
                   Inactive reason: Route Preference
                   Local AS:    100 Peer AS:    100
                   Age: 10:36      Metric2: 1
                   Task: BGP_100.7.0.0.4+57844
                   Announcement bits (2): 0-PIM.FOO-MVPN 1-mvpn global task
                   AS path: I
                   Communities: target:7.0.0.1:5
                   Import Accepted
                   Localpref: 100
                   Router ID: 7.0.0.4
                   Primary Routing Table bgp.mvpn.0
```

FIGURE 3.87

(Continued)

```
BGP     Preference: 170/-101
        Next hop type: Indirect
        Next-hop reference count: 6
        Source: 7.0.0.5
        Protocol next hop: 7.0.0.5
        Indirect next hop: 2 no-forward
        State: <Secondary NotBest Int Ext>
        Inactive reason: Not Best in its group - Router ID
        Local AS:    100 Peer AS:    100
        Age: 10:36      Metric2: 1
        Task: BGP_100.7.0.0.5+61278
        Announcement bits (2): 0-PIM.FOO-MVPN 1-mvpn global task
        AS path: I
        Communities: target:7.0.0.1:5
        Import Accepted
        Localpref: 100
        Router ID: 7.0.0.5
        Primary Routing Table bgp.mvpn.0
```

FIGURE 3.87

(*Continued*)

Next, check the Multicast forwarding table seen in Figure 3.88.


```
operator@PE1# run show multicast route instance FOO-MVPN extensive
Family: INET
Group: 238.1.1.1
    Source: 192.168.1.9/32
    Upstream interface: ge-4/0/1.0
    Session description: Unknown
    Statistics: 854 kBps, 615 pps, 474525 packets
    Next-hop ID: 1048576
    Upstream protocol: MVPN
    Route state: Active
    Forwarding state: Forwarding
    Cache lifetime/timeout: forever
    Wrong incoming interface notifications: 0

Group: 239.1.1.1
    Source: 192.168.1.9/32
    Upstream interface: ge-4/0/1.0
    Session description: Administratively Scoped
    Statistics: 1211 kBps, 872 pps, 674573 packets
    Next-hop ID: 1048577
    Upstream protocol: MVPN
    Route state: Active
    Forwarding state: Forwarding
    Cache lifetime/timeout: forever
    Wrong incoming interface notifications: 0
```

FIGURE 3.88

Checking the Multicast forwarding table.

Finally, the MVPN instance as shown in Figure 3.89 is checked.

```
operator@PE1# run show mvpn instance
MVPN instance:
Legend for provider tunnel
I-P-tnl -- inclusive provider tunnel S-P-tnl -- selective provider tunnel
Legend for c-multicast routes properties (Pr)
DS -- derived from (*, c-g)          RM -- remote VPN route
Instance : FOO-MVPN
  MVPN Mode : SPT-ONLY
  Provider tunnel: I-P-tnl:invalid:
  Neighbor                       I-P-tnl
  7.0.0.4
  7.0.0.5
C-mcast IPv4 (S:G)           Ptnl                                      St
192.168.1.9/32:238.1.1.1/32  S-RSVP-TE P2MP:7.0.0.1, 47058,7.0.0.1    RM
192.168.1.9/32:239.1.1.1/32  S-RSVP-TE P2MP:7.0.0.1, 47057,7.0.0.1    RM
```

FIGURE 3.89

Checking the MVPN instance.

3.4.3.3.9 Validations at the Egress PE Router—PE2

The same set of steps is performed on PE2 and PE3. On PE2 we see two Type 3 and corresponding Type 4 routes, since PE2 has interested receivers for groups 238.1.1.1 and 239.1.1.1 (see Figure 3.90).

```
operator@PE2# run show route table FOO-MVPN.mvpn.0
FOO-MVPN.mvpn.0: 15 destinations, 17 routes (15 active, 1 holddown, 0 hidden)
+ = Active Route, - = Last Active, * = Both
1:100:1:7.0.0.1/240
                  *[BGP/170] 00:17:29, localpref 100, from 7.0.0.1
                     AS path: I
                   > to 172.16.1.6 via ge-4/0/3.0
1:100:1:7.0.0.4/240
                  *[MVPN/70] 1d 03:30:20, metric2 1
                     Indirect
1:100:1:7.0.0.5/240
                  *[BGP/170] 1d 03:30:07, localpref 100, from 7.0.0.5
                     AS path: I
                   > to 172.16.1.2 via ge-4/0/0.0
```

FIGURE 3.90

Checking the MVPN routing table.

```
3:100:1:32:192.168.1.9:32:238.1.1.1:7.0.0.1/240
                   *[BGP/170] 00:16:28, localpref 100, from 7.0.0.1
                      AS path: I
                    > to 172.16.1.6 via ge-4/0/3.0
3:100:1:32:192.168.1.9:32:239.1.1.1:7.0.0.1/240
                   *[BGP/170] 00:16:33, localpref 100, from 7.0.0.1
                      AS path: I
                    > to 172.16.1.6 via ge-4/0/3.0
4:3:100:1:32:192.168.1.9:32:238.1.1.1:7.0.0.1:7.0.0.4/240
                   *[MVPN/70] 00:16:28, metric2 1
                      Indirect
4:3:100:1:32:192.168.1.9:32:239.1.1.1:7.0.0.1:7.0.0.4/240
                   *[MVPN/70] 00:16:33, metric2 1
                      Indirect
5:100:1:32:192.168.1.9:32:238.1.1.1/240
                   *[BGP/170] 00:16:28, localpref 100, from 7.0.0.1
                      AS path: I
                    > to 172.16.1.6 via ge-4/0/3.0
5:100:1:32:192.168.1.9:32:239.1.1.1/240
                   *[BGP/170] 00:16:33, localpref 100, from 7.0.0.1
                      AS path: I
                    > to 172.16.1.6 via ge-4/0/3.0
6:100:1:100:32:7.0.0.1:32:224.2.127.254/240
                   *[PIM/105] 00:17:29
                      Multicast (IPv4)
6:100:1:100:32:7.0.0.1:32:233.1.1.1/240
                   *[PIM/105] 00:17:29
                      Multicast (IPv4)
6:100:1:100:32:7.0.0.1:32:238.1.1.1/240
                   *[PIM/105] 00:17:29
                      Multicast (IPv4)
6:100:1:100:32:7.0.0.1:32:239.1.1.1/240
                   *[PIM/105] 00:17:29
                      Multicast (IPv4)
7:100:1:100:32:192.168.1.9:32:238.1.1.1/240
                   *[MVPN/70] 00:16:28, metric2 1
                      Multicast (IPv4)
                    [PIM/105] 00:16:28
                      Multicast (IPv4)
7:100:1:100:32:192.168.1.9:32:239.1.1.1/240
                   *[MVPN/70] 00:16:33, metric2 1
                      Multicast (IPv4)
                    [PIM/105] 00:16:32
                      Multicast (IPv4)
```

FIGURE 3.90

(*Continued*)

Some detailed outputs are seen in Figure 3.91.

Now we check the Multicast forwarding table (Figure 3.92).

Next we check the MVPN instance information (Figure 3.93).

```
operator@PE2# run show route table FOO-MVPN.mvpn.0 detail
FOO-MVPN.mvpn.0: 15 destinations, 17 routes (15 active, 1 holddown, 0 hidden)
1:100:1:7.0.0.1/240 (1 entry, 1 announced)
        *BGP        Preference: 170/-101
                    Next hop type: Indirect
                    Next-hop reference count: 10
                    Source: 7.0.0.1
                    Protocol next hop: 7.0.0.1
                    Indirect next hop: 2 no-forward
                    State: <Secondary Active Int Ext>
                    Local AS:    100 Peer AS:    100
                    Age: 19:43     Metric2: 1
                    Task: BGP_100.7.0.0.1+179
                    Announcement bits (2): 0-PIM.FOO-MVPN 1-mvpn global task
                    AS path: I
                    Communities: target:100:1
                    Import Accepted
                    Localpref: 100
                    Router ID: 7.0.0.1
                    Primary Routing Table bgp.mvpn.0

1:100:1:7.0.0.4/240 (1 entry, 1 announced)
        *MVPN       Preference: 70
                    Next hop type: Indirect
                    Next-hop reference count: 5
                    Protocol next hop: 7.0.0.4
                    Indirect next hop: 0 -
                    State: <Active Int Ext>
                    Age: 1d 3:32:34          Metric2: 1
                    Task: mvpn global task
                    Announcement bits (3): 0-PIM.FOO-MVPN 1-mvpn global task 2-BGP RT
Background
                    AS path: I

1:100:1:7.0.0.5/240 (1 entry, 1 announced)
        *BGP        Preference: 170/-101
                    Next hop type: Indirect
                    Next-hop reference count: 2
                    Source: 7.0.0.5
                    Protocol next hop: 7.0.0.5
                    Indirect next hop: 2 no-forward
                    State: <Secondary Active Int Ext>
                    Local AS:    100 Peer AS:    100
                    Age: 1d 3:32:21          Metric2: 1
                    Task: BGP_100.7.0.0.5+179
                    Announcement bits (2): 0-PIM.FOO-MVPN 1-mvpn global task
                    AS path: I
                    Communities: target:100:1
                    Import Accepted
                    Localpref: 100
                    Router ID: 7.0.0.5
                    Primary Routing Table bgp.mvpn.0

3:100:1:32:192.168.1.9:32:238.1.1.1:7.0.0.1/240 (1 entry, 1 announced)
        *BGP        Preference: 170/-101
PMSI: Flags 0x1: Label[0:0:0]: RSVP-TE: Session_13[7.0.0.1:0:47058:7.0.0.1]
```

FIGURE 3.91

Checking the MVPN routing table—Detailed outputs.

```
                  Next hop type: Indirect
                  Next-hop reference count: 10
                  Source: 7.0.0.1
                  Protocol next hop: 7.0.0.1
                  Indirect next hop: 2 no-forward
                  State: <Secondary Active Int Ext>
                  Local AS:    100 Peer AS:    100
                  Age: 18:42      Metric2: 1
                  Task: BGP_100.7.0.0.1+179
                  Announcement bits (2): 0-PIM.FOO-MVPN 1-mvpn global task
                  AS path: I
                  Communities: target:100:1
                  Import Accepted
                  Localpref: 100
                  Router ID: 7.0.0.1
                  Primary Routing Table bgp.mvpn.0

3:100:1:32:192.168.1.9:32:239.1.1.1:7.0.0.1/240 (1 entry, 1 announced)
        *BGP     Preference: 170/-101
PMSI: Flags 0x1: Label[0:0:0]: RSVP-TE: Session_13[7.0.0.1:0:47057:7.0.0.1]
                  Next hop type: Indirect
                  Next-hop reference count: 10
                  Source: 7.0.0.1
                  Protocol next hop: 7.0.0.1
                  Indirect next hop: 2 no-forward
                  State: <Secondary Active Int Ext>
                  Local AS:    100 Peer AS:    100
                  Age: 18:47      Metric2: 1
                  Task: BGP_100.7.0.0.1+179
                  Announcement bits (2): 0-PIM.FOO-MVPN 1-mvpn global task
                  AS path: I
                  Communities: target:100:1
                  Import Accepted
                  Localpref: 100
                  Router ID: 7.0.0.1
                  Primary Routing Table bgp.mvpn.0

4:3:100:1:32:192.168.1.9:32:238.1.1.1:7.0.0.1:7.0.0.4/240 (1 entry, 1 announced)
        *MVPN    Preference: 70
                  Next hop type: Indirect
                  Next-hop reference count: 5
                  Protocol next hop: 7.0.0.4
                  Indirect next hop: 0 -
                  State: <Active Int Ext>
                  Age: 18:42      Metric2: 1
                  Task: mvpn global task
                  Announcement bits (3): 0-PIM.FOO-MVPN 1-mvpn global task 2-BGP RT
Background
                  AS path: I
                  Communities: target:7.0.0.1:0

4:3:100:1:32:192.168.1.9:32:239.1.1.1:7.0.0.1:7.0.0.4/240 (1 entry, 1 announced)
        *MVPN    Preference: 70
                  Next hop type: Indirect
                  Next-hop reference count: 5
```

FIGURE 3.91

(Continued)

```
                    Protocol next hop: 7.0.0.4
                    Indirect next hop: 0 -
                    State: <Active Int Ext>
                    Age: 18:47        Metric2: 1
                    Task: mvpn global task
                    Announcement bits (3): 0-PIM.FOO-MVPN 1-mvpn global task 2-BGP RT
Background
                    AS path: I
                    Communities: target:7.0.0.1:0

5:100:1:32:192.168.1.9:32:238.1.1.1/240 (1 entry, 1 announced)
        *BGP        Preference: 170/-101
                    Next hop type: Indirect
                    Next-hop reference count: 10
                    Source: 7.0.0.1
                    Protocol next hop: 7.0.0.1
                    Indirect next hop: 2 no-forward
                    State: <Secondary Active Int Ext>
                    Local AS:    100 Peer AS:    100
                    Age: 18:42        Metric2: 1
                    Task: BGP_100.7.0.0.1+179
                    Announcement bits (2): 0-PIM.FOO-MVPN 1-mvpn global task
                    AS path: I
                    Communities: target:100:1
                    Import Accepted
                    Localpref: 100
                    Router ID: 7.0.0.1
                    Primary Routing Table bgp.mvpn.0

5:100:1:32:192.168.1.9:32:239.1.1.1/240 (1 entry, 1 announced)
        *BGP        Preference: 170/-101
                    Next hop type: Indirect
                    Next-hop reference count: 10
                    Source: 7.0.0.1
                    Protocol next hop: 7.0.0.1
                    Indirect next hop: 2 no-forward
                    State: <Secondary Active Int Ext>
                    Local AS:    100 Peer AS:    100
                    Age: 18:47        Metric2: 1
                    Task: BGP_100.7.0.0.1+179
                    Announcement bits (2): 0-PIM.FOO-MVPN 1-mvpn global task
                    AS path: I
                    Communities: target:100:1
                    Import Accepted
                    Localpref: 100
                    Router ID: 7.0.0.1
                    Primary Routing Table bgp.mvpn.0

6:100:1:100:32:7.0.0.1:32:224.2.127.254/240 (1 entry, 1 announced)
        *PIM        Preference: 105
                    Next hop type: Multicast (IPv4), Next hop index: 1048576
                    Next-hop reference count: 42
                    State: <Active Int>
                    Age: 19:43
                    Task: PIM.FOO-MVPN
```

FIGURE 3.91

(*Continued*)

```
                    Announcement bits (2): 0-PIM.FOO-MVPN 1-mvpn global task
                    AS path: I
                    Communities: no-advertise target:7.0.0.1:5

6:100:1:100:32:7.0.0.1:32:233.1.1.1/240 (1 entry, 1 announced)
        *PIM        Preference: 105
                    Next hop type: Multicast (IPv4), Next hop index: 1048576
                    Next-hop reference count: 42
                    State: <Active Int>
                    Age: 19:43
                    Task: PIM.FOO-MVPN
                    Announcement bits (2): 0-PIM.FOO-MVPN 1-mvpn global task
                    AS path: I
                    Communities: no-advertise target:7.0.0.1:5

6:100:1:100:32:7.0.0.1:32:238.1.1.1/240 (1 entry, 1 announced)
        *PIM        Preference: 105
                    Next hop type: Multicast (IPv4), Next hop index: 1048576
                    Next-hop reference count: 42
                    State: <Active Int>
                    Age: 19:43
                    Task: PIM.FOO-MVPN
                    Announcement bits (2): 0-PIM.FOO-MVPN 1-mvpn global task
                    AS path: I
                    Communities: no-advertise target:7.0.0.1:5

6:100:1:100:32:7.0.0.1:32:239.1.1.1/240 (1 entry, 1 announced)
        *PIM        Preference: 105
                    Next hop type: Multicast (IPv4), Next hop index: 1048576
                    Next-hop reference count: 42
                    State: <Active Int>
                    Age: 19:43
                    Task: PIM.FOO-MVPN
                    Announcement bits (2): 0-PIM.FOO-MVPN 1-mvpn global task
                    AS path: I
                    Communities: no-advertise target:7.0.0.1:5

7:100:1:100:32:192.168.1.9:32:238.1.1.1/240 (2 entries, 2 announced)
        *MVPN       Preference: 70
                    Next hop type: Multicast (IPv4), Next hop index: 1048576
                    Next-hop reference count: 42
                    State: <Active Int Ext>
                    Age: 18:42        Metric2: 1
                    Task: mvpn global task
                    Announcement bits (3): 0-PIM.FOO-MVPN 1-mvpn global task 2-BGP RT
Background
                    AS path: I
                    Communities: target:7.0.0.1:5
        PIM         Preference: 105
                    Next hop type: Multicast (IPv4), Next hop index: 1048576
                    Next-hop reference count: 42
                    State: <Int>
                    Inactive reason: Route Preference
                    Age: 18:42
                    Task: PIM.FOO-MVPN
```

FIGURE 3.91

(Continued)

```
            Announcement bits (2): 0-PIM.FOO-MVPN 1-mvpn global task
            AS path: I
            Communities: target:7.0.0.1:5

7:100:1:100:32:192.168.1.9:32:239.1.1.1/240 (2 entries, 2 announced)
        *MVPN    Preference: 70
                 Next hop type: Multicast (IPv4), Next hop index: 1048576
                 Next-hop reference count: 42
                 State: <Active Int Ext>
                 Age: 18:47      Metric2: 1
                 Task: mvpn global task
                 Announcement bits (3): 0-PIM.FOO-MVPN 1-mvpn global task 2-BGP RT
Background
                 AS path: I
                 Communities: target:7.0.0.1:5
        PIM      Preference: 105
                 Next hop type: Multicast (IPv4), Next hop index: 1048576
                 Next-hop reference count: 42
                 State: <Int>
                 Inactive reason: Route Preference
                 Age: 18:46
                 Task: PIM.FOO-MVPN
                 Announcement bits (2): 0-PIM.FOO-MVPN 1-mvpn global task
                 AS path: I
                 Communities: target:7.0.0.1:5
```

FIGURE 3.91

(Continued)

```
operator@PE2# run show multicast route instance FOO-MVPN extensive
Family: INET
Group: 238.1.1.1
    Source: 192.168.1.9/32
    Upstream interface: lsi.21
    Downstream interface list:
        ge-4/0/2.100
    Session description: Unknown
    Statistics: 898 kBps, 1068 pps, 1313590 packets
    Next-hop ID: 1048576
    Upstream protocol: MVPN
    Route state: Active
    Forwarding state: Forwarding
    Cache lifetime/timeout: forever
    Wrong incoming interface notifications: 0

Group: 239.1.1.1
    Source: 192.168.1.9/32
    Upstream interface: lsi.21
    Downstream interface list:
        ge-4/0/2.100
    Session description: Administratively Scoped
    Statistics: 1223 kBps, 1454 pps, 1854674 packets
    Next-hop ID: 1048576
    Upstream protocol: MVPN
    Route state: Active
    Forwarding state: Forwarding
    Cache lifetime/timeout: forever
    Wrong incoming interface notifications: 0
```

FIGURE 3.92

Checking the MVPN forwarding table.

```
operator@PE2# run show mvpn instance
MVPN instance:
Legend for provider tunnel
I-P-tnl -- inclusive provider tunnel S-P-tnl -- selective provider tunnel
Legend for c-multicast routes properties (Pr)
DS -- derived from (*, c-g)          RM -- remote VPN route
Instance : FOO-MVPN
  MVPN Mode : SPT-ONLY
  Provider tunnel: I-P-tnl:invalid:
  Neighbor                          I-P-tnl
  7.0.0.1
  7.0.0.5
C-mcast IPv4 (S:G)           Ptnl                                    St
192.168.1.9/32:238.1.1.1/32  S-RSVP-TE P2MP:7.0.0.1, 47058,7.0.0.1 DS
192.168.1.9/32:239.1.1.1/32  S-RSVP-TE P2MP:7.0.0.1, 47057,7.0.0.1 DS
```

FIGURE 3.93

Checking the MVPN forwarding table.

3.4.3.3.10 Validations at the Egress PE Router—PE3

Now we use the same set of procedures for validation on PE3 as seen in Figures 3.94 to 3.97.

```
operator@PE3# run show route table FOO-MVPN.mvpn.0
FOO-MVPN.mvpn.0: 11 destinations, 12 routes (11 active, 0 holddown, 0 hidden)
+ = Active Route, - = Last Active, * = Both

1:100:1:7.0.0.1/240
                  *[BGP/170] 00:25:04, localpref 100, from 7.0.0.1
                    AS path: I
                  > to 172.16.1.1 via ge-1/0/1.0, Push 299856
1:100:1:7.0.0.4/240
                  *[BGP/170] 1d 03:37:55, localpref 100, from 7.0.0.4
                    AS path: I
                  > to 172.16.1.1 via ge-1/0/1.0
1:100:1:7.0.0.5/240
                  *[MVPN/70] 1d 03:37:42, metric2 1
                    Indirect
3:100:1:32:192.168.1.9:32:238.1.1.1:7.0.0.1/240
                  *[BGP/170] 00:24:03, localpref 100, from 7.0.0.1
                    AS path: I
                  > to 172.16.1.1 via ge-1/0/1.0, Push 299856
3:100:1:32:192.168.1.9:32:239.1.1.1:7.0.0.1/240
                  *[BGP/170] 00:24:08, localpref 100, from 7.0.0.1
                    AS path: I
                  > to 172.16.1.1 via ge-1/0/1.0, Push 299856
4:3:100:1:32:192.168.1.9:32:239.1.1.1:7.0.0.1:7.0.0.5/240
                  *[MVPN/70] 00:24:08, metric2 1
                    Indirect
```

FIGURE 3.94

Checking the MVPN routing table.

```
5:100:1:32:192.168.1.9:32:238.1.1.1/240
                      *[BGP/170] 00:24:03, localpref 100, from 7.0.0.1
                        AS path: I
                      > to 172.16.1.1 via ge-1/0/1.0, Push 299856
5:100:1:32:192.168.1.9:32:239.1.1.1/240
                      *[BGP/170] 00:24:08, localpref 100, from 7.0.0.1
                        AS path: I
                      > to 172.16.1.1 via ge-1/0/1.0, Push 299856
6:100:1:100:32:7.0.0.1:32:224.2.127.254/240
                      *[PIM/105] 00:25:04
                        Multicast (IPv4)
6:100:1:100:32:7.0.0.1:32:239.1.1.1/240
                      *[PIM/105] 00:25:04
                        Multicast (IPv4)
7:100:1:100:32:192.168.1.9:32:239.1.1.1/240
                      *[MVPN/70] 00:24:08, metric2 1
                        Multicast (IPv4)
                      [PIM/105] 00:24:07
                        Multicast (IPv4)
```

FIGURE 3.94

(Continued)

```
operator@PE3# run show route table FOO-MVPN.mvpn.0 detail
FOO-MVPN.mvpn.0: 11 destinations, 12 routes (11 active, 0 holddown, 0 hidden)
1:100:1:7.0.0.1/240 (1 entry, 1 announced)
        *BGP    Preference: 170/-101
                Next hop type: Indirect
                Next-hop reference count: 10
                Source: 7.0.0.1
                Protocol next hop: 7.0.0.1
                Indirect next hop: 2 no-forward
                State: <Secondary Active Int Ext>
                Local AS:    100 Peer AS:    100
                Age: 26:32      Metric2: 1
                Task: BGP_100.7.0.0.1+179
                Announcement bits (2): 0-PIM.FOO-MVPN 1-mvpn global task
                AS path: I
                Communities: target:100:1
                Import Accepted
                Localpref: 100
                Router ID: 7.0.0.1
                Primary Routing Table bgp.mvpn.0

1:100:1:7.0.0.4/240 (1 entry, 1 announced)
        *BGP    Preference: 170/-101
                Next hop type: Indirect
                Next-hop reference count: 2
                Source: 7.0.0.4
                Protocol next hop: 7.0.0.4
                Indirect next hop: 2 no-forward
                State: <Secondary Active Int Ext>
```

FIGURE 3.95

Checking the MVPN routing table—Detailed outputs.

```
                    Local AS:    100 Peer AS:    100
                    Age: 1d 3:39:23        Metric2: 1
                    Task: BGP_100.7.0.0.4+63093
                    Announcement bits (2): 0-PIM.FOO-MVPN 1-mvpn global task
                    AS path: I
                    Communities: target:100:1
                    Import Accepted
                    Localpref: 100
                    Router ID: 7.0.0.4
                    Primary Routing Table bgp.mvpn.0

1:100:1:7.0.0.5/240 (1 entry, 1 announced)
        *MVPN    Preference: 70
                    Next hop type: Indirect
                    Next-hop reference count: 4
                    Protocol next hop: 7.0.0.5
                    Indirect next hop: 0 -
                    State: <Active Int Ext>
                    Age: 1d 3:39:10        Metric2: 1
                    Task: mvpn global task
                    Announcement bits (3): 0-PIM.FOO-MVPN 1-mvpn global task 2-BGP RT
Background
                    AS path: I

3:100:1:32:192.168.1.9:32:238.1.1.1:7.0.0.1/240 (1 entry, 1 announced)
        *BGP     Preference: 170/-101
PMSI: Flags 0x1: Label[0:0:0]: RSVP-TE: Session_13[7.0.0.1:0:47058:7.0.0.1]
                    Next hop type: Indirect
                    Next-hop reference count: 10
                    Source: 7.0.0.1
                    Protocol next hop: 7.0.0.1
                    Indirect next hop: 2 no-forward
                    State: <Secondary Active Int Ext>
                    Local AS:    100 Peer AS:    100
                    Age: 25:31    Metric2: 1
                    Task: BGP_100.7.0.0.1+179
                    Announcement bits (2): 0-PIM.FOO-MVPN 1-mvpn global task
                    AS path: I
                    Communities: target:100:1
                    Import Accepted
                    Localpref: 100
                    Router ID: 7.0.0.1
                    Primary Routing Table bgp.mvpn.0

3:100:1:32:192.168.1.9:32:239.1.1.1:7.0.0.1/240 (1 entry, 1 announced)
        *BGP     Preference: 170/-101
PMSI: Flags 0x1: Label[0:0:0]: RSVP-TE: Session_13[7.0.0.1:0:47057:7.0.0.1]
                    Next hop type: Indirect
                    Next-hop reference count: 10
                    Source: 7.0.0.1
                    Protocol next hop: 7.0.0.1
                    Indirect next hop: 2 no-forward
                    State: <Secondary Active Int Ext>
                    Local AS:    100 Peer AS:    100
```

FIGURE 3.95

(Continued)

```
              Age: 25:36      Metric2: 1
              Task: BGP_100.7.0.0.1+179
              Announcement bits (2): 0-PIM.FOO-MVPN 1-mvpn global task
              AS path: I
              Communities: target:100:1
              Import Accepted
              Localpref: 100
              Router ID: 7.0.0.1
              Primary Routing Table bgp.mvpn.0

4:3:100:1:32:192.168.1.9:32:239.1.1.1:7.0.0.1:7.0.0.5/240 (1 entry, 1 announced)
         *MVPN     Preference: 70
              Next hop type: Indirect
              Next-hop reference count: 4
              Protocol next hop: 7.0.0.5
              Indirect next hop: 0 -
              State: <Active Int Ext>
              Age: 25:36      Metric2: 1
              Task: mvpn global task
              Announcement bits (3): 0-PIM.FOO-MVPN 1-mvpn global task 2-BGP RT
Background
              AS path: I
              Communities: target:7.0.0.1:0

5:100:1:32:192.168.1.9:32:238.1.1.1/240 (1 entry, 1 announced)
         *BGP      Preference: 170/-101
              Next hop type: Indirect
              Next-hop reference count: 10
              Source: 7.0.0.1
              Protocol next hop: 7.0.0.1
              Indirect next hop: 2 no-forward
              State: <Secondary Active Int Ext>
              Local AS:   100 Peer AS:   100
              Age: 25:31      Metric2: 1
              Task: BGP_100.7.0.0.1+179
              Announcement bits (2): 0-PIM.FOO-MVPN 1-mvpn global task
              AS path: I
              Communities: target:100:1
              Import Accepted
              Localpref: 100
              Router ID: 7.0.0.1
              Primary Routing Table bgp.mvpn.0

5:100:1:32:192.168.1.9:32:239.1.1.1/240 (1 entry, 1 announced)
         *BGP      Preference: 170/-101
              Next hop type: Indirect
              Next-hop reference count: 10
              Source: 7.0.0.1
              Protocol next hop: 7.0.0.1
              Indirect next hop: 2 no-forward
              State: <Secondary Active Int Ext>
              Local AS:   100 Peer AS:   100
              Age: 25:36      Metric2: 1
              Task: BGP_100.7.0.0.1+179
```

FIGURE 3.95

(Continued)

```
                    Announcement bits (2): 0-PIM.FOO-MVPN 1-mvpn global task
                    AS path: I
                    Communities: target:100:1
                    Import Accepted
                    Localpref: 100
                    Router ID: 7.0.0.1
                    Primary Routing Table bgp.mvpn.0

6:100:1:100:32:7.0.0.1:32:224.2.127.254/240 (1 entry, 1 announced)
        *PIM     Preference: 105
                    Next hop type: Multicast (IPv4), Next hop index: 1048577
                    Next-hop reference count: 21
                    State: <Active Int>
                    Age: 26:32
                    Task: PIM.FOO-MVPN
                    Announcement bits (2): 0-PIM.FOO-MVPN 1-mvpn global task
                    AS path: I
                    Communities: no-advertise target:7.0.0.1:5

6:100:1:100:32:7.0.0.1:32:239.1.1.1/240 (1 entry, 1 announced)
        *PIM     Preference: 105
                    Next hop type: Multicast (IPv4), Next hop index: 1048577
                    Next-hop reference count: 21
                    State: <Active Int>
                    Age: 26:32
                    Task: PIM.FOO-MVPN
                    Announcement bits (2): 0-PIM.FOO-MVPN 1-mvpn global task
                    AS path: I
                    Communities: no-advertise target:7.0.0.1:5

7:100:1:100:32:192.168.1.9:32:239.1.1.1/240 (2 entries, 2 announced)
        *MVPN    Preference: 70
                    Next hop type: Multicast (IPv4), Next hop index: 1048577
                    Next-hop reference count: 21
                    State: <Active Int Ext>
                    Age: 25:36       Metric2: 1
                    Task: mvpn global task
                    Announcement bits (3): 0-PIM.FOO-MVPN 1-mvpn global task 2-BGP RT
Background
                    AS path: I
                    Communities: target:7.0.0.1:5
        PIM      Preference: 105
                    Next hop type: Multicast (IPv4), Next hop index: 1048577
                    Next-hop reference count: 21
                    State: <Int>
                    Inactive reason: Route Preference
                    Age: 25:35
                    Task: PIM.FOO-MVPN
                    Announcement bits (2): 0-PIM.FOO-MVPN 1-mvpn global task
                    AS path: I
                    Communities: target:7.0.0.1:5
```

FIGURE 3.95

(*Continued*)

```
operator@PE3# run show multicast route instance FOO-MVPN extensive
Family: INET
Group: 239.1.1.1
    Source: 192.168.1.9/32
    Upstream interface: lsi.1
    Downstream interface list:
        ge-1/0/2.0
    Session description: Administratively Scoped
    Statistics: 1224 kBps, 1455 pps, 2359320 packets
    Next-hop ID: 1048577
    Upstream protocol: MVPN
    Route state: Active
    Forwarding state: Forwarding
    Cache lifetime/timeout: forever
    Wrong incoming interface notifications: 0
```

FIGURE 3.96

Checking the MVPN forwarding table.

```
operator@PE3# run show mvpn instance
MVPN instance:
Legend for provider tunnel
I-P-tnl -- inclusive provider tunnel S-P-tnl -- selective provider tunnel

Legend for c-multicast routes properties (Pr)
DS -- derived from (*, c-g)         RM -- remote VPN route
Instance : FOO-MVPN
  MVPN Mode : SPT-ONLY
  Provider tunnel: I-P-tnl:invalid:
  Neighbor                          I-P-tnl
  7.0.0.1
  7.0.0.4
C-mcast IPv4 (S:G)          Ptnl                               St
192.168.1.9/32:239.1.1.1/32 S-RSVP-TE P2MP:7.0.0.1, 47057,7.0.0.1 DS
```

FIGURE 3.97

Checking the MVPN forwarding table.

3.4.4 MLDP Provider Tunnels

The details for using MLDP (Multicast LDP) as Provider Tunnels are defined in "draft-minei-mpls-ldp-p2mp.txt." In this section we will discuss the setup and signaling of MLDP P2MP LSPs. From a functional standpoint, MLDP LSPs can be used to signal both I-PMSI and S-PMSI tunnels. The only difference between MLDP and RSVP-TE is that the former cannot provide any TE-specific features such as bandwidth guarantees, built-in Link Protection, and user-defined paths based on constraints.

The setup of I-PMSI or S-PMSI tunnels is similar to the process defined in Section 3.4.3 since the attributes are attached within the BGP MVPN routes. Hence there is no additional process involved.

An MLDP P2MP LSP allows traffic from a single root (or ingress) node to be delivered to a number of leaf (or egress) nodes. Similar to RSVP-TE, only a single copy of the packet will be sent on any link traversed by the Multi Point (MP) LSP. This is accomplished without the use of a multicast protocol in the network. There can be several MP LSPs rooted at a given ingress node, each with its own identifier. The leaf nodes (Egress PEs) of the MP LSP come to know about the root node (Ingress PE) and identifier of the MP LSP to which they belong via the BGP control plane and routing announcements.

While using RSVP-TE we noticed that the Ingress PE initiates the P2MP LSP using RSVP PATH messages, which Egress PE routers respond to with appropriate Label information. With MLDP P2MP LSPs, the leaf nodes initiate P2MP LSP setup and teardown. For instance, if an Egress PE router receives a BGP Type 1 route from an Ingress PE router with an I-PMSI attribute, the Leaf initiates the setup of the P2MP LSP and also installs a forwarding state to deliver the traffic received on a P2MP LSP to wherever it needs to go. Transit nodes install the MPLS forwarding state and propagate the P2MP LSP setup (and teardown) toward the root, and the root node installs the forwarding state to map traffic into the P2MP LSP. For the setup of a P2MP LSP with LDP, we define one new protocol entity, the P2MP FEC Element, to be used in the FEC TLV. The description of the P2MP FEC Element is seen in Figure 3.98.

Parameters	Description
Tree Type	P2MP, MP2MP Up, MP2MP Down
Address Family	Root node address format (IPv4 =1 or IPv6 = 2)
Address Length	Number of octets in root address (IPv4 = 4, IPv6 = 16)
Root Node Address	Host address of MP LSP root (within MPLS core)
Opaque Value	One or more TLVs uniquely identifying MP LSP within the context of the root

FIGURE 3.98

From the context of NG-MVPNs, the LDP Opaque Value Element is not used for any applications. However, they are used in certain vendor (Non-Next-Generation Multicast VPN) mvpn implementations that use MLDP as the forwarding plane as well. This is covered in Chapter 7.

Now we can look at the setup of MLDP P2MP LSPs. As mentioned a bit earlier, an Egress PE knows the next hop for the Ingress PE connected to the multicast source, based on the BGP announcements. To receive the LSPs it needs to tell the upstream router what label it needs to use for this multicast stream. To advertise the label it will send a Label mapping to its upstream router for this multicast source. The label mapping will contain the label to be used. Since the upstream router does not need to have any knowledge of the source, it only contains an FEC to identify the P2MP tree. If the upstream router does not have any FEC state, it will create it and install the assigned downstream outgoing label. If the FEC state was created and this router is not the LSP ingress of the P2MP tree, it needs to forward a label mapping upstream. This operation continues until we reach the LSP ingress router. This process is illustrated in Figure 3.99.

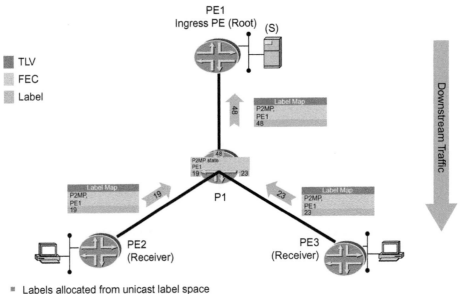

- Labels allocated from unicast label space
- Downstream on demand allocation method used

FIGURE 3.99

The forwarding process from the Ingress PE router is illustrated in Figure 3.100.

3.4.4.1 Configurations

In this section we look at the I-PMSI and S-PMSI configurations needed for MLDP as the forwarding plane. The details on control plane specific outputs remain the same as detailed in Section 3.4.3 since the same BGP control plane infrastructure is used.

The only configuration needed for building an I-PMSI MLDP Tunnel is the keyword "ldp-p2mp" (see Figure 3.101).

Next we look at the S-PMSI configuration using MLDP (see Figure 3.102). In this configuration an I-PMSI tunnel is defined for all groups as well as an S-PMSI tunnel for the C-MCAST Source and Group pair (238.1.1.1, 192.168.1.9). All possible options, such as the use of wild cards, as defined in Section 3.4.3 can be used with MLDP. An S-PMSI only setup may also be used. This is possible, since the BGP control plane is common for all of the provider tunnel types.

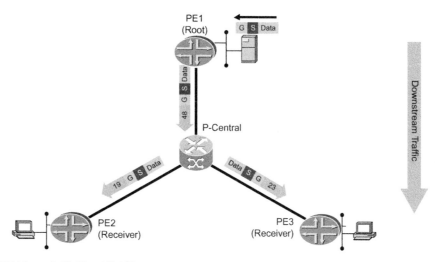

- PE-1 forwards (S, G) on MP-LSP
- Labels are swapped at each hop
  {48} → {19} and {23} at branching point

FIGURE 3.100

```
routing-instances {
FOO-MVPN {
    instance-type vrf;
    interface ge-4/0/1.0;
    interface lo0.1;
    route-distinguisher 100:1;
    provider-tunnel {
        ldp-p2mp;           ----------→ P2MP I-PMSI Tunnel
    }
    vrf-target target:100:1;
    vrf-table-label;
    protocols {
        bgp {
            family inet {
                unicast;
            }
            group peer {
                type external;
                peer-as 65005;
                neighbor 192.168.1.9;
                neighbor 192.168.1.17 {
                    peer-as 65010;
                }
            }
        }
    }
```

FIGURE 3.101

I-PMSI configuration using MLDP Provider Tunnels.

```
        pim {
            rp {
                local {
                    address 7.0.0.1;
                }
            }
            interface ge-4/0/1.0 {
                mode sparse;          →
                version 2;
            }
            interface lo0.1 {
                mode sparse;
                version 2;
            }
        }
        mvpn;
    }
}
```

FIGURE 3.101

(Continued)

```
Routing-instances {
FOO-MVPN {
    instance-type vrf;
    interface ge-4/0/1.0;
    interface lo0.1;
    route-distinguisher 100:1;
    provider-tunnel {
      ldp-p2mp; ------------→ I-PMSI Configuration
        selective { ----------→ S-PMSI Configuration
            group 238.1.1.1/32 {
                source 192.168.1.9/32 {
                    ldp-p2mp;

                }
            }
        }
    }
    vrf-target target:100:1;
    vrf-table-label;
    protocols {
        bgp {
            family inet {
                unicast;
            }
            group peer {
                type external;
                peer-as 65005;
                neighbor 192.168.1.9;
                neighbor 192.168.1.17 {
                    peer-as 65010;
                }
            }
        }
    }
```

FIGURE 3.102

I-PMSI and S-PMSI configuration.

```
        pim {
            rp {
                local {
                    address 7.0.0.1;
                }
            }
            interface ge-4/0/1.0 {
                mode sparse; →
                version 2;    →
            }
            interface lo0.1 {
                mode sparse;
                version 2;
            }
        }
        mvpn;
    }
}
```

FIGURE 3.102

(*Continued*)

Next an MVPN P-tunnel-specific output, similar to the details seen in the RSVP-TE sections, is reviewed (Figure 3.103).

```
operator@PE1> show mvpn instance extensive
MVPN instance:
Legend for provider tunnel
I-P-tnl -- inclusive provider tunnel S-P-tnl -- selective provider tunnel
Legend for c-multicast routes properties (Pr)
DS -- derived from (*, c-g)          RM -- remote VPN route
Instance: FOO-MVPN
  Provider tunnel: I-P-tnl:LDP P2MP:7.0.0.1, lsp-id 1
  Neighbor                          I-P-tnl
  7.0.0.4
  7.0.0.5
  C-mcast IPv4 (S:G)         Ptnl                        St
  192.168.1.8/32:238.2.2.2/32    LDP P2MP:7.0.0.1, lsp-id 1    RM
```

FIGURE 3.103

Checking the MVPN instance.

3.4.5 PIM-SSM Provider Tunnels

In this section, we look at a network setup using PIM-SSM-based Provider Tunnels as the Data plane along with the BGP control plane. The following setup (Figure 3.104) will be used to demonstrate the functionality.

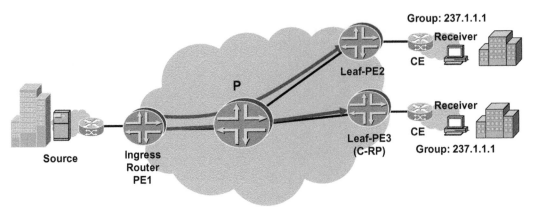

- The router "P" does not indicate a single Provider router, and indicates a Carrier Provider core that may contain many devices. A single device is just given ONLY for illustrative reasons.

FIGURE 3.104

3.4.5.1 Configurations

In the configuration, the Provider Tunnel is now configured for PIM Source Specific Multicast with a group address "232.1.1.1." This group address is the PIM Group address used in the Provider network (remember the P-Group address in Draft-Rosen Multicast VPNs) since we are now using GRE-based SSM Tunnels to create the data plane infrastructure. To enable a PIM-based infrastructure within the core, PIM has been enabled on the respective interfaces. However, there is no RP configuration within the context of PIM in the master instance because we are using SSM and not ASM or Spare Mode (see Figure 3.105).

```
protocols {
rsvp {
    interface ge-1/0/1.0;
}
mpls {
    interface ge-1/0/1.0;
    interface fe-1/1/0.0;
}
bgp {
    group PE {
        type internal;
        local-address 7.0.0.5;
        family inet-vpn {
            unicast;
        }
```

FIGURE 3.105

Ingress PE router configuration—PE1.

```
        family inet-mvpn {
            signaling;
        }
        neighbor 7.0.0.4 {
            peer-as 100;
        }
        neighbor 7.0.0.1 {
            peer-as 100;
        }
    }
}
ospf {
    area 0.0.0.0 {
        interface ge-1/0/1.0 {
            interface-type p2p;
        }
        interface lo0.0 {
            passive;
        }
        interface fe-1/1/0.0;
    }
}
ldp {
    interface ge-1/0/1.0;
    interface fe-1/1/0.0;
}
pim {
    interface all {
        version 2;
    }
}
routing-instances {
MVPN-FOO {
instance-type vrf;
interface ge-1/0/2.0;
interface lo0.1;
route-distinguisher 100:1;
provider-tunnel {
    pim-ssm {
        group-address 232.1.1.1;
    }
}
vrf-target target:100:1;
vrf-table-label;
protocols {
    bgp {
        family inet {
            unicast;
        }
        group peer {
            type external;
            peer-as 65004;
            neighbor 192.168.1.5;
        }
    }
```

FIGURE 3.105

(*Continued*)

```
        }
    pim {
        rp {
            static {
                address 7.0.0.1;
            }
        }
        interface ge-1/0/2.0 {
            mode sparse-dense;
            version 2;
        }
        interface lo0.1 {
            mode sparse-dense;
            version 2;
        }
    }
    mvpn;
        }
    }
}
```

FIGURE 3.105

(Continued)

Now we review the Egress PE router configurations (Figures 3.106 and 3.107). Only the relevant portions of the configuration are displayed for simplicity. No Provider Tunnels are configured because the egress PE routers only host receiver sites.

```
routing-instances {
MVPN-FOO {
instance-type vrf;
interface ge-4/0/2.100;
interface lo0.1;
route-distinguisher 100:1;
vrf-target target:100:1;
vrf-table-label;
protocols {
    bgp {
        family inet {
            unicast;
        }
        group peer {
            type external;
            peer-as 65003;
            neighbor 192.168.1.1;
        }
    }
    pim {
        rp {
            static {
                address 7.0.0.1;
            }
```

FIGURE 3.106

Egress PE router configuration—PE2.

```
        }
        interface ge-4/0/2.100 {
            mode sparse-dense;
            version 2;
        }
        interface lo0.1 {
            mode sparse-dense;
            version 2;
        }
    }
    mvpn;
  }
 }
}
protocols {
 pim {
  interface all {
    version 2;
  }
 }
}
```

FIGURE 3.106

(*Continued*)

```
routing-instances {
MVPN-FOO {
instance-type vrf;
interface ge-4/0/2.100;
interface lo0.1;
route-distinguisher 100:1;
vrf-target target:100:1;
vrf-table-label;
protocols {
    bgp {
        family inet {
            unicast;
        }
        group peer {
            type external;
            peer-as 65003;
            neighbor 192.168.1.1;
        }
```

FIGURE 3.107

Egress PE router configuration—PE3.

```
        }
    pim {
        rp {
            static {
                address 7.0.0.1;
            }
        }
        interface ge-4/0/2.100 {
            mode sparse-dense;
            version 2;
        }
        interface lo0.1 {
            mode sparse-dense;
            version 2;
        }
    }
    mvpn;
  }
 }
}
protocols {
 pim {
  interface all {
    version 2;
  }
 }
}
```

FIGURE 3.107

(Continued)

3.4.5.1.1 Validation of the Control Plane Prior to Traffic Generation

We start off by validating the control plane information on all of the routers prior to generating multi-cast traffic flows (Figures 3.108–3.110).

```
operator@PE1# run show route table MVPN-FOO.mvpn.0

1:100:1:7.0.0.1/240
                    *[BGP/170] 00:08:41, localpref 100, from 7.0.0.1
                      AS path: I
                    > to 172.16.1.1 via ge-1/0/1.0, Push 299808
1:100:1:7.0.0.4/240
                    *[BGP/170] 00:08:41, localpref 100, from 7.0.0.4
                      AS path: I
                    > to 172.16.1.1 via ge-1/0/1.0
1:100:1:7.0.0.5/240
                    *[MVPN/70] 00:00:22, metric2 1
                      Indirect
```

FIGURE 3.108

BGP-MVPN routing information—PE1.

```
operator@PE2# run show route table MVPN-FOO.mvpn.0
MVPN-FOO.mvpn.0: 5 destinations, 5 routes (5 active, 0 holddown, 0 hidden)
+ = Active Route, - = Last Active, * = Both
1:100:1:7.0.0.1/240
                     *[BGP/170] 00:30:07, localpref 100, from 7.0.0.1
                       AS path: I
                     > to 172.16.1.6 via ge-4/0/3.0
1:100:1:7.0.0.4/240
                     *[MVPN/70] 20:51:14, metric2 1
                       Indirect
1:100:1:7.0.0.5/240
                     *[BGP/170] 00:01:45, localpref 100, from 7.0.0.5
                       AS path: I
                     > to 172.16.1.2 via ge-4/0/0.0
6:100:1:100:32:7.0.0.1:32:237.1.1.1/240
                     *[PIM/105] 00:29:22
                       Multicast (IPv4)
```

FIGURE 3.109

BGP MVPN routing information—PE2.

```
operator@PE3# run show route table MVPN-FOO.mvpn.0

1:100:1:7.0.0.1/240
                     *[MVPN/70] 00:31:50, metric2 1
                       Indirect
1:100:1:7.0.0.4/240
                     *[BGP/170] 20:47:15, localpref 100, from 7.0.0.4
                       AS path: I
                     > to 172.16.1.5 via ge-4/0/0.0
1:100:1:7.0.0.5/240
                     *[BGP/170] 00:03:27, localpref 100, from 7.0.0.5
                       AS path: I
                     > to 172.16.1.5 via ge-4/0/0.0, Push 299776
6:100:1:100:32:7.0.0.1:32:237.1.1.1/240
                     *[PIM/105] 00:00:08
                       Multicast (IPv4)
```

FIGURE 3.110

BGP MVPN routing information—PE3.

3.4.5.1.2 Validation of the Control and Data Plane after Traffic Generation on PE1
Next we look at the respective outputs on PE1 after traffic has been generated from the C-MCAST source connected behind PE1.

In the output below PE1 receives the Type 7 routes from PE2 and PE3 and also generates a Type 5 route (Figure 3.111). Another Type 5 route, the C-RP, is received from PE3. Remember, the customer Multicast domain is still using ASM or PIM Sparse Mode.

```
operator@PE1# run show route table MVPN-FOO.mvpn.0

1:100:1:7.0.0.1/240
                      *[BGP/170] 00:23:07, localpref 100, from 7.0.0.1
                         AS path: I
                       > to 172.16.1.1 via ge-1/0/1.0, Push 299808
1:100:1:7.0.0.4/240
                      *[BGP/170] 00:23:07, localpref 100, from 7.0.0.4
                         AS path: I
                       > to 172.16.1.1 via ge-1/0/1.0
1:100:1:7.0.0.5/240
                      *[MVPN/70] 00:14:48, metric2 1
                         Indirect
5:100:1:32:192.168.1.5:32:237.1.1.1/240
                      *[PIM/105] 00:00:03
                         Multicast (IPv4)
                       [BGP/170] 00:00:03, localpref 100, from 7.0.0.1
                         AS path: I
                       > to 172.16.1.1 via ge-1/0/1.0, Push 299808
7:100:1:100:32:192.168.1.5:32:237.1.1.1/240
                      *[PIM/105] 00:00:03
                         Multicast (IPv4)
                       [BGP/170] 00:00:03, localpref 100, from 7.0.0.1
                         AS path: I
                       > to 172.16.1.1 via ge-1/0/1.0, Push 299808
                       [BGP/170] 00:00:03, localpref 100, from 7.0.0.4
                         AS path: I
                       > to 172.16.1.1 via ge-1/0/1.0
```

FIGURE 3.111

BGP MVPN routing information—PE1.

The multicast forwarding state on PE1 is seen in Figure 3.112. The downstream interface now displays "MT," which means GRE-based Multicast Tunnel Interface.

```
operator@PE1# run show multicast route instance MVPN-FOO extensive
Family: INET
Group: 237.1.1.1
    Source: 192.168.1.5/32
    Upstream interface: ge-1/0/2.0
    Downstream interface list:
        mt-0/3/0.32768 ------------> GRE interface
    Session description: Unknown
    Statistics: 75 kBps, 890 pps, 197055 packets
    Next-hop ID: 1048579
    Upstream protocol: MVPN
    Route state: Active
    Forwarding state: Forwarding
    Cache lifetime/timeout: forever
    Wrong incoming interface notifications: 0
```

FIGURE 3.112

Multicast forwarding information—PE1.

The MVPN instance-specific output is checked next (Figure 3.113). The display illustrates a PIM-SSM Tunnel being used with associated C-MCAST Source and Group Pairs. The P-tunnel also displays information on the PIM Provider Group being used in the core (232.1.1.1).

```
operator@PE1# run show mvpn instance extensive
MVPN instance:
Legend for provider tunnel
I-P-tnl -- inclusive provider tunnel S-P-tnl -- selective provider tunnel
Legend for c-multicast routes properties (Pr)
DS -- derived from (*, c-g)          RM -- remote VPN route
Instance : MVPN-FOO
  MVPN Mode : SPT-ONLY
  Provider tunnel: I-P-tnl:PIM-SSM:7.0.0.5, 232.1.1.1
  Neighbor                          I-P-tnl
  7.0.0.1
  7.0.0.4
  C-mcast IPv4 (S:G)         Ptnl                             St
  192.168.1.5/32:237.1.1.1/32  PIM-SSM:7.0.0.5, 232.1.1.1     RM
```

FIGURE 3.113

MVPN instance information—PE1.

In the output in Figure 3.114, the PIM-SSM-specific information on the PIM Master instance is checked. Remember, we are using PIM-SSM in the core, and appropriate state information would be created for the Source (Ingress PE) and Provider Multicast Group address being used (232.1.1.1).

```
operator@PE1# run show pim source detail
Instance: PIM.master Family: INET
Source 7.0.0.5 --------→ PE1
    Prefix 7.0.0.5/32
    Upstream interface Local
    Upstream neighbor Local
    Active groups:232.1.1.1 --→ P-Group Address
Instance: PIM.master Family: INET6
```

FIGURE 3.114

PIM-SSM state information—PE1.

Another interesting command as given in Figure 3.115 can validate the control plane and data plane used. Here we see the data plane, control plane (NG-MVPN), and the associated routing instance.

```
operator@PE1# run show pim mvpn
Instance            VPN-Group        Mode           Tunnel
PIM.MVPN-FOO        232.1.1.1        NG-MVPN        PIM-SSM
```

FIGURE 3.115

MVPN association.

3.4.5.1.3 Validation of the Control and Data Plane after Traffic Generation on PE2

The respective outputs on PE2, which is an Egress PE router, after traffic has been generated from the C-MCAST source connected behind PE1 are seen in Figure 3.116.

```
operator@PE2# run show route table MVPN-FOO.mvpn.0

1:100:1:7.0.0.1/240
                    *[BGP/170] 01:01:20, localpref 100, from 7.0.0.1
                      AS path: I
                    > to 172.16.1.6 via ge-4/0/3.0
1:100:1:7.0.0.4/240
                    *[MVPN/70] 21:22:27, metric2 1
                      Indirect
1:100:1:7.0.0.5/240
                    *[BGP/170] 00:32:58, localpref 100, from 7.0.0.5
                      AS path: I
                    > to 172.16.1.2 via ge-4/0/0.0
5:100:1:32:192.168.1.5:32:237.1.1.1/240
                    *[BGP/170] 00:18:12, localpref 100, from 7.0.0.1
                      AS path: I
                    > to 172.16.1.6 via ge-4/0/3.0
                     [BGP/170] 00:18:12, localpref 100, from 7.0.0.5
                      AS path: I
                    > to 172.16.1.2 via ge-4/0/0.0
6:100:1:100:32:7.0.0.1:32:237.1.1.1/240
                    *[PIM/105] 01:00:35
                      Multicast (IPv4)
7:100:1:100:32:192.168.1.5:32:237.1.1.1/240
                    *[MVPN/70] 00:18:12, metric2 1
                      Multicast (IPv4)
                     [PIM/105] 00:18:12
                      Multicast (IPv4)
```

FIGURE 3.116

BGP MVPN routing information—PE2.

Now the multicast forwarding state on PE2 is checked (Figure 3.117). The upstream interface now displays "MT," which means there is a GRE-based Multicast Tunnel Interface.

```
operator@PE2# run show multicast route instance MVPN-FOO extensive
Family: INET
Group: 237.1.1.1
    Source: 192.168.1.5/32
    Upstream interface: mt-5/3/0.49152
    Downstream interface list:
        ge-4/0/2.100
    Session description: Unknown
    Statistics: 77 kBps, 916 pps, 31783 packets
    Next-hop ID: 1048577
    Upstream protocol: MVPN
    Route state: Active
    Forwarding state: Forwarding
    Cache lifetime/timeout: forever
    Wrong incoming interface notifications: 0
```

FIGURE 3.117

Multicast forwarding information—PE2.

Next we check the MVPN instance-specific output (Figure 3.118).

```
operator@PE2# run show mvpn instance
MVPN instance:
Legend for provider tunnel
I-P-tnl -- inclusive provider tunnel S-P-tnl -- selective provider tunnel
Legend for c-multicast routes properties (Pr)
DS -- derived from (*, c-g)          RM -- remote VPN route
Instance : MVPN-FOO
  MVPN Mode : SPT-ONLY
  Provider tunnel: I-P-tnl:invalid:
  Neighbor                          I-P-tnl
  7.0.0.1
  7.0.0.5                           PIM-SSM:7.0.0.5, 232.1.1.1
  C-mcast IPv4 (S:G)      Ptnl                         St
  192.168.1.5/32:237.1.1.1/32  PIM-SSM:7.0.0.5, 232.1.1.1   DS
```

FIGURE 3.118

MVPN instance information—PE2.

In the output in Figure 3.119, we check the PIM-SSM-specific information on the PIM Master instance. Remember, we are using PIM-SSM in the core, and appropriate state information would be created for the Source (Ingress PE) and Provider Multicast Group address being used (232.1.1.1).

```
operator@PE2# run show pim source detail
Instance: PIM.master Family: INET
Source 7.0.0.5 -------> Ingress PE
    Prefix 7.0.0.5/32
    Upstream interface ge-4/0/0.0
    Upstream neighbor 172.16.1.2
    Active groups:232.1.1.1
```

FIGURE 3.119

PIM-SSM State information—PE2.

3.4.5.1.4 Validation of the Control and Data Plane after Traffic Generation on PE3

Figure 3.120 illustrates the respective outputs on PE3, which is an Egress PE router, after traffic has been generated from the C-MCAST source connected behind PE1.

```
operator@PE3# run show route table MVPN-FOO.mvpn.0

MVPN-FOO.mvpn.0: 7 destinations, 9 routes (7 active, 1 holddown, 0 hidden)
+ = Active Route, - = Last Active, * = Both

1:100:1:7.0.0.1/240
                  *[MVPN/70] 01:33:53, metric2 1
                      Indirect
```

FIGURE 3.120

BGP MVPN routing information—PE3.

```
1:100:1:7.0.0.4/240
                    *[BGP/170] 00:11:03, localpref 100, from 7.0.0.4
                      AS path: I
                    > to 172.16.1.5 via ge-4/0/0.0
1:100:1:7.0.0.5/240
                    *[BGP/170] 00:11:03, localpref 100, from 7.0.0.5
                      AS path: I
                    > to 172.16.1.5 via ge-4/0/0.0, Push 299776
5:100:1:32:192.168.1.5:32:237.1.1.1/240
                    *[PIM/105] 00:00:05
                      Multicast (IPv4)
                     [BGP/170] 00:00:05, localpref 100, from 7.0.0.5
                      AS path: I
                    > to 172.16.1.5 via ge-4/0/0.0, Push 299776
6:100:1:100:32:7.0.0.1:32:237.1.1.1/240
                    *[PIM/105] 00:11:03
                      Multicast (IPv4)
7:100:1:100:32:192.168.1.5:32:237.1.1.1/240
                    *[MVPN/70] 00:00:05, metric2 1
                      Multicast (IPv4)
                     [PIM/105] 00:00:05
                      Multicast (IPv4)
```

FIGURE 3.120

_____

(_Continued_)

The multicast forwarding state on PE2 is illustrated in Figure 3.121. The upstream interface now displays "MT," which means GRE-based Multicast Tunnel Interface.

```
operator@PE3# run show multicast route instance MVPN-FOO extensive
Family: INET
Group: 237.1.1.1
    Source: 192.168.1.5/32
    Upstream interface: mt-0/0/10.49152
    Downstream interface list:
        ge-4/0/1.0
    Session description: Unknown
    Statistics: 74 kBps, 877 pps, 462774 packets
    Next-hop ID: 1048576
    Upstream protocol: MVPN
    Route state: Active
    Forwarding state: Forwarding
    Cache lifetime/timeout: forever
    Wrong incoming interface notifications: 0
```

FIGURE 3.121

_____

Multicast forwarding information—PE3.

Now we check the MVPN instance-specific output (Figure 3.122).

In the output seen in Figure 3.123, we check the PIM-SSM-specific information on the PIM Master instance. Remember, we are using PIM-SSM in the core, and appropriate state information would be created for the Source (Ingress PE) and Provider Multicast Group address used (232.1.1.1).

```
operator@PE2# run show mvpn instance
MVPN instance:
Legend for provider tunnel
I-P-tnl -- inclusive provider tunnel S-P-tnl -- selective provider tunnel
Legend for c-multicast routes properties (Pr)
DS -- derived from (*, c-g)          RM -- remote VPN route
Instance : MVPN-FOO
  MVPN Mode : SPT-ONLY
  Provider tunnel: I-P-tnl:invalid:
  Neighbor                          I-P-tnl
  7.0.0.4
  7.0.0.5                           PIM-SSM:7.0.0.5, 232.1.1.1
  C-mcast IPv4 (S:G)        Ptnl                              St
  192.168.1.5/32:237.1.1.1/32  PIM-SSM:7.0.0.5, 232.1.1.1    DS
```

FIGURE 3.122

MVPN instance information—PE3.

```
operator@PE2# run show pim source detail
Instance: PIM.master Family: INET
Source 7.0.0.5
    Prefix 7.0.0.5/32
    Upstream interface ge-4/0/0.0
    Upstream neighbor 172.16.1.5
    Active groups:232.1.1.1
```

FIGURE 3.123

PIM-SSM state information—PE3.

3.4.5.2 Case Study for a PIM-SSM-Based Data Plane—S-PMSI Setup

In this section, the actual configurations required for creating an S-PMSI based on PIM-SSM for certain multicast groups are reviewed. In our case study, we intend to have an S-PMSI created only for group "238.1.1.1" and source "192.168.1.5." This would be between the Ingress PE router PE1 and Egress PE router PE2. The relative configurations are seen in Figure 3.124.

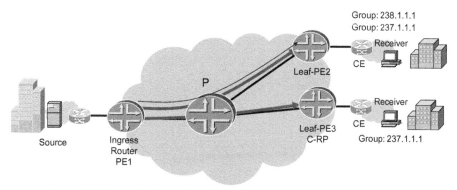

* The router "P" does not indicate a single Provider router, and indicates a
  Carrier Provider core that may contain many devices. A single device is just
  given ONLY for illustrative reasons.

FIGURE 3.124

3.4.5.2.1 Configurations

The S-PMSI configuration is only required on the Ingress PE router. The C-MCAST Source and Group pairs are defined, and the group-range for creating an appropriate P-Group address similar to the Draft-Rosen Data MDTs also has to be defined. In our example (Figure 3.125), we use group "232.1.1.2."

```
Routing-instance {
MVPN-FOO {
    instance-type vrf;
    interface ge-1/0/2.0;
    interface lo0.1;
    route-distinguisher 100:1;
    provider-tunnel {
        pim-ssm {
            group-address 232.1.1.1;
        }
        selective {
            group 238.1.1.1/32 {
                source 192.168.1.5/32 {
                    pim-ssm {
                        group-range 232.1.1.2/32;
                    }
                }
            }
        }
    }
    vrf-target target:100:1;
    vrf-table-label;
    protocols {
        bgp {
            family inet {
                unicast;
            }
            group peer {
                type external;
                peer-as 65004;
                neighbor 192.168.1.5;
            }
        }
        pim {
            rp {
                static {
                    address 7.0.0.1;
                }
            }
            interface ge-1/0/2.0 {
                mode sparse-dense;
                version 2;
            }
            interface lo0.1 {
                mode sparse-dense;
                version 2;
            }
        }
        mvpn;
    }
}
}
```

FIGURE 3.125

S-PMSI configuration on PE1.

3.4.5.2.2 Validations on PE1

The BGP MVPN routing information, after we start generating traffic to both the groups "238.1.1.1" and "237.1.1.1," is reviewed next. There is one interesting observation in the output seen in Figure 3.126. PE1 does originate a Type 3 route for the specific (C-Source, C-Group) pair that has been configured to create an S-PMSI infrastructure; however, a corresponding Type 4 route from PE2 has not been received. Non-MPLS based S-PMSI infrastructures (GRE based) will not have a Type 4 route sent by an interested receiver PE. Instead, the Type 7 route information (which indicates preference

```
operator@PE1# run show route table MVPN-FOO.mvpn.0
1:100:1:7.0.0.1/240
                    *[BGP/170] 00:57:33, localpref 100, from 7.0.0.1
                      AS path: I
                    > to 172.16.1.1 via ge-1/0/1.0, Push 299808
1:100:1:7.0.0.4/240
                    *[BGP/170] 00:59:12, localpref 100, from 7.0.0.4
                      AS path: I
                    > to 172.16.1.1 via ge-1/0/1.0
1:100:1:7.0.0.5/240
                    *[MVPN/70] 00:41:44, metric2 1
                      Indirect
3:100:1:32:192.168.1.5:32:238.1.1.1:7.0.0.5/240
                    *[MVPN/70] 00:04:11, metric2 1
                      Indirect
5:100:1:32:192.168.1.5:32:237.1.1.1/240
                    *[PIM/105] 00:04:19
                      Multicast (IPv4)
                     [BGP/170] 00:04:19, localpref 100, from 7.0.0.1
                      AS path: I
                    > to 172.16.1.1 via ge-1/0/1.0, Push 299808
5:100:1:32:192.168.1.5:32:238.1.1.1/240
                    *[PIM/105] 00:04:11
                      Multicast (IPv4)
                     [BGP/170] 00:04:11, localpref 100, from 7.0.0.1
                      AS path: I
                    > to 172.16.1.1 via ge-1/0/1.0, Push 299808
7:100:1:100:32:192.168.1.5:32:237.1.1.1/240
                    *[PIM/105] 00:04:19
                      Multicast (IPv4)
                     [BGP/170] 00:04:19, localpref 100, from 7.0.0.1
                      AS path: I
                    > to 172.16.1.1 via ge-1/0/1.0, Push 299808
                     [BGP/170] 00:04:19, localpref 100, from 7.0.0.4
                      AS path: I
                    > to 172.16.1.1 via ge-1/0/1.0
7:100:1:100:32:192.168.1.5:32:238.1.1.1/240 - Received only from PE2.
                    *[PIM/105] 00:04:11
                      Multicast (IPv4)
                     [BGP/170] 00:04:11, localpref 100, from 7.0.0.4
                      AS path: I
                    > to 172.16.1.1 via ge-1/0/1.0
```

FIGURE 3.126

BGP MVPN routing information—PE1.

or interest in a given group) will be used by the Ingress PE to create the S-PMSI. Why does an RSVP-TE P-tunnel (for instance) have the Type 4 response built in? This occurs because the RSVP-TE-based P-tunnels support the Type 4 announcements in order to support aggregation of Multicast Trees or S-PMSI Tunnels. Because of this they rely on Type 4 routes that provide more granularity in information. The topic of aggregation will be discussed in Chapter 7.

Without a Type 4 route being announced, how do we ensure that the specific (C-S, C-G) pair is using an S-PMSI Tunnel? The output seen in Figure 3.127 validates this. Here we note that traffic from source "192.168.1.5" destined for group "238.1.1.1" uses an S-PMSI (indicated as S-PIM-SSM), and traffic from the same source destined to group "237.1.1.1" used an I-PMSI infrastructure.

```
operator@PE1# run show mvpn instance
MVPN instance:
Legend for provider tunnel
I-P-tnl -- inclusive provider tunnel S-P-tnl -- selective provider tunnel
Legend for c-multicast routes properties (Pr)
DS -- derived from (*, c-g)          RM -- remote VPN route
Instance : MVPN-FOO
  MVPN Mode : SPT-ONLY
  Provider tunnel: I-P-tnl:PIM-SSM:7.0.0.5, 232.1.1.1
  Neighbor                           I-P-tnl
  7.0.0.1
  7.0.0.4
  C-mcast IPv4 (S:G)           Ptnl                         St
  192.168.1.5/32:237.1.1.1/32  PIM-SSM:7.0.0.5, 232.1.1.1   RM
  192.168.1.5/32:238.1.1.1/32  S-PIM-SSM:7.0.0.5, 232.1.1.2 RM
```

FIGURE 3.127

Checking the MVPN instance information.

Now we check the multicast forwarding state for the groups "237.1.1.1" and "238.1.1.1" (see Figure 3.128).

```
operator@PE1# run show multicast route instance MVPN-FOO extensive
Family: INET
Group: 237.1.1.1
    Source: 192.168.1.5/32
    Upstream interface: ge-1/0/2.0
    Downstream interface list:
        mt-0/3/0.32769
    Session description: Unknown
    Statistics: 47 kBps, 561 pps, 35492 packets --> Traffic being forwarded
    Next-hop ID: 1048581
    Upstream protocol: MVPN
    Route state: Active
    Forwarding state: Forwarding
    Cache lifetime/timeout: forever
    Wrong incoming interface notifications: 0
```

FIGURE 3.128

Checking the MVPN instance information.

```
Group: 238.1.1.1
    Source: 192.168.1.5/32
    Upstream interface: ge-1/0/2.0
    Downstream interface list:
        mt-0/3/0.32768
    Session description: Unknown
    Statistics: 14 kBps, 166 pps, 3765 packets -→ Traffic being forwarded.
    Next-hop ID: 1048576
    Upstream protocol: MVPN
    Route state: Active
    Forwarding state: Forwarding
    Cache lifetime/timeout: forever
    Wrong incoming interface notifications: 0
```

FIGURE 3.128

(*Continued*)

3.4.5.2.3 Validations on PE2
The outputs on the egress PE router PE2 are reviewed next. In Figure 3.129 PE2 has originated Type 7 routing information for both groups (237.1.1.1 and 238.1.1.1).

```
operator@PE2# run show route table MVPN-FOO.mvpn.0
1:100:1:7.0.0.1/240
                    *[BGP/170] 18:59:03, localpref 100, from 7.0.0.1
                     AS path: I
                    > to 172.16.1.6 via ge-4/0/3.0
1:100:1:7.0.0.4/240
                    *[MVPN/70] 1d 16:42:59, metric2 1
                     Indirect
1:100:1:7.0.0.5/240
                    *[BGP/170] 00:07:10, localpref 100, from 7.0.0.5
                     AS path: I
                    > to 172.16.1.2 via ge-4/0/0.0
3:100:1:32:192.168.1.5:32:238.1.1.1:7.0.0.5/240
                    *[BGP/170] 00:07:10, localpref 100, from 7.0.0.5
                     AS path: I
                    > to 172.16.1.2 via ge-4/0/0.0
5:100:1:32:192.168.1.5:32:237.1.1.1/240
                    *[BGP/170] 00:03:53, localpref 100, from 7.0.0.1
                     AS path: I
                    > to 172.16.1.6 via ge-4/0/3.0
                     [BGP/170] 00:03:53, localpref 100, from 7.0.0.5
                     AS path: I
                    > to 172.16.1.2 via ge-4/0/0.0
5:100:1:32:192.168.1.5:32:238.1.1.1/240
                    *[BGP/170] 00:13:11, localpref 100, from 7.0.0.1
                     AS path: I
                    > to 172.16.1.6 via ge-4/0/3.0
                     [BGP/170] 00:07:10, localpref 100, from 7.0.0.5
                     AS path: I
                    > to 172.16.1.2 via ge-4/0/0.0
```

FIGURE 3.129

Checking the MVPN instance information.

```
6:100:1:100:32:7.0.0.1:32:237.1.1.1/240
                     *[PIM/105] 18:55:42
                      Multicast (IPv4)
6:100:1:100:32:7.0.0.1:32:238.1.1.1/240
                     *[PIM/105] 18:10:45
                      Multicast (IPv4)
7:100:1:100:32:192.168.1.5:32:237.1.1.1/240
                     *[MVPN/70] 00:03:53, metric2 1
                      Multicast (IPv4)
                     [PIM/105] 00:03:53
                      Multicast (IPv4)
7:100:1:100:32:192.168.1.5:32:238.1.1.1/240
                     *[MVPN/70] 00:07:10, metric2 1
                      Multicast (IPv4)
                     [PIM/105] 00:03:10
                      Multicast (IPv4)
```

FIGURE 3.129

(Continued)

In Figure 3.130 the MVPN instance information is checked. The output clearly validates an S-PMSI and I-PMSI being set up to PE2.

```
operator@PE2# run show mvpn instance
MVPN instance:
Legend for provider tunnel
I-P-tnl -- inclusive provider tunnel S-P-tnl -- selective provider tunnel
Legend for c-multicast routes properties (Pr)
DS -- derived from (*, c-g)        RM -- remote VPN route
Instance : MVPN-FOO
  MVPN Mode : SPT-ONLY
  Provider tunnel: I-P-tnl:invalid:
  Neighbor                         I-P-tnl
  7.0.0.1
  7.0.0.5                          PIM-SSM:7.0.0.5, 232.1.1.1
  C-mcast IPv4 (S:G)        Ptnl                          St
  192.168.1.5/32:237.1.1.1/32  PIM-SSM:7.0.0.5, 232.1.1.1   DS
  192.168.1.5/32:238.1.1.1/32  S-PIM-SSM:7.0.0.5, 232.1.1.2 DS
```

FIGURE 3.130

Checking the MVPN instance information.

Finally, the multicast forwarding state can be verified for both of the C-MCAST groups (238.1.1.1 and 237.1.1.1; see Figure 3.131).

```
operator@PE2# run show multicast route instance MVPN-FOO extensive
Family: INET
Group: 237.1.1.1
    Source: 192.168.1.5/32
    Upstream interface: mt-5/3/0.49152
    Downstream interface list:
        ge-4/0/2.100
    Session description: Unknown
    Statistics: 0 kBps, 0 pps, 35490 packets
    Next-hop ID: 1048577
    Upstream protocol: MVPN
    Route state: Active
    Forwarding state: Forwarding
    Cache lifetime/timeout: forever
    Wrong incoming interface notifications: 0

Group: 238.1.1.1
    Source: 192.168.1.5/32
    Upstream interface: mt-5/3/0.49152
    Downstream interface list:
        ge-4/0/2.100
    Session description: Unknown
    Statistics: 0 kBps, 0 pps, 74065 packets
    Next-hop ID: 1048577
    Upstream protocol: MVPN
    Route state: Active
    Forwarding state: Forwarding
    Cache lifetime/timeout: forever
    Wrong incoming interface notifications: 0
```

FIGURE 3.131

Checking the multicast forwarding information.

3.4.5.2.4 Validations on PE3

The outputs on the egress PE router PE3 are checked in Figure 3.132. Here the PE3 has originated Type 7 routing information only for group (237.1.1.1).

```
operator@PE3# run show route table MVPN-FOO.mvpn.0
1:100:1:7.0.0.1/240
                    *[MVPN/70] 20:27:48, metric2 1
                        Indirect
1:100:1:7.0.0.4/240
                    *[BGP/170] 19:04:58, localpref 100, from 7.0.0.4
                        AS path: I
                    > to 172.16.1.5 via ge-4/0/0.0
1:100:1:7.0.0.5/240
                    *[BGP/170] 00:13:06, localpref 100, from 7.0.0.5
                        AS path: I
                    > to 172.16.1.5 via ge-4/0/0.0, Push 299776
```

FIGURE 3.132

Checking the MVPN instance information.

```
5:100:1:32:192.168.1.5:32:237.1.1.1/240
                    *[PIM/105] 00:00:03
                       Multicast (IPv4)
                    [BGP/170] 00:00:03, localpref 100, from 7.0.0.5
                       AS path: I
                    > to 172.16.1.5 via ge-4/0/0.0, Push 299776
6:100:1:100:32:7.0.0.1:32:237.1.1.1/240
                    *[PIM/105] 19:04:58
                       Multicast (IPv4)
7:100:1:100:32:192.168.1.5:32:237.1.1.1/240
                    *[MVPN/70] 00:00:03, metric2 1
                       Multicast (IPv4)
                    [PIM/105] 00:00:03
                       Multicast (IPv4)
```

FIGURE 3.132

(Continued)

Next the MVPN instance information is checked in Figure 3.133. The output clearly validates that only an I-PMSI has been set up to PE3.


```
operator@PE3# run show mvpn instance
MVPN instance:
Legend for provider tunnel
I-P-tnl -- inclusive provider tunnel S-P-tnl -- selective provider tunnel
Legend for c-multicast routes properties (Pr)
DS -- derived from (*, c-g)          RM -- remote VPN route
Instance : MVPN-FOO
  MVPN Mode : SPT-ONLY
  Provider tunnel: I-P-tnl:invalid:
  Neighbor                           I-P-tnl
  7.0.0.4
  7.0.0.5                            PIM-SSM:7.0.0.5, 232.1.1.1
  C-mcast IPv4 (S:G)       Ptnl                        St
  192.168.1.5/32:237.1.1.1/32  PIM-SSM:7.0.0.5, 232.1.1.1   DS
```

FIGURE 3.133

Checking the MVPN instance information.

Finally, the multicast forwarding state is checked (Figure 3.134). Traffic is being forwarded only for group "237.1.1.1."

```
operator@PE3# run show multicast route instance MVPN-FOO extensive
Family: INET
Group: 237.1.1.1
    Source: 192.168.1.5/32
    Upstream interface: mt-0/0/10.49152
    Downstream interface list:
        ge-4/0/1.0
    Session description: Unknown
    Statistics: 0 kBps, 0 pps, 999 packets
    Next-hop ID: 1048576
    Upstream protocol: MVPN
    Route state: Active
    Forwarding state: Forwarding
    Cache lifetime/timeout: forever
    Wrong incoming interface notifications: 0
```

FIGURE 3.134

Checking the multicast forwarding information.

3.4.6 PIM-SM Provider Tunnels

In this section, we take a look at a network setup using PIM-SM-based Provider Tunnels as the Data plane along with the BGP control plane. The following setup (Figure 3.135) will be used to demonstrate functionality. The setup is exactly the same as the one used for the PIM-SSM P-tunnel illustration.

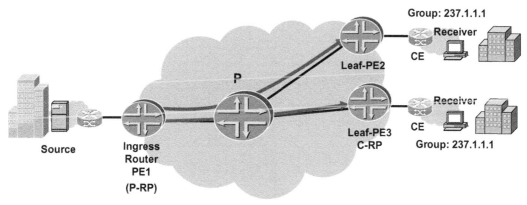

- The router "P" does not indicate a single Provider router, and indicates a Carrier Provider core that may contain many devices. A single device is just given ONLY for illustrative reasons.

FIGURE 3.135

3.4.6.1 Configurations on the PE Routers

The P-tunnel configurations are only required on the Ingress PE router. In this section we use an ASM or PIM-SM P-tunnel for the I-PMSI infrastructure so we need to configure an RP for the Provider or Master PIM instance. Remember, PIM-ASM relies on the RP to create the required infrastructure. In our configuration (see Figure 3.136), the PIM-Provider group address used is "239.1.1.2."

```
Protocols {
rsvp {
    interface ge-1/0/1.0;
}
mpls {
    interface ge-1/0/1.0;
    interface fe-1/1/0.0;
}
bgp {
    group PE {
        type internal;
        local-address 7.0.0.5;
        family inet-vpn {
            unicast;
        }
        family inet-mvpn {
            signaling;
        }
        neighbor 7.0.0.4 {
            peer-as 100;
        }
        neighbor 7.0.0.1 {
            peer-as 100;
        }
    }
}
ospf {
    area 0.0.0.0 {
        interface ge-1/0/1.0 {
            interface-type p2p;
        }
        interface lo0.0 {
            passive;
        }
    }
}
ldp {
    interface ge-1/0/1.0;
    interface fe-1/1/0.0;
}
pim {
    rp {
        local {
            address 7.0.0.5; -> Local router is RP for PIM master instance
        }
```

FIGURE 3.136

Configuration on PE1.

```
    }
    interface all {
        version 2;
    }
}
routing-instances {
MVPN-FOO {
    instance-type vrf;
    interface ge-1/0/2.0;
    interface lo0.1;
    route-distinguisher 100:1;
    provider-tunnel {
        pim-asm { ----------> PIM-ASM as the P-Tunnel
            group-address 239.1.1.2;
        }
    }
    vrf-target target:100:1;
    vrf-table-label;
    protocols {
        bgp {
            family inet {
                unicast;
            }
            group peer {
                type external;
                peer-as 65004;
                neighbor 192.168.1.5;
            }
        }
        pim {
            rp {
                static {
                    address 7.0.0.1;
                }
            }
            interface ge-1/0/2.0 {
                mode sparse-dense;
                version 2;
            }
            interface lo0.1 {
                mode sparse-dense;
                version 2;
            }
        }
        mvpn;
    }
  }
}
```

FIGURE 3.136

(*Continued*)

The configuration on Egress PE router PE2 is seen in Figure 3.137). In our configuration, the PIM-Provider group address used is "239.1.1.2," and this is identified by means of the P-tunnel configuration. Further PIM (Master instance) is configured to statically point to PE1 as the Provider RP.

```
protocols {
rsvp {
    interface so-4/1/0.0;
    interface ge-4/0/3.0;
    interface ge-4/0/0.0;
    interface ge-4/0/7.0;
}
mpls {
    interface ge-4/0/0.0;
    interface ge-4/0/5.0;
    interface ge-4/0/3.0;
}
bgp {
    group PE {
        type internal;
        local-address 7.0.0.4;
        family inet-vpn {
            unicast;
        }
        family inet-mvpn {
            signaling;
        }
        neighbor 7.0.0.5 {
            peer-as 100;
        }
        neighbor 7.0.0.1 {
            peer-as 100;
        }
    }
}
ospf {
    area 0.0.0.0 {
        interface lo0.0 {
            passive;
        }
        interface ge-4/0/0.0 {
            interface-type p2p;
        }
        interface ge-4/0/5.0 {
            interface-type p2p;
        }
        interface ge-4/0/3.0 {
            interface-type p2p;
        }
    }
}
ldp {
    interface ge-4/0/0.0;
    interface ge-4/0/3.0;
    interface ge-4/0/5.0;
    interface ge-4/0/7.0;
}
```

FIGURE 3.137

Configuration on PE2.

```
pim {
    rp {
        static {
            address 7.0.0.5;
        }
    }
    interface all {
        version 2;
    }
}
}
routing-instances {
MVPN-FOO {
instance-type vrf;
interface ge-4/0/2.100;
interface lo0.1;
route-distinguisher 100:1;
vrf-target target:100:1;
vrf-table-label;
protocols {
    bgp {
        family inet {
            unicast;
        }
        group peer {
            type external;
            peer-as 65003;
            neighbor 192.168.1.1;
        }
    }
    pim {
        rp {
            static {
                address 7.0.0.1;
            }
        }
        interface ge-4/0/2.100 {
            mode sparse-dense;
            version 2;
        }
        interface lo0.1 {
            mode sparse-dense;
            version 2;
        }
    }
    mvpn;
  }
 }
}
```

FIGURE 3.137

(Continued)

The configuration on Egress PE router PE3 is seen in Figure 3.138. In our configuration, the PIM-Provider group address used is "239.1.1.2," and this is identified by means of the P-tunnel configuration. Further PIM (Master instance) is configured to statically point to PE1 as the Provider RP.

```
protocols {
rsvp {
    interface ge-4/0/0.0;
    interface ge-0/1/0.0;
}
mpls {
    interface ge-4/0/0.0;
    interface ge-0/1/0.0;
}
bgp {
    group PE {
        type internal;
        local-address 7.0.0.1;
        family inet-vpn {
            unicast;
        }
        family inet-mvpn {
            signaling;
        }
        neighbor 7.0.0.5 {
            peer-as 100;
        }
        neighbor 7.0.0.4 {
            peer-as 100;
        }
    }
}
ospf {
    area 0.0.0.0 {
        interface lo0.0 {
            passive;
        }
        interface ge-4/0/0.0 {
            interface-type p2p;
        }
        interface ge-0/1/0.0 {
            interface-type p2p;
        }
    }
}
ldp {
    interface ge-0/1/0.0;
    interface ge-4/0/0.0;
}
pim {
    rp {
        static {
            address 7.0.0.5;
        }
    }
    interface all {
        version 2;
    }
  }
}
```

FIGURE 3.138

Configuration on PE3.

```
routing-instances {
MVPN-FOO {
instance-type vrf;
interface ge-4/0/1.0;
interface lo0.1;
route-distinguisher 100:1;
vrf-target target:100:1;
vrf-table-label;
protocols {
    bgp {
        family inet {
            unicast;
        }
        group peer {
            type external;
            export export;
            peer-as 65005;
            neighbor 192.168.1.9;
            neighbor 192.168.1.17 {
                peer-as 65010;
            }
        }
    }
    pim {
        rp {
            local {
                address 7.0.0.1;
            }
        }
        interface ge-4/0/1.0 {
            mode sparse;
            version 2;
        }
        interface lo0.1 {
            mode sparse;
            version 2;
        }
    }
    Mvpn ;
    }
  }
}
```

FIGURE 3.138

(*Continued*)

3.4.6.2 Validations on the PE1

First we check the MVPN routing table on the Ingress PE router PE1. We can see the Type 5 route originated and two Type 7 routes being received from PE2 and PE3 (Figure 3.139).

The MVPN instance output is now checked and the P-tunnel information is validated with the PIM-SM P-tunnel (Figure 3.140).

The multicast forwarding state for the group "237.1.1.1" is checked (see Figure 3.141).

```
operator@PE1# run show route table MVPN-FOO.mvpn.0
1:100:1:7.0.0.1/240
                        *[BGP/170] 00:58:48, localpref 100, from 7.0.0.1
                          AS path: I
                        > to 172.16.1.1 via ge-1/0/1.0, Push 299808
1:100:1:7.0.0.4/240
                        *[BGP/170] 00:58:51, localpref 100, from 7.0.0.4
                          AS path: I
                        > to 172.16.1.1 via ge-1/0/1.0
1:100:1:7.0.0.5/240
                        *[MVPN/70] 00:36:57, metric2 1
                          Indirect
5:100:1:32:192.168.1.5:32:237.1.1.1/240
                        *[PIM/105] 00:02:07
                          Multicast (IPv4)
                         [BGP/170] 00:02:07, localpref 100, from 7.0.0.1
                          AS path: I
                        > to 172.16.1.1 via ge-1/0/1.0, Push 299808
7:100:1:100:32:192.168.1.5:32:237.1.1.1/240
                        *[PIM/105] 00:02:07
                          Multicast (IPv4)
                         [BGP/170] 00:02:07, localpref 100, from 7.0.0.1
                          AS path: I
                        > to 172.16.1.1 via ge-1/0/1.0, Push 299808
                         [BGP/170] 00:02:07, localpref 100, from 7.0.0.4
                          AS path: I
                        > to 172.16.1.1 via ge-1/0/1.0
```

FIGURE 3.139

BGP MVPN routing information—PE1.

```
operator@PE1# run show mvpn instance
MVPN instance:
Legend for provider tunnel
I-P-tnl -- inclusive provider tunnel S-P-tnl -- selective provider tunnel
Legend for c-multicast routes properties (Pr)
DS -- derived from (*, c-g)          RM -- remote VPN route
Instance : MVPN-FOO
  MVPN Mode : SPT-ONLY
  Provider tunnel: I-P-tnl:PIM-SM:7.0.0.5, 239.1.1.2
  Neighbor                           I-P-tnl
  7.0.0.1
  7.0.0.4
  C-mcast IPv4 (S:G)           Ptnl                       St
  192.168.1.5/32:237.1.1.1/32  PIM-SM:7.0.0.5, 239.1.1.2  RM
```

FIGURE 3.140

Checking the MVPN instance information.

```
operator@PE1# run show multicast route instance MVPN-FOO extensive
Family: INET

Group: 237.1.1.1
    Source: 192.168.1.5/32
    Upstream interface: ge-1/0/2.0
    Downstream interface list:
        mt-0/3/0.32768
    Session description: Unknown
    Statistics: 0 kBps, 0 pps, 882 packets
    Next-hop ID: 1048579
    Upstream protocol: MVPN
    Route state: Active
    Forwarding state: Forwarding
    Cache lifetime/timeout: forever
    Wrong incoming interface notifications: 0
```

FIGURE 3.141

Checking the MVPN instance information.

3.4.6.3 Validations on PE2

Next we check the outputs on the egress PE router PE2 (see Figure 3.142). PE2 has originated Type 7 routing information for group "237.1.1.1."

```
operator@PE2# run show route table MVPN-FOO.mvpn.0
1:100:1:7.0.0.1/240
                    *[BGP/170] 19:54:43, localpref 100, from 7.0.0.1
                      AS path: I
                    > to 172.16.1.6 via ge-4/0/3.0
1:100:1:7.0.0.4/240
                    *[MVPN/70] 1d 17:38:39, metric2 1
                      Indirect
1:100:1:7.0.0.5/240
                    *[BGP/170] 00:41:09, localpref 100, from 7.0.0.5
                      AS path: I
                    > to 172.16.1.2 via ge-4/0/0.0
5:100:1:32:192.168.1.5:32:237.1.1.1/240
                    *[BGP/170] 00:06:19, localpref 100, from 7.0.0.1
                      AS path: I
                    > to 172.16.1.6 via ge-4/0/3.0
6:100:1:100:32:7.0.0.1:32:237.1.1.1/240
                    *[PIM/105] 19:51:22
                      Multicast (IPv4)
6:100:1:100:32:7.0.0.1:32:238.1.1.1/240
                    *[PIM/105] 19:06:25
                      Multicast (IPv4)
7:100:1:100:32:192.168.1.5:32:237.1.1.1/240
                    *[MVPN/70] 00:06:19, metric2 1
                      Multicast (IPv4)
```

FIGURE 3.142

Checking the MVPN instance information.

The MVPN instance information is checked in Figure 3.143. The output clearly validates an I-PMSI being set up to PE2.

```
operator@PE2# run show mvpn instance
MVPN instance:
Legend for provider tunnel
I-P-tnl -- inclusive provider tunnel S-P-tnl -- selective provider tunnel
Legend for c-multicast routes properties (Pr)
DS -- derived from (*, c-g)          RM -- remote VPN route
Instance : MVPN-FOO
  MVPN Mode : SPT-ONLY
  Provider tunnel: I-P-tnl:invalid:
  Neighbor                      I-P-tnl
  7.0.0.1
  7.0.0.5                       PIM-SM:7.0.0.5, 239.1.1.2
  C-mcast IPv4 (S:G)       Ptnl                        St
  192.168.1.5/32:237.1.1.1/32  PIM-SM:7.0.0.5, 239.1.1.2   DS
```

FIGURE 3.143

Checking the MVPN instance information.

Finally, the multicast forwarding state can be verified for the C-MCAST group "237.1.1.1"; (see Figure 3.144).

```
operator@PE2# run show multicast route instance MVPN-FOO extensive
Family: INET
Group: 237.1.1.1
    Source: 192.168.1.5/32
    Upstream interface: mt-5/3/0.49152
    Downstream interface list:
        ge-4/0/2.100
    Session description: Unknown
    Statistics: 0 kBps, 0 pps, 1896 packets
    Next-hop ID: 1048576
    Upstream protocol: MVPN
    Route state: Active
    Forwarding state: Forwarding
    Cache lifetime/timeout: forever
    Wrong incoming interface notifications:
```

FIGURE 3.144

Checking the multicast forwarding information.

3.4.6.4 Validations on PE3

The outputs on the egress PE router PE3 are now checked. In Figure 3.145 PE3 has originated Type 7 routing information for group "237.1.1.1."

```
operator@PE3# run show route table MVPN-FOO.mvpn.0
1:100:1:7.0.0.1/240
                        *[MVPN/70] 21:21:20, metric2 1
                            Indirect
1:100:1:7.0.0.4/240
                        *[BGP/170] 19:58:30, localpref 100, from 7.0.0.4
                            AS path: I
                        > to 172.16.1.5 via ge-4/0/0.0
1:100:1:7.0.0.5/240
                        *[BGP/170] 00:44:56, localpref 100, from 7.0.0.5
                            AS path: I
                        > to 172.16.1.5 via ge-4/0/0.0, Push 299776
5:100:1:32:192.168.1.5:32:237.1.1.1/240
                        *[PIM/105] 00:01:41
                            Multicast (IPv4)
                        [BGP/170] 00:01:41, localpref 100, from 7.0.0.5
                            AS path: I
                        > to 172.16.1.5 via ge-4/0/0.0, Push 299776
6:100:1:100:32:7.0.0.1:32:237.1.1.1/240
                        *[PIM/105] 19:58:30
                            Multicast (IPv4)
7:100:1:100:32:192.168.1.5:32:237.1.1.1/240
                        *[MVPN/70] 00:01:41, metric2 1
                            Multicast (IPv4)
                        [PIM/105] 00:01:41
                            Multicast (IPv4)
```

FIGURE 3.145

Checking the MVPN instance information.

Next is the MVPN instance information (see Figure 3.146). The output clearly validates that an I-PMSI has been set up to PE3.

```
operator@PE3# run show mvpn instance
MVPN instance:
Legend for provider tunnel
I-P-tnl -- inclusive provider tunnel S-P-tnl -- selective provider tunnel
Legend for c-multicast routes properties (Pr)
DS -- derived from (*, c-g)          RM -- remote VPN route
Instance : MVPN-FOO
  MVPN Mode : SPT-ONLY
  Provider tunnel: I-P-tnl:invalid:
  Neighbor                           I-P-tnl
  7.0.0.4
  7.0.0.5                            PIM-SM:7.0.0.5, 239.1.1.2
  C-mcast IPv4 (S:G)        Ptnl                        St
  192.168.1.5/32:237.1.1.1/32  PIM-SM:7.0.0.5, 239.1.1.2    DS
```

FIGURE 3.146

Checking the MVPN instance information.

Finally, the multicast forwarding state is checked (see Figure 3.147). Traffic is being forwarded for group "237.1.1.1."

```
operator@PE3# run show multicast route instance MVPN-FOO extensive
Family: INET
Group: 237.1.1.1
    Source: 192.168.1.5/32
    Upstream interface: mt-0/0/10.49152
    Downstream interface list:
        ge-4/0/1.0
    Session description: Unknown
    Statistics: 75 kBps, 890 pps, 184464 packets
    Next-hop ID: 1048576
    Upstream protocol: MVPN
    Route state: Active
    Forwarding state: Forwarding
    Cache lifetime/timeout: forever
    Wrong incoming interface notifications: 0
```

FIGURE 3.147

Checking the multicast forwarding information.

3.4.6.5 S-PMSI

PIM-ASM cannot provide S-PMSI tunnels that are Source Specific in nature; hence it relies on PIM-SSM for this function. Use an ASM infrastructure for the I-PMSI setup with SSM Tunnels (as illustrated in Section 3.4.5) to create S-PMSI.

3.4.7 Migration from Draft-Rosen to NG-MVPNs

In this section, the focus is on the migration of a Draft-Rosen MVPN infrastructure to a NGEN-MVPN. By now we understand the various components of a Draft-Rosen MVPN setup, which essentially uses PIM for control plane signaling and GRE for the Data Plane. In comparison, NGEN-MVPNs use BGP for a control plane, and offer a wide range of data plane options. Now we can look at the various steps involved in the migration process and, most important, the impact to customer multicast traffic during the migration process. We use the following infrastructure for illustrating the migration process (see Figure 3.148).

3.4.7.1 Step 1: Check the Existing Draft-Rosen Infrastructure

First we examine the existing multicast routing tables and forwarding infrastructure prior to starting any actual migration. We check the "inet.1"multicast routing table followed by the multicast forwarding state. PE1 is used as an example (see Figure 3.149).

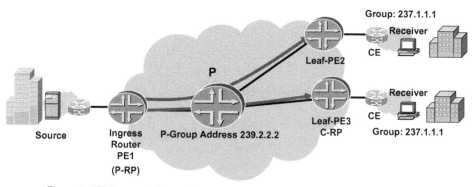

- The router "P" does not indicate a single Provider router, and indicates a Carrier Provider core that may contain many devices. A single device is just given ONLY for illustrative reasons.

FIGURE 3.148

```
operator@PE1# run show route table inet.1 detail
inet.1: 3 destinations, 3 routes (3 active, 0 holddown, 0 hidden)
239.2.2.7.0.0.1/64 (1 entry, 1 announced)
        *PIM    Preference: 105
                Next hop type: Multicast (IPv4), Next hop index: 1048579
                Next-hop reference count: 4
                State: <Active Int>
                Local AS:    100
                Age: 11:02
                Task: PIM.master
                Announcement bits (1): 0-KRT
                AS path: I

239.2.2.7.0.0.4/64 (1 entry, 1 announced)
        *PIM    Preference: 105
                Next hop type: Multicast (IPv4), Next hop index: 1048579
                Next-hop reference count: 4
                State: <Active Int>
                Local AS:    100
                Age: 0
                Task: PIM.master
                Announcement bits (1): 0-KRT
                AS path: I

239.2.2.7.0.0.5/64 (1 entry, 1 announced)
        *PIM    Preference: 105
                Next hop type: Multicast (IPv4), Next hop index: 1048577
                Next-hop reference count: 2
                State: <Active Int>
                Local AS:    100
                Age: 11:15
                Task: PIM.master
                Announcement bits (1): 0-KRT
                AS path: I
```

FIGURE 3.149

Checking the multicast routing information.

The multicast forwarding state indicates the upstream protocol used as "PIM" compared to the "MVPN" used for NG-MVPNs (see Figure 3.150).

```
operator@PE1# run show multicast route instance MVPN-FOO extensive
Family: INET
Group: 237.1.1.1
    Source: 192.168.1.5/32
    Upstream interface: ge-1/0/2.0
    Downstream interface list:
        mt-0/3/0.32768
    Session description: Unknown
    Statistics: 70 kBps, 839 pps, 6257 packets
    Next-hop ID: 1048581
    Upstream protocol: PIM
    Route state: Active
    Forwarding state: Forwarding
    Cache lifetime/timeout: 360 seconds
    Wrong incoming interface notifications: 0
```

FIGURE 3.150

Checking the multicast forwarding information.

3.4.7.2 Step 2: Enable the NG-MVPN Control and Forwarding Plane in the MVPN

Our objective is to minimize the disruption to customer traffic and provide an optimal migration. In this step, we configure the routing-instance or MVPN with the NGEN-forwarding plane. In our example, we use P2MP-RSVP-TE Tunnels. We also enable the support for NG-MVPN signaling, but only within the context of the MVPN. The configurations used are given in the following list. Note that a carrier may opt for an all-out migration within a single window—where all MVPNs across the various PE routers are migrated within a single window—or a partial migration. A partial migration accomplishes the following:

- Demonstrates the co-existence of NG-MVPN with Draft-Rosen MVPNs within the same MVPN. Some sites use NG-MVPN and some use Draft-Rosen. The key is interoperability across the two flavors.
- Provides the carrier the ability to observe the behavior of the NG framework and migrate sites in a phased manner

We would use the phased migration approach and focus on migrating the sites connected to PE1 and PE2.

The configuration of the following parameters (Figures 3.151 and 3.152) is non-disruptive to any traffic. Additions to the existing configurations are italicized (Figure 3.151).

At this stage, the multicast forwarding state for the MVPN should be examined. As seen in Figures 3.153 and 3.154, the forwarding (upstream) protocol is still PIM.

```
protocols {
ospf {
    traffic-engineering;
    area 0.0.0.0 {
        interface ge-1/0/1.0 {
            interface-type p2p;
        }
        interface lo0.0 {
            passive;
        }
        interface fe-1/1/0.0;
    }
}
mpls {
label-switched-path P2MP-RSVP-TE {
    template;
    p2mp;
}
interface ge-1/0/1.0;
interface fe-1/1/0.0;
 }
}
routing-instances {
MVPN-FOO {
instance-type vrf;
interface ge-1/0/2.0;
interface lo0.1;
route-distinguisher 100:1;
provider-tunnel {
    rsvp-te {
        label-switched-path-template {
            P2MP-RSVP-TE;
        }
    }
}
vrf-target target:100:1;
vrf-table-label;
protocols {
    bgp {
        family inet {
            unicast;
        }
        group peer {
            type external;
            peer-as 65004;
            neighbor 192.168.1.5;
        }
    }
```

FIGURE 3.151

Configuration on PE1.

```
    pim {
        vpn-group-address 239.2.2.2;
        rp {
            static {
                address 7.0.0.1;
            }
        }
        interface ge-1/0/2.0 {
            mode sparse-dense;
            version 2;
        }
        interface lo0.1 {
            mode sparse-dense;
            version 2;
        }
    }
    mvpn;
  }
 }
}
```

FIGURE 3.151

(*Continued*)

```
Protocols {
ospf {
    traffic-engineering;
    area 0.0.0.0 {
        interface lo0.0 {
            passive;
        }
        interface ge-4/0/0.0 {
            interface-type p2p;
        }
        interface ge-4/0/5.0 {
            interface-type p2p;
        }
        interface ge-4/0/3.0 {
            interface-type p2p;
        }
        interface ge-4/0/7.0 {
            interface-type p2p;
        }
    }
  }
}
routing-instances {
MVPN-FOO {
instance-type vrf;
interface ge-4/0/2.100;
interface lo0.1;
route-distinguisher 100:1;
vrf-target target:100:1;
vrf-table-label;
protocols {
```

FIGURE 3.152

Configuration on PE2.

```
    bgp {
        family inet {
            unicast;
        }
        group peer {
            type external;
            peer-as 65003;
            neighbor 192.168.1.1;
        }
    }
    pim {
        vpn-group-address 239.2.2.2;
        rp {
            static {
                address 7.0.0.1;
            }
        }
        interface ge-4/0/2.100 {
            mode sparse-dense;
            version 2;
        }
        interface lo0.1 {
            mode sparse-dense;
            version 2;
        }
    }
    mvpn;
  }
 }
}
```

FIGURE 3.152

(*Continued*)

```
operator@PE1# run show multicast route instance MVPN-FOO extensive
Family: INET

Group: 237.1.1.1
    Source: 192.168.1.5/32
    Upstream interface: ge-1/0/2.0
    Downstream interface list:
        mt-0/3/0.32768
    Session description: Unknown
    Statistics: 75 kBps, 894 pps, 3554327 packets
    Next-hop ID: 1048581
    Upstream protocol: PIM
    Route state: Active
    Forwarding state: Forwarding
    Cache lifetime/timeout: 360 seconds
    Wrong incoming interface notifications: 0
```

FIGURE 3.153

Checking the multicast forwarding information on PE1.

```
operator@PE2# run show multicast route instance MVPN-FOO extensive
Family: INET

Group: 237.1.1.1
    Source: 192.168.1.5/32
    Upstream interface: mt-5/3/0.49152
    Downstream interface list:
        ge-4/0/2.100
    Session description: Unknown
    Statistics: 74 kBps, 885 pps, 4027320 packets
    Next-hop ID: 1048577
    Upstream protocol: PIM
    Route state: Active
    Forwarding state: Forwarding
    Cache lifetime/timeout: 360 seconds
    Wrong incoming interface notifications: 0
```

FIGURE 3.154

Checking the multicast forwarding information on PE2.

3.4.7.3 Step 3: Enable BGP Support for the NG-MVPN Address Family

In this step, we enable BGP to support the "MVPN" address family on PE1 and PE2. At this point we have live C-MCAST traffic flowing from a source connected to PE1 toward receivers connected via PE2 and PE3—over the Draft-Rosen Default MDT. Since we have enabled the MVPN protocol under the "routing-instance" (and not yet under the BGP protocol) in step 2, the MVPN routing tables are created but are not advertised between PE routers since BGP is yet to be configured to support this signaling type. The MVPN routing infrastructure created on PE1 and PE2 is seen in Figures 3.155 and 3.156. The MVPN routes are created, but no routes are yet to be advertised or received.

```
operator@PE1# run show route table MVPN-FOO.mvpn.0
MVPN-FOO.mvpn.0: 3 destinations, 3 routes (3 active, 0 holddown, 0 hidden)
+ = Active Route, - = Last Active, * = Both
1:100:1:7.0.0.5/240
                    *[MVPN/70] 01:51:21, metric2 1
                        Indirect
5:100:1:32:192.168.1.5:32:237.1.1.1/240
                    *[PIM/105] 01:51:21
                        Multicast (IPv4)
7:100:1:100:32:192.168.1.5:32:237.1.1.1/240
                    *[PIM/105] 01:51:21
                        Multicast (IPv4)
```

FIGURE 3.155

MVPN routing infrastructure on PE1.

```
operator@PE2# run show route table MVPN-FOO.mvpn.0
MVPN-FOO.mvpn.0: 1 destinations, 1 routes (1 active, 0 holddown, 0 hidden)
+ = Active Route, - = Last Active, * = Both
1:100:1:7.0.0.4/240
                      *[MVPN/70] 01:54:54, metric2 1
                       Indirect
```

FIGURE 3.156

MVPN routing infrastructure on PE2.

Next we enable BGP support for the NG-MVPN control plane. This step causes the BGP neighbor to reset because the support for a new address family (AF) needs to be negotiated. During this transition, look at the multicast forwarding table on PE1, PE2, and even PE3 (Figures 3.157–3.159). If we look at PE1, the multicast forwarding state for the group is shown as "PRUNED." This is an indication of traffic outage for the given group. However, this outage is extremely minimal and based on real-life tests it can be around a few seconds depending on the various factors.

```
operator@PE1# run show multicast route instance MVPN-FOO extensive
Family: INET
Group: 237.1.1.1
    Source: 192.168.1.5/32
    Upstream interface: ge-1/0/2.0
    Session description: Unknown
    Statistics: 0 kBps, 2 pps, 56079 packets
    Next-hop ID: 0
    Upstream protocol: PIM
    Route state: Active
    Forwarding state: Pruned --> Forwarding PRUNED
    Cache lifetime/timeout: 360 seconds
    Wrong incoming interface notifications: 0
```

FIGURE 3.157

Multicast forwarding state on PE1.

```
operator@PE2# run show multicast route instance MVPN-FOO extensive
Family: INET
```

FIGURE 3.158

Multicast forwarding state on PE2.

```
operator@PE3# run show multicast route instance MVPN-FOO extensive
Family: INET
```

FIGURE 3.159

Multicast forwarding state on PE3.

After this very minimal outage of traffic (which was about a few seconds), check the multicast forwarding state on all the PE routers. Based on the outputs seen in Figures 3.160–3.162, the upstream protocol used on PE1 and PE2 has now changed to MVPN, indicating that the NGEN infrastructure is being used while PE3 still uses PIM + GRE.

```
operator@PE1# run show multicast route instance MVPN-FOO extensive
Family: INET
Group: 237.1.1.1
    Source: 192.168.1.5/32
    Upstream interface: ge-1/0/2.0
    Session description: Unknown
    Statistics: 74 kBps, 880 pps, 206802 packets
    Next-hop ID: 1048580
    Upstream protocol: MVPN --→ Control Plane protocol is NG-MVPN.
    Route state: Active
    Forwarding state: Forwarding
    Cache lifetime/timeout: forever
    Wrong incoming interface notifications: 0
```

FIGURE 3.160

Multicast forwarding state on PE1.

```
operator@PE2# run show multicast route instance MVPN-FOO extensive
Family: INET
Group: 237.1.1.1
    Source: 192.168.1.5/32
    Upstream interface: lsi.21
    Downstream interface list:
        ge-4/0/2.100
    Session description: Unknown
    Statistics: 76 kBps, 901 pps, 176771 packets
    Next-hop ID: 1048575
    Upstream protocol: MVPN --→ Control Plane protocol is NG-MVPN.
    Route state: Active
    Forwarding state: Forwarding
    Cache lifetime/timeout: forever
    Wrong incoming interface notifications: 0
```

FIGURE 3.161

Multicast forwarding state on PE2.

The NG-MVPN signaling at PE3 is finally activated. Next check the MVPN instance and routing tables on PE1, PE2, and PE3 (Figures 3.163–165). The routing tables reflect the Type 5 and Type 7 routes propagated between the PE routers.

```
operator@PE3# run show multicast route instance MVPN-FOO extensive
Family: INET
Group: 237.1.1.1
    Source: 192.168.1.5/32
    Upstream interface: mt-0/0/10.49152
    Downstream interface list:
        ge-4/0/1.0
    Session description: Unknown
    Statistics: 74 kBps, 878 pps, 216899 packets
    Next-hop ID: 1048577
    Upstream protocol: PIM -> Still uses PIM+GRE
    Route state: Active
    Forwarding state: Forwarding
    Cache lifetime/timeout: 360 seconds
    Wrong incoming interface notifications: 0
```

FIGURE 3.162

Multicast forwarding state on PE3.

```
operator@PE1# run show route table MVPN-FOO.mvpn.0
1:100:1:7.0.0.1/240
                    *[BGP/170] 02:57:06, localpref 100, from 7.0.0.1
                      AS path: I
                    > to 172.16.1.1 via ge-1/0/1.0, Push 299776
1:100:1:7.0.0.4/240
                    *[BGP/170] 1d 16:00:05, localpref 100, from 7.0.0.4
                      AS path: I
                    > to 172.16.1.1 via ge-1/0/1.0
1:100:1:7.0.0.5/240
                    *[MVPN/70] 1d 16:14:06, metric2 1
                      Indirect
5:100:1:32:192.168.1.5:32:237.1.1.1/240
                    *[PIM/105] 00:00:12
                      Multicast (IPv4)
                    [BGP/170] 00:00:12, localpref 100, from 7.0.0.1
                      AS path: I
                    > to 172.16.1.1 via ge-1/0/1.0, Push 299776
7:100:1:100:32:192.168.1.5:32:237.1.1.1/240
                    *[PIM/105] 00:00:12
                      Multicast (IPv4)
                    [BGP/170] 00:00:12, localpref 100, from 7.0.0.1
                      AS path: I
                    > to 172.16.1.1 via ge-1/0/1.0, Push 299776
                    [BGP/170] 00:00:12, localpref 100, from 7.0.0.4
                      AS path: I
                    > to 172.16.1.1 via ge-1/0/1.0
```

FIGURE 3.163

Multicast routing information—PE1.

```
operator@PE2# run show route table MVPN-FOO.mvpn.0
1:100:1:7.0.0.1/240
                        *[BGP/170] 02:58:57, localpref 100, from 7.0.0.1
                          AS path: I
                        > to 172.16.1.6 via ge-4/0/3.0
1:100:1:7.0.0.4/240
                        *[MVPN/70] 1d 16:01:57, metric2 1
                          Indirect
1:100:1:7.0.0.5/240
                        *[BGP/170] 1d 16:07:36, localpref 100, from 7.0.0.5
                          AS path: I
                        > to 172.16.1.2 via ge-4/0/0.0
5:100:1:32:192.168.1.5:32:237.1.1.1/240
                        *[BGP/170] 00:02:03, localpref 100, from 7.0.0.1
                          AS path: I
                        > to 172.16.1.6 via ge-4/0/3.0
                         [BGP/170] 00:02:03, localpref 100, from 7.0.0.5
                          AS path: I
                        > to 172.16.1.2 via ge-4/0/0.0
6:100:1:100:32:7.0.0.1:32:237.1.1.1/240
                        *[PIM/105] 1d 15:58:25
                          Multicast (IPv4)
7:100:1:100:32:192.168.1.5:32:237.1.1.1/240
                        *[MVPN/70] 00:02:03, metric2 1
                          Multicast (IPv4)
                         [PIM/105] 00:02:03
                          Multicast (IPv4)
```

FIGURE 3.164

Multicast routing information—PE2.

```
operator@PE3# run show route table MVPN-FOO.mvpn.0
1:100:1:7.0.0.1/240
                        *[MVPN/70] 03:00:08, metric2 1
                          Indirect
1:100:1:7.0.0.4/240
                        *[BGP/170] 1d 15:59:36, localpref 100, from 7.0.0.4
                          AS path: I
                        > to 172.16.1.5 via ge-4/0/0.0
1:100:1:7.0.0.5/240
                        *[BGP/170] 1d 15:59:40, localpref 100, from 7.0.0.5
                          AS path: I
                        > to 172.16.1.5 via ge-4/0/0.0, Push 299792
5:100:1:32:192.168.1.5:32:237.1.1.1/240
                        *[PIM/105] 00:03:14
                          Multicast (IPv4)
                         [BGP/170] 00:03:14, localpref 100, from 7.0.0.5
                          AS path: I
                        > to 172.16.1.5 via ge-4/0/0.0, Push 299792
6:100:1:100:32:7.0.0.1:32:237.1.1.1/240
                        *[PIM/105] 00:03:28
                          Multicast (IPv4)
7:100:1:100:32:192.168.1.5:32:237.1.1.1/240
                        *[MVPN/70] 00:03:14, metric2 1
                          Multicast (IPv4)
                         [PIM/105] 00:03:14
                          Multicast (IPv4)
```

FIGURE 3.165

Multicast routing information—PE3

The Multicast forwarding state on PE3 must now be verified (see Figure 3.166). We see that the upstream protocol is now "MVPN," indicating that the transition from PIM + GRE to NG-MVPN is now complete.

```
operator@PE3# run show multicast route instance MVPN-FOO extensive
Family: INET
Group: 237.1.1.1
    Source: 192.168.1.5/32
    Upstream interface: lsi.0
    Downstream interface list:
        ge-4/0/1.0
    Session description: Unknown
    Statistics: 77 kBps, 912 pps, 313607 packets
    Next-hop ID: 1048576
    Upstream protocol: MVPN --> MVPN being used.
    Route state: Active
    Forwarding state: Forwarding
    Cache lifetime/timeout: forever
    Wrong incoming interface notifications: 0
```

FIGURE 3.166

Multicast forwarding state on PE3.

3.4.8 NG-MVPN Extranets

At the beginning of the chapter it was mentioned that building MVPN extranets within the context of NG-MVPNs is simplified because NG-MVPNs use the same model as BGP/MPLS Unicast VPNs. Use of the BGP control plane ensures that no additional configuration is required, apart from ensuring that Extranet connectivity is established within the Layer 3 VPN, that is, via Unicast policies. The relevant portions of the configuration can be seen in Figure 3.167.

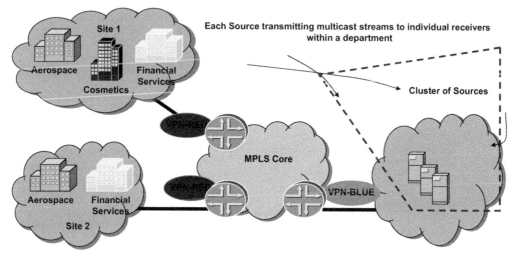

FIGURE 3.167

In this illustration, there are two VPNs: VPN-RED and VPN-BLUE. VPN-RED has a set of receivers in each of their two sites (Site 1 and Site 2). Each department within VPN-BLUE is interested in certain traffic, which is sent to a given C-MCAST group address, with sources centered at VPN-BLUE. VPN-BLUE has a set of multicast sources and hence is the sender site. To achieve multicast traffic flow across the two VPNs, extranet connectivity needs to be enabled. The relevant portions of the configurations are seen in Figure 3.168–3.170.

```
routing-instances {
VPN-BLUE {
instance-type vrf;
interface ge-4/0/2.100;
interface lo0.1;
route-distinguisher 200:1;
provider-tunnel {
    rsvp-te {
        label-switched-path-template {
            P2MP;
        }
    }
}
vrf-import import;
vrf-export export;
vrf-table-label;
protocols {
    bgp {
        family inet {
            unicast;
        }
        group peer {
            type external;
            peer-as 65003;
            neighbor 192.168.1.1;
        }
    }
    pim {
        rp {
            static {
                address 7.0.0.1;
            }
        }
        interface ge-4/0/2.100 {
            mode sparse-dense;
            version 2;
        }
        interface lo0.1 {
            mode sparse-dense;
            version 2;
        }
```

FIGURE 3.168

Configuration on PE1—Source PE at VPN-BLUE.

```
        }
      mvpn;
    }
   }
}
policy-options {
policy-statement export {
term 1 {
      then {
          community add BLUEVPN;
          accept;
      }
}
term 2 {
    then reject;
  }
}

policy-statement import {
term 1 {
    from community [ BLUEVPN REDVPN ];
    then accept;
}
term 2 {
    then reject;
  }
}
community BLUEVPN members target:200:1;
community REDVPN members target:100:1;
}
```

FIGURE 3.168

(*Continued*)

```
routing-instances {
VPN-RED {
instance-type vrf;
interface ge-4/0/1.0;
interface lo0.1;
route-distinguisher 100:1;
vrf-import import;
vrf-export export;
vrf-table-label;
protocols {
    bgp {
        family inet {
            unicast;
        }
```

FIGURE 3.169

Configuration on PE2—Receiver PE at VPN-RED.

```
            group peer {
                type external;
                export export;
                peer-as 65005;
                neighbor 192.168.1.9;
                neighbor 192.168.1.17 {
                    peer-as 65010;
                }
            }
        }
        pim {
            rp {
                local {
                    address 7.0.0.1;
                }
            }
            interface ge-4/0/1.0 {
                mode sparse;
                version 2;
            }
            interface lo0.1 {
                mode sparse;
                version 2;
            }
        }
        mvpn
    }
  }
}
policy-options {
policy-statement export {
term 1 {
    then {
        community add REDVPN;
        accept;
    }
}
term 2 {
    then reject;
  }
}

policy-statement import {
term 1 {
    from community [ REDVPN BLUEVPN ];
    then accept;
}
term 2 {
    then reject;
  }
}
community BLUEVPN members target:200:1;
community REDVPN members target:100:1;
}
```

FIGURE 3.169

(Continued)

```
routing-instances {
VPN-RED {
instance-type vrf;
interface ge-1/0/2.0;
interface lo0.1;
route-distinguisher 100:1;
vrf-import import;
vrf-export export;
vrf-table-label;
protocols {
    bgp {
        family inet {
            unicast;
        }
        group peer {
            type external;
            peer-as 65004;
            neighbor 192.168.1.5;
        }
    }
    pim {
        rp {
            static {
                address 7.0.0.1;
            }
        }
        interface ge-1/0/2.0 {
            mode sparse-dense;
            version 2;
        }
        interface lo0.1 {
            mode sparse-dense;
            version 2;
        }
    }
    mvpn
  }
 }
}
policy-options {
policy-statement export {
term 1 {
    then {
        community add REDVPN;
        accept;
    }
}
term 2 {
    then reject;
 }
}
```

FIGURE 3.170

Configuration on PE3—Receiver PE at VPN-RED.

```
policy-statement import {
term 1 {
    from community [ REDVPN BLUEVPN ];
    then accept;
}
term 2 {
    then reject;
 }
}
community BLUEVPN members target:200:1;
community REDVPN members target:100:1;
}
```

FIGURE 3.170

(Continued)

3.4.8.1 PE Router Configurations

If we look at the configuration of the various PE routers, the only difference between MVPN Intranets and Extranets is the use of appropriate policies (two policies are used on each PE router) to ensure that VPNv4 unicast routing information is available between VPNs. Once this reachability is ensured, multicast traffic flow between the VPNs is also established.

Outputs are not being provided for this section, because there is no difference in the MVPN route signaling between MVPN Intranets and Extranets.

3.4.9 Provider Router Configuration

A typical provider router configuration in the context of NG-MVPN would only be comprised of configurations relevant to the infrastructure within the core, such as IGP, MPLS, LDP, RSVP-TE (if RSVP-TE P2MP LSPs are used), PIM (if PIM P-tunnels are used), and MDLP (if P2MP LDP is used). There is no BGP-specific configuration required. A sample configuration for an MPLS Provider router supporting RSVP-TE P2MP LSPs is given in Figure 3.171.

```
Protocols {
rsvp {
    interface ge-0/2/0.0;
    interface ge-0/0/0.0;
    interface ge-0/2/1.0;
    interface ge-0/0/1.0;
}
mpls {
    interface ge-0/2/0.0;
    interface ge-0/0/0.0;
    interface ge-0/2/1.0;
    interface ge-0/0/1.0;
}
ospf {
    traffic-engineering;
    area 0.0.0.0 {
        interface ge-0/2/0.0;
        interface ge-0/0/0.0;
        interface ge-0/2/1.0;
        interface ge-0/0/1.0;
        interface lo0.0;
    }
  }
}
```

FIGURE 3.171

Provider router configuration.

3.4.10 **NG-MVPN—IPv6**

In this section configurations for extending existing NGEN-MVPN functionality to transport multicast IPv6 customer traffic over the IPv4 core network are reviewed (Figures 3.172 and 3.173). This feature does not require IPv6 support in the core. IPv6 is enabled only on PEs in VPN-instance configurations.

```
protocols {
    mld { -------------------> MLD version 2
### Only if MLD hosts are directly connected to PE.
### This is optional as MLD (version 1) is implicitedly enabled on
### all interfaces in the vpn instance
### You really need this only when version 2 is to be enabled.
        interface fe-1/3/0.0;
    }
    mpls {
        ipv6-tunneling;
        interface so-0/1/3.0;
        interface so-0/1/2.0;
    }
    bgp {
        group int {
            type internal;
            local-address 10.255.2.202;
            family inet-vpn {
                any;
            }
            family inet6-vpn {
                unicast;
            }
            family inet-mvpn {
                signaling;
            }
            family inet6-mvpn { -----> Support for IPv6 Multicast traffic
                signaling;
            }
            neighbor 10.255.2.204;
            neighbor 10.255.2.203;
        }
    }
    ospf {
        area 0.0.0.0 {
            interface so-0/1/3.0;
            interface so-0/1/2.0;
            interface lo0.0 {
                passive;
            }
        }
```

FIGURE 3.172

Provider edge router configuration for IPv6—Using PIM-ASM P-tunnels.

```
            }
        }
        ldp {
            interface so-0/1/2.0;
            interface so-0/1/3.0;
        }
        pim {
            rp {
                static {
                    address 10.255.2.203;
                }
            }
            interface lo0.0;
            interface so-0/1/3.0;
            interface so-0/1/2.0;
        }
    }
routing-instances {
    vpn_blue {
        instance-type vrf;
        interface fe-1/3/0.0;
        interface lo0.1;
        provider-tunnel {
            pim-asm { -------------→ PIM-ASM Provider Tunnel
                group-address 239.1.1.1;
            }
        }
        vrf-target target:100:200;
        vrf-table-label;
        protocols {
            pim {
                rp {
                    static {
                        address 10.12.53.12;
                        address ::10.12.53.12;
                    }
                }
                interface lo0.1;
                interface fe-1/3/0.0 {
                    priority 100;
                }
            }
            mvpn;
        }
    }
}
}
```

FIGURE 3.172

(Continued)

In this section we take a look at a configuration template using RSVP-TE I-PMSI/S-PMSI Tunnels.

```
protocols {
    rsvp {
        interface so-0/1/3.0;
        interface so-0/1/1.0;
    }
    mpls {
        ipv6-tunneling;
        label-switched-path lsp-to-e {
            to 10.255.2.204;
            p2mp p2mp-to-e;
        }
        interface so-0/1/3.0;
        interface so-0/1/1.0;
    }
    bgp {
        group int {
            type internal;
            local-address 10.255.2.202;
            family inet-vpn {
                any;
            }
            family inet6-vpn {
                unicast;
            }
            family inet-mvpn {
                signaling;
            }
            family inet6-mvpn {
                signaling;
            }
            neighbor 10.255.2.204;
            neighbor 10.255.2.203;
        }
    }
    ospf {
        traffic-engineering;
        area 0.0.0.0 {
            interface so-0/1/3.0;
            interface so-0/1/1.0;
            interface lo0.0 {
                passive;
            }
        }
    }
    ldp {
        interface so-0/1/1.0;
        interface so-0/1/3.0;
    }
}
routing-instances {
    vpn_blue {
        instance-type vrf;
        interface fe-1/3/0.0;
```

FIGURE 3.173

Provider edge router configuration for IPv6—Using RSVP-TE P-tunnels.

```
        interface lo0.1;
        provider-tunnel {
            rsvp-te {
                label-switched-path-template {
                    default-template;
                }
            }
            selective { ------->S-PMSI Tunnel
                group ffff::/16 {
                    source ::192.168.90.0/120 {
                        rsvp-te {
                            static-lsp p2mp-to-e;
                        }
                        threshold-rate 12;
                    }
                }
                group 225.0.0.0/16 {
                    source 192.168.90.0/24 {
                        rsvp-te {
                            static-lsp p2mp-to-e;
                        }
                        threshold-rate 12;
                    }
                }
            }
        }
        vrf-target target:100:200;
        vrf-table-label;
        protocols {
            pim {
                rp {
                    static {
                        address 10.12.53.12;
                        address ::10.12.53.12;
                    }
                }
                interface lo0.1;
                interface fe-1/3/0.0 {
                    priority 100;
                }

            }
            mvpn {

            }
        }
    }
}
```

FIGURE 3.173

(*Continued*)

3.4.11 Internet Multicast Using Next-Gen BGP Control Plane

In this section, we look at deploying Internet multicast over MPLS. Assume that a set of routers, running IP Multicast, are connected by an MPLS network. This solution allows these IP routers to exchange multicast state and data. It is based on a BGP control plane between the border routers for carrying multicast routing and auto-discovery information and an MPLS data plane between the border routers.

Assume that the IP network consists of Edge routers that run the multicast protocol. There are a set of Border Routers that connect to the Edge routers downstream and run IP Multicast on these interfaces. The Border Routers are connected to the MPLS core on the upstream with each other. The Border Routers form a full-mesh iBGP session to exchange multicast control state and full-mesh P2P LSPs for the data plane. The Internet Multicast IP traffic is encapsulated by the Border Routers in MPLS and carried over MPLS LSPs to other border routers, finally getting across to the edge routers.

To support IP Multicast over an MPLS network, the existing JUNOS NG-MVPN infrastructure is used. A full-mesh iBGP session is run between all border routers to exchange a multicast control state. The NLRI defined in BGP-MVPN is used to carry the multicast control state in BGP. "Ingress-replication" tunnels are configured on all of the border routers to form a full mesh of MPLS P2P LSP. These MPLS P2P LSPs are triggered dynamically when the border routers auto-discover each other through the inet-MVPN auto-discovery route defined in the NGEN framework discussed in the previous sections. The procedures to exchange control messages and data are explained in the rest of this chapter.

A new routing instance type, called "internet-multicast," is defined to support Internet Multicast over an MPLS network. Even though a new routing-instance is defined, it merely leverages the existing infrastructure to provide support for multicast in the default instance (master instance). The internet-multicast instance does not have any forwarding entries.

The following attributes are defined for the internet-multicast instance. No interfaces can be configured in the instance. The interfaces running IP Multicast on a border router will be associated with "inet.0," which is the Global routing table and not the routing instance and which is primarily for control plane procedures. Only one instance of internet-multicast can be defined. Currently, only the "MVPN" protocol is supported under the instance. A provider-tunnel can be configured in the instance for MVPN.

When the internet-multicast routing instance is configured, a VPN-label is allocated for the default instance. This label is necessary to terminate the data received on the P2P LSP in the default instance. Since data received on the LSP carry an inner VPN-label, an "lsi" interface is created dynamically in the default instance to terminate the data. Since this interface must terminate data in the default instance, packets arriving with the VPN-label are mapped to the lsi interface, which in turn strips the VPN-label, resulting in an IP lookup in the default instance's multicast RIB. The summary of these changes are described below:

- A VPN-label is allocated for the default instance when the internet-multicast instance is configured.
- The VPN-label maps to an lsi interface (which belongs to the master instance).
- The lsi interface is associated with the default instance's multicast RIB so that when the VPN-label is popped, the next IP lookup is done in the default instance.

To associate the default instance's multicast protocol with the internet-multicast instance, a knob must be configured under the multicast protocol. Currently, this knob is supported for PIM.

When a border router receives a PIM join on its IP enabled interface, an RPF lookup is done to the source address. The following rule is used to differentiate sources that are reachable through an IP interface (referred as local-source) and sources that are reachable through a different BR through the MPLS core (referred as remote-source):

If the unicast route to the source has the vrf rt-import extended community and the source-as extended community, the source is treated as a remote-source reachable through a remote Border route. If these communities are not present, the source is treated as a local-source reachable through an IP interface.

Each border router participating in BGP MPLS-based Internet multicast will auto-discover the other border routers participating in the same using Intra-AS A-D routes. The P-tunnel attribute will be used to signal whether a border router is configured to use ingress replication, that is, P2P LSPs for transporting internet-multicast traffic. The MVPN AD routes exchanged in the mpls internet-multicast context differ from the VPN context in one aspect—since the mpls-internet-multicast instance is not a vrf instance, the MVPN AD routes do not carry any target communities (in the VPN context they carry the import targets used for unicast inet-VPN routes). When a router receives such an AD route (without a target community), it accepts and imports the route if and only if the mpls-internet-multicast instance is configured.

In the mpls internet-multicast context, PIM is configured only on the IP interfaces. Since the PIM relies on the MVPN infrastructure to carry the control state between border routers, a new knob called "mpls-internet-multicast'" is introduced under PIM to achieve this. When the knob is configured, a pseudo-interface is created in the master instance to be used as the RPF interface for all remote sources reachable through the MPLS core. When a border router receives a join for a remote source in the default instance, PIM behaves as follows:

- Uses the pseudo-interface as the upstream interface
- Finds the mpls-internet-multicast instance
- Installs a C-multicast route in the instance's MVPN TIB

Since the forwarding entries and control routes are maintained in different instances, PIM sets the correct instance based on the operation.

When MVPN is configured in the mpls-internet-multicast instance rather than a vrf instance, the following behaviors are changed:

- Unicast route lookup is done in the master instance.
- MVPN forwarding entries are always created in the master instance.
- RD value of 0:0 is used for MVPN routes indicating that these routes are created by the mpls-internet-multicast instance.

When an egress Border Router receives a PIM-SSM or PIM-ASM (S, G) join, it discovers the Upstream Multicast Hop (UMH) for the S and generates a BGP Source tree C-multicast route toward the UMH. Once the ingress BR receives a C-multicast route for a (S, G), it follows the procedures in BGP-MVPN, which may result in generating a PIM join toward the source. Further, the ingress BR creates a forwarding plane state to send packets for (S, G) to all egress BRs.

If the egress BR receives a PIM-ASM (*, G) join, then the BR discovers the UMH for the C-RP. It may or may not generate a BGP shared tree C-multicast route toward the UMH, depending on whether PIM-ASM is configured using "only inter-site source trees" or "inter-site shared and source trees."

A border router creates an (S, G) or (*, G) control plane state as a result of receiving a BGP C-multicast route originated by another border router. When ingress replication is configured as the provider tunnel, the ingress BR creates an (S, G) or (*, G) forwarding entry in the Internet IP forwarding table with the P2P LSPs to all other BRs downstream along with IP enabled interfaces that have local receivers.

The inclusive ingress-replication tunnel results in a border router sending traffic, for which it has at least one remote receiver, to all other border routers. When the ingress-replication-based selective P-tunnel is configured, the ingress BR forwards the data only on LSPs that terminate at BRs that have sent C-multicast joins to the ingress BR. This ensures that the data are not flooded to BRs that are not interested in it and also ensures that an egress BR never gets duplicate data from multiple ingress BRs.

A new provider-tunnel, called ingress-replication, is implemented to support internet multicast over the mpls network and also as a new provider tunnel for multicast VPN. Ingress Replication uses unicast tunnels between the border routers to create the multicast distribution tree.

A full mesh of unicast tunnels between the BRs (and PEs in the case of multicast VPNs) is required to ensure that the inclusive provider tunnel rooted at all BRs can be established. When a BR needs to establish a multicast distribution tree to a set of egress BRs, the ingress BR replicates the data on all of the unicast tunnels terminating at the egress BRs. The unicast tunnels from the ingress BR to all of the egress BRs form the ingress replication tunnel.

Ingress Replication can be reached using different kinds of unicast tunnels such as point-to-point LSP GRE tunnels. Current ideas support only point-to-point LSP-based ingress replication. The IR provider-tunnel can be configured in two different modes:

- In the default "existing-unicast-tunnel" mode, when an application requests the addition of a destination to the IR tunnel, an existing unicast tunnel to the destination is used. If a unicast tunnel is not available, then the destination is not added to the IR tunnel. The IR module picks an existing tunnel to a destination through an mpls route lookup to the destination (in the inet.3 routing table). It also handles route changes to the destination and rebuilds the IR tunnel based on the changes in the mpls route. The IR module makes an assumption that the LSP routes in inet.3 are only for host addresses. The IR tunnel module cannot handle prefix routes currently.
- In the second mode, called "create-new-ucast-tunnel," when an application requests the addition of destination to the IR tunnel, a new unicast tunnel is created to the destination and added to the IR tunnel. The unicast tunnel will be deleted when the application requests for deletion of the destination from the IR tunnel.

When ingress-replication is used as the provider tunnel in MVPN, a downstream allocated mpls label is advertised in the intra-as AD route. This downstream allocated label is used to demultiplex the traffic arriving on the unicast tunnel to the correct MVPNs on the egress PE router. This is a requirement for a multicast VPN. However, with an mpls internet-multicast, PHP results in IP packets reaching the egress BR. Since the traffic belongs to the default instance (and not a VPN), there is no need for the inner label to demultiplex the traffic on the egress BR. But this presents a different problem. Consider the following topology:

```
if1
-- ---
/ \ /
/ if2 \ /
BR1---- ...---- BR2 --- (IP interfaces)
\ / \
\ if3/ \
-- ---
```

In this topology BR2 has three MPLS core facing interfaces: if1, if2, and if3. When the BR2 receives a join to a source connected to BR1 (remote source), BR2 must install an (S, G) forwarding entry to receive data from the MPLS core. Because multicast forwarding entries have been RPF enabled, the MVPN module must compute the correct incoming interface for the forwarding entry. Since it is not possible to determine the incoming interface on the egress BR when a unicast tunnel delivers traffic (since the tunneling protocol can compute its own path through the mpls network), there are two ways MVPN can handle RPF checks:

- Disable RPF check: The first option is to disable RPF check on routes for remote sources. This will ensure that the traffic received on the unicast tunnel is accepted by the egress BR irrespective of the incoming interface. This approach, however, breaks parts of the PIM functionality that depends on interface mismatch notification.
- Use lsi as iif: The second option is to add an inner mpls label to the traffic sent on the unicast tunnel. The egress BR uses the lsi interface to receive data on the unicast tunnel. This allows MVPN to use the lsi interface as the iif interface.

For the previously mentioned reason, a downstream allocated mpls label is always used for traffic sent on the unicast tunnels and the egress BR uses the lsi interface as the incoming interface for its forwarding entries to receive traffic from remote sources (see Figure 3.174).

Configuring the mpls-internet-multicast instance automatically creates an lsi interface in the master instance. This interface is used by MVPN as the iif for the provider tunnel.

3.4.12 Considerations for Deploying Broadcast Video/IPTV

Traditionally IPTV/Broadcast Video has been deployed both within the context of an MVPN and in the Global routing Table also known as Internet Multicast. One of the frequently asked questions is: Which is the best approach for deploying such traffic? The NG-MVPN framework based on BGP provides an operator with an excellent opportunity to deploy IPTV within an MVPN. Some of the benefits of this approach are as follows:

1. The BGP control plane with the various MVPN route types provides an opportunity to use auto-discovery of member sites and automates the provisioning of P-tunnels. This simplifies the provisioning aspect, as compared to traditional Internet Multicast schemes that relied mainly on static configurations.

```
routing-instances {
    <instance_name> {
+       instance-type mpls-internet-multicast;
        provider-tunnel {
+           ingress-replication {
+                   create-new-ucast-tunnel; /* trigger new ucast tunnel */
+               label-switched-path {      /* Use P2P unicast tunnel */
+                   label-switched-path-template { /* dynamic LSP */
+                       template <template name>; /* pre-defined template */
+                       default-template;        /* use default template */
+                   }
+               }
+           }
        }
        protocols {
            mvpn;
        }
    }
}
The following PIM configuration is necessary in order to work in a
mpls internet multicast context.

protocols {
    pim {
+       mpls-internet-multicast; /* Indicates mpls internet multicast instance
is used for PIM */
        ...
    }
}
admin@siluan> show ingress-replication mvpn
Ingress Tunnel: mvpn:1
  Application: MVPN
  Unicast tunnels
    Leaf Address      Tunnel-type     Mode      State
    10.255.245.2      P2P LSP         New       Up
```

FIGURE 3.174

Configuration template for Internet Multicast.

2. The operator can choose to use I-PMSI and S-PMSI or S-PMSI tunnels only depending on various factors such as traffic thresholds and Source/Group pairs.
3. An operator providing PIM-SSM transit services to smaller carriers and operators always faces the fear of overlapping multicast groups; this can cause undesirable effects on traffic and its users. Containing traffic within an MVPN provides a framework for ensuring individual privacy for multicast traffic on a per customer/carrier basis in such cases.
4. There is a wide range of tunnel types to choose from within the NG-MVPN framework.

3.4.13 Vendor Support for the NG-MVPN Framework

The industry including vendors and carriers has started moving toward the NG-MVPN framework due to the tremendous benefits and the paradigm shift in building multicast infrastructures that the

Next-Gen MVPN framework offers. There is a large installed base of this solution already with some of the largest service providers deploying this solution. Many customers who have used satellite infrastructures to offer High Definition Video have successfully migrated their applications (such as Broadcast/Linear video) to a converged MPLS platform using NG-MVPN thus cutting costs on OPEX.

From a vendor standpoint, Alcatel-Lucent has been supporting the NG-MVPN solution based on the BGP control plane for quite some time with some limitations on the support for the various BGP route types. For instance, only auto-discovery, that is, Type 1 BGP, routes are supported as of TiMOS release 7.0R5. Starting with TiMOS Release 8.0, Alcatel-Lucent supports a full-fledged version of the NG-MVPN framework based on the BGP control plane, which is completely interoperable with the JUNOS-based implementation. This will be further discussed in Chapter 4. Other vendors have also claimed a road map for this solution, but have not yet announced its availability.

3.5 SUMMARY

NG-MVPNs lay the foundation for a new dimension in delivery of multicast enabled applications over a converged IP/MPLS infrastructure, and define a paradigm shift in the delivery of applications that were once considered not optimal for delivery over an IP core; for example, high definition video. The BGP control plane provides an opportunity for creating new service types in the form of MVPN routing information. The vendor and carrier community have expressed great interest and support for this framework and today this is not just an emerging solution, but a well-established and mature technology with many worldwide deployments. Throughout this book, the implementations of specific nuances on Alcatel-Lucent and Cisco devices will be examined.

Next Generation Multicast VPNs on Alcatel-Lucent (TiMOS)

4.1 INTRODUCTION

Alcatel-Lucent has been supporting the NG-MVPN solution based on the BGP control plane for quite some time, with some limitations on the support for the various BGP route types. For example, only auto-discovery (i.e., Type 1 BGP) routes are supported as of TiMOS early releases. Starting with TiMOS release 8.0, TiMOS supports a complete implementation of the NG framework based on the BGP control plane.

On earlier TiMOS releases, the offerings have been limited to using PIM-ASM/SSM for the I-PMSI and SSM to create S-PMSI. Support for other Tunnel types and a fully fledged BGP control plane with support for all route types is only available in version 8.0.

4.2 BEGINNING OF NG-MVPN SUPPORT ON ALU

In this section we look at the Alcatel-Lucent TiMOS implementation. Figure 4.1 will be used to demonstrate the configuration and other details. The configuration and details provided in this figure are based on TiMOS.

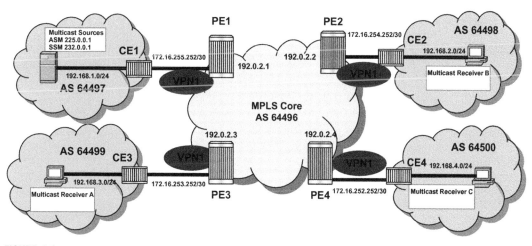

FIGURE 4.1

311

Like this illustration, multicast traffic from the source is streamed toward router CE1. Receivers connected to PE2, PE3, and PE4 are interested in joining this multicast group. CE1 to CE4 are PIM enabled routers that form a PIM adjacency with the nearest PE. Data plane traffic is transported across the I-PMSI until a configured bandwidth threshold is reached. A selective PMSI that carries data plane traffic is then signaled.

4.2.1 Provider Common Configuration

This section describes the common configuration required for each PE within the Provider multicast domain, which includes IGP and VPRN service configurations. The configuration tasks can be summarized as follows:

- *PE global configuration.* This includes configuration of the Interior Gateway Protocol (IGP; ISIS or OSPF), configuration of link layer LDP between PEs, and the configuration of BGP between PEs to facilitate VPRN route learning.
- *VPRN configuration on PEs.* This includes configuration of basic VPRN parameters (route-distinguisher, route target communities), configuration of attachment circuits toward CEs, configuration of VRF routing protocol, and any policies toward CE.
- *VRF PIM and MVPN parameters.* I-PMSI and CE configuration.

4.2.2 PE Global Configuration

This involves the following steps. On each of the PE routers, configure the appropriate router interfaces OSPF (or ISIS) and link layer LDP. For clarity, only the configuration for PE1 is shown, but PE2, PE3, and PE4 are similar (see Figure 4.2).

```
A:PE1>config router
        interface "int-pe1-pe2"
        address 192.168.1.1/30
            port 1/1/1
        exit
        interface "int-pe1-pe3"
        address 192.168.2.1/30
            port 1/1/2
        exit
        interface "system"
            address 192.0.2.1/32
        exit
        autonomous-system 64496
        ospf
            area 0.0.0.0
                interface "system"
        exit
```

FIGURE 4.2

PE router configuration.

```
            interface "int-pe1-pe2"
               interface-type point-to-point
      exit
            interface "int-pe1-pe3"
            interface-type point-to-point
               exit
         exit
      exit
      ldp
           interface-parameters
             interface "int-pe1-pe2"
             exit
             interface "int-pe1-pe3"
             exit
      exit
           targeted-session
         exit
      exit
```

FIGURE 4.2

(*Continued*)

Now we verify the OSPF and LDP adjacencies and ensure that they have been established (see Figure 4.3).

```
A:PE1# show router ospf neighbor
===============================================================================
OSPF Neighbors
===============================================================================
Interface-Name Rtr Id State Pri RetxQ TTL
-------------------------------------------------------------------------------
int-pe1-pe2 192.0.2.2 Full 1 0 31
int-pe1-pe3 192.0.2.3 Full 1 0 37
-------------------------------------------------------------------------------
No. of Neighbors: 2
===============================================================================

A:PE1 # show router ldp session
===============================================================================
LDP Sessions
===============================================================================
Peer LDP Id Adj Type State Msg Sent Msg Recv Up Time
-------------------------------------------------------------------------------
192.0.2.2:0 Link Established 8651 8651 0d 06:38:44
192.0.2.3:0 Link Established 8697 8694 0d 06:40:20
-------------------------------------------------------------------------------
No. of Sessions: 2
===============================================================================
```

FIGURE 4.3

Check OSPF and LDP adjacencies.

In Figure 4.4, we configure BGP between the Provider Edge routers.

```
A:PE1> configure router
bgp
    group "internal"
      family vpn-ipv4
      peer-as 64496
      neighbor 192.0.2.2
    exit
     neighbor 192.0.2.3
    exit
     neighbor 192.0.2.4
    exit
   exit
exit
```

FIGURE 4.4

Configuration of BGP on the PE router.

Check the status of the BGP sessions between PE routers (see Figure 4.5).

```
A:PE1# show router bgp summary
===============================================================================
BGP Router ID:192.0.2.1        As:64496        Local As:64496
===============================================================================
BGP Admin State           : Up       BGP Oper State            : Up
Total Peer Groups         : 1        Total Peers               : 3
Total BGP Paths           : 15       Total Path Memory         : 1932
Total IPv4 Remote Rts     : 0        Total IPv4 Rem. Active Rts : 0
Total IPv6 Remote Rts     : 0        Total IPv4 Rem. Active Rts : 0
Total Supressed Rts       : 0        Total Hist. Rts           : 0
Total Decay Rts           : 0

Total VPN Peer Groups     : 1        Total VPN Peers           : 1
Total VPN Local Rts       : 2
Total VPN-IPv4 Rem. Rts   : 7        Total VPN-IPv4 Rem. Act. Rts : 6
Total VPN-IPv6 Rem. Rts   : 0        Total VPN-IPv6 Rem. Act. Rts : 0
Total L2 VPN Rem. Rts     : 0        Total L2VPN Rem. Act. Rts : 0
Total VPN Supp. Rts       : 0        Total VPN Hist. Rts       : 0
Total VPN Decay Rts       : 0
Total MVPN-IPv4 Rem Rts   : 3        Total MVPN-IPv4 Rem Act Rts : 3
===============================================================================
```

FIGURE 4.5

Verifying BGP sessions.

In Figure 4.6 we enable PIM on all network interfaces, including the system interface (remember we are using PIM + GRE as the Provider Tunnel). This allows the signaling of PMSIs that transport PIM signaling within each VRF. As each I-PMSI will signal using PIM ASM, a rendezvous point (RP) is required within the global PIM configuration. A static RP is used and PE1 is selected. All PEs must be configured with this RP address as per standard ASM procedures.

```
A:PE1> configure router
bgp
    group "internal"
      family vpn-ipv4 mvpn-ipv4
      peer-as 64496
      neighbor 192.0.2.2
    exit
     neighbor 192.0.2.3
    exit
     neighbor 192.0.2.4
    exit
   exit
exit
A:PE1> Configure router
        pim
          interface "system"
          exit
          interface "int-pe1-pe2"
          exit
          interface "int-pe1-pe3"
          exit
          rp
          static
          address 192.0.2.1
          group-prefix 239.255.0.0/16
          exit
        exit
         bsr-candidate
           shutdown
         exit
        rp-candidate
         shutdown
        exit
       exit
  exit
```

FIGURE 4.6

Configuration of PIM on the PE.

Now we check the status of PIM associations and their status (see Figure 4.7).

```
A:PE1# show router pim neighbor
===============================================================================
PIM Neighbor ipv4
===============================================================================
Interface Nbr DR Prty Up Time Expiry Time Hold Time
Nbr Address
-------------------------------------------------------------------------------
int-pe1-pe2 1 0d 23:21:04 0d 00:01:15 105
192.168.1.2
int-pe1-pe3 1 0d 23:22:40 0d 00:01:34 105
192.168.2.2
-------------------------------------------------------------------------------
Neighbors : 2
===============================================================================
```

FIGURE 4.7

Check PIM status.

4.2.3 PE VPRN (VPN) Configuration

Because each PE contains a CE that will be part of the multicast VRF, it is necessary to enable PIM on each interface containing an attachment circuit toward a CE, and to configure the I-PMSI multicast tunnel for the VRF. For the BGP routes to be accepted into the VRF, a route-target community is required (vrftarget). This is configured in the "**configure service vprn 1 mvpn**" context and, in this case, is set to the same value as the "unicast vrf-target"—the "vrf-target" community as configured under the "**configure service vprn 1vrf-target**" context.

On each PE, A VPRN instance is configured as seen in Figure 4.8.

```
A:PE2# configure service vprn 1
            autonomous-system 64496
            route-distinguisher 64496:1
            auto-bind ldp
            vrf-target target:64496:1
            interface "int-pe2-ce2" create
              address 172.16.254.254/30
              sap 1/1/3:1 create
             exit
            exit
              pim
                interface "int-pe2-ce2"
            exit
            mvpn
                auto-discovery
                provider-tunnel
                inclusive
                pim asm 239.255.255.1
                exit
            exit
        exit
          vrf-target unicast
          exit
        exit
        no shutdown
```

FIGURE 4.8

PE VPRN configuration.

The multicast group address used for the PMSI must be the same on all PEs for this VPRN instance as configured in our examples with JUNOS. The presence of auto-discovery will initiate BGP updates between the PEs that contain an MVPN, such as Intra-AD MVPN routes, and are generated and advertised to each peer as illustrated in Figure 4.9.

```
A:PE1# show router bgp routes mvpn-1pv4
===============================================================================
 BGP Router ID:192.0.2.1      AS:64496       Local AS:64496
===============================================================================
 Legend -
 Status codes : u - used, s - suppressed, h - history, d - decayed, * - valid
 origin codes : i - IGP, e - BGP, ? - incomplete, > - best


===============================================================================
BGP MVPN-IPv4 Routes
===============================================================================
 Flag    RouteType          OriginatorIP          LocalPref      MED
         RD                 SourceAS                             VPNLabel
         Nexthop            SourceIP
         As-Path            GroupIP
 ------------------------------------------------------------------------------
 u*>1    Intra-Ad           192.0.2.2             100            0
         64496:1            -                                    -
         192.0.2.2          -
         NO As-Path         -

 u*>1    Intra-Ad           192.0.2.3             100            0
         64496:1            -                                    -
         192.0.2.3          -
         NO As-Path         -
 u*>1    Intra-Ad           192.0.2.4             100            0
         64496:1            -                                    -
         192.0.2.4          -
         NO As-Path         -
 ------------------------------------------------------------------------------
 Routes  : 3
===============================================================================
```

FIGURE 4.9

MVPN routing information.

Figure 4.9 shows that PE1 has received an Intra-AD route from each of the other PEs, each of which has multicast VPRN 1 configured. Examining one of the Intra-AD routes from PE2 shows that the route-target community matches the unicast VRF-target (64496:1), and also that the PMSI tree has a multicast group address of 239.255.255.1, which matches the I-PMSI group configuration on PE1. This is illustrated in Figure 4.10.

4.2.4 S-PMSI Configuration

When a configurable data threshold for a multicast group has been exceeded, multicast traffic across the Provider network can be switched to a selective PMSI (S-PMSI). This has to be configured as a separate group and must contain a threshold which, if exceeded, will see a new PMSI signaled by the PE nearest the source and traffic switched onto the S-PMSI. The configuration details are given in Figure 4.11.

```
A:PE1# show router bgp routes mvpn-1pv4 type intra-ad originator-ip 192.0.2.2 detail
===================================================================================
  BGP Router ID:192.0.2.1      AS:64496        Local AS:64496
===================================================================================
  Legend -
  Status codes : u - used, s - suppressed, h - history, d - decayed, * - valid
  origin codes : i - IGP, e - EGP, ? - incomplete, > - best
===================================================================================
BGP MVPN-IPv4 Routes
===================================================================================
Route Type     : Intra-Ad
Route Dist.    : 64496:1
Originator IP  : 192.0.2.2
Nexthop        : 192.0.2.2
From           : 192.0.2.2
Res. Nexthop   : 0.0.0.0
Local Pref.    : 100                     Interface Name : Not Available
Aggregator As  : None                    Aggregator     : None
Atomic Aggr.   : Not Atomic              MED            : 0
Community      : target:64496:1
Cluster        : No Cluster Members
Originator Id  : None                    Peer Router Id : 192.0.2.2
Flags          : Used Valid Best IGP
As-Path        : No As-Path
-----------------------------------------------------------------------------------
PMSI Tunnel Attribute :
Tunnel-type    : PIM-SM Tree        Flags                : Local Info not Required
MPLS Label     : 0X0
Sender         : 192.0.2.2          P-Group              : 239.255.255.1
-----------------------------------------------------------------------------------
-----------------------------------------------------------------------------------
Routes : 1
===================================================================================
```

FIGURE 4.10

MVPN routing information—Detailed output.

```
  *A:PE1# configure service vprn 1
                  mvpn
                    provider-tunnel
                    inclusive
                    pim asm 239.255.255.1
                   exit
                  exit
                   selective
                     data-threshold 232.0.0.0/8 1
                       pim-ssm 232.255.1.0/24
                   exit
                  exit
               exit
             no shutdown
```

FIGURE 4.11

S-PMSI configuration.

The configuration in Figure 4.12 indicates that when the traffic threshold for multicast groups covered by the range 232.0.0.0/8 exceeds 1 Kbps between a pair of PEs, an S-PMSI is signaled between the PEs. This is a separate multicast tunnel over which traffic in the given group now flows.

```
A:PE1# show router pim s-pmsi detail
===============================================================================
PIM Selective provider tunnels
===============================================================================
Md Source Address : 192.0.2.1          Md Group Address        : 232.255.1.14
Number of VPN SGs : 1                  Uptime                  : 0d 00:00:12
MT IfIndex        : 16395

VPN Group Address : 232.0.0.1          VPN Source Address      : 192.168.1.2
State             : TX Jointed         Mdt Threshold           : 1
Join Timer        : 0d 00:00:47        Holddown Timer          : 0d 00:00:47
===============================================================================
PIM Selective provider tunnels Interfaces : 1
===============================================================================
```

FIGURE 4.12

Validating S-PMSI at the Ingress Node.

In Figure 4.12, the (S, G) group is (192.168.1.2, 225.0.0.1). As the data rate has exceeded the configured MDT threshold of 1 Kbps, a new provider tunnel with a group address of 232.255.1.14 has been signaled and now carries the multicast stream. The TX Joined state indicates that the S-PMSI has been sourced at this PE–PE1. Comparing this to PE3, where a receiver is connected through a CE, indicates that it has received a join to connect the S-PMSI as seen in Figure 4.13.

```
A:PE3# show router pim s-pmsi detail
===============================================================================
PIM Selective provider tunnels
===============================================================================
Md Source Address : 192.0.2.1          Md Group Address        : 232.255.1.14
Number of VPN SGS : 1                  Uptime                  : 0d 00:00:13
MT IfIndex        : 24576              Egress Fwding Rate      : 52.8 kbps

VPN Group Address : 232.0.0.1          VPN Source Address      : 192.168.1.2
State             : RX Jointed
Expiry Timer      : 0d 00:02:31
===============================================================================
PIM Selective provider tunnels Interfaces : 1
...
===============================================================================
```

FIGURE 4.13

Validating S-PMSI at the Egress Node.

4.3 FULL-FLEDGED NG-MVPN SUPPORT ON ALU (REL 8.0)

Release 8.0 has the complete support for the NG-MVPN framework using the BGP control plane for autodiscovery and C-MCAST signaling. In the following sections, we take a look at a few case studies along with the relevant configuration details.

4.4 NG-MVPN USING PIM-SSM AS THE P-TUNNEL

In this example, we look at the PE configurations required for building PIM-SSM-based Provider Tunnels and the use of BGP for C-MCAST signaling (see Figure 4.14).

CONTEXT	COMMAND	EXPLANATION

config>router	pim
	    ssm-groups
	        group-range 239.10.0.0/16
		Add to ssm group ranges if necessary

config>router>bgp	family vpn-ipv4 mvpn-ipv4	Enable multi-protocol BGP support for MVPN signaling

config>service>vpm	mvpn
	    auto-discovery
	    c-mcast-signaling bgp
	    provider-tunnel
	        inclusive
	            pim ssm 239.10.20.1
	                no shutdown
	            exit
	        exit
	        selective
	            no auto-discovery-disable
	            data-delay-interval 3
	            data-threshold 239.1.1.0/24 1024
	            pim-ssm 232.0.1.0/24
	        exit
	    exit
	exit
		Configure MVPN parameters; I-PMSI uses PIM-SSM, and S-PMSIs use PIM-SSM

FIGURE 4.14

4.5 NEXT-GEN MVPN USING RSVP-TE P2MP LSP AS THE P-TUNNEL

In this section we look at a configuration example of an I-PMSI and S-PMSI setup using RSVP-TE as the provider tunnel (see Figure 4.15).

CONTEXT	COMMAND	EXPLANATION

config>router>mpls	lsp-template "pmsi" p2mp
	   adaptive
	   bandwidth 5
	   cspf
	   fast-reroute facility
	   no shutdown
		Create P2MP LSP template

config>router>bgp	family vpn-ipv4 mvpn-ipv4	Enable multi-protocol BGP support for MVPN signaling

config>service>vpm	mvpn
	   auto-discovery
	   c-mcast-signaling bgp
	   provider-tunnel
	      inclusive
	         rsvp
	            lsp-template "pmsi"
	         exit
	      exit
	      selective
	         no auto-discovery-disable
	         data-delay-interval 3
	         data-threshold 239.1.1.0/24 1024
	         rsvp
	            lsp-template "pmsi"
	         exit
	        exit
	      exit
	   exit
		Configure MVPN parameters; I-PMSI uses RSVP, and S-PMSIs use RSVP

FIGURE 4.15

4.6 SUMMARY

The Alcatel Lucent implementation based on TiMOS Release 8.0 completely supports the NG-MVPN framework with support for PIM-ASM, SSM, and RSVP-TE as Provider Tunnels. There is complete interoperability between other vendors, such as Juniper, who support this framework.

Internet Multicast and Multicast VPNs Based on MDLP In-Band Signaling

5.1 INTRODUCTION

Chapter 4 introduced the building blocks of Label Switched Multicast, also referred to as Next-Generation Multicast, which is the enabler for Next-Generation Multicast VPNs. It provided a deep dive into the control plane infrastructure, which is built using BGP and also the various options for enabling the data plane, such as RSVP-TE, MLDP, and PIM-SM. Each of these is standards based and interoperable across vendors.

In this chapter, we take a look at an implementation purely based on MLDP both from a control plane and data plane perspective (an MVPN application uses PIM for VPN specific multicast information; however, and this is the only exception). This implementation is based on the IETF draft "draft-wijnands-mpls-in-band-signalling-01." Note that at this time the implementation was only supported by Cisco-based platforms.

5.1.1 Terminology

Before we discuss this implementation in more detail, the various terms used throughout this chapter are listed in Table 5.1. The terms LSR and PE are used interchangeably.

Table 5.1 LSM Terminology

Term	Definition
Ingress Router (LSR/PE)	Start of MP LSP, closest to multicast source (root node)
Egress Router (LSR/PE)	End branch of MP LSP, closest to a multicast receiver (leaf node)
Upstream	Multicast traffic traveling from Egress LSR toward root
Downstream	Multicast traffic traveling from root toward Egress LSR
P2P LSP	LSP with one Ingress LSR and one Egress LSR
P2MP LSP	LSP with one Ingress LSR and one or more Egress LSR
MP2MP LSP	LSP that connects a set of leaf nodes, acting as Ingress or Egress
MP LSP	Any type of multipoint LSP
LSR	Label Switch Router

5.2 MULTICAST LDP IN-BAND SIGNALING

A few points mentioned in the early part of this chapter (even though they were discussed in previous chapters) are well worth mentioning again to refresh our memories. We are well aware that MLDP is a receiver-driven protocol. This means that a Point to Multipoint or Multipoint to Multipoint LSP is only created or joined if there is a receiver at the edge of the MPLS network that wishes to join a group. All LSPs must have a root (in the MPLS core) that will be the MPLS PE connected to the source in the IP Multicast network. The MP LSP path selection is based on the root address derived either from the BGP Next-Hop of the source, statically configured in the case of MP2MP LSPs, or by some other signaling protocol such as PIM.

Note that this draft only uses PIM for C-MCAST signaling.

5.2.1 MLDP Signaling

MLDP signaling essentially provides two functions:

- To discover the FEC (and its associated Opaque Value) for an MP LSP; FEC elements are explained in detail in the following sections
- To assign a multicast flow to an MP LSP

MLDP can use two signaling methods: In-band Signaling and Out-of-Band or Overlay Signaling (which was discussed in Chapter). However, let us do a small comparison between the two signaling options for ease of reading.

In the context of MLDP signaling, an FEC uniquely defines the MP LSP within the network, and the signaling maps the streams that will run over that MP LSP.

- In-Band Signaling
  - Opaque Value is used to map an MP LSP to an IP Multicast flow
  - Contents of the opaque value are derived from the Multicast flow
- Out-Of-Band Signaling (also referred to as Next-Generation Multicast and Multicast VPNs that use the BGP Control Plane)
  - Uses an overlay protocol (BGP) to map an MP LSP to an IP Multicast flow
  - MP LSP is created on-demand or can be pre-configured
  - Allows aggregating multicast streams onto a single MP LSP

The best way to understand how the different signaling mechanisms work is to discuss these concepts and illustrate each signaling option in detail, which will be done in the following sections.

5.2.1.1 MLDP in the Context of Next-Generation MVPNs

It is worthwhile to note that all the building blocks of MLDP (provided in the following sections) are in line with the MVPN Next-Generation draft "draft-minei-mpls-ldp-p2mp.txt"; therefore, all of the components of MLDP described in this section are also in line with the draft. However "in-band signaling," which is the focus of this section, is based on a draft that utilizes MLDP for transport, but with a modified approach in the implementation especially within the context of using a combination of MLDP Opaque values and PIM (for C-MCAST signaling) for achieving the deployment of multicast applications. Because of this it does not adhere to the Next-Generation MVPN framework. We will discuss these details as we progress in the chapter.

5.2.1.2 MLDP Topology

In the context of this draft, which uses in-band signaling, the only change is that there is no over-lay signaling protocol used for C-MCAST signaling. Both the forwarding and control plane rely on MLDP. The only exception is the deployment of Multicast-VPNs, which do use PIM for exchanging customer multicast routing information. Because of this the implementation is subject to certain con-straints that are discussed a bit later in this chapter.

There are essentially two parts to the network as shown in Figure 5.1.

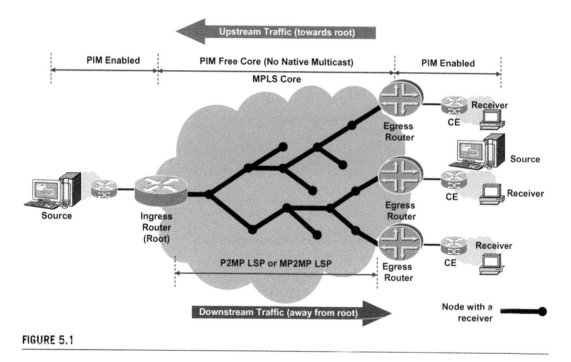

FIGURE 5.1

The MPLS core where the MP LSPs exist and the PIM enabled edge network. Therefore native IP operates on the edge of the network, while only label switching operates in the MPLS core; there is no PIM or BGP control plane necessary in the core.

Traffic flow or the data plane is similar to how MLDP operates when out-of-band signaling is used. The PE router closest to the multicast source is referred to as the ingress router as traffic comes into the MPLS core at this point. The ingress router is also the root of the MP LSP. Multicast traffic trav-els downstream (away from the root) along the MP LSP toward the receivers. The PE routers closest to the receivers are referred to as the egress router where multicast traffic leaves the MPLS core and enters the PIM domain where it is routed via normal IP Multicast. Upstream traffic travels toward the root of the tree and may include control packets and bi-directional streams. Both the ingress and egress routers participate in both the native IP Multicast domain (PIM) and the MPLS domain (MLDP).

5.2.2 FEC Elements

Central to the operation of MLDP are MP LSP Forwarding Equivalency Class (FEC) Elements. To understand FEC Elements it is important to review how LDP messages work.

The LDP protocol consists of various types of **messages** such as Hello, Initialize, and Label Mapping. We are primarily interested in the Label Mapping message as shown in Figure 5.2. It is used by MLDP to create the MP LSP hop-by-hop to the root Ingress PE router and it carries additional information known as **TLVs**. There are many types of TLVs, such as the **FEC TLV** in the Label Mapping message that maps packets onto LSPs using a label defined in the **Label TLV**. The FEC TLV contains **FEC Elements** that actually define the set of packets that will use the LSP. For example, in **unicast forwarding** an FEC Element would contain an IP prefix (or PE Loopback); therefore, any destination IP address that falls within this prefix range will use the label defined in the Label TLV, in essence sharing the same LSP (Forwarding Equivalency Class).

FIGURE 5.2

For **multicast forwarding** three FEC elements have been defined for MLDP to create various MP LSPs.

- P2MP FEC element
  - This builds point-to-multipoint SPT trees.
- MP2MP downstream FEC
  - This will build a downstream tree but is used for bi-directional trees.
- MP2MP upstream FEC element
  - This will build the upstream tree portion of the bi-directional tree.

When building an MP LSP, the FEC TLV can only contain a single FEC Element. Carried within the FEC Element TLV is the **Opaque Value TLV**. It is the Opaque Value that uniquely identifies the MP LSP and also assists in identifying the multicast streams that will forward on the MP LSP. A detailed explanation of the Opaque Value is covered in the following sections.

5.2.2.1 Multicast FEC Element Encoding

Figure 5.3 details the encoding used to define an FEC Element for MP LSPs. There are several parameters defined:

- Tree Type—Whether it is a point-to-point or bi-directional
- Address Family—The type of stream (IPv4 or IPv6) the tree is replicating; this actually defines the root address type

```
0                   1                   2                   3
0 1 2 3 4 5 6 7 8 9 0 1 2 3 4 5 6 7 8 9 0 1 2 3 4 5 6 7 8 9 0 1
```

Tree Type	Address Family	Address Length
	Root Node Address	
Opaque Value Length	Opaque Value(s)...	...

Parameters	Description
Tree Type	P2MP, MP2MP Up, MP2MP Down
Address Family	Root node address format (IPv4 = 1 or IPv6 = 2)
Address Length	Number of octets in root address (IPv4 = 4, IPv6 = 16)
Root Node Address	Host address of MP LSP root (within MPLS core)
Opaque Value	One or more TLVs uniquely identifying MP LSP within the context of the root

FIGURE 5.3

- Address Length—The length of the root address
- Root Node Address—The actual root address of the MP LSP within the MPLS core (IPv4 or IPv6)
- Opaque Value—Contains the stream information that uniquely identifies this **tree to the root**.

5.2.2.1.1 Root Address

The root address defines the root of the MP LSP and will normally be the loopback address of the ingress PE router. The root address is selected by the MLDP client application egress router and can be derived from the BGP next-hop of the IP source address, either statically configured or through some other method.

It is the root address that is used to build the MP LSP. Each LSR in the path resolves the next-hop of the root address and then sends a Label Mapping Message with the relevant Multicast FEC Element information to that next-hop. This process is executed hop-by-hop until the root is reached, resulting in a dynamically created MP LSP. The IGP is used to find the path to the root.

5.2.2.1.2 Opaque Value

Each MP LSP is identified by an opaque value used to uniquely identify the MP LSP. The Opaque Value is of variable length and combined with the root address to build the MP LSP tree. The content of the Opaque value only has meaning to the Ingress and Egress LSRs. The core P routers do not need to understand the contents but can use them to uniquely identify the MP LSP entry. The content of the Opaque Value will vary depending on the multicast application (or client) being transported. It can represent the (S, G) stream (PIM-SSM Transit) or can be an LSP identifier to define the Default/ Data MDTs in an mVPN application.

Currently four multicast applications are supported, each with its own Opaque Value format as shown in Figure 5.4.

- **IPv4 PIM-SSM transit**—Allows global PIM-SSM streams to be transported across the MPLS core. The Opaque Value contains the actual (S, G), which resides in the **global mroute** table of the Ingress and Egress PE routers.
- **IPv6 PIM-SSM Transit**—As previously discussed but for IPv6 streams in the global table.
- **Multicast VPN**—Allows VPNv4 traffic to be transported across a Default MDT (MI-PMSI)[1] or Data MDT (S-PMSI) using label switching.
- **Direct MDT or VPv4 transit**—Here the Opaque Value allows VPNv4 streams to be directly built without the existence of the Default MDT. It is when there are high-bandwidth source/sources in a static mVPN environment with many receivers.

Opaque Type	Opaque Value	Multicast Application	Signaling Method
IPV4	(S, G)	PIM-SSM transit of IPv4	In-band
IPV6	(S, G)	PIM-SSM transit of IPv6	In-band
MDT	(VPN-ID, MDT#)	mVPN Default MDT (MDT# = 0) mVPN Data MDT (MDT# > 0)	In-band
VPNv4	(S, G, RD)	Direct MDT, VPNv4 Transit	In-band
LSP ID	4 byte value	BGP assigned LSPs	Out-of-band
CsC	C-FEC	Carrier Supporting Carrier	In-band

FIGURE 5.4

In a Cisco-based implementation, all of the supported applications mentioned earlier use in-band signaling for the Opaque Value, which will be explained in the next section.

The Opaque Value uniquely identifies the MP LSP, and it may also carry the (S, G) stream information from the edge IP Multicast network. P routers in the MP LSP path do not need to parse the

---

[1] The terminology for Default and Data MDTs was changed in the latest draft http://tools.ietf.org/html/draft-ietf-l3vpn-2547bis-mcast-10. MDTs are now called Provider Multicast Service Interfaces (PMSI). There is a Multidirectional Inclusive (MI-PMSI), which is a Default MDT and a Selective (S-PMSI), which is a Data MDT. We will stick with the old terms in this chapter.

Opaque Value, but will use the value as an index into their local MP LSP database to determine the next hop(s) in which to replicate the multicast packet. However, the Ingress PE LSP (closest to the source) will decode value so that it can select the correct MP LSP for the incoming (S, G) stream. The Egress PE can use value to install the (S, G) state into the local VRF or global multicast routing table.

5.2.2.2 In-Band Signaling Operation

Figure 5.5 illustrates how in-band signaling works. It is called this because the Egress PE uses the multicast stream information to create the Opaque Value and the Ingress PE uses this Opaque value to learn which multicast flow to send on the MP LSP. Let us look at the sequence of events in the following list:

1. The Egress PE receives an (S, G) IGMP join from a receiver. It creates a label mapping message containing the FEC TLV with the Opaque Value and a label TLV based on this information. The root address in the FEC Element will be derived from the BGP next-hop or (S). All ingress PE routers will create exactly the same FEC Element.
2. The Egress PE then builds an MP LSP toward the Ingress LSP (which is the root of the tree) using the label mapping message with the downstream label {X}. At each hop along the way, the P routers will use the same FEC Element, but the downstream label will change as shown to {Y} and then {Z}. When the ingress PE receives the label mapping message, it parses the Opaque Value to extract the multicast stream information and creates the appropriate (S, G) state and mapping information.
3. When the Ingress PE receives the (S, G) stream it will then forward it onto the correct MP LSP using label {Z}.

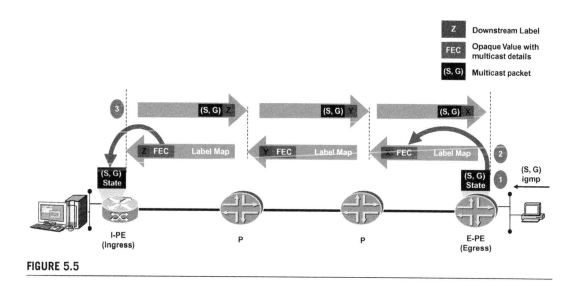

FIGURE 5.5

The constraint that in-band signaling imposes is that each stream (S, G) would need a dedicated MP LSP, which can result in scaling issues in a network where hundreds to thousands of streams can exist at any given point in time. The MVPN deployment, however, can use a single Default MDT for various traffic streams that use the MDT. This cannot be looked at as aggregation, but as an aspect that may offer some amount of similarity to the Draft-Rosen scheme from a Default MDT standpoint. This is discussed in greater detail later in this chapter.

5.2.2.3 Out-of-Band (Overlay) Signaling Operation

Figure 5.6 illustrates how overlay signaling works. It is a recap of the events discussed in Chapter 4. It is called out-of-band or overlay signaling because an overlay protocol (PIM in this implementation) signals the mapping of the IP Multicast flow to an MP LSP.

1. The Egress PE creates the FEC dynamically or through a static procedure. It then builds the MP LSP hop-by-hop to the root based on the FEC information.
2. Using overlay signaling, the Egress PE signals the Ingress PE to forward the IP Multicast stream over the MP LSP with the unique FEC value (it is also feasible that the Ingress PE could provide this information). The Ingress PE will insert the multicast information into its state table.
3. The Ingress PE then forwards the (S, G) traffic onto the tree using the mapping information it learned in the overlay signal.

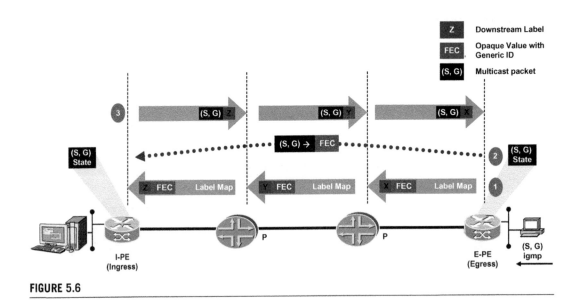

FIGURE 5.6

The advantage of the overlay signaling is that aggregate trees can be created where a single MP LSP could support many different {S, G} streams. The classic example of this is with mVPN, where a single Default MDT carries many customer streams.

In-Band Signaling	Out-of-Band Signaling

• Egress LSR assigns Opaque value
 	
   From multicast stream information
 	
• Egress LSR joins MP LSP stream
 	
   Using locally created Opaque value
 	
• Opaque value uniquely identifies LSP and signals Ingress LSR multicast stream to forward over MP LSP
 	
• 1:1 mapping of FEC → MP LSP
 	
• Use for global IPv4/IPv6 multicast
 	
• PIM-SSM/SM deployments
 	
• For video distribution
 	
   Where no TE is required
	• Egress LSR learns Opaque value
	
	   Dynamically via BGP or static
	
	• Egress LSR joins MP LSP stream
	
	   Via receiver driven or statically
	
	• Overlay signaling is used to map IP Multicast streams to the LSP
	
	• N:1 mapping of FEC → MP LSP
	
	   Can provide aggregation of FECs
	
	• Overlay signaling options can be PIM, BGP, or PORT
	
	   In mVPN, PIM used as Overlay

FIGURE 5.7

5.2.2.4 MLDP Signaling Comparison

Figure 5.7 compares the differences between the two signaling mechanisms.

In summary

- In-band signaling can be used for the following applications; however, scaling is always a factor that would need to be carefully considered.
    - Used for global table transport of IPv4 and IPv6 multicast.
    - Typical for SSM or PIM Sparse mode sources.
    - IPTV deployments where traffic engineering is not required.
    - Multicast VPN applications: PIM is used here to distribute customer multicast routing information. However, the application uses in-band signaling and opaque values to identify the default and Data MDTs. All configuration examples illustrated in subsequent sections are based on in-band signaling. Therefore the use of PIM in this context is not to be confused with out-of-band signaling.

> **NOTE**
>
> Each of these service options is discussed in detail in the following section.

- Out-of-band (overlay) signaling
    - Used where aggregation is necessary
    - In the MVPN solution where protocols such as BGP can be used as overlay

5.2.3 Point-to-Multipoint LSPs

P2MP LSPs only have a single root and it is the Ingress LSR. The P2MP LSP is created based on an interested receiver connected to the Egress LSR. The Egress LSR initiates the tree creation (or grafting onto an existing branch) by creating the FEC and Opaque Value. To receive label switched multicast packets the Egress PE indicates to the upstream router (the next hop closest to the root) what label it needs to use for this multicast source by using the label mapping message.

The upstream router does not need to have any knowledge of the source; it only needs the received FEC to identify the correct P2MP LSP. If the upstream router does not have any FEC state, then it will create it and install the assigned downstream outgoing label into the label forwarding table. If the upstream router is not the root of the tree, it must forward the label mapping message to the next hop upstream. This process repeats hop-by-hop until the root is reached.

By using downstream label allocation the router that wishes to receive the multicast traffic also assigns the label for it. The label request sent to the upstream router is like an unsolicited label mapping (the upstream did not request it). The upstream router that receives that label mapping will use the specific label to send the multicast packets downstream to the receiver. The advantage of this approach is that the router allocating the labels does not get into a situation where it has the same label for two different multicast sources, because it manages its own label space allocation locally.

5.2.3.1 Basic P2MP Operation in In-Band Signaling

This section provides an illustration on how a P2MP LSP is created using in-band signaling. Generally a P2MP LSP is used for:

- Transit of PIM SSM
- Carrying PIM transparently across the core (PIM at edge)
- Transit of PIM Sparse mode source trees
- Interconnection of the Data MDT in an mVPN
- Any One-2-Many traffic application

5.2.3.1.1 Tree Creation

Figure 5.8 shows how a P2MP tree is created and forwarded using MLDP. The diagram shows two receivers at PE-West and PE-East wishing to join the stream (S1, G2). The source (S1) is connected to PE-North, which is the root of the tree. These receivers are in the IP Multicast portion of the network (no MPLS).

When PE-West and PE-East receive the (S, G) join they will create a label mapping message that contains the FEC TLV and the downstream Label TLV.

 NOTE
For the purposes of illustration, Opaque Value of the FEC contains an abstract value.

The FEC TLV will contain the type P2MP to indicate the building of a point-to-point tree, and the root address, resolved from the BGP next-hop of (S1), will be PE-North. Since PE-West and PE-East both received the same (S1, G2) join they will create the same Opaque Value, which is 200. The FEC TLV will be the same as they are resolving to the root PE-North. The Label TLV will be allocated

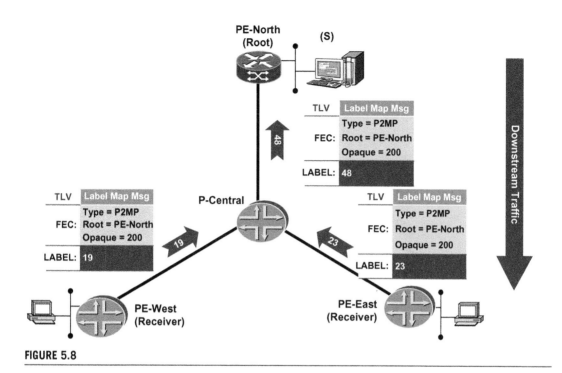

FIGURE 5.8

locally, {19} for PE-West and {23} for PE-East, and passed upstream to P-Central in the label mapping message. When P-Central receives the label mapping message it will install the labels {19} and {23} for the matching FEC (Root = PE-North, Opaque = 200) entry if it exists or create the FEC entry for the P2MP LSP. Since P-Central is not the root, it will forward the label mapping message with the same FEC (Root = PE-North, Opaque = 200) to PE-North, changing the downstream label to {48}. When PE-North receives the label mapping message it will know it is the root and extract and parse the FEC information, using this tree for any (G2) stream it receives from (S1).

✎ NOTE

- FECs created are identical for same multicast stream.
- Labels allocated from platform label space (same pool as unicast MPLS).
- Downstream on-demand allocation method used.

5.2.3.1.2 Multicast Forwarding
In Figure 5.9, traffic is forwarded downstream on a P2MP from ingress PE-North (root) to the egress PE routers, PE-West and PE-East. When PE-North receives the (S1, G2) stream it will push label {48} onto the stack as received from P-Central. At P-Central the traffic will be replicated using label {19} to PE-West and label {23} to PE-East.

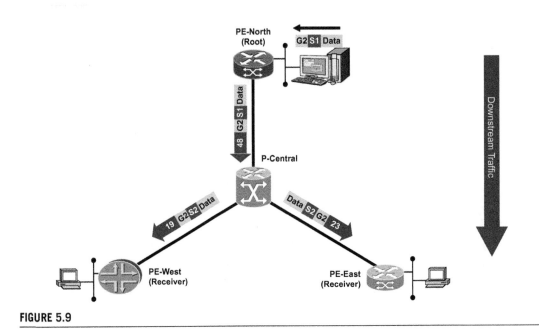

FIGURE 5.9

5.2.4 Multipoint-to-Multipoint LSPs

An MP2MP LSP allows leaf LSRs to inject packets into a tree from attached sources. This means sources can be attached to any part of the tree and traffic can travel on an upstream path (toward the root) or a downstream path (away from the root). Therefore the operation of an MP2MP LSP is similar to the way PIM Bi-Dir works. There must be an upstream path so that leaf LSRs can inject multicast packets into the tree and a downstream path so that traffic can travel back to other leafs where there are receivers.

Since we have two paths for every MP2MP tree, we also need corresponding procedures to create those paths as summarized in Figure 5.10. The following sections will explain these procedures in greater detail.

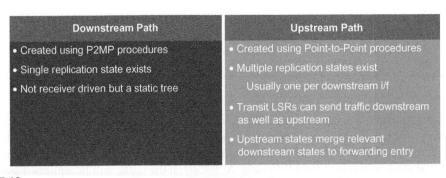

Downstream Path	Upstream Path
• Created using P2MP procedures	• Created using Point-to-Point procedures
• Single replication state exists	• Multiple replication states exist
• Not receiver driven but a static tree	Usually one per downstream i/f
	• Transit LSRs can send traffic downstream as well as upstream
	• Upstream states merge relevant downstream states to forwarding entry

FIGURE 5.10

An important aspect of an MP2MP LSP compared to a P2MP LSP is the way the downstream path is created. A P2MP LSP is receiver driven and therefore the downstream path is created dynamically because we can derive the root address from the source information (BGP next-hop).

However, with an MP2MP LSP every leaf of the tree can be a receiver and a source so it is not intuitive where the root should be placed. Any MP LSP (whether a P2MP or MP2MP) can only have one root defined; therefore, the current process to create a single root for an MP2MP LSP is to define it statically. Hence, the downstream path for an MP2MP LSP is not receiver driven, but operator created through a static configuration. The disadvantage to statically configuring a root node is that if the root node fails the tree will also fail. To address this problem a feature called "Root Node Redundancy" is available and is discussed in detail in the later sections.

5.2.4.1 *Basic MP2MP Operation*
This section illustrates how an MP2MP LSP is created using in-band signaling. Generally, an MPMP LSP is used for:

- Transit of bi-directional PIM traffic. This application is not covered in this chapter due to its complexity and the relatively small number of bi-directional PIM infrastructures deployed for non-Multicast VPN applications.
- Interconnection of Default MDT in an mVPN.
- ANY Many-2-Many traffic application.

To create an MP2MP LSP, MLDP defines two different FEC types, **MP2MP down** and **MP2MP up**, to create the downstream and upstream paths. There is a single replication state for the downstream path (from the root to the leaf nodes), and there are multiple replication states for the upstream paths (from the leaf nodes to the root). As previously mentioned, the downstream path is just like building a P2MP LSP to a root node except we need to statically define the root. The main difference is that unlike a P2MP LSP the root node may not be necessarily injecting packets into the tree. This is where the upstream path is used. Each leaf node is allowed to inject packets into the MP2MP LSP using the upstream path toward the defined root. The packets are forwarded upstream to the root node, and will be forwarded down the tree on intermediate nodes where there are receivers.

5.2.4.1.1 Downstream Path Creation
Figure 5.11 illustrates how a downstream path is created for an MP2MP LSP. As mentioned previously, it is created in much the same way as a P2MP LSP but with a static root manually configured on all the leaves (not receiver driven). The diagram in Figure 5.11 shows that PE-North has been chosen as the root for the downstream path. There is a source (S1) at PE-East with receivers as PE-West and PE-NWest. A label mapping message is sent from all Edge LSRs toward the static root. The FEC TLV created will be identical on all leaves participating in this tree. The tree type will be set to "MP Down," the root will be statically configured, and the contents of the Opaque Value will be derived based on the multicast application it is supporting (more examples of this are discussed in Section 5.3.6).

The label mapping message is forwarded hop-by-hop toward the root, with the downstream label changing at each hop (the FEC remains the same). There is a single replication state in each LSR representing the downstream path of the MP2MP LSP.

5.2.4.1.2 Upstream Path Creation
Figure 5.12 illustrates how an upstream path is created for an MP2MP LSP. When an upstream LSR receives an FEC TLV with the type "MP2MP Down," it will respond with a label mapping message

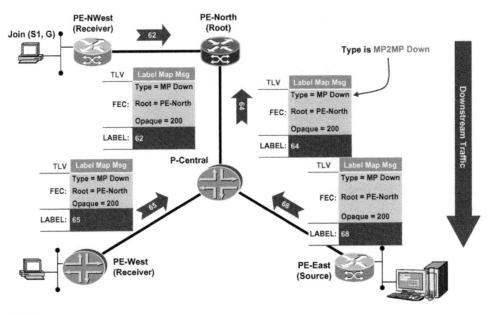

FIGURE 5.11

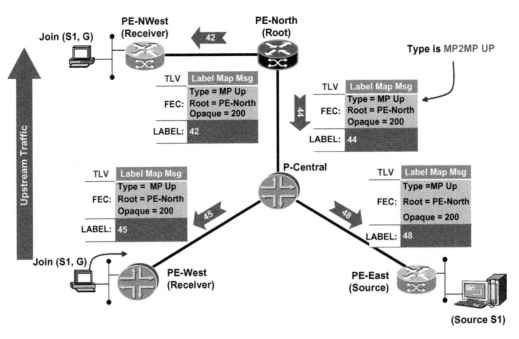

FIGURE 5.12

using the same Opaque Value and Root. This label mapping message will have the FEC TLV type of "MP2MP Up and contains the label the leaf LSR will use to inject traffic into the tree upstream toward the root.

A separate upstream replication state will exist in the forwarding table for each downstream interface (i.e., interfaces where a leaf LSR is connected). In Figure 5.12 P-Central has allocated an upstream label {45} and {48} for both of the downstream entries it received for PE-West and PE-East.

5.2.4.1.3 Downstream and Upstream State Entries

Figure 5.13 shows the resultant upstream and downstream state entries created for the node P-Central among its three interfaces. As can be seen for the downstream state, there is a *single* entry in the LFIB for the label {64} with two outgoing labels {65} and {68} replicating to PE-West and PE-East. Therefore any multicast traffic traveling downstream from the direction of the root will come into P-Central with label {64}.

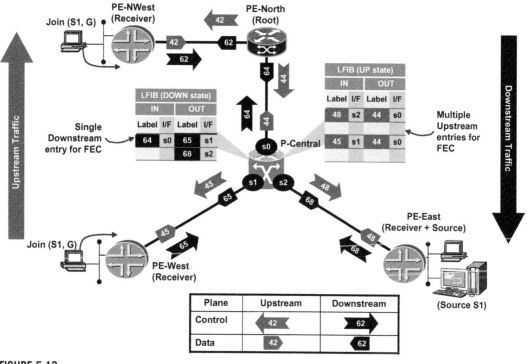

FIGURE 5.13

On the other hand, there are *multiple* entries for each upstream state. For each upstream label P-Central received it created a separate entry in the LFIB. If source (S1) at PE-East were to begin transmitting it would use the label {48} to send traffic upstream toward P-Central.

5.2.4.1.4 Merging States and Multicast Forwarding

After the upstream states have been created, packets can then travel toward the root of the tree from the leaves. However, while forwarding packets upstream on an MP2MP tree, we want to avoid depending on the root to send the packets downstream to interested receivers. If there are intermediate nodes on the upstream path that have receivers, it is desirable that we send packets downstream at this point. This is achieved by merging the downstream and upstream state entries as shown in Figure 5.14. Each upstream state will copy the interfaces from the downstream state O-list, except if it is the same as its incoming interface. The merging rule is as follows:

If (Upstate IN I/F) = (Downstate Out I/F) then do not merge the entry

This rule is necessary to prevent multicast traffic from being sent back where it came from. For example, let us examine the s2 interface of P-Central shown in Figure 5.13. On S2 P-Central has sent an upstream label {48} toward PE-East; therefore, when PE-East sends multicast traffic upstream, it will come into s2 P-Central using label {48}. P-Central also has a downstream label {68} on s2 received from PE-East. This means that when P-Central wishes to send multicast traffic to PE-East it will push {68} onto the stack and forward it out s2. However, we want to avoid doing this if label {48} comes in on s2 to prevent a loop.

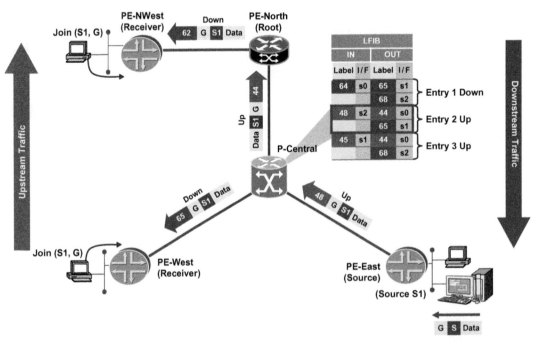

FIGURE 5.14

The end result of the merging is a table as shown in Figure 5.14. The merged table consists of three entries: a single replication state for the downstream and multiple replication states representing each upstream entry. This occurs because the downstream state is created used P2MP procedures while the upstream states are created using P2P procedures.

✎ **NOTE**

The end result of the table is that every leaf node will have an upstream and downstream label; therefore, it can send and receive traffic bi-directionally.

When source (S1) at PE-East begins to transmit, PE-East will push label {48} on the packets and send it upstream toward the root. Upon receipt of this packet, P-Central consults the forwarding table for {48} and sees two entries in the o-List. P-Central knows from this information that it is an intermediate node for a downstream receiver at PE-West. The packet is then replicated upstream out interface s0 using label {44} toward the root and also downstream out interface s1 using label {65} toward PE-West. Once the packet reaches the root, it will then be replicated down the remaining portion of the tree. In the example, PE-North pushes label {62} onto the stack and forwards it to PE-NWest.

Figure 5.15 illustrates that every leaf LSR (regardless whether it has a connected source or not) on an MP2MP tree will have a distinct P2P upstream LSP back to the root. Along the way P2P LSP is merged with the P2MP downstream tree to create the MP2MP tree. Therefore, as traffic travels upstream toward the root it will then be passed downstream at each branch point where there is edge LSR.

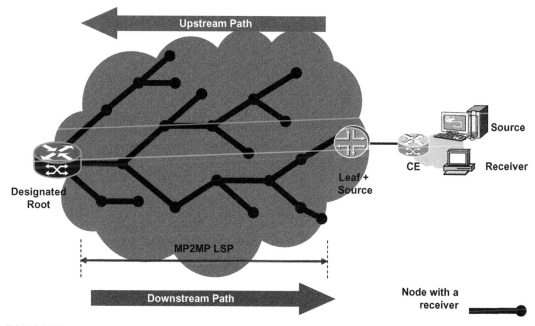

FIGURE 5.15

5.2.5 Root Node Redundancy

The root node is a single point of failure for any MP LSP, whether this is P2MP or MP2MP. The problem is particularly severe for MP2MP LSPs. In the case of MP2MP LSPs, all leaf nodes must use the same root node to set up the MP2MP LSP; otherwise the traffic sourced by some leafs will not be received by others. The root address can be configured statically for MP2MP LSPs or learned dynamically for P2MP LSPs. The procedure used depends on the MLDP client application (see Figure 5.4), for example, PIM-SSM or Multicast VPN.

 NOTE

MLDP can only learn about a root from the client application.

The requirements to address root node failure include:

- A redundancy mechanism in the event of a root failure
- Fast convergence in selecting the new root

5.2.5.1 P2MP Root Node Redundancy

As previously mentioned, for a P2MP LSP, MLDP depends on the client application to provide the root address. For the currently supported applications such as PIM-SSM Transit, Data MDT, and Direct MDT, the root address is derived from the BGP next-hop associated with the source IP address.

Providing redundancy for a root failure on a P2MP LSP is relatively straightforward. If the root of a tree (BGP-next-hop of the source) fails, then a new BGP prefix must be chosen assuming there is a new next-hop available. The root of an existing P2MP LSP cannot be changed; therefore, a new tree must be built and the old tree removed. The convergence time of swapping to a new root is totally dependent upon BGP convergence to replace the next-hop.

5.2.5.2 MP2MP Root Node Redundancy

For MP2MP LSPs the current method is to configure the root statically. If the root fails, there is no dynamic way to restore to a new root as is achieved with P2MP LSPs. The solution, however, involves assigning *multiple* roots to the leaf LSR.

To provide root node redundancy for an MP2MP leaf LSR, the following rules are followed:

- The leaf LSR is statically configured with the same set of root
- The leaf LSR joins all configured roots (multiple MP2MP LSPs)
- A leaf LSR will receive traffic from all roots
- A leaf LSR will transmit traffic to only one selected root
- The root selection policy is local to the leaf LSR
  - Currently based on IGP selection (closest root or best metric)

To illustrate this concept consider the scenario in Figure 5.16. The dark lines show the P2P upstream paths for each of the leaves. There are two MP2MP trees, with different roots, but the same set of receivers. Both trees have the same Opaque Value (200) but different roots. Leaf A, B, and C will join both trees at Root 1 and Root 2. In the figure, Leaf A chooses Root 1 as its primary root; therefore, its source traffic will be transmitted down the FEC 200, Root 1 tree. Leaf C chooses Root 2 as its primary root; therefore, its source traffic will be transmitted down the FEC 200, Root 2 tree. Since leaf LSRs are joined to both trees, they can receive traffic on either of the MP2MP LSPs regardless of which root was chosen by the source leaf LSR.

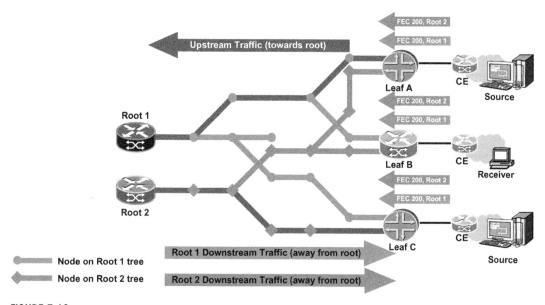

FIGURE 5.16

Load balancing on a source basis is possible to distribute the load between root nodes. In theory many root nodes can be configured. The disadvantage is that more LSP states are created in the network. There is a trade-off between redundancy and consumed resources in the network.

In Figure 5.17, Leaf C has lost its path to Root 2 due to a link failure. Because Leaf C is also connected to an MP2MP tree at Root 2, it will revert to that root and continue to transmit multicast packets. Switching to the new root is dependent on the speed of IGP convergence. The actual root selection policy (whether you use Root 1...N first) is a local leaf policy. The selection method is currently based on IGP distance.

Finally, an MP2MP LSP is created for *each root*. MLDP supports multipath load balancing on the tree in both the upstream and downstream directions.

5.2.5.2.1 M2MP Anycast Root Node Redundancy
The Anycast[2] technique can be used to provide root node redundancy in an MP2MP LSP. Figure 5.18 shows two roots available for a particular FEC. Both roots share the same loopback address 10.1.1.1; however, each has a different mask. Root 2 injects 10.1.1.1 with a mask of /32, whereas Root 1

---

[2]Anycast for root node redundancy is basically exploiting a configuration trick rather than a purposely built feature.

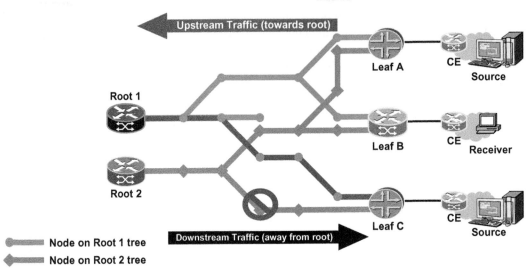

FIGURE 5.17

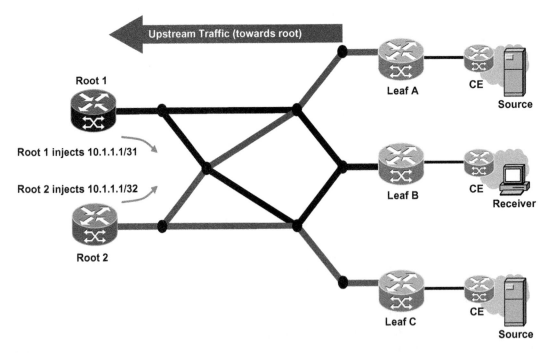

FIGURE 5.18

injects a /31 mask. Since the longest match is preferred, Root 2 will be chosen by the leaf LSRs to inject traffic from the source.

Figure 5.19 shows a failure of Root 2. In this case, the /32 route will be withdrawn and the next best preferred. Therefore Root 1 will be chosen by all leaves for injecting multicast source streams.

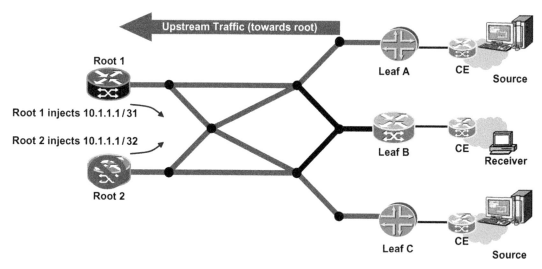

FIGURE 5.19

In summary:

- If the preferred root fails:
  - Traffic is rerouted to the next best root based on the mask length.
- All MP2MP LSPs will prefer the same root node.
- There is a single MP2MP LSP at any given time.
  - No hot standby path.
- No load balancing over the Anycast Roots.

5.2.6 **LSP Virtual Interfaces**

The LSP Virtual Interface (LSP-VIF) represents the head- and tail-ends of the MP LSPs and appears as an RPF or outbound interface in the global or VRF mroute table. LSP-VIFs are dynamically created on the Ingress and Egress LSRs for P2MP and MP2MP LSPs and are not created on P routers. The LSP-VIFs are set to unnumbered with an IPv4 or IPv6 enabled interface on the router (preferably a loopback is used).

A single LSP-VIF can have multiple adjacencies with each adjacency representing a unique MP LSP. The LSP-VIF can be considered as an NMBA interface, with one interface and may "virtual circuit" trees as shown in Figure 5.20. At the head-end of an LSP we only need to create one default

LSP-VIF interface. There is no need for an LSP-VIF interface per LSP or egress PE. Multiple LSPs will share the same LSP-VIF interface. Each LSP will have its own unique adjacency on the default LSP-VIF interface.

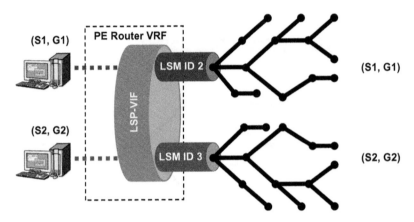

FIGURE 5.20

This example shows a VRF that holds two sources: (S1, G1) and (S2, G2). Only a single LSP-VIF will be created in the VRF, but each source within that VRF will use a different P2MP LSP. All P2MP LSPs associated with this VRF will be reachable through the same LSP-VIF.

5.2.7 MLDP Commands
5.2.7.1 Command Summary
Tables 5.2–5.5 summarize all of the commands related to the configuration of MLDP.

> **NOTE**
> The syntax and output of these commands may vary from the actual release and version of the code. The document will be updated accordingly.

5.2.7.2 Command Details
This section provides an in-depth view of all of the available IOS commands associated with MLDP configuration.

5.2.7.2.1 [no] mpls MLDP
MLDP is enabled by default, and this command disables the MLDP process. The "no" form of the command will appear in the running-config.

Table 5.2 Global Command Summary

Global Commands

[no] mpls MLDP enable

[no] mpls MLDP logging notifications

[no] mpls MLDP forwarding recursive

[no] ip(v6) multicast mpls MLDP range <acl>[1]

[no] ip multicast mpls traffic-eng [range <acl>]

[no] ip multicast vrf <vrf name> mpls MLDP [range <acl>][1]

[no] ip(v6) pim mpls source <interface>

[no] mpls MLDP multipath upstream

[no] mpls MLDP multipath downstream

[1]*Hidden command.*

Table 5.3 VRF Command Summary

Local Commands

[no] mdt default mpls MLDP <ip-address-of-root>

[no] mdt data mpls MLDP <# data-mdts> threshold <kbps>

[no] mdt preference [pim] [MLDP]

[no] mdt direct[1]

[1]*Hidden command.*

Table 5.4 Show Command Summary

Show Commands

show mpls MLDP database id <LSM ID>

show mpls MLDP database opaque_type

  [IPv4 <source> <group>]
  [IPv6 <source> <group>]
  [mdt <VPN iD> <MDT number>]
  [vpnv4 <source> <group> <RD>]
  [<Type number>]

show mpls MLDP database

show mpls MLDP neighbors

show mpls MLDP label release

show mpls MLDP root

show ip multicast mpls vif

show ip multicast mpls mrib-client [ipv4] [ipv6][1]

show ip multicast mpls vrf <vrf name> mrib-client [ipv4] [ipv6][1]

show ip multicast mpls vrf <vrf name> mrib-client [ipv4] [ipv6][1]

[1]*Hidden command.*

Table 5.5 Debug Command Summary
Debug Commands
debug mpls MLDP generic
debug mpls MLDP all
debug mpls MLDP mfi
debug mpls MLDP mrib
debug mpls MLDP gr
debug mpls MLDP neighbor
debug mpls MLDP packet
debug mpls MLDP filter opaque_type
[ipv4 <source> <group>] [ipv6 <source> <group>]
[mdt <VPN ID> <MDT number>]
[VPNv4 <source> <group> <RD>]
<Type number>

[no] mpls MLDP forwarding recursive MLDP has two ways to resolve the next-hop used for forwarding labeled packets. Without this command enabled MLDP resolves the outgoing interface based on the next-hop to the downstream LSR. If mpls MLDP forwarding recursive is configured, the outgoing interface is resolved by the MFI using P2P LSPs. Then MLDP uses recursive forwarding over a P2P LSP. That means a P2P LSP for the next-hop needs to be available in the MFI. This configuration needs to be enabled to make MLDP FRR back up over a TE tunnel when possible. Recursion will be enabled by default, and the no form of the command will appear in the running-config.

5.2.7.2.2 [no] mpls MLDP multipath upstream
If there are multiple paths available to reach the root of an MP-LSP, we use an algorithm to select a path such that we are load balancing different LSPs over the available paths. The algorithm used to influence the paths selection calculates a 32-bit CRC of the total FEC length of the LSP, and then does a "crc32_value mod number_of_paths." The result of this calculation identifies the path. If this command is disabled the path with the highest next-hop IP address is used to reach the root.

5.2.7.2.3 [no] mpls MLDP multipath downstream
If there are multiple downstream paths to reach an LDP peer we load balance the branches of the LSPs over these paths. The assignment of the downstream paths to the LSPs is done in a circular way. If this command is disabled, the path with the highest next-hop IP address is used.

5.2.7.2.4 [no] ip(v6) multicast mpls MLDP range <acl>
This command enables transit IPv4 or IPv6 multicast over an MLDP built P2MP LSP. Using the <acl>, an access-list can be configured to enable transit service for a specific set of multicast stream(s). The ACL is a named or extended access-list that can be filter based on source and/or group. This command needs to be configured on the egress PE as well as the ingress PE, but the ACL only has an effect on those sources for which this PE is the egress.

5.2.7.2.5 [no] IP Multicast mpls Traffic-eng [Range <acl>]
This command enabled transit IP4 multicast over an RSVP-TE built P2MP LSP. Using the <acl>, an access-list can be configured to enable transit service for a specific set of multicast stream(s). The ACL is a named or extended access list that can filter based on source and/or group. This command needs to be configured only on the egress PE.

5.2.7.2.6 [no] IP Multicast vrf <vrf name> mpls MLDP Range <acl>
This command enables transit VPNv4 multicast over a P2MP LSP. Using the <acl>, an access-list can be configured to enable transit service for a specific set of multicast stream(s). The ACL is a named or extended access list that can filter based on source and/or group. This command needs to be configured on the egress PE as well as the ingress PE, but the ACL only has an effect for which sources this PE is the egress.

5.2.7.2.7 [no] IP(v6) pim mpls Source <interface>
For transit multicast service a virtual interface (LSP-VIF) is created as head- and tail-end of the tunnel to interact with PIM. This interface is created automatically on demand and is configured to be unnumbered with an interface on the router that is configured with an IPv4 or IPv6 address. This command is used to configure the interface that is used as an unnumbered interface for the virtual interface. Without this command a virtual interface will not be created. This command needs to be configured in combination with IP Multicast mpls MLDP and IP Multicast mpls traffic-eng.

5.2.7.2.8 [no] mdt Default mpls MLDP <ip-address-of-root>
This command specifies that the Default MDT should be constructed using MLDP. By default MLDP uses an MP2MP LSP to build the default MDT. An IP address must be given that specifies the root of the MP2MP tree.

Multiple commands such as these may be entered for the same VPN and FEC-ID but with different Root addresses. When multiple commands such as these are configured, MLDP automatically uses root node redundancy procedure for this MP2MP LSP.

5.2.7.2.9 [no] mdt Data mpls MLDP <# data-mdts> Threshold <kbps>
The existing mdt data CLI is extended to take the mpls MLDP keyword. When specified it indicates that the Data MDTs for the VRF should be signaled via MLDP. In addition, by default Data MDTs are P2MP Trees rooted at the tree that initiates the MDT switchover. The user also configures the number of Data MDTs that he or she wants the VPN to use. The threshold keyword is used to supply a rate in kilobits per second. If the traffic rate for a given stream is above the threshold rate, it is switched over to use a Data MDT.

5.2.7.2.10 [no] mdt Preference [pim] [MLDP]
For MVPN migration strategy we allow PIM MDTs to be configured parallel to MLDP MDTs. To influence the path selection in the mroute table we can use this command to give preference to a certain tree type. If this command is not configured then PIM is preferred over MLDP. The order in which the keywords "pim" and "MLDP" are entered gives the preference. The first keyword has the higher preference.

5.2.7.2.11 show mpls MLDP database

This command shows the MLDP database. It also shows the FEC, the opaque value of the FEC decoded (if the router understands it), and the replication clients associated with it.

5.2.7.2.12 show mpls MLDP database id <LSD ID>

This command shows an entry in the MLDP database using the hexadecimal LSM system ID.

5.2.7.2.13 show mpls MLDP database id opaque_type <Type>

This command shows an entry in the MLDP database using the opaque type, which can consist of multiple fields that can be used to refine the selection. Supported types include:

- IPv4 <source> <group>
- IPv6 <source> <group>
- mdt <VPN ID> <MDT number>
- VPNv4 <source> <group> <RD>
- <Type number>

5.2.7.2.14 show mpls MLDP neighbors

This command displays the MLDP Peers known to the router. It displays the identity address, which is the address used to create the LDP TCP peering. It also displays information about next-hop, interface, LDP graceful restart status, and uptime.

5.2.7.2.15 show mpls MLDP label release

This command displays labels that are withdrawn and pending to be released to the system.

5.2.7.2.16 show mpls MLDP root

This command displays the root data structure. The root is a common entry between multiple LSPs.

5.2.7.2.17 show IP Multicast mpls vif

This command shows the virtual interfaces that are created on the router. Interfaces are identified by an addrtype address.

5.2.7.2.18 show IP Multicast mpls mrib-client [ipv4] [ipv6] and show IP Multicast vrf <vrf-name> mrib-client [ipv4] [ipv6]

These commands display the routes, which the MLDP PE function has learned from the IPv4 MRIBs. These are the routes for which MLDP Multipoint LSPs are set up. Also these routes are signaled via MLDP in-band signaling.

5.2.7.3 Debug Commands

The following sections detail the debug commands supported.

5.2.7.3.1 debug mpls MLDP all

Turns on all MLDP-related debugging.

5.2.7.3.2 debug mpls MLDP generic

Turns on Generic MLDP debugging.

5.2.7.3.3 debug mpls MLDP mfi

Turns on debugging for MLDP/MFI interactions.

5.2.7.3.4 debug mpls MLDP mrib

Turns on debugging for MLDP/MRIB interactions.

5.2.7.3.5 debug mpls MLDP gr

Turns on debugging for MLDP Graceful Restart events.

5.2.7.3.6 debug mpls MLDP neighbor

Turns on debugging for MLDP neighbor events.

5.2.7.3.7 debug mpls MLDP packet

Turns on debugging or MLDP generated MPLS control plane packets, such as PIM Hellos going over an MPLS tunnel.

5.2.7.3.8 debug mpls MLDP filter opaque_type <type>

A debug filter that applies to the MLDP debug commands with keyword generic mfi, mrib, and gr. Using this command filtering can be done using the opaque type. The following types are supported:

- IPv4 <source> <group>
- IPv6 <source> <group>
- mdt <VPN ID> <MDT number>
- VPNv4 <source> <group> <RD>
- <Type number>

5.3 MLDP CONFIGURATION EXAMPLES

This chapter provides configuration details and outputs for four multicast applications (or clients) initially supported by MLDP as discussed in Section . To recap, MLDP will transport multicast packets for the following applications

- PIM-SSM transit of IPv4
- PIM-SSM transit of IPv6
- Multicast VPN
- Direct MDT or VPNv4 transit

For each of these applications, the corresponding Opaque Value used in the FEC TLV has a particular format that will be covered in each configuration example.

 NOTE

All the examples use in-band signaling, which is currently the only method supported on Cisco platforms.

5.3.1 Reference Network

Figure 5.21 shows the simple reference network that will be used for the various configuration scenarios. Four routers make up the MPLS portion of the network: three edge LSRs such as PE-North, PE-West, and PE-East and a core router P-Central. There are also three CE routers in VPN Green that are running IP Multicast using PIM within the VPN.

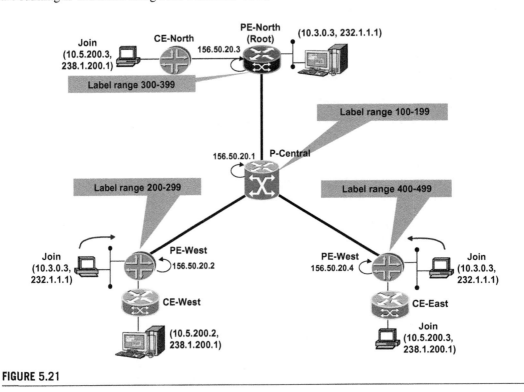

FIGURE 5.21

The core routers also have a directly attached source (10.3.0.3, 232.1.1.1) at PE-North and receivers at PE-West and PE-East operating in the global table.

To assist in clarifying the examples, each router is configured with a separate label range so we can tell where the label originated from as seen in Table 5.6.

Table 5.6 Reference Label Ranges		
Router	**Label Range**	**Loopback Address**
P-Central	100–199	156.50.20.1
PE-West	200–299	156.50.20.2
PE-North	300–399	156.50.20.3
PE-East	400–499	156.50.30.4

5.3.2 **Enabling MLDP**

The MLDP capability is enabled by default. Since it is an extension to LDP, MLDP will reuse the LDP adjacencies already established for unicast. It does not need any additional configuration on P routers; however, some application specific configuration is necessary on PE routers.

To allow the head- and tail-end of LSPs to be created, an LSP-VIF must be associated with an interface on the PE router using the command in Figure 5.22.

```
ip pim mpls source Loopback0
```

FIGURE 5.22

Associating MLDP with loopback.

MLDP can be specifically disabled using the command in Figure 5.23.

```
no mpls MLDP
```

FIGURE 5.23

Disabling MLDP.

 NOTE

If you disable/enable MLDP on a P router label bindings are automatically relearned by triggering an MLDP wildcard request message to adjacent LDP peers. On ingress and egress PE routers you need to manually re-enable MLDP configurations for MVPN and transit IPv4/IPv6.

5.3.3 **MLDP Capabilities**

Figure 5.24 shows the capabilities available at PE-West that it will advertise to its LDP peers. This is an enhancement to the LDP session establishment. In this example, PE-West is capable of supporting P2MP and MP2MP LSPs.

```
PE-West# show mpls ldp capabilities

LDP Capabilities - [<description> (<type>)]
-----------------------------------------------------------
    [Dynamic Announcement (0x0506)]
    [MLDP Point-to-Multipoint (0x0508)]
    [MLDP Multipoint-to-Multipoint (0x0509)]
    [Typed Wildcard (0x0970)]
```

FIGURE 5.24

MLDP capabilities.

5.3.4 MLDP Database

The MLDP database exists on every LSR participating in MLDP and contains detailed information about head-end, transit, and tail-end MP LSPs on the local LSR. The MLDP database is consulted to see whether an MP LSP branch exists or needs to be created toward the root when a label mapping message is received.

Each MLDP database entry gets a unique system ID represented as a hexadecimal number. The database entry is actually identified and indexed by the variable length FEC value consisting of the root and opaque value. However, this value can be quite long and unreadable, as can be seen in Figure 5.26. For that reason a unique system ID is used in show and debug commands to reference a database entry.

The options for displaying specific MLDP database entries based on the opaque encoding are shown in Figure 5.25.

```
PE#sh mpls MLDP db opaque_type ?
  <0-65535>  Opaque type value
  ipv4       IPv4 opaque type
  ipv6       IPv6 opaque type
  mdt        MDT opaque type
  vpnv4      VPNv4 opaque type
```

FIGURE 5.25

MLDP database display options.

Each of these options corresponds to an application/client supported by MLDP. Figure 5.26 shows a sample entry that includes the contents of the FEC TLV, the decoded Opaque Value (remember it differs depending on the application), and the local label (212) assigned for this part of the tree (which will be passed to the upstream neighbor).

```
PE-West#show mpls MLDP database
  LSM ID              : 17000007
  Uptime              : 02:21:34
  Tree type           : P2MP
  FEC Root            : 156.50.20.3   (we are leaf)
  Opaque length       : 11 bytes
  Opaque value        : 0200080A 030003E8 0101019C
  Opaque decoded      : [ipv4 10.3.0.3 232.1.1.1]
  Upstream peer ID    : 156.50.20.1:0, Label local (D): 212    active
  Path Set ID         : 85000009
  Replication client(s):
  MRIBv4(0)        uptime: 02:21:34
                   intrf: Lspvif2
```

FIGURE 5.26

MLDP database.

5.3.5 **PIM-SSM Transit Application**

PIM-SSM transit supports the forwarding of (S, G) states at the IP edge across the MPLS core. It can be summarized as follows:

- Supports (S, G) transit for both IPv4 and IPv6 multicast
- Carried across MPLS core using a P2MP LSP
- Opaque value comprises the (S, G) value of the transit stream
- Signaling is done in-band
- Source prefixes (at PEs) are distributed using BGP
- Root derived from BGP next-hop of source
- No PIM necessary in MPLS core
    - PIM at edge
    - P2MP LSP in core

✏ **NOTE**

The examples covered are for IPv4 traffic.

5.3.5.1 *Scenario*

Figure 5.27 shows the example network for PIM-SSM transit. PE-North is connected to a source in the IP network transmitting the stream (10.3.0.3, 232.1.1.1). Both PE-West and PE-East have received

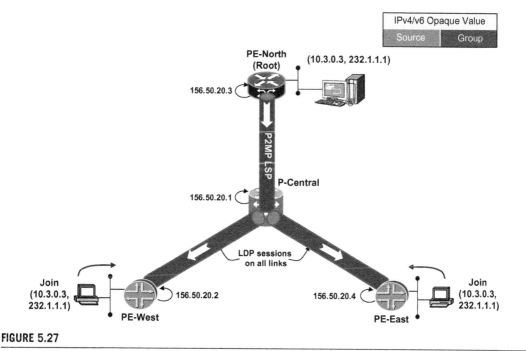

FIGURE 5.27

SSM join for (10.3.0.3, 232.1.1.1) and will build a P2MP tree rooted at PE-North. The Opaque Value format is (S, G).

 NOTE

This solution can only work if the Egress LSR knows both the S and the G values that must reside in the global multicast route table.

5.3.5.2 Configuration

Figure 5.28 shows the configuration for all three PE routers. The first command allows the creation of the LSP-VIF, which will be associated with loopback 0. The second command then instructs MLDP to allow the transport of (S, G) traffic across the P2MP LSP. There is an optional range access control list that allows selective (S, G) across the P2MP LSP. This is useful if you want some (S, G) to be label switched and others to use native PIM (if needed).

The Ethernet 0/0 interface faces the customer IP Multicast network and is configured with PIM. The core facing interface Serial 4/0 only runs MPLS; there is no native multicast.

```
ip pim mpls source Loopback0
ip multicast mpls MLDP [range <acl>]
ip pim ssm default
!
interface Ethernet0/0
 ip address 10.3.0.1 255.255.255.0
 ip pim sparse-mode
end
!
interface Serial4/0
 description Circuit to P-Central
 ip address 156.50.10.6 255.255.255.252
 mpls ip
```

FIGURE 5.28

PIM-SSM configuration.

This configuration would be consistent among all of the edge routers supporting PIM-SSM transit.

5.3.5.3 PIM Free Core

PIM-SSM transit allows the core of the MPLS network to be completely free of an IP Multicast control plane such as PIM. As shown in Figure 5.29, only MP-BGP is required to redistribute the IP address/prefix of the source networks to all PE routers in the network. This allows MLDP to use the BGP next-hop of the source to derive the root of the P2MP LSP.

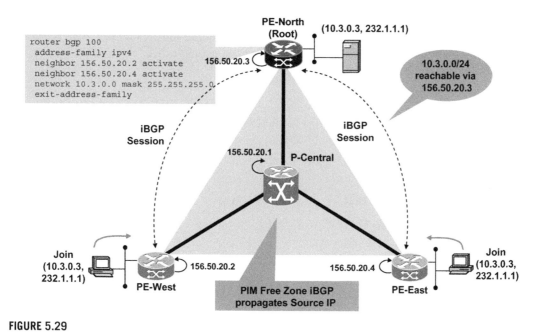

FIGURE 5.29

5.3.5.4 LDP Peers

The LDP peer is found using the unicast Reachability information of the root IP address. The root address is looked up in the unicast RIB. The next-hop that is returned is then used to find the LDP neighbor. In Figure 5.30, to find the next hop LDP peer for source 10.3.0.3, PE-West looks up the routing table. The next hop returned is 156.50.20.3, which is the root of the tree. The MLDP root information is then examined to determine the next hop (there is only one) to the LDP peer, which is 156.50.20.1. Figure 5.30 also shows an FEC count of 3 representing the various applications using MLDP.

```
PE-West#show ip route
B        10.3.0.0 [200/0] via 156.50.20.3, 18:28:28

PE-West#show mpls MLDP root 156.50.20.3

 Root node    : 156.50.20.3
  Metric      : 129
  Distance    : 110
  Interface   : Serial4/0 (via unicast RT)
  FEC count   : 3
  Path count  : 1
  Path(s)     : 156.50.10.1     LDP nbr: 156.50.20.1:0     Serial4/0
```

FIGURE 5.30

LDP peer.

Figure 5.31 shows the MLDP neighbors. If this entry does not appear after LDP session establishment it means that MLDP has been disabled (no mpls MLDP). The entry shows that there is a single path to receive multicast from and that there are five separate streams active.

```
PE-West#show mpls MLDP neighbor

MLDP peer ID    : 156.50.20.1:0, uptime 02:35:07 Up,
  Target Adj    : No
  Session hndl  : 1
  Upstream count : 5
  Branch count  : 0
  Path count    : 1
  Path(s)       : 156.50.10.1      LDP Serial4/0
  Nhop count    : 1
  Nhop list     : 156.50.10.1
```

FIGURE 5.31

MLDP neighbors.

5.3.5.5 P2MP LSP Creation
Figure 5.32 shows the label mapping messages used to create the P2MP LSP for (10.3.0.3, 232.1.1.1).

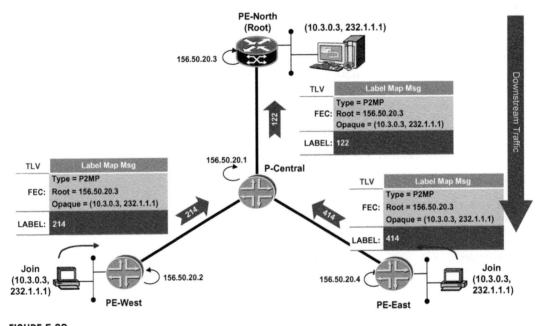

FIGURE 5.32

When PE-West and PE-East receive the join request, a P2MP label mapping message is created with the FEC containing the Opaque Value of (10.3.0.3, 232.1.1.1) using the BGP next-hop 156.50.20.3 as the root. Both Egress PE routers know they must create a P2MP LSP for the (S, G) because of the **IP Multicast mpls MLDP [range <acl>]** command configured. The tree is set up with three downstream labels {214} from PE-West and {414} from PE-East, which is merged into {122} from P-Central. Therefore, when the ingress LSR PE-North receives a multicast packet from the source 10.3.0.3, it will push {122} onto the stack.

5.3.5.6 In-Band Signaling of SSM Multicast State

When PE-North receives the label mapping message from P-Central it not only knows the label {122}, but it needs to push onto the stack; it also learns about the actual (S, G) state it needs to insert into the multicast route table and map to the outbound LSP-VIF. This is due to in-band signaling as shown in Figure 5.33. When PE-West receives the IGMP request from the source, it inserts (10.3.0.3, 232.1.1.1) into the multicast state table and then creates an FEC TLV with the Opaque Value and the root. On receipt of the label mapping message, PE-North will parse the Opaque Value and extract the (S, G), which it will then insert into its own multicast state table. By using in-band signaling in the label mapping message, no other control mechanism such as BGP is required to signal the multicast state across the MPLS core.

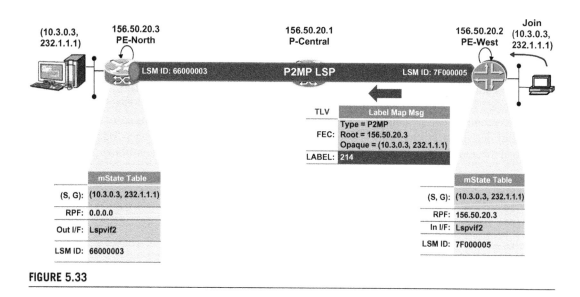

FIGURE 5.33

In summary, the FEC TLV with Opaque Value does several things:

- Uniquely identifies the MP LSP
- Creates an LSP path to the root
- Creates the multicast (S, G) state at the ingress router

5.3.5.7 mRoute and LSP-VIF Entry

Figure 5.34 shows the multicast route also known as the mroute entry for (10.3.0.3, 232.1.1.1) at PE-West. For MLDP the RPF interface should always point to an LSP-VIF, in this case Lspvif2. Looking at the VIF entries, we can see that the next-hop for Lspvif2 is 156.50.20.3, which is the root of the tree (you will not see the actual physical next hop in this entry). The application supported for Lspvif2 shows MLDP in the global (default) table.

```
PE-West#show ip mroute 232.1.1.1 10.3.0.3
(10.3.0.3, 232.1.1.1), 17:43:34/00:02:51, flags: sTI
  Incoming interface: Lspvif2, RPF nbr 156.50.20.3
  Outgoing interface list:
    Ethernet0/0, Forward/Sparse, 15:49:06/00:02:51

PE-West#show ip multicast mpls vif

Interface    Next-hop        Application    Ref-Count    Table / VRF name
Lspvif2      156.50.20.3     MLDP           N/A          default
Lspvif1      0.0.0.0         MDT            N/A          1    (vrf green)
Lspvif0      0.0.0.0         MDT            N/A          2    (vrf red)
```

FIGURE 5.34

Mroute and LSP-VIF entry.

5.3.5.8 MLDP Database Entry—PE-West

Figure 5.35 shows the MLDP database entry for the (10.3.0.3, 232.1.1.1) P2MP LSP. The Opaque Type searched for is the PIM-SSM IPv4 (S, G). The system ID allocated is 7F000005, which means all output commands referencing this entry will use this system. The root for this entry is 156.50.20.3 (PE-North) derived from the BGP next-hop of 10.3.0.3 and the decoded Opaque value is the type (IPv4) and the actual (S, G). The local label allocated by PE-West for this tree is {214}. Note the (D)

```
PE-West# show mpls MLDP database opaque_type ipv4 10.3.0.3 232.1.1.1
  LSM ID              : 7F000005
  Uptime              : 02:46:53
  Tree type           : P2MP
  FEC Root            : 156.50.20.3  (we are leaf)
  Opaque length       : 11 bytes
  Opaque value        : 0200080A 030003E8 0101019C
  Opaque decoded      : [ipv4 10.3.0.3 232.1.1.1]
  Upstream peer ID    : 156.50.20.1:0, Label local (D): 214   active
  Path Set ID         : 85000009
  Replication client(s):
  MRIBv4(0)       uptime: 02:46:53
                  intrf: Lspvif2
```

FIGURE 5.35

PIM-SSM database entry—PE-West.

on the entry; this signifies it is a downstream label, meaning PE-West will advertise it to the upstream peer 156.50.20.1 (P-Central). P-Central will then use {214} as the downstream label toward PE-West when it has traffic to forward for the multicast stream. MRIBv4 is the single replication client on this entry. Traffic coming in from Lspvif2 will be replicated into the global MRIBv4 and passed to the IP Multicast receiver in the PIM domain.

5.3.5.9 MLDP Database Entry—P-Central

Figure 5.36 shows the MLDP database entry at P-Central. Notice that the raw FEC value is identical to the database entry as PE-West, because it is the same P2MP tree when used in conjunction with the same root (156.50.20.3). The system ID, 24000003, is of local significance to the router. There are two outgoing replication clients for this tree to PE-West (next-hop interface address 156.50.10.2) and PE-East (next-hop interface address 156.50.10.10). The downstream label {214} will be used to PE-West as this is the label P-Central received in Figure 5.35. Finally, the local label {122} allocated to this tree will be passed upstream to PE-North.

```
P-Central#show mpls MLDP database opaque_type ipv4 10.3.0.3 232.1.1.1
  LSM ID              : 24000003
  Uptime              : 02:50:59
  Tree type           : P2MP
  FEC Root            : 156.50.20.3
  Opaque length       : 11 bytes
  Opaque value        : 0200080A 030003E8 0101019C
  Opaque decoded      : [ipv4 10.3.0.3 232.1.1.1]
  Upstream peer ID    : 156.50.20.3:0, Label local (D): 122   active
  Path Set ID         : 84000011
  Replication client(s):
  156.50.20.4:0   uptime: 02:50:59
                  remote label (D): 414
                  nhop: 156.50.10.10 intrf: Serial6/0 ← PE-East
  156.50.20.2:0   uptime: 02:50:58
                  remote label (D): 214
                  nhop: 156.50.10.2 intrf: Serial4/0  ← PE-West
```

FIGURE 5.36

PIM-SSM database entry—P-Central.

5.3.5.10 MLDP Database Entry—PE-North

Figure 5.37 shows the database entry for PE-North. Note that PE-North is aware it is the root because 156.50.20.3 matches an address on one of its interfaces; therefore, there will be no upstream peer nor a local (D) label allocated for the tree. There is only one replicated client, label {122} toward P-Central (next-hop interface address 156.50.10.5).

5.3.5.11 Label Forwarding Entries

Figure 5.38 shows the resultant LFIB entry at P-Central, PE-West, and PE-East for the P2MP LSP. Since P-Central is a branch point for the tree there will be two branches for its local label entry {122}. Multicast traffic coming in with label {122} will be replicated with {414} and {214}. The

```
PE-North# show mpls MLDP database opaque_type ipv4
  LSM ID              : B00000E
  Uptime              : 00:06:07
  Tree type           : P2MP
  FEC Root            : 156.50.20.3 (we are the root)
  Opaque length       : 11 bytes
  Opaque value        : 0200080A 030003E8 0101019C
  Opaque decoded      : [ipv4 10.3.0.3 232.1.1.1]
  Upstream peer ID    : None
  Path Set ID         : 57000014
  Replication client(s):
  156.50.20.1:0   uptime: 00:06:07
                  remote label (D): 122
                  nhop: 156.50.10.5 intrf: Serial4/0
```

FIGURE 5.37

PIM-SSM database entry—PE-North.

```
P-Central#show mpls for label 122
Local      Outgoing    Prefix            Bytes Label    Outgoing    Next Hop
Label      Label       or Tunnel Id      Switched       interface
122        414         [ipv4 10.3.0.3 232.1.1.1]    \
                                         11191776       Se6/0       point2point
           214         [ipv4 10.3.0.3 232.1.1.1]    \
                                         11191776       Se4/0       point2point

PE-West#show mpls for label 212
Local      Outgoing    Prefix            Bytes Label    Outgoing    Next Hop
Label      Label       or Tunnel Id      Switched       interface
214  [T]   No Label    [ipv4 10.3.0.3 232.1.1.1]    \
                                         12050226       aggregate

PE-East#show mpls for label 416
Local      Outgoing    Prefix            Bytes Label    Outgoing    Next Hop
Label      Label       or Tunnel Id      Switched       interface
414  [T]   No Label    [ipv4 10.3.0.3 232.1.1.1]    \
                                         12076402       aggregate
```

FIGURE 5.38

PIM-SSM LFIB entries.

tunnel ID contains the opaque value detailed in Figure 5.36. As can be seen, both branches have received the indicated bytes of multicast traffic.

5.3.6 Multicast VPN Application

The Multicast VPN solution (mVPN) is based on Multicast Distribution Trees (MDT), which are tunnels built over a core network. Customer multicast traffic is then transported/tunneled via these MDTs. The mVPN architecture has been designed to be independent of the tunneling mechanism used to create the MDTs.

MLDP creates the MDTs as follows:

- The Default MDT uses MP2MP LSPs
  - Supports low bandwidth and control traffic between VRFs
- The Data MDT uses P2MP LSPs
  - Supports single high bandwidth source stream from a VRF

All other operation of mVPN remains the same regardless of the tunneling mechanism:

- PIM neighbors in a VRF are seen across an LSP-VIF
- VPN multicast state is signaled by PIM

The only difference when using MLDP is that the MDT Group address used in the mGRE (Draft-Rosen) solution is replaced with a VPN-ID.

5.3.6.1 *Default MDT*

This section discusses how the Default MDT is created using MP2MP procedures in MLDP.

5.3.6.1.1 Scenario

Figure 5.39 shows the Default MDT scenario. The Opaque Value used to signal a Default MDT consists of two parameters. The first parameter is the VPN-ID and the MDT number in the format (<VPN-ID>, 0), where <VPN-ID> is a manually configured 32-bit number that uniquely identifies this VPN. The second parameter is the MDT number for this VPN, and for the Default MDT it is set to zero.

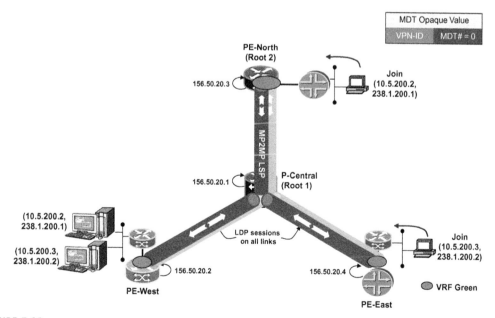

FIGURE 5.39

In this scenario each of the three PE routers belongs to VPN Green (they have the same VPN-ID). Each PE router with the same VPN-ID will join the same MP2MP tree. Also, the PE routers have created a primary MP2MP tree rooted at P-Central (Root 1) and a backup MP2MP tree rooted at PE-North (Root 2). There are two sources at PE-West and interested receivers at both PE-North and PE-East. PE-West will choose one of the MP2MP trees to transmit the customer VPN traffic, while all PE routers can receive traffic on either of the MP2MP trees.

5.3.6.1.2 Configuration

Figure 5.40 shows the configuration for the Default MDT. This configuration is consistent for every PE-router participating in the same VPN-ID. As mentioned, the "vpn id 100:2" command replaces the MDT Group Address used with the mGRE (Draft-Rosen) transport method and is defined in RFC 2685. To provide redundancy, two Default MDT trees are statically configured and rooted at P-Central and PE-North. The selection as to which MP2MP tree the Default MDT will use at a particular PE-Router is determined by IGP metrics. An MP2MP LSP is implicit for the Default MDT.

```
ip pim mpls source Loopback0
ip multicast-routing
ip multicast-routing vrf green
ip pim vrf green mpls source Loopback0 ← Seems to work without this
!
ip vrf green
 rd 100:2
 vpn id 100:2
 route-target export 200:2
 route-target import 200:2
 mdt default mpls MLDP 156.50.20.1 (P-Central)
 mdt default mpls MLDP 156.50.20.3 (PE-North)
```

FIGURE 5.40

Default MDT configuration.

5.3.6.1.3 LSP Downstream

Figures 5.41 and 5.42 show the downstream tree creation for each of the roots. Note that each PE router configured with VPN-ID 100:2 creates the same FEC TLV, but with a different root and downstream labels per MP2MP tree. The FEC Type will be "MP2MP Down," which prompts the receiving LSR to respond with an upstream label mapping message to create the Upstream Path.

5.3.6.1.4 LSP Upstream

Figures 5.43 and 5.44 show the upstream LSP creation for the Default MDTs. For each downstream label received a corresponding upstream label is sent. In Figure 5.43, P-Central sends out three upstream labels—{111}, {109}, and {105}—to each downstream directly connected neighbor (remember downstream is away from the root). The process for PE-North is the same except that it only sends a single upstream label {313} as there is only one directly connected downstream neighbor.

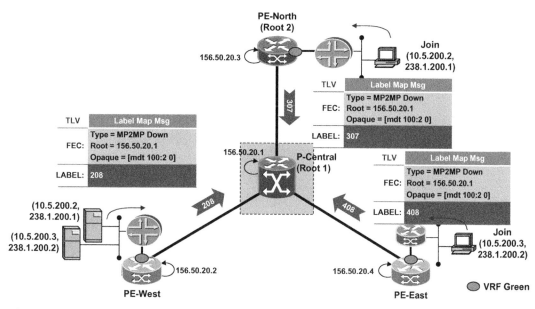

FIGURE 5.41

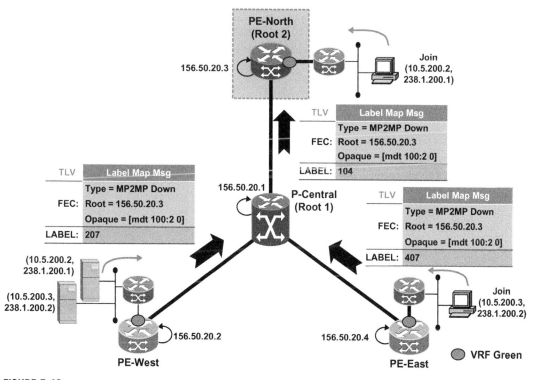

FIGURE 5.42

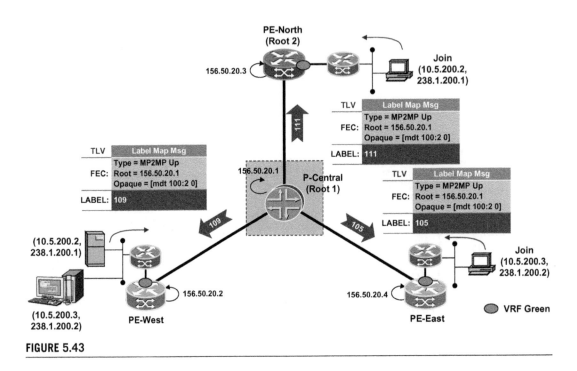

FIGURE 5.43

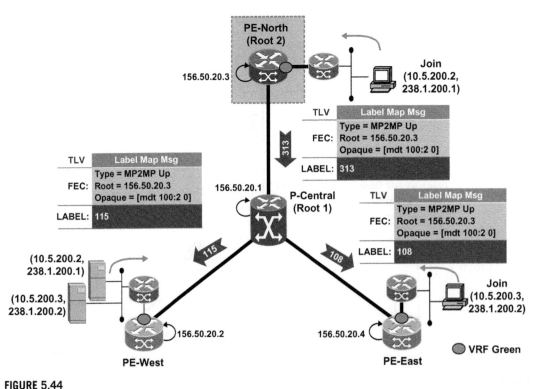

FIGURE 5.44

5.3.6.1.5 PIM Overlay Signaling of VPN Multicast State

The signaling of a multicast state within a VPN is via PIM. It is called overlay signaling because the PIM session runs over the MP LSP and maps the VPN multicast flow to the LSP. In the mVPN solution a PIM adjacency is created between PE routers and the multicast states within a VRF are populated over the PIM sessions. When using MLDP, the PIM session runs over an LSP-VIF inter-face. Figure 5.45 shows PIM signaling running over the Default MDT MP2MP LSP. Access to the MP2MP LSP is via the LSP-VIF, which can see all the leaf PE routers at the ends of branches, much like a LAN interface. In Figure 5.45, PE-East sends a downstream label mapping message to the root, P-Central, which in turn sends an upstream label mapping message to PE-West. This creates the LSP between the two leaf PE routers. A PIM session can then be activated over the top of the LSP, allow-ing the (S, G) states and control messages to be signaled between PE-West and PE-East. In this case PE-East receives a join for (10.5.200.3, 238.1.200.2) within VRF Green, which it inserts into the mroute table. The join is then sent via the PIM session to PE-West (BGP next-hop of 10.5.200.3), which populates its VRF Green mroute table. This process is identical if an mGRE (Draft-Rosen) tun-nel was used.

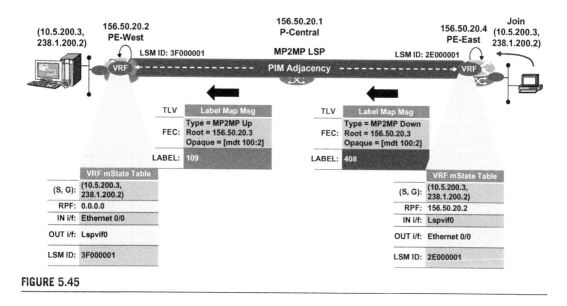

FIGURE 5.45

In summary:

- FEC TLV + label mapping message creates the MP2MP LSP
- PIM over MP2MP LSP creates the state within VPN

5.3.6.1.6 PIM Adjacencies

PIM operates over the LSP-VIF as if it is a regular tunnel interface. That means PIM Hellos are exchanged over the LSP-VIF to establish PIM adjacencies over the default MDT. Figure 5.46 shows the three PIM adjacencies in VRF Green of PE-East. The first is the adjacency to the receiver network over s6/0, while the next two are the adjacencies to PE-West and PE-North over the MP2MP LSP via Lspvif0.

> **NOTE**
>
> Notice that the same Lspvif0 is used for both MP2MP LSPs (different roots); therefore, Lspvif0 has two adjacencies. The source streams in VRF Green will be transmitted to the primary root.

```
PE-East#show ip pim vrf green neighbor
192.168.10.18    Serial6/0        04:53:19/00:01:18 v2 1 / G
156.50.20.3      Lspvif0          04:52:32/00:01:28 v2 1 / B S P G
156.50.20.2      Lspvif0          04:52:32/00:01:17 v2 1 / B S P G

PE-East#show ip mroute vrf green 238.1.200.2 10.5.200.3
(10.5.200.3, 238.1.200.2), 04:54:18/00:02:40, flags: sT
  Incoming interface: Lspvif0, RPF nbr 156.50.20.2
  Outgoing interface list:
    Serial6/0, Forward/Sparse-Dense, 04:54:18/00:02:40
```

FIGURE 5.46

PIM adjacencies.

The output also shows the (S, G) entry for VRF Green. The stream 238.1.200.2 has the RPF interface of LSPvif0 and the neighbor 156.50.20.2, which is PE-West.

5.3.6.1.7 MLDP Database Entry—PE-East

Figure 5.47 shows the database entries for the MP2MP trees supporting the Default MDT at PE-East. The database is searched by Opaque Value "mdt 100:2," which results in information for two MP2MP trees (one for each root) being returned. Both trees have different system IDs and use the same Opaque Value [mdt 100:2 0], but with different roots. The last "0" in the Opaque Value indicates this tree is a Default MDT. Entry 79000004 shows it is the primary MP2MP tree; therefore, PE-East will transmit all source multicast traffic on this LSP, while B2000006 will be the backup root. Note that interface Lspvif0 represents both MP2MP LSPs. The Local Label (D) is the downstream label allocated by PE-East for this tree. In other words, traffic from the root will be received with either label {408} (Primary Tree) or {407} (Backup Tree). The Remote Label (U) is the label that PE-East will use to send traffic into the tree upstream toward the root, either {105} for the Primary Tree or {108} for the Backup Tree. Both of these labels in the 100 series were received from P-Central.

```
PE-East#show mpls MLDP database  opaque_type mdt 100:2
  LSM ID              : 79000004 (RNR LSM ID: 5)
  Uptime              : 00:29:18
  Tree type           : MP2MP
  FEC Root            : 156.50.20.1  (we are leaf)
  Opaque length       : 14 bytes
  Opaque value        : 07000B00 01000000 00020000 00009C
  Opaque decoded      : [mdt 100:2 0]
  Upstream peer ID    : 156.50.20.1:0, Label local (D): 408  remote (U): 105 active
  RNR active LSP       : (this entry)
  Candidate RNR ID(s): 79000004
  Path Set ID         : 9E000007
  Replication client(s):
  MDT               uptime: 00:29:18    Path Set ID: CF000008
                    intrf: Lspvif0 (vrf green)

  LSM ID              : B2000006 (RNR LSM ID: 5)
  Uptime              : 00:29:18
  Tree type           : MP2MP
  FEC Root            : 156.50.20.3  (we are leaf)
  Opaque length       : 14 bytes
  Opaque value        : 07000B00 01000000 00020000 00009C
  Opaque decoded      : [mdt 100:2 0]
  Upstream peer ID    : 156.50.20.1:0, Label local (D): 407  remote (U): 108 active
  RNR active LSP       : 79000004 (root: 156.50.20.1)
  Path Set ID         : 63000005
  Replication client(s):
  MDT               uptime: 00:29:18    Path Set ID: 25000006
                    intrf: Lspvif0 (vrf green)
```

FIGURE 5.47

Default MDT database entry.

5.3.6.1.8 Label Forwarding Entry—P-Central (Root 1)

Figure 5.48 shows the VRF Green (MDT 100:2) MLDP database entry 1F000001 for the primary MP2MP LSP, which is P-Central. Since the local router P-Central is the root there is no upstream peer ID; therefore, no labels are allocated locally. However, there are three replication clients representing each of the three PE routers—PE-North, PE-West, and PE-East. In the replication entry *looking from the perspective of the root* there are two types of labels:

- Remote label (D)—Labels received from remote peers that are downstream to the root (remember traffic flows downstream away from the root)
- Local label (U)—Labels provided by P-Central to its neighbors to be used as upstream labels (sending traffic to the root). It is easy to tell this as the labels all start in the 100 range, which we have configured for P-Central to use. P-Central sends these labels out when it receives an FEC with the type = "MP2MP Down"

From the labels received and sent in the replication entries, the LFIB is created. The LFIB has one entry per upstream path and one entry per downstream path. Since P-Central is the root, there are only upstream entries in the LFIB that have been merged with the corresponding downstream labels. For example, label {105} is the label P-Central sent to PE-East to send source traffic upstream (see Figure 5.43). Traffic received from PE-East will then be replicated using the downstream labels {307} to PE-West and {208} to PE-North.

```
P-Central#show mpls MLDP database opaque_type mdt 100:2
  LSM ID               : 1F000001
  Uptime               : 00:42:03
  Tree type            : MP2MP
  FEC Root             : 156.50.20.1 (we are the root)
  Opaque length        : 14 bytes
  Opaque value         : 07000B00 01000000 00020000 00009C
  Opaque decoded       : [mdt 100:2 0]
  Upstream peer ID     : None
  Path Set ID          : B4000007
  Replication client(s):
  156.50.20.2:0   uptime: 00:42:03    Path Set ID: AC000008
                  remote label (D): 208  local label (U): 109
                  nhop: 156.50.10.2 intrf: Serial4/0
  156.50.20.3:0   uptime: 00:42:02    Path Set ID: E00000C
                  remote label (D): 307  local label (U): 111
                  nhop: 156.50.10.6 intrf: Serial5/0
  156.50.20.4:0   uptime: 00:41:44    Path Set ID: 3D000010
                  remote label (D): 408  local label (U): 105
                  nhop: 156.50.10.10 intrf: Serial6/0

P-Central#show mpls forwarding-table | inc 1F000001
  105    307         MLDP:1F000001    38468       Se5/0      point2point
         208         MLDP:1F000001    38468       Se4/0      point2point
  109    307         MLDP:1F000001    34738       Se5/0      point2point
         408         MLDP:1F000001    34738       Se6/0      point2point
  111    408         MLDP:1F000001    282         Se6/0      point2point
         208         MLDP:1F000001    282         Se4/0      point2point
```

FIGURE 5.48

Default MDT LFIB—Root 1.

Figure 5.49 shows the entry on P-Central for the MP2MP LSP rooted at PE-North (backup root). In this tree P-Central is a branch of the tree, not a root; therefore, there are some minor differences to note:

- The upstream peer ID is PE-North, therefore, P-Central has allocated label {104} in the downstream direction toward PE-North and subsequently, PE-North has responded with an upstream label of {313}.
- The replication shows two entries representing PE-East and PE-West.
- The merged LFIB shows two entries:
  - A downstream entry label {104} receiving traffic from Root 2 (PE-North) which is then directed further downstream using labels {207} PE-West and {407} PE-East
  - Two upstream entries {108} and {115} receiving traffic from the leaves and directing it either downstream {207} and {407} or upstream using label {313}

```
Central_P#show mpls MLDP database opaque_type mdt 100:2
LSM ID              : E6000004
 Uptime             : 00:42:03
 Tree type          : MP2MP
 FEC Root           : 156.50.20.3
 Opaque length      : 14 bytes
 Opaque value       : 07000B00 01000000 00020000 00009C
 Opaque decoded     : [mdt 100:2 0]
 Upstream peer ID   : 156.50.20.3:0, Label local (D): 104  remote (U): 313 active
 Path Set ID        : 48000003
 Replication client(s):
 156.50.20.2:0   uptime: 00:42:03     Path Set ID: CF000004
                 remote label (D): 207  local label (U): 115
                 nhop: 156.50.10.2 intrf: Serial4/0
 156.50.20.4:0   uptime: 00:41:44     Path Set ID: 5800000E
                 remote label (D): 407  local label (U): 108
                 nhop: 156.50.10.10 intrf: Serial6/0

Central_P# show mpls forwarding-table | inc E6000004
104   207         MLDP:E6000004    251228     Se4/0    point2point
      407         MLDP:E6000004    251334     Se6/0    point2point
108   207         MLDP:E6000004    0          Se4/0    point2point
      313         MLDP:E6000004    0          Se5/0    point2point
115   313         MLDP:E6000004    0          Se5/0    point2point
      407         MLDP:E6000004    0          Se6/0    point2point
```

FIGURE 5.49

Default MDT LFIB—Root 2.

5.3.6.2 Data MDT

An mVPN traffic that exceeds a certain threshold can move off the Default MDT onto a Data MDT. This section discusses how a Data MDT is formed using MLDP.

5.3.6.2.1 Scenario

Figure 5.50 shows the Data MDT scenario. The Opaque Value used to signal a Data MDT consists of two parameters—the VPN-ID and the MDT number in the format (<VPN-ID>, MDT# > 0)—where <VPN-ID> is a manually configured 32-bit number that uniquely identifies this VPN. The second parameter is the unique Data MDT number for this VPN, which is a number greater than zero.

In this scenario two receivers at PE-North and PE-East are interested in two sources at PE-West. Assume the source 10.5.200.3 exceeds the threshold on the Default MDT. When this happens, PE-West will send out an MDT Join TLV over the Default MDT MP2MP LSP advising all PE routers that a new Data MDT is being created.

Since PE-East has an interested receiver in VPN Green, it will build an MP LSP using the P2MP procedures discussed back to PE-West, which will be the root of the tree. PE-North does not have a receiver for 10.5.200.3; therefore, it will just cache the Join TLV.

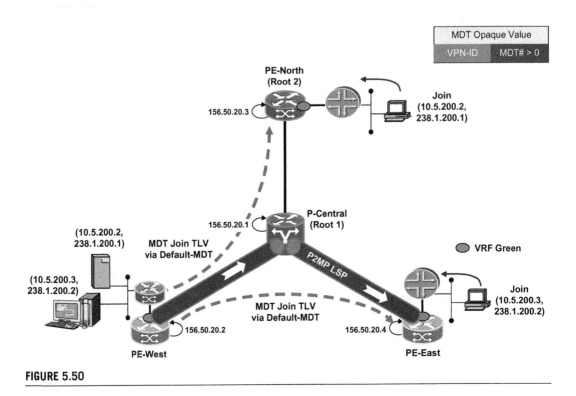

FIGURE 5.50

5.3.6.2.2 Configuration

Figure 5.51 shows the Data MDT configuration for all the PE routers. The "mdt data" commands are the only additional command necessary. The first command allows a maximum of 60 Data MDTs to be created, while the second command sets the threshold. If the number of Data MDTs exceeds 60 then the Data MDTs will be reused the same way they are for the mGRE (Draft-Rosen) tunnel method (the one with the lowest refcount).

```
ip pim vrf green mpls source Loopback0
!
ip vrf green
 rd 100:2
 vpn id 100:2
 route-target export 200:2
 route-target import 200:2
 mdt default mpls MLDP 156.50.20.1 (P-Central)
 mdt default mpls MLDP 156.50.20.3 (PE-North)
 mdt data mpls MLDP 60
 mdt data threshold 1
```

FIGURE 5.51

Data MDT configuration.

5.3.6.2.3 VRF mRoute Table—PE-West

Figure 5.52 shows the VRF Green mroute table on PE-West *before* the high bandwidth source exceeds the threshold. At this point there are two streams, representing each of the two VPN sources at PE-West, on a single MP2MP LSP (System ID D8000000). The LSP represents the Default MDT accessed via Lspvif0.

```
PE-West#show ip mroute vrf green verbose
...
(10.5.200.2, 238.1.200.1), 00:00:25/00:03:29, flags: sT
  Incoming interface: Serial6/0, RPF nbr 192.168.10.6
  Outgoing interface list:
    Lspvif0, LSM MDT: D8000000 (default),Forward/Sparse-Dense, ...
(10.5.200.3, 238.1.200.2), 00:11:14/00:02:48, flags: sT
  Incoming interface: Serial6/0, RPF nbr 192.168.10.6
  Outgoing interface list:
    Lspvif0, LSM MDT: D8000000 (default),Forward/Sparse-Dense, ...
```

FIGURE 5.52

VRF mRoute table before threshold.

Figure 5.53 shows the output after the source transmission exceeds the threshold. PE-West sends an MDT Join TLV to signal the creation of a Data MDT. In this case the Data MDT number is "1"; therefore PE-East will send a label mapping message back to PE-West with an FEC TLV containing root = PE-West, Opaque Value = (mdt <vpn-id> 1). The System ID is now changed to 4E000003 signaling a different LSP; however, the LSP-VIF is still Lspvif0. The (S, G) entry also has the "y" flag set indicating this stream has switched to a Data MDT.

```
PE-West# show ip mroute vrf green 10.5.200.3 238.1.200.2 verbose
...
(10.5.200.3, 238.1.200.2), 00:00:08/00:03:27, flags: sTy
  Incoming interface: Serial6/0, RPF nbr 192.168.10.6
    MDT TX nr: 1 LSM-ID 4E000003
  Outgoing interface list:
    Lspvif0, LSM MDT: 4E000003 (data) Forward/Sparse-Dense,
```

FIGURE 5.53

VRF mRoute table after threshold.

5.3.6.2.4 LSP-VIF Adjacencies—PE-West

The LSP Virtual interface was discussed in Section . It is treated as an NBMA interface, with each "virtual circuit" representing a unique MP LSP forwarding instance. The correct adjacency is selected when sending the multicast packet. Figure 5.54 shows the application of that concept on PE-West. There is a single Lspvif0 interface, but it has three adjacencies as follows:

- 4E000003 is the single Data MDT created for (10.5.200.3, 238.1.200.2)
- 58000000 is the Default MDT (backup root)
- D8000000 is the Default MDT (primary root)

```
PE-West#show adjacency lspvif 0
Protocol Interface              Address
IP        Lspvif0               4E000003(5)
IP        Lspvif0               58000000(4)
IP        Lspvif0               D8000000(3)
```

FIGURE 5.54

LSP VIF adjacencies.

5.3.6.2.5 MLDP Database Entries

Figure 5.55 shows the MLDP entry for the Data MDT (4E000003) on the ingress router PE-West. Points to note about this entry include:

- The tree type is P2MP with PE-West (156.50.20.2) as the root.
- The Opaque Value is [mdt 100:2 1] denoting the first Data MDT.
- There are no labels allocated, because it is the root.
- There are two replication client entries on this tree:
  - Label {112} will be used to send the traffic downstream (since PE-West is the root) toward PE-East (via P-Central).
  - The MDT entry is an internal construct.

```
PE-West# show mpls MLDP database id 4E000003
LSM ID              : 4E000003
 Uptime             : 00:04:46
 Tree type          : P2MP
 FEC Root           : 156.50.20.2 (we are the root) (we are leaf)
 Opaque length      : 14 bytes
 Opaque value       : 07000B00 01000000 00020000 00019C
 Opaque decoded     : [mdt 100:2 1]
 Upstream peer ID   : None
 Path Set ID        : 1500000A
 Replication client(s):
 MDT                      uptime: 00:04:46
                          intrf: Lspvif0 (vrf green)
 156.50.20.1:0            uptime: 00:04:46
                          remote label (D): 112
                          nhop: 156.50.10.1 intrf: Serial4/0
```

FIGURE 5.55

Data MDT database entry PE-West.

Figure 5.56 shows the database entry for the Data MDT on PE-East, the egress router. Also shown is the MDT join TLV that was sent from PE-West over the Default MDT. The MDT join TLV contains all the necessary information to allow PE-East to create a label mapping message P2MP LSP back to the root of PE-West. Label {414} will be used by P-Central to send traffic to PE-East.

```
*Feb 19 04:43:24.039: PIM(1): MDT join TLV received for
(10.5.200.3,238.1.200.2)
*Feb 19 04:43:24.039: MLDP: LDP root 156.50.20.2 added
*Feb 19 04:43:24.039: MLDP: [mdt 100:2 1] label mapping msg sent to
156.50.20.1:0

PE-East#show mpls MLDP database opaque_type mdt 100:2 1
  LSM ID                : 9E000004
  Uptime                : 00:13:54
  Tree type             : P2MP
  FEC Root              : 156.50.20.2   (we are leaf)
  Opaque length         : 14 bytes
  Opaque value          : 07000B00 01000000 00020000 00019C
  Opaque decoded        : [mdt 100:2 1]
  Upstream peer ID      : 156.50.20.1:0, Label local (D): 414    active
  Path Set ID           : BE00000A
  Replication client(s):
  MDT                   uptime: 00:13:54
                        intrf: Lspvif0 (vrf green)
```

FIGURE 5.56

Data MDT database entry—PE-East.

5.3.6.3 Label Forwarding Entries
Figure 5.57 shows the LFIB entry for the Data MDT as it passes through P-Central and PE-East. The Tunnel ID used for the LSP is the opaque value [mdt 100:2 1].

```
P-Central#show mpls for label 112
Local       Outgoing    Prefix          Bytes Label    Outgoing    Next Hop
Label       Label       or Tunnel Id    Switched       interface
112         414         [mdt 100:2 1]   2993584        Se6/0       point2point

PE-East#show mpls for label 400
Local       Outgoing    Prefix          Bytes Label    Outgoing    Next Hop
Label       Label       or Tunnel Id    Switched       interface
414    [T]  No Label    [mdt 100:2 1][V] 3297312       aggregate/green
```

FIGURE 5.57

Data MDT LFIB for P-Central and PE-East.

5.3.6.4 Direct MDT (VPNv4) Application

The Direct MDT or VPNv4 Transit is very similar in its operation to the PIM-SSM Transit application. The difference is that a direct MDT is VPN specific and uses the RD along with the (S, G) in the Opaque Value to make an MP LSP unique. Direct MDT uses in-band signaling; that is, the Opaque Value is derived from the multicast flow and is used to signal the mapping between the LSP and the VPN multicast flow.

With mVPN, you normally need a Default MDT for control traffic (PIM) and low bandwidth sources. The Default MDT would then be used to send Join TLV to signal a move to a Data MDT. Direct MDT does not require the Default MDT mechanism and its associated PIM signaling to create what looks and behaves like a Data MDT; instead it uses a P2MP LSP with in-band signaling. There is no PIM adjacency running over the Direct MDT LSP.

The Direct MDT application would benefit Multicast VPNs, where the there are limited high bandwidth sources constantly sending traffic to a number of receivers spread around the MPLS network. Another benefit of Direct MDTs is that they support the building of extranet P2MP LSPs, which will be discussed further in the chapter. The VPN (S, G) states can be selectively filtered to use a Direct MDT or Default/Data MDTs.

In summary, Direct MDTs:

- Are similar to IPv4 transit LSP but for VPN traffic
  - Use in-band signaling of (S, G) along with RD in Opaque Value
- Do not use Default/Data MDT control planes
- Use VPN Multicast state signaled in-band like IPv4 transit
  - One P2MP LSP per (S, G) state within VPN (SSM Only)
- Have extranet multicast streams that are supported
- Can be used in conjunction with Default/Data MDTs
  - (S, G) operation can be selective within VPN
  - Either over Direct MDT or Default MDT
- Are useful for VPNs with a limited number of states

5.3.6.4.1 Scenario

Figure 5.58 shows the Direct MDT scenario. This example shows the same VRF Green with two sources at PE-West and receivers at PE-North and PE-East. Through Direct MDT, instead of creating a Default MDT, we can just set up two permanent P2MP LSPs directly to the root at PE-West for each of the sources. Once set up, the P2MP LSPs will remain in the MPLS core until manually removed. There is no need for a Default MDT. The MP LSP creation is very similar to that of the in-band P2MP LSP procedures for PIM-SSM Transit, except that the Opaque Value will contain the RD of the VPN along with the (S, G).

5.3.6.4.2 Configuration

Figure 5.59 shows the configuration for a Direct MDT on VRF Green. This configuration will be consistent among all PE routers of the same VPN. The "mdt direct" command under the VRF configuration enables the feature and is necessary on both the ingress and egress routers to enable a connection to the MRIB. The egress PE router learns about multicast routes to build a P2MP LSP, the ingress PE populates the MRIB with multicast routes it learns from MLDP.

The "MLDP range" command associated with VRF Green signals that only (S, G) in ACL 100 will operate over a Direct MDT. In this case it is the two hosts and their groups at PE-West.

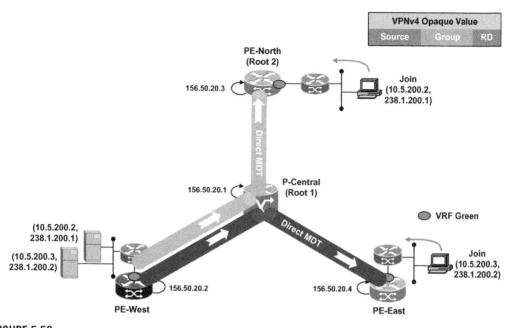

FIGURE 5.58

```
ip pim vrf green mpls source Loopback0
ip multicast vrf green mpls MLDP range 100
!
access-list 100 permit ip host 10.5.200.2 host 238.1.200.1
access-list 100 permit ip host 10.5.200.3 host 238.1.200.2
!
ip vrf green
 rd 100:2
 vpn id 100:2
 route-target export 200:2
 route-target import 200:2
 mdt default MLDP mp2mp 156.50.20.1 (P-Central)
 mdt default MLDP mp2mp 156.50.20.3 (PE-North)
 mdt direct
 mdt data MLDP 60 threshold 1
```

FIGURE 5.59

Direct MDT configuration.

5.3.6.4.3 P2MP LSP Creation

Figure 5.60 shows the resultant P2MP LSP creation for each of the sources. The item to note is the format of the Opaque Value. Looking at the entry from PE-East, we can see the value is (10.5.200.3 238.1.200.2 100:2). The 100:2 is the route distinguisher associated with VRF Green. It is used to uniquely identify the P2MP LSP in the MPLS core and also, since we are using in-band signaling, allows PE-West to parse the Opaque Value to know which VRF it should associate this P2MP LSP with.

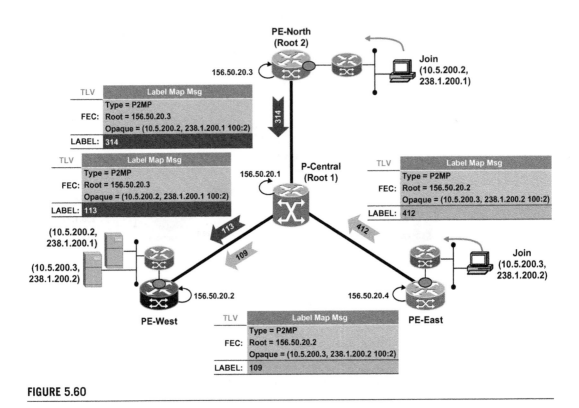

FIGURE 5.60

5.3.6.4.4 In-Band Signaling of VPN Multicast State

Figure 5.61 shows in-band signaling of the VPN (S, G) state for a Direct MDT. The process is identical to that of PIM-SSM except that the head- and tail-ends of the P2MP LSP are associated with a VRF. PE-West parses the received Opaque Value and uses the RD to look up the correct VRF (in this case VRF Green) to install the (S, G) into the MRIB. It then knows to associate (10.5.200.3, 238.1.200.2) with the P2MP LSP on o-list Lspvif0.

5.3.6.4.5 VRF mRoute—PE-East Egress

Figure 5.62 shows information about the stream (10.5.200.3, 238.1.200.2) at PE-East where a receiver is connected in VRF Green. Since this (S, G) matches the ACL a Direct MDT will be created. The RD is resolved by looking up the BGP information for the source 10.5.200.3. As seen, the Opaque Value can then be derived using RD = 100:2, Root = 156.50.20.2 (which is the BGP next-hop).

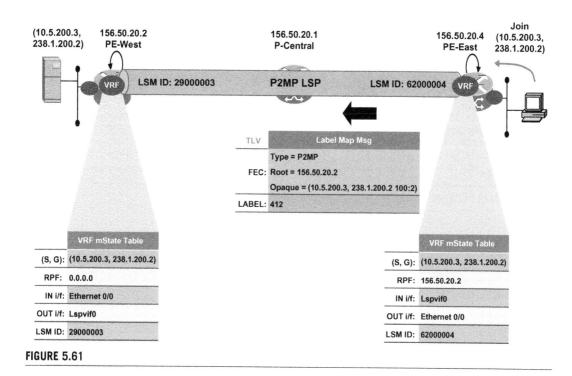

FIGURE 5.61

```
PE-East#show ip mroute vrf green ssm
(10.5.200.3, 238.1.200.2), 08:14:48/00:03:27, flags: sT
  Incoming interface: Lspvif3, RPF nbr 156.50.20.2
  Outgoing interface list:
    Serial6/0, Forward/Sparse-Dense, 08:14:48/00:03:27

PE-East#show ip bgp vpnv4 all 10.5.200.0
BGP routing table entry for 100:2:10.5.200.0/24, version 10
Paths: (1 available, best #1, no table)
  Not advertised to any peer
  Local
    156.50.20.2 (metric 129) from 156.50.20.2 (156.50.20.2)
      Origin incomplete, metric 0, localpref 100, valid, internal, best
      Extended Community: RT:200:2
      mpls labels in/out nolabel/210
```

FIGURE 5.62

mRoute and BGP table.

5.3.6.4.6 VRF mRoute—PE-West Ingress

Figure 5.63 shows the VRF Green mRoute table at PE-West. There are two entries, one for each multicast source. Notice that the LSP-VIF is the same for each entry, Lspvif2, but the System ID is different (29000003, D8000002), representing the different P2MP LSP reach through Lspvif2.

```
PE-West#show ip mroute vrf green ssm
(10.5.200.2, 238.1.200.1), 09:32:34/00:2:54, flags: sTI
  Incoming interface: Serial6/0, RPF nbr 192.168.10.6
  Outgoing interface list:
    Lspvif2, LSM ID: 29000003, Forward/Sparse, 09:32:34/00:02:28

(10.5.200.3, 238.1.200.2), 09:32:35/00:02:31, flags: sTI
  Incoming interface: Serial6/0, RPF nbr 192.168.10.6
  Outgoing interface list:
    Lspvif2, LSM ID: D8000002, Forward/Sparse, 09:32:35/00:02:28
```

FIGURE 5.63

mRoute table at PE-West.

5.3.6.4.7 MLDP Database Entry—PE-West Ingress

Figure 5.64 shows the PE-West database entries for the Opaque Type VPNv4 for Direct MDTs. As expected, there are two entries that correspond to each source. Note that the format of the Opaque Value includes the type "vpnv4," the (S, G), and the RD (100:2).

```
PE-West# show mpls MLDP database opaque_type vpnv4
  System ID         : 29000003
  Uptime            : 09:45:29
  FEC tree type     : P2MP
  FEC length        : 28 bytes
  FEC value         : 00000001 00000003 0A05C802 EE01C801 00000064 00000002
9C321402
  FEC Root          : 156.50.20.2 (we are the root)
  Opaque decoded    : [vpnv4 10.5.200.2 238.1.200.1 100:2]
  Upstream peer ID  : none
  Local label (D)   : no_label
  Replication client(s):
  156.50.20.1:0   uptime: 09:45:29   remote label (D): 113   nhop: 156.50.10.1

  System ID         : D8000002
  Uptime            : 09:45:30
  FEC tree type     : P2MP
  FEC length        : 28 bytes
  FEC value         : 00000001 00000003 0A05C803 EE01C802 00000064 00000002
9C321402
  FEC Root          : 156.50.20.2 (we are the root)
  Opaque decoded    : [vpnv4 10.5.200.3 238.1.200.2 100:2]
  Upstream peer ID  : none
  Local label (D)   : no_label
  Replication client(s):
  156.50.20.1:0   uptime: 09:45:30   remote label (D): 109   nhop: 156.50.10.1
```

FIGURE 5.64

Direct MDT database entries at PE-West.

5.3.6.5 *Direct MDT Extranets*

With Direct MDT Extranets, a P2MP LSP is built through the core using the source and group of the multicast stream and the RD of the ingress PE. The RD is found by doing a route lookup using the source in the BGP table. Using the BGP prefix that is returned from the route lookup, original RD of the ingress PE can be found. The MP LSP is created using the (S, G, RD) state in the core network. In the case of extranets, if a particular source needs to be joined in from a different VRF, the standard unicast import/exports RTs may be used to join a multicast stream that is in a different VRF.

In summary:

- Multicast extranets are simple to form with Direct MDT.
- Source routes can be imported from different VRF.
  - Using standard route-target mechanisms for extranet
- (S, G, RD) P2MP LSP is formed in core.
  - By doing BGP lookup to get source RD
- RD is then used to create (S, G) in source VRF, which is in a different VRF to receiver VRF.

5.3.6.5.1 Configuration

Figure 5.65 shows a typical extranet configuration used with a unicast VPN. In this case, assume VRF Green has the source and VRF Red has an interested receiver. VRF Green will export a route-target of 200:2, while VRF Red will import rt 200:2. This populates VRF Red with routes from VRF Green including the multicast source subnet or host. MDT Direct is also enabled on both VRF as well as the appropriate commands to allow MP LSPs to be created.

```
ip vrf green
 rd 100:2
 vpn id 100:2
 route-target export 200:2
 route-target import 200:2
 mdt direct
!
ip vrf red
 rd 100:1
 vpn id 100:1
 route-target export 100:1
 route-target import 100:1
 route-target import 200:2
 mdt direct
!
ip multicast vrf green mpls MLDP range 100
ip multicast vrf green mpls source Loopback0
ip multicast vrf red mpls MLDP range 100
ip multicast vrf red mpls source Loopback0
access-list 100 permit ip host 10.5.200.2 host 238.1.200.1
access-list 100 permit ip host 10.5.200.3 host 238.1.200.2
```

FIGURE 5.65

Extranet configuration.

5.3.6.5.2 MROUTE and MLDP Database

When VRF Red receives an IGMP join, it will create a label mapping message with (S, G, RD). The RD will be derived from the BGP entry for 10.5.200.3 in VRF Red. Since it imported 10.5.200.3 from VRF Green, it will have the RD value from VRF Green; therefore, it can create the correct FEC to join the MP LSP rooted at VRF Green. Figure 5.66 shows the MLDP database entry for the stream (10.5.200.3, 238.1.200.2) with the RD of 100:2. Since VRF Red was aware of all this information it becomes a replication client of the P2MP LSP as shown in the last line of the output.

```
PE-East#show ip mroute vrf red ssm
(10.5.200.3, 238.1.200.2), 01:20:08/00:02:32, flags: sT
  Incoming interface: Lspvif4, RPF nbr 156.50.20.2
  Outgoing interface list:
    Serial5/0, Forward/Sparse, 01:20:08/00:02:32

PE-East#show mpls MLDP database opaque_type vpnv4
  System ID            : EF000003
  Uptime               : 12:36:17
  FEC tree type        : P2MP
  FEC length           : 28 bytes
  FEC value            : 00000001 00000003 0A05C803 EE01C802 00000064 00000002
9C321402
  FEC Root             : 156.50.20.2  (we are leaf)
  Opaque decoded       : [vpnv4 10.5.200.3 238.1.200.2 100:2]
  Upstream peer ID     : 156.50.20.1:0
  Local label (D)      : 412
  Replication client(s):
  MRIBv4(1)       uptime: 12:36:17   intrf: Lspvif3 (vrf green)
  MRIBv4(3)       uptime: 00:34:46   intrf: Lspvif4 (vrf red)
```

FIGURE 5.66

Extranet MLDP database.

5.4 SUMMARY

As mentioned earlier, this draft does not support aggregation of multicast streams. This is likely to pose many challenges to an operator who intends to deploy a large-scale Multicast environment. In an MVPN environment, the Default MDT may offer aggregation as available in the Draft-Rosen MVPNs; however, if the provider moves to a Data MDT (S-PMSI), aggregation of multiple streams within the S-PMSI is not possible.

The draft "draft-ietf-mpls-mldp-in-band-signaling" itself mentions the following:

Each IP Multicast tree is mapped one-to-one to a P2MP or MP2MP LSP in the MPLS network. This type of service works well if the number of LSPs created is under control of the MPLS network operator, or if the number of LSPs for a particular service is known to be limited in number.

In the context of the MVPN service, the carrier does not have control over the number of multicast streams used by an MVPN customer; thus, it cannot control the number of LSPs required by the in-band signaling. Therefore it is fair to mention that this implementation would serve carriers intending to deploy small- to medium-sized multicast environments.

Application: IPTV

6.1 INTRODUCTION

"IPTV" is a term that means different things to different people. The acronym is defined as "Internet Protocol Television," which would mean that any form of video carried over Internet Protocol, either part of the way or the entire distance, would qualify as IPTV.

Further video content has multiple applications, the most obvious of which is broadcast TV. Broadcast TV is one application that can be deployed using multicast, which is the main theme of this book. Other video applications such as video-on-demand (VoD) are at the transport layer unicast applications, which are not of significant interest to the current discussion. Other "multicast-oriented" applications of IPTV are distance education as adapted in the academic or corporate environments, conference webcasts that are increasingly deployed both in corporate environment and in the case of industry events, and so forth.

IPTV is a classic case of voice, video, and data convergence, which would replace the numerous networks run by service providers with a single terrestrial infrastructure. For the end user this translates to a single "pipe" into the house that provides bundled communication and entertainment services at a lower price point. Whereas convergence does bring in its own efficiencies of the transport infrastructure, there are other aspects that differentiate IPTV services from commercial and user-experience points of view.

Targeted advertising, for instance, is a domain that has made significant technical progress in the last decade. Amazon, Google, and other major companies have made this into a science and have reaped commercial benefits with exponential returns. With IPTV, the technology makes it possible for "ad insertion" at varying levels of granularity: regional (Northeast during a snowfall for instance), subregional (state-wide where political primaries are in progress), and potentially with some progress to demographic segments based on their Internet usage patterns. IPTV then, is no longer simple television on IP; it is now a fundamentally different service.

Similarly, having IPTV provided on the same pipe as the broadband connection allows service providers to receive user input. Feedback from the user can be transmitted "upstream" where it can be processed. Examples of this could be purchase of advertised products, feedback on programming, or even user-behavior patterns that can be sent back automatically from the STBs/CPEs to the service providers. It would also be possible for users to select the categories of ads in which they would be interested. Such interaction opens up other avenues as well, such as dynamic content creation from the user end. It also allows for "browsing" options within the EPG choices, which can create more of an Internet feel "pulling" content of interest rather than the traditional "push" mode of TV broadcasting.

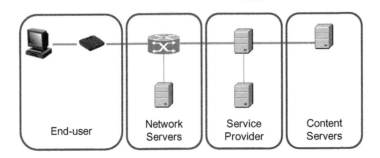

End-user   Network Servers   Service Provider   Content Servers

FIGURE 6.1

The focus of this chapter is to discuss IPTV as an application in a multicast environment. In a simplistic way, IPTV architecture can be broken down into four domains (see Figure 6.1):

1. **Content Domain:** In the IPTV world this domain is where the content is generated. These could be studios or individuals who in turn provide this content to the service providers who broadcast this content to end users. The content domain is outside of the scope of this discussion.
2. **Head-end Domain:** This part of the architecture deals with the aggregation of content that is to be sent to the end user. The head-end section of the architecture contains functions such as content preparation, personalization, and back-end functions such as subscription management. Content preparation would entail the generation of multimedia content in a digital format, the necessary storage infrastructure for VoD content, the necessary satellite infrastructure to receive content from other networks, and so forth. Personalization of EPG and customer profile management are personalization functions.
3. **Transport Network Domain:** Usage of multicast technologies in the transport infrastructure for the purpose of transporting IPTV content is the area of focus for this chapter. As transport network is studied in further detail, it is broken down into the long-haul transport and the last-mile (access) infrastructures. The standards associated with IPTV transport, aspects such as quality of experience (QoE) and how IP quality of service (QoS), are tweaked to provide the necessary support, and some of the challenges relating to the implementation such as ensuring minimal channel change time (zap time) are discussed as a part of Section.
4. **Home Network Domain:** This aspect of the IPTV architecture deals with the STBs/CPEs deployed at the end-user premises to facilitate IPTV. CPEs are far more sophisticated than the STBs with an F-connector. Today's smart clients have decoding, storage, and networking as well as Web-based client interfaces bundled into a single device.

6.2 IPTV STANDARDS

IPTV architecture for each major operator is a walled garden, with a customer-engineered solution from the head end to the end user. Multi-service operators (MSOs) most often rely on the capabilities of the vendor equipment about what services can or cannot be offered and service flexibility is curtailed by the product road maps. While such a situation is unavoidable in the nascent stages of the technology adaptation life cycle, it invariably stifles the "evolution" of the services in response to the market dynamics. The traditional voice telecommunication service is a classic example of the benefits that accrue when open, standards-based architecture allows innovation and propels growth.

There are several standards bodies working on IPTV so that the architectural building blocks have well-defined interfaces that can interoperate across multiple vendors. This maturing of technology is necessary for the IPTV ecosystem to evolve. Instead of having to deploy a monolithic IPTV solution, it is increasingly possible for the MSOs to mix-and-match a variety of technologies to offer optimized solutions. The rest of this section deals with the standards bodies that contribute to IPTV.

6.2.1 **ITU-T**

"ITU will take the lead in international standardization for IPTV with the announcement that it is to form a Focus Group on IPTV (IPTV FG)." With this simple announcement in April 2006, ITU began its work in the IPTV domain. At the seventh and final meeting of IPTV FG in December 2008, the first set of global standards was announced. The IPTV Global Standards Initiative (IPTV GSI) was announced with the intent of carrying forward this standardization work in collaboration with other standards bodies such as DSL Forum, ETSI TISPAN, IIF, and so forth.

The Next Generation Network (NGN) Architecture specified by ITU-T in Y.2001, Y.2011, and Y.2012 (Next Generation Networks—Frameworks and Functional Architecture Models) has been the bible of the vendors and service providers around the world. This framework has been the reference for the development of the current transport infrastructure built by carriers around the world. This model has been used as the underlying blueprint for the evolution of IPTV network architecture.

Y.19XX standards of ITU-T are focused on *IPTV Over NGN*. Y.1901 (Requirements for the Support of IPTV Services) specifies the high-level requirements to support IPTV services. These include IPTV requirements for service offering, network-related aspects, QoS and QoE, service and content protection, end system, middleware, and content.

The contribution of ITU-T spans the diverse areas of activities within the IPTV domain: home network, transport network, middleware, content protection, QoE, and so forth. Some of the recommendations in these areas are listed in Table 6.1.

Table 6.1 Selected IPTV Standards/Recommendations by ITU-T

Domain	Recommendation	Title
IPTV general	Y.1901	Requirement for the support of IPTV services
	Y.1910	IPTV functional architecture
IPTV QoE/QoS	G.1080	IPTV QoE
	G.1081	Performance monitoring
IPTV network management	Y.IPTV-TM	Traffic management capabilities for supporting IPTV services
	Y.iptvintwrm	IPTV services over interworking over NGN
Home network	H.622.1	Home network
	H.IPTV-RM	Home network remote management

Contributions of ITU-T related to the architecture and the different components of the architecture are discussed later in this chapter.

6.2.2 Broadband Forum

Earlier called DSL Forum, this organization has been rechristened Broadband Forum. They have been publishing "Technical Reports" that serve as standards and reference documents for the industry.

The areas of interest of the Broadband Forum include:

- Access transport technologies
- Broadband in the home network
- Network management
- Testing and interoperability focused on multivendor interoperability

6.2.3 ETSI TISPAN

Since its creation in 2003, ETSI TISPAN (Telecommunications and Internet converged Services and Protocols for Advanced Networking) has been the key standardization body in creating the NGN specifications. To further enhance the IPTV support by the NGN, TISPAN defines the architecture and reference points of a customer network device for IMS-based IPTV services.

6.2.4 Other Organizations Influencing IPTV Evolution

Table 6.2 Organizations Influencing IPTV Evolution

Organization	Areas of Work
Digital Living Network Alliance (DLNA)	Interoperability certification for home network products
Digital Video Broadcasting (DVB) project	Mobile TV, metadata, interactive apps, content and service protection
IETF	Primarily IP-transport-related standards
Home Gateway Initiative (HGI)	Hardware and Software for home gateway, home network
Open IPTV forum (OIPF)	IPTV services, seamless interoperability between vendors
Universal plug and play forum	Media distribution, QoS, home network

6.3 NGN REFERENCE ARCHITECTURE

ITU-T published the first NGN Network Reference Architecture (Y.2012) in 2006. It built upon the earlier standards of Y.2010 and Y.2011, and its purpose was to provide a standardized communication framework that would eventually serve as a replacement to the ISDN and PSTN.

At a simplistic level the architecture broke down the communication framework that contained two strata: a "services stratum" and a "transport stratum" (see Figure 6.2). One of the restrictive features of legacy telecommunication architectures was that the transport infrastructure and the services that ran over it were intertwined to the extent that the vendor providing the gear for the transport was the only one who could provide new services over the transport infrastructure. This dependency gradually declined with the onset of IN services in the PSTN, but the overall architecture was still too monolithic and restrictive; particularly compared to the IP-centric architectures that were unleashed with the Internet. This architecture was first released by ITU-T as a part of the Y.2011 recommendation in 2004.

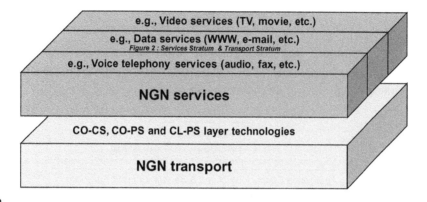

FIGURE 6.2

The advantage of the separation of the services and the transport layers was that as long as the interface between the two layers was clearly defined, each layer could be built independent of the other. Transport-layer devices such as routers, switches, and DWDM equipment could be purchased from any number of vendors. The services functions such as resource allocation, application support, and so forth could be provided by any number of software entities. This approach releases the service provider from the road map constraints of any specific vendor. This approach also triggers innovation as any number of vendors can focus on their specific areas of competence and develop products that meet the interface requirements specified by ITU-T. The communication domain truly then moves from the realm of the big telecom vendor firms to an open arena where small, medium, or large players can develop products according to their domain competence.

The NGN reference architecture was later built on this two-layer framework by providing for two important extensions:

1. The first extension provided three important "interface definitions": user-to-network interface, network-to-network interface, and application to network interface.
2. The second major enhancement to the earlier architecture was to further subdivide the NGN transport and NGN service layers into more detailed functional building blocks.

6.3.1 Network Interface Definitions

The first interface definition is the User Network Interface (UNI), which defined the connectivity of the end-user equipment (i.e., CPE) at the physical layer to the NGN transport layer. The UNI also defined the logical interface of the end-user equipment to the "services layer." Through this interface the user could request a modification of the services provided by the NGN (increase of bandwidth, better QoS, etc.)

The second interface defined the Network-to-Network Interface (NNI), which defined how NGNs interface each other. Interconnection border gateway, network signaling interworking, and other such functions are clearly defined to facilitate the interconnection.

The third interface is Application-to-Network Interface (ANI), which is between the applications that provide the services functions. The ANI defines the application support and services support functions.

6.3.2 Services, Transport, and Management Functions

The two-strata architecture discussed earlier was elaborated further in the Y.2012 standard. Figure 6.3 shows how the transport and services layers contain other functions.

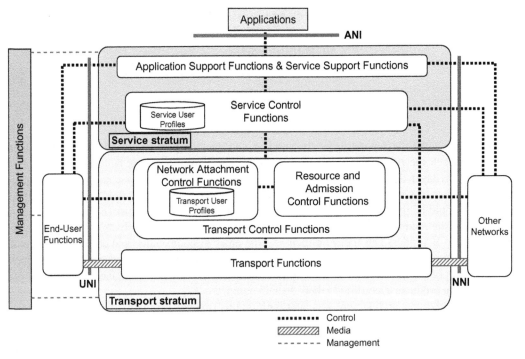

FIGURE 6.3

The network stratum in actuality is broken up along different lines for different purposes. For instance, with IPTV-related traffic this stratum can be viewed as being made up of the Access transport function and Core transport function. Access transport would involve technologies such as GPON, WIMAX, and so forth, whereas Core transport would be made up of technologies such as DWDM. At the protocol level, the access technologies of relevance would be VPLS, TDM encapsulation, and so forth; whereas on the core part it would be traffic engineering tunnels in the MPLS network.

The Network Attachment Control Function (NACF), for instance, would include functions such as:

- IP Address provisioning
- User Authentication
- Access Network configuration based on user profiles, etc.

The Resource Admission Control Function (RACF) provides an abstract view of the transport network to the service control functions in a component- and hardware-agnostic way. It performs policy-based resource control upon request from the service layer. If a user accessing the network has an access speed of 20 Mbps, the resource control function passes instructions to the transport layer RACF, which in turn sends the instructions to the devices that will restrict the bandwidth to 20 Mbps. At the time of provisioning, a similar approach would allow the RACF to determine whether the required resources should offer the required service. For instance, with a unicast IPTV service such as VoD the transport infrastructure has to be validated to check if the required bandwidth is available on all the network segments of the network from the source to the end user. If the resources are not available, the RACF communicates to the services layer that the service is unavailable at the required QoS levels at that particular time.

The Management Function is an overlay function that plugs into both the service and the transport strata. Each service has to be provided at the expected quality, security, and reliability assuring this is the role of the Management Function.

6.4 IPTV REFERENCE ARCHITECTURE FRAMEWORK

There are three architectural approaches outlined for IPTV by the ITU-T Y.1910 standard. All of these approaches are based on the NGN Reference architecture published in the Y.2011 and Y.2012 standards. These three approaches are

1. **Non-NGN IPTV Functional Architecture:** This architecture is fundamentally a framework that recognizes that there are several diverse IPTV solutions that have evolved since the mid-1990s. There are legacy technologies and protocols that have already been modified to provide IPTV services by different vendors.
2. **NGN-based non-IMS Functional Architecture**: This architecture uses the NGN reference framework as outlined in Y.2012. A brief discussion of this NGN reference architecture is provided next to serve as a reference for the IPTV architecture based on it.
3. **NGN-based IMS Functional Architecture**: This architecture uses components of NGN architecture including the IMS component to support the provisioning of the IPTV services along with other IMS services as required.

Figure 6.4 provides a high-level overview of the IPTV Functional architecture framework.

Similarities between the NGN functional architecture and the proposed IPTV functional architecture become quite apparent. The two architectures have the Transport Function below, and the Services Function above that. The UNI from the NGN architecture becomes the End-User Functions block. The ANI has become an integral part of the architecture, since in this case IPTV is the application. In the ITU-T NGN architecture, the Application layer was more generic, and was meant to accommodate voice, video, data, and any kind of application across all of these areas. Two other functional blocks appear in this architecture, which are not a part of the NGN framework: the Content

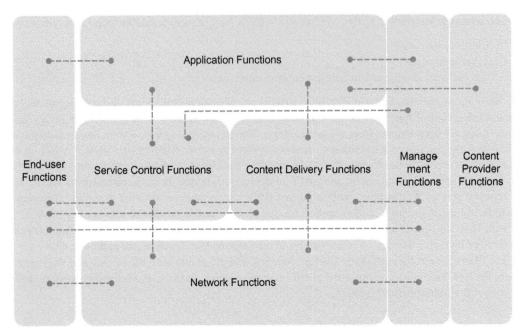

FIGURE 6.4

Delivery Functions block and the Content Provider Functions block. All of these Functional blocks are described in the following list:

End-User Functions: This block performs the mediation between the end user and the IPTV infrastructure.

Application Functions: Facilitates the end-user interaction with the content. For broadcast TV it could be a simple channel selection. For Pay-Per-View items this function allows the end user to pay for and view the content.

Service Control Functions: Allow the necessary functions to request and release network and services resources required to support the IPTV Services.

Content Delivery Functions: Make it possible to receive the content from the application functions, store, process, and deliver it to the end-user functions using other functional elements.

Network Functions: This functional block provides the IP transport infrastructure that interconnects all of the other functional elements at the physical level. It is this block that is of interest to the present discussion.

The following section delves into the detail of the Network function and elaborates on all of the relevant technologies and architectures.

Management Functions: This functional block provides all the necessary network, services, and application management infrastructure.

Content Provider Functions: This function is the content source of the video programming distributed to the end user.

All three architectural approaches outlined for IPTV by the ITU-T Y.1910 standard follow this reference architecture: Non-NGN IPTV functional architecture, NGN-based non-IMS functional architecture, and NGN-based IMS functional architecture. They build upon the reference architecture. The subcomponents and the interfaces in each of the three functional architectures may have some differences, but the overall framework applies to all three of them. The following sections briefly discuss the details of the three functional architectures.

6.4.1 Network Function in the IPTV Reference Architecture

The Network Function block in the IPTV Reference Architecture refers to the physical connectivity of the network. All other sections of the network deal with logical activity. All of the details pertaining to OSI Layers 1–3 (Physical, Data Link, and Network) are addressed as a part of the Network Function in the IPTV Reference Architecture. The transport infrastructure is subdivided into the access and core domains.

In the IPTV network transport domain it is the access networks that are of significant importance. The access networks offer diverse options of technology ranging from DSL to WiMax. These topics are covered in more detail in the following section.

The core networks provide city- or nation-wide connectivity. The connectivity from the head end to the local area of service is made possible through the core network. The physical topology of the core networks could be either a partial-mesh or a ring. The underlying physical connectivity would be through fiber lit up by DWDM equipment. The details of the topology and the protocols are discussed in more detail in the following section.

6.5 ACCESS NETWORKS FOR IPTV

The access network technologies are variedly referred to as the "last mile" or the "first mile." The most common access technologies for IPTV are xDSL, Cable, and FTTx. GPON, Wi-Fi, WiMax, and other technologies are still nascent in their use as IPTV access networks. Their usage and deployment will no doubt increase in the future, but it is unlikely that they will challenge DSL in the near future. The dominance of mobile-based TV using WiMax or LTE as a last-mile technology is still a few years away, particularly due to infrastructural bottlenecks on the Mobile Backhaul side, which are yet to be resolved. Based on different research reports, the approximate global penetration of access technologies is shown in Figure 6.5.

From an IP Multicasting point of view, the access technologies of interest are xDSL and FTTx. Wireless broadband is a domain yet nascent, and multicasting in wireless areas is the subject of Chapter 8.

Further discussion in this chapter focuses on a combination of xDSL in the last mile, Carrier Ethernet in the access, and aggregation sections of the network and IP/MPLS backbone in the core network. This topology covers one of the most common deployment scenarios in the current networks around the world.

6.5.1 xDSL in the Access

Globally the most widely deployed telecom infrastructure over the last hundred years is the copper line to the end customers. With declining voice revenues, telecom operators around the world are under pressure to generate revenues through other services. DSL technology allows telecom operators

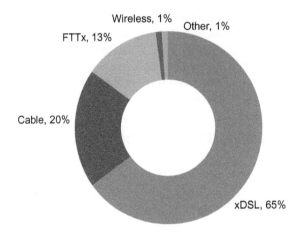

FIGURE 6.5

to run high-speed data and video services over their copper in the last mile. Because of this, telecoms have been eager to embrace the DSL technology and leverage it for providing both Internet access and IPTV.

Typical IPTV connectivity for DSL customers in the last mile is seen in Figure 6.6.

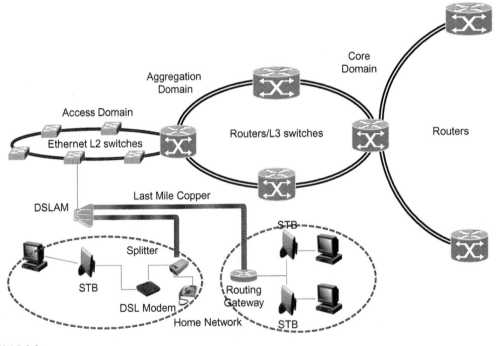

FIGURE 6.6

The DSLAM is in the POP of the network provider. From here the connectivity to the customer premises is through the copper lines (the twisted pair). At the customer premises there is a splitter separating the data and voice lines. The data line is connected to the DSL modem, the IPTV STB connects to the DSL modem, and the IPTV connects to the STB. In some cases where there are multiple IPTVs in a single dwelling, there may be a routing gateway that aggregates the multiple STBs. The WAN architecture shown earlier is an example of the Carrier Ethernet.

The throughput achieved with DSL has evolved over the years. Although the initial download speeds of DSL were in the order of 2 Mbps, now technologies such as VDSL2 offer download speeds of close to 100 Mbps over limited distances.

Figure 6.7 shows the download speeds for the common DSL technologies. The exact throughput on a DSL line could vary vastly with distance. For instance, VDSL can experience download speeds of 100 Mbps at short distances, whereas there is an exponential degradation of throughput with distance. There are a significant number of technical aspects to DSL, but these are outside the scope of the current work. The focus here is to look at the connectivity in the Network Function block of the IPTV reference architecture and understand the application of multicast for IPTV at the access layer.

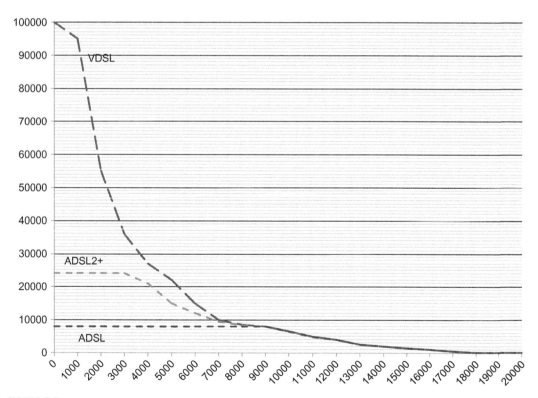

FIGURE 6.7

6.5.2 Source Specific Multicast

Source Specific Multicast (SSM) is a multicast protocol optimized for one too many applications. The approach adopted by SSM is to have the membership on the basis of an (S, G) pair—referred to as a *channel*. S indicates the unicast source from which the data is forwarded and G represents the specific multicast group on that source. There can be multiple channels, each with a different group (G) associated with the same source (S).

In SSM, it is assumed that the subscriber knows the address of the source out-of-band. SSM establishes the shortest path between the source and the receiver from the time of subscription and is therefore very efficient. This is in contrast to PIM-SM, which relied on a Rendezvous Point that helped any interested receiver determine the path to the multicast source of interest and then the establishment of the shortest path between the source and the receiver. Internet Group Multicast Protocol (IGMP) is used for the members of the multicast group to join or leave.

SSM continues to use some of the supporting mechanisms common to other protocols. Multicast forwarding is based on source addresses, unlike unicast forwarding which relies on destination addresses. In unicast routing, the router looks up the destination address and forwards the packet on the interface, which is associated with the most optimal path toward the destination. In multicast forwarding, the forwarding is essentially based on membership to a given channel. In large, redundant topologies it is easy to conceive that any device in the path could receive copies of the same traffic through multiple interfaces. Loop-free forwarding is accomplished by verifying that the source address of any packet received on an interface has a corresponding routing entry for the reverse path. All other copies of this traffic received from other interfaces are discarded.

Other mechanisms used in SSM include Designated Router (DR) selection in case of multiple devices on the same LAN desiring the membership of the same channel.

The SSM Group (G) multicast address is in the range of 232.0.0.0 and 232.255.255.255.

6.5.3 IGMPv3

Internet Group Multicast Protocol is the protocol used in IPTV networks to facilitate acquiring and relinquishing membership into multicast groups. When there is a multicast stream available in the network, any receiver (STB in the case of IPTV) would need to JOIN the multicast group to receive the multicast traffic. Similarly, when this traffic is no longer of interest, the receiver would send a LEAVE message to stop receiving the multicast traffic. These JOIN and LEAVE messages are a part of the overall multicast control framework that is made possible by IGMP.

Originally specified in RFC 1112, IGMP became more popular for IPTV in its later versions IGMPv2 (RFC 2236) and IGMPv3 (RFC 3376). IGMPv3 is now popular, and it is expected that all new IPTV standards will assume the use of IGMPv3.

6.5.4 SSM and IGMPv3: Initial Join in IPTV Network

The sequence of events that triggers the initial join of an STB into an IPTV network is shown in Figure 6.8. When the IPTV switches on, the STB detects the channel request and sends an IGMP Host Report. This is forwarded up to the DR. This router detects the neighbor to which it should forward the reverse path traffic and sends the JOIN (S, G) message upstream. The IP WAN/MAN network forwards the JOIN (S, G) messages until they reach the router to which the source is connected. As the JOIN (S, G) message flows through the routing domain, the shortest path tree (SPT) is constructed across the network to the router connecting to the content source.

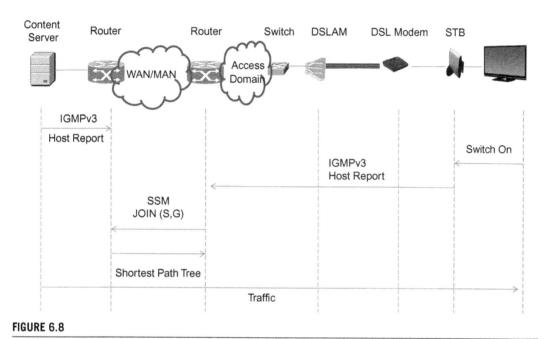

FIGURE 6.8

The traffic flow then begins through the network from the source, along the SPT to the DSLAM, and finally to the STB and the IPTV.

6.5.5 SSM and IGMPv3: Channel Zap

Whenever a user switches channels the duration between the channel change request (pressing the buttons on the remote) and the steady transmission of the desired channel is referred to as the channel zap time. The signaling that takes place during the channel zap is shown in the Figure 6.9.

When the user changes channels, there is a LEAVE signal associated with the channel he is currently viewing and a JOIN signal associated with the new channel that is to be received. In IGMPv3 with optimized signaling it is possible to combine both these LEAVE and JOIN messages into a single message and send it to the network. Once the network elements receive this message, the traffic associated with the present channel is stopped to this DSLAM and the traffic associated with the new channel is transmitted to this DSLAM.

Further discussion on the components of channel zap time and the acceptable boundaries are in Section 6.6.

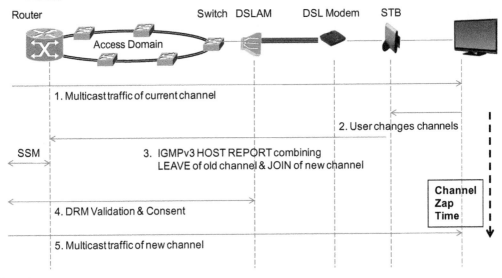

FIGURE 6.9

6.5.6 IGMP Snooping

As the number of channels and the number of customers increase on an IPTV network, the control traffic on the network increases. The number of JOIN and LEAVE messages along with other control traffic increases significantly with the implementation of IGMP snooping,

In the previous section it was discussed how for any channel change the control traffic reaches the nearest router and from there the channel traffic is sent to the IPTV. Figure 6.10 shows the efficiencies achieved through IGMP snooping.

When Channel 23 is requested for the first time, the signaling arrives right up to the DR and when this channel has not been previously subscribed to, the signaling goes all the way up to the router connected to the source. However, when the channel is requested on subsequent occasions, then the DSLAM replicates the channel and forwards it over to the new customer. The signaling is truncated at the DSLAM.

The impact on the traffic is shown in Figure 6.11. Without IGMP snooping two distinct streams of traffic make their way through the network from the L-3 domain, but with IGMP snooping the DSLAM replicates the traffic at the edge of the network. This increases the efficiency of the access network.

6.6 NETWORK DESIGN CONSIDERATIONS FOR IPTV

In this section the overall end-to-end network requirements for the successful deployment of IPTV are reviewed. The common principles that apply to any IP network design would be as relevant for a network built for offering IPTV service.

Some of the key considerations in a large-scale network design include: bandwidth computation, QoS and QoE, network resiliency, traffic engineering, VLAN configuration, and so forth. In this section we address each of these design considerations and the associated trade-offs.

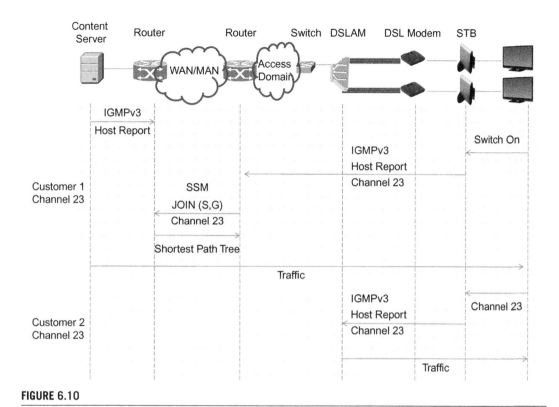

FIGURE 6.10

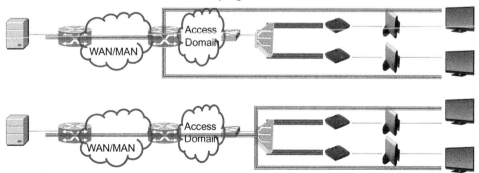

IPTV Streams without IGMP snooping

IPTV Streams with IGMP snooping

FIGURE 6.11

6.6.1 Bandwidth Requirement for IPTV

MPEG-2 is the most widely deployed encoding format for video content. From a bandwidth point of view, a single MPEG-2-encoded SDTV stream would consume 6 Mbps and an HDTV channel would need about 19 Mbps.

MPEG-4, originally introduced in 1998, has evolved through a series of amendments, and today it offers an encoding at almost half the bandwidth of MPEG-2. With an SD channel possible at 2 Mbps and an HD channel at 9 Mbps, MPEG-4 (Part 10 of H.264) has been particularly useful for the proliferation of HD channels over IPTV networks. It is possible to get SD and HD channels at lower bandwidth than indicated, but in such scenarios the quality of the video content would be somewhat degraded.

Figure 6.12 shows the bandwidth requirements of MPEG-4-encoded HD and SD channels over DSL transmission speeds. It shows the overlap of the two aspects: xDSL bandwidth capability over long distances and the SDTV/HDTV bandwidth requirement. This overlay gives an indication of what access technology would be suitable over different distances to offer SD and HD IPTV services.

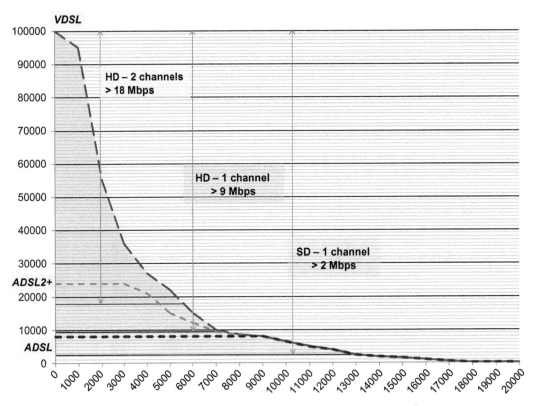

FIGURE 6.12

When designing a network for IPTV the end-to-end bandwidth requirements need to be calculated with these numbers in mind. From the head end through the core network and the aggregate network it is acceptable to assume that each IPTV channel is only transmitted once, irrespective of the number of receivers subscribing to any particular channel. So the bandwidth requirement in the core and aggregation of the network would be the sum total of the SD and HD channel bandwidth requirements.

In the access, however, it is possible to achieve bandwidth efficiencies through subscription to specific channels. Any given DSLAM need not receive the total volume of traffic of all of the channels. It would receive a subset of the channels depending on what the end users connecting to the DSLAM would have requested. The exact percentage varies with the size of the DSLAM. For instance, a deployment of NSN 16-slot hiX 5635 can serve up to 1,000 ADSL2 + subscribers. In such high-density deployments where thousands of subscribers are connected, it is possible that all of the channels would also be received by the DSLAM. In low-density deployments such as rural areas, where a few hundred subscribers are connected to the DSLAM, it is possible that only 50% of the total channels offered are requested by the DSLAM so the traffic would be considerably lower. This subscription ratio also depends on the number of free and paid-for channels.

IGMP snooping and proxy routing are enabled in the network to optimize the data and control traffic. With IGMP snooping, the traffic is forwarded within the DSLAM only to the ports that have requested a particular channel.

For example, a service provider offering 100 SD channels would need a bandwidth of 200 Mbps through the core. If a combination of 100 SD channels and 50 HD channels is offered, then the bandwidth requirement would be in the range of 550 Mbps.

Another key design parameter in IPTV networks is VoD traffic. In a deployment of say, 15,000 subscribers, even a 5% subscription to VoD would result in about 750 VoD transmissions. As mentioned earlier, VoD traffic is unicast, where each stream is separate and would consume bandwidth with no optimization possible, and 750 such transmissions at 2 Mbps would result in a 1.5 Gbps bandwidth usage. If the VoD service offers HD channels, the corresponding bandwidth requirement would be closer to 7 Gbps.

Bandwidth sizing for the core, aggregation, and access networks would need to take this into account. The exact percentage of VoD subscribers varies widely across geographies, and 5 to 10% would be the range for reasonable estimation.

6.6.2 IPv4 Address Usage Guidelines

In the classical allocation of IP addresses, the class D range of addresses—224.0.0.0 to 239.255.255.255—was reserved for multicast usage. RFC 2365 recommends how the address space should be 239.0.0.0/8 is used. Table 6.3 shows the usage of the entire class D address space.

It is best for operators to apply to the respective NIC for IP address space and use the space allocated.

The deployment of IP addresses within the network is done using DHCP servers. The servers may be centrally located along with the rest of the protected infrastructure such as DNS hardware, billing infrastructure, and so forth. The IP network components between the STB and the DHCP server act as DHCP relays, so the IP address is allocated to the STB by the server.

Table 6.3 IP Address Usage Guidelines

From	To	Description
224.0.0.0	224.0.0.255	Local link scope addresses
224.0.1.0	224.0.1.255	Internetwork control block
224.0.2.0	224.0.255.255	Ad hoc block
224.1.0.0	224.1.255.255	Unassigned
224.2.0.0	224.2.255.255	SDP/SAP block
224.3.0.0	231.255.255.255	Unassigned
232.0.0.0	232.255.255.255	SSM block
233.0.0.0	232.255.255.255	GLOP block
234.0.0.0	238.255.255.255	Unassigned
239.0.0.0	239.255.255.255	Administratively scoped block

6.6.3 GLOP Addressing

During the evolution of multicast IP address allocation, a quick and easy way was invented to allocate a /24 IP address range to each of the operators who already had an AS. This was conceived as a quick way to allocate multicast addresses, while the overall global multicast IP allocation strategy evolved in tune with the emerging multicast application requirements. Defined in RFC 2770 originally, and later in RFC 3180, GLOP addressing takes a clever approach.

This approach uses the address block 233/8 (233.0.0.0 to 233.255.255.255). The first octet remains as 233 for all operators. The fourth octet is variable from 0 to 255, providing each operator 254 individual addresses. The second and third octets are derived from the operator's AS number, which is traditionally a four-digit decimal number. This number is converted into 16 bits (padding zeros as the higher order bits if necessary).

Here is an example using AS 9829:

Decimal notation	9829
Binary notation	100110 01100101 (14 bits)
Modified binary notation	00100110 01100101 (adjusted to 16 bits)
Derived second and third octets	38.101
Derived IP addresses	233.38.101.0 to 233.38.101.255

This approach allowed operators with a registered AS number to immediately use a /24 globally unique address range for multicast applications. No further application for multicast address or allocation from the NICs was necessary.

For any operators that did not have their own AS number, it was possible to "lease" the AS number of their upstream provider and use this address range.

While GLOP addressing allowed users to derive IP addresses quickly, it is still not a sufficiently scalable address space for a service like IPTV, which is expected to have more than tens of thousands of users.

GLOP is not an acronym. It was a random word used to refer to this scheme when this method was invented, and its use has just continued.

6.6.4 **IPv6 Multicast Address Allocation**

The 128-bit IPv6 address space has an allocation specific to multicast. The range of addresses represented by FF00::/8, where the first octet is represented by all 1s (1111 1111), has been reserved for multicast allocation. The details of the allocation of the 128 bits are shown in Figure 6.13.

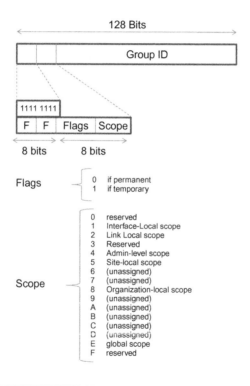

FIGURE 6.13

For dynamic IP address allocation DHCPv6 has been defined in RFC 3315. With Link Local Addresses that can be created during initialization, STBs and other CPE devices (DHCP Clients) can use a well-known multicast address to discover and communicate with DHCP servers or relay agents on their link.

The flags field in Figure 6.13 is set to 1 for all dynamic address allocations (temporary allocation). This will distinguish the dynamically allocated addresses from the permanently assigned multicast addresses.

6.6.5 VLAN Design

TR-101, a standard published by DSL Forum, proposes two ways to connect Broadband DSL users to the aggregation network: have one VLAN per subscriber or have one VLAN per service in the network. These are also referred to as 1:1 and N:1 modes. VLANs allow segregation of traffic either by service type or by customer, or a combination of both. VLAN usage and definitions are in the IEEE 802.1Q standard.

6.6.5.1 Dedicated VLAN per Service

Another way to define the VLANs is to have one VLAN across the network per service. Services such as High Speed Internet (HSI) access and Voice Over IP (VoIP) each have a dedicated VLAN. This design enables efficient use of bandwidth, particularly in the case of a multicasting service. The network QoS can be set on a per-service basis and is easily implementable across the network. Similarly, the bandwidth in the core of the network can be reserved on a per-service basis.

This approach is limited because all subscribers are treated on par. Policies are applied on a per-service basis and they apply to all the subscribers of that service.

6.6.5.2 Dedicated VLAN per Subscriber

This approach is subscriber-centric. Each customer has his own dedicated VLAN and all the services are routed to him through this single VLAN. However, the 12 bits reserved for the VLAN ID in the Ethernet frame restrict the total VLANs in a given system to a total of 4096 (4 K) VLANs, of which 4,095 are usable. A total number of 4,095 customers across a network would be an impractical limitation; therefore, this approach uses stacked VLANs (see Figure 6.14).

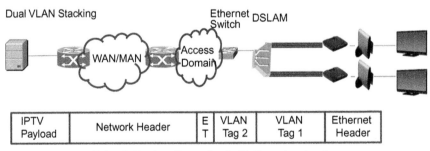

Network Header : For routing traffic through network
ET : Ether Type
VLAN Tag 2 : Indentifies the DSLAM
VLAN Tag 1 : Indentifies the subscriber

FIGURE 6.14

Stacked VLANs would use about 4 K IDs for DSLAMs and another 4 K IDs per each DSLAM to identify users. The inner VLAN tag identifies the port to which the user is connected on the DSLAM. The outer VLAN identifies the DSLAM in the network. This would allow the network to scale beyond the 4 K restriction. IEEE 802.1ad defines the Double Tagged Frame.

6.6.5.3 Hybrid VLAN Architecture

To overcome the weaknesses of the C-VLAN and S-VLAN architectures a combination of these two approaches is used (see Figure 6.15). This combination provides the strengths of both architectures. In this hybrid architecture, the S-VLANs are used to carry traffic of multicast services optimally. This S-VLAN is also referred to as M-VLAN, indicating that it carries multicast traffic.

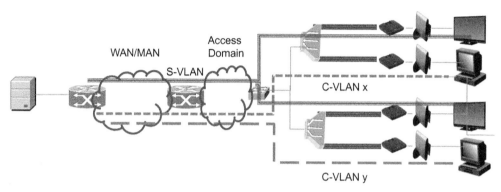

FIGURE 6.15

The C-VLANs carry customer specific traffic of other unicast services, such as VoIP, Internet Access, and so forth. The C-VLAN approach is suitable with unicast-centric services. A significant weakness of a "C-VLAN-only" model is that each subscriber receives a unicast stream of each of the services, which would make it inefficient in terms of bandwidth usage. Multiple data streams, one for each customer, are carried across the network.

6.6.6 QoS and QoE

The evolution of the IP Quality of Service (QoS) paradigm has been central to the evolution of multiservice IP networks. In this section we cover the technicalities of QoS and also the Quality of Experience (QoE), which is a more common measure to evaluate the performance of IPTV service over a network.

Service providers offering end-user services such as IPTV and VoIP need to be acutely aware that there is a significant subjective component in the perception of service. ITU-T Recommendation G.1000, Communications Quality of Service: A Framework and Definitions, points out that there are four viewpoints regarding QoS and QoE, and these are shown in Figure 6.16.

On the right are the service provider's efforts to define *ideal QoS* framework for his services and below that the actual *achieved QoS*. Often the ideal QoS scenario is difficult to achieve due to various design and operational factors. Multi-vendor deployments often achieve a QoS, which is the lowest common denominator for all the equipment. Most often the number of queues, the buffers at the

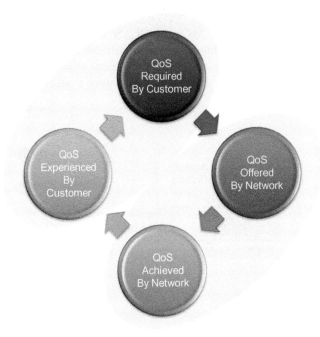

FIGURE 6.16

ports, the traffic shaping mechanisms, and so forth vary between vendors or even across product families within the same vendor. This results in a suboptimal QoS achieved by the service provider.

On the left in Figure 6.16 is the *perceived QOE* of the end customer. The experience of the customer depends on the actual QoS achieved by the service provider. There is a subjective element to the perception of the customer, and the experience in turn sets the end-users' expectation regarding the *desired QOE*.

A comprehensive analysis of the QoE and QoS would include performance measurements across all four domains of IPTV: the content domain, the head-end domain, the transport domain, and the home network domain. However, in this section the focus is primarily on the transport domain.

6.6.6.1 QoS

The QoS metrics that impact the network performance are built around jitter and packet loss. The Differentiated Services model (RFCs 2475, 3270) provided the Per-Hop Behavior (PHB) definitions that allowed packets to be marked with Diff Serv Code Points (DSCPs). Packets with the same DSCP markings would be treated identically in terms of prioritization and this allowed multiple services to be mapped to DSCPs, and based on these markings the scheduling, queuing, policing, or shaping behavior at a particular hop would be determined.

The DiffServ framework broadly classifies PHB into two categories: Expedited Forwarding (RFC 2598) and Assured Forwarding (RFC 2597). Expedited Forwarding would be applied for traffic that needs low-latency treatment in the network. Examples of traffic in this category would be Voice and

Video. Assured Forwarding classification is meant for traffic that prioritizes data integrity at the cost of latency. In MPLS networks it is common to have multiple classes of Assured Forwarding traffic, which provide the operators with the option of offering multiple categories of QoS.

Table 6.4 shows how the various services offered in a triple-play network are assigned DSCP values to ensure that there is a network-wide prioritization of the services.

Table 6.4 DSCP Values for Different Services

Service	Category	DSCP Values	Description
Routing protocols		48	Low delay, low loss, no over-subscription
VoIP, other real-time traffic	EF	46	Low delay, low loss, low jitter, no over-subscription
Multicast video	AF-3	32	Low delay, low loss, low over-subscription, sequence preservation
VoD	AF-2	24	Low delay, low loss, low over-subscription, sequence preservation
Business data (in contract)	AF-1	16	Low loss, medium over-subscription
Business data (out of contract)		8	Low loss, medium over-subscription
Best effort		0	High over-subscription

6.6.6.2 QoE

While QoS provides the underlying technology constructs, which allows prioritization of different services, the performance of the services with respect to the customer experience is measured by the Quality of Experience framework. QoE is agnostic to the underlying architecture and technologies. It solely focuses on the experience of the end user; therefore it is a subjective measurement. Subjective measurements of QoE are often taken by surveying focus groups of end users, so that the aggregate response may be indicative of how the service will be perceived by all of the end users. Some of the factors that influence this perception include Channel Zap time, pixilation, blurring, frame-freezes, and so forth.

6.6.6.3 Channel Zap Time

As described earlier in Section 6.5, Channel Zap Time is the duration from the time the user presses the channel change button until there is a steady state audio and video display of the desired channel.

Channel Zap Time has three underlying components:

IGMP Processing Delay: Once the user presses the desired channel, the STB generates two IGMP requests—an IGMP Leave message for the existing multicast group and an IGMP Join request to the desired channel's multicast group address through an IGMP Join Message. Once the new Join request the closest SSM domain, the traffic stream is directed to the end user. IGMP Processing Delay is normally less than 100 msec.

Buffering Delay: Once the traffic for a new channel begins to arrive at the STB, the STB will initially buffer the content. This buffering allows the video stream to be uninterrupted, even when there is jitter in the IP transport layer. For this reason these buffers are called De-jitter Buffers. These buffers can store video content of 100–500 msec.

Decoding Delay: After the STB fills the content of the de-jitter buffers, it starts decoding the content and renders them on the TV screen. The delay here includes I-frame acquisition delay as well as codec decoding delay. The overall contribution of this component is close to 100 msec.

To ensure satisfactory QoE, the overall Channel Zap Time should be less than 2 seconds.

6.6.6.4 Media Delivery Index

Since subjective methods are expensive and time-consuming, objective methods have been evolved to measure QoE. The media delivery index (MDI) is represented by using two values: the Delay Factor (DF) and the Media Loss Rate (MLR). The purpose of MDI is to represent both the instantaneous as well as the long-term behavior of networks carrying streaming video. Defined in RFC 4445, A Proposed Media Delivery Index (MDI), it is an indicator of the de-jitter buffer sizes that are required at STBs, and it also provides an indication of the packet loss in the network.

The MDI is comprised of two indices: DF and MLR. The MDI is shown as a combination of the two.

6.6.6.4.1 Delay Factor

For an STB, for instance, it has been discussed how there is a need for de-jitter buffers. When the video traffic arrives at the STB from the network the content is first stored in the de-jitter buffers. Since the network conditions are variable, the arriving stream will not be steady, but will vary between a minimum and a maximum (Amax, Amin). When the payload is being decoded and rendered to the screen, the de-jitter buffers are being emptied steadily (B). The difference between these two, X (defined as A − B), would also then vary between a maximum and a minimum.

Delay Factor is then mathematically defined as:

$$DF = (Max (X) - Min (X))/Media\ Rate$$

Delay factor at any given point in the network is the amount of time the media stream will need to buffer (e.g., 100 msec of video), so that the end-user QoE does not degrade because of delays in the video stream.

6.6.6.4.2 Media Loss Rate

Media loss rate is the count of the lost or out-of-order packets over a pre-specified time interval. It is common to measure this on a per second basis. It is important to note that the packets referred to here are not IP packets, but the MPEG Transport stream packets. So the loss of a single IP packet could result in the loss of seven MPEG transport stream packets.

As a practical example in a given service provider network when measured at different points, there may be different MDI values. Normally the lower the MDI values the better the QoE is for the end user. However, since MDI is a combination of two parameters, it gets difficult to compare. For instance, an MDI of 100:5 is better than an MDI of 150:20. However, due to transient conditions, if one has two MDI values of 50:20 and 100:5, then it would be a little more complex to analyze which would yield better QoE.

6.6.7 **Network Characteristics**

High availability and network resiliency are key aspects of network design for any service provider network. The ideal goal of the network design should be to provide uninterrupted services without quality degradation, even in the event of one or multiple link- or node-level network component failures.

6.6.7.1 *Convergence Time*

In Wide Area Networks this resiliency is achieved through a variety of ways. The network topology is created as a partial mesh with each core router having three or more links connecting to other core routers. It is important to ensure that no core router is isolated when there are one or more fiber cuts. Similarly at the aggregate layer, at least two if not more connections are preferred. At the optical layer, it should be validated that there are at least two or more alternate physical paths over which any core router is connected to any other core routers. This is path diversification.

Aside from the network topology, the Interior Gateway Protocol (IGP) plays a key role in the recovery of the network in the event of a failure. The IGP re-establishes the network reachability through alternate path computation. IS-IS and OSPF are both widely used in IPTV networks. Depending on the size of the network, IGP makes it possible for traffic flows to be re-established in a few hundred milliseconds. However, this recovery time is insufficient to meet the performance requirements of IPTV service, where the necessary recovery time is less than 100 msec and preferably around 50 msec. The convergence of the multicast protocols is dependent on the convergence of the unicast protocol.

To further improve the recovery times, bi-directional forwarding (BFD; RFC 5880 to RFC 5885) is one of the options available for deployment. BFD is often used as a trigger for MPLS Fast Reroute. It has been observed that BFD brings down the restoration time by 50% or more, compared to networks that only run IGP.

6.6.7.2 *Payload Corruption*

Due to the transient network conditions, there are different ways in which payload is corrupted in the IPTV environment. Out-of-sequence packets, dropped or lost IP packets, corrupted IP packets, and so forth result in the IPTV image being compromised.

Normally out-of-order packets are a result of multiple parallel paths being available or a transient state when there is a link failure and alternate paths are chosen. The STB's buffer packets, before they are rendered on to the screen and normally when the out-of-order packets arrive very close to each other, are sequenced correctly and then rendered on to the screen.

Dropped packets in IPTV degrade the overall quality of the video. The latest compression techniques such as H.264 are extremely sensitive to dropped packets. A few dropped packets cause a fairly serious disruption to the audio and video. Unlike data transmission, IPTV packet drops cannot be corrected by Transport Layer protocols such as TCP. The time taken for retransmission is often so long that the retransmitted packets arrive after the video has been rendered.

It would be difficult for a network to be designed where all the transient conditions are prevented. However, if IPTV is the dominant application of the network, to that extent the architecture can be optimized to suit the network characteristics most desirable in an IPTV transport network. For instance, the capacity can be large close to the source and reduce toward the edge of the network. The design may also accommodate the network architecture. Alternate paths between the source and set of receivers should be of equal bandwidth. In a multiservice network, a specific QoS class may be assigned for IPTV traffic to ensure that all IPTV traffic receives the same preference, and also that burstiness of any other application does not impact the flow of IPTV traffic.

6.7 CONCLUSION

IPTV is an application that involves multiple technologies. ITU-T, DSL Forum, IETF, and ETSI are among the organizations contributing actively to the IPTV evolution. A combination of Carrier Ethernet in the core and aggregation and DSL in the access is a common transport architecture for IPTV delivery. SSM and IGMPv3 are protocols that together provide the necessary support for users to Join and Leave multicast groups. Quality of service and quality of experience are important parameters in the area of IPTV. Unlike in the data world, the end-user sensitivity to video is quite high so it is necessary for the network to be optimized for video delivery. All of these topics have been discussed in this chapter in varying degrees of detail.

Multicast for VPLS and Carrier Ethernet Networks

7.1 INTRODUCTION

In previous chapters, we discussed the various options available for deploying Multicast for BGP MPLS VPNs, starting from the earlier Draft-Rosen implementation to the Next Generation framework. In this chapter we look at the possible options available for offering Multicast in a carrier Ethernet environment, with VPLS as the carrier infrastructure used to offer various services to end customers.

7.2 VIRTUAL PRIVATE LAN SERVICE AKA VPLS

Before we get into VPLS, let us briefly look at MPLS Layer 2 VPNs, also referred to as Point-Point services.

A point-to-point L2VPN circuit, as defined by the PWE3 working group, is a provider service that offers a point-to-point service infrastructure over an IP/MPLS packet switched network. The PWE3 working group of the IETF describes mechanisms for delivering L2 VPN services across a packet switched IP/MPLS network. The basic reference model is outlined in Figure 7.1.

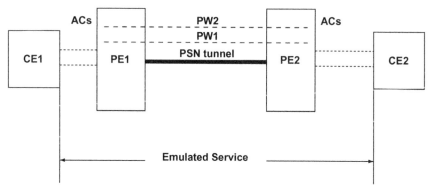

FIGURE 7.1

A pseudo-wire (PW) is a connection between two provider edge (PE) devices that connects two attachment circuits (ACs). An AC can be a Frame Relay DLCI, an ATM VPI/VCI, an Ethernet port, a VLAN, an HDLC, a PPP connection on a physical interface, a PPP session from an L2TP tunnel, an MPLS LSP, and so forth. During the setup of a PW, the two PE routers will be configured or will automatically exchange information about the service to be emulated so that later they know how to process packets coming from the other end. The PE routers use Targeted LDP sessions for setting the PW. After a PW is set up between two PE routers, frames received by one PE from an AC are encapsulated and sent over the PW to the remote PE, where native frames are reconstructed and forwarded to the other CE.

From a data plane perspective, different PWs in the same Packet Switched Network (PSN) tunnel are identified using a multiplexing field. This multiplexing field is an MPLS label, and the encapsulation of the customer frames over these (MPLS) connections or PWs is defined in the IETF Pseudo-Wire Encapsulation Edge to Edge (PWE3) working group. PSN tunnels are implemented in the provider's network as MPLS LSPs (RSVP, LDP), or using IP-in-IP (GRE). Figure 7.2 illustrates the protocol stack in the core of the provider's network for Ethernet frames.

Byte4	Byte3	Byte2	Byte1

CRC			
CRC			
Data			
Protocol ID		Source MAC address	
Source MAC address			
Destination MAC address			
Destination MAC address		MPLS VC Label	
MPLS VC Label		MPLS PSN Tunnel Label	
MPLS PSN Tunnel Label		Protocol ID	
Source MAC address			
Source MAC address		Destination MAC address	
Destination MAC address			

FIGURE 7.2

Next we review Virtual Private LAN Services (VPLS), also known as multipoint-to-multipoint Ethernet L2VPN, which is a provider service that emulates the full functionality of a traditional Local Area Network (LAN). A VPLS makes it possible to interconnect several LAN segments over a PSN and makes the remote LAN segments behave as one single LAN. The same PSN is able to offer separate VPLS services to different customers. Figure 7.3 is an example of the VPLS reference model.

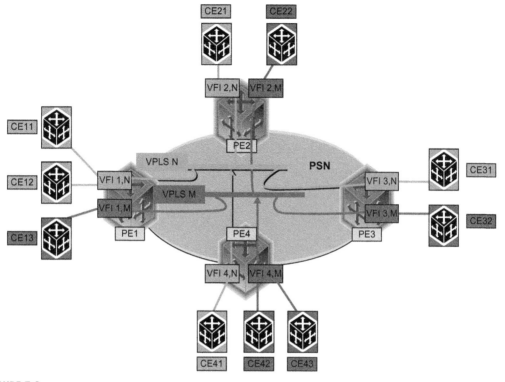

FIGURE 7.3

Figure 7.3 illustrates an IP/MPLS backbone network (PSN operated by a service provider. The backbone network offers a VPLS service to two VPN customers: an orange customer and a red customer. A customer has different private sites that it wants to interconnect at the Ethernet layer. Customer sites are connected to the SP's backbone via ACs between Customer Edge (CE) devices and PE devices. As such, a VPN can be represented by a collection of CE devices: in Figure 7.3 the orange L2VPN N consists of <CE11, CE12, CE21, CE31, CE41> while the red L2VPN M consists of <CE13, CE22, CE32, CE42, CE43>.

Like in all PE-based VPNs, with VPLS the CE devices are unaffected by the service: a VPLS CE can be a standard router, Ethernet bridge, or host. It is the PE device that implements VPLS specific functions. Indeed, the PE device needs to implement a separate Virtual Forwarding Instance (VFI) for every VPLS to which it is attached. This is also known as Virtual Switched Instance (VSI), which is the equivalent of VRF tables for MPLS Layer 3 VPNs. Such a VFI has physical direct interfaces to attached CE devices that belong to the considered VPLS, and virtual interfaces or PWs that are point-to-point connections from the considered VFI to remote VFIs that belong to the same VPLS and are located in other PE devices. These PWs are carried from one PE to another PE via PSN Tunnels. From a data plane perspective, different PWs in the same PSN tunnel are identified using a multiplexing field. This multiplexing field is an MPLS label, and the encapsulation of the customer Ethernet frames over these (MPLS) connections or PWs is defined in the IETF PWE3 working group. PSN tunnels are implemented in the provider's network as MPLS LSPs (RSVP, LDP), or using IP-in-IP (GRE). Figure 7.4 shows the protocol stack in the core of the provider's network.

Byte4	Byte3	Byte2	Byte1

CRC			
CRC			
Data			
Protocol ID		Source MAC address	
Source MAC address			
Destination MAC address			
Destination MAC address		MPLS VC Label	
MPLS VC Label		MPLS PSN Tunnel Label	
MPLS PSN Tunnel Label		Protocol ID	
Source MAC address			
Source MAC address		Destination MAC address	
Destination MAC address			

FIGURE 7.4

Draft-Rosen MVPNs represent themselves as emulated LANs. Each MVPN has a logical PIM interface, and will form an adjacency to every other PIM interface across PE routers within the same MVPN.

Note that with VPLS, it is assumed there is a full mesh of PSN tunnels between the network's PE devices, and that for every VPLS instance there is a full mesh of PWs between the VFIs that belong to that VPLS. The IETF Layer 2 VPN Working Group has produced two separate VPLS standards documented in RFC 4761 and RFC 4762 (see Kompella and Rekhter, 2007; Lasserre and Kompella, 2007). These two RFCs define almost identical approaches with respect to the VPLS data plane, but specify significantly different approaches to implementing the VPLS control planes.

7.2.1 VPLS Control Plane

The VPLS control plane has two primary functions: autodiscovery and signaling. Discovery refers to the process of finding all PE routers that participate in a given VPLS instance. A PE router can be configured with the identities of all the other PE routers in a given VPLS instance, or the PE router can use a protocol to discover the other PE routers. The latter method is called autodiscovery. After discovery occurs, each pair of PE routers in a VPLS network must be able to establish PWs to each other, and in the event of membership change, the PE router must be able to tear down the established PWs. This process is known as signaling. Signaling is also used to transmit certain characteristics of the PW that a PE router sets up for a given VPLS.

7.2.1.1 BGP-VPLS Control Plane

The BGP-VPLS control plane, as defined by RFC 4761, is similar to that for Layer 2 and Layer 3 (see Kompella, 2006; Rosen and Rekhter, 2006). It defines a means for a PE router to discover which remote PE routers are members of a given VPLS (autodiscovery), and for a PE router to know which PW label a given remote PE router will use when sending the data to the local PE router (signaling). With the BGP-VPLS control plane, BGP carries enough information to provide the autodiscovery and signaling functions simultaneously. This is illustrated in Figure 7.5.

Auto-Discovery: PE-A Announces to other PEs (or RR) that it has VPLS Instance M for VPLS domain RED

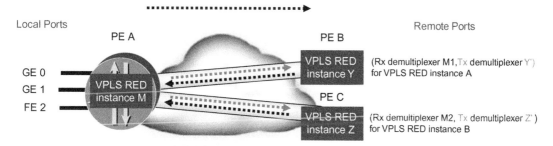

Signaling: PE-A Announce to other PEs which demultiplexers (M1 & M2) should be used to send it traffic (Rx)

- A VPLS Domain is a set of VPLS Instances.
- Each VPLS Instance consists of:
    - Local Ports
    - Remote Ports
        - Each connects a VPLS Instance
        - Requires a set of pseudo-wires, one to send traffic and one to receive

FIGURE 7.5

The details for demultiplexer fields will be discussed in the following sections. As in the BGP scheme for Layer 2 and Layer 3 VPNs, a route target is configured on each PE router for each VPLS present on the PE router. The route target is the same for a particular VPLS across all PE routers and is used to identify the VPLS instance to which an incoming BGP message pertains. For each VPLS on each PE router, an identifier is configured, known as a site identifier. Each PE router involved in a particular VPLS must be configured with a unique site identifier. The site identifier is the same as the Virtual Edge Identifier (VEID; one per VPLS Instance per PE irrespective of how many local ports belong to that VPLS) referred to in RFC 4761. A label block is a set of demultiplexer labels used to reach a given VPLS site within a set of remote sites. The PE router uses a label block to send a single common update message to establish a PW with multiple PE routers, instead of having to send an individual message to each PE router. A number of illustrations are provided in the following sections that elaborate on this.

Note: Each PE router creates a Virtual Connection Table (VCT) per VPLS instance. The VCT is similar to the VFI (referred to in the earlier sections of this chapter). Hence the acronyms VCT and VFI are used interchangeably in this chapter.

In the first illustration, let us look at a JUNOS Configuration snippet describing the basic setup of a BGP-based VPLS instance. The configuration given in Figure 7.6 is exactly like the configuration for BGP MPLS Layer 3 VPNs with the exception of the keyword "VPLS" defined under the protocols hierarchy, which in the case of BGP MPLS VPNs would be BGP/OSPF/RIP and so forth.

```
routing-instances vpnA { // Configuration for VPN A
    instance-type vpls;    // vpls
    interface ge-0/0/0.0;  // multipoint Ethernet interface
    route-distinguisher 1234:5.6.7.8;
    route-target 1234:8765; // set Route Target to 1234:8765
    protocols {            // PE-CE protocol
        vpls {
            site-range 20;
            site CE-A3 {
                site-idenfier 3;
            }
        }
    }
}
```

FIGURE 7.6

Let us look at a sample illustration (Figure 7.7) of a two-site VPLS instance created between two PE routers. This would clarify each of the configuration statements provided in Figure 7.6 and their relevance.

In Figure 7.7, a label base of "2000" is allocated by PE2 for a given VPLS instance—VPLS RED. PE3 uses the label base "3000" for the same VPLS instance. In Figure 7.8, the role of the label base is illustrated.

In Figure 7.8 the PE2 has been allotted 3002 by PE3, as the Inner label to be used to reach Site 3 on PE3. Similarly, PE3 will use 2003 as the Inner label for reaching Site 2 on PE2. Another label would be used by each of the PE routers, if they need to connect to another site within the same VPLS instance (VPLS RED) on another PE. The MPLS outer labels are also displayed in PE2's VFT (Label 640).

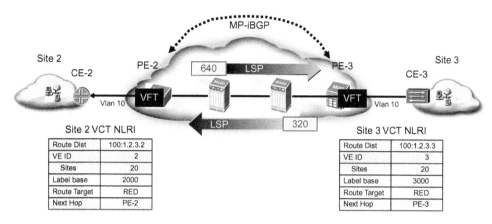

Site 2 VCT NLRI

Route Dist	100:1.2.3.2
VE ID	2
Sites	20
Label base	2000
Route Target	RED
Next Hop	PE-2

Site 3 VCT NLRI

Route Dist	100:1.2.3.3
VE ID	3
Sites	20
Label base	3000
Route Target	RED
Next Hop	PE-3

- PE-PE VCT distribution using Multi-Protocol BGP (RFC 2858)
  - Requires full-mesh MP-iBGP or Route Reflectors
  - Route Distinguisher: "uniquifies" VCT information
  - Route Target: determines VPN topology
  - Analogous to CE-PE routes advertisements in RFC2547 VPNs
  - One single LNRI advertisement per VPLS instance per PE is sufficient

FIGURE 7.7

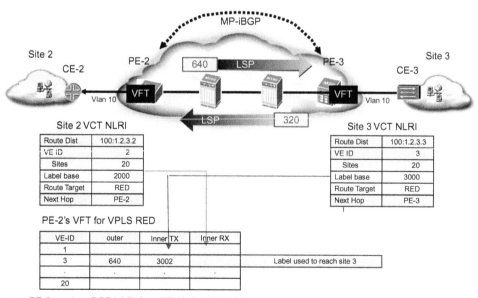

Site 2 VCT NLRI

Route Dist	100:1.2.3.2
VE ID	2
Sites	20
Label base	2000
Route Target	RED
Next Hop	PE-2

Site 3 VCT NLRI

Route Dist	100:1.2.3.3
VE ID	3
Sites	20
Label base	3000
Route Target	RED
Next Hop	PE-3

PE-2's VFT for VPLS RED

VE-ID	outer	Inner TX	Inner RX
1			
3	640	3002	Label used to reach site 3
.	.	.	.
20			

- PE-2 receives BGP NLRI from PE-3's for RED VPLS instance site 3

FIGURE 7.8

If there are more PE routers added to VPLS instance RED, different label blocks are used by each of them. This is illustrated in Figure 7.9 as well.

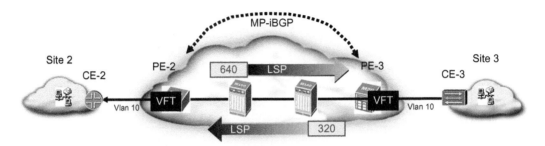

VE-ID	outer	Inner TX	Inner RX
1	600	5002	2001
3	640	3002	2003
.	.	.	.
15	670	9002	2020

PE-2's VFT for VPLS RED

VE-ID	outer	Inner TX	Inner RX
1	320	5003	3001
2	320	2003	3002
.	.	.	.
15	360	9003	2020

PE-3's VFT for VPLS RED

- A full mesh of pseudo-wires are set up between all VPLS instances for VPLS RED

FIGURE 7.9

After examining PE2's VFT, we see that site-id "1" and site-id "15" have different MPLS outer and inner labels. This indicates that those sites belong to different PE routers. This is the same for PE3.

7.2.1.2 LDP-VPLS Control Plane

In contrast to the BGP-VPLS control plane, the LDP-VPLS control plane provides signaling, but not autodiscovery (more on this in the following sections). In this control plane, LDP is used to signal the PWs that are used to interconnect the VPLS instances of a given customer on the PE routers. The LDP signaling scheme for VPLS is similar to the LDP scheme for point-to-point Layer 2 connections (see Martini et al., 2006). In the absence of an autodiscovery mechanism, the identities of all the remote PE routers that are part of a VPLS instance must be configured on each PE router manually.

The virtual circuit identifier (VCID), which is in the point-to-point Layer 2 connection used to identify a specific PW, is configured to be the same for a particular VPLS instance on all PE routers. Hence, the VCID enables a PE router to identify the VPLS instance to which the LDP message refers as shown in Figure 7.10.

7.2.1.3 LDP-VPLS and BGP-VPLS Forwarding Plane

Forwarding plane procedures, at least for unicast and to some extent for multicast (which will appear later in Section), are the same for both BGP VPLS and LDP VPLS. For each VPLS, a PE VPLS data plane functions as a learning bridge and supports all of the standard bridge operations, such as MAC address learning, aging, and flooding. All the PWs established by BGP or LDP signaling and the local CE router ports of a VPLS instance constitute the logical ports of a bridge domain.

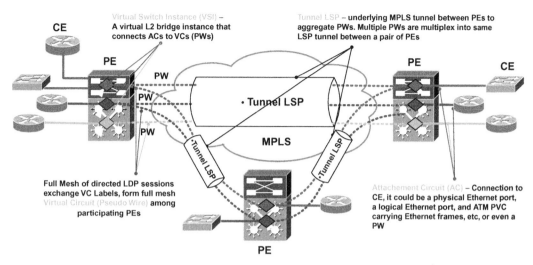

FIGURE 7.10

A MAC forwarding table is created for each VPLS instance on a PE router. This table is populated using a source MAC address learning function and is used to forward unicast VPLS traffic based on the destination MAC address of the received frame. The control plane of VPLS does not need to advertise and distribute reachability information; instead it uses address learning of the standard bridge function in the data plane to provide reachability. Just like an Ethernet switch, the VPLS floods all of the received Ethernet packets with unknown unicast addresses, broadcast addresses, and multicast addresses to all ports (all the ports and PWs associated with the VPLS instance).

To forward a packet, a PE must be able to establish an MAC Forwarding Database. Different from the BGP/MPLS Layer 3 VPN that uses the route advertisement mechanism to establish a routing table in the control plane, the VPLS uses the standard bridge learning function to establish the FDB in the forwarding plane. The MAC address FDB is established by MAC address learning, including the learning of packets from UNI/Attachment Circuit and the learning of packets from PWs. The MAC address learning process involves two parts:

- Remote MAC address learning associated with PWs connected to remote PE routers
- Local MAC address learning of the port directly connected to the user (AC)

The MAC learning process starts with a user having MAC Address A and IP address "1.1.1.2" trying to reach MAC address B connected to a remote PE. The ingress PE floods the packet across all PWs for the relevant VPLS instance (if the destination MAC address is unknown). In this case, one of the PE routers responds to the ARP request originated by the sender PC/client with its MAC address. The Ingress PE builds its MAC database with the relevant MAC-Address-PW/Remote PE for future usage. Figure 7.11 also shows that another participating PE router, within the context of the same VPLS instance, also builds its MAC FDB with an entry for MAC A.

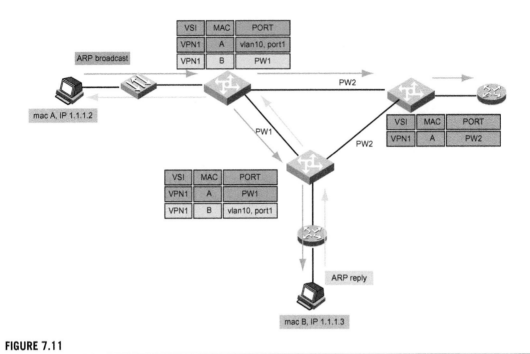

FIGURE 7.11

7.2.1.4 Autodiscovery for LDP-VPLS

It was discussed in the previous section that LDP-based VPLS traditionally relied on manual and static configurations on all participating PE routers. For instance, if a new customer with 20 sites is to be provisioned in the network, then each PE router will need to be configured with all of the customer specific details such as the VCID to facilitate the PW creation between each PE router for the given customer. Further, if a new customer site is added to the existing 20 sites, then all the PE routers will need to be configured to identify this new site and this process has to be performed manually. This can be an operational nightmare in a large carrier network, since the number of touch points for provisioning new sites/customers can be very intensive.

LDP-VPLS can now rely on BGP for Auto-Discovery (AD) purposes. BGP AD is a framework for automatically discovering, connecting, and maintaining the end points for a VPLS instance. BGP AD provides one-touch provisioning for LDP VPLS where all of the related PEs are discovered automatically. The service provider can make use of existing BGP policies to regulate the exchanges between PEs. This procedure does not require carriers to uproot their existing VPLS deployments and to change the signaling protocol, just to provide discovery functions. The BGP protocol establishes neighbor relationships between configured peers. An OPEN message is sent after the completion of the three-way TCP handshake. This OPEN message contains information about the BGP peer sending the message. It contains an Autonomous System Number, BGP version, timer information, and operational parameters including capabilities. The capabilities of a peer are exchanged using two numerical values, the Address Family Identifier (AFI) and Subsequent Address Family Identifier

(SAFI) numbers. These numbers are allocated by the Internet Assigned Numbers Authority (IANA). A peer that announces a capability AFI 65 (L2VPN) and SAFI 25 (BGP VPLS) indicates support for BGP AD. The complete list of AFI and SAFI allocations can be found by following these URLs: http://www.iana.org/assignments/address-family-numbers and http://www.iana.org/assignments/safi-namespace.

Following the establishment of the peer relationship, the discovery process begins as soon as a new VPLS service is provisioned on the PE. Two VPLS identifiers are used to indicate the VPLS membership and the individual VPLS instance:

1. VPLS-ID—Membership information, unique network-wide identifier; the same value is assigned for all VPLS Switch/Forwarding Instances belonging to the same VPLS; encodable and carried as a BGP Extended Community in one of the following formats:
   - Two-octet AS specific Extended Community
   - IPv4 address specific Extended Community
2. VSI-ID—unique identifier for each individual VSI/VFI, built by concatenating a Route Distinguisher (RD) with a 4-byte identifier (usually the System IP of the VPLS PE); encoded and carried as a BGP VPLS NLRI, i.e., RD:IP

To advertise this information BGP AD employs a simplified version of the BGP VPLS NLRI, where just the RD and the next 4 bytes (VE id and VE Block Offset) are used to identify the VPLS instance. There is no need for Label Block and Label Size fields as Targeted-LDP (T-LDP) will take care of signaling the service labels later. The format of the BGP AD NLRI is very similar with the one used for BGP MPLS Layer 3 VPNs, as depicted in Figure 7.12. The system IP may be used for the last 4 bytes of the VSI id, further simplifying the addressing and the provisioning process.

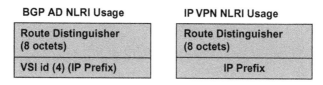

FIGURE 7.12

Network Layer Reachability Information (NLRI) is exchanged between BGP peers, indicating how to reach prefixes. The NLRI is used with VPLS to tell PE peers how to reach the VSI, rather than specific prefixes. The advertisement includes the BGP Next Hop and a Route Target (RT). The BGP next hop indicates the VSI location, and it will be used in the next step to determine which signaling session is to be used for PW signaling. The RT, also coded as an extended community, can be used to build a VPLS full mesh or an H-VPLS hierarchy through the use of BGP import/export policies. BGP is only used to discover VPN end points and exchange reachability information. It is not used to signal the PW labels. This task remains the responsibility of T-LDP.

Two LDP FEC elements are defined in RFC 4447 (PW Setup and Maintenance Using LDP). The original PWid FEC element 128 (0x80) employs a 32-bit field to identify the virtual circuit ID, and it was used extensively in the initial and early VPLS deployments. The simple format is easy to understand, but it does not provide the required structure for BGP AD function. To support BGP AD and other new applications a new Layer 2 FEC Element, the Generalized FEC (0x81), is required.[1]

The Generalized PWid FEC Element has been designed for autodiscovery applications. It provides a field, the Address Group Identifier (AGI), that can be used to signal membership information, that is, VPLS-id in the VPLS case. Separate address fields are provided for the source and target end points called Source Attachment Individual Identifier (SAII) and, respectively, Target Attachment Individual Identifier (TAII). These are the VSI-ids for the two instances that are supposed to be connected through the signaled PW.

The detailed format for FEC 129 is depicted in Figure 7.13.

```
 0                   1                   2                   3
 0 1 2 3 4 5 6 7 8 9 0 1 2 3 4 5 6 7 8 9 0 1 2 3 4 5 6 7 8 9 0 1
+-+-+-+-+-+-+-+-+-+-+-+-+-+-+-+-+-+-+-+-+-+-+-+-+-+-+-+-+-+-+-+-+
|Gen PWid (0x81)|C|         PW Type           | PW info Length|
+-+-+-+-+-+-+-+-+-+-+-+-+-+-+-+-+-+-+-+-+-+-+-+-+-+-+-+-+-+-+-+-+
|   AGI Type    |    Length     |     Value                   |
+-+-+-+-+-+-+-+-+-+-+-+-+-+-+-+-+-+-+-+-+-+-+-+-+-+-+-+-+-+-+-+-+
~                    AGI Value (contd.)                        ~
|                                                             |
+-+-+-+-+-+-+-+-+-+-+-+-+-+-+-+-+-+-+-+-+-+-+-+-+-+-+-+-+-+-+-+-+
|   AII Type    |    Length     |     Value                   |
+-+-+-+-+-+-+-+-+-+-+-+-+-+-+-+-+-+-+-+-+-+-+-+-+-+-+-+-+-+-+-+-+
~                    SAII Value (contd.)                       ~
|                                                             |
+-+-+-+-+-+-+-+-+-+-+-+-+-+-+-+-+-+-+-+-+-+-+-+-+-+-+-+-+-+-+-+-+
|   AII Type    |    Length     |     Value                   |
+-+-+-+-+-+-+-+-+-+-+-+-+-+-+-+-+-+-+-+-+-+-+-+-+-+-+-+-+-+-+-+-+
~                    TAII Value (contd.)                       ~
|                                                             |
+-+-+-+-+-+-+-+-+-+-+-+-+-+-+-+-+-+-+-+-+-+-+-+-+-+-+-+-+-+-+-+-+
```

FIGURE 7.13

Each of the FEC fields is designed as a sub-TLV equipped with its own type and length providing support for new applications. To accommodate the BGP AD information model, the following FEC formats are used:

- AGI (type 1) is identical in format and content with the BGP Extended Community attribute used to carry the VPLS-ID value.

---

[1] More detailed information for each FEC can be found in Sections 5.2.2 (0x80) and 5.3 (0x81) of RFC 4447.

- Source AII (type 1) is a 4-byte value destined to carry the local VSI-id (outgoing NLRI minus the RD).
- Target AII (type 1) is a 4-byte value destined to carry the remote VSI-id (incoming NLRI minus the RD).

BGP is responsible for discovering the location of VSIs that share the same VPLS membership. LDP protocol is responsible for setting up the PW infrastructure between the related VSIs by exchanging service specific labels between them. Once the local VPLS information is provisioned in the PE, the related PEs participating in the same VPLS are identified through BGP AD exchanges. A list of far end PEs is generated and will trigger LDP specific functions, that is, the creation, if required, of the necessary T-LDP sessions to these PEs and the exchange of the service specific VPN labels. The steps for the BGP AD process and LDP session establishment and label exchange are shown in Figure 7.14.

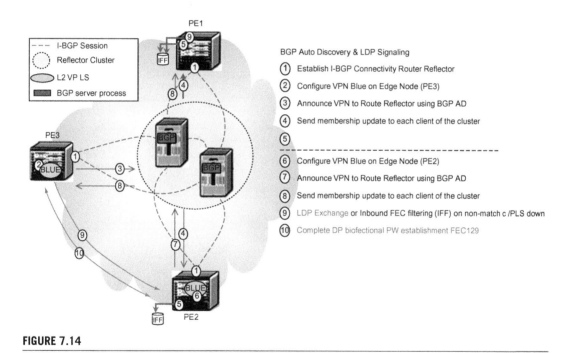

FIGURE 7.14

Implementations allow for manually provisioned and auto-discovered PWs to co-exist in the same VPLS instance, that is, both FEC128 and FEC129 are supported. This allows for gradual introduction of autodiscovery into an existing VPLS deployment. Because FEC128 and 129 represent different addressing schemes, it is important to make sure that just one of them is used at any point between the same two VPLS instances. Otherwise, both PWs may become active, causing a loop that might adversely impact the correct functioning of the service. Hence, it is recommended to disable the FEC128 PW as soon as the FEC129 addressing scheme is introduced in a portion of the network. Alternatively, a Layer 2 protocol such as RSTP may be used during the migration as a safety mechanism to provide additional protection against operational errors.

7.2.1.5 Autodiscovery for LDP-VPLS—Implementation Details

In this section we look at some implementation specific details. We will only use a TiMOS (Alcatel-Lucent) specific configuration to understand the concepts discussed. We will not illustrate other vendor implementations (JUNOS or Cisco IOS/XR), since the objective of this section is to help relate the various building blocks to understanding what level of configuration detail is required for BGP AD. Therefore we choose to use TiMOS for illustrative purposes.

Based on Figure 7.15, assume PE6 was previously configured with VPLS 100 as indicated by the configuration's lines in the upper right. The BGP AD process will commence after PE134 is configured with the VPLS 100 instance as shown in the upper left. This shows a very basic and simple BGP AD configuration. The minimum requirement for enabling BGP AD on a VPLS instance is configuring the VPLS-id and point to a pw-template.

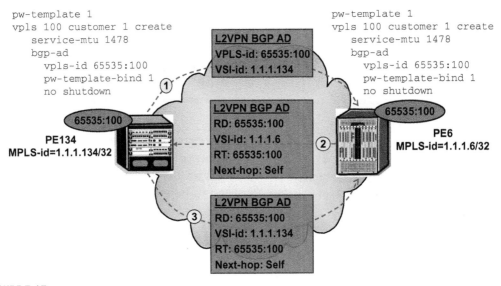

FIGURE 7.15

In many cases VPLS connectivity is based on a PW mesh. To reduce the configuration requirement, the BGP values can be automatically generated using the vpls-id and the PE router-id. By default, the lower 6 bytes of the vpls-id will be used to generate the RD and the RT values. The VSI-id value is generated from the PE router-id. All of these parameters are configurable and can be coded to suit the customer's requirements and build different topologies. In Figure 7.15, a VPLS instance named (Customer 1) with a service-identifier of "100" is created. BGP AD is configured along with the VPLS-ID for this instance, which is configured as "65535:100." This is similar to the RD in the context of a BGP/MPLS VPN. The MTU SIZE is also set to 1478 bytes.

The command "PW-Template" is defined under the top level service command and specifies whether to use an automatically generated Service Distribution Path (SDP). By definition, an SDP acts as a logical way of directing traffic from one PE to another through a unidirectional service tunnel.

An SDP originating on one node terminates at a destination node, which then directs incoming traffic to the correct egress Service Access Point (SAP as known in TimOS) or UNI. The easiest way to refer to an SDP is to consider it as the equivalent of a PW. An SDP can automatically be created using a PW-Template or by manual configuration, wherein each VPLS customer/instance can be associated with a given SDP. Two types of SDPs used in a VPLS deployment are

- **Spoke SDP:** Flooded traffic received on the Spoke SDP is replicated on all ports within the same VPLS instance, with Split Horizon assumed.
- **Mesh SDP:** Flooded traffic received on any Mesh SDP is replicated to all ports within the same VPLS instance, with the exception of not being forwarded on any Mesh SDP.

More on the SDP deployment will be discussed in the subsequent sections.

Next we will look at commands. The command given below provides the set of parameters required for establishing the PW binding as described in the following sections:

```
PERs6>config>service# pw-template 1 create
  - [no] pw-template <policy-id> [use-provisioned-sdp]

 <policy-id>          : [1..2147483647]
 <use-provisioned-s*> : keyword


 [no] accounting-pol* - Configure accounting-policy to be used
 [no] collect-stats   - Enable/disable statistics collection
 [no] disable-aging   - Enable/disable aging of MAC addresses
 [no] disable-learni* - Enable/disable learning of new MAC addresses
 [no] discard-unknow* - Enable/disable discarding of frames with unknown
                        source MAC address
      egress          + Spoke SDP binding egress configuration
      igmp-snooping   + Configure IGMP snooping parameters
      ingress         + Spoke SDP binding ingress configuration
 [no] limit-mac-move  - Configure mac move
 [no] mac-pinning     - Enable/disable MAC address pinning on this spoke SDP
 [no] max-nbr-mac-ad* - Configure the maximum number of MAC entries in the FDB
                        from this SDP
 [no] split-horizon-* + Configure a split horizon group
      vc-type         - Configure VC type
 [no] vlan-vc-tag     - Configure VLAN VC tag
```

FIGURE 7.16

Commands for PW Binding.

A pw-template-bind command configured within the VPLS service under the bgp-ad subcommand is a pointer to the pw-template that should be used. If a VPLS service does not specify an import-rt list, then that binding applies to all route targets accepted by that VPLS. The pw-template-bind command can select a different template on a per import-rt basis. Further, it is possible to specify specific pw-templates for some route targets with a VPLS service and use the single pw-template-bind command to address all unspecified but accepted imported targets. Referring back to the previous configuration, the pw-template-bind 1 binds template 1 with a set of given characteristics to a particular VPLS instance. The various command options are given next.

```
PERs6>config>service>vpls>bgp-ad# pw-template-bind
  - pw-template-bind <policy-id> [split-horizon-group <group-name>] [import-rt
    {ext-community, ...(upto 5 max)}]
  - no pw-template-bind <policy-id>

  <policy-id>          : [1..2147483647]
  <group-name>         : [32 chars max]
  <ext-community>      : target:{<ip-addr:comm-val>|<as-number:ext-comm-val>}
                         ip-addr       - a.b.c.d
                         comm-val      - [0..65535]
                         as-number     - [1..65535]
                         ext-comm-val  - [0..4294967295]
```

FIGURE 7.17

Options for the PW-Template command.

It is important to understand the significance of the split-horizon group used by the pw-template. Traditionally, when a VPLS instance is manually created the PWs are automatically placed in a common split-horizon group to prevent forwarding between the PWs in the VPLS instances. This prevents loops that would have otherwise occurred in the Layer 2 service. When automatically discovering VPLS service using BGP AD, the service provider has the option of associating the autodiscovered PWs with a split-horizon group to control the forwarding between PWs.

T-LDP is triggered once the VPN end points have been discovered using BGP. The T-LDP session between the PEs is established when one does not exist. The Far-End IP address required for the T-LDP identification is gleaned from the BGP AD next hop information. The pw-template and pw-template-bind configuration statements are used to establish the automatic SDP or to map to the appropriate SDP (if there is a PW already established between two PE routers, and a new site is coming up on one of these PEs). The FEC129 content is built using the following values:

- AGI from the locally configured VPLS-id
- SAII from the locally configured VSI-id
- TAII from the VSI-id contained in the last 4 bytes of the received BGP NLRI

Figure 7.18 shows the different detailed phases of the LDP signaling path, post BGP AD completion. It also indicates how some fields can be auto generated when they are not specified in the configuration.

The next configuration shows the different detailed phases of the LDP signaling path, post BGP AD completion. It also indicates how some fields can be auto generated when they are not specified in the configuration. The first command seen will display the LDP peering relationships that have been established. The type of adjacency is displayed in the "Adj Type" column, and the type is "Both", meaning link and targeted sessions have been successfully established.

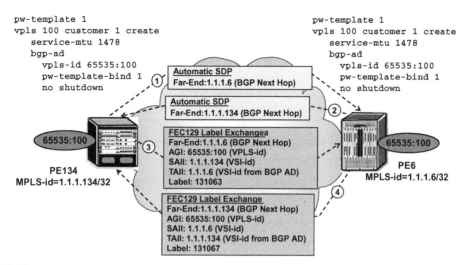

FIGURE 7.18

```
PE6# show router ldp session
================================================================================
LDP Sessions
================================================================================
Peer LDP Id        Adj Type   State        Msg Sent  Msg Recv  Up Time
--------------------------------------------------------------------------------
1.1.1.134:0        Both       Established  21482     21482     0d 15:38:44
--------------------------------------------------------------------------------
No. of Sessions: 1
================================================================================
```

FIGURE 7.19

Verifying the LDP Session.

The second command shows the specific LDP service label information broken up per FEC Element type, 128 or 129, basis. The information for FEC Element 129 includes the AGI, SAII, and the TAII.

```
PE# show router ldp bindings fec-type services
================================================================================
LDP LSR ID: 1.1.1.6
================================================================================
Legend: U - Label In Use, N - Label Not In Use, W - Label Withdrawn
        S - Status Signaled Up,  D - Status Signaled Down
        E - Epipe Service, V - VPLS Service, M - Mirror Service
        A - Apipe Service, F - Fpipe Service, I - IES Service, R - VPRN service
        P - Ipipe Service, C - Cpipe Service
        TLV - (Type, Length: Value)
================================================================================
```

FIGURE 7.20

Verifying LDP Bindings.

```
LDP Service FEC128 Bindings
===============================================================================
Type   VCId      SvcId     SDPId  Peer          IngLbl  EgrLbl  LMTU  RMTU
-------------------------------------------------------------------------------
No Matching Entries Found


===============================================================================
LDP Service FEC129 Bindings
===============================================================================
AGI                                SAII               TAII
Type             SvcId     SDPId   Peer          IngLbl  EgrLbl  LMTU  RMTU
-------------------------------------------------------------------------------
65535:100                          1.1.1.6            1.1.1.134
V-Eth            100       17406   1.1.1.134     131063U 131067S 1464  1464
-------------------------------------------------------------------------------
No. of FEC129s: 1
===============================================================================
```

FIGURE 7.20

(Continued)

The FEC129 output just shown illustrates the various details including the AGI/Type, SAII, and TAII. The SDP-ID is basically a number assigned to the PW or SDP between the two PE routers for the given VPLS instance.

The second command illustrates the specific LDP service label information broken up per FEC Element type, 128 or 129, basis. The information for FEC Element 129 includes the AGI, SAII, and the TAII. To further understand specific topologies and their implementations regarding BGP AD, a few use cases will be reviewed a little later in the chapter.

7.2.2 Characteristics of LDP VPLS

To enable VPLS, all PE routers connected to common VPLS customers must be able to exchange VPLS signaling information among them. As the number of PE routers in the network increases, scaling this signaling component of the VPLS control plane becomes essential.

For LDP-VPLS signaling, the exchange of VPLS signaling information is accomplished by setting up a full mesh of targeted LDP sessions between each pair of PE routers that have at least one VPLS in common. A brief description of T-LDP (Targeted LDP) is provided below.

Normally, LDP sessions are set up between directly connected LSRs. In a network in which the IGP routes need to be labeled, this is sufficient, because the label switching of packets is hop per hop. Therefore, if the label bindings are advertised hop per hop for the IGP routes, the LSPs are set up. However, in some cases, a remote or targeted LDP session is needed. This is an LDP session between LSRs that are not directly connected. Examples in which the targeted LDP session is needed are VPLS and Layer 2 VPN services are being offered. Targeted LDP sessions are different because during the discovery phase hellos are unicast to the LDP peer rather than using multicast.

As the size of the VPLS network grows, the number of LDP targeted sessions increases exponentially on the order of $O(N^2)$, where N is the number of LDP-VPLS PE routers in the network.

Maintenance of all of these LDP sessions creates an additional load on the control plane of PE routers in the VPLS network. The operational challenge resulting from the $O(N^2)$ increase in LDP sessions becomes even more noticeable when a service provider authenticates the sessions using Message Digest 5 (MD5), because MD5 keys must be configured on each end of every LDP session. Adding a new PE router or deleting an existing one becomes a cumbersome task because the configuration on each of the PE routers in the network must be modified. Figure 7.21 illustrates the full-mesh problem in LDP-VPLS.

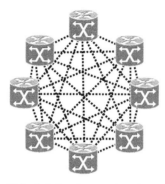

- Potential signaling overhead
- Full PW mesh from the edge
- Packet replication done at the edge

FIGURE 7.21

To address the control plane scaling issues when using a Flat-VPLS model as illustrated in Figure 7.21, a hierarchy should be defined within the VPLS domain to avoid a full mesh of PWs between every PE router that caters to a given VPLS customer. This method of creating a hierarchy is known as Hierarchical VPLS (H-VPLS).

H-VPLS tries, to some extent, to mitigate the full-mesh requirement by creating a two-level hierarchy of hub-and-spoke devices. Using an H-VPLS model, service providers can deploy Multi-Tenant Units (MTUs) in multi-tenant buildings to serve the various enterprises in these buildings; each enterprise can potentially belong to a different VPLS VPN. Service providers then need to aggregate the MTU traffic toward the PE device in the central office or point of presence (POP).

In Figure 7.22 we refer to two VPLS customers that are hosted on the same PE router, which acts as a Virtual Bridge (VB) for both of these customers.

A traditional MTU is an Ethernet device that supports all Layer 2 switching functions, including the normal bridging functions of learning and replication on all of its ports; it is typically dedicated to one enterprise. It is also technically possible to extend the VPLS functionality to the MTUs. In this case, the MTUs act like PE devices, leading to a large number of MTUs participating in the VPLS. In a network with numerous PEs/MTUs, this would lead to scalability limitations in terms of the number of PWs to be maintained. H-VPLS here can be used to introduce a hierarchy, eliminating the need for a full mesh of PWs between all participating devices. Hierarchy is achieved by augmenting the base

VPLS' core mesh of PE-to-PE PWs (referred to as hub PWs) with access PWs (called spoke PWs) to form a two-tier hierarchical VPLS model, as shown in Figure 7.22.

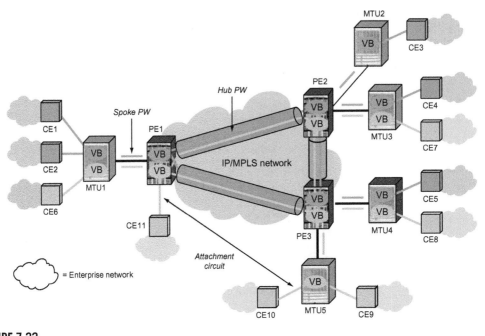

FIGURE 7.22

As per Figure 7.22, spoke PWs are created between the MTUs and the PE routers. The Hub-PW in this context refers to the PWs between PE routers in the core. These are typically Mesh-SDPs.

H-VPLS also offers certain operational advantages by centralizing the major functions (i.e., VPLS end-point auto-discovery, participating in a routed backbone, maintaining a full mesh of tunnel LSPs and multiple full meshes of PWs) in the PoP PE routers. This makes it possible to use lower cost, low-maintenance MTU devices, reducing the overall capital expenditure and operating expenses because typically there are an order of magnitude more MTU devices than PE routers. Another operational advantage offered by H-VPLS along with BGP AD is centralized provisioning, with fewer elements to touch when turning up service for a customer. Adding a new MTU device requires some configuration of the local PE router but does not require any signaling to other PE routers or MTU devices, simplifying the provisioning process.

In H-VPLS, a CE is attached to an MTU through an attachment circuit. An AC from a specific customer is associated (by configuration) with a virtual bridge that is dedicated to that customer within the considered MTU. An AC may be a physical or a virtual LAN (VLAN) tagged logical port. In the basic scenario, an MTU has one uplink to a PE. This uplink contains one spoke PW (Spoke SDP) for each VPLS served by the MTU. The end points of this spoke PW are an MTU and a PE. As per Figure 7.22, the uplink between MTU1 and PE1 carries two PWs because MTU1 has two VPLS customers attached.

7.2.3 Use Cases for LDP-VPLS and BGP AD

7.2.3.1 Full-Mesh VPLS

The full mesh is likely the most common VPLS topology deployed. It provides a full mesh of direct connection between all nodes in a VPLS. It is also the simplest to configure for BGP AD. This provides a logical starting point on which other configurations will build. Here, BGP AD is used to connect MTUs1, PERs4, and MTUs2 in a full mesh. Figure 7.23 shows the VPLS service VPN200 instantiated on the three nodes.

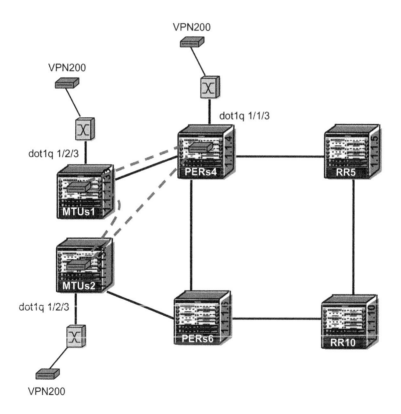

FIGURE 7.23

A similar BGP AD configuration is used on all three nodes participating in VPN 200. The service difference is the port on which the access port or UNI (referred to as SAP in TiMOS) is configured. Therefore, only the configuration for MTUs1 is presented next.

```
MTUs1
pw-template 1 create
    split-horizon-group "mesh"
    exit
exit
vpls 200 customer 1 create
    service-mtu 1478
    bgp-ad
       vpls-id 65535:200
       pw-template-bind 1
       no shutdown
    exit
    exit
    stp
      shutdown
    exit
    sap 1/2/3:200 create
    exit
    no shutdown
exit
```

FIGURE 7.24

BGP AD Configuration.

The basic service display has been extended to include the BGP-AD service information and any automatically generated SDP.

```
MTUs1# show service id 200 base
===============================================================================
Service Basic Information
===============================================================================
Service Id         : 200             Vpn Id             : 0
Service Type       : VPLS
Customer Id        : 1
Last Status Change: 01/18/2008 06:19:22
Last Mgmt Change   : 01/18/2008 08:05:51
Admin State        : Up              Oper State         : Up
MTU                : 1478            Def. Mesh VC Id    : 200
SAP Count          : 1               SDP Bind Count     : 2
Snd Flush on Fail : Disabled         Host Conn Verify   : Disabled
Def. Gateway IP    : None
Def. Gateway MAC   : None
-------------------------------------------------------------------------------
BGP Auto-discovery Information
-------------------------------------------------------------------------------
Admin State        : Up              Vpls Id            : 65535:200
Route Dist         : 65535:200       Prefix             : 1.1.1.133 -->vsi-id
Rte-Target Import : None             Rte-Target Export : None
L2-Auto-Bind Plcy : 1               L2-Auto-Bind SHG   : None
Vsi-Import         : None
Vsi-Export         : None
-------------------------------------------------------------------------------
```

FIGURE 7.25

Checking the service.

```
Service Access & Destination Points
-------------------------------------------------------------------------
Identifier                            Type      AdmMTU  OprMTU  Adm  Opr
-------------------------------------------------------------------------
sap:1/2/3:200                         q-tag     1518    1518    Up   Up
sdp:17406:4294967295 SB(1.1.1.4)      BgpAd     0       1492    Up   Up
sdp:17407:4294967295 SB(1.1.1.134)    BgpAd     0       1492    Up   Up
-------------------------------------------------------------------------
[<sap-id>] indicates a Managed SAP
=========================================================================
```

FIGURE 7.25

(Continued)

The standard SDP show commands are used to view the relationship of the service to the SDP regardless of whether they were created automatically following the BGP AD process or manually.

```
MTUs1# show service sdp-using
=========================================================================
SDP Using
=========================================================================
SvcId      SdpId             Type    Far End        Opr S* I.Label  E.Label
-------------------------------------------------------------------------
200        17406:4294967295  BgpAd   1.1.1.4        Up     131064   131063
200        17407:4294967295  BgpAd   1.1.1.134      Up     131063   131064
-------------------------------------------------------------------------
Number of SDPs : 2
-------------------------------------------------------------------------
=========================================================================
* indicates that the corresponding row element may have been truncated.
```

FIGURE 7.26

Checking the SDP.

The LDP binding command has been extended to include the Generic PWid FEC Element (0x81/129). This display includes all of the LDP specific attributes for the VPLS instance including the AGI, SAII, and TAII signaling options.

```
MTUs1# show router ldp bindings service-id 200
=========================================================================
LDP LSR ID: 1.1.1.133
=========================================================================
Legend: U - Label In Use, N - Label Not In Use, W - Label Withdrawn
        S - Status Signaled Up,  D - Status Signaled Down
        E - Epipe Service, V - VPLS Service, M - Mirror Service
        A - Apipe Service, F - Fpipe Service, I - IES Service, R - VPRN service
        P - Ipipe Service, C - Cpipe Service
        TLV - (Type, Length: Value)
=========================================================================
```

FIGURE 7.27

LDP specific attributes.

```
LDP Service FEC128 Bindings
===============================================================================

===============================================================================
LDP Service FEC129 Bindings
===============================================================================
AGI                                   SAII                TAII
Type            SvcId     SDPId  Peer         IngLbl EgrLbl LMTU  RMTU
-------------------------------------------------------------------------------
65535:200                             1.1.1.133           1.1.1.4
V-Eth           200       17406  1.1.1.4      131064U 131063S 1464  1464

65535:200                             1.1.1.133           1.1.1.134
V-Eth           200       17407  1.1.1.134    131063U 131064S 1464  1464


-------------------------------------------------------------------------------
No. of FEC129s: 2
===============================================================================
===============================================================================
```

FIGURE 7.27

(*Continued*)

Specific L2VPN AD routes are stored in the BGP RIB IN and RIB OUT tables. MTUs1 receives two L2VPN AD routes for VPN 200 for PERs4, one advertised from each route reflector. Only one of these will be actively used. To determine the L2VPN AD routes advertised from MTUs1 (RIB OUT), use the local loopback address as the prefix.

```
*A:MTUs1# show router bgp routes l2-vpn 1.1.1.4/32 hunt → Remote PE
===============================================================================
 BGP Router ID : 1.1.1.133       AS : 65535    Local AS : 65535
===============================================================================
 Legend -
 Status codes : u - used, s - suppressed, h - history, d - decayed, * - valid
 Origin codes : i - IGP, e - EGP, ? - incomplete, > - best


===============================================================================
BGP L2VPN-AD Routes
===============================================================================
-------------------------------------------------------------------------------
RIB In Entries
-------------------------------------------------------------------------------
Network         : 1.1.1.4/32
Nexthop         : 1.1.1.4
Route Dist.     : 65535:200
```

FIGURE 7.28

Checking the L2VPN routes.

```
From           : 1.1.1.10
Res. Nexthop   : 0.0.0.0
Local Pref.    : 100                Interface Name : NotAvailable
Aggregator AS  : None               Aggregator     : None
Atomic Aggr.   : Not Atomic         MED            : 0
Community      : target:65535:200  l2-vpn:65535:200
Cluster        : 1.1.1.5
Originator Id  : 1.1.1.4            Peer Router Id : 1.1.1.10
Flags          : Used  Valid  Best  IGP
AS-Path        : No As-Path

Network        : 1.1.1.4/32
Nexthop        : 1.1.1.4
Route Dist.    : 65535:200
From           : 1.1.1.5
Res. Nexthop   : 0.0.0.0
Local Pref.    : 100                Interface Name : NotAvailable
Aggregator AS  : None               Aggregator     : None
Atomic Aggr.   : Not Atomic         MED            : 0
Community      : target:65535:200  l2-vpn:65535:200
Cluster        : 1.1.1.5
Originator Id  : 1.1.1.4            Peer Router Id : 1.1.1.5
Flags          : Valid  IGP
AS-Path        : No As-Path


-------------------------------------------------------------------------
RIB Out Entries
-------------------------------------------------------------------------
```

FIGURE 7.28

(Continued)

7.2.3.2 Mixed FEC128 and FEC129 Configurations

There are numerous cases that may require carriers to mix manually configured end point environments with discovered Layer 2 services using BGP AD. Some of these may include:

- H-VPLS solutions where the carrier does not want to deploy BGP to the edge nodes but still wants the benefits of MPLS to the edge
- Mixed operational models used by different operational bodies inside the same carrier
- During a migration from manually provisioned services to a discovered operational model

Next, let us look at the following case study and Figure 7.29.

VPN 100 will follow the H-VPLS solution. Manually configured PWs connect the MTU nodes to the PE nodes and BGP AD is used to build the full mesh between the PE-rs nodes. PERs4 contains both the PWid FEC Element (0x80/128) and the Generalized PWid FEC Element (0x81/129). MTUs1 uses the standard configuration for a VPLS, including the SDP and the service definition.

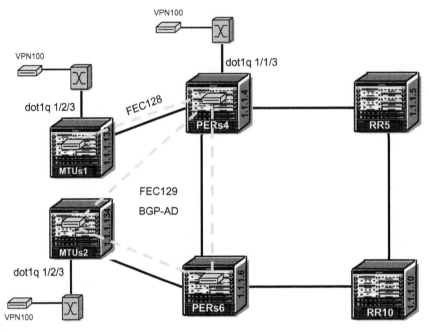

FIGURE 7.29

```
MTUs1
sdp 14 mpls create ---→SDP config
    far-end 1.1.1.4 → Remote PE
    ldp -→T-LDP enabled
    keep-alive
      shutdown
    exit
    no shutdown
exit
vpls 100 customer 1 create
    service-mtu 1478
    stp
        shutdown
    exit
    sap 1/2/3:100 create
    exit
    spoke-sdp 14:100 create
    exit
     no shutdown
exit
```

FIGURE 7.30

MTU Configuration.

As stated earlier, PERs4 includes the manual service configuration for VPN 100 facing MTUs1 and BGP AD facing the other nodes in the full mesh. The standard configuration for FEC128 only node (MTUs1), is highlighted in red.

```
PERs4
sdp 41 mpls create
    far-end 1.1.1.133
    ldp
    keep-alive
        shutdown
    exit
    no shutdown
exit
pw-template 1 create
    split-horizon-group "mesh"
    exit
exit
vpls 100 customer 1 create
    service-mtu 1478
    bgp-ad
        vpls-id 65535:100
        pw-template-bind 1
    no shutdown
    exit
    stp
      shutdown
    exit
    sap 1/1/3:100 create
    exit
    spoke-sdp 41:100 create
    exit
    no shutdown
exit
```

FIGURE 7.31

PERs configuration.

The other two nodes participating in the VPN 100 full mesh only require BGP AD configuration for the service. Here PERs6, PERs4, and MTUs2 have a full mesh of PW between them, and MTUs1 is only connected to PERs4.

```
MTUs2                                    PERs6
pw-template 1 create                     pw-template 1 create
    split-horizon-group "mesh"               split-horizon-group "mesh"
    exit                                     exit
exit                                     exit
```

FIGURE 7.32

MTU and PERs configurations.

```
vpls 100 customer 1 create              vpls 100 customer 1 create
    service-mtu 1478                         service-mtu 1478
    bgp-ad                                  bgp-ad
       vpls-id 65535:100                       vpls-id 65535:100
       pw-template-bind 1                      pw-template-bind 1
       no shutdown                             no shutdown
    exit                                    exit
     stp                                    stp
      shutdown                                shutdown
    exit                                    exit
    sap 1/2/3:100 create                    no shutdown
    exit                                exit
    no shutdown
exit
```

FIGURE 7.32

(Continued)

Next, operational commands will be illustrated. The basic service display command has been extended to include the BGP-AD service information and any automatically generated SDP.

```
PERs-4# show service id 100 base
===============================================================================
Service Basic Information
===============================================================================
Service Id          : 100          Vpn Id             : 0
Service Type        : VPLS
Customer Id         : 1
Last Status Change: 01/18/2008 09:06:45
Last Mgmt Change  : 01/18/2008 09:08:15
Admin State         : Up           Oper State         : Up
MTU                 : 1478         Def. Mesh VC Id    : 100
SAP Count           : 1            SDP Bind Count     : 3
Snd Flush on Fail : Disabled       Host Conn Verify   : Disabled
Def. Gateway IP     : None
Def. Gateway MAC    : None


-------------------------------------------------------------------------------
BGP Auto-discovery Information
-------------------------------------------------------------------------------
Admin State         : Up           Vpls Id            : 65535:100
Route Dist          : 65535:100    Prefix             : 1.1.1.4
Rte-Target Import : None           Rte-Target Export : None
L2-Auto-Bind Plcy : 1             L2-Auto-Bind SHG  : None
```

FIGURE 7.33

Checking the service ID.

```
Vsi-Import        : None
Vsi-Export        : None

-------------------------------------------------------------------
Service Access & Destination Points
-------------------------------------------------------------------
Identifier                            Type      AdmMTU  OprMTU  Adm  Opr
-------------------------------------------------------------------
sap:1/1/3:100                         q-tag     1518    1518    Up   Up
sdp:41:100 S(1.1.1.133)               n/a       0       1492    Up   Up
sdp:17405:4294967295 SB(1.1.1.6)      BgpAd     0       1556    Up   Up
sdp:17407:4294967294 SB(1.1.1.134)    BgpAd     0       1556    Up   Up
-------------------------------------------------------------------
[<sap-id>] indicates a Managed SAP
===================================================================
```

FIGURE 7.33

(*Continued*)

The standard SDP show commands are used to view the relationship of the service to the SDP regardless of whether they were created automatically following the BGP AD process or created manually.

```
PERs-4# show service sdp-using
===================================================================
SDP Using
===================================================================
SvcId      SdpId              Type     Far End       Opr  S*  I.Label  E.Label
-------------------------------------------------------------------
100        41:100             Spoke    1.1.1.133     Up       131062   131065
100        17405:4294967295   BgpAd    1.1.1.6       Up       131060   131064
100        17407:4294967294   BgpAd    1.1.1.134     Up       131061   131063
-------------------------------------------------------------------
Number of SDPs : 3
-------------------------------------------------------------------
```

FIGURE 7.34

Checking the SDP.

The LDP binding command has been extended to include the Generic PWid FEC Element (0x81/129). This display includes all of the LDP specific attributes for the VPLS instance including the AGI, SAII, and TAII signaling options.

```
PERs-4# show router ldp bindings service-id 100
==============================================================================
LDP LSR ID: 1.1.1.4
==============================================================================
Legend: U - Label In Use, N - Label Not In Use, W - Label Withdrawn
        S - Status Signaled Up,  D - Status Signaled Down
        E - Epipe Service, V - VPLS Service, M - Mirror Service
        A - Apipe Service, F - Fpipe Service, I - IES Service, R - VPRN service
        P - Ipipe Service, C - Cpipe Service
        TLV - (Type, Length: Value)
==============================================================================
LDP Service FEC128 Bindings
==============================================================================
Type    VCId        SvcId      SDPId  Peer          IngLbl  EgrLbl  LMTU  RMTU
------------------------------------------------------------------------------
V-Eth   100         100        41     1.1.1.133     131062U 131065S 1464  1464
------------------------------------------------------------------------------
No. of VC Labels: 1


==============================================================================
LDP Service FEC129 Bindings
==============================================================================
AGI                            SAII              TAII
Type                SvcId      SDPId  Peer          IngLbl  EgrLbl  LMTU  RMTU
------------------------------------------------------------------------------
65535:100                      1.1.1.4           1.1.1.6
V-Eth               100        17405  1.1.1.6       131060U 131064S 1464  1464

65535:100                      1.1.1.4           1.1.1.134
V-Eth               100        17407  1.1.1.134     131061U 131063S 1464  1464


------------------------------------------------------------------------------
No. of FEC129s: 2
==============================================================================
```

FIGURE 7.35

Checking LDP bindings.

7.2.3.3 H-VPLS Configurations

As VPLS networks expand, some carriers will deploy a hierarchical solution model, H-VPLS. In this case MTU-s nodes single homed to one PE node can make use of BGP AD to automatically discover the VPN memberships. Membership is derived from the configured VPLS-id. The corresponding topology is built based on import and export route targets. H-VPLS topologies require each PE-rs to export and import a unique route target to/from the MTU-s nodes for which it is responsible. This means a PE-rs node is required to import and export two different route targets, one for all the MTU-s nodes connected to it and one for the full mesh connecting it to other PE-rs nodes. The PE-rs nodes must map the two different route targets to different pw-templates configured at the service level. The MTU-s PWs must be able to switch between themselves, the SAPs, and the mesh. The PWs that form the mesh can only forward to SAPs and MTU-s PWs and not to other mesh PWs. Figure 7.36 shows the import and export requirements for the H-VPLS solution.

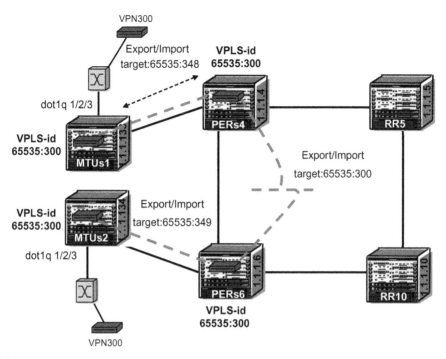

FIGURE 7.36

```
MTUs1
pw-template 2 create
exit
vpls 300 customer 1 create
     service-mtu 1478
     bgp-ad
       vpls-id 65535:300
       route-target export target:65535:348 import target:65535:348
       pw-template-bind 2
       no shutdown
     exit
     stp
       shutdown
     exit
     sap 1/2/3:300 create
     exit
     no shutdown
   exit
```

FIGURE 7.37

MTU Configuration.

```
MTUs2
pw-template 2 create
exit
vpls 300 customer 1 create
    service-mtu 1478
    bgp-ad
       vpls-id 65535:300
       route-target export target:65535:349 import target:65535:349
       pw-template-bind 2
       no shutdown
    exit
    stp
      shutdown
    exit
    sap 1/2/3:300 create
    exit
    no shutdown
exit
```

FIGURE 7.38

MTU Configuration.

```
PERs4
Router Policy Configuration
---------------------------
community "mesh-300" members "target:65535:300"
community "h-vpls300" members "target:65535:300" "target:65535:348"
community "spoke-300" members "target:65535:348"
policy-statement "h-vpls300-exp"
    entry 10
        action accept
            community add "h-vpls300"
        exit
    exit
exit
policy-statement "h-vpls300-imp"
    entry 10
      from
            community "mesh-300"
      exit
      action accept
      exit
    exit
    entry 20
        from
            community "spoke-300"
      exit
      action accept
      exit
    exit
exit
```

FIGURE 7.39

PERs Configuration.

```
Service Configuration
--------------------
pw-template 1 create
    split-horizon-group "mesh"
    exit
exit
    pw-template 2 create
    exit

vpls 300 customer 1 create
    service-mtu 1478
    bgp-ad
        vsi-export "h-vpls300-exp"
        vsi-import "h-vpls300-imp"
        vpls-id 65535:300
        pw-template-bind 1 import-rt "target:65535:300"
        pw-template-bind 2 import-rt "target:65535:348"
        no shutdown
    exit
    split-horizon-group "mesh" create
    exit
    stp
        shutdown
    exit
    no shutdown
exit
```

FIGURE 7.39

(*Continued*)

The PE router, being a Hub for the MTUs devices in the Metro domain and having fully meshed PWs between other PEs in the core, is configured with an export policy that adds two RTs (one is imported by the MTUs acting as Spoke sites and the other is imported by PEs acting as Hub sites for their respective Metro domains consisting of MTUs). PERs4 is configured next with appropriate import and export policies, and also associates a Mesh-SDP to other PEs (PERs6) and a Spoke SDP to MTUs1. It is important to remember that flooded traffic from MTUs1 (using a Spoke SDP) will be flooded to PERs6 via the Mesh SDP. Similarly, traffic from PERs6 received via a Mesh SDP will be flooded to MTUs1 via the Spoke SDP. This ensures that MTUs1 learns about the MAC address behind MTUs2 via only PERs4, and therefore only has a single PW/SDP to PERs4. Traffic between MTUs1 and MTUs2 is switched via PERs4. What we have achieved here is a "reduction in the number of PWs between devices using a hierarchy."

The display output for VPN 300 is from the perspective of PERs4. Notice that there is no SDP connection between PERs4 and MTUs2. Similarly, there is no connection between MTUs1 and PERs6. Since there is no common import/export between these pairs of nodes, there is no automatically established SDP.

```
PERs6
Router Policy Configuration
--------------------------
community "mesh-300" members "target:65535:300"
community "h-vpls300" members "target:65535:300" "target:65535:349"
community "spoke-300" members "target:65535:34"
policy-statement "h-vpls300-exp"
    entry 10
        action accept
            community add "h-vpls300"
        exit
    exit
exit
policy-statement "h-vpls300-imp"
    entry 10
      from
            community "mesh-300"
      exit
      action accept
      exit
    exit
    entry 20
        from
            community "spoke-300"
      exit
      action accept
      exit
    exit
exit


Service Configuration
---------------------
pw-template 1 create
    split-horizon-group "mesh"
    exit
exit
pw-template 2 create
exit
vpls 300 customer 1 create
    service-mtu 1478
    bgp-ad
        vsi-export "h-vpls300-exp"
        vsi-import "h-vpls300-imp"
        vpls-id 65535:300
        pw-template-bind 1 import-rt "target:65535:300"
        pw-template-bind 2 import-rt "target:65535:349"
        no shutdown
    exit
    split-horizon-group "mesh" create
    exit
    stp
      shutdown
    exit
    no shutdown
  exit
```

FIGURE 7.40

PERs configuration.

```
PERs-4# show service id 300 base
===============================================================================
Service Basic Information
===============================================================================
Service Id          : 300            Vpn Id              : 0
Service Type        : VPLS
Customer Id         : 1
Last Status Change: 01/18/2008 09:15:59
Last Mgmt Change   : 01/18/2008 09:19:01
Admin State         : Up             Oper State          : Up
MTU                 : 1478           Def. Mesh VC Id     : 300
SAP Count           : 0              SDP Bind Count      : 2
Snd Flush on Fail   : Disabled       Host Conn Verify    : Disabled
Def. Gateway IP     : None
Def. Gateway MAC    : None


-------------------------------------------------------------------------------
BGP Auto-discovery Information
-------------------------------------------------------------------------------
Admin State         : Up             Vpls Id             : 65535:300
Route Dist          : 65535:300      Prefix              : 1.1.1.4
Rte-Target Import   : None           Rte-Target Export   : None
L2-Auto-Bind Plcy   : 1              L2-Auto-Bind SHG    : None
Vsi-Import          : h-vpls300-imp
Vsi-Export          : h-vpls300-exp
-------------------------------------------------------------------------------
Service Access & Destination Points
-------------------------------------------------------------------------------
Identifier                          Type       AdmMTU  OprMTU  Adm  Opr
-------------------------------------------------------------------------------
sdp:17405:4294967294 SB(1.1.1.6)    BgpAd      0       1556    Up   Up
sdp:17406:4294967294 SB(1.1.1.133)  BgpAd      0       1492    Up   Up
===============================================================================


PERs-4# show service sdp-using
===============================================================================
SDP Using
===============================================================================
SvcId    SdpId            Type    Far End       Opr S* I.Label  E.Label
-------------------------------------------------------------------------------
300      17405:4294967294 BgpAd   1.1.1.6       Up     131058   131062
300      17406:4294967294 BgpAd   1.1.1.133     Up     131059   131062
-------------------------------------------------------------------------------
Number of SDPs : 2
-------------------------------------------------------------------------------
===============================================================================
* indicates that the corresponding row element may have been truncated.
```

FIGURE 7.41

Checking the service.

```
PERs-4# show router ldp bindings service-id 300
==================================================================
LDP LSR ID: 1.1.1.4
==================================================================
Legend: U - Label In Use, N - Label Not In Use, W - Label Withdrawn
        S - Status Signaled Up,  D - Status Signaled Down
        E - Epipe Service, V - VPLS Service, M - Mirror Service
        A - Apipe Service, F - Fpipe Service, I - IES Service, R - VPRN service
        P - Ipipe Service, C - Cpipe Service
        TLV - (Type, Length: Value)
==================================================================
LDP Service FEC128 Bindings
==================================================================
Type    VCId      SvcId     SDPId  Peer            IngLbl  EgrLbl  LMTU  RMTU
------------------------------------------------------------------
No Matching Entries Found
==================================================================


==================================================================
LDP Service FEC129 Bindings
==================================================================
AGI                         SAII              TAII
Type    SvcId     SDPId  Peer            IngLbl  EgrLbl  LMTU  RMTU
------------------------------------------------------------------
65535:300                   1.1.1.4           1.1.1.6
V-Eth   300       17405  1.1.1.6         131058U 131062S 1464  1464

65535:300                   1.1.1.4           1.1.1.133
V-Eth   300       17406  1.1.1.133       131059U 131062S 1464  1464


------------------------------------------------------------------
No. of FEC129s: 2
==================================================================
```

FIGURE 7.42

Checking the LDP bindings.

Slightly different from the previous cases, the L2VPN routes advertised from PERs4 will be explored, such as RIB OUT from IP address 1.1.1.4/32. PERs4 sends L2VPN AD routes to each route reflector server. Each of those route reflectors will propagate that information to all of their I-BGP clients. For each of the receiving clients I-BGP peers will determine whether or not to accept the L2VPN route based on match VPLS-id and a corresponding import route target. To determine the L2VPN routes received by PERs4 from other peers (RIB IN), use the specific remote peers /32 prefix. PERs4 imports and exports two route targets: 65535:348, which corresponds to MTUs1, and 65535:300, which corresponds to the full mesh to which PERs6 belongs. However, since BGP is based on reflecting information to all peers equally, all BGP peers would receive these advertisements—in this case, one from each route reflector. However, only those specifically configured with the VPLS-id and matching import route-target would install the routes and trigger complementary action like T-LDP sessions and service label exchanges.

```
PERs-4# show router bgp routes l2-vpn 1.1.1.4/32 hunt
===============================================================================
 BGP Router ID : 1.1.1.4          AS : 65535    Local AS : 65535
===============================================================================
 Legend -
 Status codes  : u - used, s - suppressed, h - history, d - decayed, * - valid
 Origin codes  : i - IGP, e - EGP, ? - incomplete, > - best


===============================================================================
BGP L2VPN-AD Routes
===============================================================================
-------------------------------------------------------------------------------
RIB Out Entries
-------------------------------------------------------------------------------
Network        : 1.1.1.4/32
Nexthop        : 1.1.1.4
Route Dist.    : 65535:300
To             : 1.1.1.10
Res. Nexthop   : n/a
Local Pref.    : 100                Interface Name : NotAvailable
Aggregator AS  : None               Aggregator     : None
Atomic Aggr.   : Not Atomic         MED            : 0
Community      : target:65535:300  target:65535:348  l2-vpn:65535:300
Cluster        : No Cluster Members
Originator Id  : None               Peer Router Id : 1.1.1.10
Origin         : IGP
AS-Path        : No As-Path

Network        : 1.1.1.4/32
Nexthop        : 1.1.1.4
Route Dist.    : 65535:300
To             : 1.1.1.5
Res. Nexthop   : n/a
Local Pref.    : 100                Interface Name : NotAvailable
Aggregator AS  : None               Aggregator     : None
Atomic Aggr.   : Not Atomic         MED            : 0
Community      : target:65535:300  target:65535:348  l2-vpn:65535:300
Cluster        : No Cluster Members
Originator Id  : None               Peer Router Id : 1.1.1.5
Origin         : IGP
AS-Path        : No As-Path


-------------------------------------------------------------------------------
RIB In Entries
-------------------------------------------------------------------------------
```

FIGURE 7.43

Checking the BGP routes.

7.2.3.4 Hub-and Spoke-VPLS Configurations

Carriers can also take advantage of hub-and-spoke models that may allow them to best utilize their network resources. These types of solutions appear to the customer as full-mesh solutions. In this backhaul case, the carrier can select different PE nodes to switch traffic rather than building any to any direct logical connections. For example, all CPE connections to the same PE can communicate directly. However, the different PEs would communicate through a central hub PE, rather than building a logical full mesh. This would emulate an H-VPLS model. As per Figure 7.44, MTUs1 and MTUs2 are logically connected to PERs4 via PWs (Spoke SDPs), even though MTUs2 is physically connected to PERs6. Therefore, both MTUs would learn about other sites (MAC addresses) only via PERs4. This would also include any sites that may be connected via PERs6. Similarly, traffic forwarding will also be via PERs4 only.

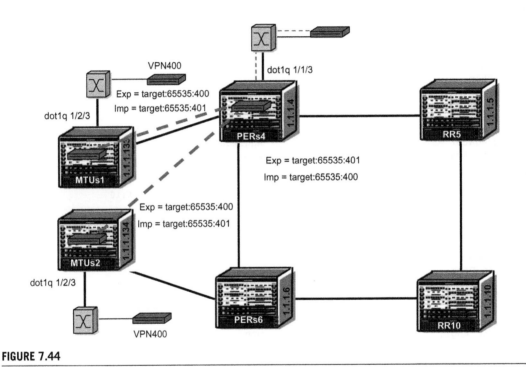

FIGURE 7.44

The configurations are presented here.

```
MTUs1
pw-template 2 create
exit
vpls 400 customer 1 create
    service-mtu 1478
    bgp-ad
        vpls-id 65535:400
```

FIGURE 7.45

MTU Configuration.

```
        route-target export target:65535:400 import target:65535:401
        pw-template-bind 2
        no shutdown
    exit
    stp
      shutdown
    exit
    sap 1/2/3:400 create
    exit
    no shutdown
  exit
```

FIGURE 7.45

(*Continued*)

```
MTUs2
pw-template 2 create
exit
vpls 400 customer 1 create
    service-mtu 1478
    bgp-ad
        vpls-id 65535:400
        route-target export target:65535:400 import target:65535:401
        pw-template-bind 2
        no shutdown
    exit
    stp
      shutdown
    exit
    sap 1/2/3:400 create
    exit
    no shutdown
exit

PERs4
pw-template 2 create
exit
vpls 400 customer 1 create
    service-mtu 1478
    bgp-ad
        vpls-id 65535:400
        route-target export target:65535:401 import target:65535:400
        pw-template-bind 2
        no shutdown
    exit
    stp
      shutdown
    exit
    sap 1/1/3:400 create
    exit
    no shutdown
exit
```

FIGURE 7.46

MTU Configuration.

There are many different models that can be constructed with router targets and router policy. BGP AD does not hamper the ability to build these topologies. There are discovered connections between PERs4 and the two MTU nodes. The MTU nodes do not connect directly because each only imports the route target exported by the hub, that is, "65535:401." The various operational commands are given next.

```
PERs-4# show service id 400 base
===============================================================================
Service Basic Information
===============================================================================
Service Id         : 400           Vpn Id            : 0
Service Type       : VPLS
Customer Id        : 1
Last Status Change: 01/23/2008 13:43:30
Last Mgmt Change  : 01/23/2008 14:16:22
Admin State        : Up            Oper State        : Up
MTU                : 1478          Def. Mesh VC Id   : 400
SAP Count          : 2            SDP Bind Count    : 2
Snd Flush on Fail : Disabled       Host Conn Verify  : Disabled
Def. Gateway IP    : None
Def. Gateway MAC   : None


-------------------------------------------------------------------------------
BGP Auto-discovery Information
-------------------------------------------------------------------------------
Admin State        : Up            Vpls Id           : 65535:400
Route Dist         : 65535:400     Prefix            : 1.1.1.4
Rte-Target Import : 65535:400      Rte-Target Export : 65535:401
L2-Auto-Bind Plcy : 2             L2-Auto-Bind SHG  : None
Vsi-Import         : None
Vsi-Export         : None


-------------------------------------------------------------------------------
Service Access & Destination Points
-------------------------------------------------------------------------------
Identifier                        Type   AdmMTU OprMTU Adm  Opr
-------------------------------------------------------------------------------
sap:1/1/3:400                     q-tag   1518   1518   Up   Up
sdp:17406:4294967295 SB(1.1.1.133) BgpAd   0     1492   Up   Up
sdp:17407:4294967295 SB(1.1.1.134) BgpAd   0     1556   Up   Up
-------------------------------------------------------------------------------
[<sap-id>] indicates a Managed SAP
===============================================================================
```

FIGURE 7.47

Checking the service ID.

```
PERs-4# show service sdp-using
================================================================================
SDP Using
================================================================================
SvcId       SdpId              Type    Far End       Opr S* I.Label  E.Label
--------------------------------------------------------------------------------
400         17406:4294967295   BgpAd   1.1.1.133     Up     131065   131065
400         17407:4294967295   BgpAd   1.1.1.134     Up     131063   131070
--------------------------------------------------------------------------------
Number of SDPs : 2
--------------------------------------------------------------------------------
================================================================================
* indicates that the corresponding row element may have been truncated.
```

FIGURE 7.48

Checking the SDP.

```
PERs-4# show router ldp bindings service-id 400
================================================================================
LDP LSR ID: 1.1.1.4
================================================================================
Legend: U - Label In Use, N - Label Not In Use, W - Label Withdrawn
        S - Status Signaled Up,  D - Status Signaled Down
        E - Epipe Service, V - VPLS Service, M - Mirror Service
        A - Apipe Service, F - Fpipe Service, I - IES Service, R - VPRN service
        P - Ipipe Service, C - Cpipe Service
        TLV - (Type, Length: Value)
================================================================================
LDP Service FEC128 Bindings
================================================================================
Type   VCId        SvcId      SDPId  Peer          IngLbl  EgrLbl  LMTU  RMTU
--------------------------------------------------------------------------------
No Matching Entries Found
================================================================================


================================================================================
LDP Service FEC129 Bindings
================================================================================
AGI                            SAII              TAII
Type               SvcId   SDPId  Peer           IngLbl  EgrLbl  LMTU  RMTU
--------------------------------------------------------------------------------
65535:400                          1.1.1.4                  1.1.1.133
V-Eth              400     17406   1.1.1.133      131065U 131065S 1464  1464

65535:400                          1.1.1.4                  1.1.1.134
V-Eth              400     17407   1.1.1.134      131063U 131070S 1464  1464

--------------------------------------------------------------------------------
No. of FEC129s: 2
================================================================================
```

FIGURE 7.49

Checking the LDP bindings.

```
PERs-4# show router bgp routes l2-vpn 1.1.1.4/32 hunt
===============================================================================
 BGP Router ID : 1.1.1.4           AS : 65535   Local AS : 65535
===============================================================================
 Legend -
 Status codes  : u - used, s - suppressed, h - history, d - decayed, * - valid
 Origin codes  : i - IGP, e - EGP, ? - incomplete, > - best


===============================================================================
BGP L2VPN-AD Routes
===============================================================================
-------------------------------------------------------------------------------
RIB In Entries
-------------------------------------------------------------------------------


-------------------------------------------------------------------------------
RIB Out Entries
-------------------------------------------------------------------------------
Network         : 1.1.1.4/32
Nexthop         : 1.1.1.4
Route Dist.     : 65535:400
To              : 1.1.1.5
Res. Nexthop    : n/a
Local Pref.     : 100              Interface Name : NotAvailable
Aggregator AS   : None             Aggregator     : None
Atomic Aggr.    : Not Atomic       MED            : 0
Community       : target:65535:401   l2-vpn:65535:400
Cluster         : No Cluster Members
Originator Id   : None             Peer Router Id : 1.1.1.5
Origin          : IGP
AS-Path         : No As-Path

Network         : 1.1.1.4/32
Nexthop         : 1.1.1.4
Route Dist.     : 65535:400
To              : 1.1.1.10
Res. Nexthop    : n/a
Local Pref.     : 100              Interface Name : NotAvailable
Aggregator AS   : None             Aggregator     : None
Atomic Aggr.    : Not Atomic       MED            : 0
Community       : target:65535:401   l2-vpn:65535:400
Cluster         : No Cluster Members
Originator Id   : None             Peer Router Id : 1.1.1.10
Origin          : IGP
AS-Path         : No As-Path


-------------------------------------------------------------------------------
Routes : 2
===============================================================================
```

FIGURE 7.50

Checking the L2VPN routes.

To determine the L2VPN routes received by PERs4 from other peers (RIB IN), use the specific remote peers /32 prefix. PERs4, the hub, imports the route target 65535:400, which is being exported by all of the spokes. Next we can see which L2VPN routes were received from MTUs1.

```
*A:PERs-4# show router bgp routes l2-vpn 1.1.1.133/32 hunt
===============================================================================
 BGP Router ID : 1.1.1.4            AS : 65535    Local AS : 65535
===============================================================================
 Legend -
 Status codes  : u - used, s - suppressed, h - history, d - decayed, * - valid
 Origin codes  : i - IGP, e - EGP, ? - incomplete, > - best


===============================================================================
BGP L2VPN-AD Routes
===============================================================================
-------------------------------------------------------------------------------
RIB In Entries
-------------------------------------------------------------------------------
Network        : 1.1.1.133/32
Nexthop        : 1.1.1.133
Route Dist.    : 65535:400
From           : 1.1.1.10
Res. Nexthop   : 0.0.0.0
Local Pref.    : 100                Interface Name : NotAvailable
Aggregator AS  : None               Aggregator     : None
Atomic Aggr.   : Not Atomic         MED            : 0
Community      : target:65535:400   l2-vpn:65535:400
Cluster        : 1.1.1.5
Originator Id  : 1.1.1.133          Peer Router Id : 1.1.1.10
Flags          : Used  Valid  Best  IGP
AS-Path        : No As-Path

Network        : 1.1.1.133/32
Nexthop        : 1.1.1.133
Route Dist.    : 65535:400
From           : 1.1.1.5
Res. Nexthop   : 0.0.0.0
Local Pref.    : 100                Interface Name : NotAvailable
Aggregator AS  : None               Aggregator     : None
Atomic Aggr.   : Not Atomic         MED            : 0
Community      : target:65535:400   l2-vpn:65535:400
Cluster        : 1.1.1.5
Originator Id  : 1.1.1.133          Peer Router Id : 1.1.1.5
Flags          : Valid  IGP
AS-Path        : No As-Path


-------------------------------------------------------------------------------
RIB Out Entries
-------------------------------------------------------------------------------
-------------------------------------------------------------------------------
Routes : 2
===============================================================================
```

FIGURE 7.51

Checking the BGP routes.

7.2.4 H-VPLS—Point to Remember

H-VPLS is an attempt to scale the control plane by reducing the number of LDP-based PWs that need to be created in the network. However, this could potentially create scaling problems on the PE devices (i.e., if the PE devices are acting as Hub sites). For example, even if the PE router does not host any VPLS sites for a given instance, it has to now maintain state information and MAC tables for the customer to offload burden from the MTU devices. Therefore, a solution to address a control plane scaling issue can now potentially affect the data plane scalability. In certain topologies, even MPLS Provider routers would need to act as Hub sites. This is true when the MTU devices act only as Layer 2 switches and the PE routers host VPLS instances. Figure 7.52 helps us to understand this further.

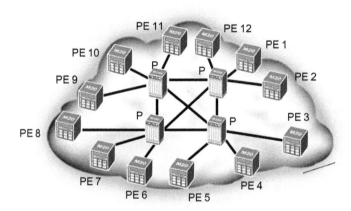

- The 12x12 mesh of PEs has become a 4x4 mesh of Ps
- However, each P router needs to learn 3 times as many MACs, and also has to be VPLS-aware, and do traffic replication for flooding and broadcast
  - This is especially bad as P routers should have no VPN state!

FIGURE 7.52

7.2.5 LDP-BGP VPLS Interworking

Currently, both LDP VPLS and BGP VPLS are widely deployed in service provider networks. Two key business drivers for LDP-BGP VPLS interworking are the need to scale and the need to extend the VPLS networks.

7.2.5.1 Scaling the VPLS Network

As the VPLS network expands, the LDP-VPLS control plane imposes certain scalability concerns as discussed earlier. In comparison, the BGP-VPLS control plane easily enables the VPLS network to scale to support new VPLS customers and to include more sites for existing VPLS customers. One option for scaling the VPLS network, when there is an existing LDP-VPLS deployment, is to abandon the LDP-VPLS control plane entirely and transition the VPLS network to the BGP-VPLS control plane. However, this approach may not be feasible for a number of reasons, including the following two constraints:

- Legacy PE routers may not support a BGP signaling mechanism. To protect the current investment, replacing the existing PE routers may not be a viable option.
- Operating overhead and possible disruption to the VPLS network for existing customers may undermine a transition from the LDP-VPLS control plane to BGP VPLS.

Another option for scaling VPLS when there is an existing LDP-VPLS deployment is to cap the existing LDP-VPLS deployment and to expand the VPLS network using the BGP control plane. With this approach, both LDP- and BGP-VPLS control planes, including the signaling mechanisms, must co-exist in the network, and there must be interworking between the two control plane mechanisms.

To be able to offer a regional or national VPLS network, service providers are seeking scalable ways to extend the reach of VPLS beyond a single LDP-VPLS metro domain. One mechanism is the use of BGP VPLS in the WAN to interconnect multiple LDP-VPLS metro domains. This approach requires a new inter-domain technique, because the currently defined solutions for multiple ASs require that all domains run the same signaling protocol. One of the critical requirements for such a deployment model is ensuring that the existing PE routers in the metro domains that are running the LDP-VPLS control plane do not require any changes or upgrades. A second requirement is the extension of VPLS without significant additional load on the control plane of the LDP-VPLS PE routers in the metro network. This solution meets the previous requirements and enables service providers to use a single protocol, BGP, in the WAN to offer multiple MPLS VPN services, including VPLS and Layer 2 and Layer 3 VPNs. Moreover, because only a single protocol is used, provisioning the system can provide operating efficiency.

With basic LDP-BGP VPLS interworking, newly added PE routers in the network support both the LDP and BGP control planes, including the corresponding signaling mechanisms required. These newly added PE routers use the BGP-VPLS control plane when communicating with each other, and use the LDP-VPLS control plane to communicate with the existing PE routers running LDP VPLS.

This deployment model facilitates expansion of existing VPLS customer sites, enabling a service provider to add new sites to BGP-VPLS PE routers while keeping the existing sites unchanged on the LDP-VPLS PE routers. A key feature of this interworking mechanism is that no changes are made to the currently defined LDP-VPLS control plane (RFC 4762; see Lasserre and Kompella, 2007). The LDP-VPLS "only" routers continue to communicate using the LDP-VPLS control plane. From their perspective, the newly added BGP-VPLS PE routers are simply LDP-VPLS PE routers. The BGP-VPLS routers, on the other hand, use both the BGP-VPLS and LDP-VPLS control planes. They use the BGP-VPLS control plane between them for autodiscovery and for signaling, establishing an internal BGP (IBGP) session between themselves or via a Route Reflector. They also use LDP-VPLS signaling to communicate with the LDP-VPLS "only" routers, establishing LDP sessions with the existing PE routers. For all VPLS customers that have sites only on either the existing LDP-VPLS PE routers or the newly added BGP-VPLS PE routers, VPLS is set up using only a single control plane and a single signaling protocol.

The LDP-BGP VPLS model employs two groups of PE routers. All PE routers in the first group run only the LDP-VPLS control plane among themselves, whereas all PE routers in the second group run only the BGP-VPLS control plane among themselves. These two groups are interconnected through a single PE router, referred to as the interworking PE router, which runs both LDP-VPLS and BGP-VPLS control planes. Figure 7.53 shows how the LDP-VPLS network is expanded using the BGP control plane in a scalable model.

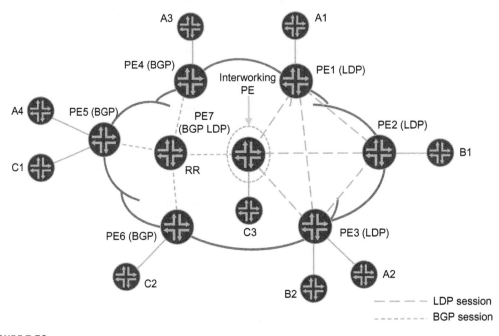

FIGURE 7.53

In Figure 7.53, the PE1, PE2, and PE3 routers are existing PE routers supporting only the LDP-VPLS control plane. The newly added PE routers (PE4, PE5, and PE6) support the BGP control plane. The PE7 router is the interworking PE router, supporting both LDP and BGP control planes and the interworking between these two distinct control planes. The existing LDP-VPLS PE routers and the newly added BGP-VPLS PE routers are isolated into two groups. The PE7 router is part of both groups and plays the vital role of interconnecting them. For example, VPLS Customer A has multiple sites in both the LDP- and BGP-VPLS groups. Customer A's Sites A1 and A2 are connected to the LDP PE routers, and Sites A3 and A4 are connected to the BGP PE routers. The PE7 router provides the LDP-BGP VPLS interworking function and stitches the PWs created by the signaling components of the two different control planes. PE routers in the BGP-VPLS group are provisioned only for the BGP-VPLS control plane. From their perspective, the interworking PE router (PE7) is a standard BGP-VPLS peer, and they are unaware of the existence of the PE routers that are part of the LDP-VPLS group behind the interworking PE router. Legacy PE routers in the LDP-VPLS group are provisioned only for the LDP-VPLS control plane. From their perspective, the interworking PE router (PE7) is a standard LDP-VPLS peer, and they are unaware of the existence of the PE routers that are part of the BGP-VPLS group behind router PE7.

Containing all of the existing LDP-VPLS PE routers in a single group caps the LDP-VPLS deployment and allows network expansion to occur in the BGP-VPLS group without creating additional control plane or data plane overhead on existing LDP-VPLS PE routers. Moreover, this method eliminates a fundamental problem with the previous method—the requirement that all BGP-VPLS PE routers also operate in the LDP-VPLS control plane. In some network designs, containing all of the LDP-VPLS PE routers in a single group may not be feasible because of geographical limitations or other administrative reasons. In such environments, multiple groups of PE routers can run the LDP-VPLS control plane and a single group of PE routers can run the BGP-VPLS control plane, which interconnects all the LDP-VPLS control plane groups through multiple interworking PE routers.

Interconnecting multiple metro networks using BGP VPLS is the most efficient and scalable way to extend VPLS beyond the metro network. Figure 7.54 shows how basic inter-domain LDP-BGP VPLS interworking techniques can be expanded to interconnect multiple LDP-VPLS domains using the BGP-VPLS control plane in the WAN. The existing PE routers in domains Metro X and Metro Y are not aware that the border routers C-ASBR1 and C-ASBR2 are extending their domain reach using the BGP-VPLS control plane in the WAN.

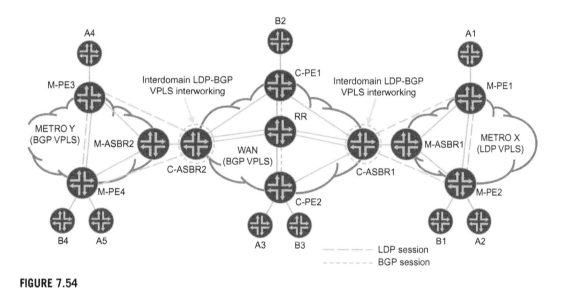

FIGURE 7.54

The basic LDP-BGP VPLS interworking method (single domain consisting of both LDP and BGP VPLS PEs) requires minimal configuration changes on the existing LDP-VPLS PE routers. However, new PE routers added as part of the network expansion must support both LDP VPLS and BGP VPLS. The support on the new PE routers is the essence of what is needed for basic LDP-BGP VPLS interworking to succeed. Because the new PE routers support both LDP VPLS and BGP VPLS, they can establish PWs using both the LDP and BGP signaling mechanisms. These PWs can be created for VPLS customers with sites attached to both existing LDP-VPLS routers and the newly added BGP-VPLS routers. A full mesh of PWs is created between the existing LDP-VPLS PE routers and the newly added BGP-VPLS PE router. As a result, data plane operations on all PE routers adhere to the split-horizon forwarding rule, and the VPLS traffic is not switched between PWs. Additionally, no changes are required to the existing LDP or BGP control plane procedures.

Scalable LDP-BGP VPLS interworking entails dividing all PE routers from a VPLS network into two groups so that one group contains all of the LDP-VPLS PE routers and the other group contains all the BGP-VPLS PE routers. One PE router, referred to as the interworking PE router, is part of both groups. All other PE routers can be part of only one group. This method requires that only the interworking PE router supports and operates both the LDP- and BGP-VPLS control planes. All other PE routers support and operate either the LDP-VPLS or the BGP-VPLS control plane, depending on the group to which they belong.

7.2.5.2 Case Study—Connecting LDP and BGP VPLS Metro Domains

Next is a sample case study where two metro domains, one using LD-VPLS and the other BGP-VPLS, are interconnected via a BGP-VPLS Interworking PE. The configuration used to illustrate the various concepts discussed earlier is based on JUNOS (see Figure 7.55).

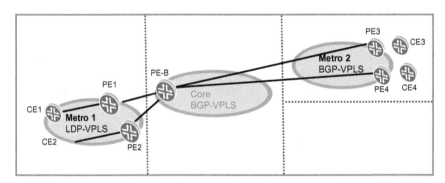

FIGURE 7.55

We will start with the CE router configuration shown in Figure 7.56. The only configuration needed here is the interface and IP Subnet details.

```
interfaces {
    ge-1/2/1 {
      unit 0 {
        family inet {
        address 10.12.31.1/24;
       }
      }
     }
   }
```

FIGURE 7.56

Router CE3 configuration.

On Router PE3, we configure the router for VPLS by configuring BGP, MPLS, OSPF, and LDP. (These protocols are the basis for most Layer 2 VPN-related applications, including VPLS.) This configuration includes the signaling statement at the [edit protocols bgp group *group-name* family l2vpn] hierarchy level.

The command "encapsulation VPLS" is used on Ethernet CE-Facing interfaces that have VPLS enabled, and it is supposed to accept packets carrying standard Tag Protocol ID (TPID) values. If the interface needs to accept VLAN (Tagged) packets, then encapsulation "vlan-vpls" is used. The family "vpls" statement enables the interface with the VPLS address family. The statement "family l2vpn signaling" enables BGP signaling for VPLS. All services (L2VPN, L3VPN, VPLS, etc.) are configured under the routing-instances hierarchy. In this case, a VPLS instance named "ABCCORP" is configured along with the RD and VRF Targets, respectively. Remember, BGP-VPLS relies on route-targets for discovery and the association of a remote PE to an instance. Once again, the same procedure is used as in BGP/MPLS VPNs. The "site-range" defines the number of sites that can exist in a VPLS instance. The site-name is a generic name and can be used to identify the site. The site-id configured on each PE needs to be unique per VPLS domain. Each site within a given PE participating in the same VPLS instance needs to have a unique site ID as well. The "site-range" specifies the maximum number of sites for the VPLS instance (see Figure 7.57).

```
[edit]
interfaces {
     so-0/2/1 {
      unit 0 {
        family inet {
        address 10.12.100.10/30;
      }
        family mpls;
     }
     so-0/2/2 {
        unit 0 {
          family inet {
            address 10.12.100.21/30;
      }
        family mpls;
       }
     }
     ge-1/3/1 { ----------> CE Facing interface
     encapsulation ethernet-vpls; ->
     unit 0 {
       family vpls;
        }
       }
      }
    }
  protocols {
       mpls {
        interface all;
       }
```

FIGURE 7.57

Router PE3 configuration.

```
            bgp {
             log-updown;
              group int {
              type internal;
              local-address 10.255.170.96;
              family l2vpn {
              signaling;
            }
             neighbor 10.255.170.98;
             neighbor 10.255.170.102;
            }
            }
            ospf {
             area 0.0.0.0 {
             interface so-0/2/1.0;
             interface so-0/2/2.0;
             interface lo0.0 {
             passive;
             }
            }
            }
            ldp {
             interface so-0/2/1.0;
             interface so-0/2/2.0;
             }
            }
        }
        routing-instances {
            ABCCORP {
             instance-type vpls;
             interface ge-1/3/1.0;
             route-distinguisher 10.255.170.96:1;
             vrf-target target:1:2;
             protocols {
              vpls {
                site-range 10;
                site 1 {
                 site-identifier 3;
              }
             }
            }
            }

            ge-1/2/1 {
              unit 0 {
                family inet {
                address 10.12.31.1/24;
              }
             }
            }
```

FIGURE 7.57

(Continued)

Router PE4 would have an identical configuration similar to PE3, with its respective "site-id," "RD," and "RT," so it is not illustrated again.

Now we move to the important portion, the Interconnect PE router, which connects the BGP and LDP VPLS domains. There are two portions of the configurations, both defined under the VPLS instance "ABCCORP." The first portion is the participation of the PE-B with the BGP VPLS domain. The second portion is the participation within the LDP domain. The command "vpls-id" is used to identify the virtual circuit identifier used for the VPLS routing instance. This statement is a part of the configuration that enables LDP signaling for VPLS. The VPLS-ID needs to be the same for all PE routers for the same VPLS instance; therefore, it needs to be globally unique.

We have seen that a single VPLS routing instance can encompass one set of PE routers that uses BGP for signaling and another set of PE routers that uses LDP for signaling. Within each set, all of the PE routers are fully meshed in both the control and data planes and have a bi-directional PW to each of the other routers in the set. However, the BGP-signaled routers cannot be directly connected to the LDP-signaled routers, so this is where the Interconnect/Border PE router is used.

In the control plane, each fully meshed set of PE routers in a VPLS routing instance is called a PE router mesh group. The border PE router must be reachable by and have bi-directional PWs to all of the PE routers that are a part of the VPLS routing instance—both the LDP- and BGP-signaled routers. To configure LDP BGP interworking for VPLS, include the mesh-group statement in the VPLS routing instance configuration of the PE border router. This is illustrated in Figure 7.58. The "neighbor" statement identifies each LDP-VPLS PE statically and builds PWs to each of them.

You can configure multiple mesh-groups to map each fully meshed LDP- or BGP-signaled VPLS domain to a mesh group. In the data plane, the border router maintains a common MAC table used to forward traffic between the LDP- and BGP-signaled mesh groups. When forwarding any VPLS traffic received over a PE router's PW, the border router assures that traffic is not forwarded back to the PE routers in the same mesh group as the originating PE router; for instance, if there are two LDP-Meshed groups configured, where each Mesh group has its own set of PE routers that are fully meshed with each other and the Interconnect PE router at the control plane. So if a CE connected to an LDP-VPLS Mesh-Group1 sends a frame whose destination MAC address is on LDP-VPLS Mesh-group2, the Ingress PE router will receive the frame and perform a MAC address lookup. The MAC address will not be in its MAC table, so it will flood the frame to the other PEs in the LDP-VPLS Mesh-Group1, which from its perspective, are the only members of the VPLS network. When the Interconnect PE receives the data, it will not find the MAC address in its MAC table, so it will flood the frame to all of the BGP-VPLS PE routers and LD-VPLS PE routers in Mesh-Group2, but not back to Mesh-Group1. The PE routers will then perform a MAC-table lookup and will flood the data to their CE routers.

```
[edit]

interfaces {
    fe-0/0/3 {
      unit 0 {
        family inet {
        address 10.12.100.13/30;
```

FIGURE 7.58

Router PEB configuration.

```
                              }
                                family mpls;
                              }
                            }
                            t1-0/1/2 {
                             unit 0 {
                               family inet {
                               address 10.12.100.1/30;
                             }
                               family mpls;
                             }
                            }
                            t1-0/1/3 {
                             unit 0 {
                               family inet {
                                 address 10.12.100.5/30;
                             }
                               family mpls;
                             }
                            }
                            so-0/2/2 {
                             unit 0 {
                               family inet {
                                 address 10.12.100.9/30;
                             }
                                family mpls;
                             }
                             }
                        }
                        protocols {
                              mpls {
                                interface all;
                              }
                              bgp {
                               log-updown;
                               group int {
                                type internal;
                                local-address 10.255.170.98;
                                family l2vpn {
                                  signaling;
                               }
                                 neighbor 10.255.170.96;
                                 neighbor 10.255.170.102;
                               }
                              }
                              ospf {
                                area 0.0.0.0 {
                                  interface t1-0/1/2.0;
                                  interface t1-0/1/3.0;
                                  interface so-0/2/2.0;
                                  interface fe-0/0/3.0;
```

FIGURE 7.58

(Continued)

```
                              interface lo0.0 {
                                passive;
                              }
                            }
                          }
                          ldp {
                           interface fe-0/0/3.0;
                           interface t1-0/1/2.0;
                           interface t1-0/1/3.0;
                           interface so-0/2/2.0;
                           interface lo0.0;
                          }
                        }
                        routing-instances {
                            ABCCORP {
                            instance-type vpls;
                             route-distinguisher 10.255.170.98:1;
                             vrf-target target:1:2;
                             protocols {
                              vpls {
                              site-range 10;
                               site 1 {
                                site-identifier 1;
                            }
                               vpls-id 101;
                                 mesh-group ldp-1 {
                                  neighbor 10.255.170.106;
                                  neighbor 10.255.170.104;
                               }
                              }
                             }
```

FIGURE 7.58

(*Continued*)

Next we move on to the configuration of the LDP PE router, PE1. This configuration (Figure 7.59) does not include any BGP specific statements or any mesh-group definitions. Only the "vpls-id" and "neighbor" statements are used. Router PEB is also configured to participate in the LDP-VPLS instance. PE2 would have an identical configuration to PE1, so it is not illustrated.

```
                      [edit]
                        interfaces {
                            fe-0/0/3 {
                             encapsulation ethernet-vpls;
                             unit 0 {
                             family vpls;
                            }
                           }
```

FIGURE 7.59

Router PE1 configuration.

```
        t1-0/1/0 {
          unit 0 {
            family inet {
            address 10.12.100.2/30;
          }
            family mpls;
          }
        }
        t1-1/1/1 {
          unit 0 {
            family inet {
            address 10.12.100.17/30;
          }
            family mpls;
          }
        }
      }
    protocols {
        mpls {
         interface all;
        }
        ospf {
         area 0.0.0.0 {
          interface t1-0/1/0.0;
          interface t1-1/1/1.0;
          interface lo0.0 {
          passive;
          }
         }
        }
        ldp {
          interface t1-0/1/0.0;
          interface t1-1/1/1.0;
          interface lo0.0;
        }
    }
    routing-instances {
        ABCCORP {
        instance-type vpls;
        interface fe-0/0/3.0;
          protocols {
            vpls {
              vpls-id 101;
              neighbor 10.255.170.98;
              neighbor 10.255.170.104;
          }
         }
        }
      }
```

FIGURE 7.59

(*Continued*)

Figure 7.60 can be used to validate and verify the BGP and LDP interworking state on PEB.

```
user@B>show vpls connections
Layer-2 VPN connections:

Legend for connection status (St)
EI -- encapsulation invalid       NC -- interface encapsulation not CCC/TCC/VPLS
EM -- encapsulation mismatch      WE -- interface and instance encaps not same
VC-Dn -- Virtual circuit down     NP -- interface hardware not present
CM -- control-word mismatch       -> -- only outbound connection is up
CN -- circuit not provisioned     <- -- only inbound connection is up
OR -- out of range                Up -- operational
OL -- no outgoing label           Dn -- down
LD -- local site signaled down    CF -- call admission control failure
RD -- remote site signaled down   SC -- local and remote site ID collision LN --
local site not designated  LM -- local site ID not minimum designated RN --
remote site not designated RM -- remote site ID not minimum designated XX --
unknown connection status  IL -- no incoming label
MM -- MTU mismatch                MI -- Mesh-Group ID not availble

Legend for interface status
Up -- operational
Dn -- down

Instance: v1
BGP-VPLS State
  Local site: 1 (1)
    connection-site         Type  St     Time last up        # Up trans
    3                       rmt   Up     Jan 21 16:38:47 2011          1
      Local interface: vt-0/3/0.1048834, Status: Up, Encapsulation: VPLS
        Description: Intf - vpls v1 local site 1 remote site 3
      Remote PE: 10.255.170.96, Negotiated control-word: No
      Incoming label: 800258, Outgoing label: 800000
    4                       rmt   Up     Jan 21 16:38:54 2011          1
      Local interface: vt-0/3/0.1048835, Status: Up, Encapsulation: VPLS
        Description: Intf - vpls v1 local site 1 remote site 4
      Remote PE: 10.255.170.102, Negotiated control-word: No
      Incoming label: 800259, Outgoing label: 800000
LDP-VPLS State
VPLS-id: 101
  Mesh-group connections: m1
    Neighbor                Type  St     Time last up        # Up trans
    10.255.170.104(vpls-id 101) rmt Up   Jan 21 16:38:40 2011          1
      Local interface: vt-0/3/0.1048833, Status: Up, Encapsulation: ETHERNET
        Description: Intf - vpls v1 neighbor 10.255.170.104 vpls-id 101
      Remote PE: 10.255.170.104, Negotiated control-word: No
      Incoming label: 800001, Outgoing label: 800000
    10.255.170.106(vpls-id 101) rmt Up   Jan 21 16:38:39 2011          1
      Local interface: vt-0/3/0.1048832, Status: Up, Encapsulation: ETHERNET
        Description: Intf - vpls v1 neighbor 10.255.170.106 vpls-id 101
      Remote PE: 10.255.170.106, Negotiated control-word: No
      Incoming label: 800000, Outgoing label: 800000
```

FIGURE 7.60

Verifying the BGP and LDP interworking.

7.2.6 Multicast Traffic in VPLS

In each VPLS routing instance, a dedicated point-to-multipoint (P2MP) LSP can be configured to carry all unknown unicast, broadcast, and multicast traffic. Enabling this feature increases the efficiency of the network, because duplicate copies of flooded traffic do not have to be created for each PE router in the VPLS routing instance. Figure 7.61 shows how flooded traffic reaches PE routers in a VPLS routing instance when a P2MP LSP is not configured for flooding. In this figure, PE1 needs to forward 100 Mbps of Multicast traffic. Since there are three recipient PE routers (PE2, PE3, and PE4), PE1 creates three copies of traffic, which are now 300 Mbps in bandwidth. Further P1 sends 200 Mbps of traffic toward P2, since PE2 and PE3 are behind P2, and sends one copy (100 Mbps) toward PE4. Finally, P2 sends the actual traffic (a copy each) to the receivers.

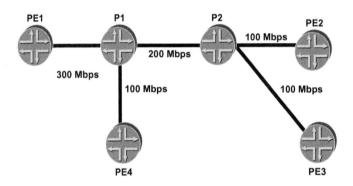

FIGURE 7.61

In a large network with high volumes of Multicast, Unknown Unicast/Broadcast traffic, this can be a very costly affair, since bandwidth consumption would be very high.

In contrast, if the VPLS instance is configured to use a P2MP LSP, the Ingress PE router only creates a single copy of the unknown traffic that needs to be flooded. Each Node in the P2MP LSP path creates only a single copy for their respective branch nodes, and this process is followed in the entire network. Based on Figure 7.62, we see a huge reduction in bandwidth utilization, which offers significant cost savings to an operator.

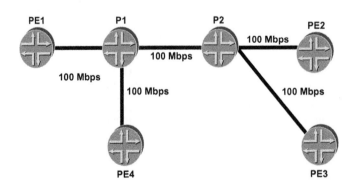

FIGURE 7.62

Some sample configurations based on JUNOS are shown in Figure 7.63. In this configuration, a P2MP Label-Switched Template has been associated with the VPLS instance.

```
[edit]
routing-instances {
   GOLD {
    instance-type vpls;
     interface ge-1/0/0.1;
     route-distinguisher 1.1.1.1:1;
      provider-tunnel {
        rsvp-te {
          label-switched-path-template {
             vpls-GOLD-p2mp-template;
      }
    }
  }
       vrf-target target:65000:1;
       protocols {
         vpls {
         site-range 8;
          site CE1 {
            site-identifier 1;
      }
    }
   }
  }
protocols {
mpls {
  label-switched-path vpls-GOLD-p2mp-template {
    template;
    link-protection;
     p2mp;
  }
interface all;
interface fxp0.0 {
  disable;
 }
 }
 }
```

FIGURE 7.63

VPLS P2MP configuration.

The following show commands can be used to view the association of the P2MP LSP with the VPLS instance. The first command displays the BGP table with all of the route information for PE routers that are part of the same VPLS instance (see Figure 7.64). The second command shows details of the VPLS instance (see Figure 7.65).

```
admin@PEA# show route table GOLD.l2vpn.0 extensive
GOLD.l2vpn.0: 5 destinations, 5 routes (5 active, 0 holddown, 0 hidden)
1.1.1.1:1:1:1/96 (1 entry, 1 announced)
*BGP    Preference: 170/-65536
Route Distinguisher: 1.1.1.1:1
PMSI: Flags 0:RSVP-TE:label[0:0:0]:Session_13[1.1.1.1:0:9519:1.1.1.1]
Next hop type: Indirect
Next-hop reference count: 4
Source: 7.7.7.7
Protocol next hop: 1.1.1.1
Indirect next hop: 2 no-forward
State: <Secondary Active Int Ext>
Local AS: 65000 Peer AS: 65000
Age: 2:30:44 Metric2: 1
Task: BGP_65000.7.7.7.7+179
Announcement bits (1): 0-GOLD-l2vpn
AS path: I (Originator) Cluster list: 7.7.7.7
AS path: Originator ID: 1.1.1.1
Communities: target:65000:1 Layer2-info: encaps:VPLS, control flags:, mtu: 0,
site
preference: 65535
Import Accepted
Label-base: 262145, range: 8
Localpref: 65535
Router ID: 7.7.7.7
Primary Routing Table bgp.l2vpn.0
Indirect next hops: 1
Protocol next hop: 1.1.1.1 Metric: 3
Indirect next hop: 2 no-forward
Indirect path forwarding next hops: 1
Next hop type: Router
Next hop: 10.10.8.2 via xe-0/1/0.0 weight 0x1
1.1.1.1/32 Originating RIB: inet.3
Metric: 3 Node path count: 1
Forwarding nexthops: 1
Nexthop: 10.10.8.2 via xe-0/1/0.0
[Output Truncated]
```

FIGURE 7.64

BGP information for participating PE routers.

```
admin@PEA# show vpls connections extensive
...
Instance: GOLD
Local site: CE3 (3)
Number of local interfaces: 1
Number of local interfaces up: 1
IRB interface present: no
ge-1/0/0.1
lsi.1048832 1 Intf - vpls GOLD local site 3 remote site 1
lsi.1048833 2 Intf - vpls GOLD local site 3 remote site 2
Interface flags: VC-Down
lsi.1048834 5 Intf - vpls GOLD local site 3 remote site 5
```

FIGURE 7.65

VPLS instance information.

```
Interface flags: VC-Down
Label-base Offset Range Preference
262145 1 8 65535
connection-site Type St Time last up # Up trans
1 rmt Up Nov 16 11:22:01 2010 1
Remote PE: 1.1.1.1, Negotiated control-word: No
Incoming label: 262145, Outgoing label: 262147
Local interface: lsi.1048832, Status: Up, Encapsulation: VPLS
Description: Intf - vpls GOLD local site 3 remote site 1
RSVP-TE P2MP lsp:
Egress branch LSP: 3.3.3.3:1.1.1.1:1:vpls:GOLD, State: Up
Connection History:
Nov 16 11:22:54 2009 PE route changed
Nov 16 11:22:01 2009 status update timer
Nov 16 11:22:01 2009 PE route changed
Nov 16 11:22:01 2009 Out lbl Update 262147
Nov 16 11:22:01 2009 In lbl Update 262145
Nov 16 11:22:01 2009 loc intf up lsi.1048832
3 rmt RN
5 rmt RD
Ingress RSVP-TE P2MP LSP: vpls-GOLD, Flood next-hop ID: 616
```

FIGURE 7.65

(*Continued*)

7.2.6.1 Selective Trees for Multicast in VPLS

Creating a P2MP tree within the context of VPLS to overcome the limitations of handling multicast flooding uses Inclusive P-tunnels. In other words, traffic is still delivered to PE routers that do not have any interested receivers. While the present model does offer extremely significant bandwidth savings, the need for more optimal multicast delivery always exists.

The following extracts from the Internet draft "draft-ietf-l2vpn-vpls-mcast-08.txt" specify procedures for delivering multicast traffic for VPLS, including the use of selective trees.

> *Once a PE decides to bind a set of VPLSs or customer multicast groups to an Inclusive P-Multicast tree or a Selective P-Multicast tree, it needs to announce this binding to other PEs in the network. This procedure is referred to as Inclusive P-Multicast tree or Selective P-Multicast tree binding distribution and is performed using BGP.*

> *If an Inclusive P-Multicast tree is used to instantiate the provider tunnel for VPLS multicast on the PE, the advertising PE MUST advertise the type and the identity of the P-Multicast tree in the PMSI Tunnel attribute.*

> *Selective trees provide a PE the ability to create separate P-Multicast trees for certain <C-S, C-G> streams. The source PE, that originates the Selective tree, and the egress PEs, MUST use the Selective tree for the <C-S, C-G> streams that are mapped to it. This may require the source and egress PEs to switch to the Selective tree from an Inclusive tree if they were already using an Inclusive tree for the <C-S, C-G> streams mapped to the Selective tree. Once a source PE decides to set up a Selective tree, it MUST announce the mapping of the <C-S, C-G> streams (which may be in different VPLSs) that are mapped to the tree to the other PEs using BGP. After the egress PEs*

receive the announcement, they set up their forwarding path to receive traffic on the Selective tree if they have one or more receivers interested in the <C-S, C-G> streams mapped to the tree. Setting up the forwarding path requires setting up the demultiplexing forwarding entries based on the top MPLS label (if there is no inner label) or the inner label (if present). The egress PEs MAY perform this switch to the Selective tree once the advertisement from the ingress PE is received or wait for a pre-configured timer to do so, after receiving the advertisement, when the P2MP LSP protocol is mLDP. When the P2MP LSP protocol is P2MP RSVP-TE, an egress PE MUST perform this switch to the Selective tree only after the advertisement from the ingress PE is received and the RSVP-TE P2MP LSP has been set up to the egress PE. This switch MAY be done after waiting for a pre-configured timer after these two steps have been accomplished. A source PE MUST use the following approach to decide when to start transmitting data on the Selective tree, if it was already using an Inclusive tree. A certain preconfigured delay after advertising the <C-S, C-G> streams mapped to a Selective tree, and the source PE begins to send traffic on the Selective tree. At this point it stops to send traffic for the <C-S, C-G> streams, which are mapped on the Selective tree, on the Inclusive tree. This traffic is instead transmitted on a Selective tree.

In a nutshell, the draft is about setting up a complete infrastructure to deliver multicast traffic using selective trees, which is very similar to the Next-Gen MVPN framework, and once again relies on the same BGP procedures for creating the control plane infrastructure. VPLS PEs rely on PIM/IGMP snooping on the PE-CE interfaces to build multicast state information.

7.2.7 Multicast in a Wholesale Model

In this section we look at some of the building blocks of a residential broadband network used for offering wholesale services. We will also take a closer look at how multicast is used with building blocks for delivering IPTV traffic for end users.

7.2.7.1 Background

Early Internet access required that each subscriber dial up from the PC to a bank of Remote Access Servers (RAS), which in turn were connected to the Internet. Point-to-Point Protocol (PPP), already used on leased lines, was adopted to enable the operator to more easily manage subscriber connections. Special software, including the PPP protocol stack, had to be installed on each PC. After establishing the connection, the subscriber would then log in using the operator-provided PPP userid.

This model quickly evolved in several ways. First, dedicated "broadband" access such as DSL replaced dial-up service, providing an "always on" connection. The dial-up modem was replaced by the DSL modem, while the dial-up RAS servers were replaced by the Broadband Remote Access Server (B-RAS). Residential gateways (RGs) were also introduced to allow multiple PCs within a site to connect to the broadband network. RGs have since evolved to provide a wide range of functions including firewall and wireless (802.1b/g/n Wi-Fi) connectivity. In addition, the RG became the termination point for the PPP connection, eliminating the need for special PC software to be installed.

These new broadband networks were built with two key assumptions. First, only a small percentage of subscribers would be using bandwidth at any given time; even if many subscribers log onto the network concurrently, few subscribers would hit the "enter" key at the exact same time. Second, traffic is TCP-based and not real time. If a packet is lost due to network congestion, TCP will determine this and retransmit the packets. Based on these assumptions, the network could be "over-subscribed."

For example, if 50 subscribers sign up for service at 1 Mbps, then the network does not need to support 50 Mbps of throughput. Instead, the network can be designed to support much lower traffic volumes. Assuming 50:1 over-subscription, this network would only need to support 1 Mbps. Basic broadband architecture was initially defined by DSL Forum TR-025 (November 1999). This specification assumed only one service, Internet Access (or "data"), was provided to subscribers. DSL Forum TR-059 (September 2003) introduced Quality of Service (QoS), allowing broadband networks to deliver Voice over IP (VoIP) as well as data. Since VoIP is a small percentage of the overall traffic, its introduction did not significantly alter the broadband delivery landscape. It is also worth noting that these standards specified ATM as the Layer 2 protocol on the broadband network.

7.2.7.2 *Delivering Broadband Services*
There are four primary methods for delivering "always on" broadband service across a wire-line network:

- Digital Subscriber Line (DSL): Uses the installed telephone wires, sending broadband information on a different frequency from the existing voice service. It is the preferred method of incumbent providers of local phone service. There are numerous generations of xDSL used for residential service, including VDSL2 (most recent), ADSL2 +, ADSL2, and ADSL. These primarily offer asymmetric (different upstream/downstream speeds) residential broadband service. Other DSL variations such as HDSL and SDSL provide symmetric speeds and are targeted at business applications. (VDSL2 also supports symmetric operation.) The head end to a DSL system is the Digital Subscriber Line Access Multiplexer (**DSLAM**). The demarcation device at the customer premise is a **DSL modem**. DSL service models are defined by the Broadband Forum (formerly called the DSL Forum). DSL is the most widely deployed broadband technology worldwide.
- **Active Ethernet:** Active Ethernet uses traditional Ethernet technology to deliver broadband service across a fiber network. Since active Ethernet does not provide a separate channel for existing voice service, VoIP phones (or TDM-to-VoIP equipment in the home) are required. In addition, sending full-speed (100 Mbps typically) Ethernet requires significant power, which must often be distributed to Ethernet switches and optical repeaters located in cabinets outside of the central office. Therefore, early active Ethernet deployments have been used in densely populated areas.
- **Passive Optical Networking (PON):** PON is the middle ground solution. Like active Ethernet, PON uses fiber to deliver services. It provides higher speed than DSL, but lower speed than active Ethernet. A key advantage is that PON does not require any powered equipment outside of the central office. Each fiber that leaves the central office is split by a non-powered optical splitter, which then has a point-to-point connection to each subscriber. PON provides higher speed to each subscriber, but requires a higher investment. PON technologies fall into three families:
  - **GPON (most recent), BPON, and APON:** These are defined by the Full Service Access Network (FSAN) Group. BPON is considered the minimum requirement for supporting high-bandwidth IPTV, which is also fueling the growth of GPON.
- **Ethernet PON (EPON):** Provides similar capabilities but uses Ethernet standards. These are defined by the IEEE. Gigabit Ethernet PON (GEPON) is the highest speed version.

The head end to a PON system is an Optical Line Terminator (OLT). The demarcation device at the customer premises is an Optical Network Terminator (ONT). The ONT provides subscriber-side ports for connecting Ethernet (RJ-45), telephone wires (RJ-11), and/or coaxial cable (F-connector).

Hybrid Fiber Coax (HFC) is a Multi-System Operators (MSO; better known as "cable TV operators") that offer broadband service via their HFC network. Services leave the central office via a fiber, which is then converted outside of the CO to a coaxial cable "tree," which reaches multiple subscribers. Broadband traffic is carried using the DOCSIS standard defined by CableLabs. The demarcation device is a cable modem, which talks to a Cable Modem Termination System (CMTS) at the head end.

Many implementations use existing copper to deliver signal to the premises, but fiber is increasingly being pushed closer to the subscriber. The term "fiber to the x (FTTx)" is used to describe how far into the network fiber is used. Either PON or active Ethernet can be used on the fiber portion, while xDSL is typically used on the copper portion. A single fiber may support multiple copper-based subscribers. Terms include:

- **Fiber to the Premises (FTTP), Fiber to the Home (FTTH),** and **Fiber to the Business (FTTB):** Fiber extends all the way to the customer's location. PON is most common for residential access, although active Ethernet can be used in dense areas such as apartment complexes. Active Ethernet is more common for delivering services to businesses.
- **Fiber to the Curb (FTTC):** Fiber is extended most of the way to the subscriber, including perhaps to the basement of a multi-tenant building. Existing copper is used for the last few hundred feet/meters. In the United States, the legal definition of FTTC is that the fiber is run within 500 feet (150 m) of the premises. This is because broadband operators that deploy FTTC/FTTH are not obligated to lease subscriber access to other carriers.
- **Fiber to the Node/Neighborhood (FTTN):** Fiber is extended to within a few thousand feet of the subscriber and converted to xDSL for the remaining run to the subscriber.
- **Fiber to the Exchange (FTTE):** Describes a typical CO-based xDSL implementation in which fiber is used to deliver traffic to the CO, and xDSL is used on the existing local loop.

Pushing fiber further into the network costs more but increases the access speed to each subscriber.

7.2.7.3 Subscriber Management

Subscriber management is the ability to dynamically learn about subscribers and to control the subscribers' access to network resources. This allows operators to offer multiple service options such as selecting from a variety of upstream/downstream connection speeds, and controlling access to (and billing for) services such as Internet Access, gaming, VoIP and IPTV. Most often subscriber information is stored centrally in a RADIUS server.

When the subscriber logs into the network using PPP, the B-RAS checks with the server about which services each subscriber can access. The B-RAS receives this information and adjusts its parameters accordingly. For example, a VoIP subscriber could automatically have separate queues set aside to support VoIP traffic, and these packets would be marked as high priority to ensure that they traverse the network successfully. Often the PPP login is programmed into the RG (or PC software), so the subscriber is unaware of this process.

If the network does not use PPP, the subscriber verification process is triggered by a DHCP address assignment request. Subscriber information is stored in the DHCP server and sent down to the B-RAS by appending DHCP "option" fields to DHCP flows. The challenge here is that the B-RAS does not know which MSAN port, and hence which subscriber, originated the request. There are various solutions to solve this:

- Have the MSAN append a field to the initial DHCP request specifying the MSAN node, slot, and port or VCI/VPI from which the request originated. The network can then use this information to determine which subscriber made the request. This is known as DHCP Option 82.
- Have a separate VLAN for each subscriber. Again, the network can check its database to determine which subscriber made the request.

Have the MSAN, rather than the B-RAS, communicate to the DHCP server.

The process of identifying the subscriber, determining what resources the subscriber has access to, and tracking usage is called Authentication, Authorization, and Accounting (AAA). The device (B-RAS or MSAN) that receives the subscriber's request for network access and communicates to the AAA (RADIUS or DHCP) server is called a proxy.

7.2.7.4 IPTV

The IP client for IPTV service is the set-top box (STB), and subscriber control is provided by the network middleware. Each STB has middleware client software, which in turn talks to a centralized middleware server controlled by the operator. Information about the services that each subscriber has access to is stored in the middleware server's database. When the STB is powered on or re-booted, it identifies itself to the server, which in turn downloads the appropriate configuration to the STB (or updates the pre-loaded software). This configuration controls which services the STB can access, including which channels can be viewed. Which configuration file is downloaded to the STB is determined by which service package the subscriber pays for.

This model moves subscriber control into the IP client, minimizing the need for "network-based" control. There are numerous IPTV middleware providers including Microsoft (MediaRoom), Myrio (TotalManage), Minerva (iTVManager), and Cascade. The STB is typically a dedicated hardware device, although recently PC software has been introduced that allows it to provide all capabilities of the STB. In the emerging standards, the network middleware server is called the IPTV Control Server (ICS).

In addition to the network middleware, key components of the IPTV head end include:

- **Acquisition systems:** Used to receive and decode the television signal from the satellite. Different acquisition systems are used for different content (SD/HD/music) and transmission techniques (analog/digital).
- **Encoders:** Compress the television signal and/or wrap the content in an IP header. (Content downloaded from satellites may require encoding, or may have been encoded before being sent to the satellite). Common formats for the compressed, or encoded, signal include MPEG2, MPEG4, and VC-1 (also known as Windows Media Version 9).
- **Conditional access (CA) systems:** Encrypt the signal to prevent the subscriber from viewing channels/services that have not been purchased. The latest evolution is Digital Rights Management (DRM) systems, which also control when the content can be viewed and whether or not it can be copied. In cable networks, the comparable process is called scrambling.
- **Video on Demand (VoD) systems:** Store content in a central library that can then push copies out to distributed servers.
- **Emergency Alert System (EAS):** Required only in the United States, it has a mechanism for providing emergency information to the general public, such as for an impending natural disaster.

In addition, there are several optional but noteworthy capabilities:

- Digital Program Insertion (DPI, not to be confused with Deep Packet Inspection, which shares the same acronym) or Ad Insertion systems are used by operators to overlay ads paid for by local businesses. This revenue stream generates several billion dollars annually for the North American cable TV industry, and is being adopted by broadband operators.
- Video caching systems provide faster channel change ("zapping") time and also yield fewer screen defects.
- Forward Error Correction (FEC) systems add information to the stream, which allows the STB to detect and correct errors that may have been introduced as the signal traversed the network.

Since there are few control plane standards and many vendors in the mix, the concept of an "eco-system" becomes important. Individual suppliers perform two- and three-way interoperability testing. For example, a middleware system may be tested with an STB and may perform a separate test with the VoD and CA systems. Since this is insufficient to ensure a complete working system, systems integrators become important players in assisting broadband operators with putting together the total solution.

Traditional television service, where specific shows are shown at specific times, is referred to as "linear" programming. Content that is viewed only occasionally or by few viewers is referred to as "long tail" content.

7.2.7.5 IPTV Locations/Placement

Like most services, not all IPTV-related equipment resides at a single site. Generally, equipment resides in four locations. Note that different vendors and operators use different terminology.

- **Super Head-End (SHE):** Centralized location where a large operator will receive and process "national" (or international) broadcast TV channels as well as VoD content. The operator may also insert some ads here, typically commercials advocating their own service such as telling you how easy it is to use the VoD service. A large operator will have two SHEs.
- **Local Head-End (LHE)/Video Hub Office (VHO):** Channels received at the SHE are distributed to this regional data center. "Local" ads sold by the operator are inserted here, and the middleware server and conditional access systems typically also reside here. Local broadcast channels (also known as OTA or "over the air" or "off-air" channels) are also received, processed, and encoded here. Copies of VoD content are often pushed down to VoD servers (caches) located here, and subscriber requests to view VoD content are served from this location.
- **Video Serving Office (VSO):** Central office closest to the subscriber. MSANs may reside here, and there may also be video caching equipment here.
- **Outside Plant (OSP):** MSANs and fiber splitters may also reside in environmentally controlled cabinets or even placed on telephone poles. MSANs in the outside plant typically connect back to an aggregation device in the nearest VSO. MSANs deployed in the OSP are often referred to as Remote Terminals (RTs).

To minimize operational expenses, one goal is to centralize equipment whenever possible. However, bandwidth and equipment scaling restrictions force some equipment to be pushed out into the network.

Regional providers often do not have a separate SHE; instead they perform all SHE/VHO functions at a single location.

7.2.7.6 Standardizing IPTV Delivery

IPTV stressed the existing broadband connectivity model. First, PPP is not well suited to deliver a single stream to multiple subscribers ("multicast"). Second, Ethernet is emerging as the networking technology of choice for the WAN, especially for high-bandwidth applications such as IPTV.

DSL Forum TR-101 defines the technologies for delivering IPTV service as well as for using Ethernet as the underlying network technology instead of ATM. Unlike the previous DSL Forum implementation standards, TR-101 provides numerous alternatives rather than dictating a single approach. Some of the key alternatives include:

- Ethernet delivery using the N:1 (or services VLAN or S-VLAN) or 1:1 (customer VLAN or C-VLAN) model. Service VLANs deliver each service (voice, video, and data) to a dedicated client such as a PC or STB and allocate a fixed amount of bandwidth to each service. Customer VLANs deliver all services to each subscriber via a single logical connection (Ethernet VLAN), allowing all bandwidth to be shared among all services.
- In addition to PPP, the operator could use the simpler (but less functional) IP over Ethernet (IPoE) model. The DHCP proponents argue that the "PPP login" is no longer required, and PPP does not support multicast IPTV well. However, this simplistic argument downplays many of PPP's benefits. PPPoE and DHCP can be used concurrently to deliver different services, even to the same subscriber.
- Use of a single B-RAS to support all traffic (single edge) or the ability to use a separate edge router to support IPTV traffic (multi-edge).

7.2.7.7 Broadband Network Overview

This section discusses the network elements that comprise the residential broadband access network. One of the many possible topologies (split multi-edge) is depicted in Figure 7.66 to illustrate the key components:

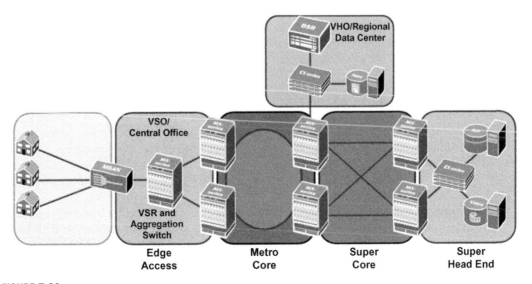

FIGURE 7.66

Equipment discussed in this section includes edge routers, which are the upstream termination point of the "access" network. Different types of edge routers are

- **Broadband Services Router (BSR):** All Internet traffic flows through the BSR. Other traffic including VoIP and IPTV may also flow through this device.
- **Video Services Router (VSR):** This optional edge router supports only IPTV-related traffic (possibly including VoD).
- **MSAN:** Aggregates traffic from multiple subscribers; this is most often a DSLAM or OLT.
- **Ethernet aggregation switch:** Aggregates traffic from multiple MSANs.
- **Data center switch:** Consolidates traffic in the various data centers such as the SHE and VHO.

The edge router is the demarcation point between the "access network" and the "core network." There are two types of edge routers:

- **BSR:** Initially targeted at High Speed Internet Access, the BSR also supports all other services including VoIP, IPTV, and gaming. The BSR is an evolution of the B-RAS.
- **VSR:** Capabilities are a subset of those provided by a BSR and support only bi-directional traffic destined for the STB. This includes IPTV and VoD streams as well as associated control traffic such as IGMP and electronic program guide (EPG) updates.

The following describe the BSR and VSR function in more detail. They can be combined into two fundamental designs:

- **Single Edge:** All traffic between a given subscriber and the MSAN flows through a single BSR. This is a widely deployed design as it provides the operator with a single point of control for all traffic, simplifying operations resulting in the lowest operating expense, notably for large customers.
- **Dual Edge (or more generically, multi-edge):** This alternative adds the VSR, and traffic to/from the MSAN goes through different edge routers. Video traffic goes through a VSR, while all other traffic typically goes through a BSR.

A BSR is the edge router that traditionally supports primarily Internet-bound traffic. It replaces and provides a superset of the functionality provided by a B-RAS. The key BSR functions can be split into two areas:

1. High Speed Internet Access (HSIA) support
   - **Subscriber management:** BSR communicates with the RADIUS server to enforce which services each subscriber can access. For example, one subscriber may have signed up for 1-Mbps Internet access service, and another may have signed up for 10-Mbps access.
   - **PPPoX termination:** If PPPoX encapsulation is used on the network, the BSR terminates the PPP session before forwarding traffic upstream. This is the function provided by the traditional B-RAS.
   - **Bandwidth management:** The BSR manages traffic to each subscriber, ensuring that each subscriber gets its fair share and that VoIP traffic receives priority. In addition, the BSR looks at aggregate bandwidth to the MSAN in making traffic forwarding decisions.
2. IPTV support: In addition, a BSR supporting IPTV traffic should also provide the following:
   - **IGMP support:** The BSR must respond to IGMP requests by starting/stopping sending multicast groups as requested by the downstream MSANs.

- **Advanced bandwidth management:** Adding high-bandwidth multicast IPTV and VoD exacerbates the traffic management challenge. Traffic must be managed to each subscriber individually and to all subscribers in aggregate (to a given MSAN or out the BSR port), assuring high quality service delivery.

A BSR is designed to support voice, video, and data traffic to thousands of low-speed subscribers with high over-subscription rates. Because the VSR does not need to manage over-subscribed traffic or balance bandwidth among multiple applications, it is less expensive than BSR.

7.2.7.8 BSR/VSR Placement
7.2.7.8.1 Single Edge
In a single edge network, there are two places where the BSR can be placed:

- **Distributed single edge:** The edge router is located out in the network, typically in the CO closest to the subscriber. MSANs are connected directly to the BSR (single edge) or via an Ethernet switch(es). This is mostly deployed in Tier 1 and regionally focused Tier 2s, which have a large number of COs and high IPTV service penetration.
- **Centralized single edge:** The edge router is more centrally located, typically at one location per region (with a possible backup site). MSANs are connected via ring or mesh networks back to the BSR. This design is used by Tier 1s that do not offer IPTV service or have low penetration. It is also popular with Tier 3 operators as well as Tier 2 operators with decentralized operations or low penetration rates.

In general, adding IPTV service pushes to IP edge outward (from a *centralized* model to a *distributed* model).

7.2.7.8.2 Multi-Edge
Using a multi-edge design, in which a separate VSR is used for video traffic, introduces additional design alternatives:

- **Co-located multi-edge:** The BSR and VSR can also be in the same location. It is simply a matter of using an Ethernet switch to direct traffic in the CO to the appropriate edge routers. A single device can serve as both Ethernet switch and VSR.
- **Split multi-edge:** The VSR and BSR may be at different locations. Typically the BSR is located centrally while the VSR is distributed.

7.2.7.9 MSAN
The defining function of the MSAN is that it aggregates traffic from multiple subscribers. At the physical level, the MSAN also converts from the last-mile technology (such as ADSL) to Ethernet. Common MSANs include DSLAMs (used in xDSL networks), OLT (for PON/FTTx networks), and Ethernet switches (for active Ethernet connections). Modern MSANs often support all of these connections as well as provide connections for additional circuits such as POTS or T1.

Each MSAN may be directly connected to the BSR/VSR, or traffic may be aggregated together by an intermediate device. There are three methods for connecting MSANs to the BSR/VSR.

It is possible to use different methods in different portions of the network. In addition, there may be multiple layers of traffic aggregation. For example, an MSAN may connect to a Central Office

Terminal (COT), which in turn connects to an Ethernet Aggregation Switch, or multiple levels of Ethernet aggregation switches can exist. Whether or not to use a switch is strictly a financial decision; it may be cheaper to aggregate traffic than to purchase additional ports on the edge router and/or WDM equipment.

There are three MSAN Aggregation models:

Direct Connect: Each MSAN has a point-to-point link to the BSR. If there is an intermediate central office, traffic from multiple MSANs may be combined onto a single fiber connection using WDM. Although the MSAN could potentially have a second link to a VSR, this requires that the MSAN has the ability to determine on which link to forward traffic. This means that an "L3 MSAN" must be used. This is almost never done when using a multi-edge model.

Ethernet Aggregation Switch: As the name implies, it is simply an Ethernet switch that aggregates (point-to-point) traffic from multiple downstream MSANs in a single connection to the MSAN. Typically this is done when to aggregate traffic from lower speed MSANs (e.g., 1 Gbps) into a higher speed connection to the BSR/VSR (e.g., 10 Gbps).

Ring Aggregation: In a ring topology, the remote MSAN that connects to subscribers is an RT. This device may be located in the OSP or in a remote CO. Traffic then traverses the ring until it reaches the COT, which is the head end of the ring. The COT then has a point-to-point connection to the BSR/VSR. To the BSR/VSR, the COT appears to be an Ethernet switch. One important point is that the RT and COT must support the same ring resiliency protocol.

7.2.7.10 VLAN Architectures for IPTV

There are three VLAN approaches to delivering multiple services including multicast IPTV to subscribers:

1. **Service (N:1) VLAN (S-VLAN):** In this model there is one VLAN *per service,* which carries traffic *for this service* to all subscribers. Each service requires adding a new VLAN, and bandwidth is typically allocated to each service. The S-VLAN model allows different groups (within the broadband provider or external application providers) to manage a given service. Historically, it is difficult for the BSR to associate all traffic belonging to a single subscriber. The MSAN provides simple QoS enforcement, forwarding the VoIP traffic to each subscriber before sending the Internet traffic (see Figure 7.67).

2. **"Pure" Customer (1:1) VLAN (C-VLAN):** In this model, there is one VLAN *per subscriber* which carries *all traffic to this one subscriber.* Having a single VLAN per subscriber simplifies operations by providing a 1:1 mapping of technology (VLANs) to subscribers, allowing the broadband operator to understand what applications a given subscriber is using at any given time. This model requires that the edge router be able to support several thousand VLANs, requiring a more scalable edge router. Since there is one VLAN per subscriber that carries all traffic to this one subscriber, this implementation is not affected by adding IPTV (or any other new) service. Using a pure C-VLAN model consumes more bandwidth since a single television channel being viewed by multiple subscribers would need to be carried across the network several times—once on each C-VLAN.

3. **"Hybrid" Customer VLAN with Multicast VLAN:** This model combines the best of the previous two by using one VLAN per subscriber to carry unicast traffic, plus one shared multicast VLAN (M-VLAN) for carrying broadcast (multicast) television traffic. *When the term C-VLAN*

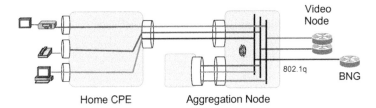

Video Node

802.1q

BNG

Home CPE   Aggregation Node

- Service connectivity and forwarding
    Single VLAN per service
    Service prioritization, Ethernet CoS-based

FIGURE 7.67

is used casually, it most often refers to this implementation. It is possible to use both the pure and hybrid C-VLAN models in different portions of the network, depending upon available bandwidth and MSAN capabilities.

Most deployments prefer using one of the C-VLAN models (pure or hybrid) because of the operational simplification. However, many MSANs cannot support the C-VLAN models because they are limited in the number of VLANs they can support, and this needs to be considered.

The previous VLAN alternatives are used between the edge router and MSAN. However, the MSAN may modify the VLAN before forwarding it to the subscriber. For example, the VLAN identifiers can be carried within the ATM VCs or can be removed. The value of keeping the VLAN header is that it carries the IEEE 802.1p Ethernet priority bits, which can be added to upstream traffic by the RG. This allows the DSLAM to easily identify and prioritize more important traffic such as control and VoIP traffic. Typically, VLAN identifier 0 (zero) is used for this purpose.

In a C-VLAN design, the DSLAM may modify the VLAN identifier so that the same VLAN is sent to each subscriber. This allows the operator to use the same DSL modem/RG configuration for all subscribers, without the need to program a different VLAN into each unit.

7.2.7.11 Customer VLANs and Ethernet Aggregation
The 12-bit VLAN identifier supports up to 4,095 subscribers. When using an aggregation switch with a C-VLAN topology, there are two situations to consider:

1. If there are (and always will be) less than 4,095 subscribers connected to a single BSR port, then the aggregation switch can transparently pass all VLANs.
2. If there may be more than 4,095 subscribers per BSR port, then VLAN stacking (IEEE 802.1ad, also known as Q-in-Q) must be used.

In the last model, the traffic from the BSR to the switch includes two VLAN tags: an outer tag identifying the destination MSAN, and an inner tag identifying the subscriber on that MSAN. For downstream traffic, the Ethernet switch uses the outer tag to determine which port to forward the traffic to and will pop this tag before forwarding the traffic. The reverse process happens for upstream traffic.

VLAN stacking is not needed for S-VLANs or on the M-VLAN. For the hybrid (C-VLAN with M-VLAN) model, the Ethernet switch must be able to pop/push tags onto C-VLAN traffic while not modifying the M-VLAN packets.

7.2.7.12 IGMP Models

In an IPTV network, channel changes are performed by having the STB send IGMP commands that tell an upstream device (MSAN or BSR) which multicast groups to start or stop sending to the subscriber. In addition, IGMP hosts periodically ask the STBs to notify them about which channels (multicast groups) are receiving. There are several different implementations:

- **Static IGMP:** All multicast channels are sent to the MSAN. When the MSAN receives an IGMP request to start/stop sending a channel, it performs the request and then throws away the IGMP packet.
- **IGMP Proxy:** Only multicast channels currently being viewed are sent to the MSAN. If the MSAN receives a request to view a channel that is not currently being forwarded to the MSAN, it will forward the request upstream. The upstream device does not see all channel change requests from each subscriber.
- **IGMP Snooping:** Only multicast channels currently being viewed are sent to the MSAN. The MSAN forwards all IGMP requests upstream unaltered, even if it is already receiving the channel. The upstream device therefore sees all channel change requests from each subscriber. Using IGMP snooping allows the BSR to use its knowledge of each multicast group's bandwidth requirement to adjust the bandwidth available to unicast traffic.
- **IGMP Passthrough (do nothing):** The MSAN can "do nothing" and transparently pass the IGMP packet upstream.

IGMP hosts (sources) also periodically verify that they are sending the correct traffic by requesting that each client send information about what multicast group it wants to receive. The responses to this "IGMP query" can result is a substantial upstream traffic burst. IGMPv2 is the minimum level required to support IPTV, and it is the most widely deployed. Emerging standards specify IGMPv3.

7.2.7.13 OIF Mapping and Reverse OIF Mapping

When using the hybrid C-VLAN/M-VLAN model, one must decide which VLAN to use for forwarding IGMP traffic. There are two options:

- **OIF mapping:** IGMP packets are forwarded on the C-VLAN. The major advantage to this is that the edge router can send IGMP queries individually to each subscriber, spacing them out over an extended period to avoid severe upstream traffic bursts. However, only a few MSANs support IGMP traffic on a different VLAN than multicast traffic.
- **Reverse OIF mapping:** IGMP packets are forwarded on the M-VLAN. This model is supported by any MSAN that supports the C-VLAN/M-VLAN model, but is subject to severe upstream traffic bursts as all subscribers respond to any IGMP query sent on the M-VLAN.

7.2.7.14 VLAN and IGMP Interactions

Based upon the previous models, a few combinations of C-VLAN and M-VLAN have emerged:

- **C-VLAN and M-VLAN with IGMP Snooping:** This is one of the most widely deployed solutions, since it allows the BSR to understand exactly what channels it needs to send to each

DSLAM. Each subscriber has a dedicated customer VLAN (C-VLAN) that carries unicast traffic such as Internet Access. In addition, a shared multicast VLAN (M-VLAN) carries IPTV traffic to each subscriber. This allows a single copy of each channel to be sent across the network. You want the BSR to see the IGMP requests so that it can adjust the bandwidth available to best-efforts traffic and avoid downstream congestion, packet loss, and the associated retransmissions. The BSR coordinates traffic to each subscriber across the two types of VLANs, so it can adjust unicast bandwidth based on the channels being watched. *This model is most widely deployed by Tier 1 operators.*

- **S-VLAN with IGMP Proxy/Static IGMP:** This is more in line with the classic "triple play" solution where bandwidth is dedicated to each service. The network has no awareness of the service; instead it simply attempts to pass all offered traffic to each subscriber. *This model is most widely deployed by Tier 3 operators and multi-edge Tier 1 deployments.*
- **C-VLAN, with IGMP Passthrough:** All IPTV traffic is sent on the C-VLAN. The downside is that if multiple subscribers are watching the same channel, then multiple copies are sent (each on a separate VLAN). *This model is most widely deployed by operators that (a) deliver multicast IPTV via out-of-band methods, such as by using RF overlay, and (b) expect unicast video (VoD, network PVR, Internet-based videos) to quickly become the largest bandwidth user.* In this case, it makes sense to use this model and eliminate multicast from the access network.

7.2.7.15 PPP and DHCP

There are two ways that broadband traffic may be encapsulated on a broadband network.

PPP: Early DSL Forum specifications (TR-025, TR-059) mandate the use of PPP encapsulation on broadband networks using PPP over ATM (PPPoA). Now TR-101 allows PPPoE. Key PPP capabilities include:

- Session establishment phase including a login process: This allows the subscribers to identify themselves to the network, in turn allowing the network to determine which services the subscribers are entitled to access.
- Logical point-to-point connection: The key PPP field is the session identifier, which is a unique value assigned to each subscriber.
- Keep-alive mechanism: PPP can determine a network outage or degradation, including sending information at a lower speed if necessary.

Historically, there is one PPP connection to each subscriber for HSIA and a separate PPP connection to each subscriber for VoIP.

DHCP/IPoE: The DSL Forum (TR-101) allows broadband providers to use DHCP and other protocols instead of PPP (e.g., 802.1X may be used if a network sign-on is required). The term "IP over Ethernet (IPoE)" is used to describe this alternative.

7.3 SUMMARY

In this chapter we reviewed the various models for building VPLS infrastructures and the mechanisms for delivering multicast. We also detailed the building blocks of a broadband wholesale network and some widely deployed architectures for delivering multi-play services.

Mobile Video Multicast

8.1 INTRODUCTION

Over the past decade the growth of cell phone users has been exponential. By 2010, the number of cell phone users was at 5 billion, which is about 72% of the total human population on this planet. The convergence of entertainment, communication, and information (through the Internet) along with the ubiquity of cell phones influences our lifestyle in ways hitherto only imagined. "Any application, anytime, anywhere, any screen" is a reality that is unfolding quickly. Whether it is corporate e-mail, watching an NFL game, or a phone call to a friend, all of this is possible through any number of interfaces from an LCD TV at home to the mobile handset on the go.

In this context, mobile video is considered to be the next biggest challenge that faces the communication industry. It is already accepted in wire-line communication network design that video content would be the most dominant traffic by 2015. This is reflected in the design choices and Quality of Service (QoS) paradigms being adopted in the wire-line communication networks. However, mobile communication networks deployed widely do not share the same design maturity regarding video traffic.

This chapter explores the standards and technologies that form the basis for supporting mobile video and the underlying multicast architecture that would be required to carry broadcast video channels over mobile networks. Varying degrees of progress have been made in the different aspects of multicast video under mobility. Some of the discussions outline the current solutions, while others indicate the problems yet to be solved and possible solutions that may be explored.

8.2 MULTIMEDIA BROADCAST MULTICAST SERVICE

Mobile Broadcast and Multicast Service (MBMS) was conceived as a service that would make it possible for efficient use of radio and network resources while transmitting audio and video content to a large group of end users. MBMS was first introduced in 2004 as a part of the 3GPP R6 specifications. MBMS is a unidirectional point-to-multipoint (PTMP) service.

Figure 8.1 depicts the MBMS architecture ratified by 3GPP as a part of 23.246 specifications. This architecture largely builds on the GPRS architecture and introduces a few entities relevant to MBMS service. The Broadcast Multicast Service Center (BM-SC) connects to the MBMS content providers and transmits and schedules MBMS services. The Gi interface between the BM-SC and the GGSN carries the data packets and the GMB interface carries the signaling traffic. The data from the content providers both within the provider's network and also over the Internet are routed through the BM-SC.

As a part of Release 9, two new elements were introduced in specification 36.440: Multicell/multicast Coordination Entity (MCE) and MBMS Gateway (MBMS GW). The MCE is a logical entity within the eNodeB responsible for the allocation of time and frequency resources for MBMS

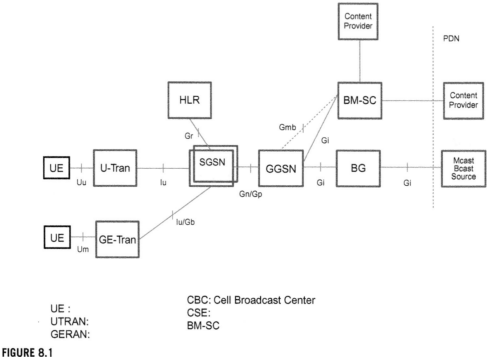

UE :
UTRAN:
GERAN:

CBC: Cell Broadcast Center
CSE:
BM-SC

FIGURE 8.1

services. The MBMS Gateway entity is responsible for transmission of the multicast content to eNodeBs. As a part of the LTE, MBMS has further advanced as Evolved MBMS (E-MBMS).

The design of MBMS is such that UEs receive other services such as voice calls and signaling information, while receiving MBMS data flow. When the UE is already attached and receiving MBMS services, it is also possible for the UE to receive notification about other MBMS services (see Figure 8.2).

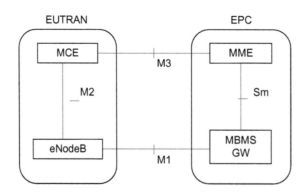

FIGURE 8.2

MBMS architecture has been designed to interoperate with IETF multicast standards and support IETF multicast addressing.

MBMS operates in two modes: broadcast and multicast. From a service point of view, the difference is self-explanatory. The MBMS standard defines the service subscription process in the two modes of operation as seen in Figure 8.3.

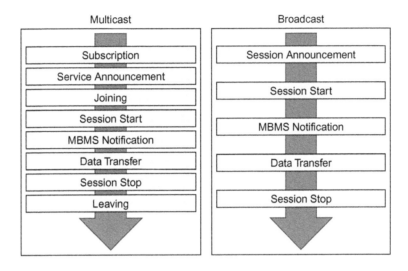

FIGURE 8.3

Because multicast service is only sent to a subgroup of users that are only interested in that specific service, there is a Subscription, Joining, and Leaving. With broadcast service, it is sent to all of the users, so there are only service specific phases involving announcement, session start, and session stop. The actual traffic flow in the MBMS environment is shown in Figure 8.4.

Data flow is along the network elements that have a UE subscribed to the multicast traffic. NodeBs that do not have UEs subscribed to multicast service would not receive the data stream. This approach conserves both network and radio resources.

Without the MBMS functionality, broadcast in the cellular domain would be multiple unicasts, as shown in Figure 8.5. This would overload the entire network resources, wireless and wire-line included.

With MBMS, however, the broadcast traffic would actually be carried as a single stream up to the farthest extent possible where it is replicated into multiple streams, as illustrated in Figure 8.6.

The SGSN, for instance, sends multiple copies of the traffic, one to each of the RNCs. This conserves the network resources substantially both in the wireless and the radio domains.

The MBMS architecture provides the infrastructure necessary for several applications to be created for the end users. Some of the services envisaged include video clips, file and music download, streaming audio and video services, localized emergency broadcasts, weather updates, and so forth.

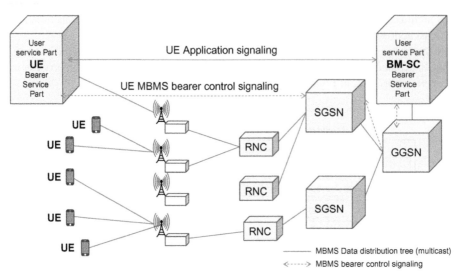

FIGURE 8.4

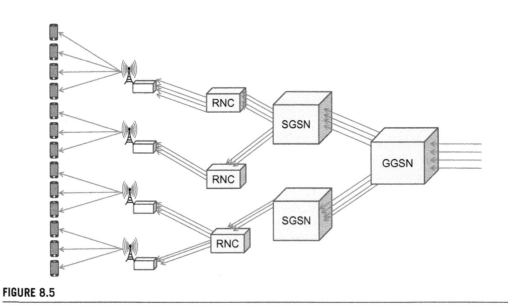

FIGURE 8.5

Different kinds of content including audio, pictures, video, and text (URLs, etc.) are supported. The bandwidth supported for MBMS at 5 MHz would allow over 20 channels to simultaneously be transmitted. However, for broadcast television applications for continuous streaming, DVB-H may offer a more compelling alternative.

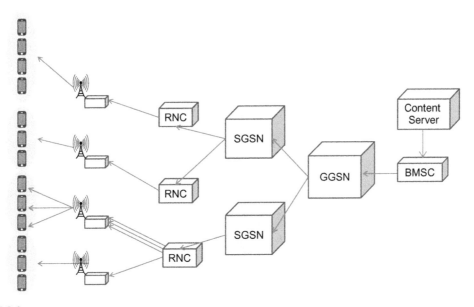

FIGURE 8.6

8.3 **DVB-H**

Digital Video Broadcast Handheld (DVB-H) is a technology pioneered for efficient deployment of broadcast services in the mobile environment. To receive DVB-H transmissions, cell phones need a DVB-H receiver. Today several vendors such as Nokia, LG, Samsung, and so forth have DVB-H enabled phones available commercially.

DVB-H is a unidirectional broadcast infrastructure. However, IP Datacast (IPDC) over DVB-H standard brings together the broadcast and the cellular mobile infrastructure for bi-directional interactivity. This section briefly covers the overall architecture of DVB-H, keeping in mind that IPDC over DVB-H would probably be the most dominant form of mobile video in the future (see Figure 8.7).

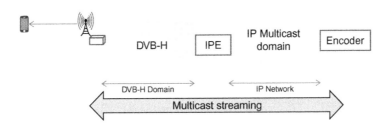

FIGURE 8.7

DVB-H standards focus upon the OSI Layers 1 and 2 focusing on radio transmission and the integrity of the data sent. IPDC over DVB-H specifications define the standards for OSI layers 3–7.

The core terrestrial network in the DVB architecture is IP based. The IP Encapsulator (IPE) entity acts as the interface between the DVB-H broadcast network and the IP network. The IP network design is per the best practices associated with the IETF standards, while the DVB-H standards define the components pertaining to the DVB-H broadcast network.

Figure 8.8 shows a more detailed level of the functional architecture of IPDC over DVB-H.

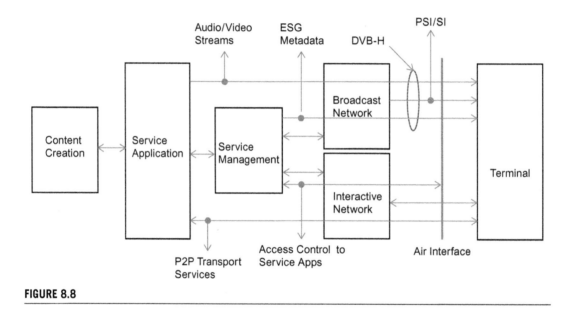

FIGURE 8.8

IPDC over DVB-H standards also define rules for DVB-H specific Program Specific Information (PSI)/Service Information (SI) signaling. Electronic Services Guide (ESG) specification is also a part of this standard.

It is expected that going forward DVB-H networks would cater to large user groups scattered over wide geographies, whereas hybrid networks with DVB-H and mobile infrastructure would cater to small but higher revenue generating subgroups with interactive television services. In 2008, DVB-H was chosen as the preferred mobile television standard (ahead of Qualcomm's MediaFLO and DMB).

8.4 MULTICAST LISTENER DISCOVERY VERSION 2 (MLDv2)

MLDv2 is a protocol used by IPv6 routers and is outlined in RFC 3810. Using MLDv2, the routers keep track of the multicast receivers connected to the different interfaces. Exchanging this information, the routers forward to each other only multicast packets relevant to the streams that are of interest to their neighbors. Multicast routers keep the state information pertinent to multicast address per attached link. The information is updated between the routers through Query mechanisms that indicate which routers are members of a given multicast group.

General Queries are periodically sent out by routers to learn multicast address listener information from attached links, and the response information (Current State Report) is used to build a Multicast Address Listener state for that link. Based on this information the relevant multicast streams are forwarded on the attached link. Multicast Address and Source Specific Query is used to verify that no listeners on a link listen to traffic from a specific set of sources.

MLDv2 as opposed to MLDv1 has enhancements specifically tailored to support Source Specific Multicast (SSM). These include support for "source filtering"—the ability to receive multicast stream "only" from specified source addresses or from "all but" specified source addresses.

MLD and MLDv2 were originally designed with fixed senders and receivers in mind. The default timers were designed by taking into account existing multicast protocols and IGPs. When applied to a mobile environment, MLD timers would need to be tweaked because the latencies introduced in the network due to the multicast routing table re-computation required sender and receiver mobility accountability.

The application requirements of multicast video do impose stringent requirements on the expected network performance. For instance, channel zap time expectation of end users is around 2 seconds and anything exceeding 4 seconds would be interpreted as application failure by the end user. Any tweaking to the MLD default timers should take these sensitivities into account.

MLDv2 is important in the environment of multicast mobility. When the user migrates across the network, network elements use MLDv2 to indicate interest in multicast traffic and terminate subscription to multicast streams that are of no further interest.

8.5 MULTICAST MOBILITY

Earlier in this chapter MBMS and DVH were briefly covered. These are the two important technologies central to the future of mobile video. In the preceding sections the focus was on the end-to-end connectivity for video over mobile phones. However, when it comes to the issues of mobility, there has been limited progress in the areas of multicast mobility over the past several years. The issues are complex, and for any solution to work there has to be wide acceptance from different stakeholders in the end-to-end architecture. The focus of this chapter is the implication of mobile video and the mobility of the user in terms of the efficiency of data transmission in the wire-line network.

Mobility violates one of the fundamental assumptions on which TCP/IP has been able to grow in popularity. Any end point in the TCP/IP network is identified by an IP address, and several such end points in a LAN are aggregated into a subnet. Several such subnets are aggregated together and their address is announced via the gateway to the Internet with a suitable prefix. Any router in the Internet would know that to reach the end point they would need to send the traffic to the gateway router that announces the relevant network address prefix. This approach worked well as long as the end points remained static within a network.

8.5.1 Receiver Mobility

With mobility the end points freely move from one network to another. Initially an end point would be in the Home Network. Subsequently it would move to a different part of the network or at times to a different "Foreign Network" (with a different gateway router). However, because the original address of the end point belongs to a subnet announced by the Home Agent to the rest of the Internet, all the IP traffic destined for the end point goes to the Home Network. This continues even after the end point moves to a different network.

Triangular forwarding is a problem introduced when such mobility occurs. It indicates a situation where data is first routed to the Home Agent (the gateway router in the home network to which the subscriber originally belongs), from where the traffic is forwarded to the Foreign Agent (the gateway router in the visiting/foreign network), and then to the end user. This triangular forwarding causes routing inefficiencies, increases latency in the sessions, and has the potential to disrupt the sessions in progress (see Figure 8.9).

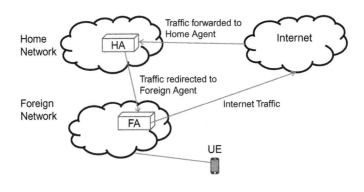

FIGURE 8.9

As a part of IPv6 with "Care Of Address" this problem is resolved. When the first few packets are received by the Home Agent, it informs the sender that the end station is now "Care Of" the Foreign Agent. The sender will then route all further traffic directly to the Foreign Agent bypassing the Home Agent.

Applying the triangular problem to multicast would have two implications: sender mobility and receiver mobility. The focus of the discussion in this section is on receiver mobility. In a multicast environment, sources are normally unaware of the receivers and the underlying logical or physical network topologies. There is no communication from the receiver to sender to indicate to the sender that the receiver's location has changed within the network. So one of the problems of mobility in multicast is that with the mobility of the receiver, the sender may continue to send traffic to the receiver's original location without noticing its mobility. The receiver, on the other hand, loses connectivity in such a scenario and drops out of the receiver group.

When the receiver moves to a new network several scenarios are possible:

1. The Foreign Networks that the receiver of the multicast group moves into may already have members that have subscribed to this multicast group and several other members may be receiving the multicast stream.

2. Multicast service is available in general; however, the specific multicast group to which the receiver has subscribed may not be available in the Foreign Network. This would mean that the existing distribution trees of the Home Network may be rejoined with suboptimal routing. The Visiting Network receives the multicast traffic but through the Home Network. This somewhat reflects the Triangular Routing problem described earlier. However, since the multicast service is enabled a single stream from the Home to Network to the Foreign Network would be sufficient, and it would later be replicated as needed within the Foreign Network.

3. The new network may not support multicast at all and a tunnel may be established to connect to the Home Network to receive the traffic from the desired group.

The receiver needs a real-time handover that needs to transfer the multicast membership context from its old to its new point of attachment. The delay in the handover can result in the disruption of the multicast session.

On the network infrastructure side, support to multicast mobility is a complex task. When the receiver moves rapidly in the network, it is necessary to arrive at routing convergence quickly so that there is no session disruption, and also to optimize use of the network infrastructure resources. It is also necessary to avoid stream multiplication issues that can potentially arise from redundant data forwarding in the infrastructure. Packet duplication and out-of-order packet delivery are also possible when the infrastructure is not optimized for mobility of multicast receivers. It is also necessary for the network infrastructure and the billing systems to ensure that the mobility management does not cause erroneous subscription or double billing (when the receiver's session is not terminated at the Home Network, even after it arrives at the Foreign Network and the billing begins in the Foreign Network).

An ideal scenario for the network infrastructure is that the mobility management is handled at the network periphery and the network infrastructure should be agnostic to whether the receiver has a wired or wireless connection. However, in practice this has yet to be accomplished.

8.5.2 Source Mobility

In SSM it is expected that the receiver knows the address of the source and establishes channel membership through a subscription to the (S, G) channel. However, for the SSM source identification to continue to remain relevant, the receivers must be MIPv6 aware so that the Home Agent Address is correctly mapped to the current Care Of Address. Even after the source handover, significant complexities remain in the infrastructure routing. A change of source address would need the relevant changes in all of the infrastructure elements and the receivers of that group. Any updates regarding an SSM source routing should not be in violation of the unicast routing tables; otherwise this would lead to routing loops and also create security holes in the SSM mobility scenario. SSM mobility, therefore, should be implemented to make route identification and route convergence possible within a reasonable time so that the application level performance would not be degraded.

Multiple approaches are under consideration for arriving at resolution of the problems that arise out of source mobility in SSM. One approach (Lee, 2006) suggests state-update mechanisms for reusing major parts of established trees. Another (Thaler) approach suggests using a binding cache. Initial session announcements and changes of source addresses are distributed periodically to clients via an additional multicast control tree. Source tree handovers are then activated on listener requests. Several other approaches are outlined in RFC 5757.

8.6 CONCLUSION

The topic of multicast mobility continues to be a subject of research in diverse areas. There are several proposals in each of these areas, and which ones would dominate the future deployments remains to be seen.

DVB-H and MBMS may be viewed as competing in some areas and complementing each other in some areas. The commercial viability, ease of use, and so forth are areas without clear answers. A recent government study in Europe recommended against having multiple DVB-H operators in each area to ensure efficient use of the spectrum. On the other hand, an oligopoly or a monopoly of this nature would impact the quality of programming (typically reduces it), and subsequently the user interest may shift toward MBMS if it offered better programming. Similar issues pertain to receiver and source mobility. Technology is not the only dominant determinant in the mobile multicast domain; there are regulatory, technical, and social aspects that are yet to play out and the verdict is still out as to what form this technology will eventually take.

Summary

We started this book with the building blocks of IP Multicast and eventually moved on to understanding real-world applications that use multicast as a foundation for creating revenue-generating products with those applications. We visited the need for multicast VPNs and the Draft-Rosen model, before we moved on to the NG-MVPNs and spoke about another draft known as in-band signaling. Finally, we covered multicast delivery and the NG-MVPN framework from the context of VPLS and Ethernet-based services. I think it is a good time to summarize a few key aspects regarding this technology and talk about what is next and where we go from here. We are human beings and, more important, professionals who are keen to know the best fit for our present needs as well as what the future offers. The following is a list of what makes the NG-MVPN framework an effective platform for delivering multicast:

1. Scalable and modular BGP control plane that can be extended to suit different service needs
2. P2MP LSPs that can use MPLS as a foundation and offer all the benefits unicast traffic enjoyed to multicast applications such as Bandwidth Reservation, Traffic Protection
3. Single infrastructure—reduced OPEX
4. Bandwidth savings
5. Suits all applications that exist
6. Industry acceptance, which makes integration easy
7. Simplifies OAM—Autodiscovery and Automatic creation of Provider Tunnels

9.1 FUTURE ENHANCEMENTS

In this section, we discuss some of the areas where the MVPN framework is making progress. One of the key areas is in the space of P2MP LSP Aggregation. P2MP Aggregation would offer the following:

1. To improve scalability of the data plane by reducing the MPLS forwarding state for P2MP LSPs
2. To improve scalability of the control plane by reducing the overhead associated with maintaining the MPLS forwarding state for P2MP LSPs by reducing the MPLS forwarding state for P2MP LSPs
3. For the same reasons as point-to-point/multipoint-to-point LSP aggregation with unicast
4. Need for a highly dynamic handling of user-generated multicast messages on access and aggregation nodes, while keeping the core network stable and minimizing state changes triggered by such messages (see draft-leymann-mpls-seamless-mpls-00)

But how do we aggregate P2MP LSPs? To answer this, see the details in the following list:

1. By nesting several P2MP inner LSPs inside a common outer P2MP LSP and forming a P2MP LSP hierarchy

2. By using the MPLS label stack construct

3. The same as for point-to-point/multipoint-to-point LSP hierarchy with unicast

Figures 9.1–9.3 illustrate the different steps.

Step 1:

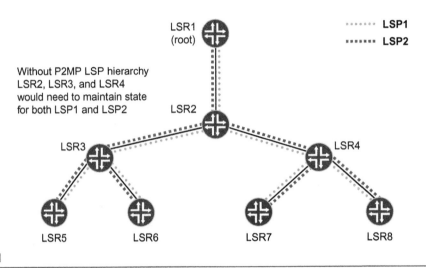

FIGURE 9.1

Step 2:

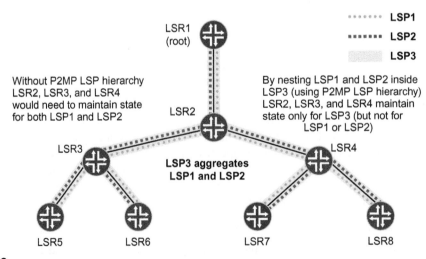

FIGURE 9.2

Step 3:

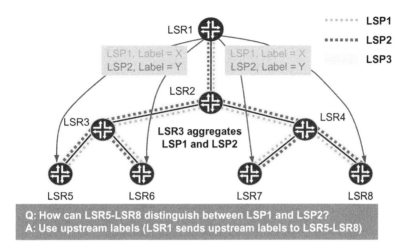

FIGURE 9.3

Several (inner) P2MP LSPs may be nested inside one (outer) P2MP LSP Root of the outer P2MP LSP, which assigns a distinct (upstream) label to each inner P2MP LSP. It also communicates this assignment/binding to all the leaves of the outer LSP; for example, LSR1 communicates to LSR5–LSR8 label X for LSP1 and label Y for LSP2. Leaves of the outer P2MP LSP use the label binding information received from the root to distinguish among different inner P2MP LSPs. For example, LSR5–LSR8 uses label X to identify traffic on LSP1 and label Y to identify traffic on LSP2.

So far we showed aggregation of fully congruent P2MP LSPs. Two or more P2MP LSPs are said to be fully congruent if they have the same root and the same set of leaf nodes. For P2MP LSPs carrying services such as MVPN, Multicast VPLS, and Internet multicast, restricting P2MP LSP hierarchy to only fully congruent P2MP LSPs may significantly limit the overall benefits of P2MP LSP hierarchy, because only a (small) fraction of such P2MP LSPs may be fully congruent. To increase the overall benefits of P2MP LSP hierarchy, the notion of aggregation of partially congruent P2MP LSPs is introduced. Two or more P2MP LSPs are said to be partially congruent if they have the same root and a common subset of the leaf nodes, yet some of the leaf nodes may not be common to all these P2MP LSPs.

Figures 9.4 and 9.5 depict this concept in detail.

Several (inner) P2MP LSPs may be nested inside one (outer) P2MP LSP, even if the set of the leaf nodes of each of these (inner) P2MP LSPs is not exactly the same and even if these LSPs are just partially but not fully congruent; for example, LSP1 and LSP2.

The benefits of the P2MP LSP hierarchy are broadened by applying it to a broader set of P2MP LSPs by relaxing the full congruency constraint on the set of P2MP LSPs that could be aggregated and allowing aggregation of partially congruent P2MP LSPs. This results in a less efficient use of bandwidth compared to the case of aggregating fully congruent (inner) P2MP LSPs; for example, LSP8 discards LSP1 traffic and LSP6 discards LSP2 traffic.

To reduce bandwidth inefficiencies the root of the aggregated P2MP LSPs needs to know the leaf nodes of these P2MP LSPs—the root needs to perform "leaf tracking." We have to remember that the

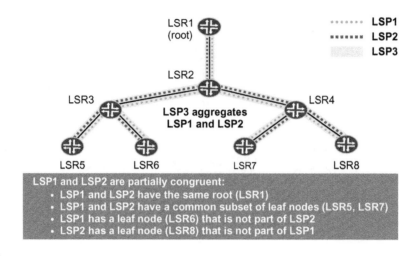

FIGURE 9.4

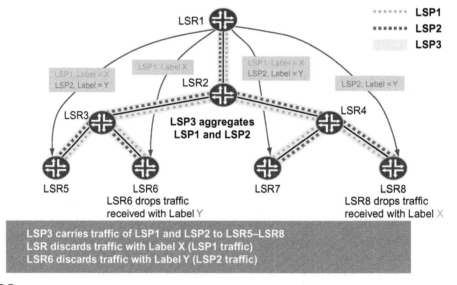

FIGURE 9.5

smaller the fraction of the common leaf nodes relative to the rest of the leaf nodes, the more bandwidth inefficiency.

9.2 CONCLUSION

This is just the beginning of an extremely interesting phase in Multicast VPN deployment.

References

CBMS 1026 v1.0.0 Rev 1/TM 3095 Rev 2. IPDC in DVB-H: Technical Requirements.

DVB Document A092r3. (April 2009). Digital Video Broadcasting (DVB), DVB-H Implementation Guidelines. ETSI EN 302 304 V1.1.1. (November 2004). Digital Video Broadcasting (DVB), Transmission System for Handheld Terminals (DVB-H).

ETSI EN 469 304 V1.1.1. (May 2006). Digital Video Broadcasting (DVB), IP Datacast over DVB-H: Architecture.

ETSI TR 102 473 V1.1.1. (April 2006). Digital Video Broadcasting (DVB), IP Datacast over DVB-H: Use Cases and Services.

Held, G. (2007). *Understanding IPTV*. Auerbach Publications.

HR-1. (July 2006). Assuring Quality of Experience For IPTV, Heavy Reading Whitepaper.

ITU-T Y.1901. (January 2009). IPTV Over NGN Series: Requirements for the support of IPTV services.

ITU-T Y.1910. (September 2008). IPTV Over NGN Series: IPTV functional architecture.

ITU-T Y.2011. (October 2004). General principles and general reference model for Next Generation Networks.

ITU-T Y.2012. (September 2004). Functional requirements and architecture of the NGN Release 1.

JNPR-1. (October 2007). Introduction to IGMP for IPTV Networks, Juniper Networks.

JNPR-2. *** Source Specific Multicast, Chapter 15, Junos Multicast Protocols Configuration Guide.

Kasim, A., Adhikari, P., & Chen, N., et al. (2008). *Delivering carrier ethernet*. New York: McGraw-Hill.

Kotternick, (October 2007). Mobile TV—A study by EU Policy Department (Economic & Scientific Policy) for the European Parliament's committee on Industry Research and Energy 0(ITRE), IP/A/ITRE/ST/2007-087/ LOT 2/C1/SC2.

Lee, H., Han, S., & Hong, J. (2006). Efficient mechanism for source mobility in Source Specific Multicast. In K. Kawahara & I. Chong (Eds.), *Proceedings of ICOIN2006* (Vol. 3961, pp. 82–91). Berlin: Springer-Verlag.

Minoli, D. (2008). *IP multicast with applications to IPTV and mobile DVB-H*. New York: Wiley-IEEE Press.

O'Neill, A. (2002). *Mobility management and ip multicast*, in press.

O'Driscoll, G. (2008). *Next Generation IPTV services and technologies*. New York: Wiley.

Blake, Black, et al. (December 1998). RFC 2475: An architecture for differentiated services.

Armitage, Schulter, at al. (January 1999). RFC 2491: IPv6 over Non-Broadcast Multiple Access (NBMA) networks.

Heinane, Baker et al. (June 1999). RFC 2597: Assured forwarding PHB group.

Jacobons, Nichols, et al. (June 1999). RFC 2598: An expedited forwarding PHB.

Le Faucheur, Davie, et al. (May 2002). RFC 3270: Multi-Protocol Label Switching (MPLS) support of differentiated services.

Cain, Deering, Kouvelas, Fenner, & Thyagarajan (October 2002). RFC 3376: Internet Group Management Protocol, Version 3.

Bhattacharyya, S. (July 2003). RFC 3569: An overview of Source-Specific Multicast (SSM).

Meyer, Lothberg (September 2001). RFC 3180: GLOP addressing in 233/8.

Droms, Bound, et al. (July 2003). RFC 3315: Dynamic Host Configuration Protocol for IPv6 (DHCPv6).

Vida, (June 2004). RFC 3810: Multicast Listener Discovery Version 2 (MLDv2) for IPv6.

Welch, Clark (April 2006). RFC 4445: A proposed Media Delivery Index (MDI).

Katz, Ward (June 2010). RFC 5880: Bi-directional Forwarding Detection (BFD).

Katz, Ward (June 2010). RFC 5881: Bi-directional Forwarding Detection (BFD) for IPv4 and IPv6 (Single Hop).

Katz, Ward (June 2010). RFC 5882: Generic application of Bi-directional Forwarding Detection (BFD).

Katz, Ward, (June 2010). RFC 5883: Bi-directional Forwarding Detection (BFD) for Multihop Paths.

Aggarwal, Kompella et al. (June 2010). RFC 5884: Bi-directional Forwarding Detection (BFD) for MPLS Label Switched Paths (LSPs).

Nadeau, Pignataro (June 2010). RFC 5885: Bi-directional Forwarding Detection (BFD) for the Pseudowire Virtual Circuit Connectivity Verification (VCCV).

Holbrook, Cain, Haberman (June 2006). RFC 4604: Using Internet Group Management Protocol Version 3 (IGMPv3) and Multicast Listener Discovery Protocol Version 2 (MLDv2) for Source Specific Multicast.

Savola, (January 2008). RFC 5110: Overview of the internet multicast routing architecture.

Schmidt, Waehlisch, Fairhurst (February 2010). RFC 5757: Multicast mobility in Mobile IP Version 6 (MIPv6): Problem statement and brief survey.

Simpson, W. (2008). *Video Over IP: A practical guide to technology and applications*. Amsterdam: Elsevier.

Choen, Shrum (April 2006). TR-101: Technical Report 101, DSL Forum, Migration to Ethernet Based DSL Aggregation.

Yomamoto, (October 2009). Standardization trends of IPTV and activities undertaken by OKI, Oki Technical Review, Special Issue on Networks.

Subject Index

Printed and bound by CPI Group (UK) Ltd, Croydon, CR0 4YY

03/10/2024

01040319-0006